ORDNANCE SURVEY

STREET ATLAS
West Sussex

Contents

IV *Key to maps*

VI *Administrative boundaries*

1 *Street maps*

208 *Index explanation and abbreviations*

209 *Index of towns, villages and rural localities*

210 *Index of street names*

PHILIP'S

First edition published 1988
Fourth edition published 1994 by

Ordnance Survey and Philip's
Romsey Road, Maybush, Southampton SO9 4DH
Philip's, an imprint of Reed Consumer Books Limited
Michelin House, 81 Fulham Road, London, SW3 6RB
and Auckland, Melbourne, Singapore and Toronto

ISBN 0-540-05876-9 (Philip's, hardback)
ISBN 0-540-05877-7 (Philip's, softback)
ISBN 0-319-00413-9 (Ordnance Survey, hardback)
ISBN 0-319-00414-7 (Ordnance Survey, softback)

To the best of the Publishers' knowledge, the information in this atlas was correct at the time of going to press. No responsibility can be accepted for any errors or their consequences.

The representation in this atlas of a road, track or path is no evidence of the existence of a right of way.

Printed in Great Britain by
Butler & Tanner Ltd, Frome and London

Key to map symbols

	British Rail station
	London transport station
	Private railway station
	Bus or coach station
	Heliport
	Police station (may not be open 24 hours)
	Hospital with casualty facilities (may not be open 24 hours)
	Post office
+	**Place of worship**
	Important building
P	**Parking**
120	**Adjoining page indicator**
	Motorway or dual carriageway
A27(T)	**Main or through road** (with Department of Transport number)
	Gate or obstruction to traffic (restrictions may not apply at all times or to all vehicles)
	Footpath
	Bridleway
	Path
	Track

The representation in this atlas of a road, track or path is no evidence of the existence of a right of way

Amb Sta	**Ambulance station**	LC	**Level crossing**
Coll	**College**	Liby	**Library**
FB	**Footbridge**	Mus	**Museum**
F Sta	**Fire station**	Sch	**School**
Hospl	**Hospital**	TH	**Town hall**

0 ¼ ½ ¾ 1mile

0 250m 500m 250m 1 Kilometre

The scale of the maps is 3½ inches to 1 mile (1:18103)

Key to map pages

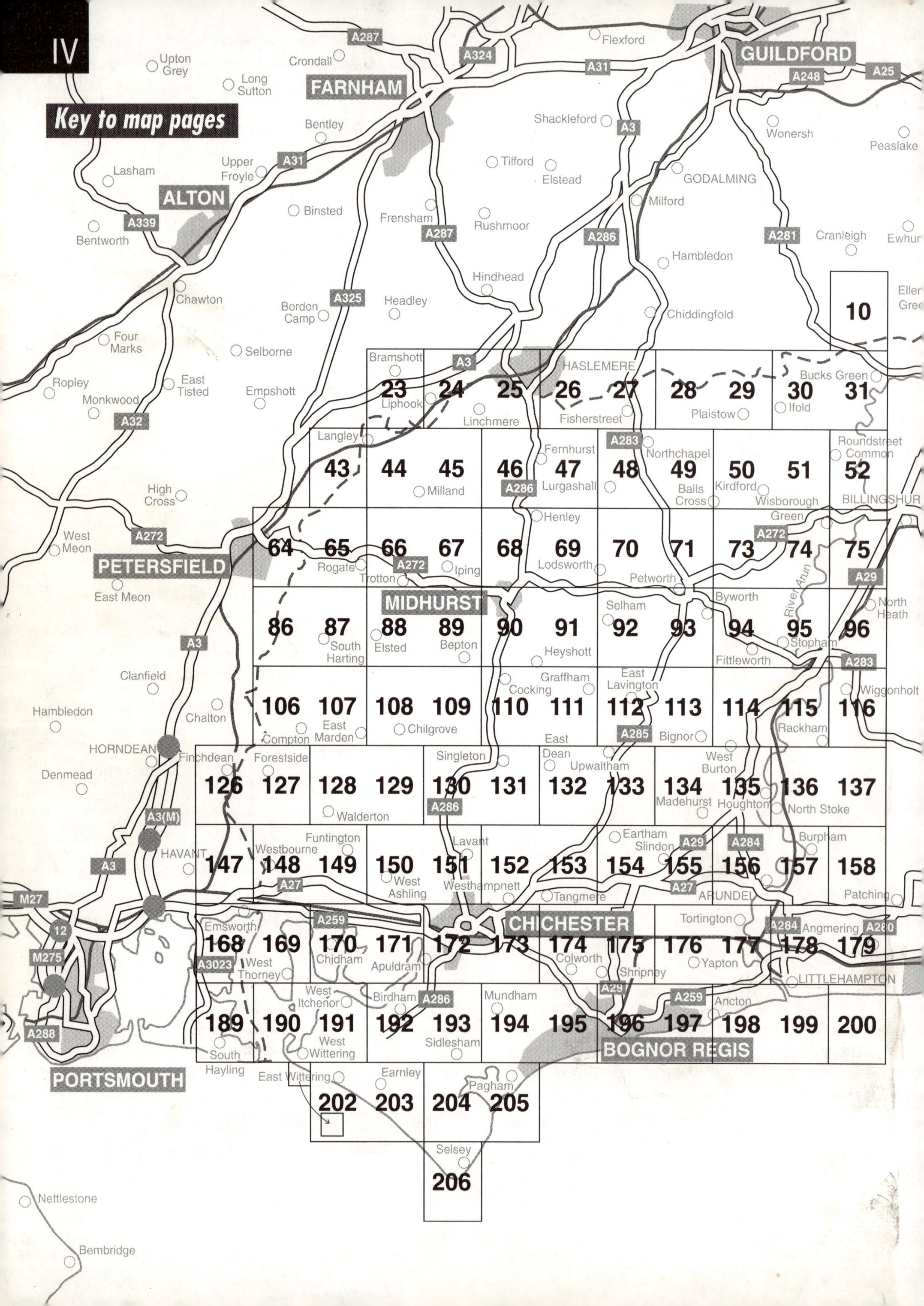

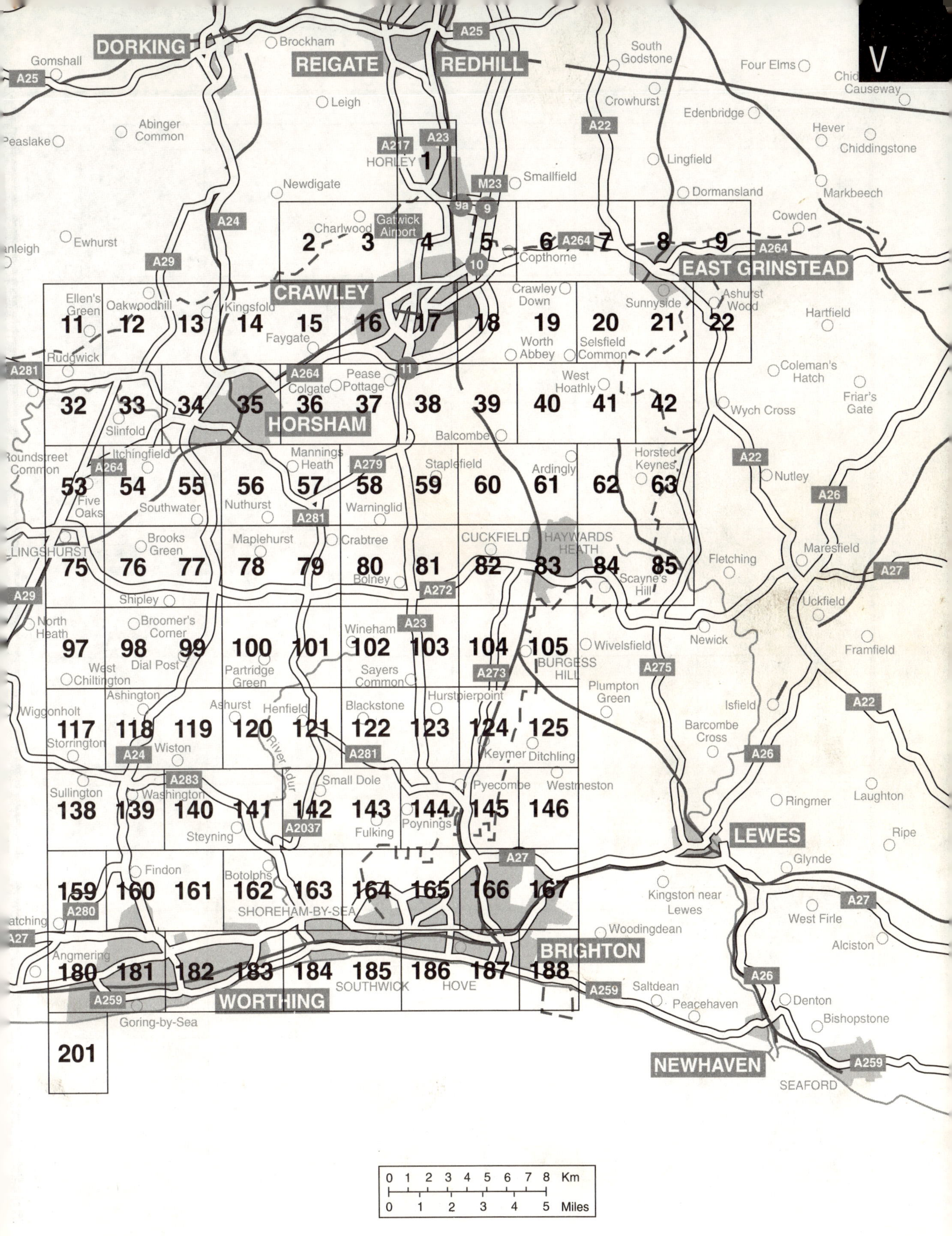
DORKING
REIGATE
REDHILL
Brockham
Gomshall
South Godstone
Four Elms
Chid
Causeway
Leigh
Crowhurst
Edenbridge
Abinger Common
Peaslake
Hever
Chiddingstone
Lingfield
HORLEY
Smallfield
Newdigate
Dormansland
Markbeech
Cowden
Charlwood
Gatwick Airport
Ewhurst
Copthorne
EAST GRINSTEAD
CRAWLEY
Crawley Down
Ashurst Wood
Ellen's Green
Oakwoodhill
Kingsfold
Sunnyside
Hartfield
Faygate
Worth Abbey
Selsfield Common
Rudgwick
Coleman's Hatch
Pease Pottage
Colgate
West Hoathly
Friar's Gate
Wych Cross
HORSHAM
Slinfold
Balcombe
Roundstreet Common
Itchingfield
Mannings Heath
Staplefield
Horsted Keynes
Ardingly
Nutley
Five Oaks
Southwater
Nuthurst
Warninglid
Brooks Green
Maplehurst
Crabtree
CUCKFIELD
HAYWARDS HEATH
Maresfield
Fletching
Bolney
Scayne's Hill
Shipley
Uckfield
North Heath
Broomer's Corner
Wineham
Newick
Wivelsfield
Framfield
West Chiltington
Dial Post
Partridge Green
Sayers Common
BURGESS HILL
Plumpton Green
Ashington
Ashurst
Henfield
Blackstone
Hurstpierpoint
Isfield
Wiggonholt
Barcombe Cross
Storrington
Wiston
River Adur
Keymer
Ditchling
Sullington
Washington
Small Dole
Pyecombe
Westmeston
Ringmer
Laughton
Steyning
Fulking
Poynings
LEWES
Ripe
Findon
Botolphs
Glynde
SHOREHAM-BY-SEA
Kingston near Lewes
West Firle
Woodingdean
Angmering
BRIGHTON
Alciston
SOUTHWICK
HOVE
Saltdean
Peacehaven
Denton
Bishopstone
WORTHING
Goring-by-Sea
NEWHAVEN
SEAFORD
A25
A217
A23
M23
A22
A24
A29
A264
A281
A279
A272
A273
A275
A26
A27
A283
A2037
A280
A259
9a
9
10
11
1 2 3 4 5 6 7 8 9
11 12 13 14 15 16 17 18 19 20 21 22
32 33 34 35 36 37 38 39 40 41 42
53 54 55 56 57 58 59 60 61 62 63
75 76 77 78 79 80 81 82 83 84 85
97 98 99 100 101 102 103 104 105
117 118 119 120 121 122 123 124 125
138 139 140 141 142 143 144 145 146
159 160 161 162 163 164 165 166 167
180 181 182 183 184 185 186 187 188
201
0 1 2 3 4 5 6 7 8 Km
0 1 2 3 4 5 Miles

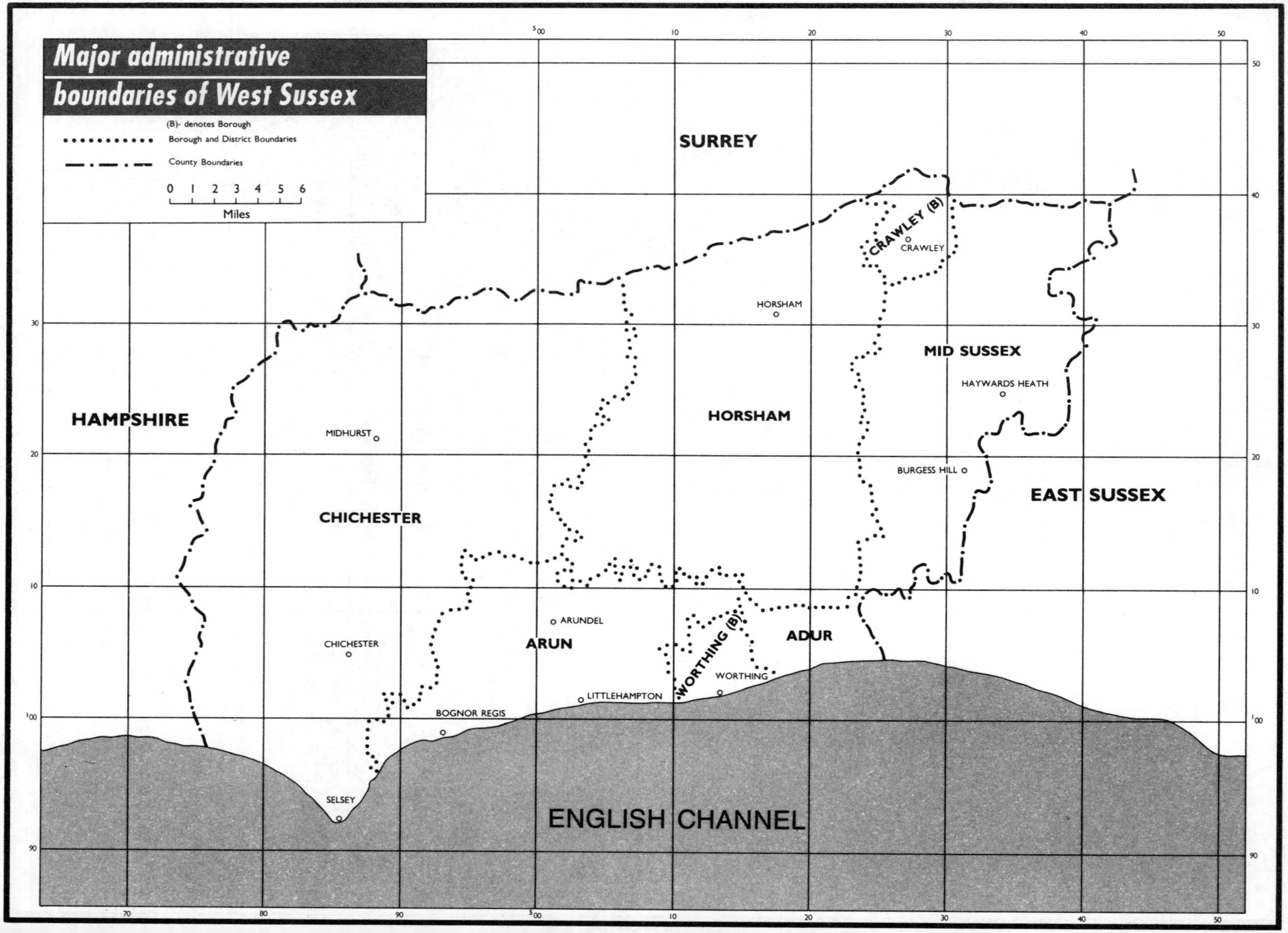
Major administrative
boundaries of West Sussex
(B)- denotes Borough
Borough and District Boundaries
County Boundaries
0 1 2 3 4 5 6
Miles
SURREY
HAMPSHIRE
CHICHESTER
HORSHAM
MID SUSSEX
EAST SUSSEX
ARUN
ADUR
CRAWLEY (B)
WORTHING (B)
CRAWLEY
HORSHAM
HAYWARDS HEATH
BURGESS HILL
MIDHURST
CHICHESTER
ARUNDEL
LITTLEHAMPTON
WORTHING
BOGNOR REGIS
SELSEY
ENGLISH CHANNEL

not continued, see key diagram

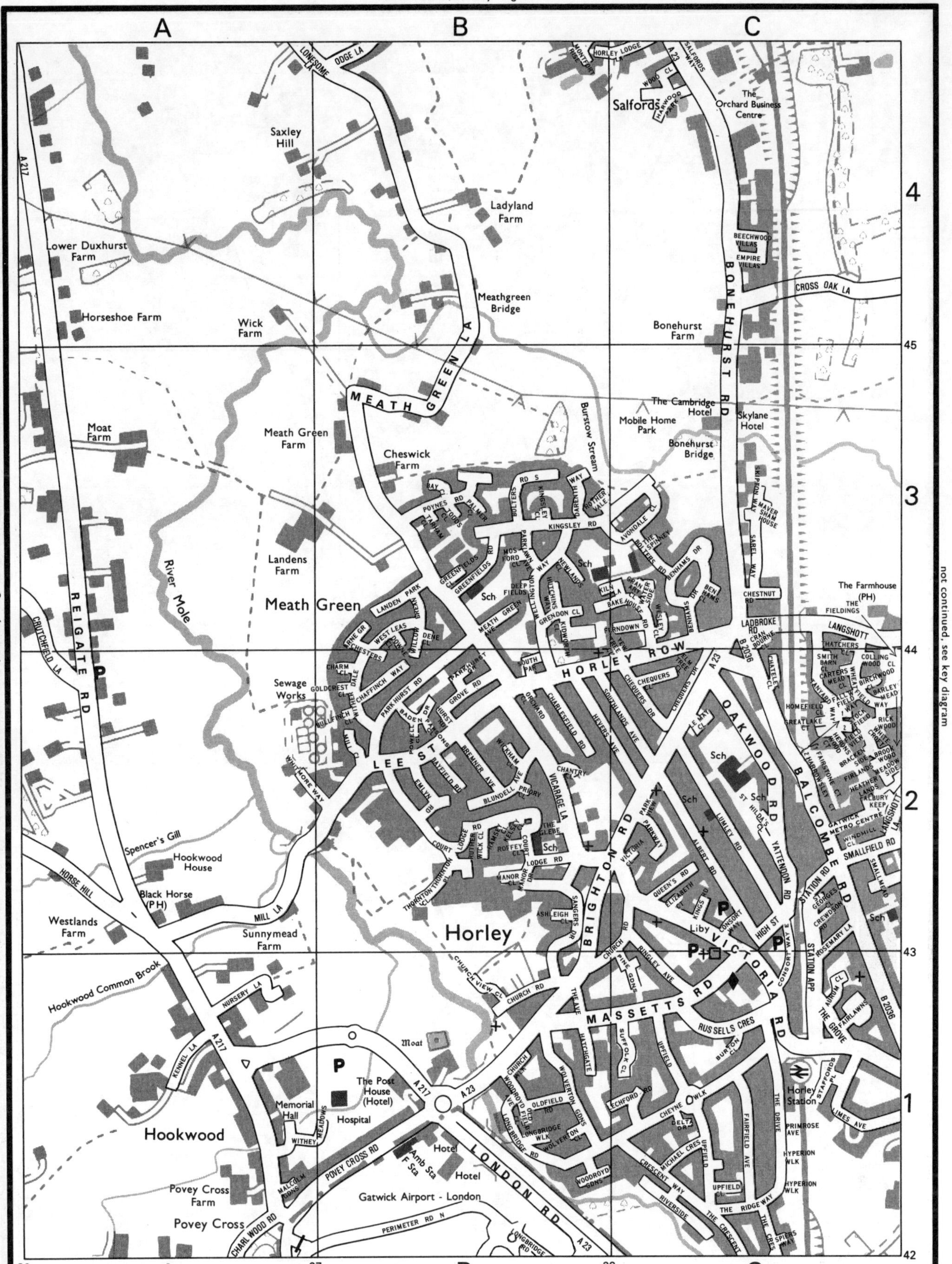

not continued, see key diagram

not continued, see key diagram

4

not continued, see key diagram

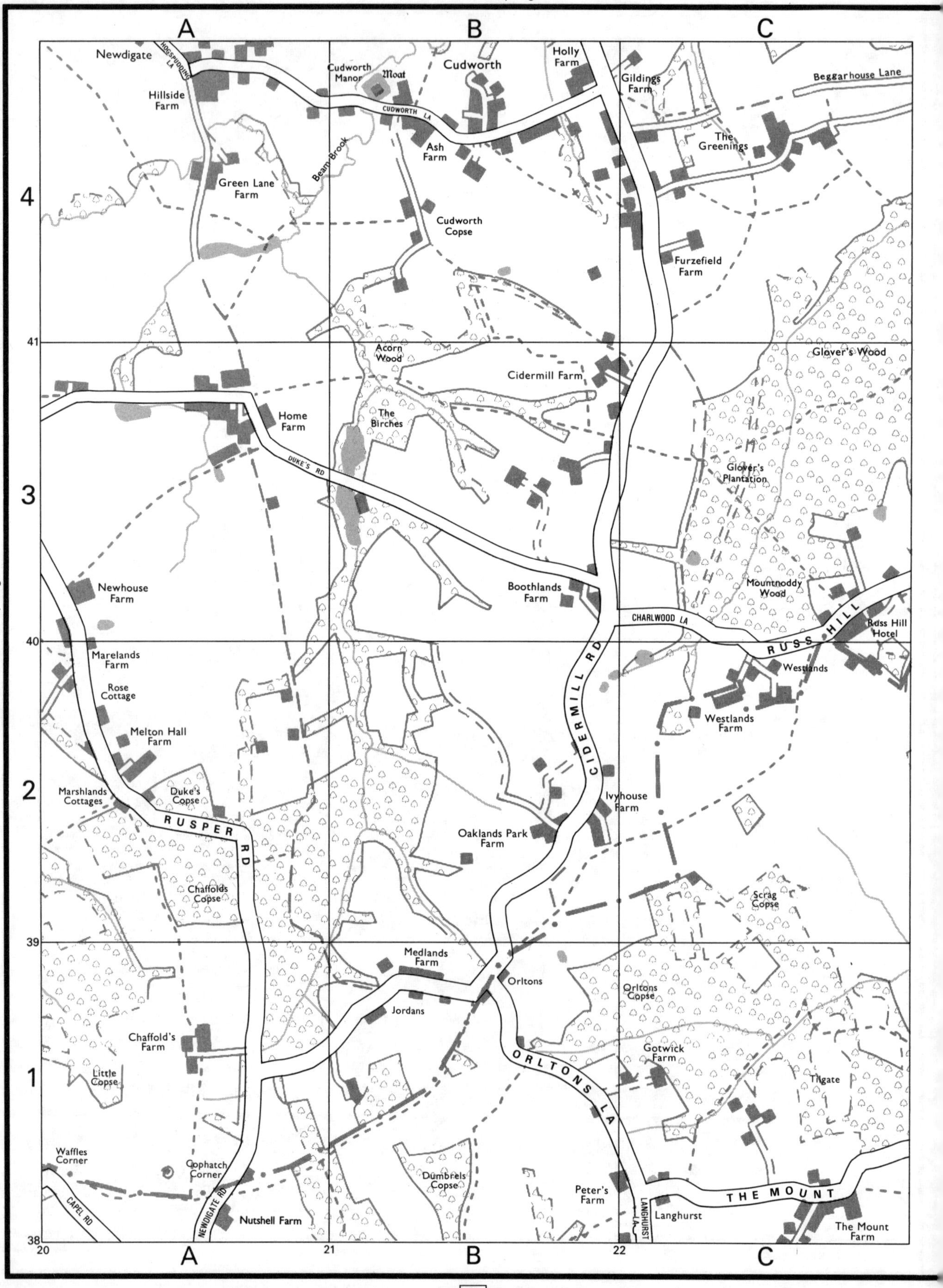

not continued, see key diagram

15

not continued, see key diagram

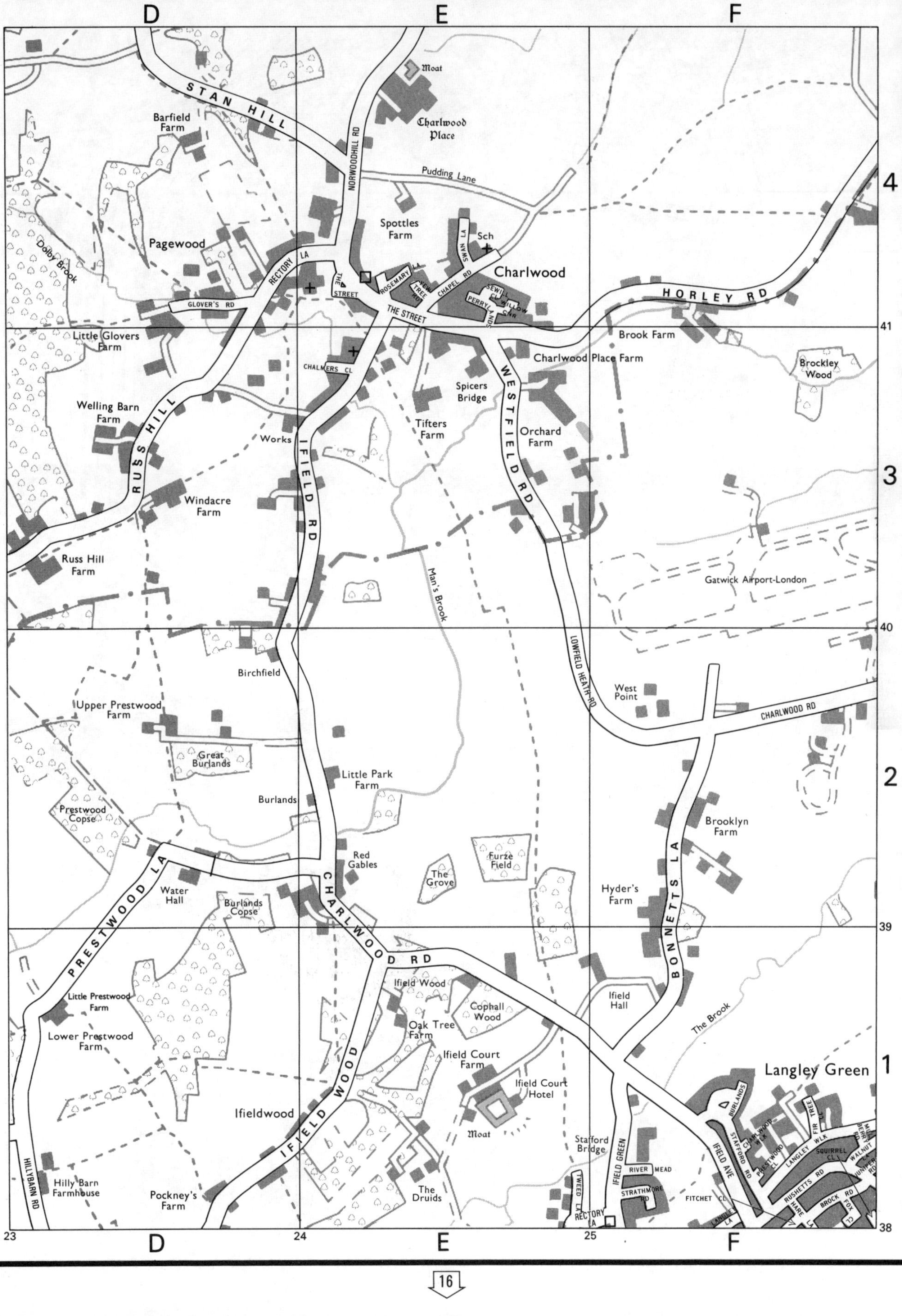

4

1

3

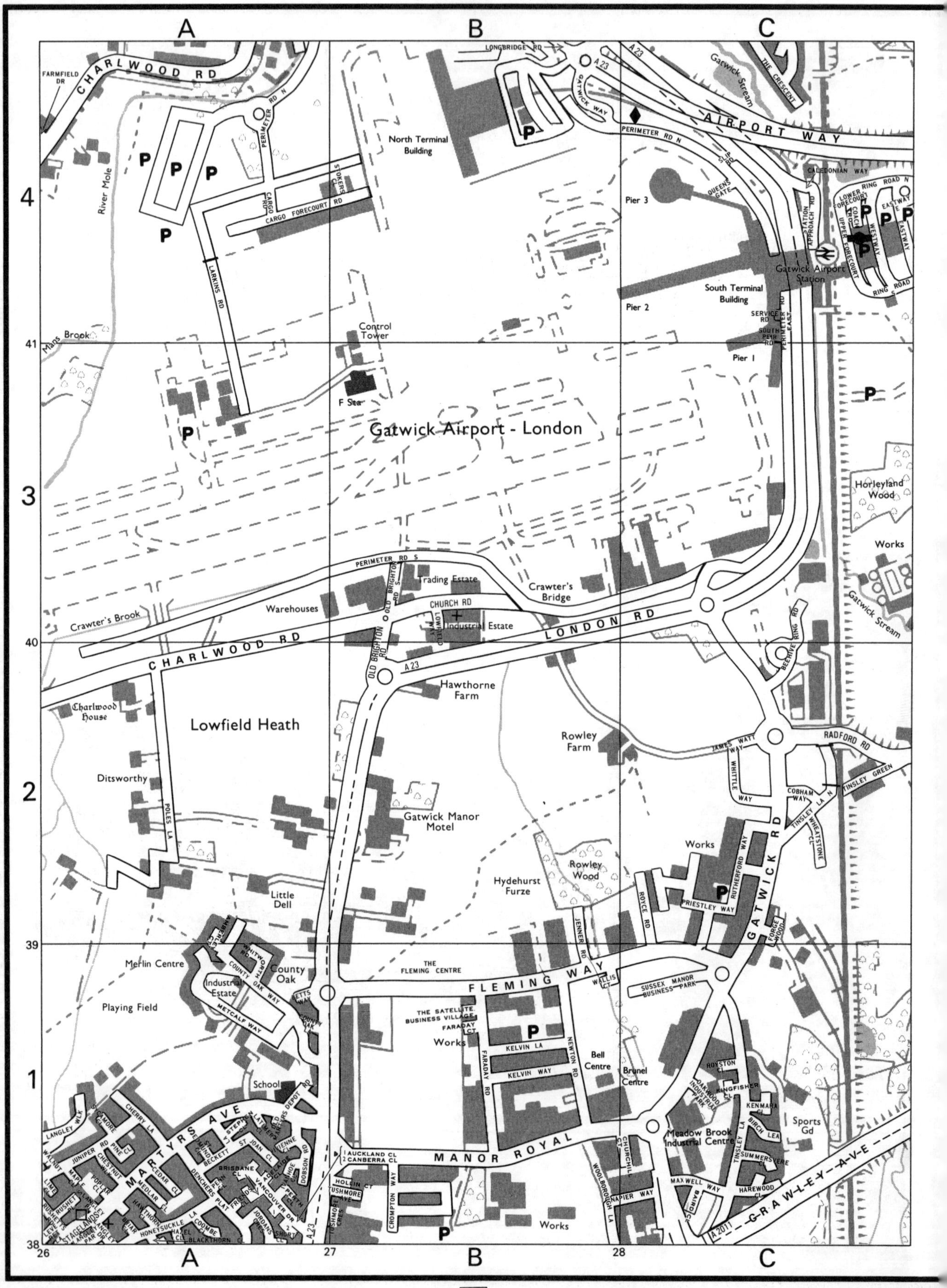
A
B
C
FARMFIELD DR
CHARLWOOD RD
LONGBRIDGE RD
A 23
GATWICK WAY
AIRPORT WAY
PERIMETER RD N
Gatwick Stream
THE CRESCENT
North Terminal Building
CARGO RD
STOKERS CL
CARGO FORECOURT RD
River Mole
LARKINS RD
Pier 3
QUEENS GATE
CALEDONIAN WAY
LOWER FORECOURT
RING ROAD
EASTWAY
WESTWAY
STATION APPROACH
UPPER FORECOURT
Gatwick Airport Station
South Terminal Building
Pier 2
SERVICE RD
SOUTH PERIMETER RD
PERIMETER RD EAST
Pier 1
Mans Brook
Control Tower
F Sta
Gatwick Airport - London
Horleyland Wood
Works
PERIMETER RD S
Trading Estate
Crawter's Bridge
Warehouses
CHURCH RD
OLD BRIGHTON RD
LOWFIELD WAY
Industrial Estate
Crawter's Brook
LONDON RD
CHARLWOOD RD
BEEHIVE RING RD
Charlwood House
Lowfield Heath
Hawthorne Farm
Rowley Farm
JAMES WATT WAY
RADFORD RD
WHITTLE WAY
COBHAM WAY
TINSLEY GREEN
TINSLEY LA N
WHEATSTONE CL
Ditsworthy
POLES LA
Gatwick Manor Motel
Works
Rowley Wood
Hydehurst Furze
RUTHERFORD WAY
GATWICK RD
PRIESTLEY WAY
ROYCE RD
JENNER RD
FORGE WOOD
Little Dell
Merlin Centre
County Oak
COUNTY OAK WAY
Industrial Estate
METCALF WAY
Playing Field
THE FLEMING CENTRE
FLEMING WAY
WALLIS CT
SUSSEX MANOR BUSINESS PARK
THE SATELLITE BUSINESS VILLAGE
FARADAY CT
Works
KELVIN LA
KELVIN WAY
NEWTON RD
FARADAY RD
Bell Centre
Brunel Centre
ROYSTON CL
KINGFISHER CL
OAKWOOD INDUSTRIAL PARK
KENMARA CT
BIRCH LEA
Sports Gd
School
CHERRY LA
MARTYRS AVE
LANGLEY WLK
JUNIPER RD
PINE CL
CHESTNUT
POPLAR CL
CEDAR CL
MEDLAR CL
HAWTHORN
HONEYSUCKLE LA
HAZEL
BLACKTHORN CL
COOMBE
DENCHERS PLAT
BECKETT
ST JOAN CL
BRISBANE
VANCOUVER DR
JORDANS
SHORT
DOBSON RD
1 AUCKLAND CL
2 CANBERRA CL
HOLLIN CT
TUSHMORE AVE
TUSHMORE CRES
CROMPTON WAY
MANOR ROYAL
CHURCHILL CT
WOOLBOROUGH LA
NAPIER WAY
Meadow Brook Industrial Centre
TINSLEY LA
SUMMERSVERE
MAXWELL WAY
HAREWOOD
A 2011
CRAWLEY AVE
Works
STAGELANDS
A 23
4
41
3
40
2
39
1
38
26
27
28

17

not continued, see key diagram

9

not continued, see key diagram

5

19

not continued, see key diagram

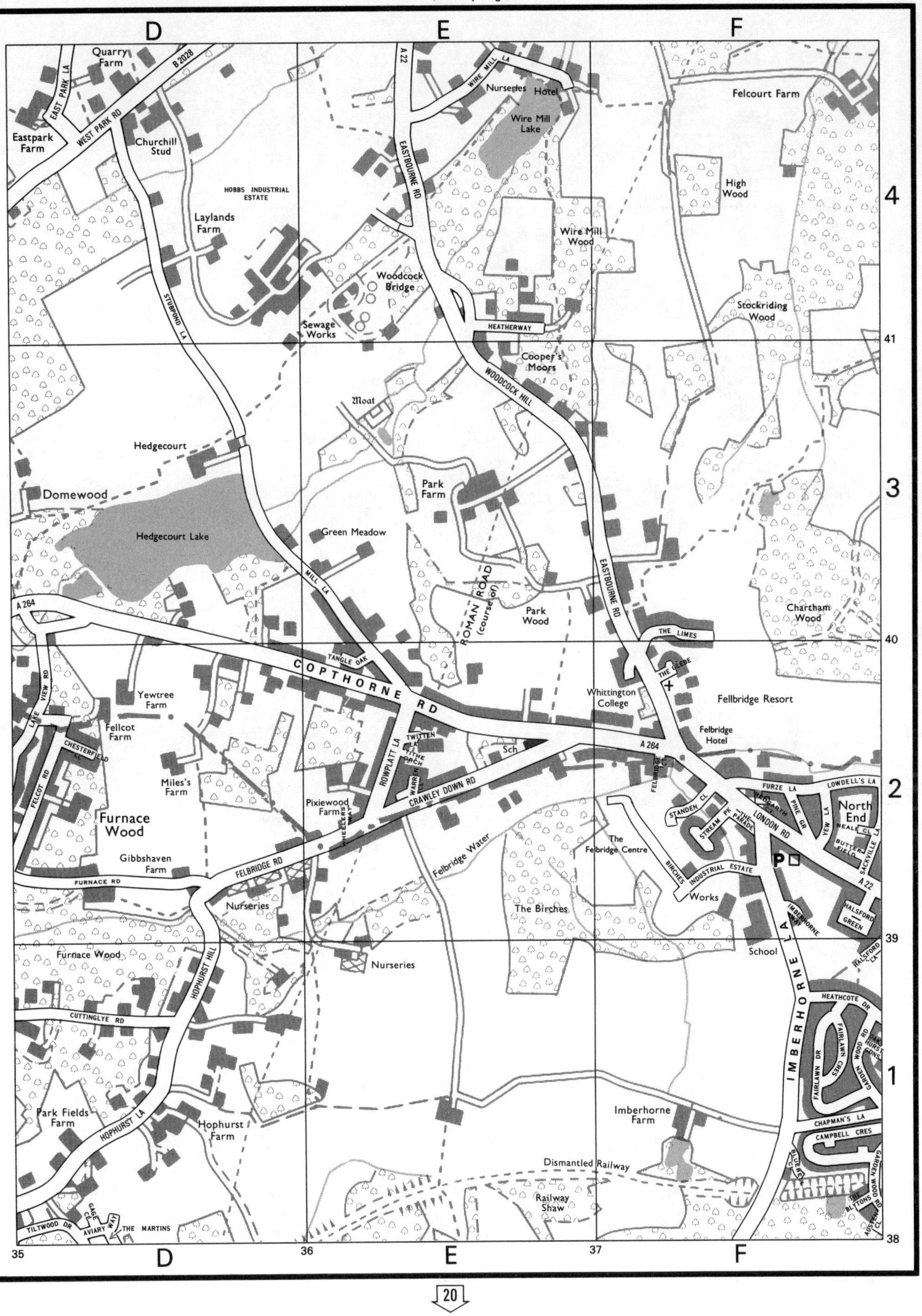

20

not continued, see key diagram

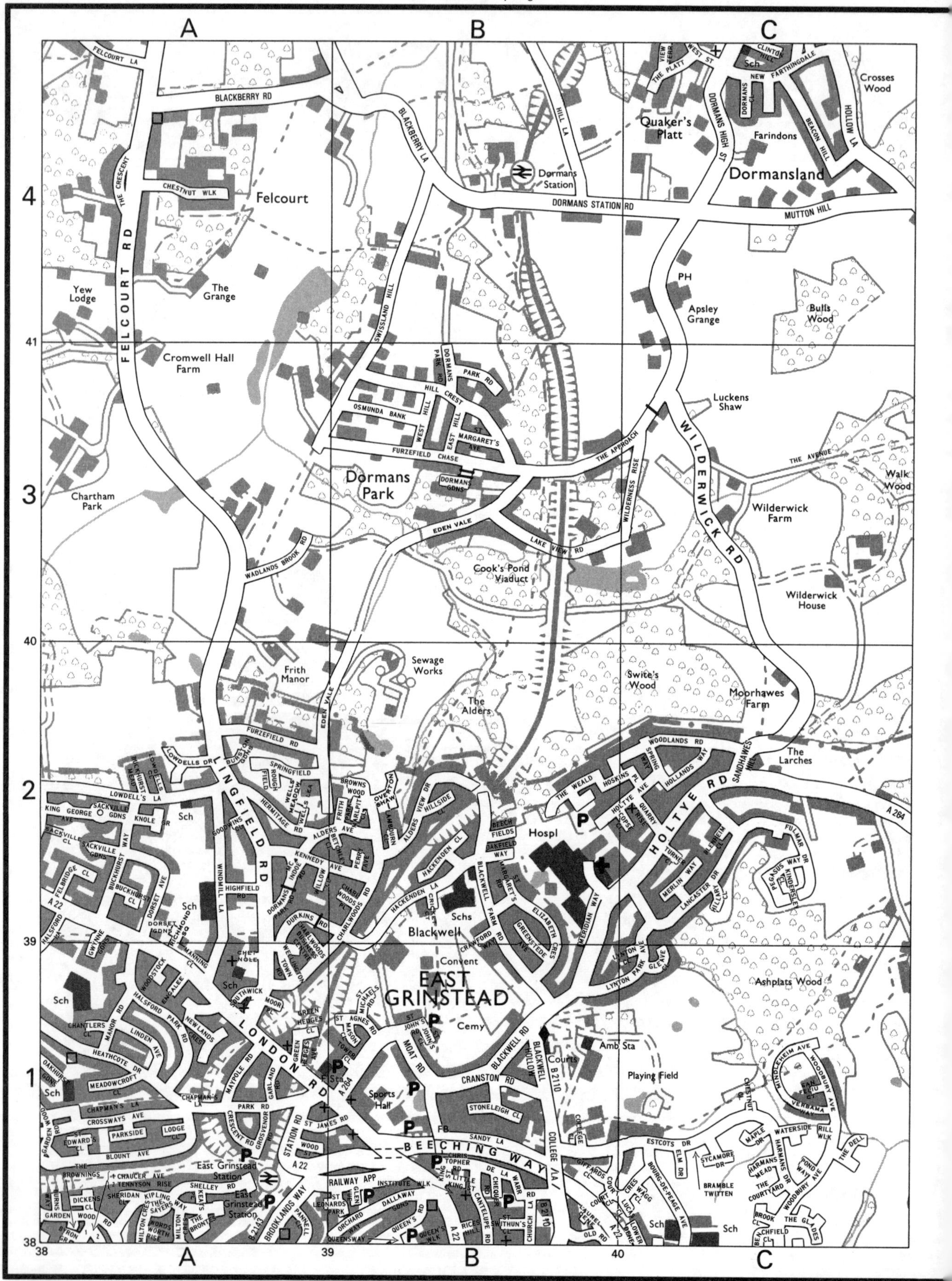

7

not continued, see key diagram

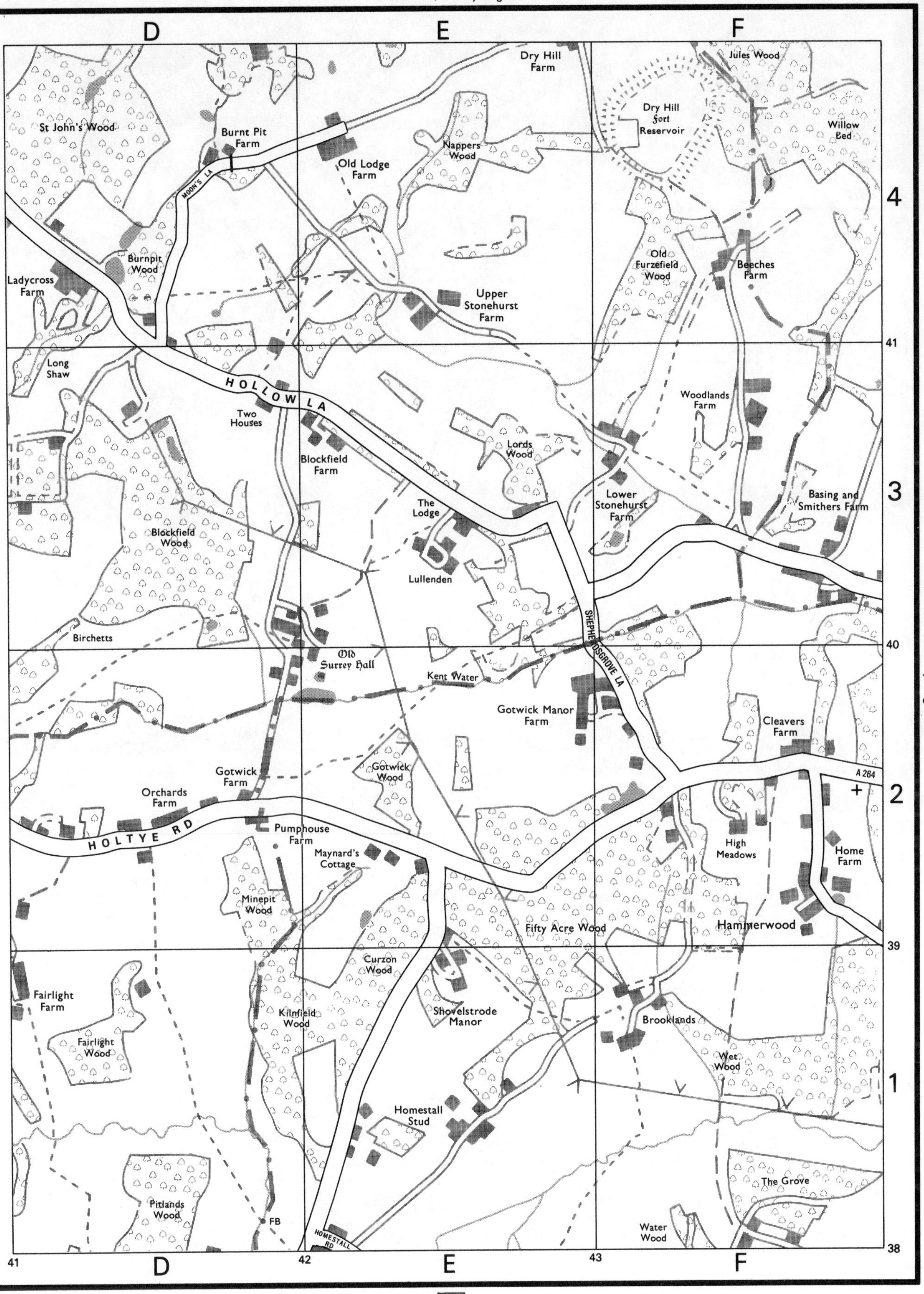

not continued, see key diagram

not continued, see key diagram

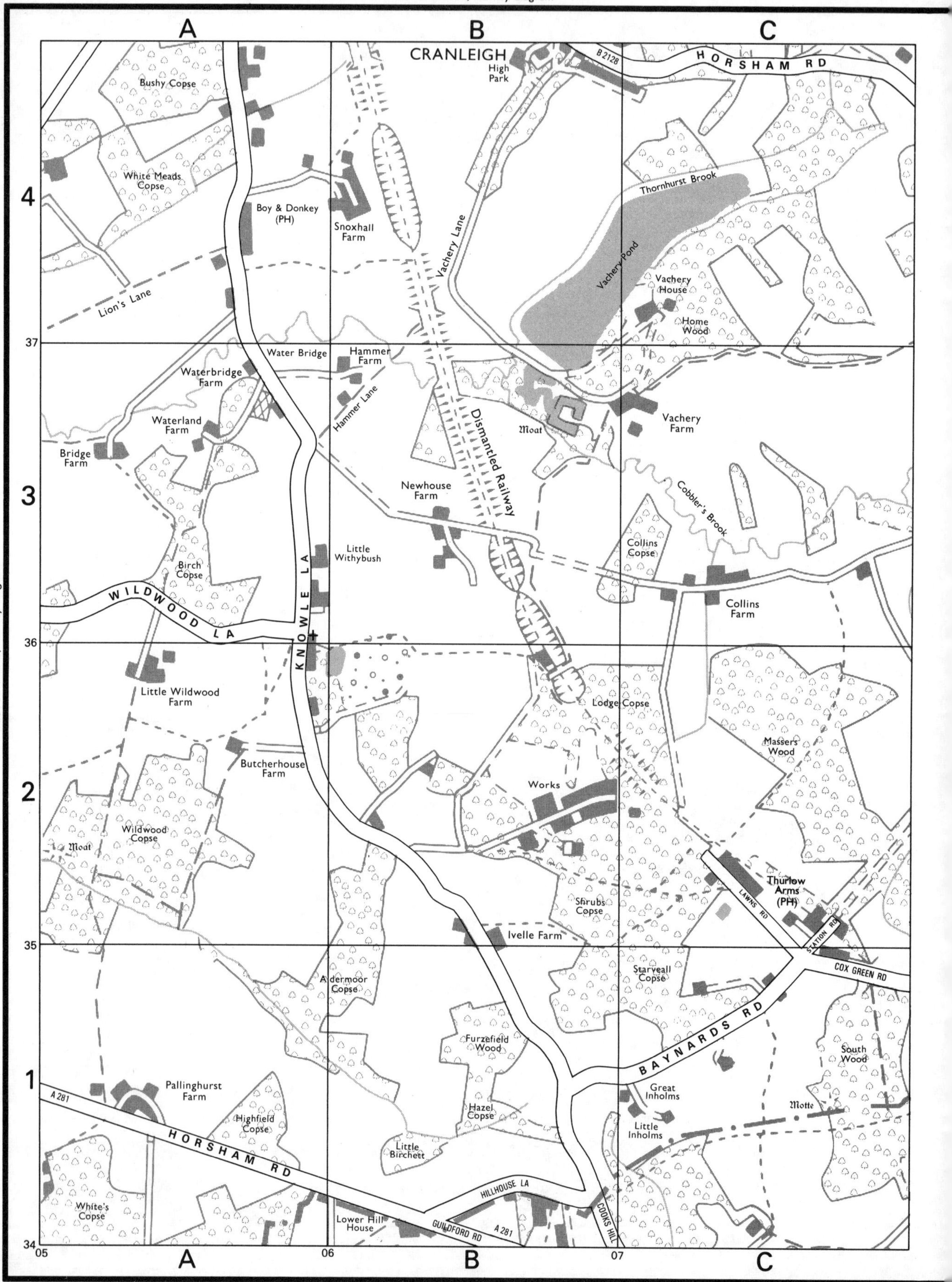

not continued, see key diagram

31

not continued, see key diagram

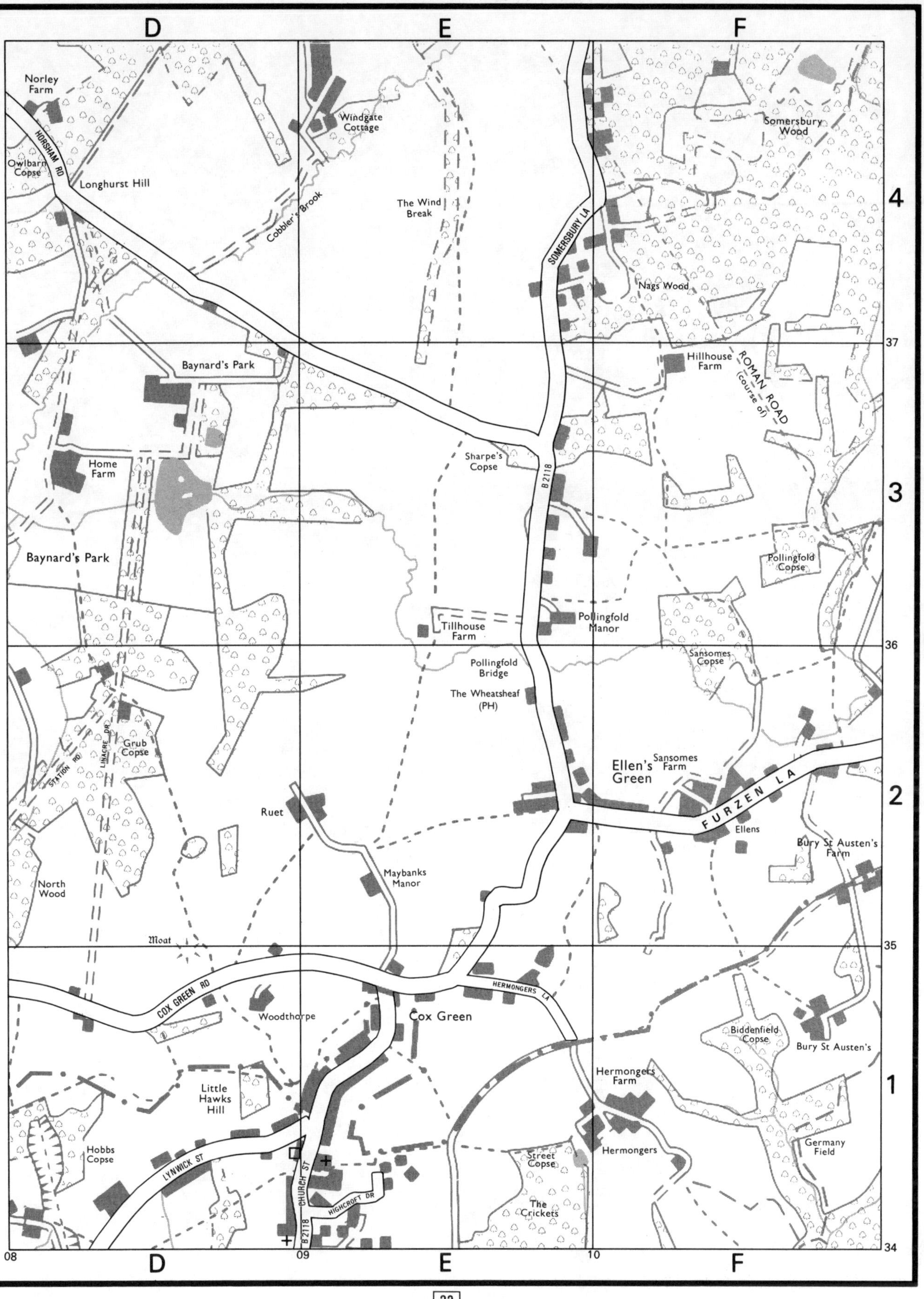

12

32

not continued, see key diagram

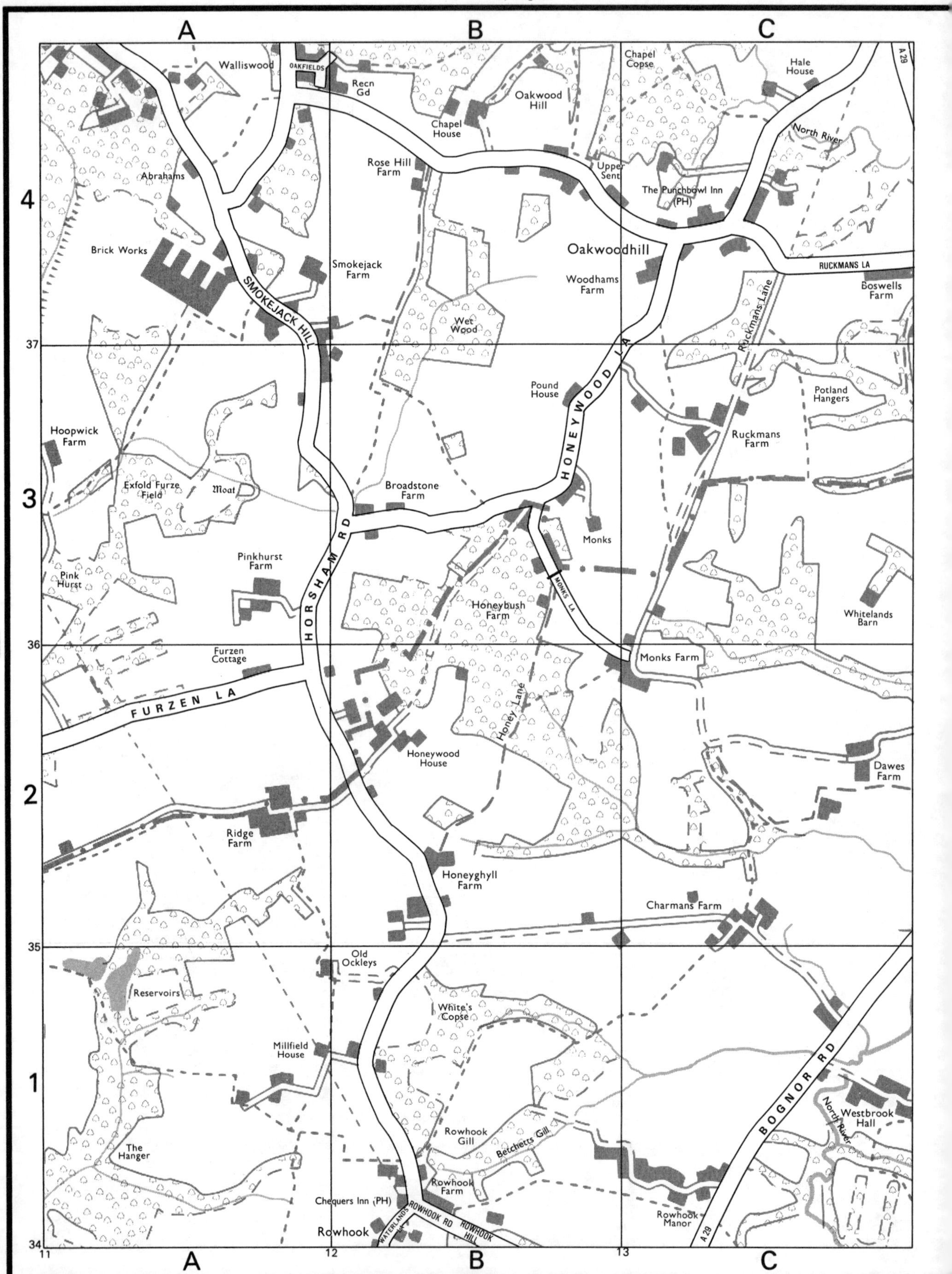

11

not continued, see key diagram

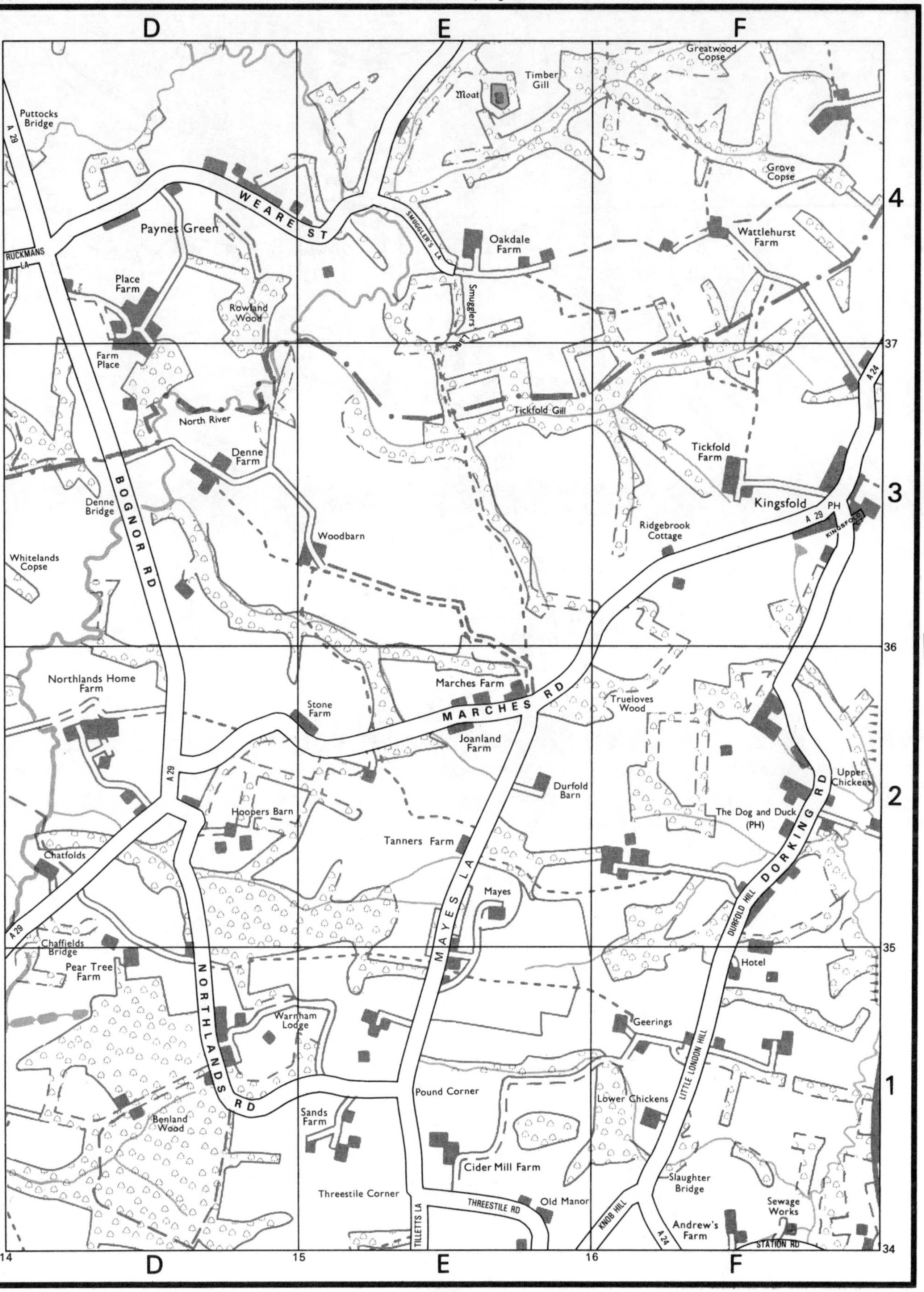

14

34

not continued, see key diagram

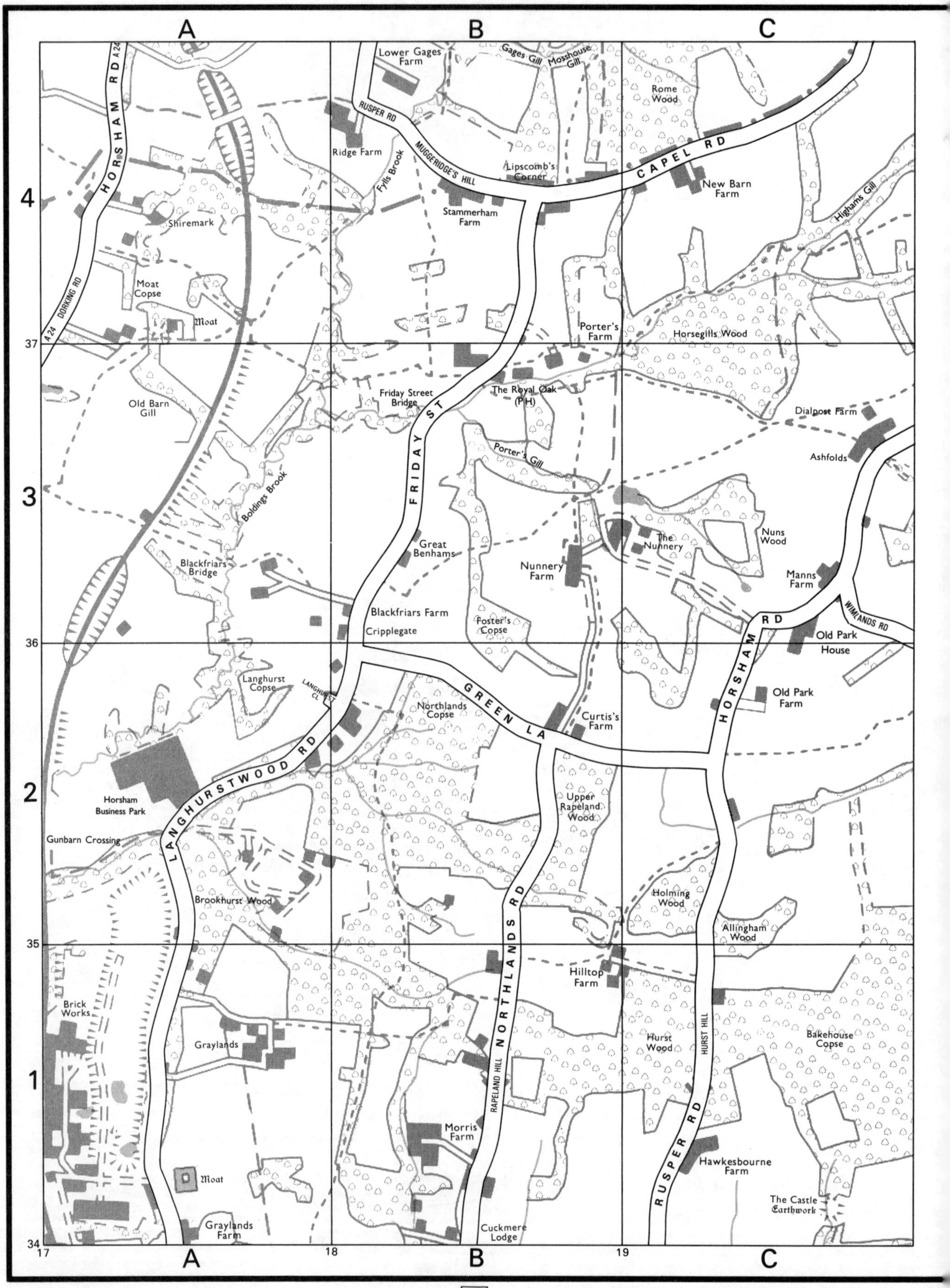

13

35

2
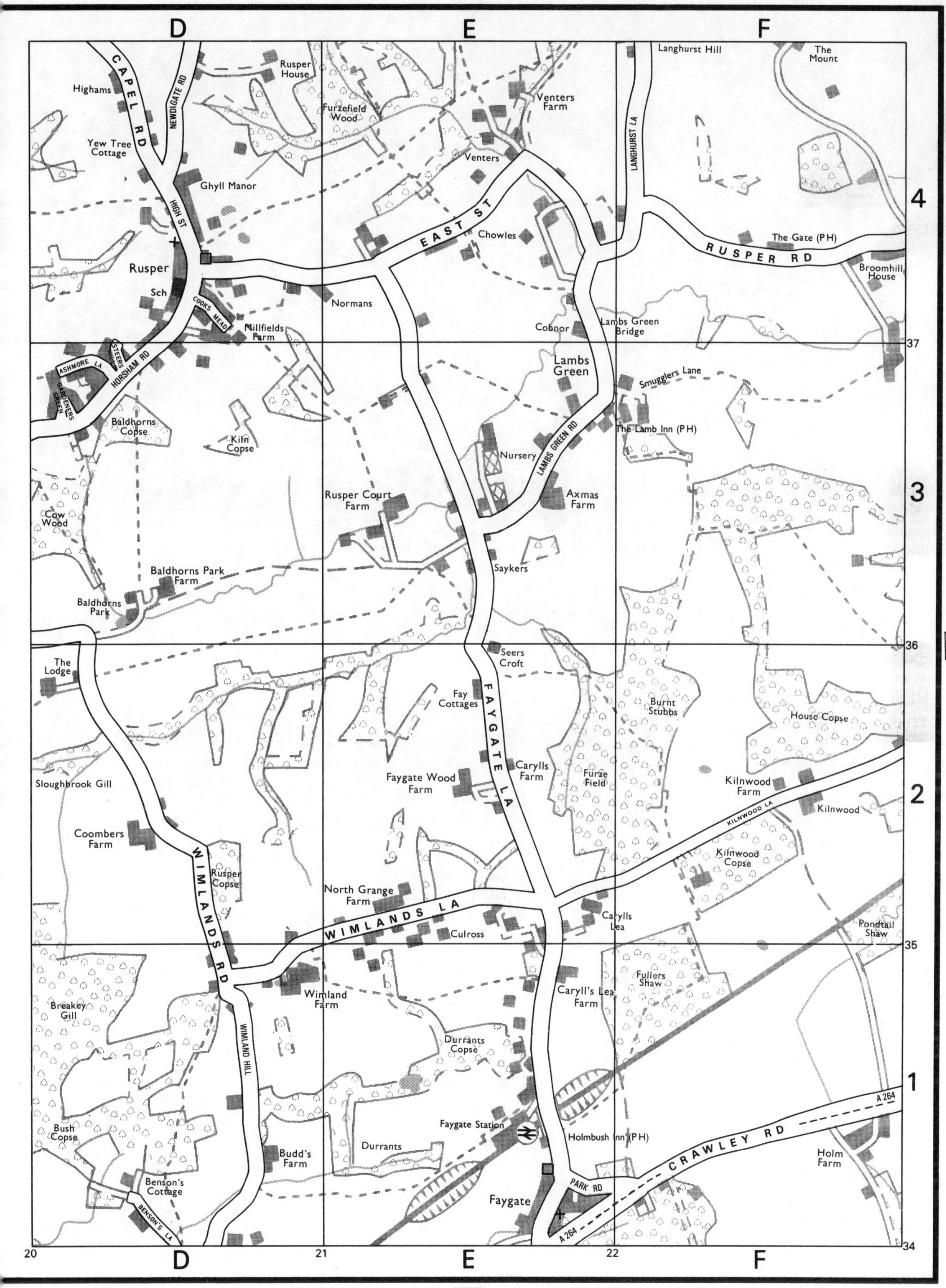
D
E
F
D
E
F
4
3
2
1
37
36
35
34
20
21
22
Langhurst Hill
The Mount
Rusper House
Highams
Venters Farm
Furzefield Wood
CAPEL RD
NEWDIGATE RD
Yew Tree Cottage
LANGHURST LA
Venters
Ghyll Manor
HIGH ST
EAST ST
Chowles
The Gate (PH)
RUSPER RD
Rusper
Broomhill House
Sch
COOKS MEAD
Normans
Millfields Farm
Cobnor
Lambs Green Bridge
ASHMORE LA
STEERS HILL
HORSHAM RD
GARDENERS GREEN
Lambs Green
Smugglers Lane
LAMBS GREEN RD
The Lamb Inn (PH)
Baldhorns Copse
Kiln Copse
Nursery
Rusper Court Farm
Axmas Farm
Cow Wood
Saykers
Baldhorns Park Farm
Baldhorns Park
The Lodge
Seers Croft
Fay Cottages
FAYGATE LA
Burnt Stubbs
House Copse
Carylls Farm
Faygate Wood Farm
Furze Field
Sloughbrook Gill
Kilnwood Farm
Kilnwood
KILNWOOD LA
Coombers Farm
Kilnwood Copse
WIMLANDS RD
Rusper Copse
North Grange Farm
WIMLANDS LA
Carylls Lea
Culross
Pondtail Shaw
Fullers Shaw
Wimland Farm
Caryll's Lea Farm
Breakey Gill
WIMLAND HILL
Durrants Copse
A 264
Faygate Station
Holmbush Inn (PH)
CRAWLEY RD
Bush Copse
Durrants
Budd's Farm
Holm Farm
Benson's Cottage
PARK RD
BENSON'S LA
Faygate
A 264
16
36

3

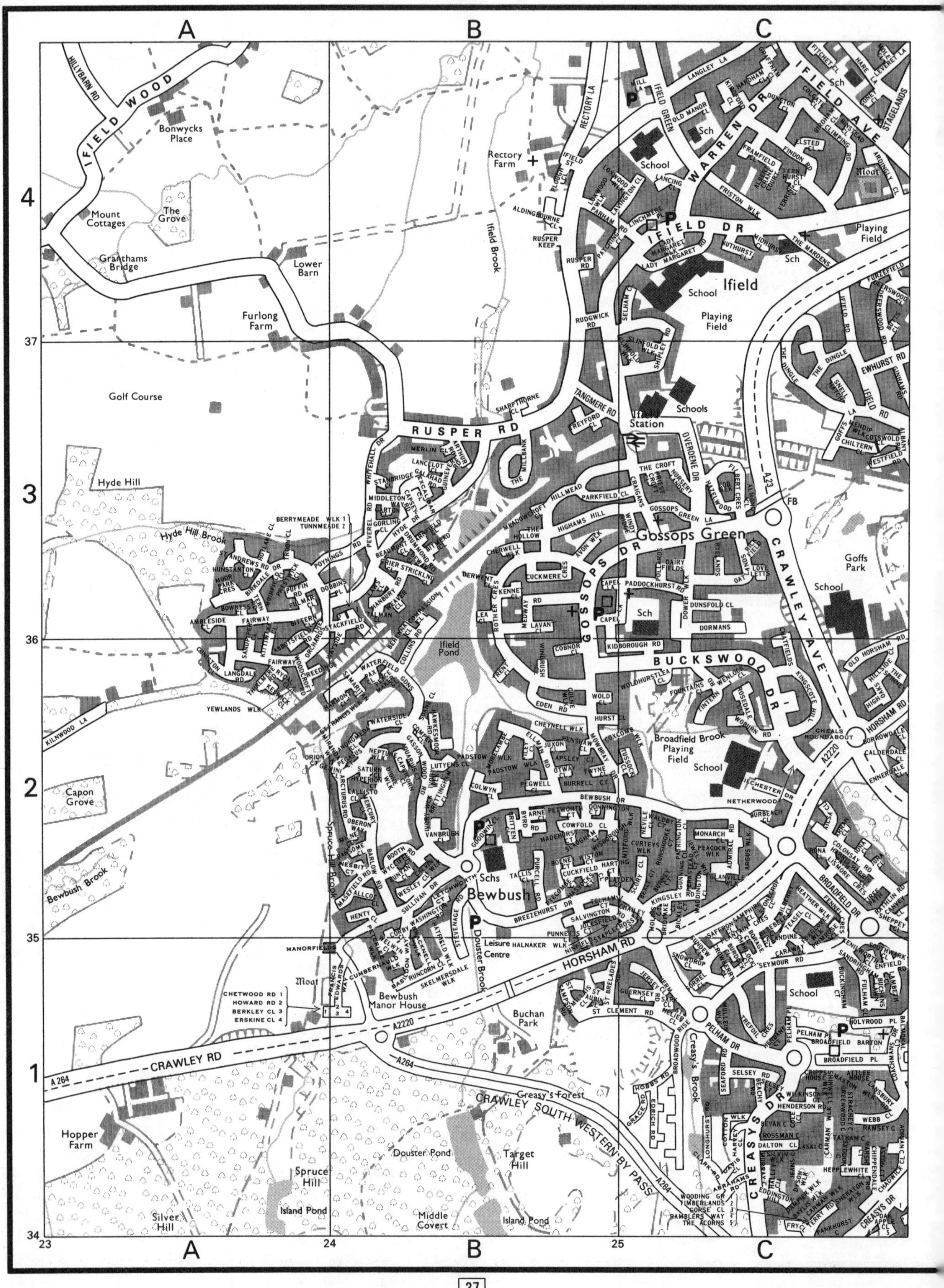
A
B
C
4
3
2
1
37
36
35
34
23
24
25
IFIELD WOOD
HILLYBARN RD
Bonwycks Place
Mount Cottages
The Grove
Granthams Bridge
Lower Barn
Furlong Farm
Rectory Farm
Ifield Brook
Golf Course
RUSPER RD
Hyde Hill
Hyde Hill Brook
Ifield Pond
Ifield Station
Ifield
IFIELD DR
IFIELD AVE
WARREN DR
School
Schools
Playing Field
Gossops Green
GOSSOPS DR
BUCKSWOOD DR
CRAWLEY AVE
Goffs Park
Broadfield Brook Playing Field
CHEALS ROUNDABOUT
HORSHAM RD
Capon Grove
Bewbush Brook
Spruce Hill Brook
Bewbush
Leisure Centre
Douster Brook
Bewbush Manor House
Moat
Buchan Park
Creasy's Brook
CRAWLEY RD
A 264
A2220
A23
Greasy's Forest
CRAWLEY SOUTH WESTERN BY PASS
Hopper Farm
Douster Pond
Target Hill
Spruce Hill
Island Pond
Middle Covert
Silver Hill
CREASYS DR
PELHAM DR
BROADFIELD DR
KILNWOOD LA
YEWLANDS WLK

15

37

4

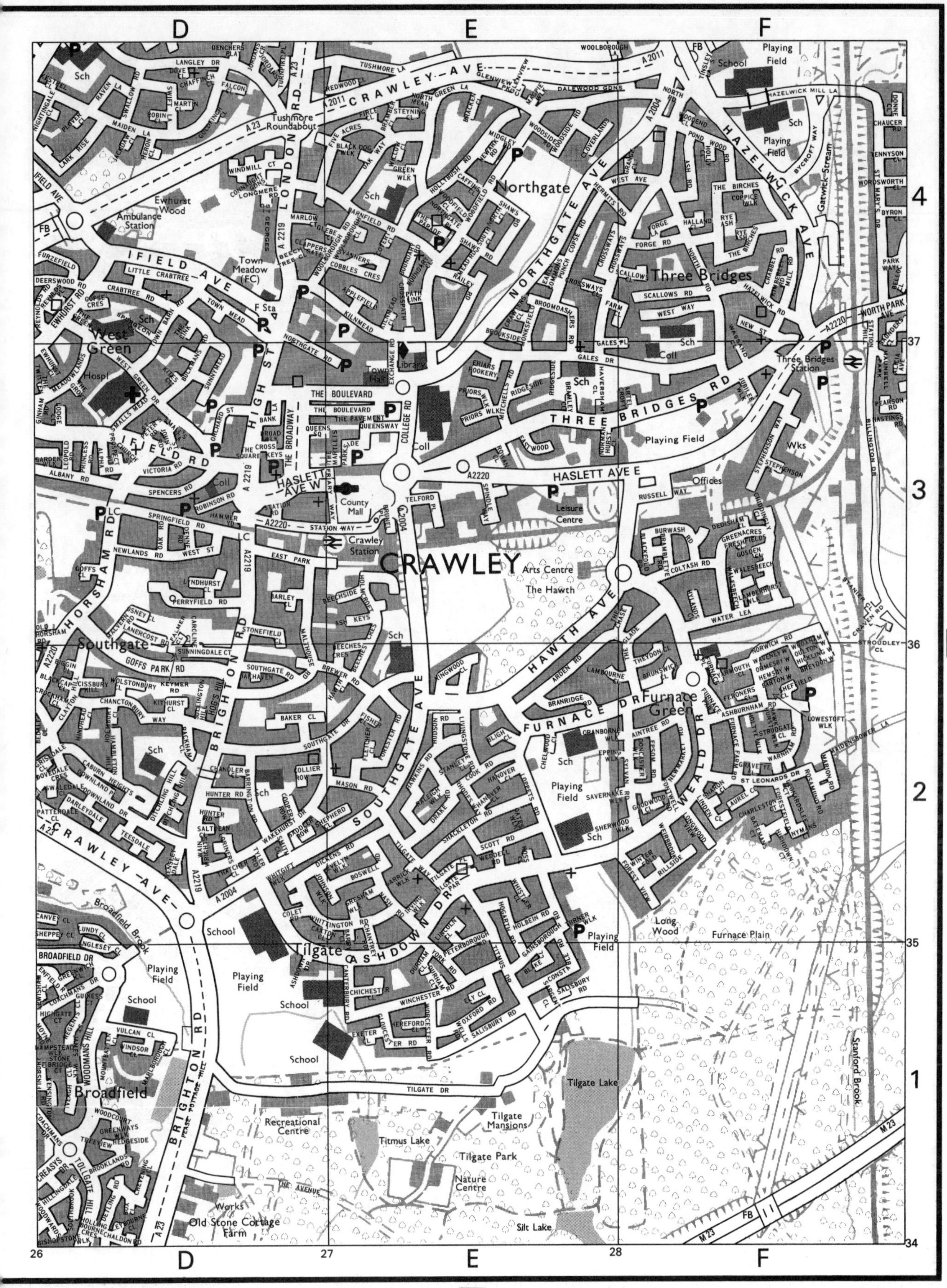

D
E
F
4
3
2
1
37
36
35
34
26
27
28
CRAWLEY
Northgate
Three Bridges
West Green
Southgate
Furnace Green
Tilgate
Broadfield
Tushmore Roundabout
Ewhurst Wood
Ambulance Station
Town Meadow (FC)
F Sta
Library
Town Hall
Coll
County Mall
Crawley Station
Three Bridges Station
Leisure Centre
Arts Centre
The Hawth
Playing Field
Sch
School
Hospl
Offices
Wks
Long Wood
Furnace Plain
Tilgate Lake
Tilgate Mansions
Titmus Lake
Tilgate Park
Nature Centre
Silt Lake
Recreational Centre
Works
Old Stone Cottage Farm
Stanford Brook
Broadfield Brook
Gatwick Stream
CRAWLEY AVE
IFIELD AVE
IFIELD RD
LONDON RD
HIGH ST
NORTHGATE AVE
THREE BRIDGES RD
HASLETT AVE E
HASLETT AVE W
STATION WAY
HAZELWICK AVE
HAWTH AVE
SOUTHGATE AVE
FURNACE DR
WEALD DR
ASHDOWN DR
BRIGHTON RD
HORSHAM RD
TILGATE DR
THE BOULEVARD
THE BROADWAY
COLLEGE RD
A23
A2011
A2004
A2219
A2220
M23

18

38

5

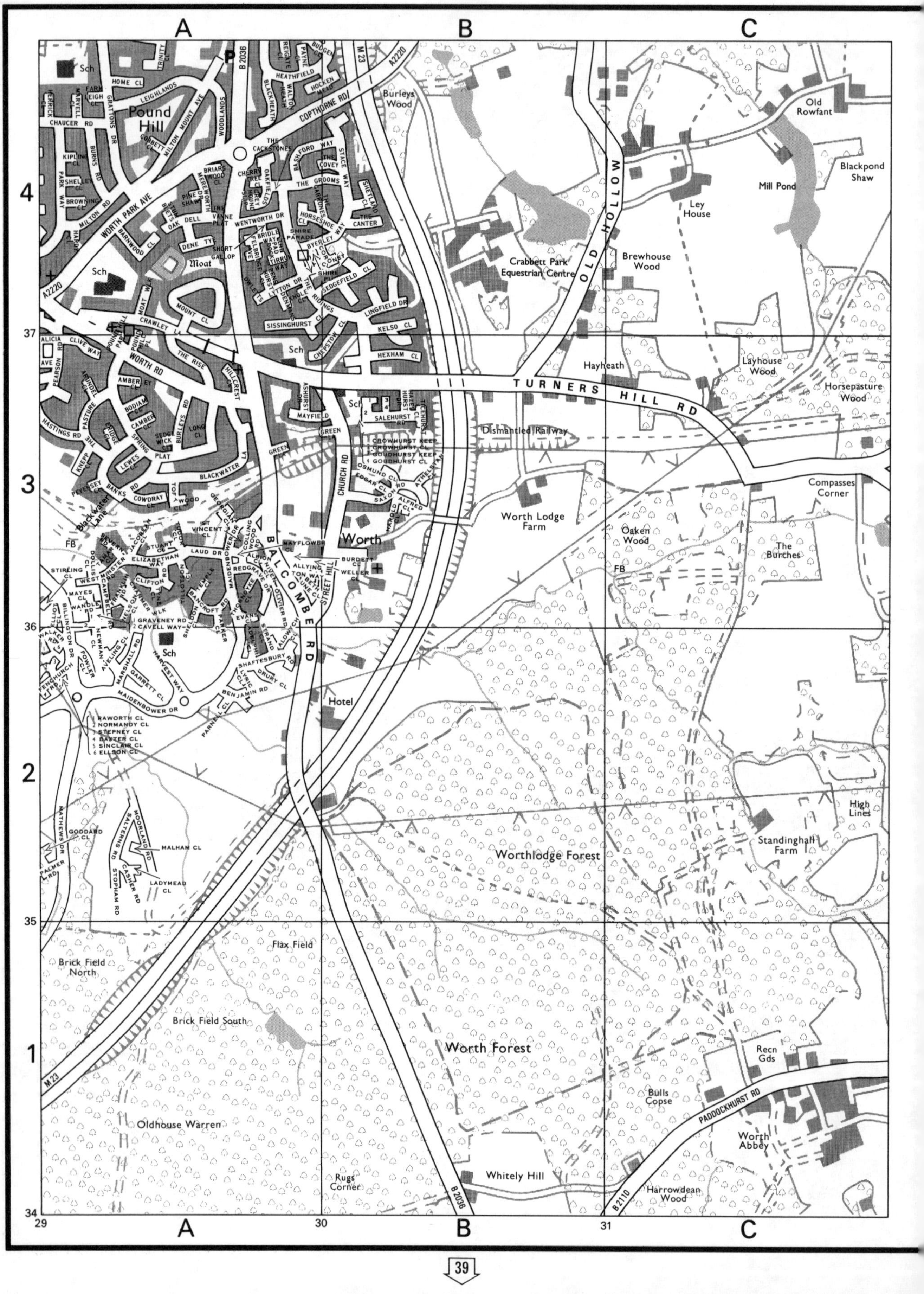
A
B
C
4
3
2
1
37
36
35
34
29
30
31
Pound Hill
Sch
Moat
Worth
Hotel
M 23
A2220
B 2036
B2110
COPTHORNE RD
WORTH PARK AVE
WORTH RD
CRAWLEY LA
BALCOMBE RD
CHURCH RD
STREET HILL
TURNERS HILL RD
OLD HOLLOW
PADDOCKHURST RD
MAIDENBOWER DR
BLACKWATER LA
Blackwater Lane
THE RISE
HILLCREST
FB
Burleys Wood
Crabbett Park Equestrian Centre
Brewhouse Wood
Ley House
Old Rowfant
Mill Pond
Blackpond Shaw
Hayheath
Layhouse Wood
Horsepasture Wood
Dismantled Railway
Compasses Corner
Worth Lodge Farm
Oaken Wood
The Burches
High Lines
Standinghall Farm
Worthlodge Forest
Worth Forest
Flax Field
Brick Field North
Brick Field South
Oldhouse Warren
Rugs Corner
Whitely Hill
Harrowdean Wood
Bulls Copse
Recn Gds
Worth Abbey
1 RAWORTH CL
2 NORMANDY CL
3 STEPNEY CL
4 BAXTER CL
5 SINCLAIR CL
6 ELLSON CL
1 GRAVENEY RD
2 CAVELL WAY
CROWHURST KEEP
CROWHURST CL
GOUDHURST KEEP
GOUDHURST CL
MALHAM CL
LADYMEAD CL
GODDARD CL
MOORLAND RD
STOPHAM RD
CASHER RD
SALTERNS RD
MATHEWS DR
PALMER RD

17

39

6
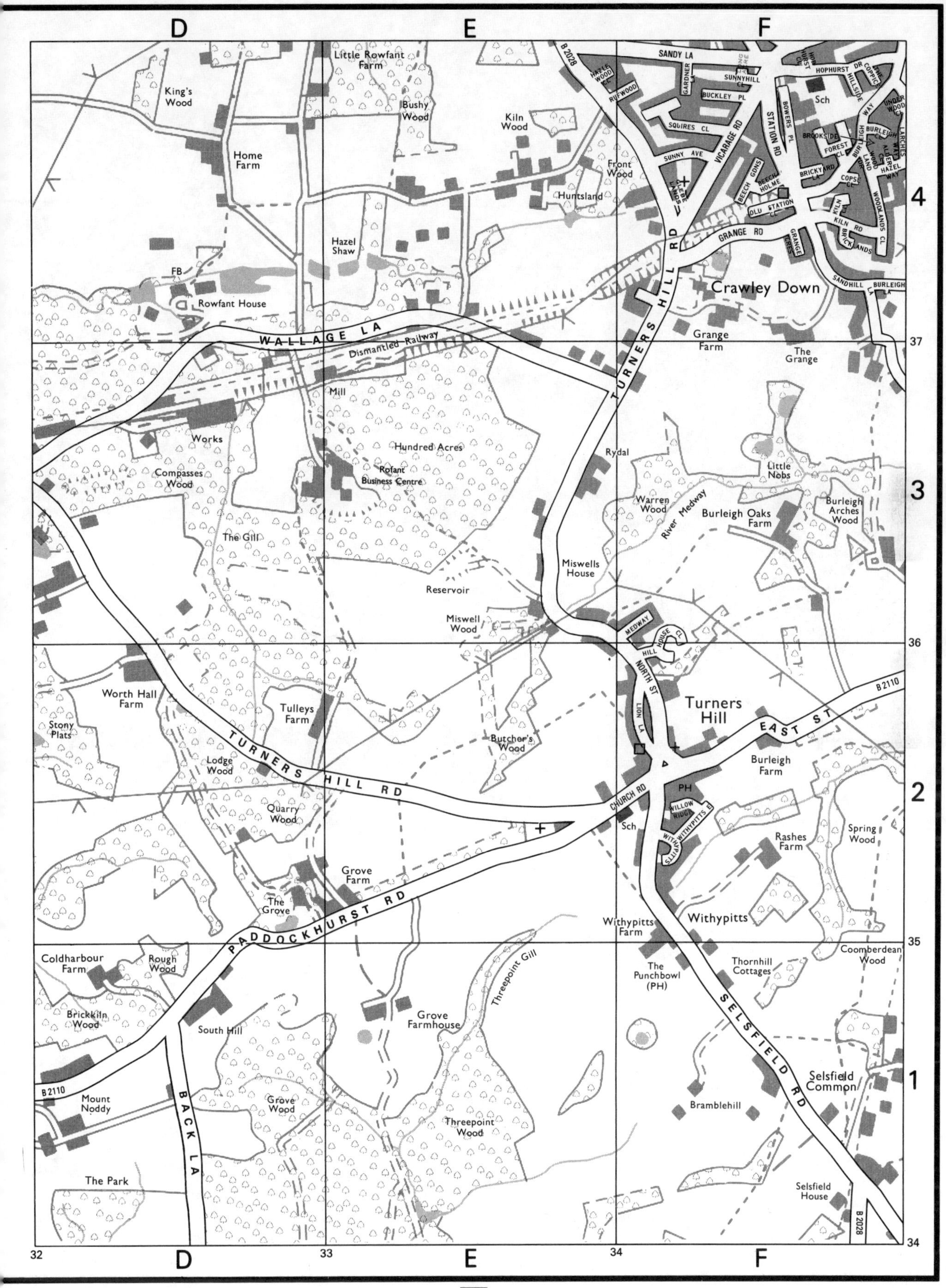

D
E
F
Little Rowfant Farm
King's Wood
Bushy Wood
Kiln Wood
Home Farm
Front Wood
Huntsland
Hazel Shaw
FB
Rowfant House
WALLAGE LA
Dismantled Railway
Mill
Works
Hundred Acres
Rofant Business Centre
Compasses Wood
The Gill
Reservoir
Miswell Wood
Miswells House
Rydal
Warren Wood
River Medway
Burleigh Oaks Farm
Little Nobs
Burleigh Arches Wood
Crawley Down
Grange Farm
The Grange
SANDY LA
Sch
STATION RD
VICARAGE RD
GRANGE RD
TURNERS HILL RD
B 2028
Worth Hall Farm
Stony Plats
Tulleys Farm
Lodge Wood
TURNERS HILL RD
Butcher's Wood
Turners Hill
EAST ST
NORTH ST
CHURCH RD
B2110
Burleigh Farm
PH
Sch
Quarry Wood
Grove Farm
The Grove
PADDOCKHURST RD
Rashes Farm
Spring Wood
Withypitts
Withypitts Farm
Coldharbour Farm
Rough Wood
Brickkiln Wood
South Hill
Grove Farmhouse
Threepoint Gill
The Punchbowl (PH)
Thornhill Cottages
Coomberdean Wood
SELSFIELD RD
Selsfield Common
Bramblehill
Mount Noddy
BACK LA
Grove Wood
Threepoint Wood
The Park
Selsfield House
4
3
2
1
37
36
35
34
32
33
34

20
40

7

19

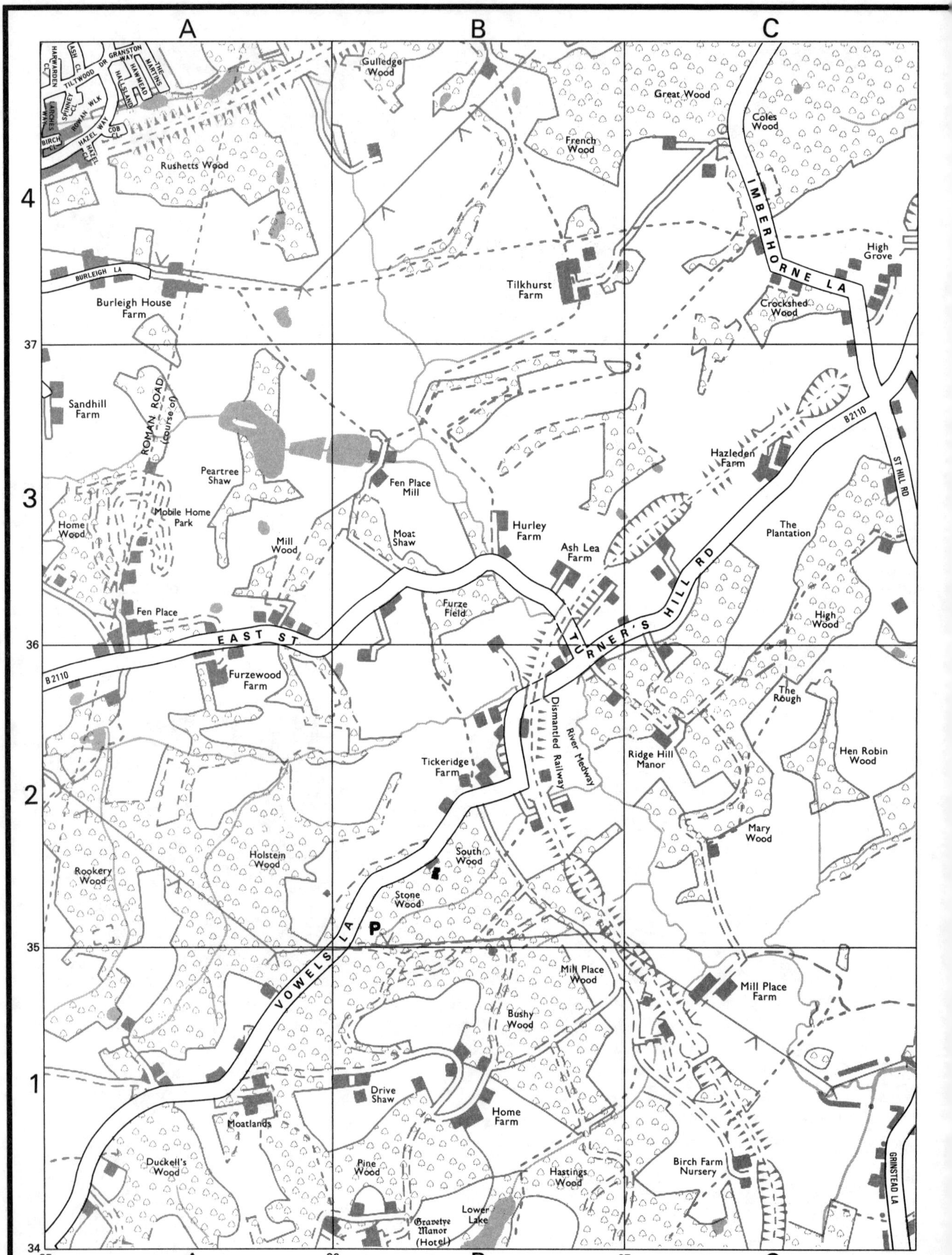
A
B
C
4
3
2
1
37
36
35
34
Gulledge Wood
Great Wood
Coles Wood
French Wood
Rushetts Wood
HARWARDEN CL
ASH CL
TILTWOOD DR
GRANSTON WAY
THE MARTINS
HAWMEAD
HALLSLAND
SPINNEY CL
ARCHES WAY
ROWAN WLK
BIRCH CL
HAZEL WAY
HAZEL CL
COB CL
IMBERHORNE LA
High Grove
BURLEIGH LA
Burleigh House Farm
Tilkhurst Farm
Crockshed Wood
Sandhill Farm
ROMAN ROAD (course of)
Peartree Shaw
Fen Place Mill
B2110
Hazleden Farm
ST HILL RD
Mobile Home Park
Home Wood
Mill Wood
Moat Shaw
Hurley Farm
Ash Lea Farm
The Plantation
Fen Place
Furze Field
TURNER'S HILL RD
High Wood
EAST ST
Furzewood Farm
The Rough
Dismantled Railway
River Medway
Ridge Hill Manor
Hen Robin Wood
Tickeridge Farm
Mary Wood
Rookery Wood
Holstein Wood
South Wood
Stone Wood
VOWELS LA
P
Mill Place Wood
Mill Place Farm
Bushy Wood
Drive Shaw
Home Farm
Moatlands
Duckell's Wood
Pine Wood
Hastings Wood
Birch Farm Nursery
GRINSTEAD LA
Lower Lake
Gravetye Manor (Hotel)
35
36
37
A
B
C

41

8

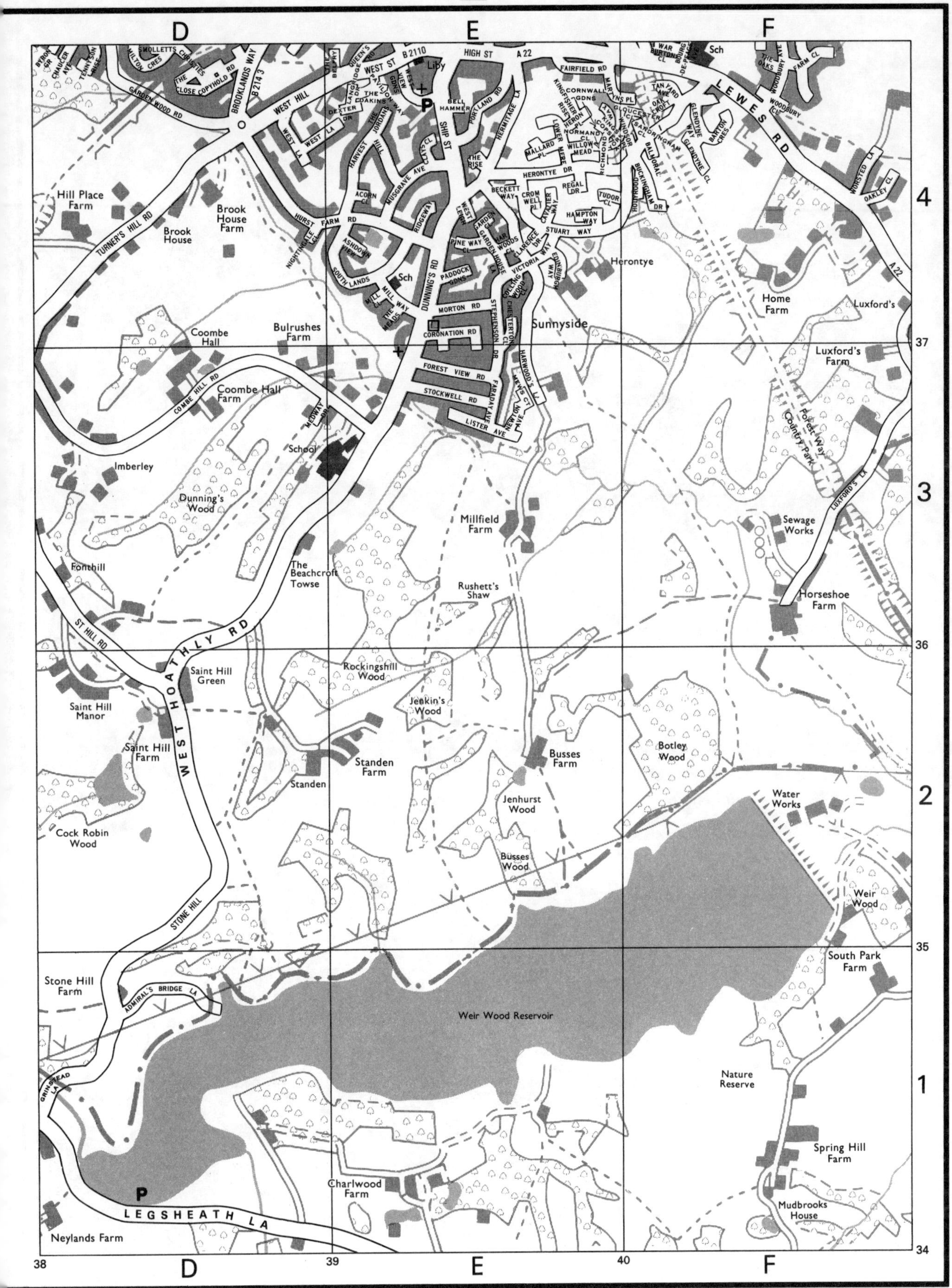

D
E
F
HIGH ST
A 22
WEST ST
B 2110
Liby
FAIRFIELD RD
Sch
LEWES RD
BROOKLANDS WAY
B 2143
WEST HILL
GARDEN WOOD RD
WEST LA
HARVEST HILL
MUSGRAVE AVE
SHIP ST
HERMITAGE LA
HERONTYE DR
STUART WAY
Hill Place Farm
Brook House Farm
Brook House
TURNER'S HILL RD
HURST FARM RD
RIDGEWAY
SOUTH LANDS
ASHDOWN VIEW
NIGHTINGALE CL
Sch
MILL WAY
DUNNING'S RD
MORTON RD
CORONATION RD
FOREST VIEW RD
STOCKWELL RD
LISTER AVE
FARADAY AVE
STEPHENSON DR
VICTORIA WAY
HARWOOD'S LA
Herontye
Home Farm
Luxford's
Luxford's Farm
A 22
4
Coombe Hall
Bulrushes Farm
Sunnyside
Coombe Hall Farm
COMBE HILL RD
MEDWAY DR
School
Imberley
Dunning's Wood
Forest Way Country Park
LUXFORD'S LA
3
Millfield Farm
Sewage Works
Fonthill
The Beachcroft Towse
Rushett's Shaw
Horseshoe Farm
ST HILL RD
WEST HOATHLY RD
Saint Hill Green
Rockingshill Wood
Saint Hill Manor
Jenkin's Wood
Saint Hill Farm
Standen Farm
Standen
Busses Farm
Botley Wood
Water Works
2
Cock Robin Wood
Jenhurst Wood
Busses Wood
Weir Wood
STONE HILL
Stone Hill Farm
ADMIRAL'S BRIDGE LA
South Park Farm
Weir Wood Reservoir
Nature Reserve
1
GRINSTEAD LA
Spring Hill Farm
Charlwood Farm
P
LEGSHEATH LA
Mudbrooks House
Neylands Farm
38
39
40
34
35
36
37
D
E
F

22

42

9

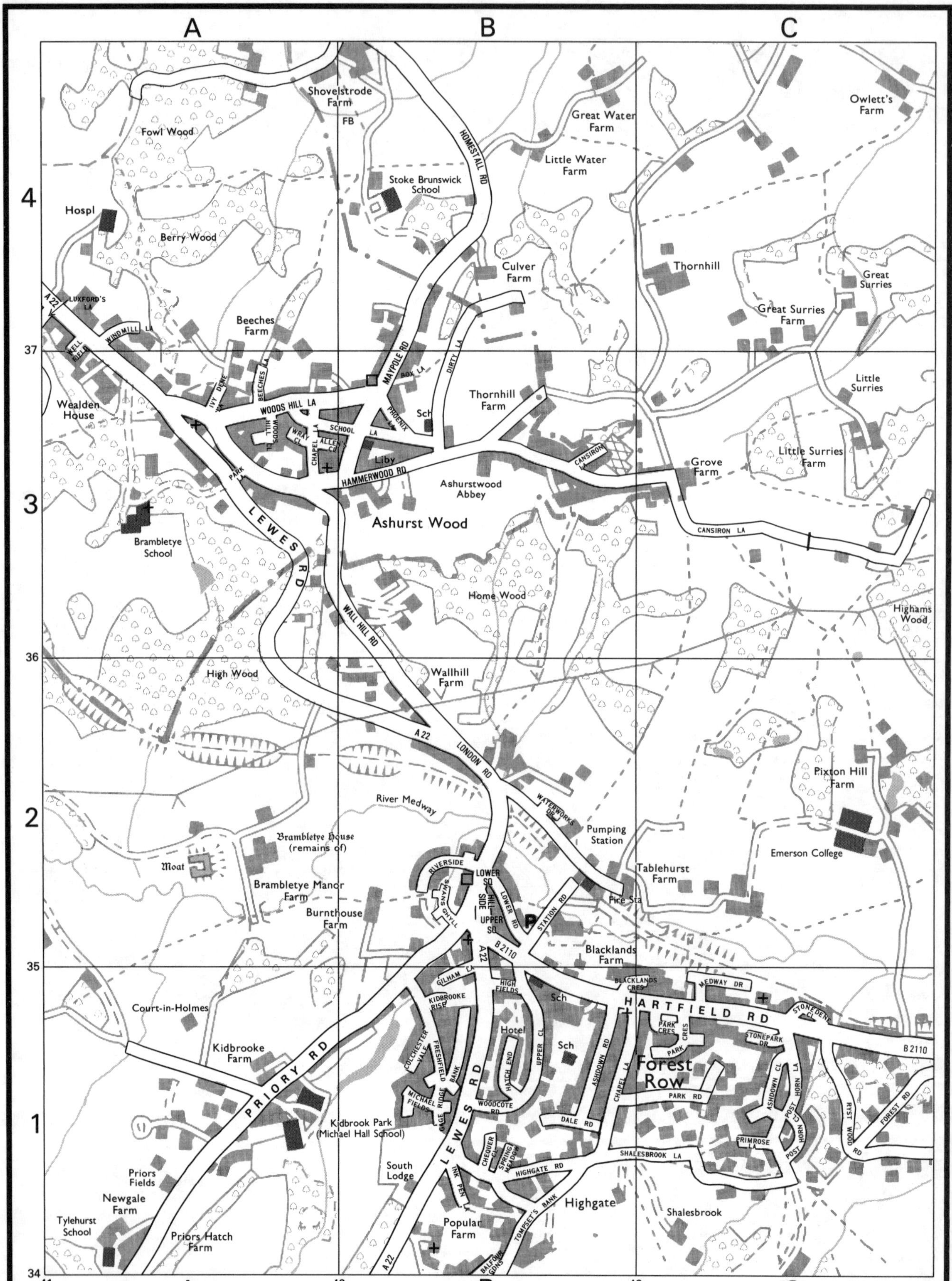

21

not continued, see key diagram

not continued, see key diagram

not continued, see key diagram

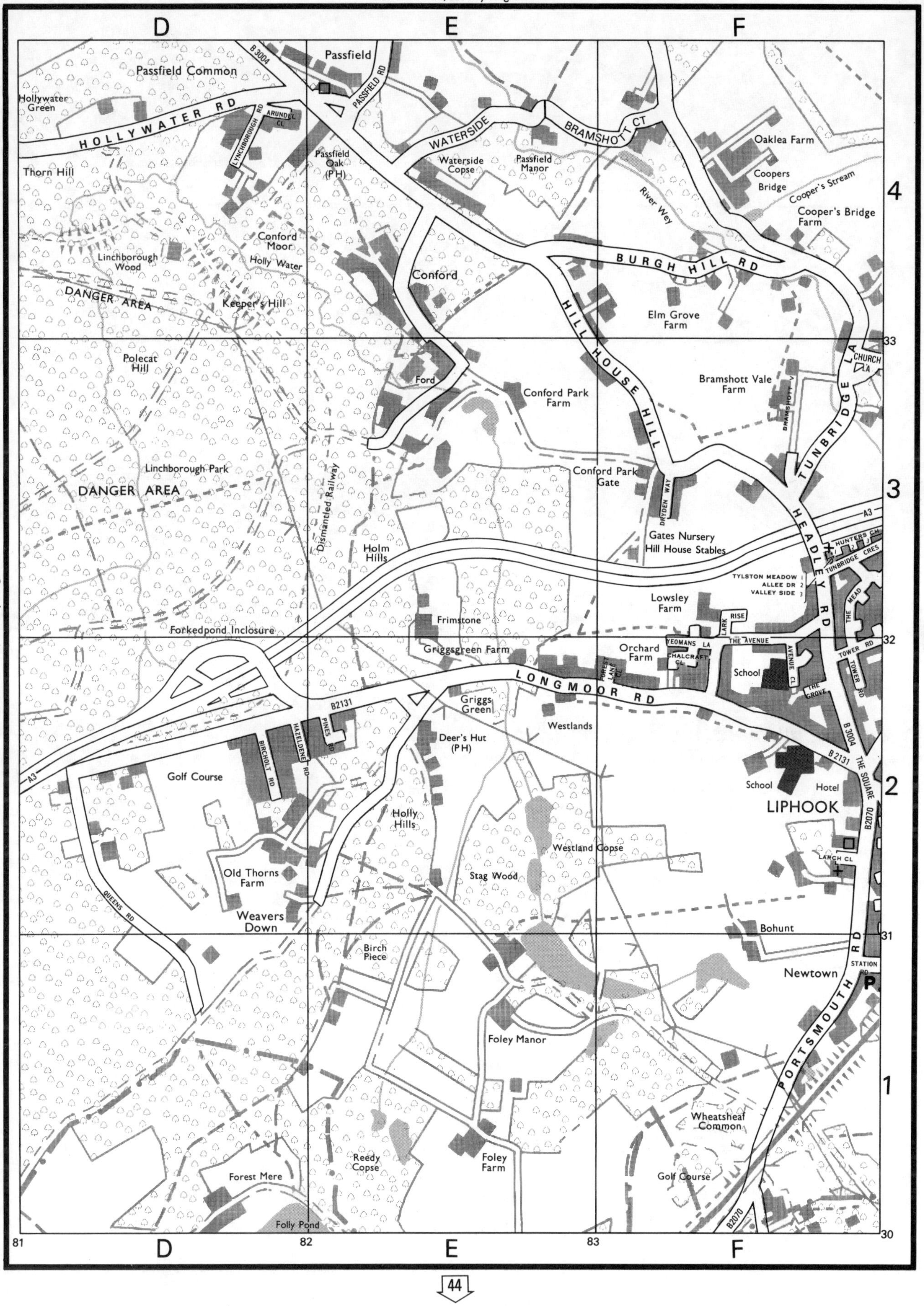

24

not continued, see key diagram

44

not continued, see key diagram

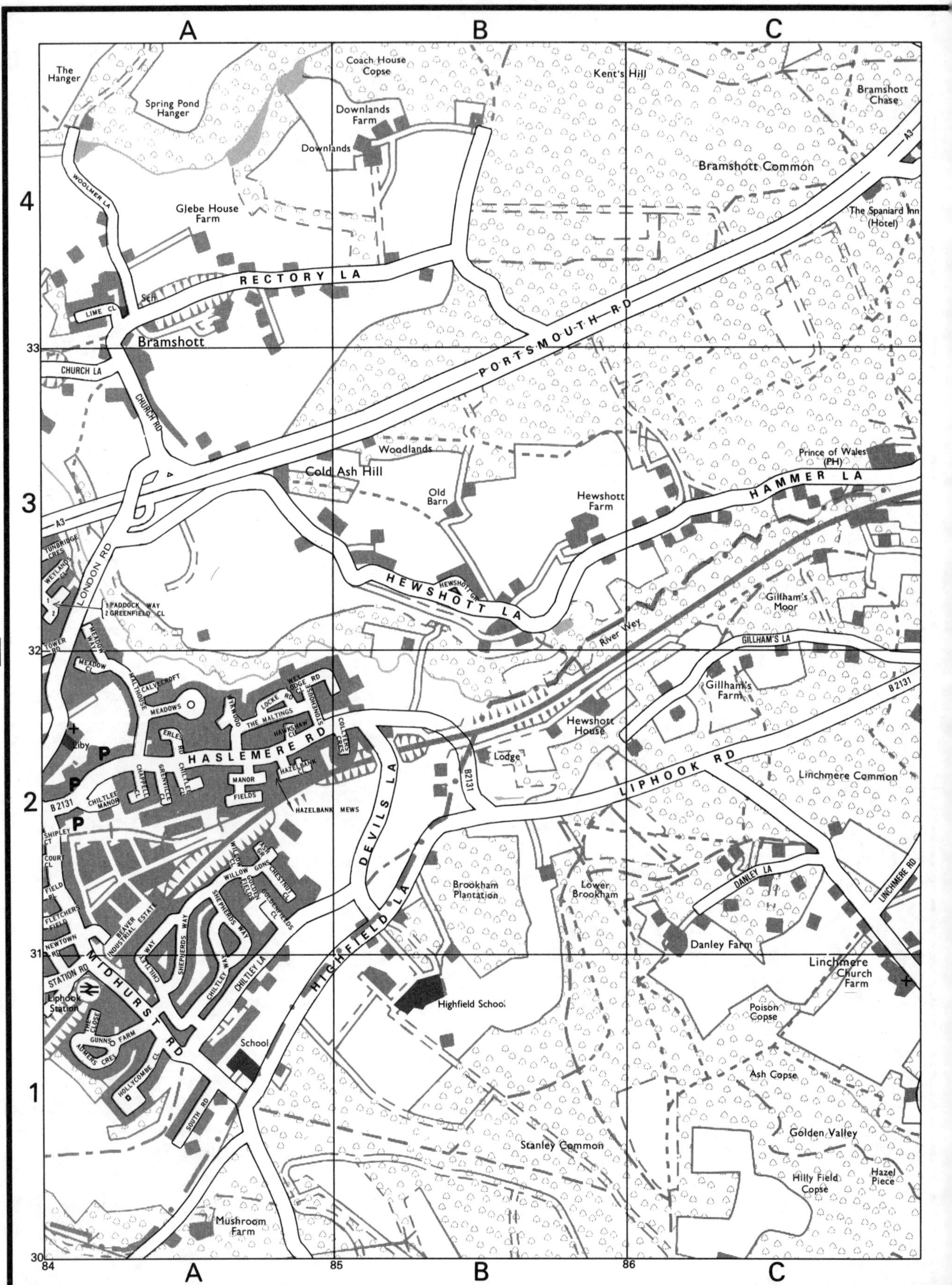

23

not continued, see key diagram

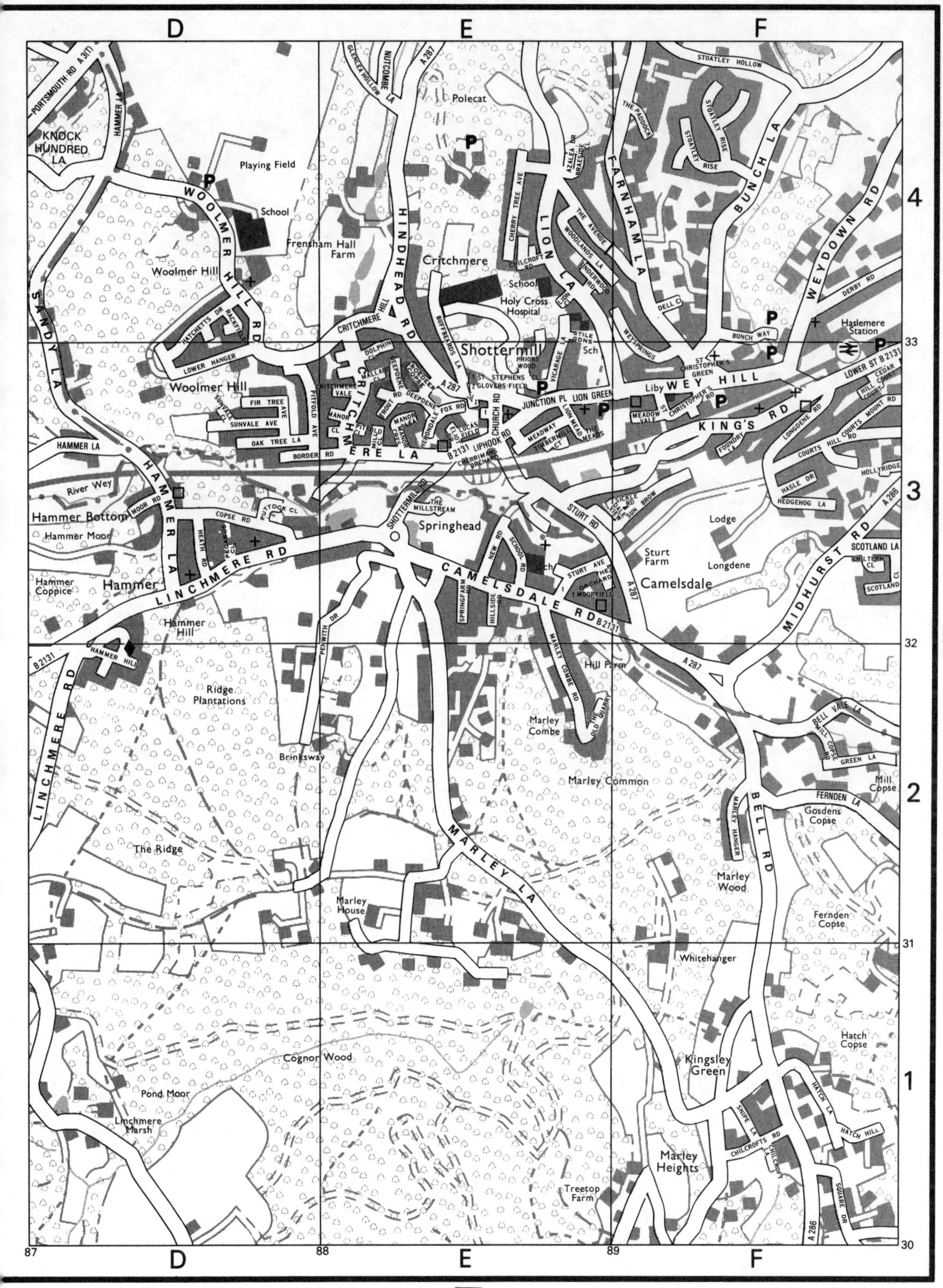

26

46

not continued, see key diagram

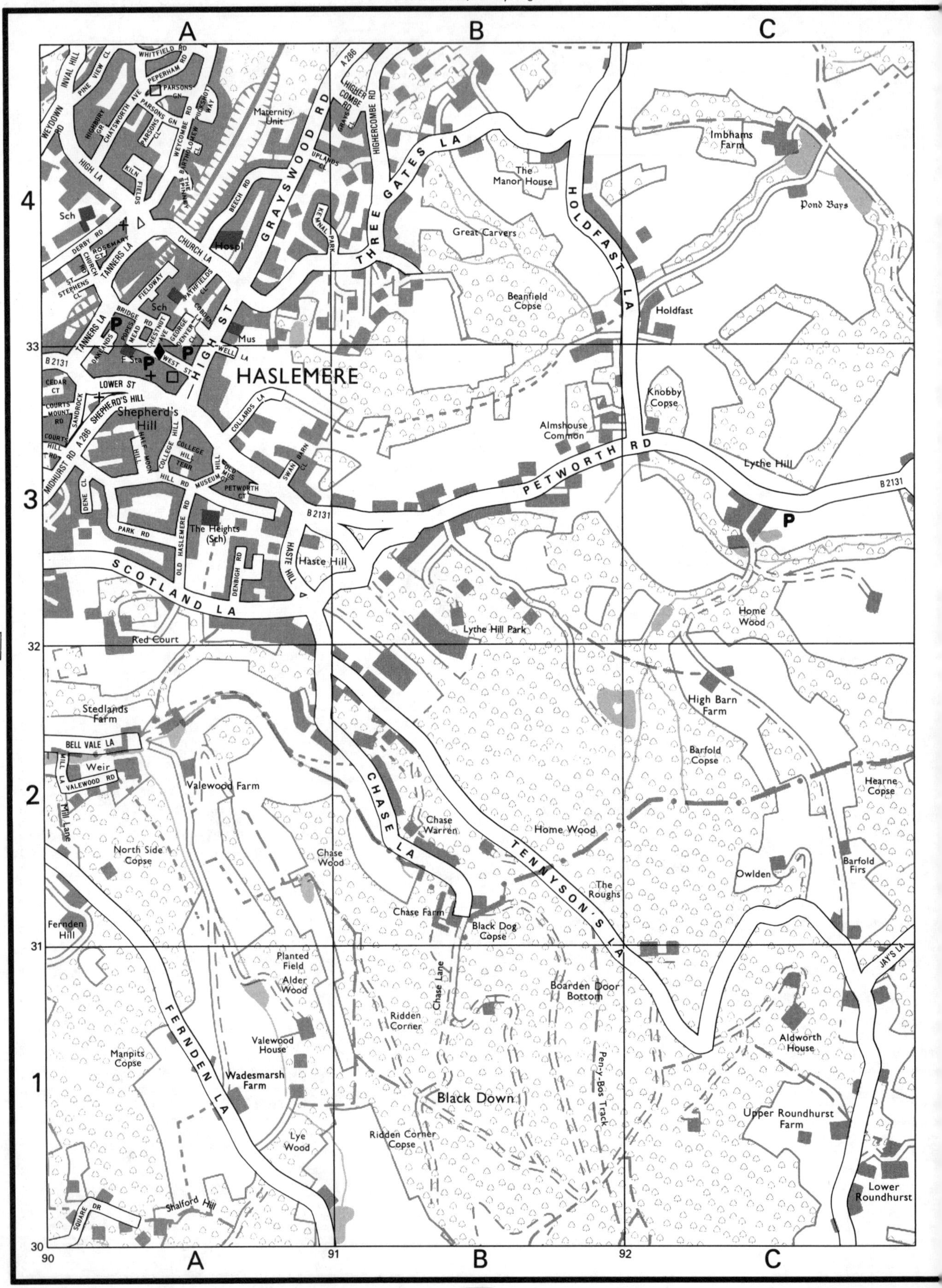

25

47

not continued, see key diagram

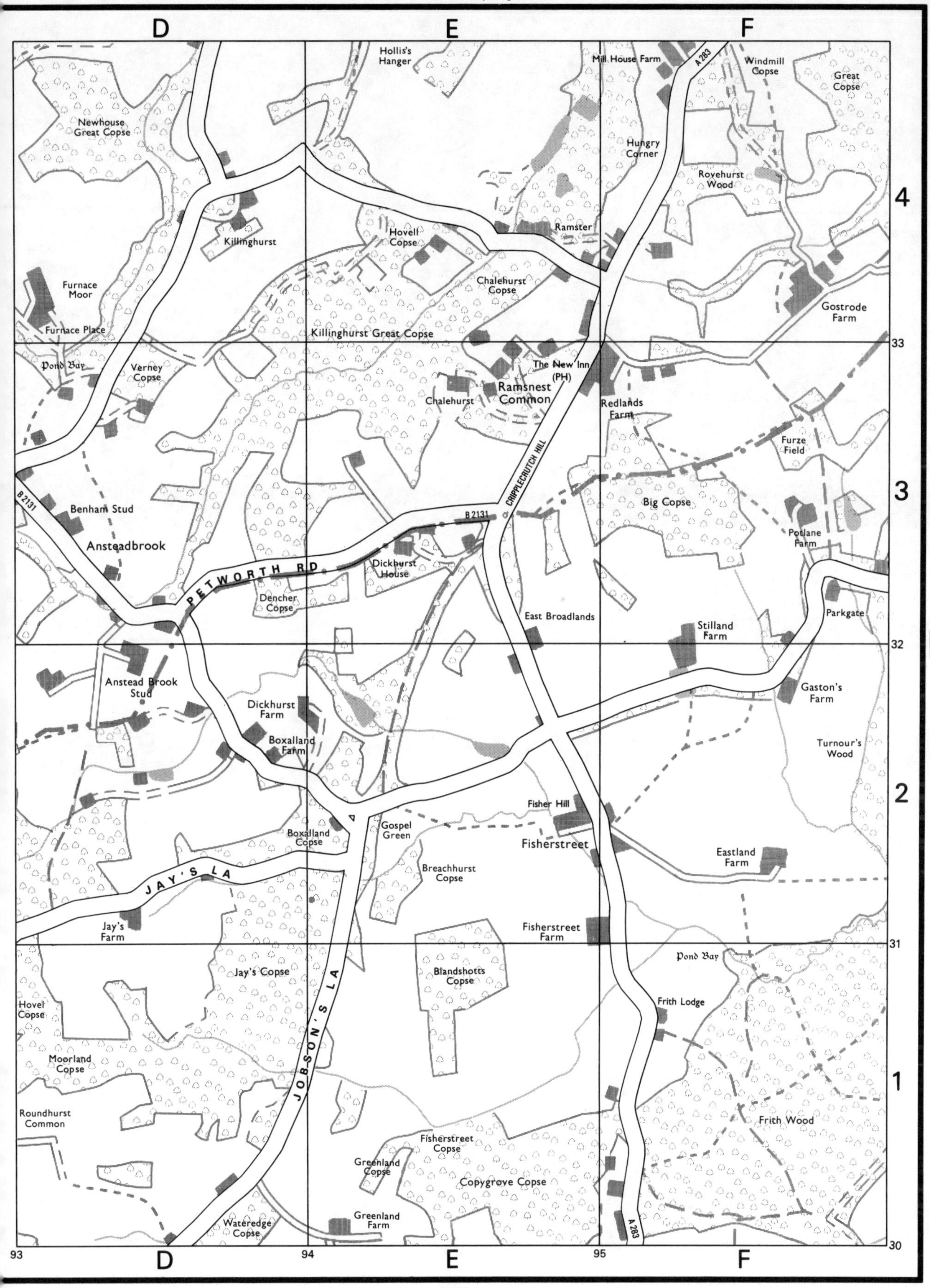

28

48

not continued, see key diagram

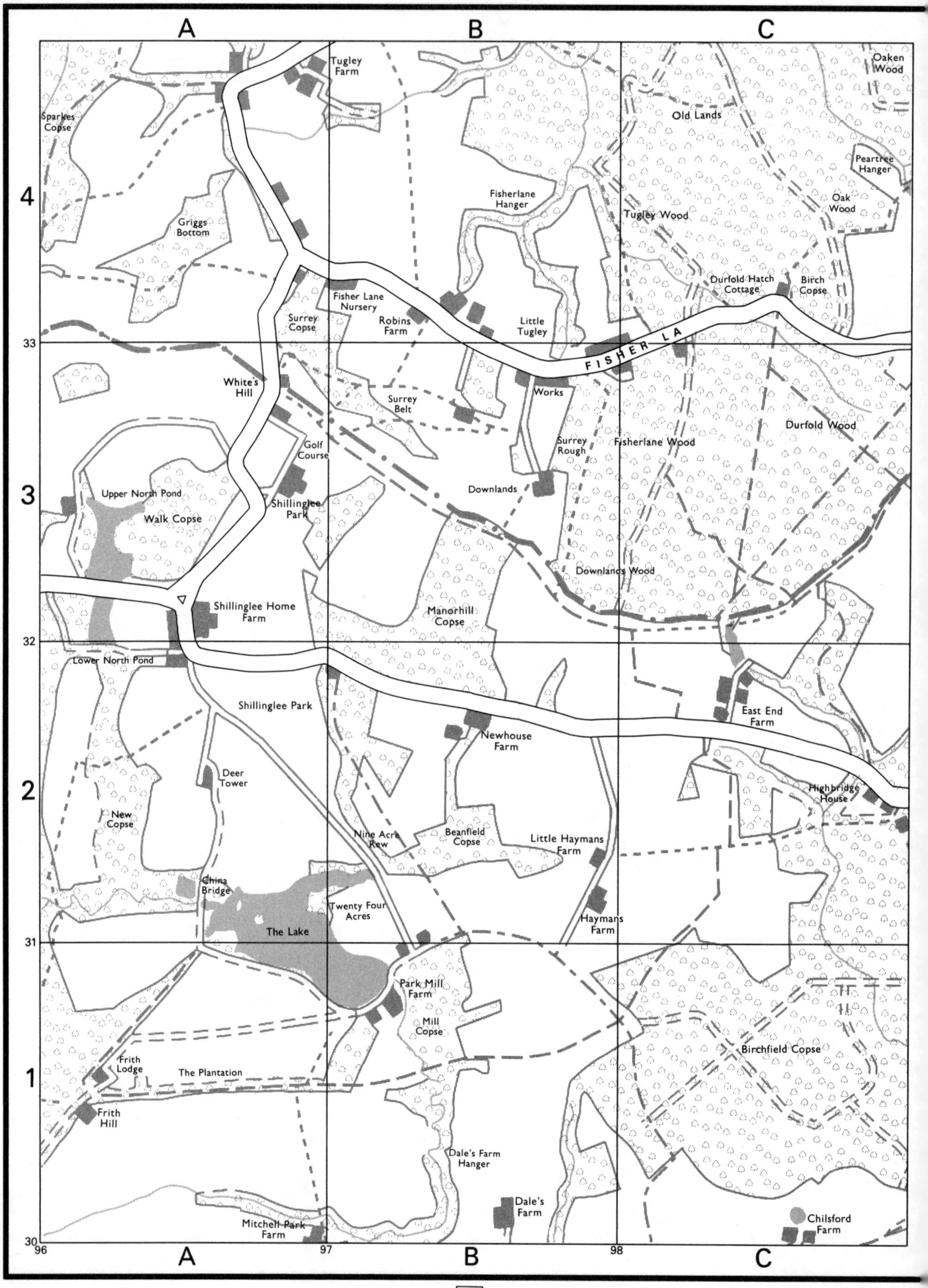

27

49

not continued, see key diagram

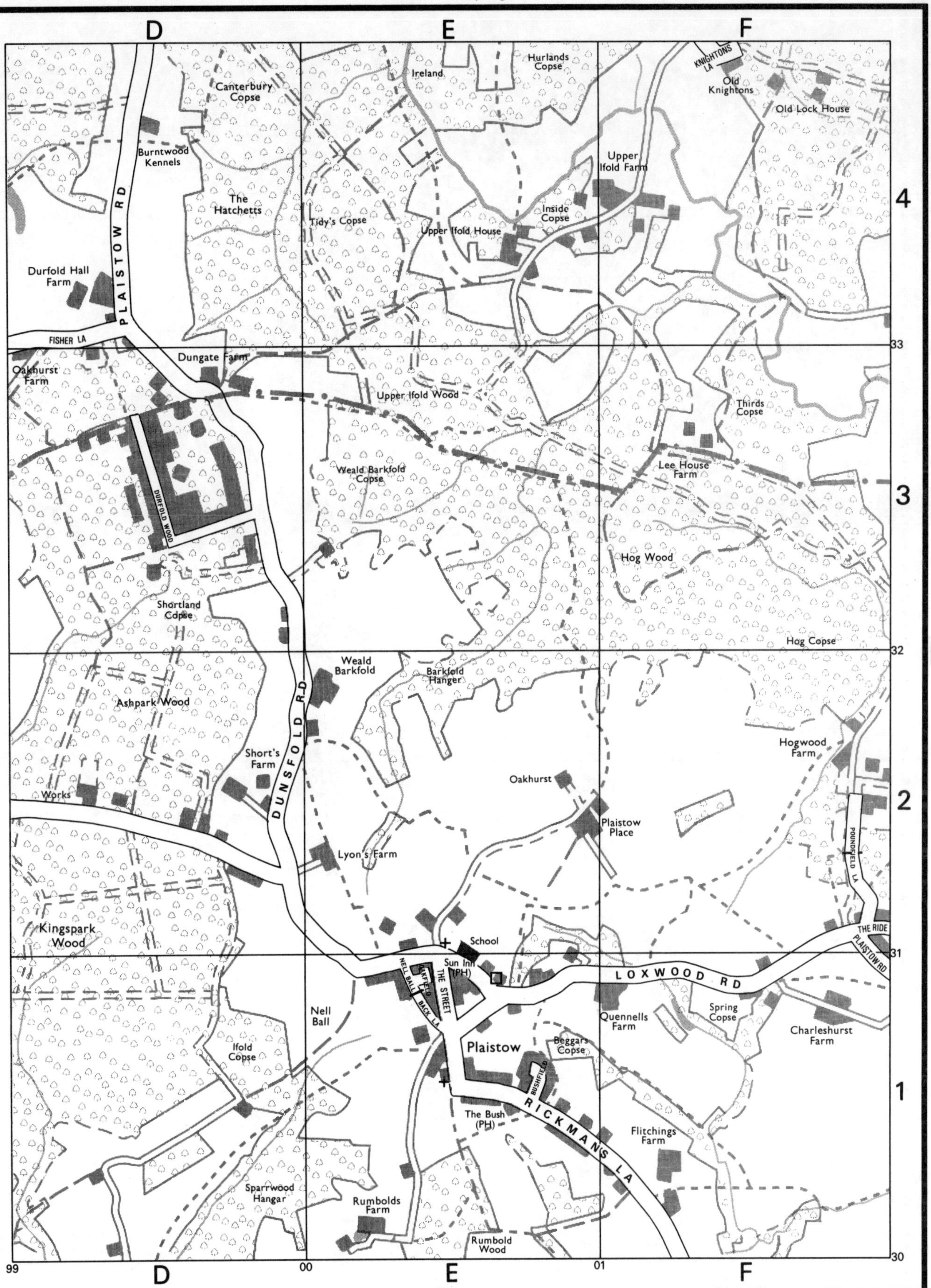

30

50

not continued, see key diagram

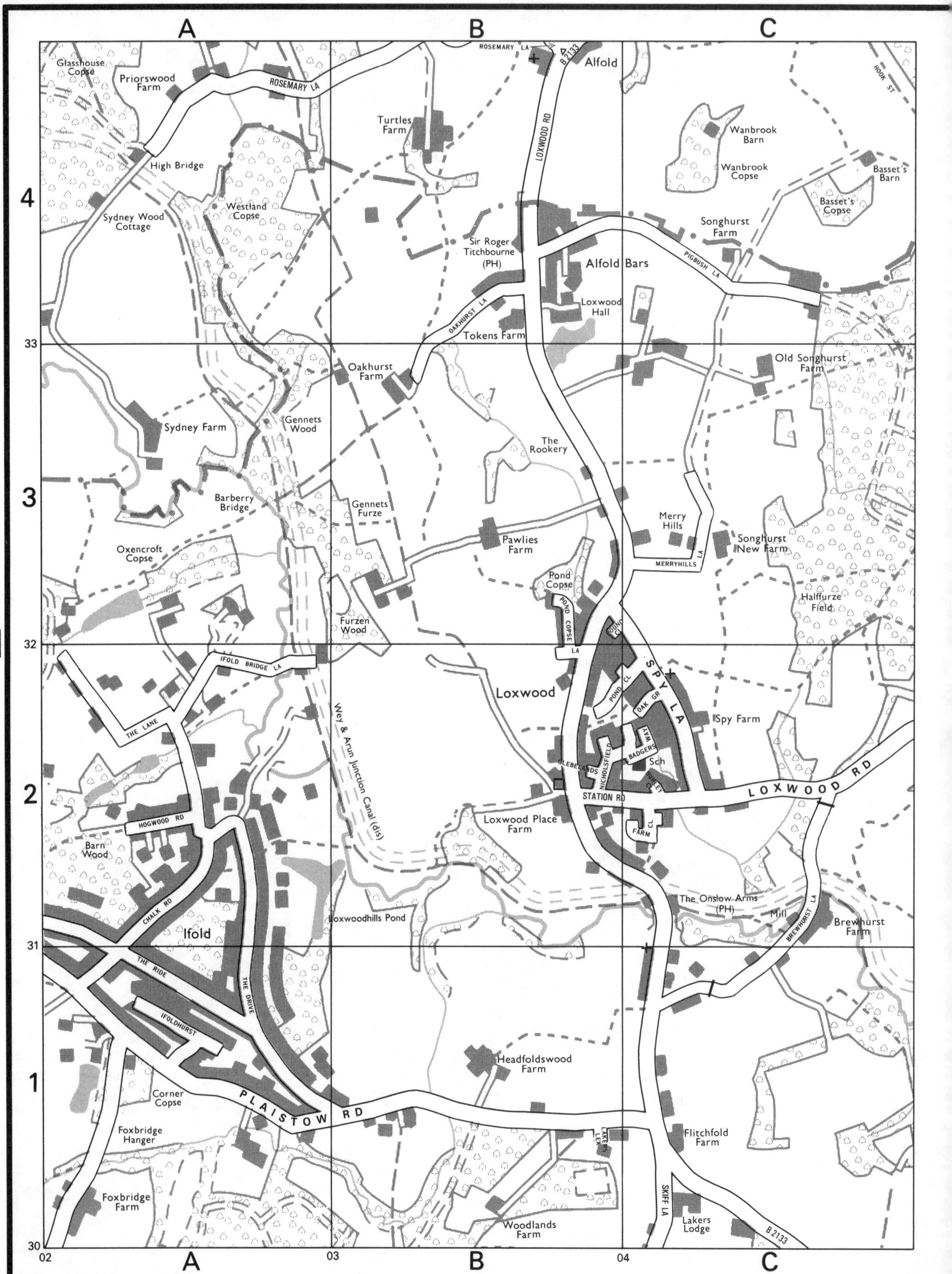

51

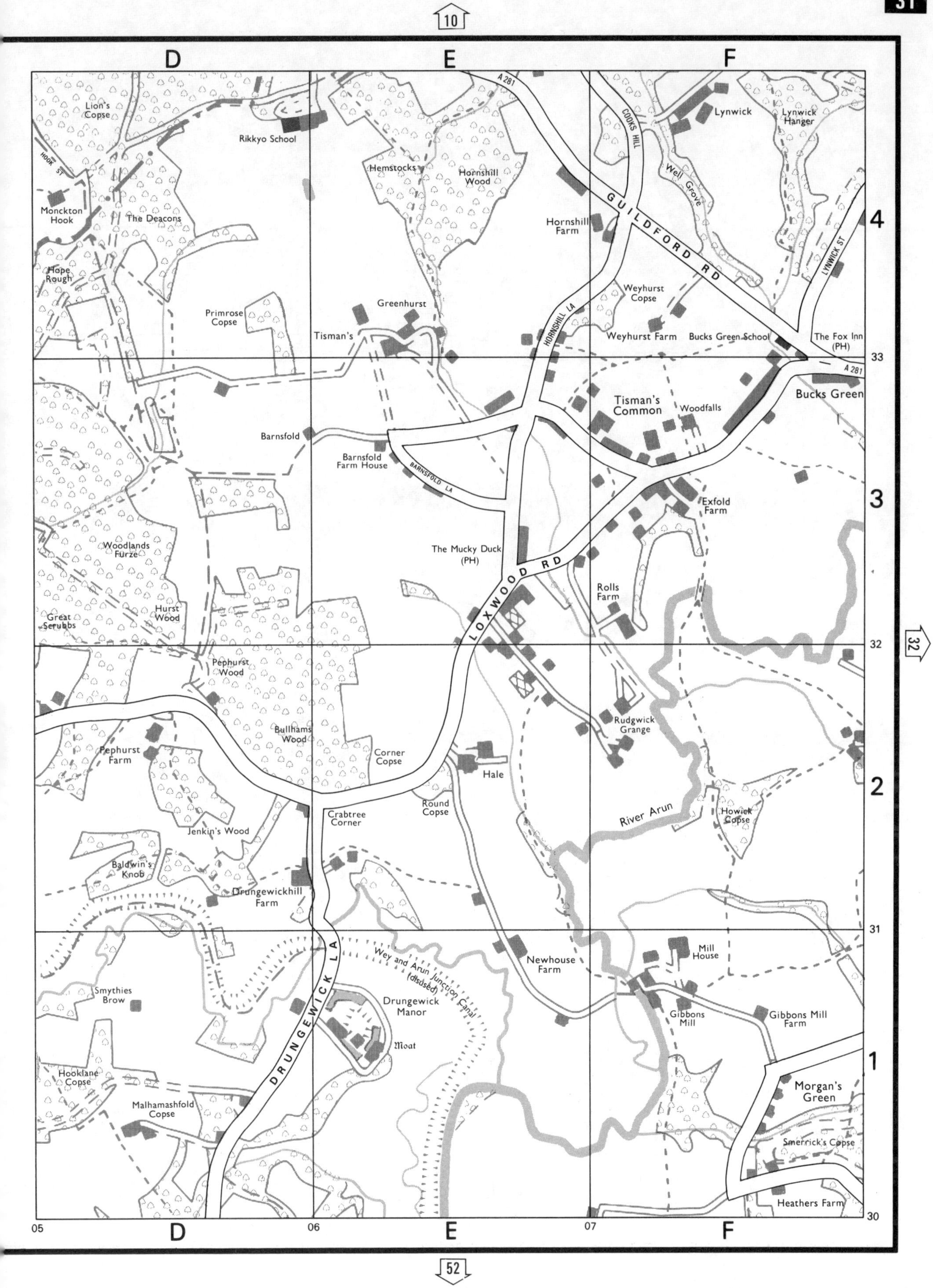
10
D
E
F
Lion's Copse
Rikkyo School
Hook St
Monckton Hook
The Deacons
Hope Rough
Primrose Copse
Hemstocks
Hornshill Wood
A 281
Cooks Hill
Lynwick
Lynwick Hanger
Well Grove
Guildford Rd
Hornshill Farm
Lynwick St
Greenhurst
Tisman's
Hornshill La
Weyhurst Copse
Weyhurst Farm
Bucks Green School
The Fox Inn (PH)
Bucks Green
Tisman's Common
Woodfalls
Barnsfold
Barnsfold Farm House
Barnsfold La
Exfold Farm
Woodlands Furze
The Mucky Duck (PH)
Loxwood Rd
Rolls Farm
Hurst Wood
Great Scrubbs
Pephurst Wood
Rudgwick Grange
Bullhams Wood
Pephurst Farm
Corner Copse
Hale
Crabtree Corner
Round Copse
River Arun
Howick Copse
Jenkin's Wood
Baldwin's Knob
Drungewickhill Farm
Mill House
Newhouse Farm
Wey and Arun Junction Canal (disused)
Smythies Brow
Drungewick Manor
Drungewick La
Gibbons Mill
Gibbons Mill Farm
Moat
Hooklane Copse
Morgan's Green
Malhamashfold Copse
Smerrick's Copse
Heathers Farm
4
3
2
1
33
32
31
30
05
06
07
32
52

11

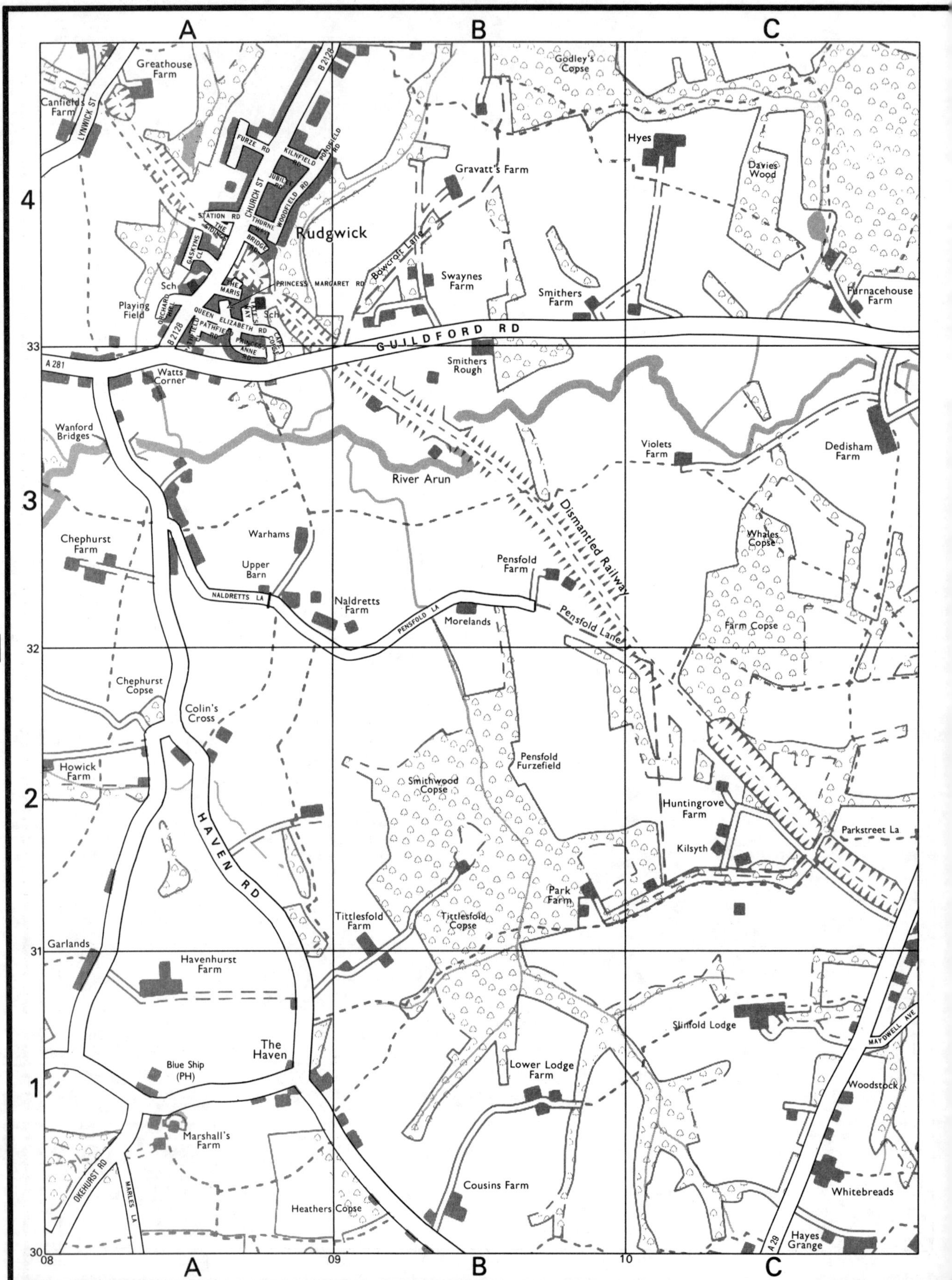
A
B
C
4
3
2
1
33
32
31
30
08
09
10
Greathouse Farm
Canfields Farm
LYNWICK ST
B 2128
FURZE RD
KILNFIELD RD
PONDFIELD RD
JUBILEE RD
WOODFIELD RD
CHURCH ST
STATION RD
THE SIDINGS
THURNE WAY
BRIDGE RD
GASKYNS CL
Rudgwick
THE MARIS
PRINCESS MARGARET RD
QUEEN ELIZABETH RD
PATHFIELD RD
PRINCESS ANNE RD
ORCHARD HILL
Sch
Playing Field
Godley's Copse
Hyes
Davies Wood
Gravatt's Farm
Bowcroft Lane
Swaynes Farm
Smithers Farm
Furnacehouse Farm
GUILDFORD RD
A 281
Smithers Rough
Watts Corner
Wanford Bridges
River Arun
Violets Farm
Dedisham Farm
Dismantled Railway
Chephurst Farm
Warhams
Whales Copse
Upper Barn
Pensfold Farm
NALDRETTS LA
Naldretts Farm
PENSFOLD LA
Morelands
Pensfold Lane
Farm Copse
Chephurst Copse
Colin's Cross
Howick Farm
Pensfold Furzefield
Smithwood Copse
Huntingrove Farm
Parkstreet La
Kilsyth
HAVEN RD
Park Farm
Tittlesfold Farm
Tittlesfold Copse
Garlands
Havenhurst Farm
Slinfold Lodge
MAYDOWELL AVE
The Haven
Blue Ship (PH)
Lower Lodge Farm
Woodstock
Marshall's Farm
OKEHURST RD
MARLES LA
Cousins Farm
Whitebreads
Heathers Copse
A 29
Hayes Grange

31

53

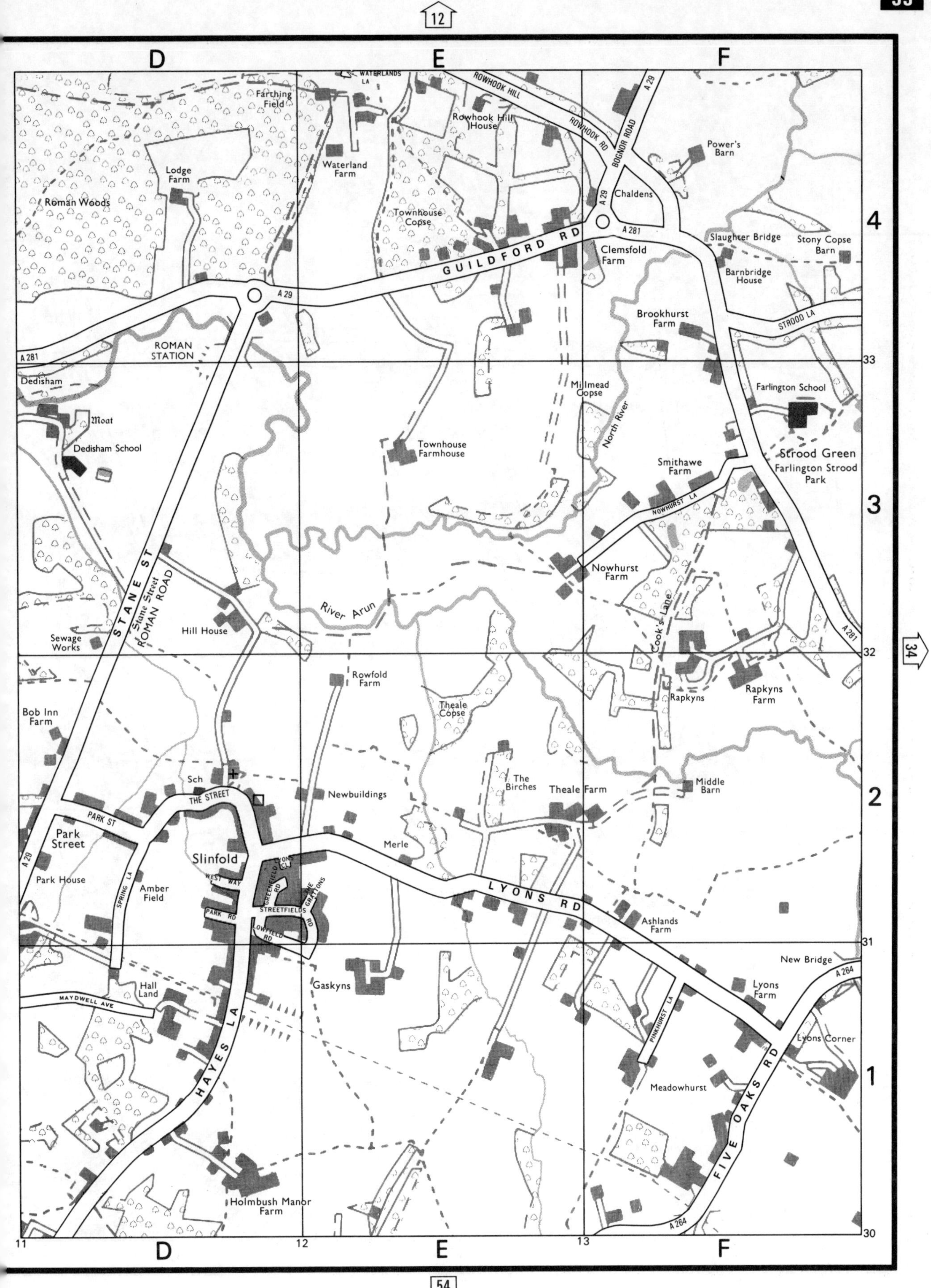
12
D
E
F
4
3
2
1
33
32
31
30
11
12
13
34
54
Farthing Field
Waterland Farm
Rowhook Hill House
ROWHOOK HILL
ROWHOOK RD
BOGNOR ROAD
A 29
Power's Barn
Lodge Farm
Roman Woods
Townhouse Copse
Chaldens
A 281
GUILDFORD RD
Clemsfold Farm
Slaughter Bridge
Stony Copse Barn
Barnbridge House
Brookhurst Farm
STROOD LA
ROMAN STATION
Dedisham
Millmead Copse
North River
Farlington School
Moat
Dedisham School
Townhouse Farmhouse
Strood Green
Farlington Strood Park
Smithawe Farm
NOWHURST LA
Nowhurst Farm
STANE ST
Stane Street
ROMAN ROAD
River Arun
Cook's Lane
Sewage Works
Hill House
Rowfold Farm
Rapkyns
Rapkyns Farm
Bob Inn Farm
Theale Copse
The Birches
Theale Farm
Middle Barn
Sch
THE STREET
Newbuildings
PARK ST
Park Street
Merle
Slinfold
WEST WAY
GREENFIELDS
LYONS CL
THE GRATTONS
STREETFIELDS
PARK RD
LOWFIELD RD
LYONS RD
Park House
SPRING LA
Amber Field
Ashlands Farm
New Bridge
Gaskyns
Hall Land
MAYDWELL AVE
A 264
Lyons Farm
PINKHURST LA
Lyons Corner
HAYES LA
FIVE OAKS RD
Meadowhurst
Holmbush Manor Farm

13

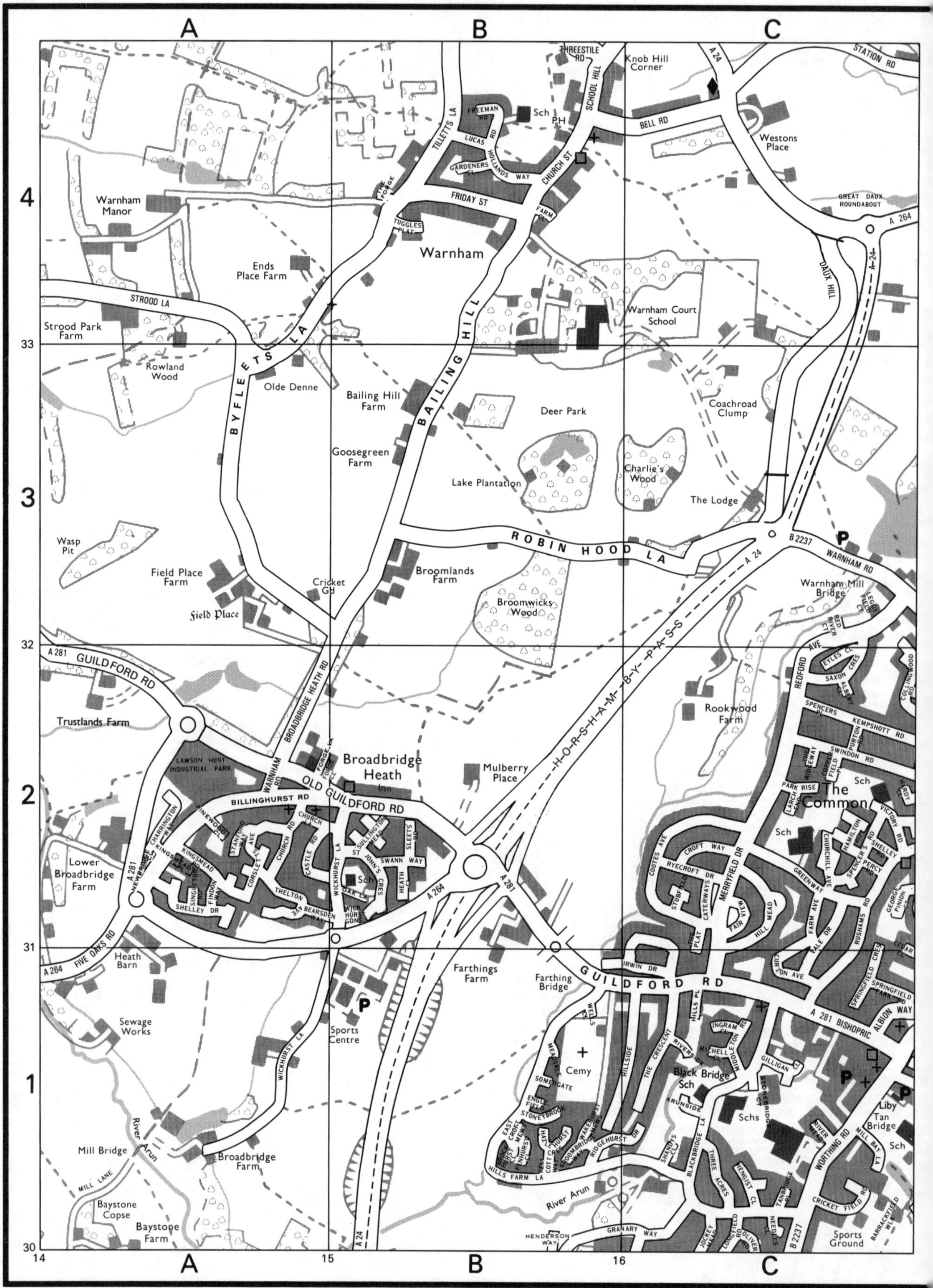
A
B
C
4
3
2
1
33
32
31
30
14
15
16
Warnham Manor
Ends Place Farm
STROOD LA
Strood Park Farm
Rowland Wood
BYFLEETS LA
Olde Denne
Bailing Hill Farm
BAILING HILL
Goosegreen Farm
Warnham
TILLETTS LA
FREEMAN RD
LUCAS RD
GARDENERS CL
HOLLANDS WAY
FRIDAY ST
THE FORGE
TUGGLES PLAT
Sch
PH
SCHOOL HILL
CHURCH ST
FARM CL
THREESTILE RD
Knob Hill Corner
BELL RD
A 24
STATION RD
Westons Place
GREAT DAUX ROUNDABOUT
A 264
DAUX HILL
Warnham Court School
Deer Park
Coachroad Clump
Lake Plantation
Charlie's Wood
The Lodge
ROBIN HOOD LA
B 2237
WARNHAM RD
P
Wasp Pit
Field Place Farm
Field Place
Cricket Gd
Broomlands Farm
Broomwicks Wood
Warnham Mill Bridge
HORSHAM BY-PASS
A 281
GUILDFORD RD
Trustlands Farm
BROADBRIDGE HEATH RD
LAWSON HUNT INDUSTRIAL PARK
WARNHAM RD
FORGE CL
Broadbridge Heath
Inn
Mulberry Place
Rookwood Farm
OLD GUILDFORD RD
BILLINGHURST RD
CHURCH RD
CASTLE RD
WICKHURST LA
SULLINGTON MEAD
ST JOHN'S CRES
SWANN WAY
SLEETS RD
HEATH CL
OAK LA
THELTON AVE
BEARSDEN WAY
WICKHURST GDNS
CHARRINGTON WAY
PINEWOOD CL
KINGSMEAD
STANFORD WAY
CORSLETT AVE
SINGLETON RD
FINDON WAY
SHELLEY DR
NEWBRIDGE RD
Lower Broadbridge Farm
FIVE OAKS RD
Heath Barn
Sewage Works
WICKHURST LA
Sports Centre
Farthings Farm
Farthing Bridge
River Arun
Mill Bridge
MILL LANE
Broadbridge Farm
Baystone Copse
Baystone Farm
REDFORD AVE
EYLES CL
SAXON CRES
ALBERY CL
SPENCERS PL
KEMPSHOTT RD
SWINDON RD
COLLINGWOOD RD
PARK RISE
The Common
Sch
HARDY CL
VICTORY RD
SHELLEY RD
CHURCHILL AVE
HAMILTON RD
PERCY RD
COOTES AVE
CROFT WAY
RYECROFT DR
MERRYFIELD DR
STUBFIELD
CATERWAYS
THE PLAT
FAIR VIEW
HILL MEAD
GREENWAY
FARM AVE
DALE DR
RUSHAMS RD
CURSON AVE
IRWIN DR
GUILDFORD RD
HILLS PL
A 281 BISHOPRIC
ALBION WAY
SPRINGFIELD PARK RD
INGRAM CL
MIDDLETON RD
MITCHELL CL
RIVERSIDE
THE CRESCENT
HILLSIDE
WELLS CL
MEADVALE
SOMERGATE
Cemy
Black Bridge Sch
GILLIGAN CL
ARUNSIDE
STONEYBROOK
ENGLEFIELD
EAST CROFT MEWS
RIDGEHURST DR
HILLS FARM LA
SHANDYS CL
BLACKBRIDGE LA
THREE ACRES
HENGIST CL
Schs
RIVER MEAD
WORTHING RD
MILL BAY LA
Liby
Tan Bridge
Sch
River Arun
HENDERSON WAY
GRANARY WAY
JOCKEY MEAD
LONGFIELD RD
OLIVER RD
NEEDLES CL
B 2237
CRICKET FIELD RD
BARRACKFIELD WLK
Sports Ground

33

55

14

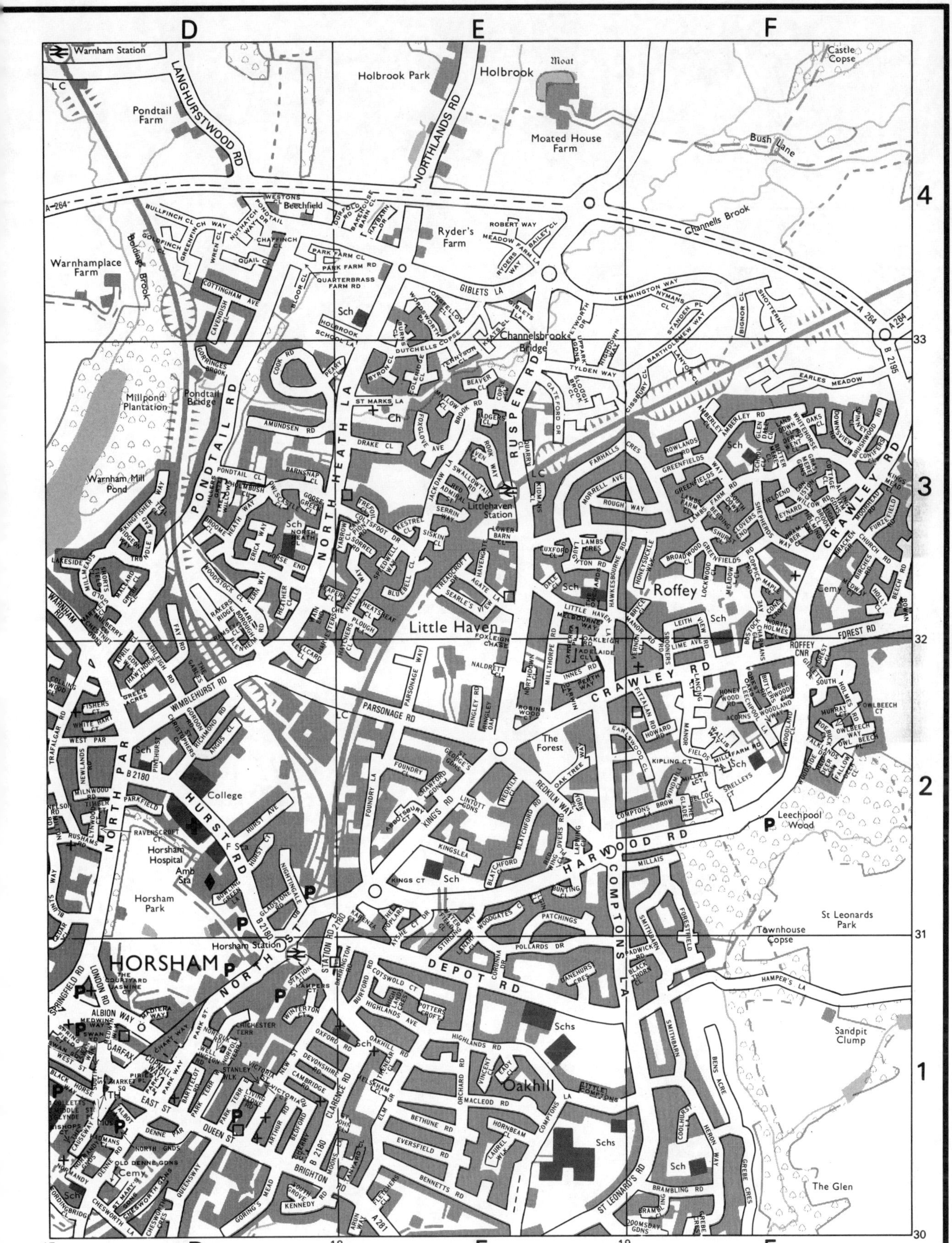

D
E
F
Warnham Station
Holbrook Park
Holbrook
Moat
Castle Copse
Pondtail Farm
LANGHURSTWOOD RD
NORTHLANDS RD
Moated House Farm
Bush Lane
A 264
Beechfield
Ryder's Farm
Channells Brook
Warnhamplace Farm
Boldings Brook
GIBLETS LA
Sch
Channelsbrook Bridge
Millpond Plantation
Pondtail Bridge
PONDTAIL RD
NORTH HEATH LA
RUSPER RD
Warnham Mill Pond
Littlehaven Station
Roffey
Little Haven
CRAWLEY RD
FOREST RD
PARSONAGE RD
The Forest
College
HURST RD
Horsham Hospital
Horsham Park
NORTH PAR
Leechpool Wood
HARWOOD RD
COMPTONS LA
St Leonards Park
Townhouse Copse
Horsham Station
HORSHAM
NORTH ST
DEPOT RD
Sandpit Clump
Schs
Oakhill
Cemy
The Glen
ST LEONARD'S RD
BRIGHTON RD
QUEEN ST
EAST ST
CARFAX
4
3
2
1
33
32
31
30
17
18
19

36

56

15

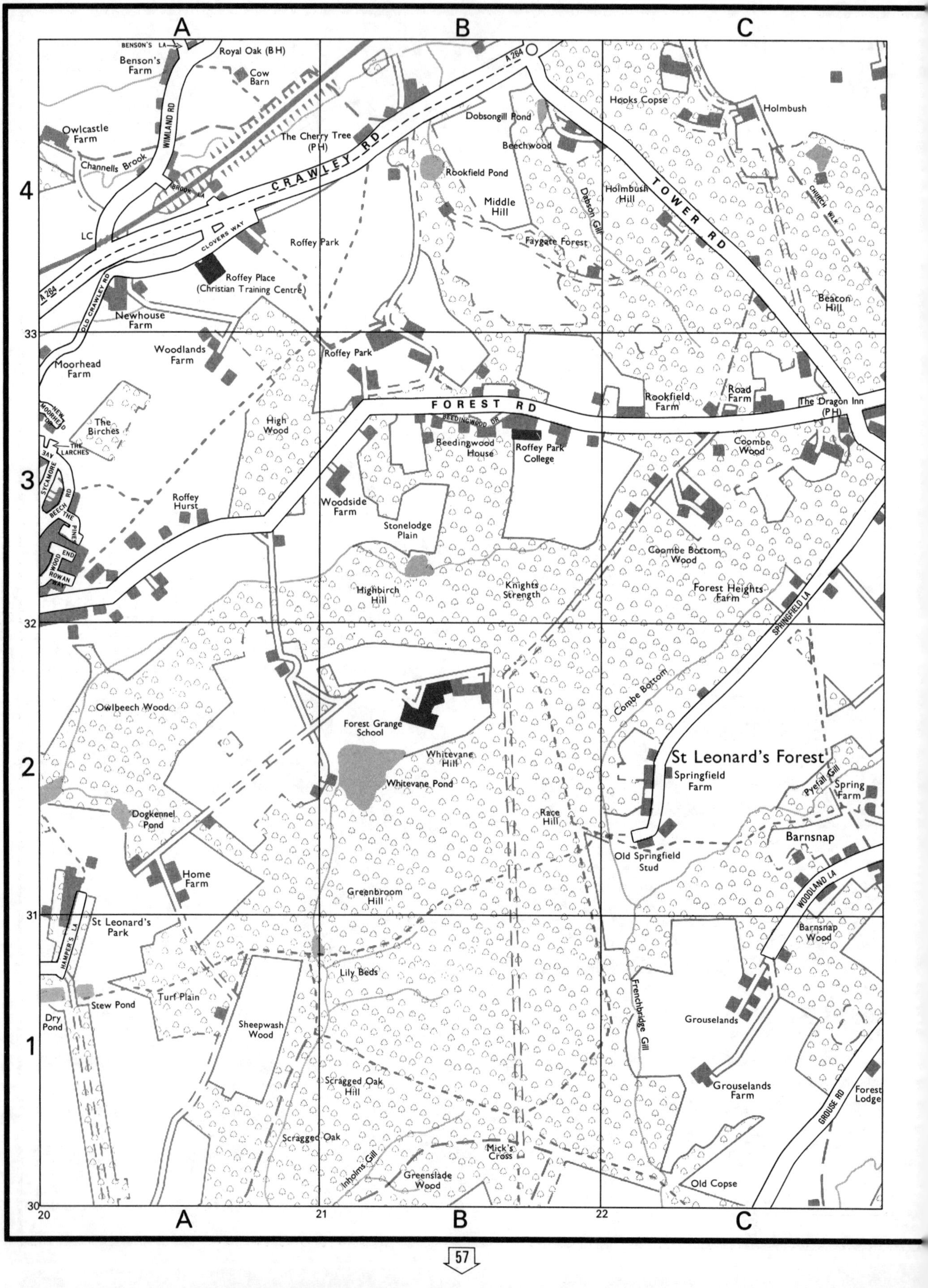
A
B
C
BENSON'S LA
Benson's Farm
Royal Oak (BH)
Cow Barn
A 264
Hooks Copse
Holmbush
Owlcastle Farm
WIMLAND RD
Dobsongill Pond
The Cherry Tree (PH)
Beechwood
Channells Brook
CRAWLEY RD
Rookfield Pond
BROOK LA
Holmbush Hill
TOWER RD
CHURCH WLK
Middle Hill
Dobson Gill
LC
CLOVERS WAY
Roffey Park
Faygate Forest
Roffey Place
(Christian Training Centre)
OLD CRAWLEY RD
Beacon Hill
Newhouse Farm
Woodlands Farm
Roffey Park
Moorhead Farm
FOREST RD
Road Farm
Rookfield Farm
The Dragon Inn (PH)
BEEDINGWOOD DR
NEW MOORHEAD DR
The Birches
High Wood
Beedingwood House
Roffey Park College
Coombe Wood
THE LARCHES
AVE
SYCAMORE
Roffey Hurst
Woodside Farm
BEECH RD
THE PINES
Stonelodge Plain
Coombe Bottom Wood
WOOD END
ROWAN WAY
Highbirch Hill
Knights Strength
Forest Heights Farm
SPRINGFIELD LA
Combe Bottom
Owlbeech Wood
Forest Grange School
St Leonard's Forest
Whitevane Hill
Springfield Farm
Pyefall Gill
Spring Farm
Whitevane Pond
Dogkennel Pond
Race Hill
Barnsnap
Old Springfield Stud
Home Farm
WOODLAND LA
Greenbroom Hill
St Leonard's Park
HAMPER'S LA
Barnsnap Wood
Lily Beds
Turf Plain
Stew Pond
Frenchbridge Gill
Dry Pond
Sheepwash Wood
Grouselands
Scragged Oak Hill
Grouselands Farm
Forest Lodge
GROUSE RD
Scragged Oak
Mick's Cross
Inholms Gill
Greenslade Wood
Old Copse
1
2
3
4
20
21
22
30
31
32
33
35

57

16

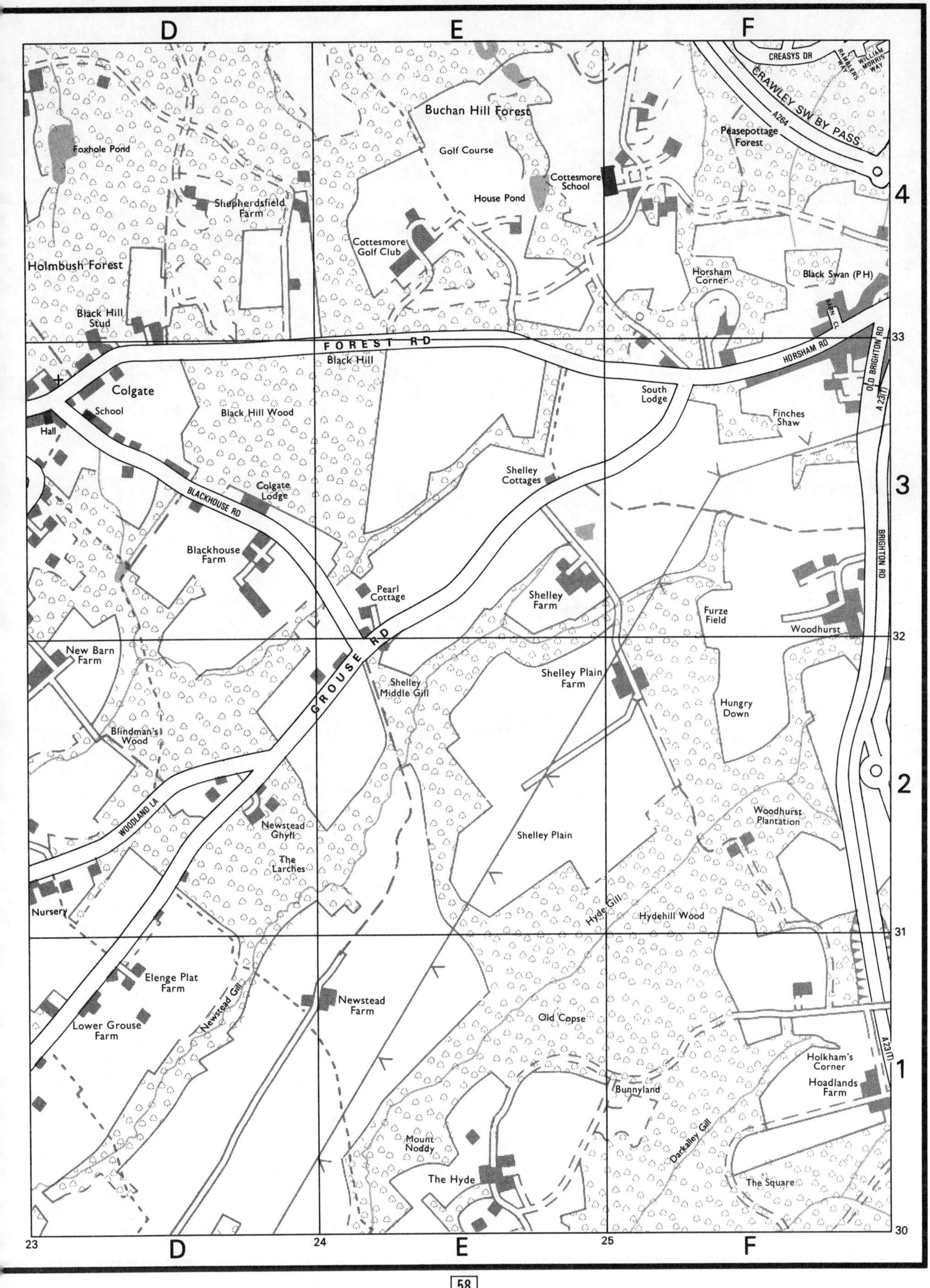
D
E
F
Buchan Hill Forest
Golf Course
Foxhole Pond
Cottesmore School
House Pond
Shepherdsfield Farm
Cottesmore Golf Club
Holmbush Forest
Black Hill Stud
CREASYS DR
RAMBLERS WAY
WILLIAM MORRIS WAY
CRAWLEY SW BY PASS
A264
Peasepottage Forest
4
Horsham Corner
Black Swan (PH)
BARN CL
FOREST RD
Black Hill
HORSHAM RD
OLD BRIGHTON RD
A 23(T)
33
Colgate
School
Hall
Black Hill Wood
South Lodge
Finches Shaw
Shelley Cottages
3
BLACKHOUSE RD
Colgate Lodge
Blackhouse Farm
BRIGHTON RD
Pearl Cottage
Shelley Farm
Furze Field
Woodhurst
32
New Barn Farm
GROUSE RD
Shelley Middle Gill
Shelley Plain Farm
Hungry Down
Blindman's Wood
2
Woodhurst Plantation
WOODLAND LA
Newstead Ghyll
Shelley Plain
The Larches
Nursery
Hyde Gill
Hydehill Wood
31
Elenge Plat Farm
Newstead Gill
Newstead Farm
Lower Grouse Farm
Old Copse
A23(T)
Holkham's Corner
Hoadlands Farm
1
Bunnyland
Darkalley Gill
Mount Noddy
The Hyde
The Square
30
23
24
25
D
E
F

38

58

17

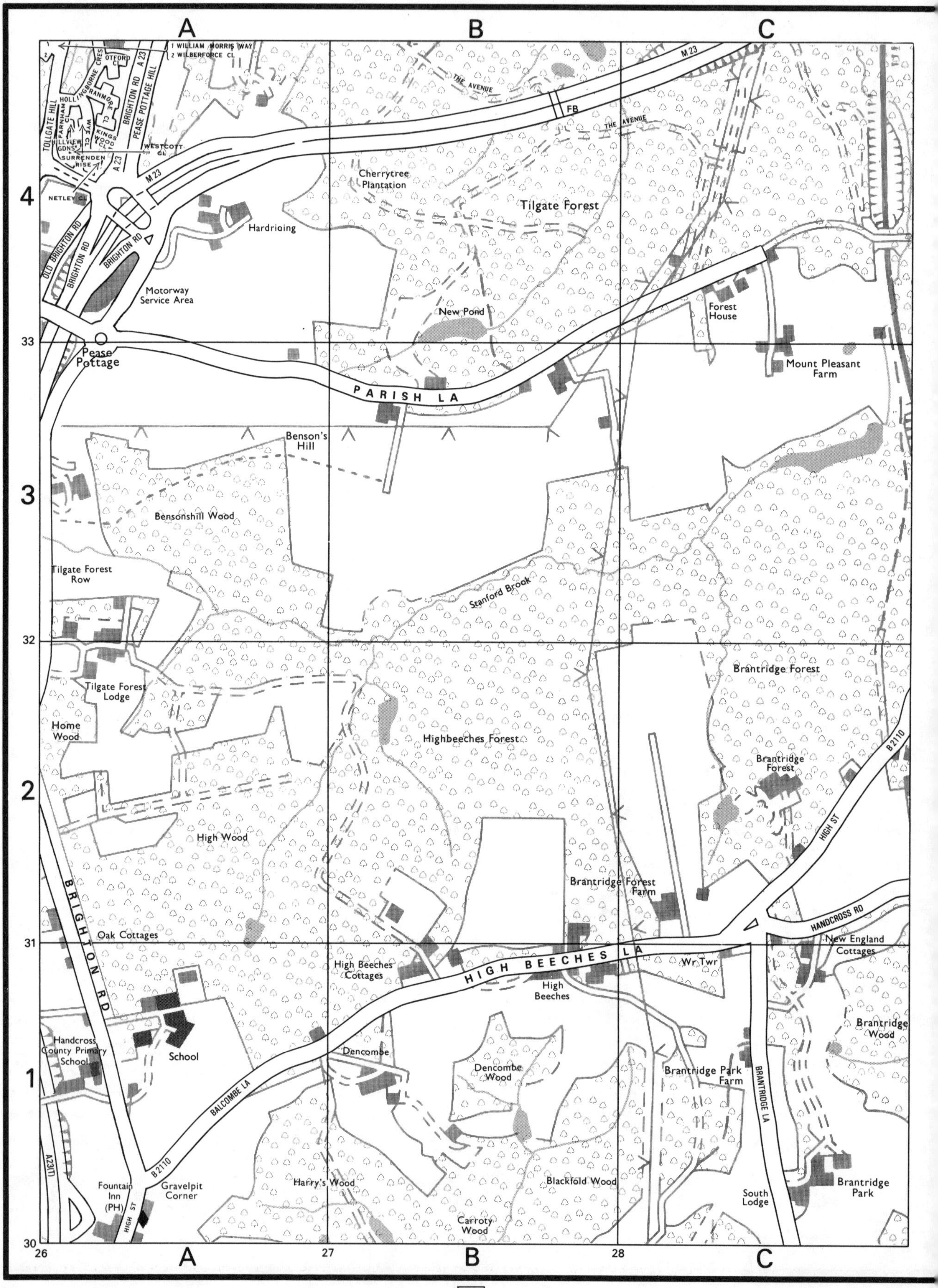
A
B
C
4
3
2
1
33
32
31
30
26
27
28
1 WILLIAM MORRIS WAY
2 WILBERFORCE CL
OTFORD CL
HOLLINGBORNE CRES
RANMORE CL
BRIGHTON RD
A 23
PEASE POTTAGE HILL
TOLLGATE HILL
FARNHAM CL
WYE CL
KINGS WOOD CL
HILLVIEW GDNS
SURRENDEN RISE
WESTCOTT CL
NETLEY CL
M 23
OLD BRIGHTON RD
Hardriding
Motorway Service Area
Pease Pottage
THE AVENUE
FB
Cherrytree Plantation
Tilgate Forest
New Pond
Forest House
Mount Pleasant Farm
PARISH LA
Benson's Hill
Bensonshill Wood
Tilgate Forest Row
Stanford Brook
Tilgate Forest Lodge
Home Wood
Brantridge Forest
Highbeeches Forest
Brantridge Forest
B2110
High Wood
HIGH ST
Brantridge Forest Farm
HANDCROSS RD
Oak Cottages
New England Cottages
HIGH BEECHES LA
Wr Twr
High Beeches Cottages
High Beeches
Handcross County Primary School
School
Dencombe
Dencombe Wood
Brantridge Wood
BRIGHTON RD
BALCOMBE LA
Brantridge Park Farm
BRANTRIDGE LA
A23(T)
B2110
Fountain Inn (PH)
Gravelpit Corner
HIGH ST
Harry's Wood
Blackfold Wood
Carroty Wood
South Lodge
Brantridge Park

37

59

18

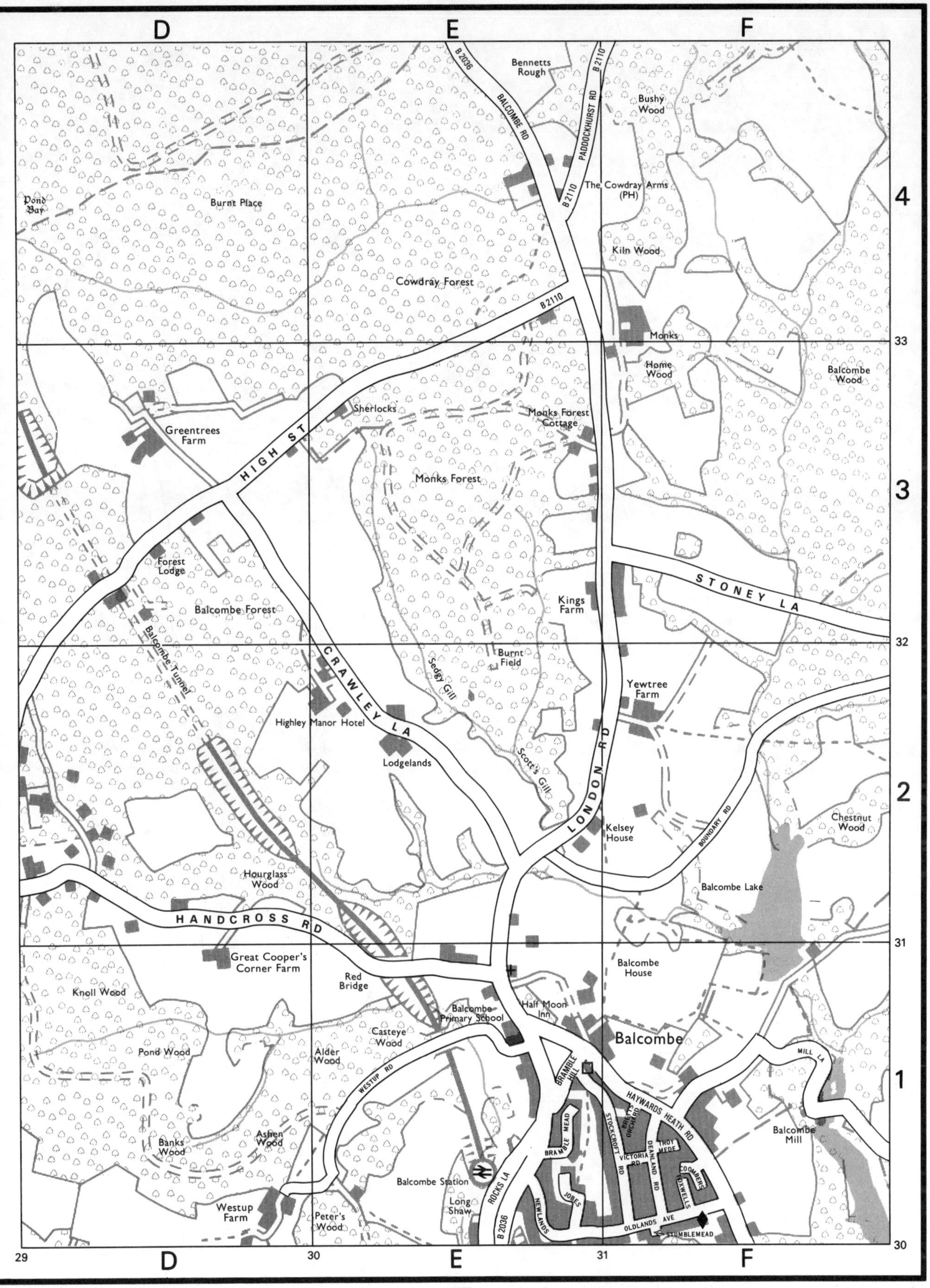

D
E
F
4
3
2
1
33
32
31
30
29
30
31
Pond Bay
Burnt Place
Bennetts Rough
B 2036
BALCOMBE RD
B 2110
PADDOCKHURST RD
Bushy Wood
The Cowdray Arms (PH)
Kiln Wood
Cowdray Forest
B 2110
Monks
Home Wood
Balcombe Wood
Sherlocks
Monks Forest Cottage
Greentrees Farm
HIGH ST
Monks Forest
STONEY LA
Forest Lodge
Balcombe Forest
Kings Farm
Balcombe Tunnel
CRAWLEY LA
Burnt Field
Sedgy Gill
Yewtree Farm
Highley Manor Hotel
Lodgelands
Scott's Gill
LONDON RD
BOUNDARY RD
Chestnut Wood
Kelsey House
Hourglass Wood
Balcombe Lake
HANDCROSS RD
Great Cooper's Corner Farm
Red Bridge
Balcombe House
Knoll Wood
Half Moon Inn
Balcombe Primary School
Balcombe
Casteye Wood
Pond Wood
Alder Wood
WESTUP RD
BRAMBLE HILL
MILL LA
HAYWARDS HEATH RD
BRAMBLE MEAD
STOCKCROFT RD
BRISTS ORCHARD
DEANLAND RD
TROY MEDE
VICTORIA RD
COOMBERS
FOXWELLS
Balcombe Mill
Banks Wood
Ashen Wood
Balcombe Station
Long Shaw
ROCKS LA
NEWLANDS
JOBES
OLDLANDS AVE
STUMBLEMEAD
B 2036
Westup Farm
Peter's Wood

40

60

19

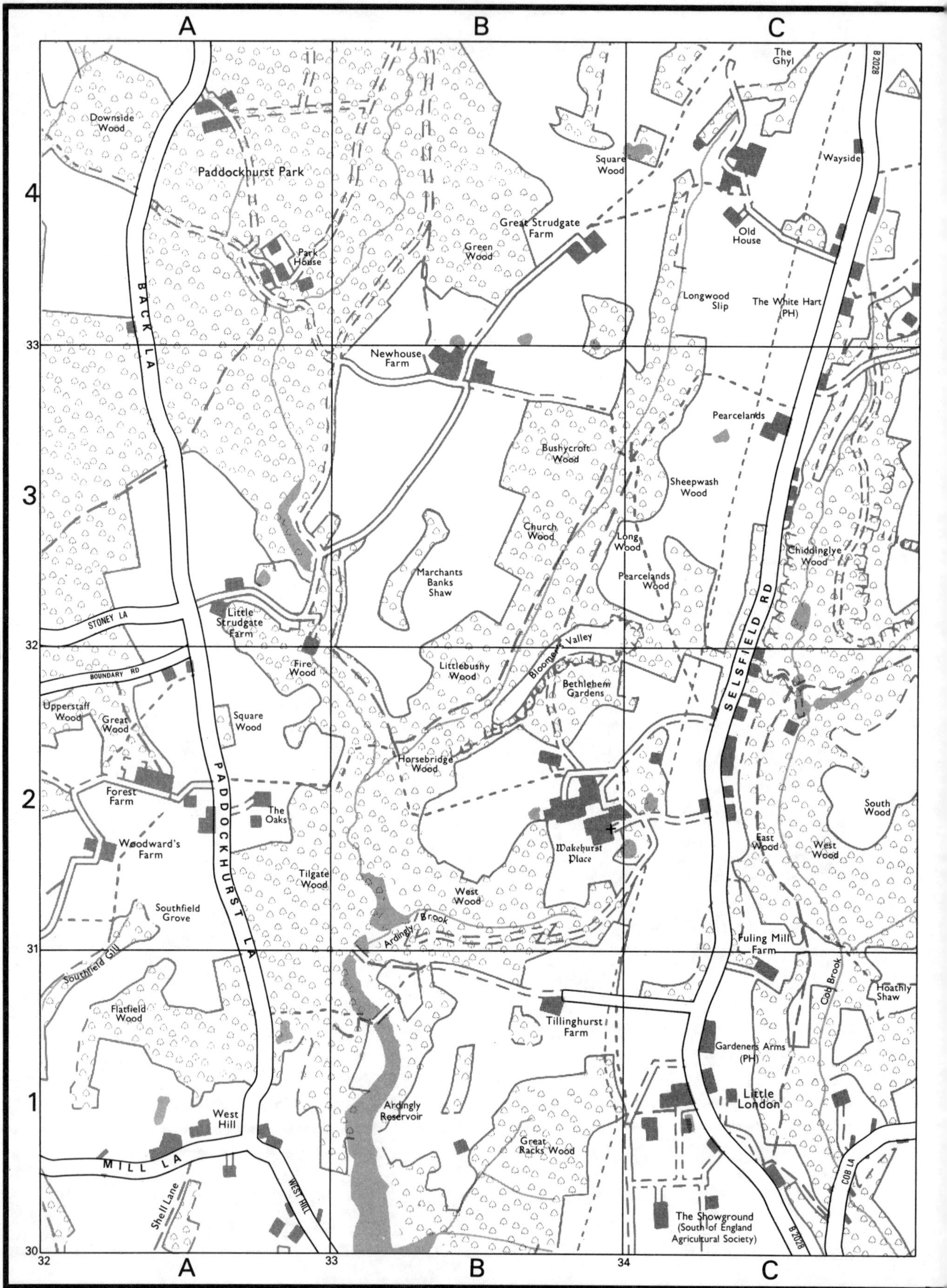
A
B
C
4
3
2
1
32
33
34
30
31
Downside Wood
Paddockhurst Park
Park House
BACK LA
Green Wood
Great Strudgate Farm
Square Wood
The Ghyl
B 2028
Wayside
Old House
Longwood Slip
The White Hart (PH)
Newhouse Farm
Pearcelands
Bushycroft Wood
Sheepwash Wood
Church Wood
Long Wood
Marchants Banks Shaw
Pearcelands Wood
Chiddinglye Wood
STONEY LA
Little Strudgate Farm
Fire Wood
Littlebushy Wood
Bloomers Valley
Bethlehem Gardens
SELSFIELD RD
BOUNDARY RD
Upperstaff Wood
Great Wood
Square Wood
Horsebridge Wood
Forest Farm
The Oaks
PADDOCKHURST LA
Wakehurst Place
South Wood
East Wood
West Wood
Woodward's Farm
Tilgate Wood
West Wood
Southfield Grove
Ardingly Brook
Fuling Mill Farm
Southfield Gill
Cob Brook
Hoathly Shaw
Flatfield Wood
Tillinghurst Farm
Gardeners Arms (PH)
Little London
Ardingly Reservoir
West Hill
MILL LA
Great Racks Wood
COB LA
Shell Lane
WEST HILL
The Showground (South of England Agricultural Society)
B 2028

39

61

20

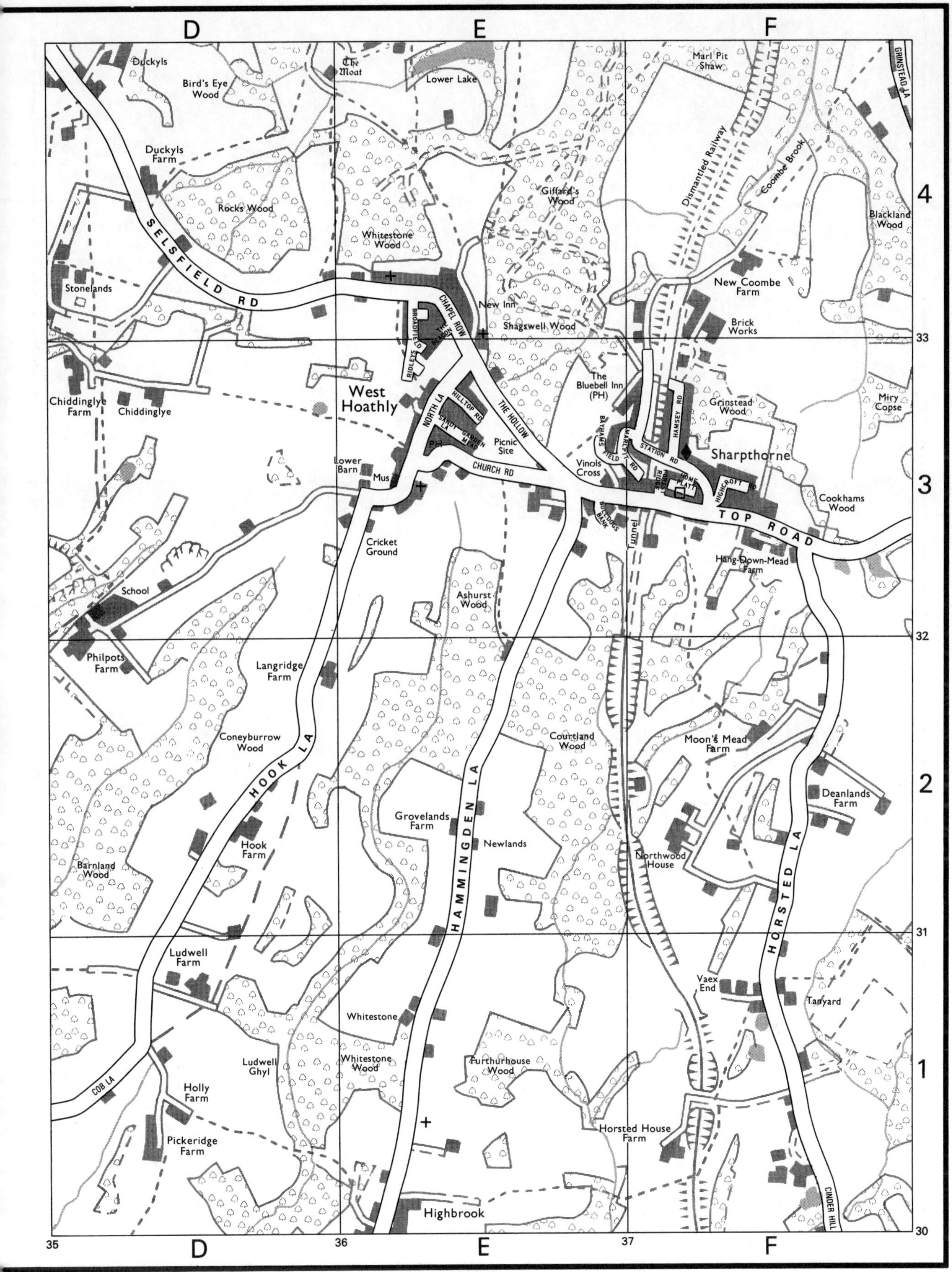
D
E
F
Duckyls
Bird's Eye Wood
The Moat
Lower Lake
Marl Pit Shaw
GRINSTEAD LA
Duckyls Farm
Rocks Wood
Whitestone Wood
Giffard's Wood
Dismantled Railway
Coombe Brook
Blackland Wood
4
SELSFIELD RD
Stonelands
New Coombe Farm
CHAPEL ROW
New Inn
Shagswell Wood
Brick Works
BROADFIELD
THE BEACON
SLEETS
RIDING
33
Chiddinglye Farm
Chiddinglye
West Hoathly
NORTH LA
HILLTOP RD
SANDY LA
GARDEN MEAD
THE HOLLOW
PH
Picnic Site
The Bluebell Inn (PH)
Grinstead Wood
Miry Copse
HAMSEY RD
BAYHAMS FIELD
MARLPIT RD
STATION RD
Sharpthorne
Lower Barn
Mus
CHURCH RD
Vinols Cross
FOREST RIDGE
HOME PLATT
HIGHCROFT RD
Cookhams Wood
3
BULLDOGS BANK
TOP ROAD
Tunnel
Cricket Ground
Hang-Down-Mead Farm
School
Ashurst Wood
32
Philpots Farm
Langridge Farm
Coneyburrow Wood
Courtland Wood
Moon's Mead Farm
2
HOOK LA
Deanlands Farm
Grovelands Farm
Newlands
Hook Farm
Northwood House
Barnland Wood
HAMMINGDEN LA
HORSTED LA
31
Ludwell Farm
Vaex End
Tanyard
Whitestone
COB LA
Ludwell Ghyl
Whitestone Wood
Furthurhouse Wood
1
Holly Farm
Pickeridge Farm
Horsted House Farm
CINDER HILL
Highbrook
30
35
36
37
D
E
F

42

62

21

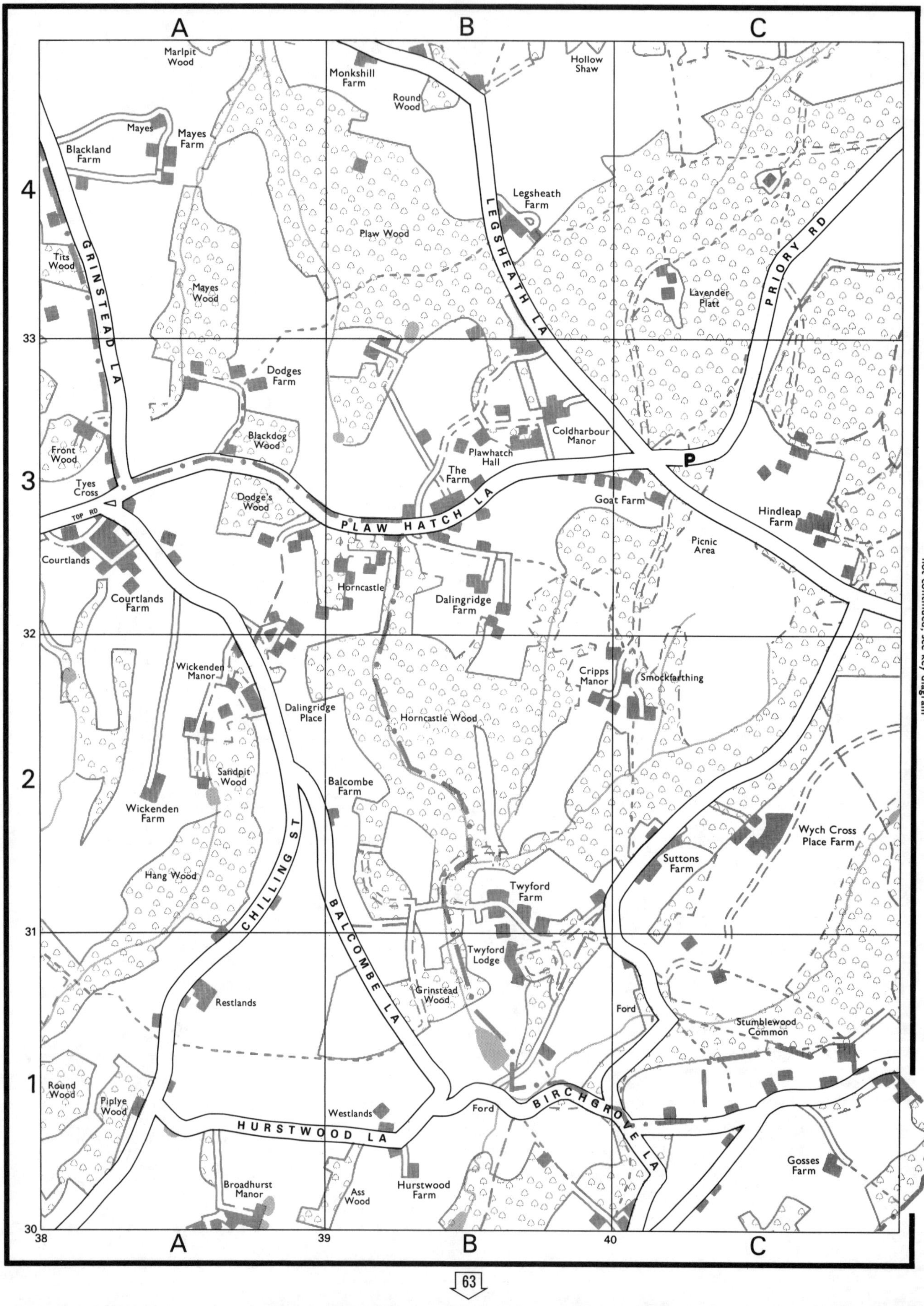

41

not continued, see key diagram

63

not continued, see key diagram

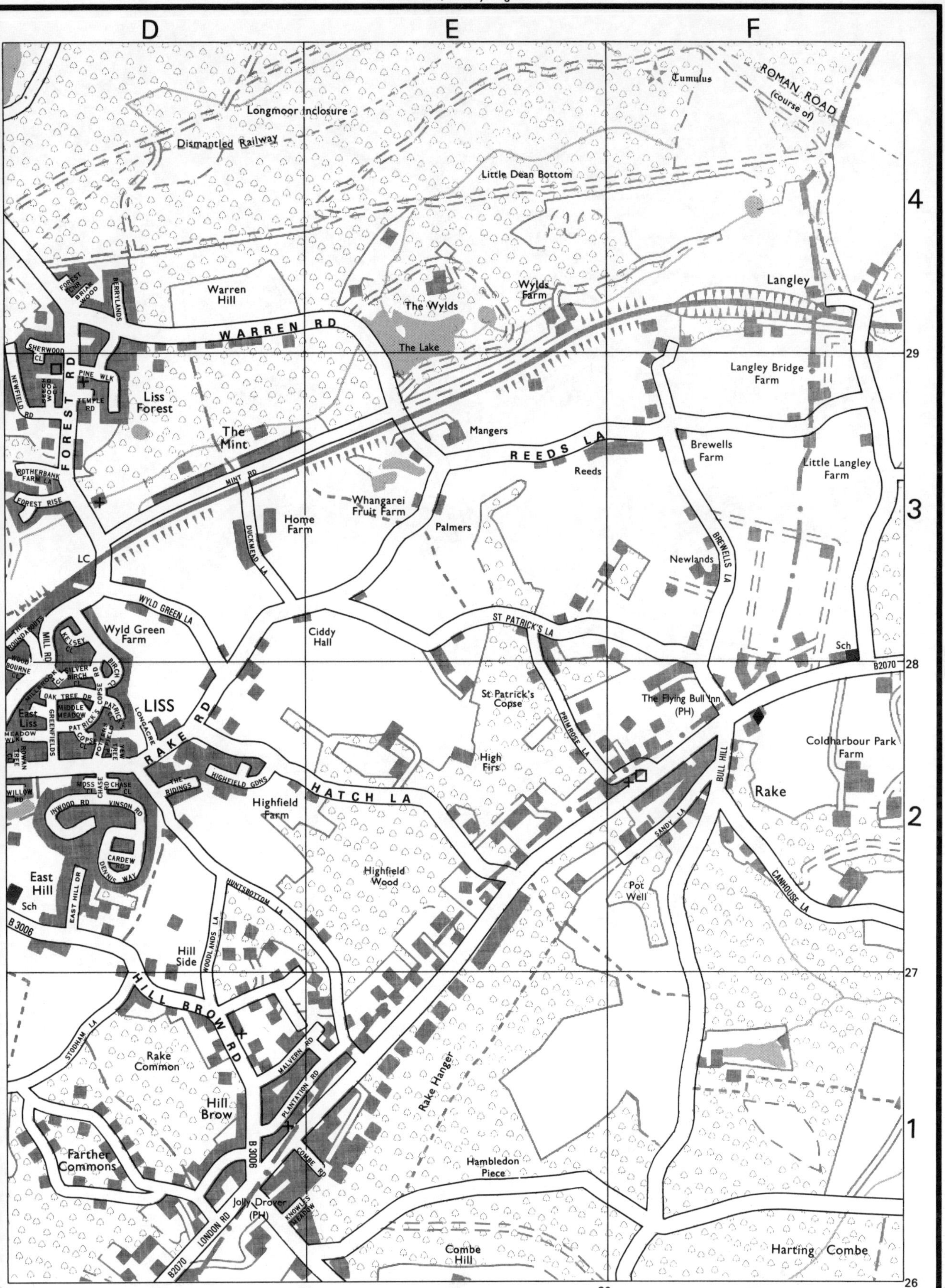

44

23

43

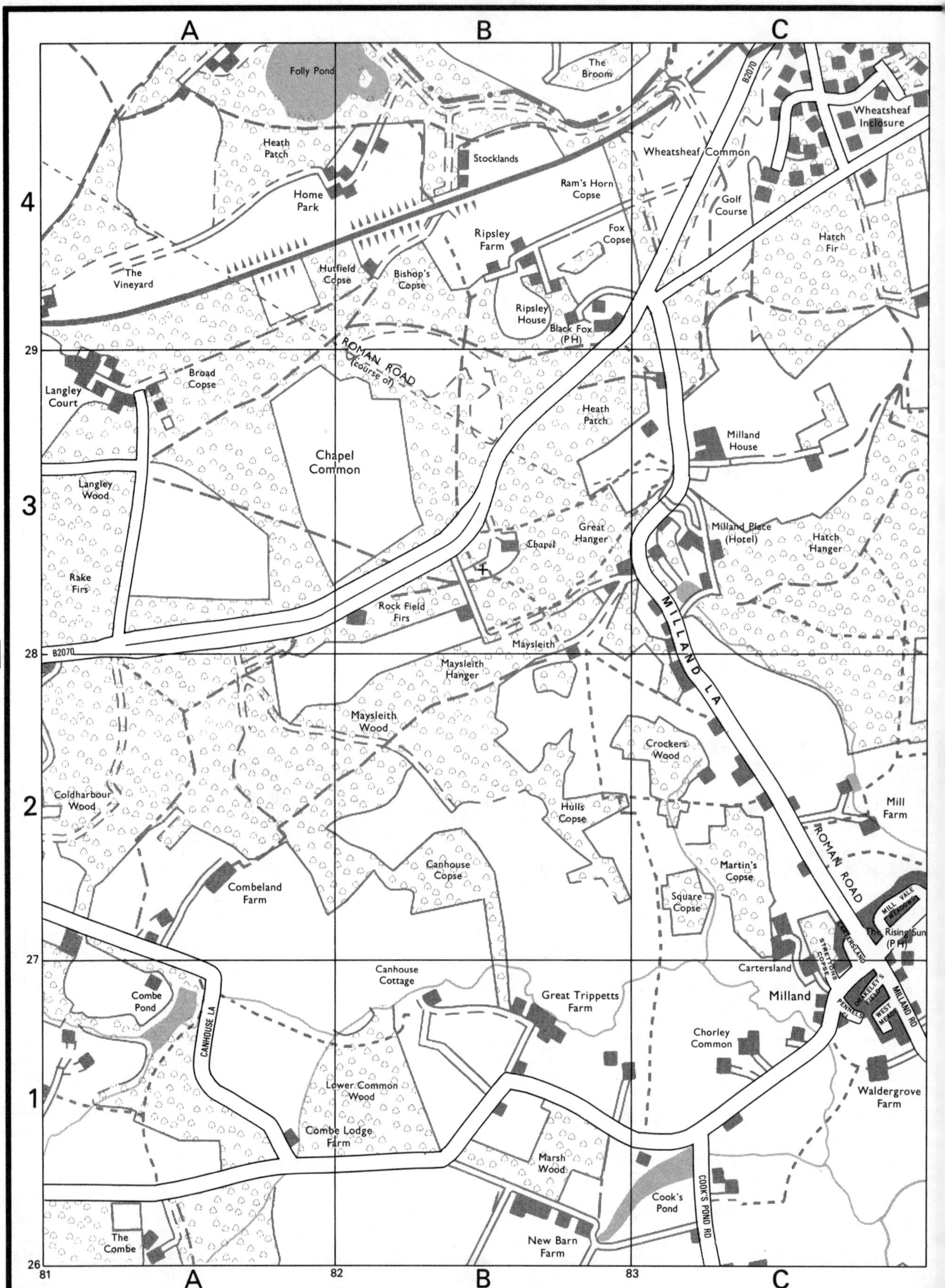

A
B
C
4
3
2
1
29
28
27
26
81
82
83
Folly Pond
The Broom
B2070
Wheatsheaf Inclosure
Heath Patch
Stocklands
Wheatsheaf Common
Home Park
Ram's Horn Copse
Golf Course
Ripsley Farm
Fox Copse
Hatch Fir
The Vineyard
Hutfield Copse
Bishop's Copse
Ripsley House
Black Fox (PH)
ROMAN ROAD (course of)
Langley Court
Broad Copse
Heath Patch
Milland House
Chapel Common
Langley Wood
Great Hanger
Milland Place (Hotel)
Hatch Hanger
Chapel
Rake Firs
Rock Field Firs
MILLAND LA
B2070
Maysleith
Maysleith Hanger
Maysleith Wood
Crockers Wood
Coldharbour Wood
Hulls Copse
Mill Farm
ROMAN ROAD
Canhouse Copse
Martin's Copse
Combeland Farm
Square Copse
MILL VALE MEADOWS
CARTERSLAND
STRETTONS COPSE
The Rising Sun (PH)
Canhouse Cottage
Cartersland
Combe Pond
Great Trippetts Farm
Milland
DRAKELEY'S FIELD
PENNELS CL
WEST MEADE
MILLAND RD
CANHOUSE LA
Chorley Common
Lower Common Wood
Waldergrove Farm
Combe Lodge Farm
Marsh Wood
Cook's Pond
COOK'S POND RD
The Combe
New Barn Farm

66

24

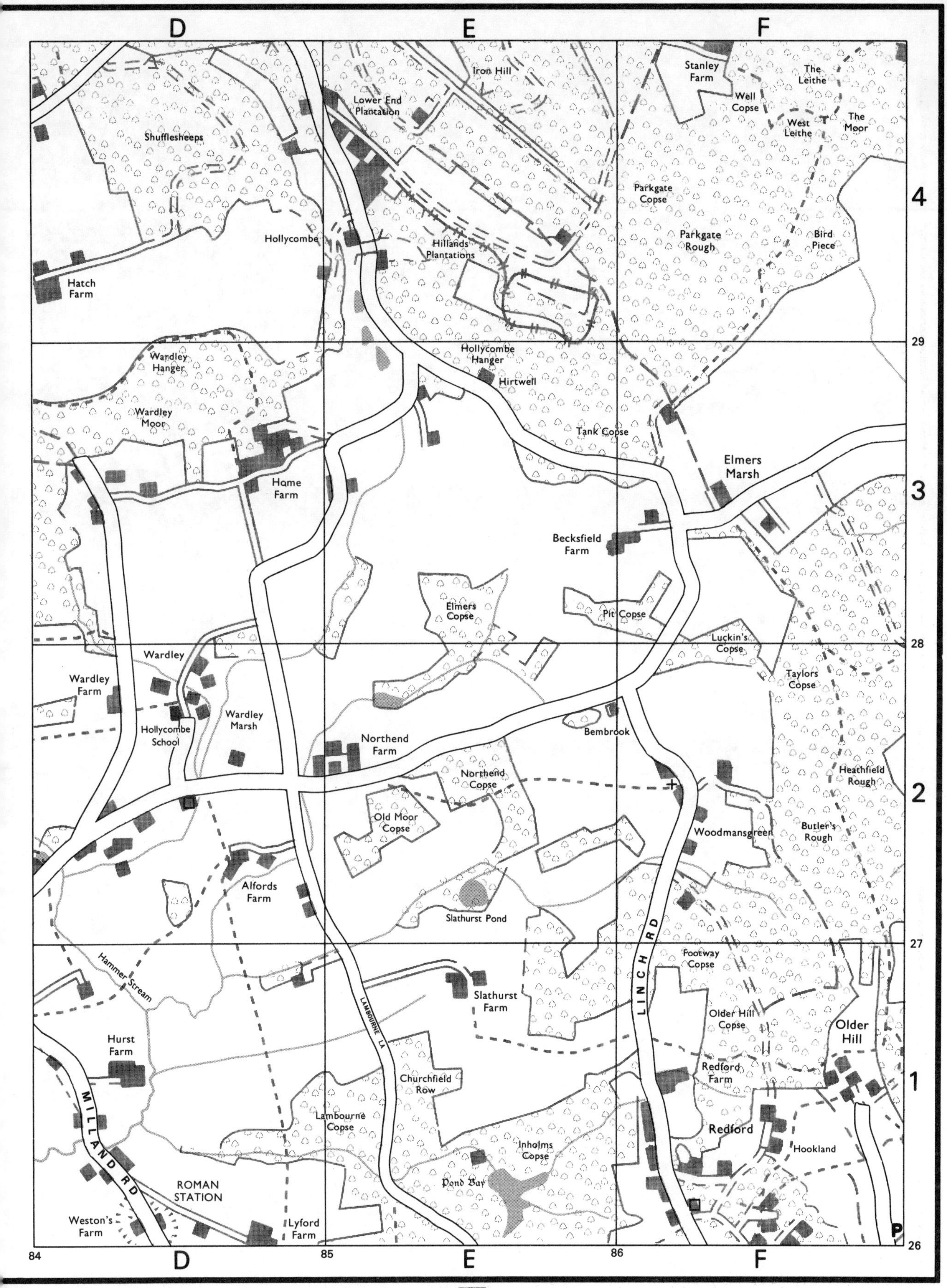
D
E
F
Iron Hill
Stanley Farm
The Leithe
Lower End Plantation
Well Copse
West Leithe
The Moor
Shufflesheeps
Parkgate Copse
Parkgate Rough
Bird Piece
Hollycombe
Hillands Plantations
Hatch Farm
Wardley Hanger
Hollycombe Hanger
Hirtwell
Wardley Moor
Tank Copse
Elmers Marsh
Home Farm
Becksfield Farm
Elmers Copse
Pit Copse
Luckin's Copse
Wardley
Wardley Farm
Taylors Copse
Wardley Marsh
Hollycombe School
Bembrook
Northend Farm
Heathfield Rough
Northend Copse
Old Moor Copse
Woodmansgreen
Butler's Rough
Alfords Farm
Slathurst Pond
Footway Copse
Hammer Stream
LINCH RD
LAMBOURNE LA
Slathurst Farm
Older Hill Copse
Older Hill
Hurst Farm
Redford Farm
Churchfield Row
Redford
MILLAND RD
Lambourne Copse
Inholms Copse
Hookland
Pond Bay
ROMAN STATION
Weston's Farm
Lyford Farm
P
4
29
3
28
2
27
1
26
84
85
86
D
E
F

46

67

25

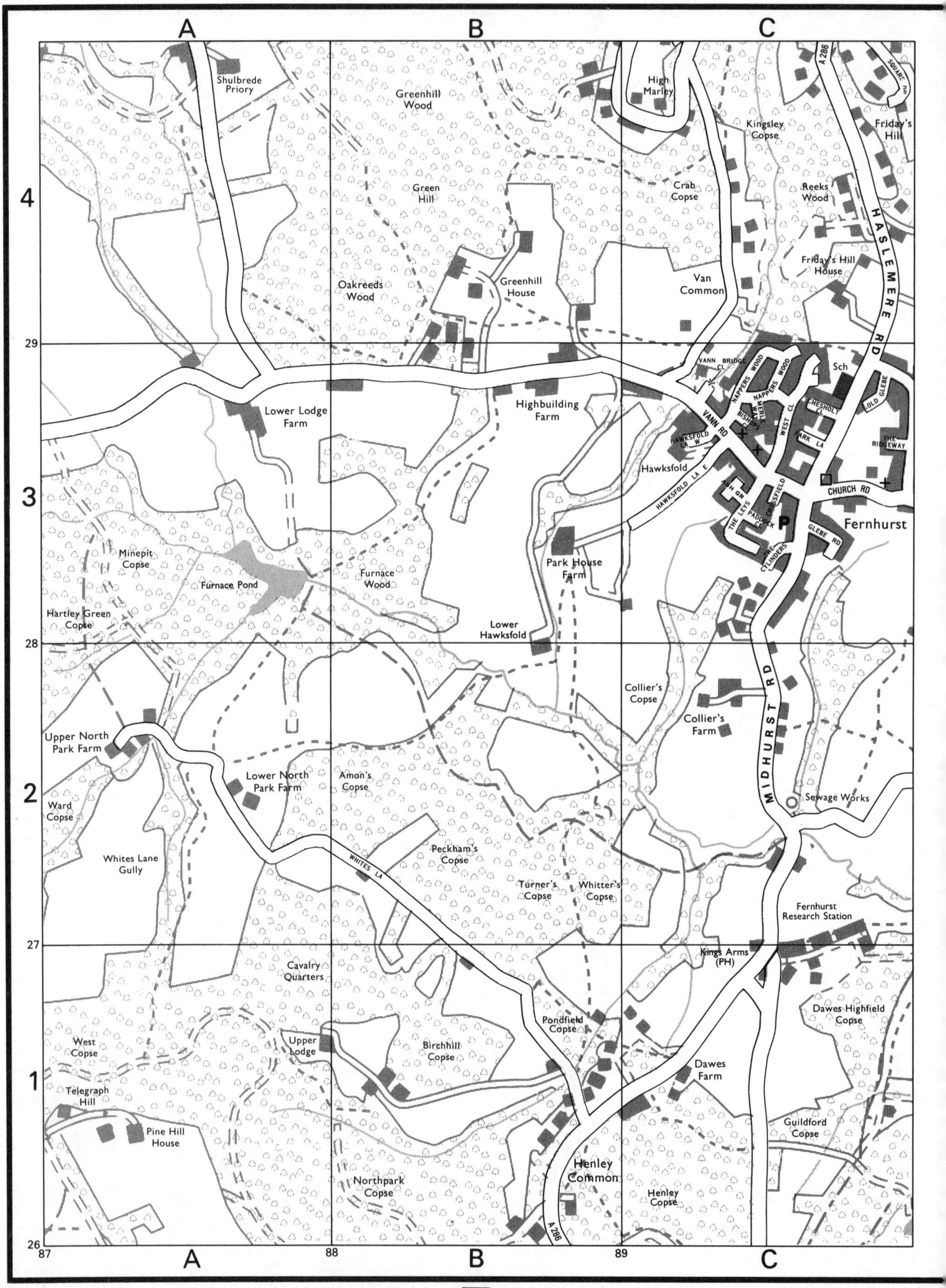
A
B
C
4
3
2
1
29
28
27
26
87
88
89
Shulbrede Priory
Greenhill Wood
High Marley
Kingsley Copse
Friday's Hill
Green Hill
Crab Copse
Reeks Wood
HASLEMERE RD
Oakreeds Wood
Greenhill House
Van Common
Friday's Hill House
A 286
SQUARE DR
VANN BRIDGE CL
NAPPERS WOOD
NAPPERS WOOD
MERLE WAY
BISHOPS CL
WEST CL
CHESHOLT CL
OLD GLEBE
PARK LA
THE RIDGEWAY
Sch
VANN RD
HAWKSFOLD LA W
HAWKSFOLD LA E
Hawksfold
ASH GR
THE LEYS
PADDOCK CL
CROSSFIELD
THE CYLINDERS
GLEBE RD
CHURCH RD
Fernhurst
Lower Lodge Farm
Highbuilding Farm
Minepit Copse
Furnace Pond
Furnace Wood
Park House Farm
Hartley Green Copse
Lower Hawksfold
Collier's Copse
Collier's Farm
MIDHURST RD
Upper North Park Farm
Lower North Park Farm
Amon's Copse
Ward Copse
Sewage Works
Whites Lane Gully
WHITES LA
Peckham's Copse
Turner's Copse
Whitter's Copse
Fernhurst Research Station
Cavalry Quarters
Kings Arms (PH)
Pondfield Copse
Dawes Highfield Copse
West Copse
Upper Lodge
Birchhill Copse
Dawes Farm
Telegraph Hill
Pine Hill House
Guildford Copse
Henley Common
Northpark Copse
Henley Copse
A 286

45

68

26

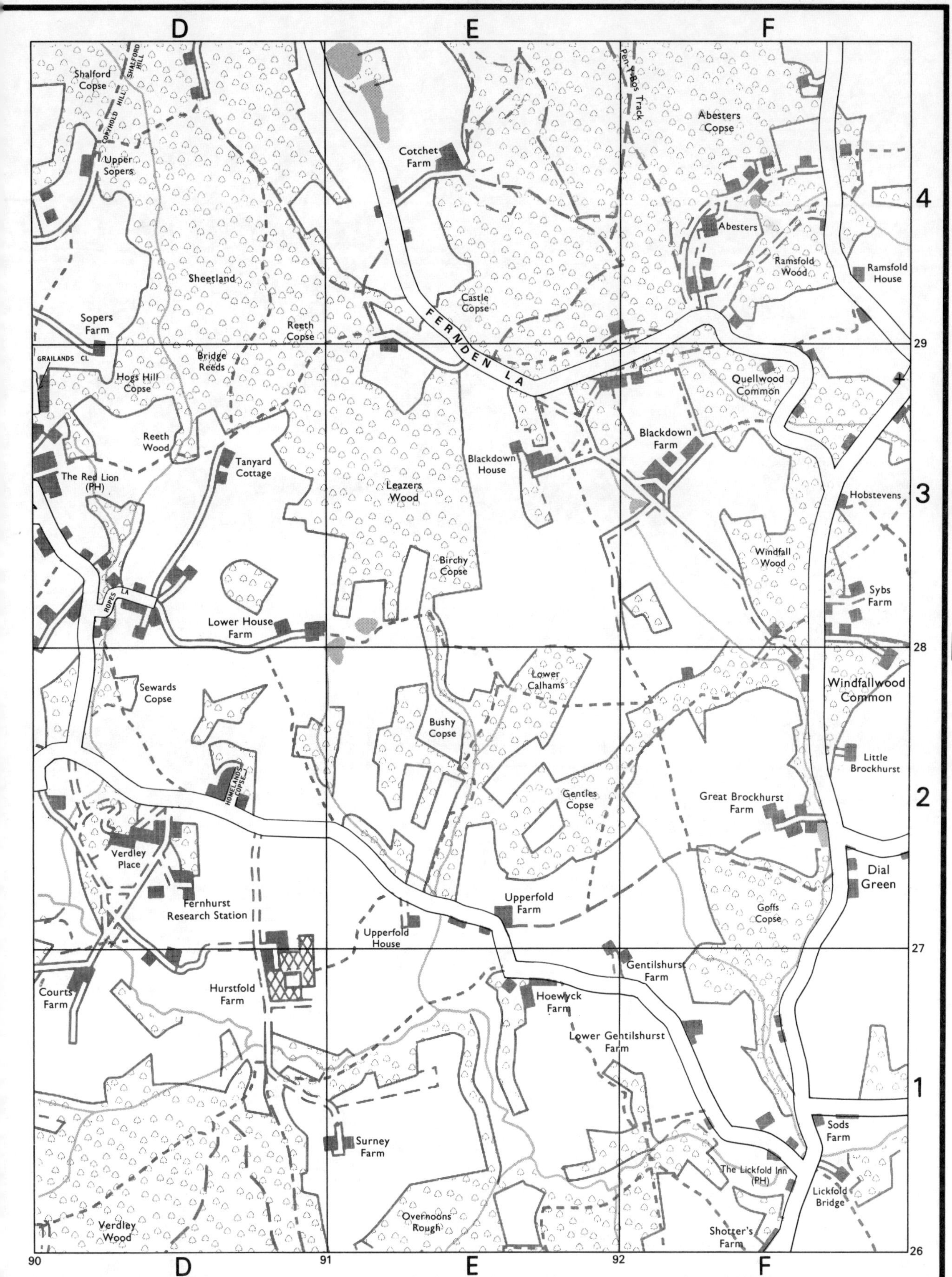
D
E
F
Shalford Copse
SHALFORD HILL
COPYHOLD HILL
Upper Sopers
Cotchet Farm
Pen-Y-Bos Track
Abesters Copse
Abesters
Ramsfold Wood
Ramsfold House
Sheetland
Sopers Farm
Reeth Copse
Castle Copse
FERNDEN LA
GRAILANDS CL
Bridge Reeds
Hogs Hill Copse
Quellwood Common
Reeth Wood
Blackdown Farm
Blackdown House
Tanyard Cottage
The Red Lion (PH)
Leazers Wood
Hobstevens
Windfall Wood
Birchy Copse
Sybs Farm
ROPES LA
Lower House Farm
Lower Calhams
Windfallwood Common
Sewards Copse
Bushy Copse
Little Brockhurst
Gentles Copse
HOMELANDS COPSE
Great Brockhurst Farm
Verdley Place
Dial Green
Upperfold Farm
Fernhurst Research Station
Goffs Copse
Upperfold House
Gentilshurst Farm
Courts Farm
Hurstfold Farm
Hoewyck Farm
Lower Gentilshurst Farm
Sods Farm
Surney Farm
The Lickfold Inn (PH)
Lickfold Bridge
Overnoons Rough
Verdley Wood
Shotter's Farm
4
3
2
1
29
28
27
26
90
91
92

48

69

27

47

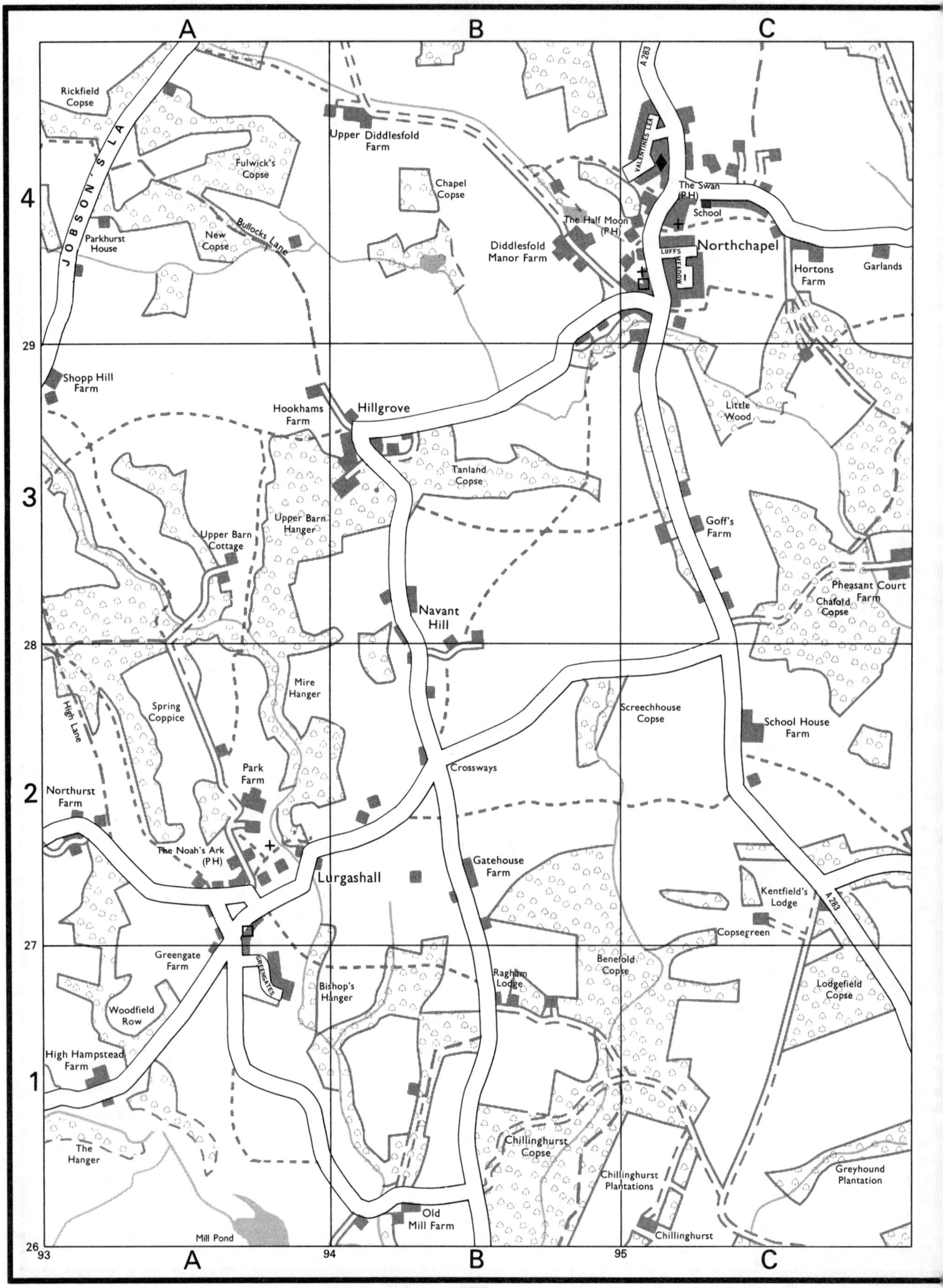

A
B
C
4
3
2
1
29
28
27
26
93
94
95
Rickfield Copse
JOBSON'S LA
Fulwick's Copse
Bullocks Lane
Parkhurst House
New Copse
Upper Diddlesfold Farm
Chapel Copse
Diddlesfold Manor Farm
The Half Moon (PH)
A 283
VALENTINES LEA
The Swan (PH)
School
Northchapel
LUFFS MEADOW
Hortons Farm
Garlands
Shopp Hill Farm
Hookhams Farm
Hillgrove
Little Wood
Tanland Copse
Upper Barn Hanger
Upper Barn Cottage
Goff's Farm
Pheasant Court Farm
Chafold Copse
Navant Hill
Mire Hanger
Spring Coppice
High Lane
Screechhouse Copse
School House Farm
Park Farm
Crossways
Northurst Farm
The Noah's Ark (PH)
Lurgashall
Gatehouse Farm
Kentfield's Lodge
Copsegreen
Greengate Farm
GREENGATES
Bishop's Hanger
Ragham Lodge
Benefold Copse
Lodgefield Copse
Woodfield Row
High Hampstead Farm
The Hanger
Chillinghurst Copse
Chillinghurst Plantations
Greyhound Plantation
Old Mill Farm
Mill Pond
Chillinghurst

70

28

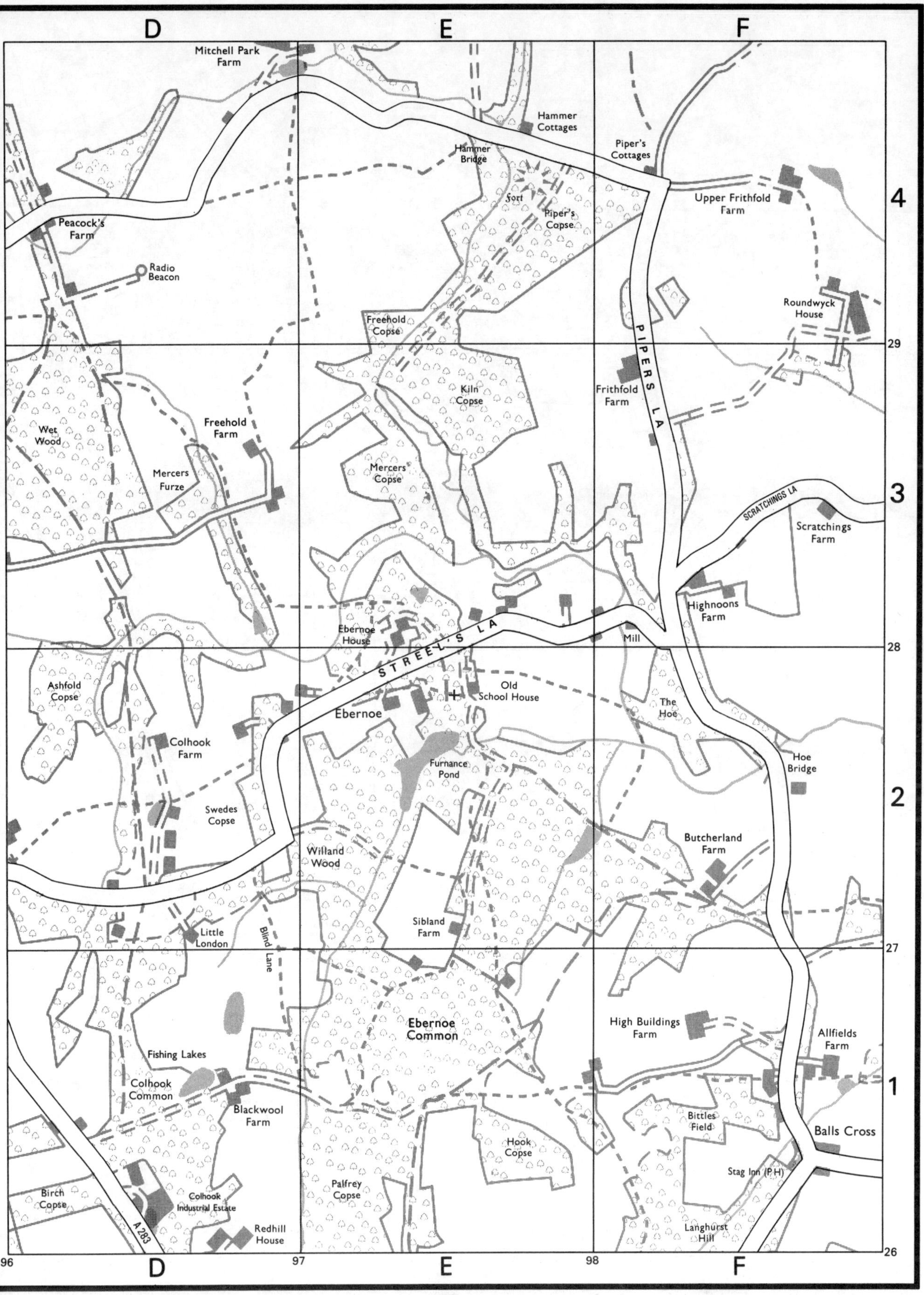
D
E
F
Mitchell Park Farm
Hammer Cottages
Hammer Bridge
Piper's Cottages
Fort
Piper's Copse
Upper Frithfold Farm
4
Peacock's Farm
Radio Beacon
Roundwyck House
Freehold Copse
PIPERS LA
29
Kiln Copse
Frithfold Farm
Wet Wood
Freehold Farm
Mercers Furze
Mercers Copse
3
SCRATCHINGS LA
Scratchings Farm
Highnoons Farm
Ebernoe House
STREEL'S LA
Mill
28
Ashfold Copse
Old School House
Ebernoe
The Hoe
Colhook Farm
Furnance Pond
Hoe Bridge
Swedes Copse
2
Willand Wood
Butcherland Farm
Sibland Farm
Little London
Blind Lane
27
Ebernoe Common
High Buildings Farm
Allfields Farm
Fishing Lakes
1
Colhook Common
Blackwool Farm
Bittles Field
Balls Cross
Hook Copse
Stag Inn (PH)
Birch Copse
Colhook Industrial Estate
Palfrey Copse
A 283
Redhill House
Langhurst Hill
26
96
97
98
D
E
F

50

71

29

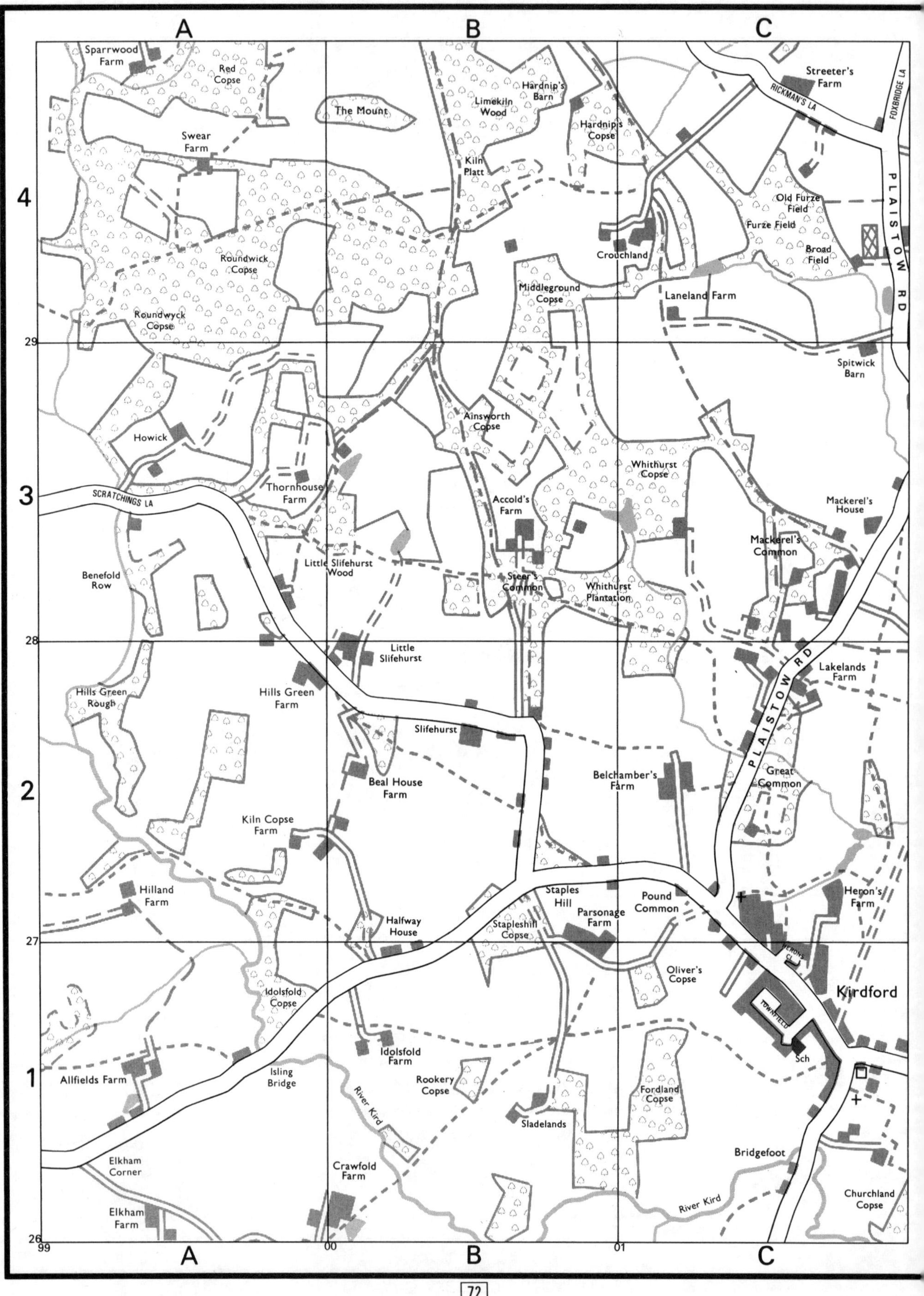
A
B
C
Sparrwood Farm
Red Copse
The Mount
Limekiln Wood
Hardnip's Barn
Hardnip's Copse
Streeter's Farm
RICKMAN'S LA
FOXBRIDGE LA
Swear Farm
Kiln Platt
Old Furze Field
Furze Field
Broad Field
PLAISTOW RD
Crouchland
Roundwick Copse
Middleground Copse
Laneland Farm
Roundwyck Copse
Spitwick Barn
Ainsworth Copse
Howick
Whithurst Copse
Thornhouse Farm
SCRATCHINGS LA
Accold's Farm
Mackerel's House
Mackerel's Common
Benefold Row
Little Slifehurst Wood
Steer's Common
Whithurst Plantation
Little Slifehurst
Lakelands Farm
Hills Green Rough
Hills Green Farm
PLAISTOW RD
Slifehurst
Belchamber's Farm
Great Common
Beal House Farm
Kiln Copse Farm
Hilland Farm
Staples Hill
Pound Common
Heron's Farm
Halfway House
Parsonage Farm
Stapleshill Copse
HERONS CL
Oliver's Copse
Idolsfold Copse
Kirdford
TOWNFIELD
Sch
Idolsfold Farm
Allfields Farm
Isling Bridge
Rookery Copse
River Kird
Fordland Copse
Sladelands
Bridgefoot
Elkham Corner
Crawfold Farm
River Kird
Churchland Copse
Elkham Farm
4
3
2
1
29
28
27
26
99
00
01

49

72

30
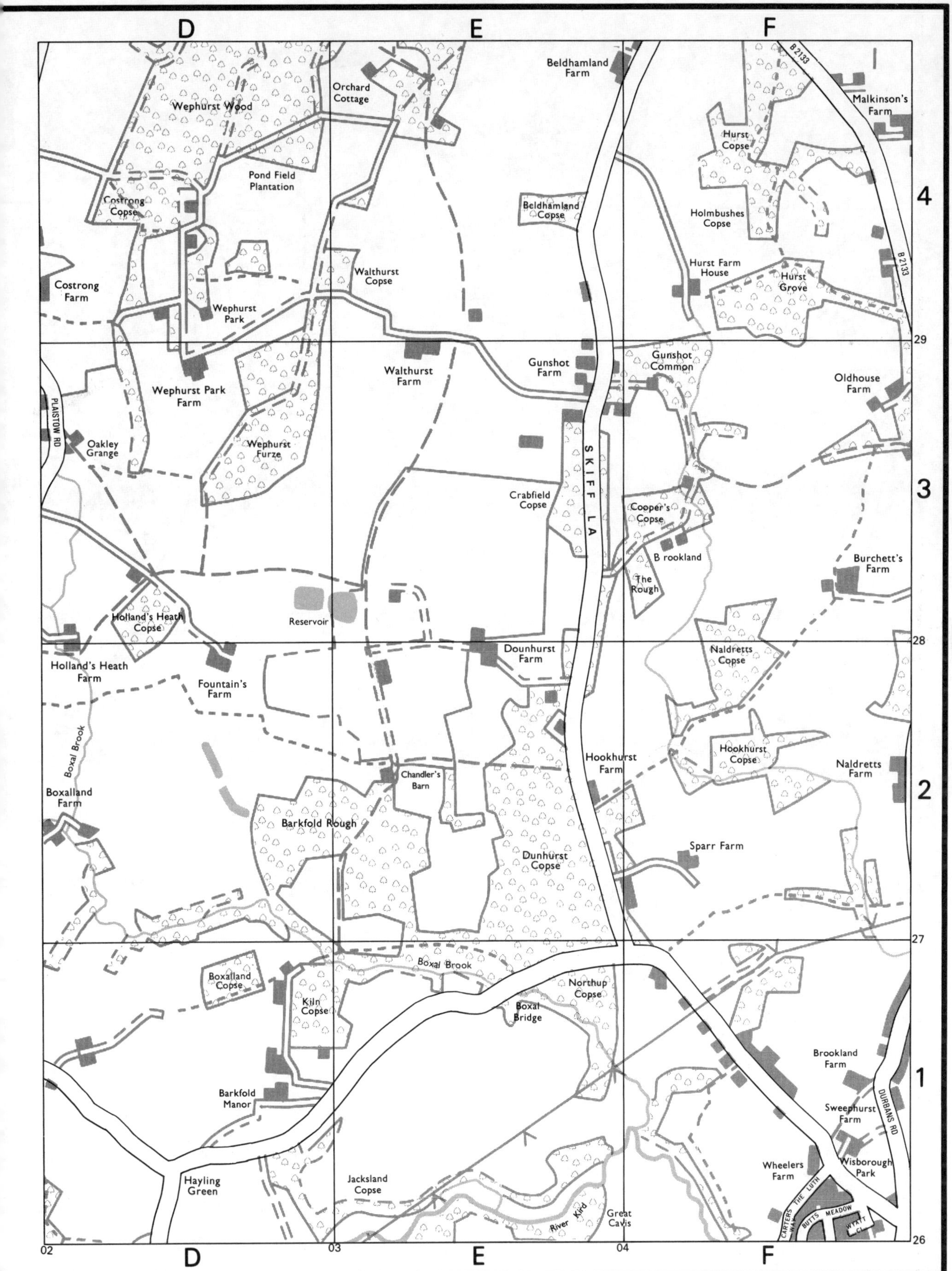
D
E
F
Beldhamland Farm
Orchard Cottage
Wephurst Wood
Malkinson's Farm
Hurst Copse
Pond Field Plantation
Costrong Copse
Beldhamland Copse
Holmbushes Copse
B2133
4
Costrong Farm
Walthurst Copse
Hurst Farm House
Hurst Grove
Wephurst Park
29
Gunshot Farm
Gunshot Common
Walthurst Farm
Oldhouse Farm
Wephurst Park Farm
PLAISTOW RD
Oakley Grange
Wephurst Furze
SKIFF LA
3
Crabfield Copse
Cooper's Copse
Brookland
Burchett's Farm
The Rough
Holland's Heath Copse
Reservoir
28
Dounhurst Farm
Naldretts Copse
Holland's Heath Farm
Fountain's Farm
Boxal Brook
Hookhurst Farm
Hookhurst Copse
Naldretts Farm
Boxalland Farm
Chandler's Barn
2
Barkfold Rough
Sparr Farm
Dunhurst Copse
27
Boxal Brook
Boxalland Copse
Northup Copse
Kiln Copse
Boxal Bridge
Brookland Farm
1
DURBANS RD
Barkfold Manor
Sweephurst Farm
Wheelers Farm
Wisborough Park
Hayling Green
Jacksland Copse
THE LUTH
CARTERS WAY
BUTTS MEADOW
WYATT CL
River Kird
Great Cavis
26
02
03
04
52
73

31

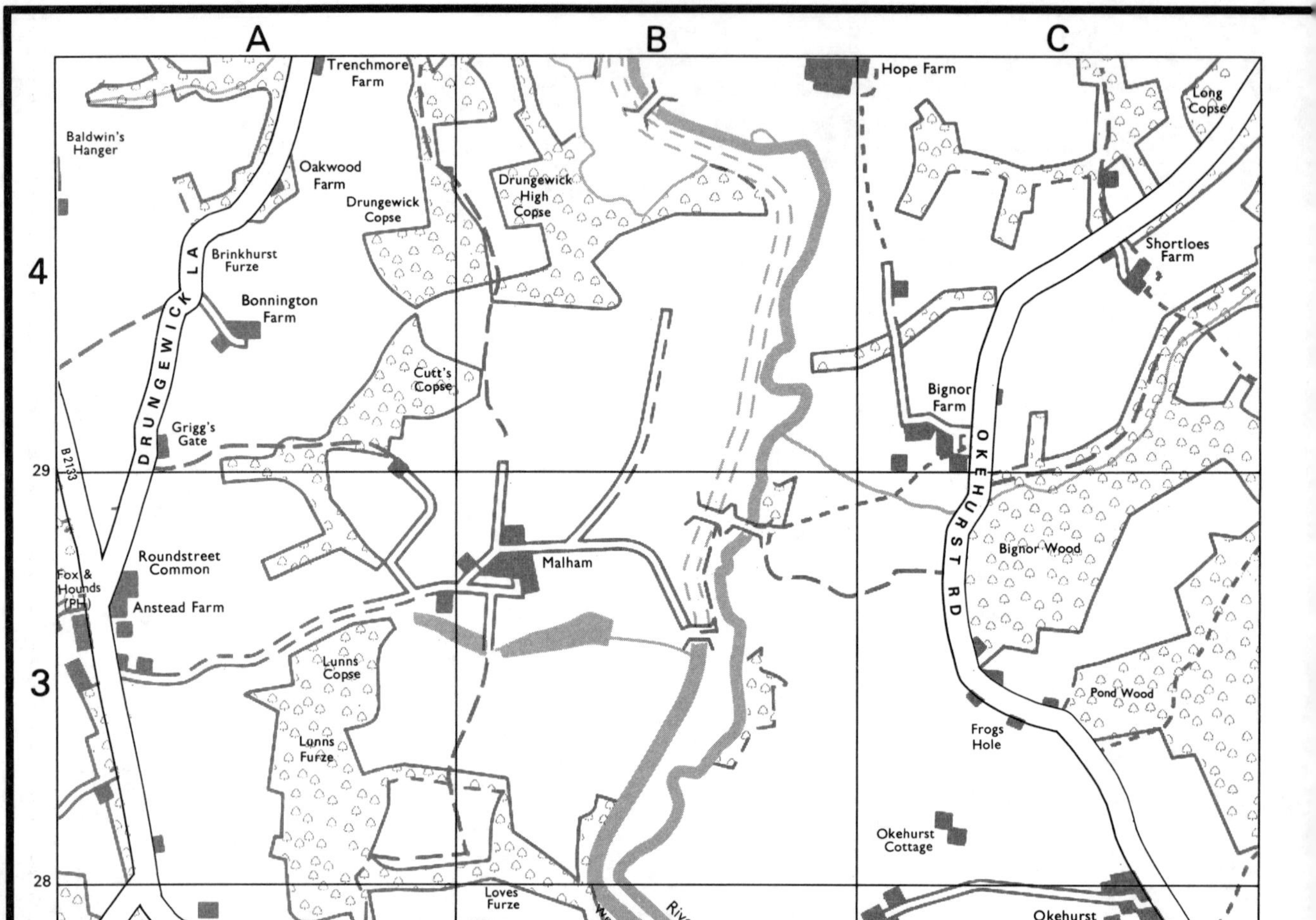

A
B
C
Trenchmore Farm
Hope Farm
Long Copse
Baldwin's Hanger
Oakwood Farm
Drungewick High Copse
Drungewick Copse
DRUNGEWICK LA
Brinkhurst Furze
Shortloes Farm
Bonnington Farm
Cutt's Copse
Bignor Farm
Grigg's Gate
B2133
OKEHURST RD
Bignor Wood
Roundstreet Common
Malham
Fox & Hounds (PH)
Anstead Farm
Lunns Copse
Pond Wood
Frogs Hole
Lunns Furze
Okehurst Cottage
Loves Furze
Okehurst
River Arun
Wey and Arun Junction Canal (disused)
Smale Farm
OKEHURST LA
Bittles Wood
Sole Copse
Naldretts Court
Loves Farm
NEWPOUND
Works
Paplands Farm
Hampshires
Sole Farm
Newpound Common
DURBANS RD
ROWNER RD
Stroodland Farm
The Bat & Ball (PH)
Rowner Farm
Howfold Farm
NEWPOUND LA
Eaton Copse
Hughes's Hill
Northlands Farm
The Cricketers Arms (PH)
B2133
4
3
2
1
29
28
27
26
05
06
07

51

74

32

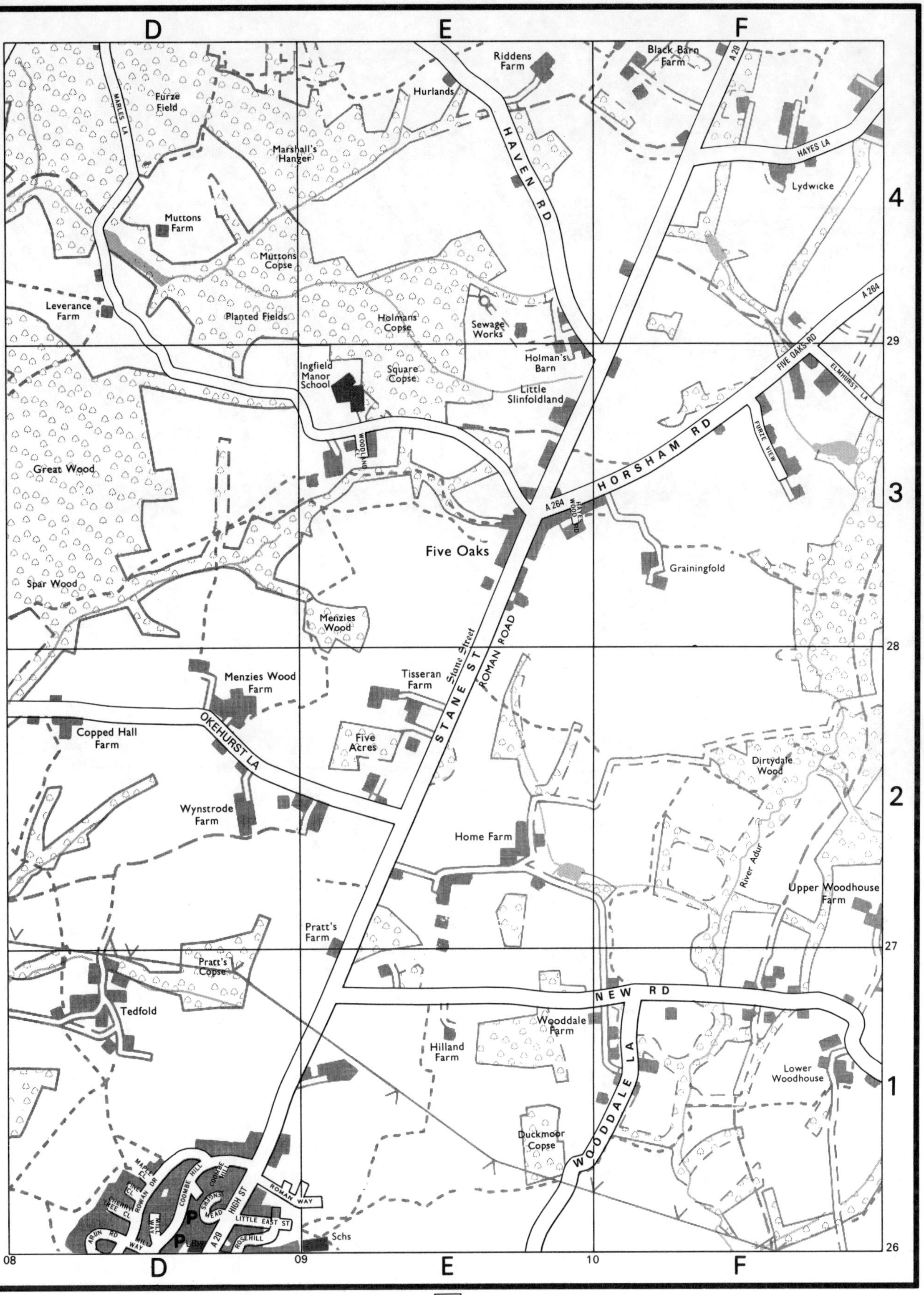

D
E
F
Black Barn Farm
Riddens Farm
Hurlands
Furze Field
MARLES LA
Marshall's Hanger
HAVEN RD
A 29
HAYES LA
Lydwicke
Muttons Farm
Muttons Copse
Leverance Farm
Planted Fields
Holmans Copse
Sewage Works
A 264
FIVE OAKS RD
ELMHURST LA
Ingfield Manor School
Square Copse
Holman's Barn
Little Slinfoldland
WOODLAND CL
HORSHAM RD
FURZE VIEW
Great Wood
HAYES WOOD RD
Five Oaks
Grainingfold
Spar Wood
Menzies Wood
Stane Street
STANE ST
ROMAN ROAD
Tisseran Farm
Menzies Wood Farm
Copped Hall Farm
OKEHURST LA
Five Acres
Dirtydale Wood
Wynstrode Farm
Home Farm
River Adur
Upper Woodhouse Farm
Pratt's Farm
Pratt's Copse
Tedfold
NEW RD
Wooddale Farm
Hilland Farm
Lower Woodhouse
WOODDALE LA
Duckmoor Copse
MAPLE CL
COOMBE HILL
ROWAN DR
CHERRY TREE CL
ARUN RD
MILL WAY
HIGH ST
ROMAN WAY
LITTLE EAST ST
ROSEHILL
A 29
Schs
4
3
2
1
29
28
27
26
08
09
10

54

75

33

53

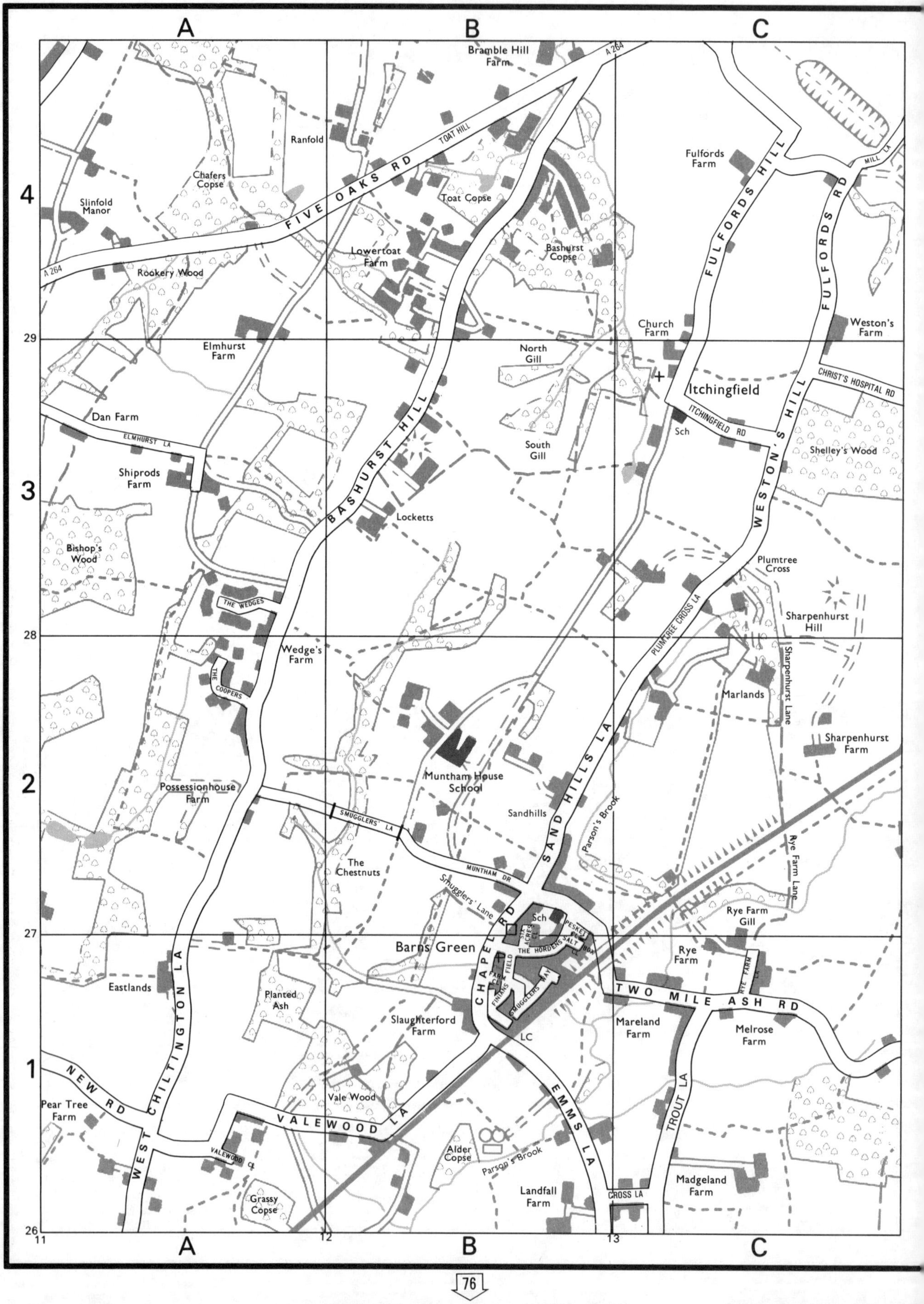

A
B
C
4
3
2
1
29
28
27
26
11
12
13
Bramble Hill Farm
A 264
Ranfold
TOAT HILL
FIVE OAKS RD
Chafers Copse
Slinfold Manor
Toat Copse
Fulfords Farm
FULFORDS HILL
FULFORDS RD
MILL LA
Lowertoat Farm
Bashurst Copse
Rookery Wood
Church Farm
Weston's Farm
Elmhurst Farm
North Gill
CHRIST'S HOSPITAL RD
Itchingfield
Dan Farm
ELMHURST LA
ITCHINGFIELD RD
Sch
South Gill
Shelley's Wood
Shiprods Farm
BASHURST HILL
WESTON'S HILL
Locketts
Bishop's Wood
Plumtree Cross
THE WEDGES
PLUMTREE CROSS LA
Sharpenhurst Hill
Wedge's Farm
THE COOPERS
Marlands
Sharpenhurst Lane
Sharpenhurst Farm
Muntham House School
Possessionhouse Farm
SMUGGLERS' LA
Sandhills
SAND HILLS LA
Parson's Brook
Rye Farm Lane
The Chestnuts
MUNTHAM DR
Smugglers' Lane
Sch
Rye Farm Gill
SIX ACRES CL
PESKETT CL
THE HORDENS
Barns Green
CHAPEL RD
FIELD
FINIANS
SMUGGLERS' WAY
Rye Farm
RYE FARM LA
Eastlands
TWO MILE ASH RD
Planted Ash
Slaughterford Farm
Mareland Farm
Melrose Farm
LC
WEST CHILTINGTON LA
NEW RD
EMMS LA
TROUT LA
Pear Tree Farm
Vale Wood
VALEWOOD LA
Alder Copse
Parson's Brook
VALEWOOD CL
Landfall Farm
Madgeland Farm
CROSS LA
Grassy Copse
A
B
C

76

34

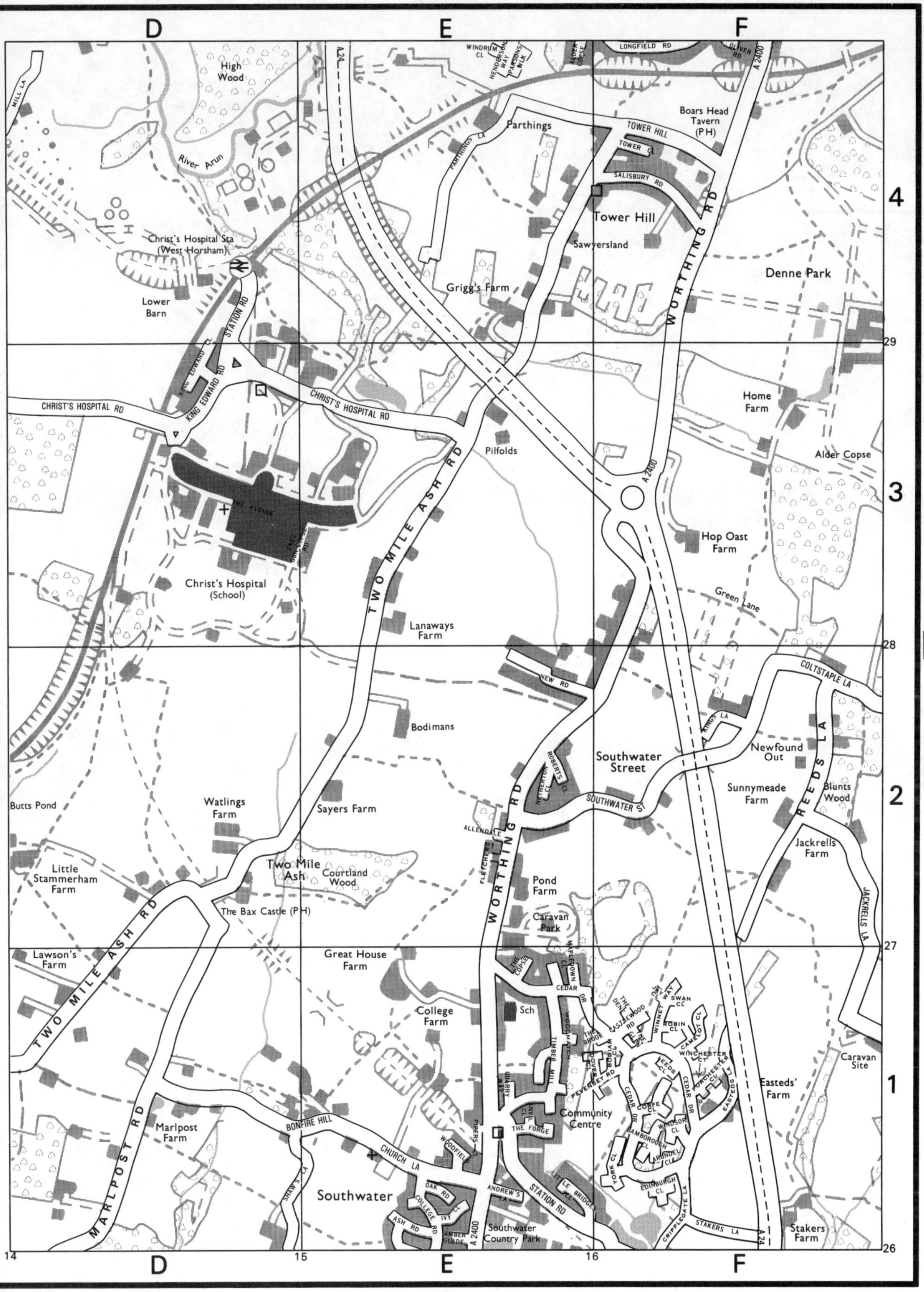
D
E
F
High Wood
MILL LA
River Arun
Christ's Hospital Sta (West Horsham)
Lower Barn
STATION RD
KING EDWARD CL
KING EDWARD RD
CHRIST'S HOSPITAL RD
THE AVENUE
EAST QUADRANGLE RD
Christ's Hospital (School)
A24
WINDRUM CL
HENDERSON WAY
PARSONS WLK
ALDER COPSE
LONGFIELD RD
OLIVER RD
A2400
Parthings
PARTHINGS LA
TOWER HILL
TOWER CL
SALISBURY RD
Boars Head Tavern (PH)
Tower Hill
Sawyersland
Grigg's Farm
WORTHING RD
Denne Park
Home Farm
Pilfolds
Alder Copse
TWO MILE ASH RD
Hop Oast Farm
Green Lane
Lanaways Farm
NEW RD
COLTSTAPLE LA
KINGS LA
Bodimans
ROBERTS CL
NETHERTON CL
Southwater Street
Newfound Out
REEDS LA
Sunnymeade Farm
Blunts Wood
SOUTHWATER ST
Butts Pond
Watlings Farm
Sayers Farm
ALLENDALE
Jackrells Farm
JACKRELLS LA
Little Stammerham Farm
Two Mile Ash
Courtland Wood
FLETCHERS
Pond Farm
The Bax Castle (PH)
Caravan Park
Lawson's Farm
Great House Farm
THE COPSE
MAPLEDOWN CL
CEDAR DR
College Farm
Sch
WOODMATCH
TIMBER MILL
THE BROOK
CASTLEWOOD RD
WINNET WAY
SWAN CL
ROBIN CL
CAMELOT CL
WINCHESTER CT
Caravan Site
QUARRY WAY
PEVENSEY RD
LEEDS CL
DORCHESTER CT
EASTEDS LA
Easteds' Farm
Marlpost Farm
BONFIRE HILL
PIPERS LA
THE FORGE
Community Centre
CORFE CL
WINDSOR CL
BAMBOROUGH CL
ARUNDEL CL
YORK CL
MARLPOST RD
SHAW'S LA
CHURCH LA
WOODFIELD
Southwater
OAK RD
COLLEGE RD
IVY CL
ASH RD
AMBER GLADE
ANDREW'S LA
STATION RD
LITTLE BRIDGE PCE
EDINBURGH CL
CRIPPLEGATE LA
STAKERS LA
Southwater Country Park
Stakers Farm
29
28
27
26
14
15
16
4
3
2
1

56

77

35

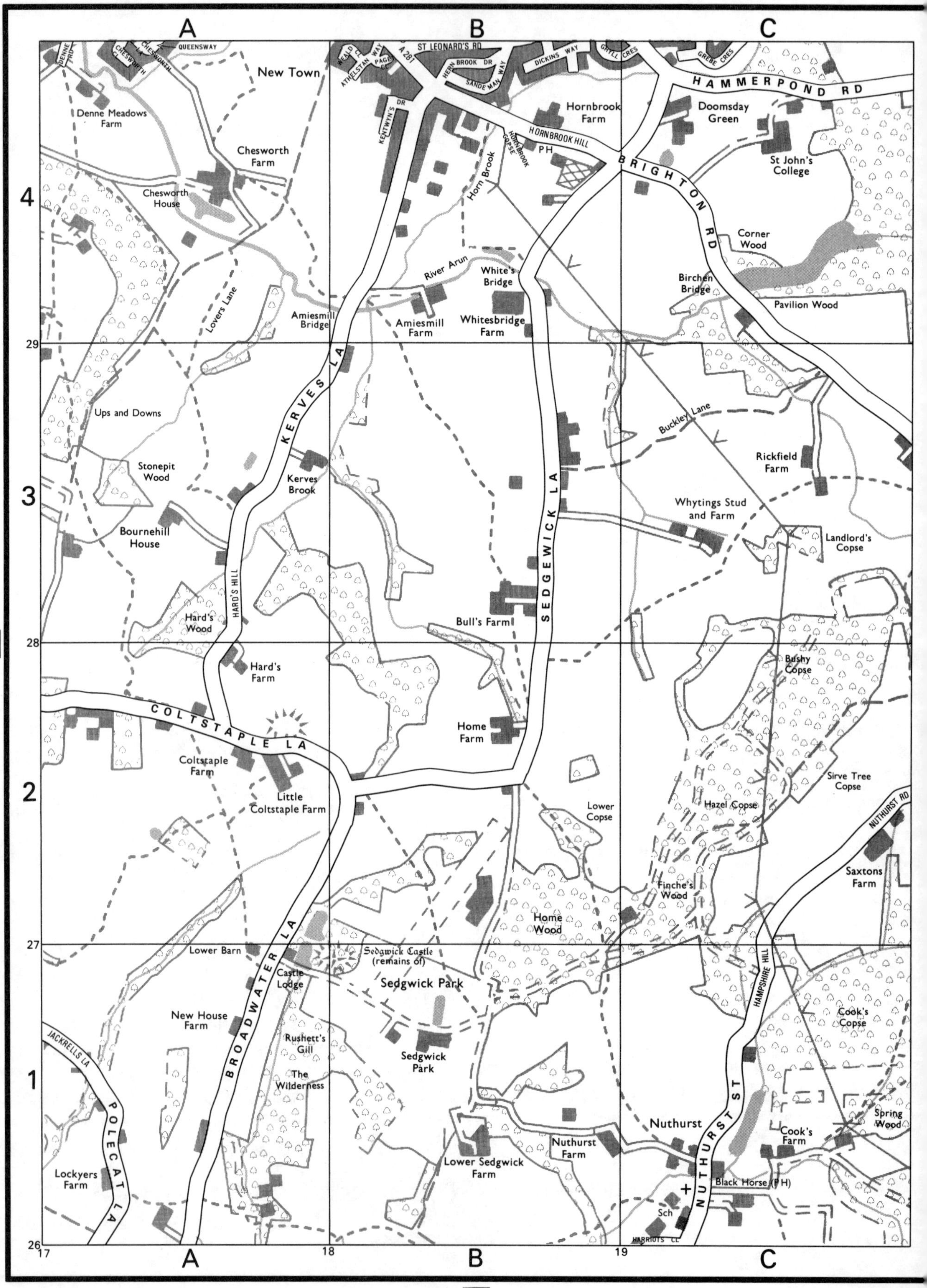
A
B
C
QUEENSWAY
DENNE RD
CHESWORTH
New Town
ST LEONARD'S RD
A 281
WEALD CL
ATHELSTAN WAY
PAGE CT
HERN BROOK DR
SANDEMAN WAY
DICKINS WAY
GHYLL CRES
GREBE CRES
HAMMERPOND RD
Denne Meadows Farm
KENTWYN'S DR
Hornbrook Farm
Doomsday Green
HORNBROOK HILL
HORNBROOK COPSE
PH
Chesworth Farm
Horn Brook
BRIGHTON RD
St John's College
Chesworth House
4
Corner Wood
River Arun
White's Bridge
Birchen Bridge
Lovers Lane
Pavilion Wood
Amiesmill Bridge
Amiesmill Farm
Whitesbridge Farm
29
KERVES LA
Ups and Downs
Buckley Lane
Rickfield Farm
Stonepit Wood
Kerves Brook
3
SEDGEWICK LA
Whytings Stud and Farm
Bournehill House
Landlord's Copse
HARD'S HILL
Hard's Wood
Bull's Farm
28
Hard's Farm
Bushy Copse
COLTSTAPLE LA
Home Farm
Coltstaple Farm
Sirve Tree Copse
2
Little Coltstaple Farm
Lower Copse
Hazel Copse
NUTHURST RD
Saxtons Farm
Finche's Wood
Home Wood
27
Lower Barn
Sedgwick Castle (remains of)
Castle Lodge
Sedgwick Park
HAMPSHIRE HILL
New House Farm
Cook's Copse
JACKRELLS LA
BROADWATER LA
Rushett's Gill
Sedgwick Park
1
The Wilderness
NUTHURST ST
POLECAT LA
Nuthurst
Spring Wood
Cook's Farm
Nuthurst Farm
Lockyers Farm
Lower Sedgwick Farm
Black Horse (PH)
Sch
HARRIOTS CL
26
17
18
19

55

78

36

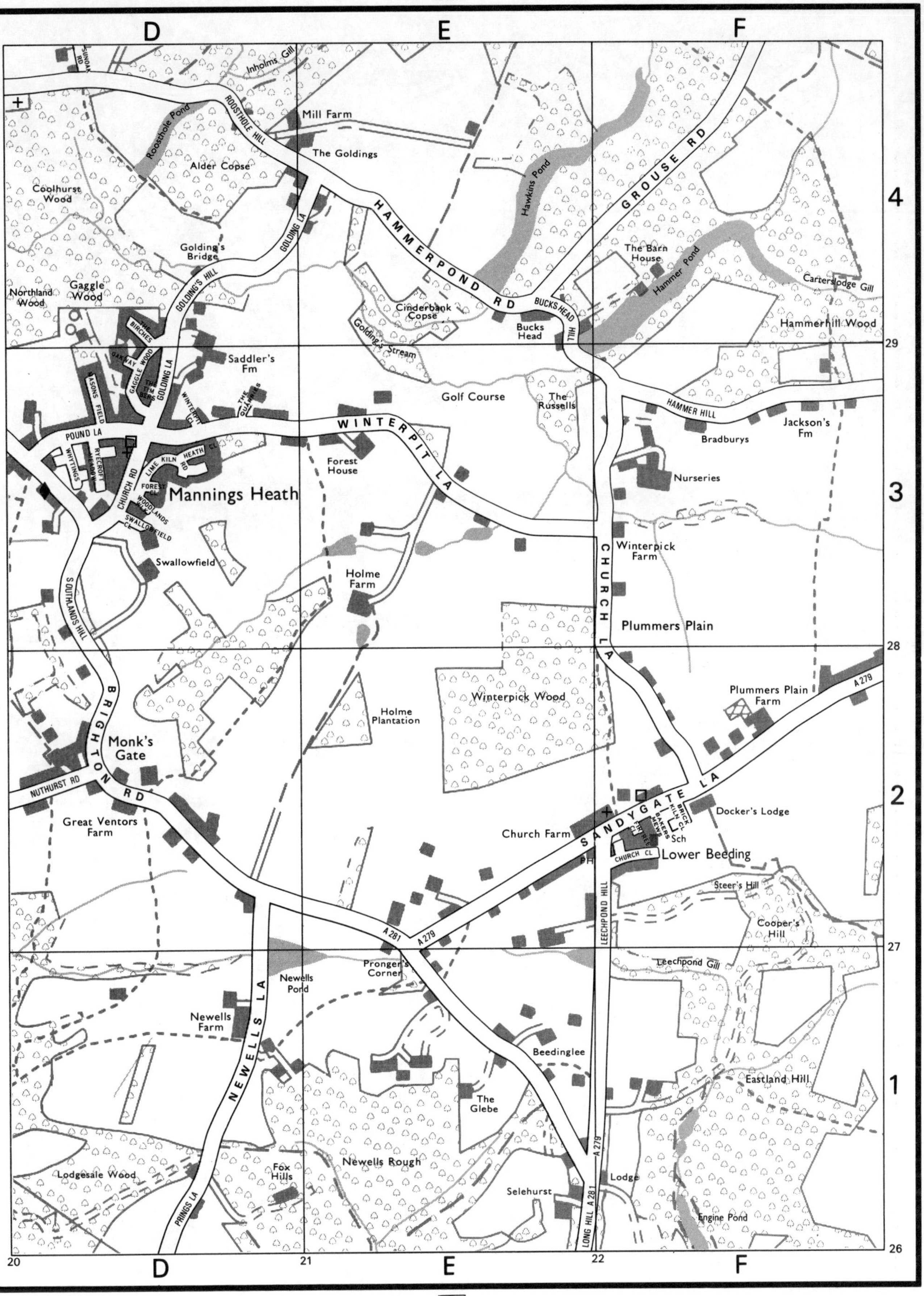
D
E
F
Inholms Gill
Mill Farm
Roosthole Pond
ROOSTHOLE HILL
The Goldings
Alder Copse
Coolhurst Wood
HAMMERPOND RD
Hawkins Pond
GROUSE RD
GOLDING LA
Golding's Bridge
GOLDING'S HILL
Northland Wood
Gaggle Wood
The Barn House
Hammer Pond
Carterslodge Gill
Cinderbank Copse
BUCKS HEAD HILL
Bucks Head
Hammerhill Wood
Golding's Stream
Saddler's Fm
Golf Course
The Russells
HAMMER HILL
Jackson's Fm
Bradburys
WINTERPIT LA
POUND LA
Forest House
Nurseries
Mannings Heath
CHURCH RD
Swallowfield
Winterpick Farm
CHURCH LA
Holme Farm
Plummers Plain
SOUTHLANDS HILL
Winterpick Wood
Plummers Plain Farm
A 279
Holme Plantation
BRIGHTON RD
Monk's Gate
NUTHURST RD
SANDYGATE LA
Docker's Lodge
Great Ventors Farm
Church Farm
Sch
CHURCH CL
Lower Beeding
PH
Steer's Hill
LEECHPOND HILL
Cooper's Hill
A 281
Prongers Corner
Leechpond Gill
Newells Pond
Newells Farm
NEWELLS LA
Beedinglee
Eastland Hill
The Glebe
Newells Rough
Lodgesale Wood
Fox Hills
Selehurst
Lodge
LONG HILL A 281
Engine Pond
PRINGS LA
4
3
2
1
29
28
27
26
20
21
22

58

79

37

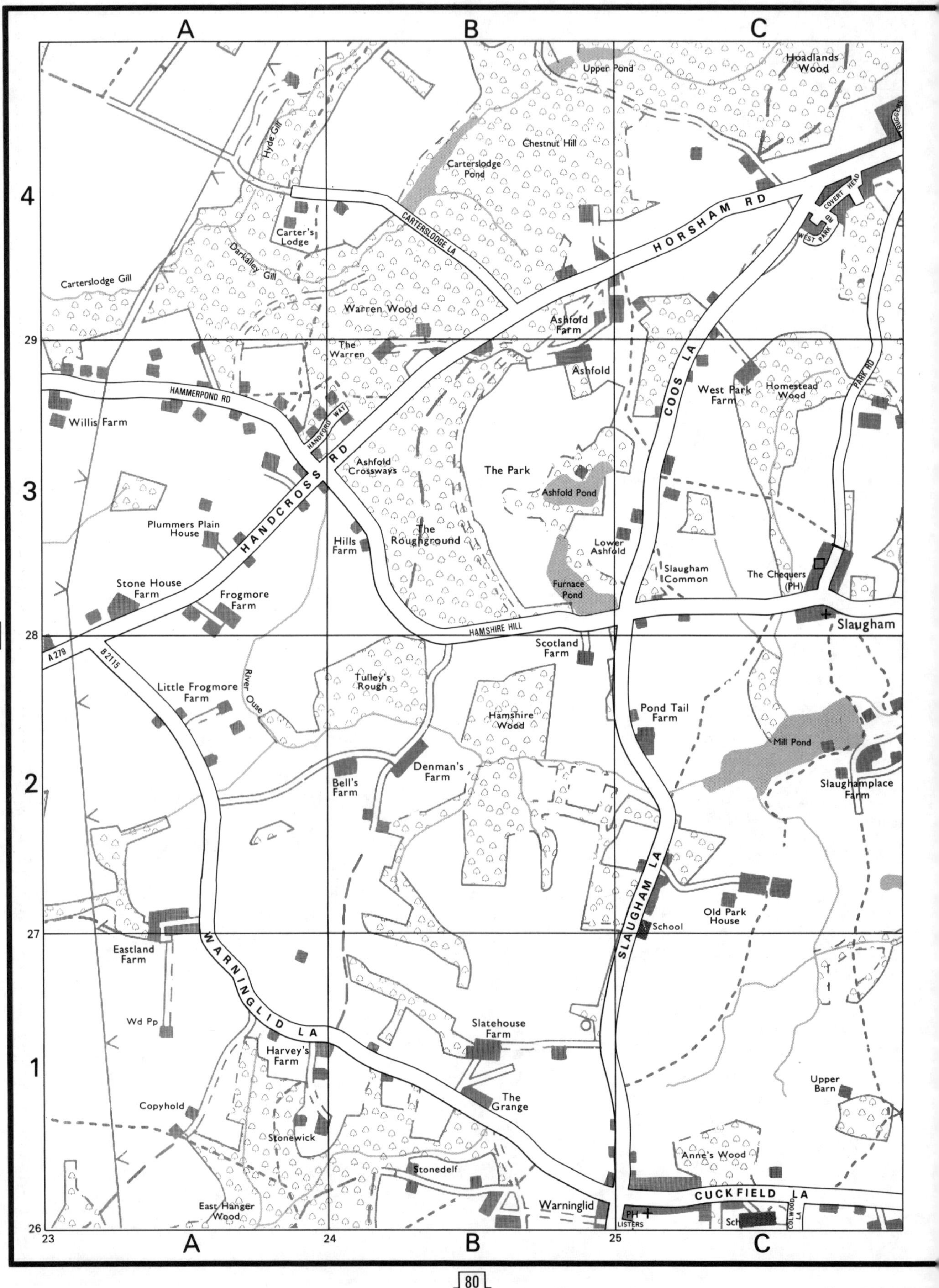

A
B
C
4
3
2
1
29
28
27
26
23
24
25
Upper Pond
Hoadlands Wood
Chestnut Hill
Carterslodge Pond
Hyde Gill
Carter's Lodge
CARTERSLODGE LA
HORSHAM RD
COVERT HEAD
WEST PARK RD
Darkalley Gill
Carterslodge Gill
Warren Wood
Ashfold Farm
The Warren
Ashfold
HAMMERPOND RD
Willis Farm
HANDFORD WAY
West Park Farm
Homestead Wood
PARK RD
COOS LA
Ashfold Crossways
The Park
Ashfold Pond
HANDCROSS RD
Plummers Plain House
Hills Farm
The Roughground
Lower Ashfold
Slaugham Common
The Chequers (PH)
Stone House Farm
Frogmore Farm
Furnace Pond
HAMSHIRE HILL
Slaugham
A 279
B 2115
Scotland Farm
Little Frogmore Farm
River Ouse
Tulley's Rough
Hamshire Wood
Pond Tail Farm
Mill Pond
Denman's Farm
Bell's Farm
Slaughamplace Farm
SLAUGHAM LA
Old Park House
School
Eastland Farm
WARNINGLID LA
Wd Pp
Slatehouse Farm
Harvey's Farm
Upper Barn
Copyhold
The Grange
Stonewick
Anne's Wood
Stonedelf
CUCKFIELD LA
East Hanger Wood
Warninglid
PH
LISTERS
COLWOOD LA
A
B
C

57

80

38
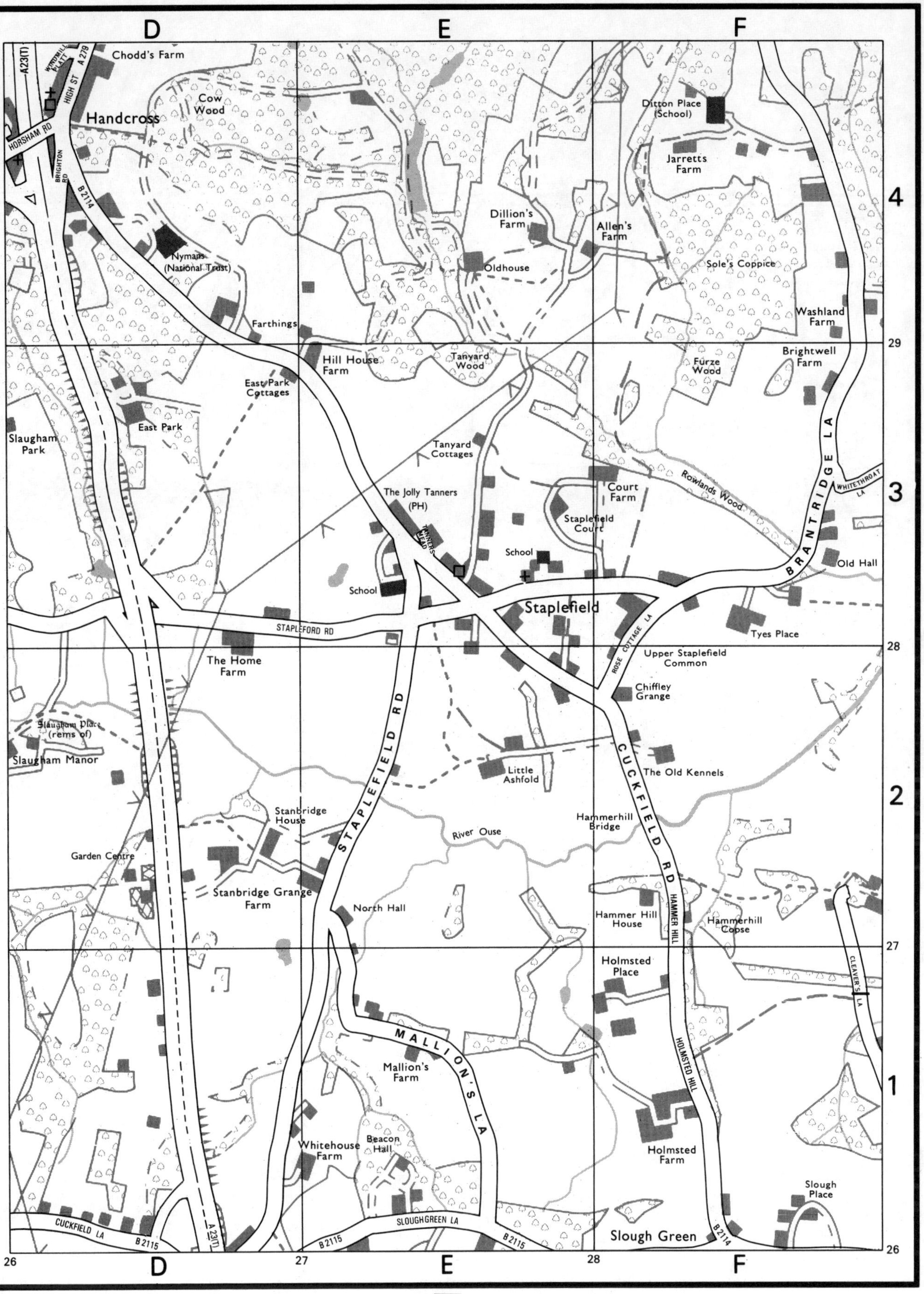
D
E
F
Chodd's Farm
Handcross
Cow Wood
HORSHAM RD
HIGH ST
A279
A23(T)
BRIGHTON RD
B2114
Nymans (National Trust)
Farthings
Ditton Place (School)
Jarretts Farm
Dillion's Farm
Allen's Farm
Oldhouse
Sole's Coppice
Washland Farm
Hill House Farm
Tanyard Wood
Furze Wood
Brightwell Farm
East Park Cottages
East Park
Slaugham Park
Tanyard Cottages
Rowlands Wood
The Jolly Tanners (PH)
Court Farm
Staplefield Court
BRANTRIDGE LA
WHITETHROAT LA
School
Old Hall
School
Staplefield
STAPLEFORD RD
ROSE COTTAGE LA
Tyes Place
The Home Farm
Upper Staplefield Common
Chiffley Grange
Slaugham Place (rems of)
Slaugham Manor
STAPLEFIELD RD
CUCKFIELD RD
The Old Kennels
Little Ashfold
Stanbridge House
Hammerhill Bridge
River Ouse
Garden Centre
Stanbridge Grange Farm
North Hall
HAMMER HILL
Hammer Hill House
Hammerhill Copse
Holmsted Place
CLEAVER'S LA
MALLION'S LA
Mallion's Farm
HOLMSTED HILL
Whitehouse Farm
Beacon Hall
Holmsted Farm
Slough Place
CUCKFIELD LA
B2115
SLOUGHGREEN LA
Slough Green
B2114
4
3
2
1
29
28
27
26
27
28
60
81

39

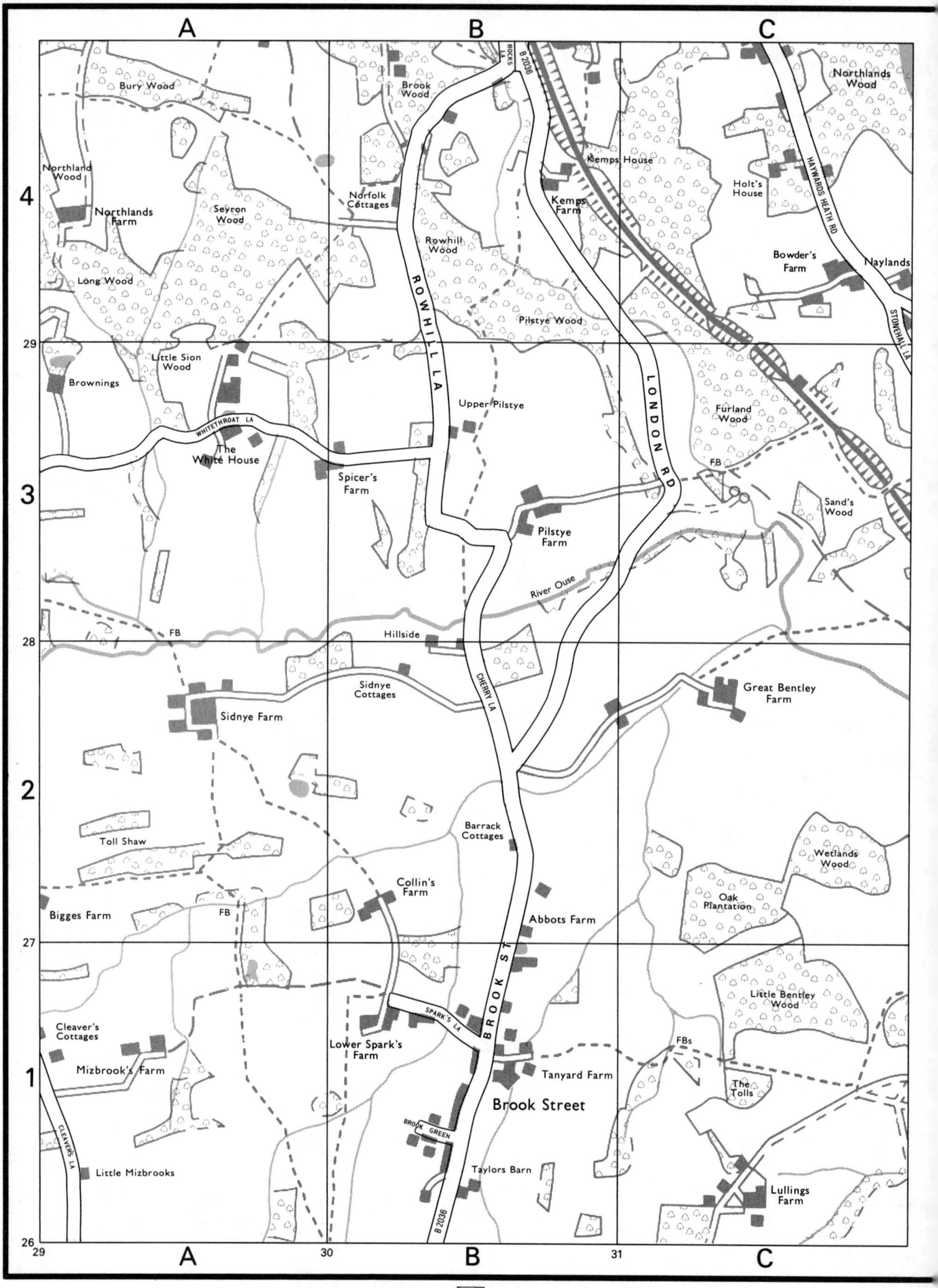
A
B
C
4
3
2
1
29
28
27
26
29
30
31
Bury Wood
Brook Wood
ROCKS LA
B 2036
Northlands Wood
Northland Wood
Northlands Farm
Seyron Wood
Norfolk Cottages
Kemps House
Kemps Farm
Holt's House
HAYWARDS HEATH RD
Rowhill Wood
Bowder's Farm
Naylands
Long Wood
ROWHILL LA
Pilstye Wood
STONEHALL LA
Little Sion Wood
Brownings
LONDON RD
Upper Pilstye
Furland Wood
WHITETHROAT LA
The White House
Spicer's Farm
FB
Sand's Wood
Pilstye Farm
River Ouse
FB
Hillside
CHERRY LA
Great Bentley Farm
Sidnye Cottages
Sidnye Farm
Barrack Cottages
Toll Shaw
Wetlands Wood
Collin's Farm
Oak Plantation
Bigges Farm
FB
Abbots Farm
BROOK ST
Little Bentley Wood
SPARK'S LA
Cleaver's Cottages
Lower Spark's Farm
FBs
Mizbrook's Farm
Tanyard Farm
The Tolls
Brook Street
CLEAVERS LA
BROOK GREEN
Little Mizbrooks
Taylors Barn
Lullings Farm
B 2036

59

82

40

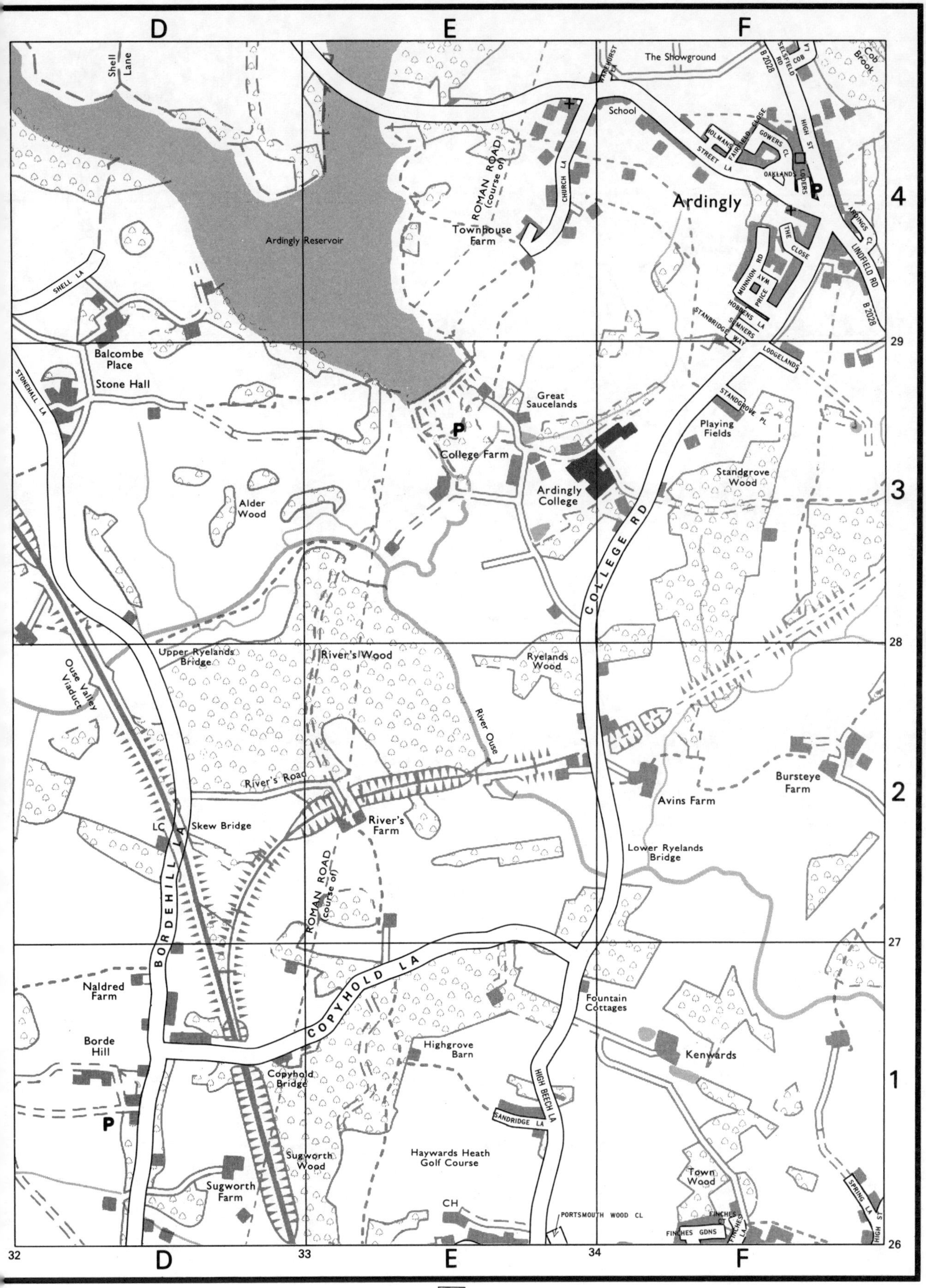

D
E
F
Shell Lane
The Showground
School
Ardingly
Ardingly Reservoir
ROMAN ROAD (course of)
Townhouse Farm
CHURCH LA
STREET LA
HOLMANS
FAIRFIELD CLOSE
GOWERS CL
OAKLANDS
LODGERS
HIGH ST
SELSFIELD RD
B 2028
COB LA
Cob Brook
ARDINGS CL
THE CLOSE
LINDFIELD RD
MUNNION RD
PRICE WAY
HOBBENS LA
SUMNERS
STANBRIDGE WAY
LODGELANDS
STANDGROVE PL
SHELL LA
Balcombe Place
Stone Hall
STONEHALL LA
Great Saucelands
College Farm
Playing Fields
Standgrove Wood
Alder Wood
Ardingly College
COLLEGE RD
Upper Ryelands Bridge
River's Wood
Ryelands Wood
Ouse Valley Viaduct
River Ouse
River's Road
Bursteye Farm
Avins Farm
LC
Skew Bridge
River's Farm
Lower Ryelands Bridge
BORDEHILL LA
ROMAN ROAD (course of)
COPYHOLD LA
Naldred Farm
Fountain Cottages
Borde Hill
Highgrove Barn
Kenwards
Copyhold Bridge
HIGH BEECH LA
SANDRIDGE LA
Haywards Heath Golf Course
Sugworth Wood
Sugworth Farm
Town Wood
CH
SPRING LA
PORTSMOUTH WOOD CL
FINCHES CL
FINCHES LA
FINCHES GDNS
HIGH ST
4
3
2
1
29
28
27
26
32
33
34

62

83

41

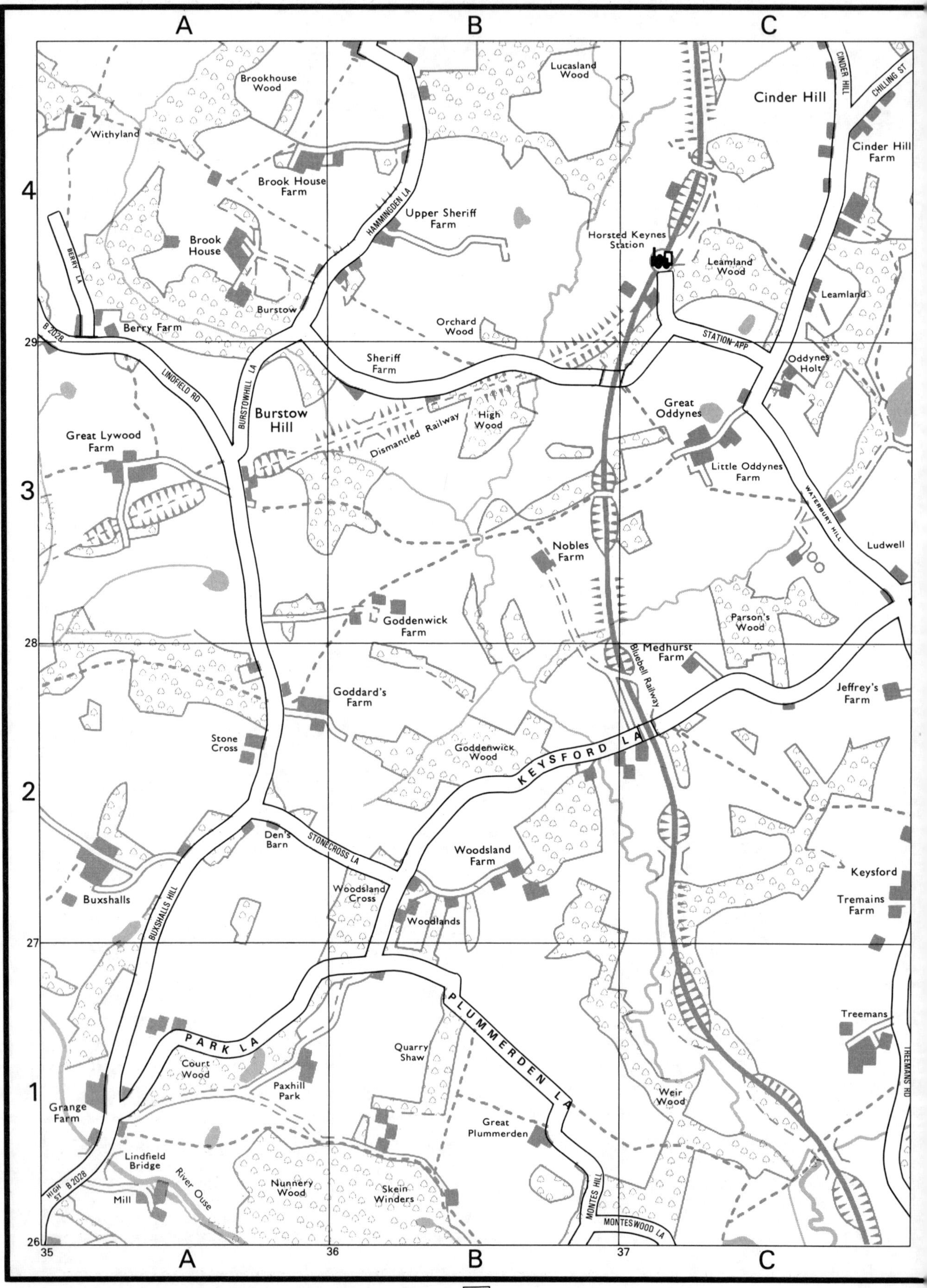
A
B
C
4
3
2
1
29
28
27
26
35
36
37
Brookhouse Wood
Lucasland Wood
Cinder Hill
CINDER HILL
CHILLING ST
Withyland
Cinder Hill Farm
Brook House Farm
HAMMINGDEN LA
Upper Sheriff Farm
Horsted Keynes Station
BERRY LA
Brook House
Leamland Wood
Leamland
Burstow
Orchard Wood
STATION APP
B 2028
Berry Farm
Sheriff Farm
Oddynes Holt
LINDFIELD RD
BURSTOWHILL LA
Burstow Hill
Great Oddynes
High Wood
Dismantled Railway
Great Lywood Farm
Little Oddynes Farm
WATERBURY HILL
Nobles Farm
Ludwell
Parson's Wood
Goddenwick Farm
Medhurst Farm
Bluebell Railway
Jeffrey's Farm
Goddard's Farm
Stone Cross
KEYSFORD LA
Goddenwick Wood
Den's Barn
STONECROSS LA
Woodsland Farm
Keysford
Buxshalls
BUXSHALLS HILL
Woodsland Cross
Tremains Farm
Woodlands
PLUMMERDEN LA
Treemans
PARK LA
Quarry Shaw
TREEMANS RD
Court Wood
Paxhill Park
Grange Farm
Weir Wood
Great Plummerden
Lindfield Bridge
River Ouse
HIGH ST
B 2028
Nunnery Wood
Skein Winders
Mill
MONTES HILL
MONTESWOOD LA

61

84

42

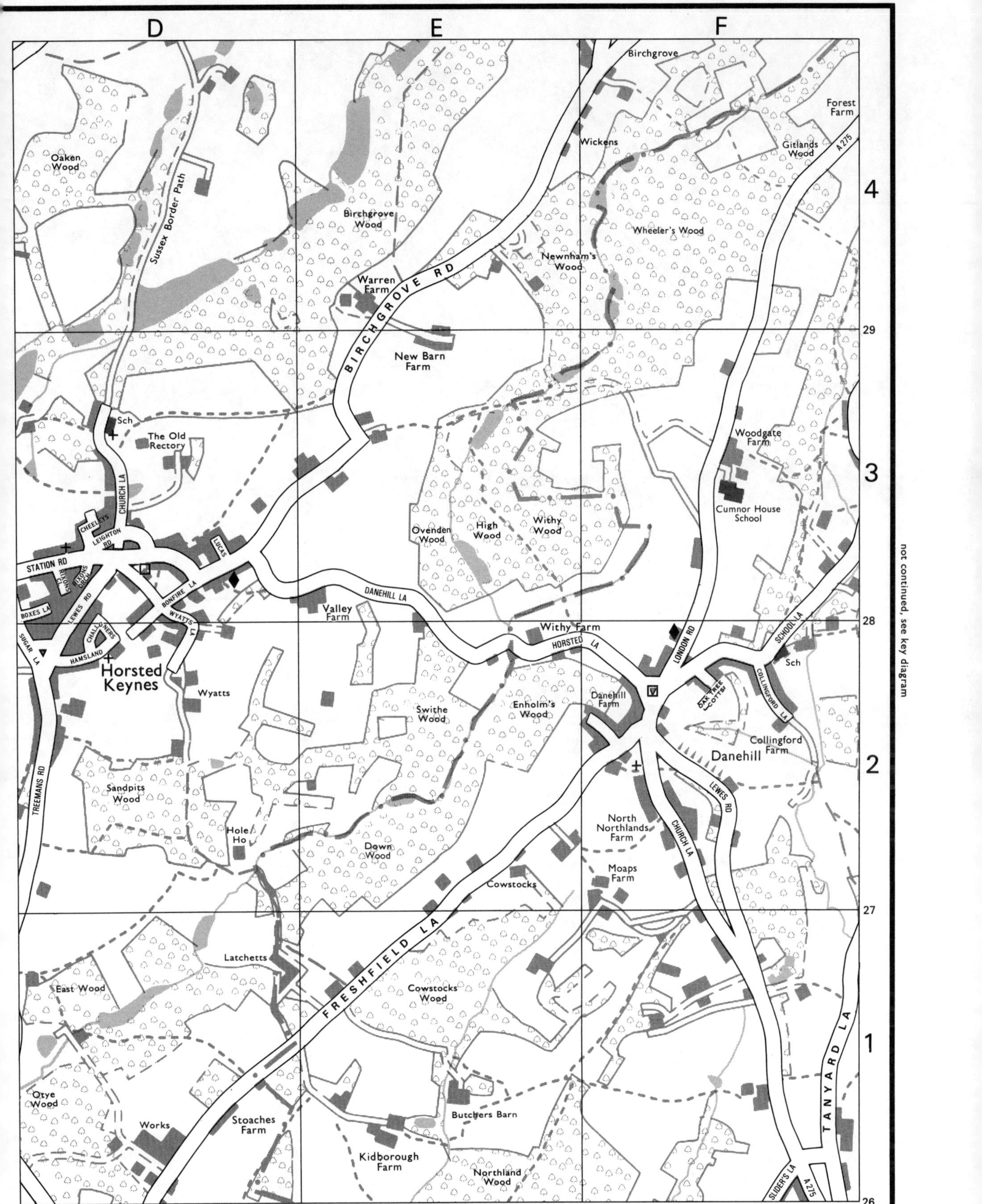
D
E
F
Oaken Wood
Sussex Border Path
Birchgrove Wood
Birchgrove
Wickens
Forest Farm
Gitlands Wood
A 275
Wheeler's Wood
Newnham's Wood
Warren Farm
BIRCHGROVE RD
New Barn Farm
Sch
The Old Rectory
CHURCH LA
CHEELEYS
LEIGHTON RD
LUCAS
STATION RD
BONFIRE LA
LEWES RD
BOXES LA
WYATTS LA
CHALLONERS
HAMSLAND
SUGAR LA
Horsted Keynes
Wyatts
DANEHILL LA
Valley Farm
Ovenden Wood
High Wood
Withy Wood
Woodgate Farm
Cumnor House School
Withy Farm
HORSTED LA
LONDON RD
SCHOOL LA
Sch
COLLINGFORD LA
OAK TREE COTTS
Danehill Farm
Enholm's Wood
Swithe Wood
Collingford Farm
Danehill
LEWES RD
Sandpits Wood
TREEMANS RD
Hole Ho
Down Wood
North Northlands Farm
CHURCH LA
Moaps Farm
Cowstocks
Latchetts
FRESHFIELD LA
East Wood
Cowstocks Wood
TANYARD LA
Otye Wood
Works
Stoaches Farm
Butchers Barn
Kidborough Farm
Northland Wood
SLIDER'S LA
A 275
4
3
2
1
29
28
27
26
38
39
40
D
E
F
not continued, see key diagram

85

not continued, see key diagram

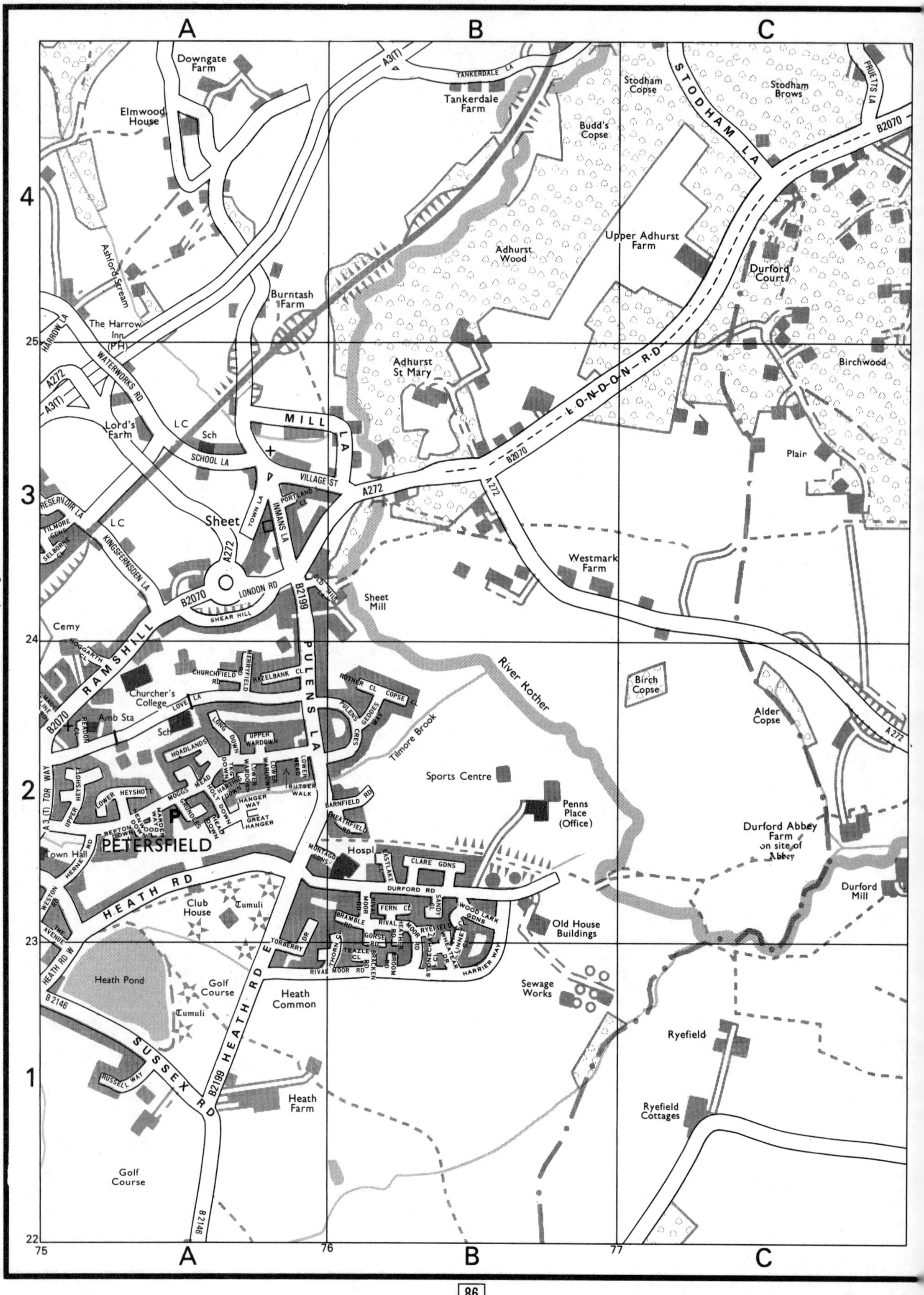

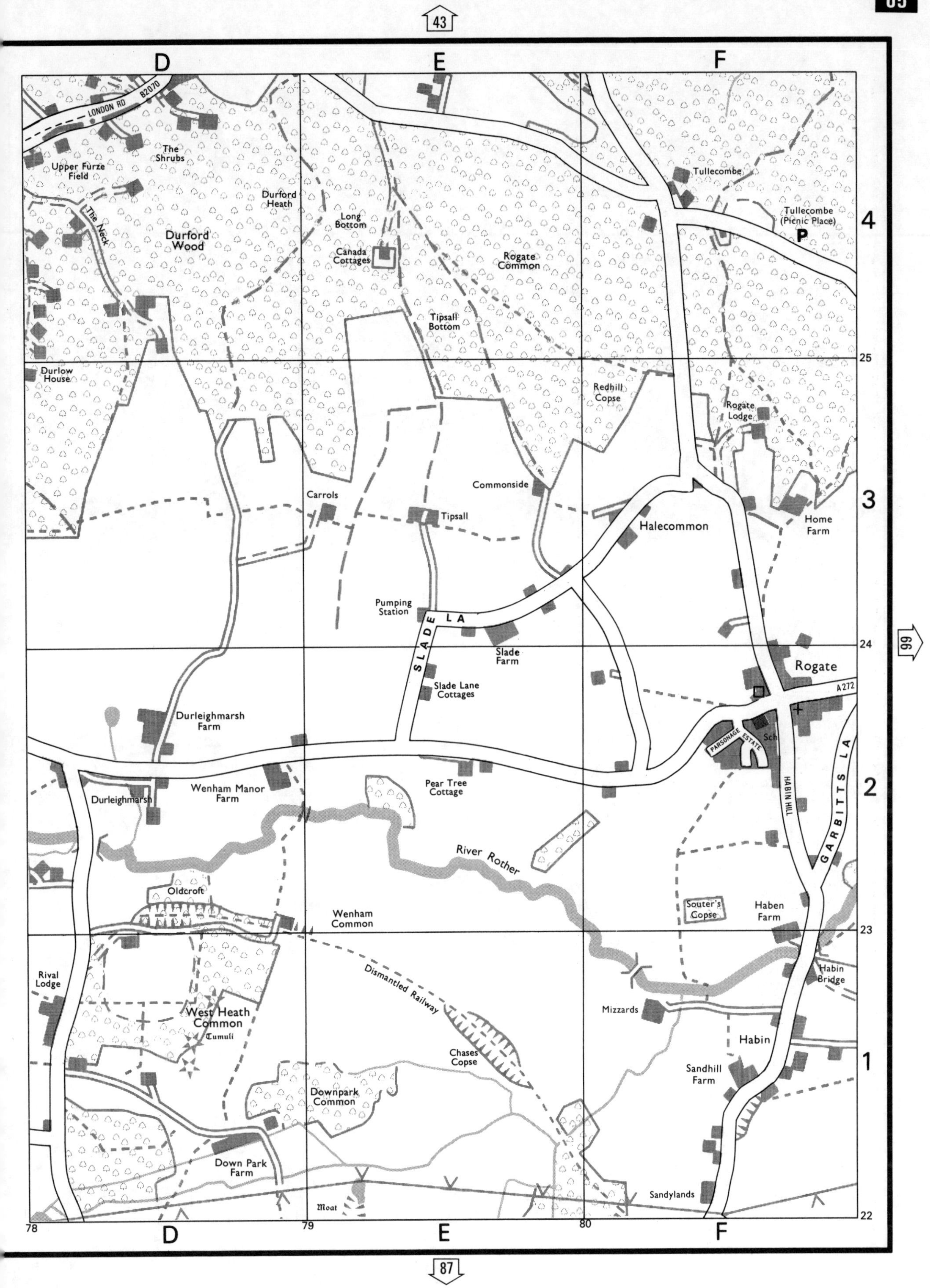
43
D
E
F
LONDON RD
B2070
The Shrubs
Upper Furze Field
Durford Heath
The Neck
Durford Wood
Long Bottom
Canada Cottages
Rogate Common
Tullecombe
Tullecombe (Picnic Place)
P
4
Tipsall Bottom
25
Durlow House
Redhill Copse
Rogate Lodge
Commonside
Carrols
Tipsall
3
Halecommon
Home Farm
Pumping Station
SLADE LA
Slade Farm
24
66
Rogate
Slade Lane Cottages
A272
Durleighmarsh Farm
PARSONAGE ESTATE
Sch
Pear Tree Cottage
HABIN HILL
GARBITTS LA
2
Wenham Manor Farm
Durleighmarsh
River Rother
Oldcroft
Souter's Copse
Haben Farm
Wenham Common
23
Rival Lodge
Dismantled Railway
Habin Bridge
West Heath Common
Tumuli
Mizzards
Habin
Chases Copse
1
Sandhill Farm
Downpark Common
Down Park Farm
Moat
Sandylands
22
78
79
80
D
E
F
87

44

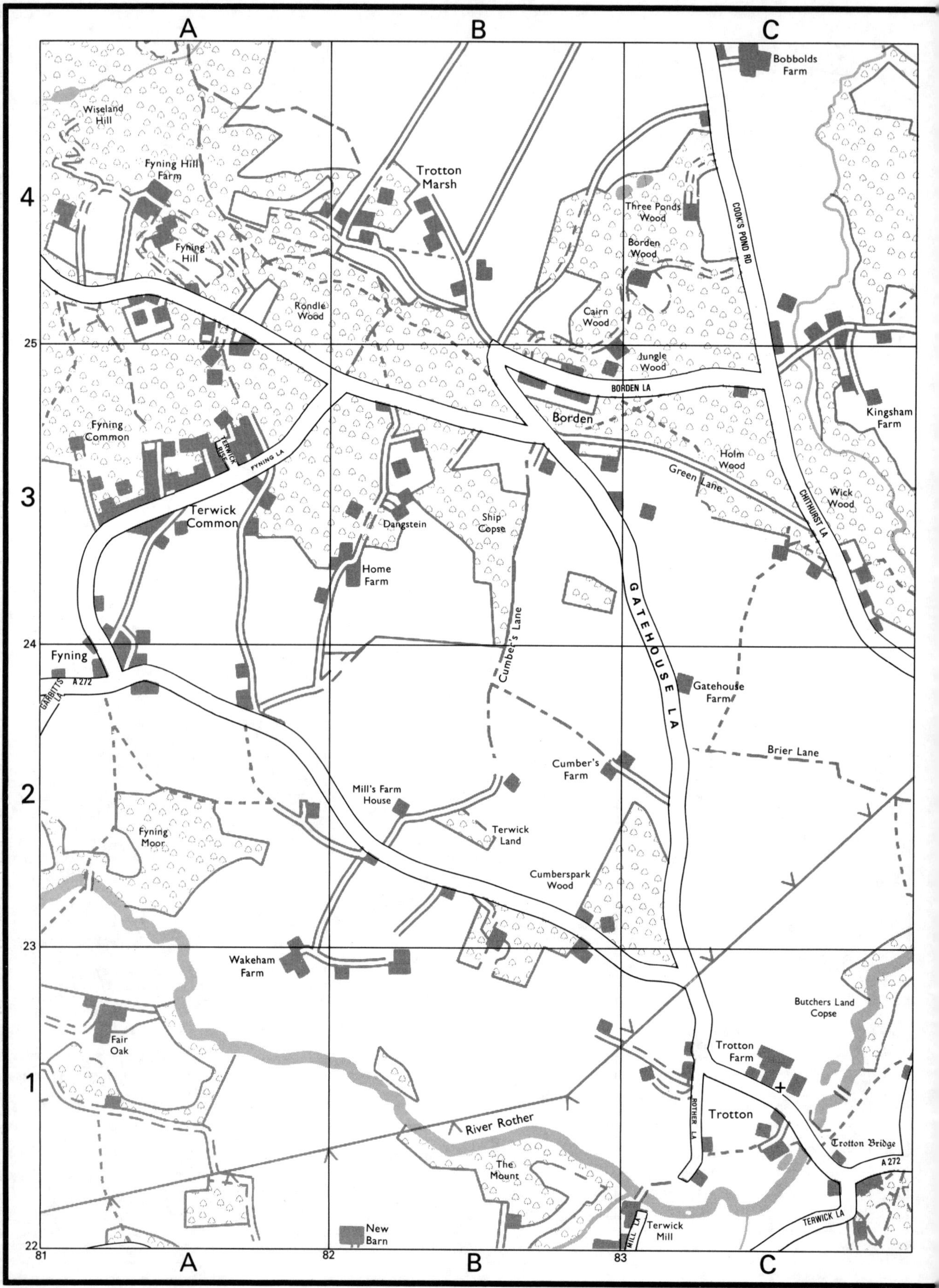
A
B
C
4
3
2
1
25
24
23
22
81
82
83
Wiseland Hill
Fyning Hill Farm
Fyning Hill
Rondle Wood
Trotton Marsh
Bobbolds Farm
Three Ponds Wood
Borden Wood
COOK'S POND RD
Cairn Wood
Jungle Wood
BORDEN LA
Borden
Kingsham Farm
Fyning Common
TERWICK RISE
FYNING LA
Holm Wood
Green Lane
Wick Wood
CHITHURST LA
Terwick Common
Dangstein
Ship Copse
Home Farm
GATEHOUSE LA
Cumber's Lane
Fyning
A 272
GARBITTS LA
Gatehouse Farm
Brier Lane
Cumber's Farm
Mill's Farm House
Fyning Moor
Terwick Land
Cumberspark Wood
Wakeham Farm
Butchers Land Copse
Fair Oak
Trotton Farm
Trotton
ROTHER LA
River Rother
Trotton Bridge
The Mount
TERWICK LA
New Barn
MILL LA
Terwick Mill

65

88

45

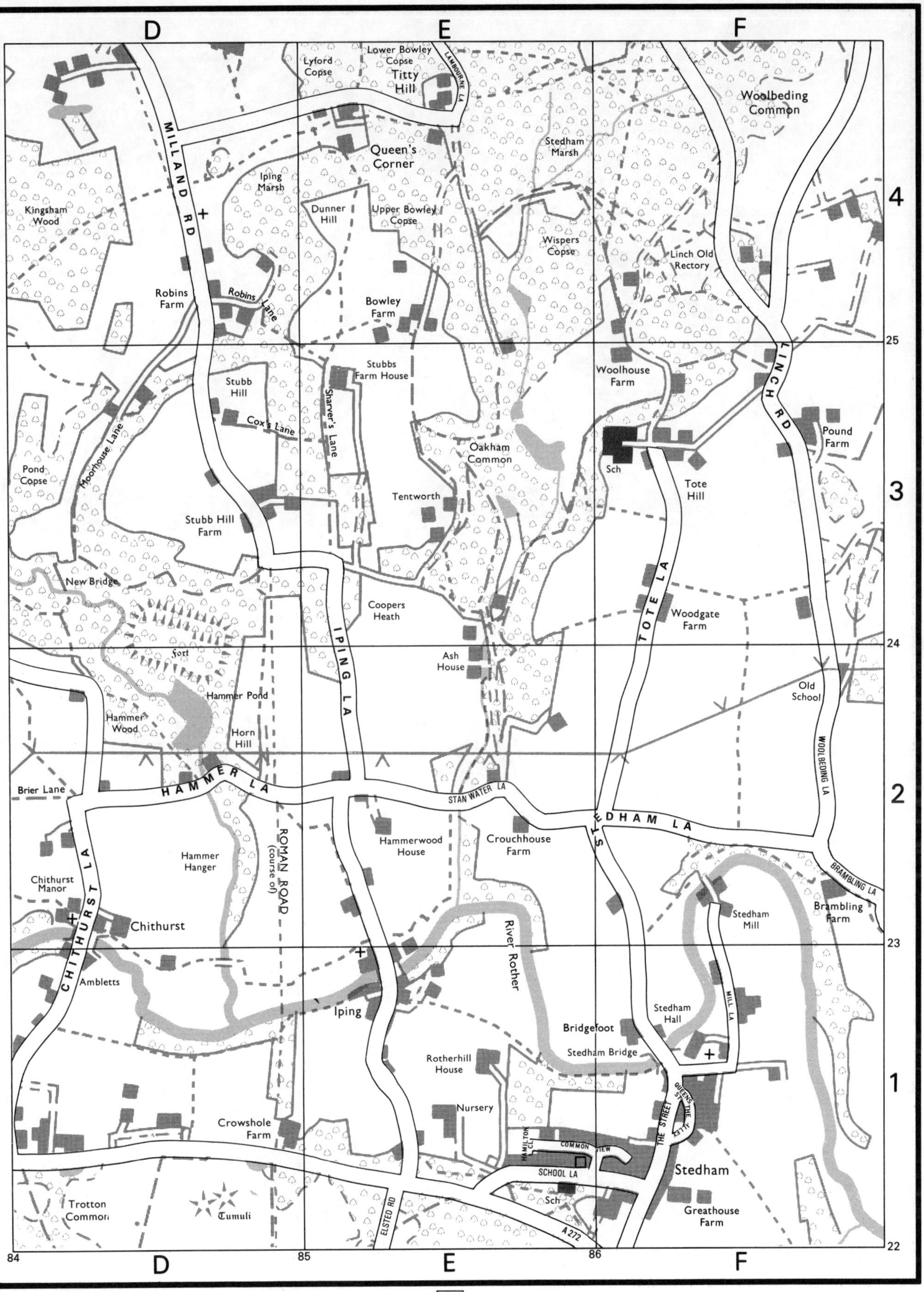

D
E
F
Lyford Copse
Lower Bowley Copse
Titty Hill
LAMBOURNE LA
Woolbeding Common
MILLAND RD
Queen's Corner
Stedham Marsh
Iping Marsh
Kingsham Wood
Dunner Hill
Upper Bowley Copse
Wispers Copse
Linch Old Rectory
Robins Farm
Robins Lane
Bowley Farm
Stubbs Farm House
Woolhouse Farm
LINCH RD
Stubb Hill
Sharver's Lane
Cox's Lane
Moorhouse Lane
Oakham Common
Sch
Pound Farm
Pond Copse
Tote Hill
Tentworth
Stubb Hill Farm
New Bridge
Coopers Heath
TOTE LA
Woodgate Farm
IPING LA
Fort
Ash House
Old School
Hammer Pond
Hammer Wood
Horn Hill
WOOLBEDING LA
Brier Lane
HAMMER LA
STAN WATER LA
STEDHAM LA
ROMAN ROAD (course of)
Hammer Hanger
Hammerwood House
Crouchhouse Farm
BRAMBLING LA
Chithurst Manor
CHITHURST LA
Chithurst
River Rother
Stedham Mill
Brambling Farm
Ambletts
Iping
MILL LA
Stedham Hall
Bridgefoot
Stedham Bridge
Rotherhill House
Nursery
Crowshole Farm
HAMILTON CL
COMMON VIEW
QUEENS THE ST
THE STREET
SCHOOL LA
Stedham
Sch
Greathouse Farm
ELSTED RD
A 272
Trotton Common
Tumuli
84
85
86
25
24
23
22
1
2
3
4

68

89

46

67

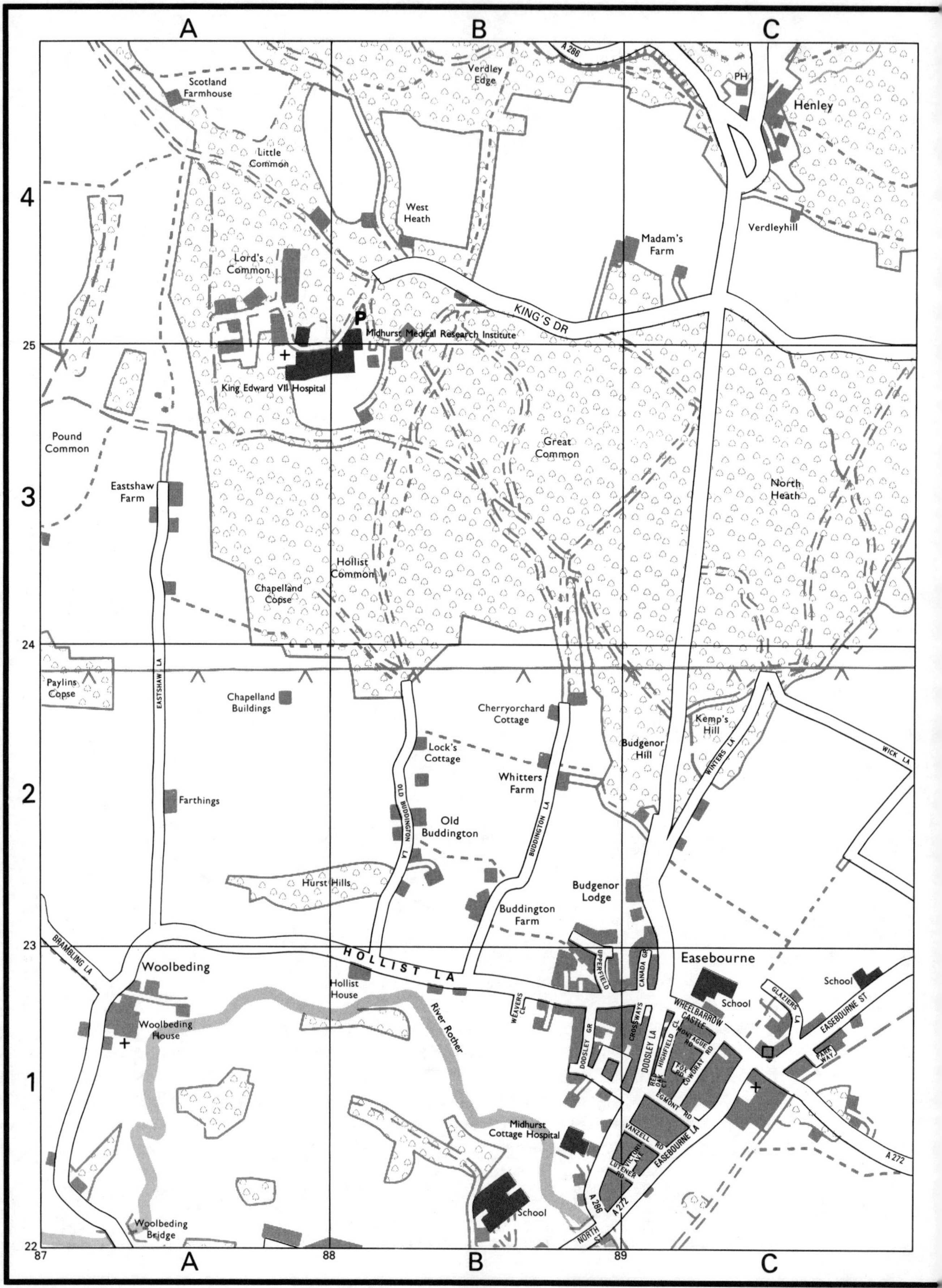

A
B
C
4
3
2
1
25
24
23
22
87
88
89
Scotland Farmhouse
Little Common
Verdley Edge
A 286
PH
Henley
West Heath
Lord's Common
Madam's Farm
Verdleyhill
KING'S DR
P
Midhurst Medical Research Institute
King Edward VII Hospital
Pound Common
Great Common
North Heath
Eastshaw Farm
Hollist Common
Chapelland Copse
Paylins Copse
EASTSHAW LA
Chapelland Buildings
Cherryorchard Cottage
Kemp's Hill
Lock's Cottage
Budgenor Hill
WINTERS LA
WICK LA
Whitters Farm
Farthings
OLD BUDDINGTON LA
Old Buddington
BUDDINGTON LA
Hurst Hills
Budgenor Lodge
Buddington Farm
BRAMBLING LA
HOLLIST LA
UPPERFIELD
CANADA GR
Easebourne
Woolbeding
Hollist House
School
WEAVERS CL
WHEELBARROW CASTLE
GLAZIERS LA
River Rother
Woolbeding House
DODSLEY GR
CROSSWAYS
DODSLEY LA
HIGHFIELD CL
MONTAGUE RD
EASEBOURNE ST
PARK WAY
RED OAK
FOX RD
COWDRAY RD
EGMONT RD
Midhurst Cottage Hospital
VANZELL RD
VICTORIA AVE
EASEBOURNE LA
LUTENER RD
A 272
A 286
NORTH ST
Woolbeding Bridge

90

47

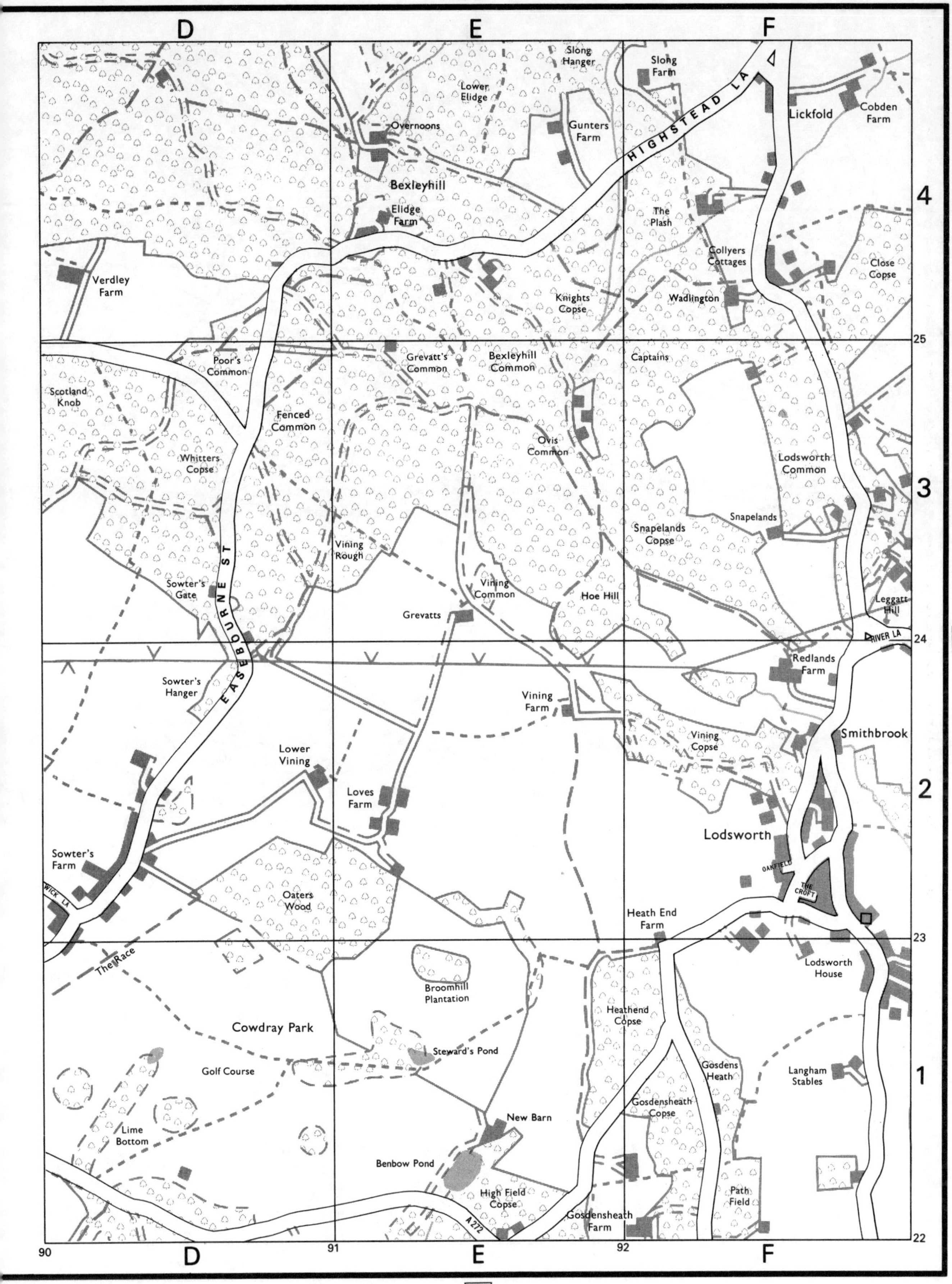
D
E
F
Slong Hanger
Slong Farm
Lower Elidge
Overnoons
Gunters Farm
HIGHSTEAD LA
Lickfold
Cobden Farm
Bexleyhill
4
Elidge Farm
The Plash
Collyers Cottages
Close Copse
Verdley Farm
Knights Copse
Wadlington
25
Poor's Common
Grevatt's Common
Bexleyhill Common
Captains
Scotland Knob
Fenced Common
Ovis Common
Lodsworth Common
Whitters Copse
3
Snapelands
Snapelands Copse
Vining Rough
EASEBOURNE ST
Sowter's Gate
Vining Common
Hoe Hill
Leggatt Hill
Grevatts
RIVER LA
24
Redlands Farm
Sowter's Hanger
Vining Farm
Smithbrook
Vining Copse
Lower Vining
Loves Farm
2
Lodsworth
Sowter's Farm
OAKFIELD
THE CROFT
WICK LA
Oaters Wood
Heath End Farm
23
The Race
Broomhill Plantation
Lodsworth House
Heathend Copse
Cowdray Park
Steward's Pond
Golf Course
Gosdens Heath
Langham Stables
1
Gosdensheath Copse
New Barn
Lime Bottom
Benbow Pond
High Field Copse
A 272
Path Field
Gosdensheath Farm
22
90
91
92
D
E
F

70

91

48

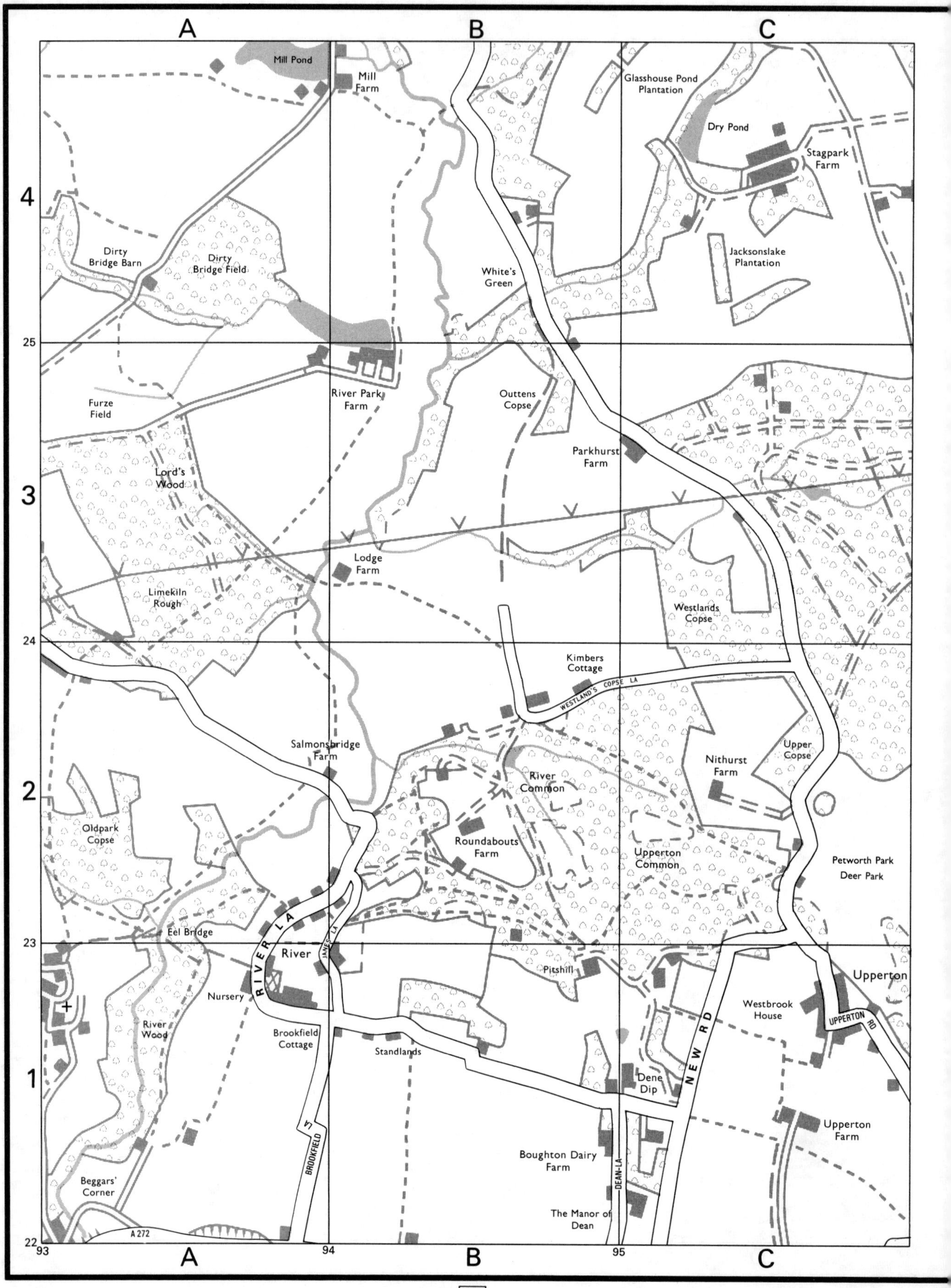
A
B
C
4
3
2
1
25
24
23
22
93
94
95
Mill Pond
Mill Farm
Glasshouse Pond Plantation
Dry Pond
Stagpark Farm
Jacksonslake Plantation
Dirty Bridge Barn
Dirty Bridge Field
White's Green
Furze Field
River Park Farm
Outtens Copse
Parkhurst Farm
Lord's Wood
Lodge Farm
Limekiln Rough
Westlands Copse
Kimbers Cottage
WESTLAND'S COPSE LA
Salmonsbridge Farm
River Common
Nithurst Farm
Upper Copse
Oldpark Copse
Roundabouts Farm
Upperton Common
Petworth Park Deer Park
Eel Bridge
RIVER LA
JAMES LA
River
Pitshill
Upperton
Nursery
Westbrook House
UPPERTON RD
River Wood
Brookfield Cottage
Standlands
NEW RD
Dene Dip
Upperton Farm
Boughton Dairy Farm
BROOKFIELD
DEAN LA
Beggars' Corner
The Manor of Dean
A 272

69

92

49

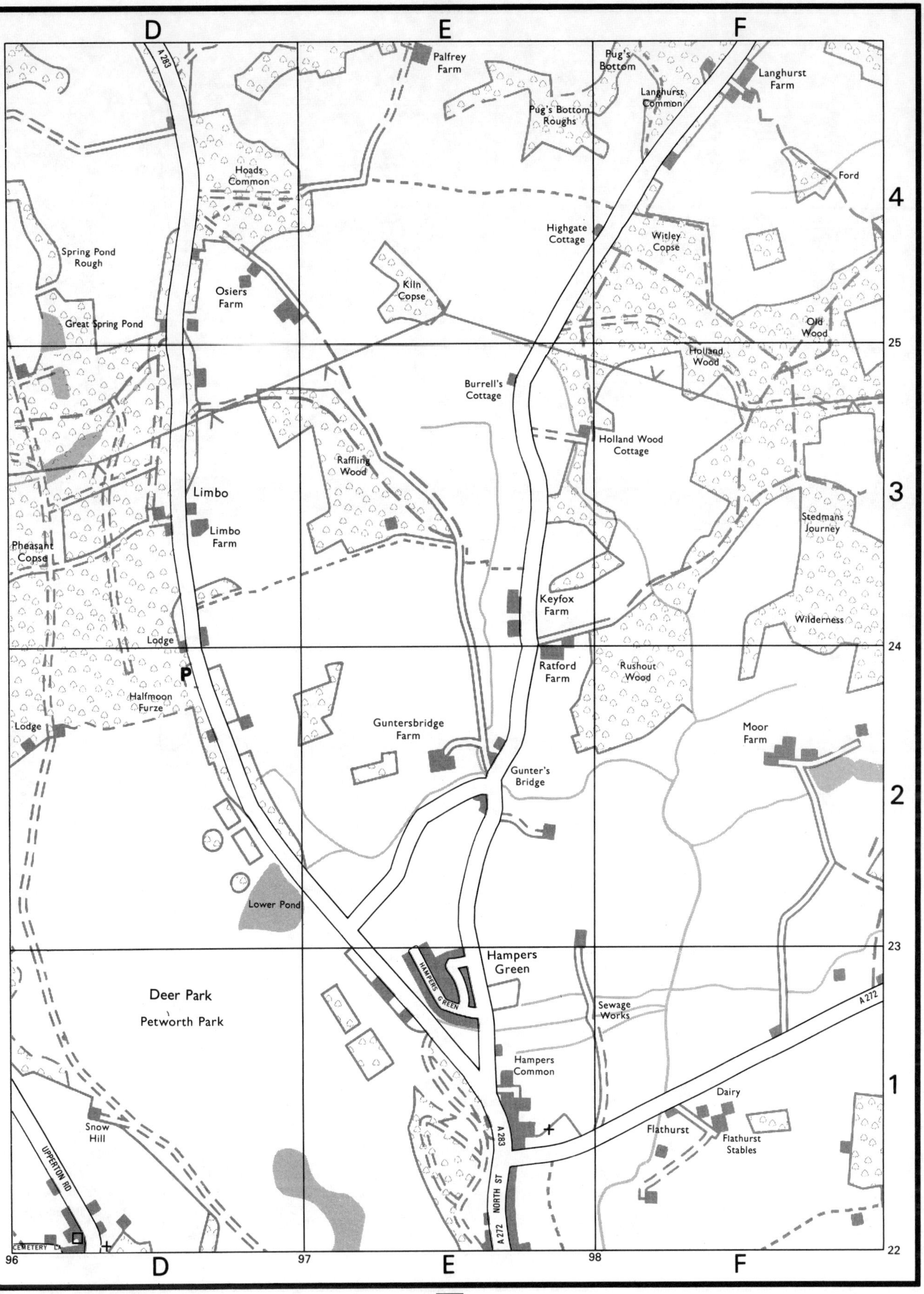
D
E
F
A 283
Palfrey Farm
Pug's Bottom
Langhurst Farm
Langhurst Common
Pug's Bottom Roughs
Hoads Common
Ford
4
Highgate Cottage
Witley Copse
Spring Pond Rough
Osiers Farm
Kiln Copse
Great Spring Pond
Old Wood
25
Holland Wood
Burrell's Cottage
Holland Wood Cottage
Raffling Wood
3
Limbo
Limbo Farm
Stedmans Journey
Pheasant Copse
Keyfox Farm
Wilderness
Lodge
24
P
Ratford Farm
Rushout Wood
Halfmoon Furze
Lodge
Guntersbridge Farm
Moor Farm
Gunter's Bridge
2
Lower Pond
23
Hampers Green
HAMPERS GREEN
Deer Park
Petworth Park
Sewage Works
A 272
Hampers Common
1
Dairy
Snow Hill
Flathurst
Flathurst Stables
A 283
UPPERTON RD
NORTH ST
A 272
CEMETERY LA
22
96
97
98
D
E
F

72

93

50

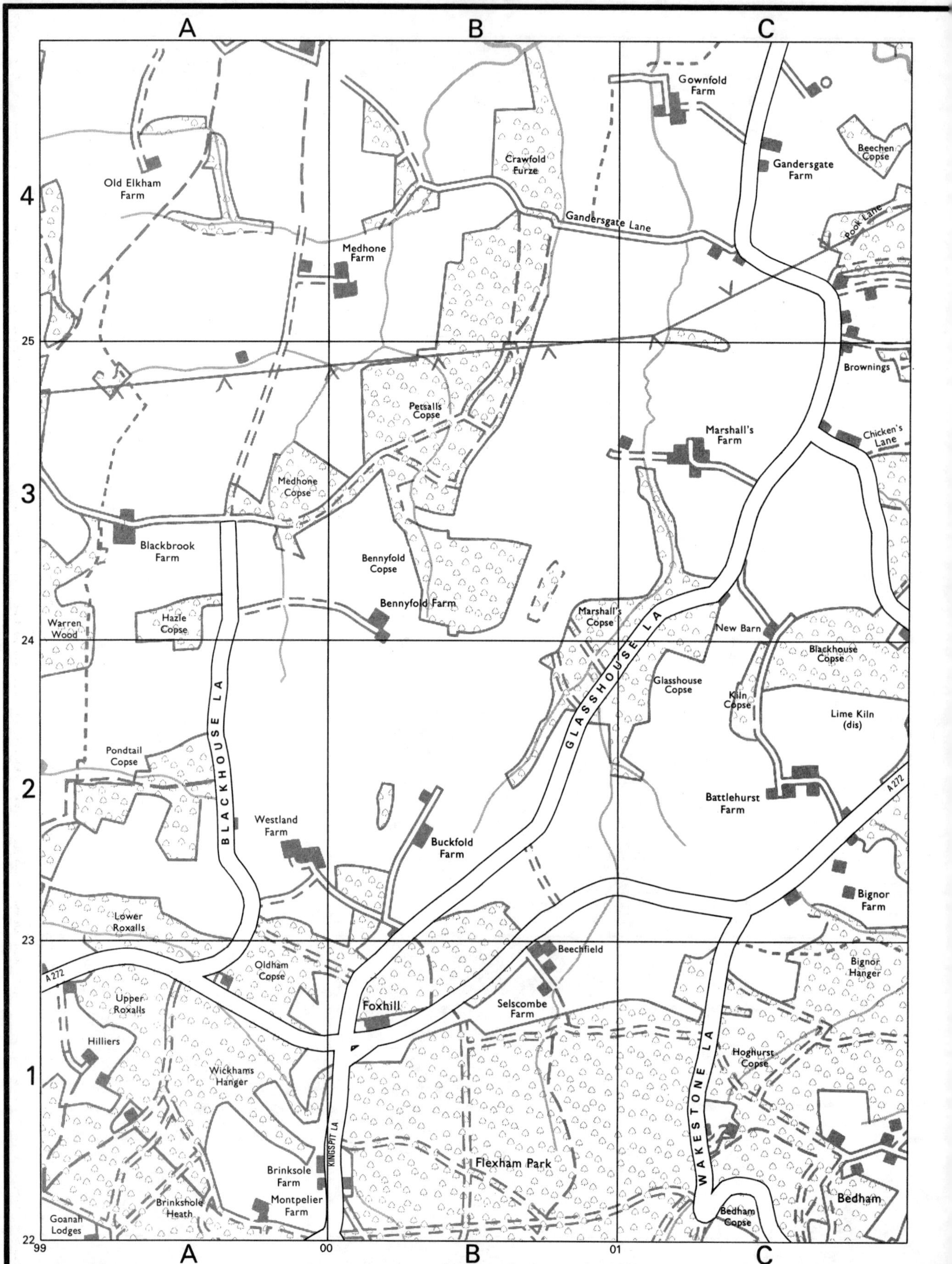
A
B
C
4
3
2
1
25
24
23
22
99
00
01
Gownfold Farm
Beechen Copse
Gandersgate Farm
Old Elkham Farm
Crawfold Furze
Gandersgate Lane
Pook Lane
Medhone Farm
Browning's
Petsalls Copse
Marshall's Farm
Chicken's Lane
Medhone Copse
Blackbrook Farm
Bennyfold Copse
Bennyfold Farm
Hazle Copse
Warren Wood
Marshall's Copse
New Barn
Blackhouse Copse
GLASSHOUSE LA
Glasshouse Copse
Kiln Copse
Lime Kiln (dis)
BLACKHOUSE LA
Pondtail Copse
Battlehurst Farm
A 272
Westland Farm
Buckfold Farm
Bignor Farm
Lower Roxalls
Beechfield
Bignor Hanger
A 272
Oldham Copse
Upper Roxalls
Foxhill
Selscombe Farm
Hilliers
Hoghurst Copse
Wickhams Hanger
WAKESTONE LA
KINGSPIT LA
Flexham Park
Brinksole Farm
Montpelier Farm
Brinkshole Heath
Bedham
Goanah Lodges
Bedham Copse

71

94

51

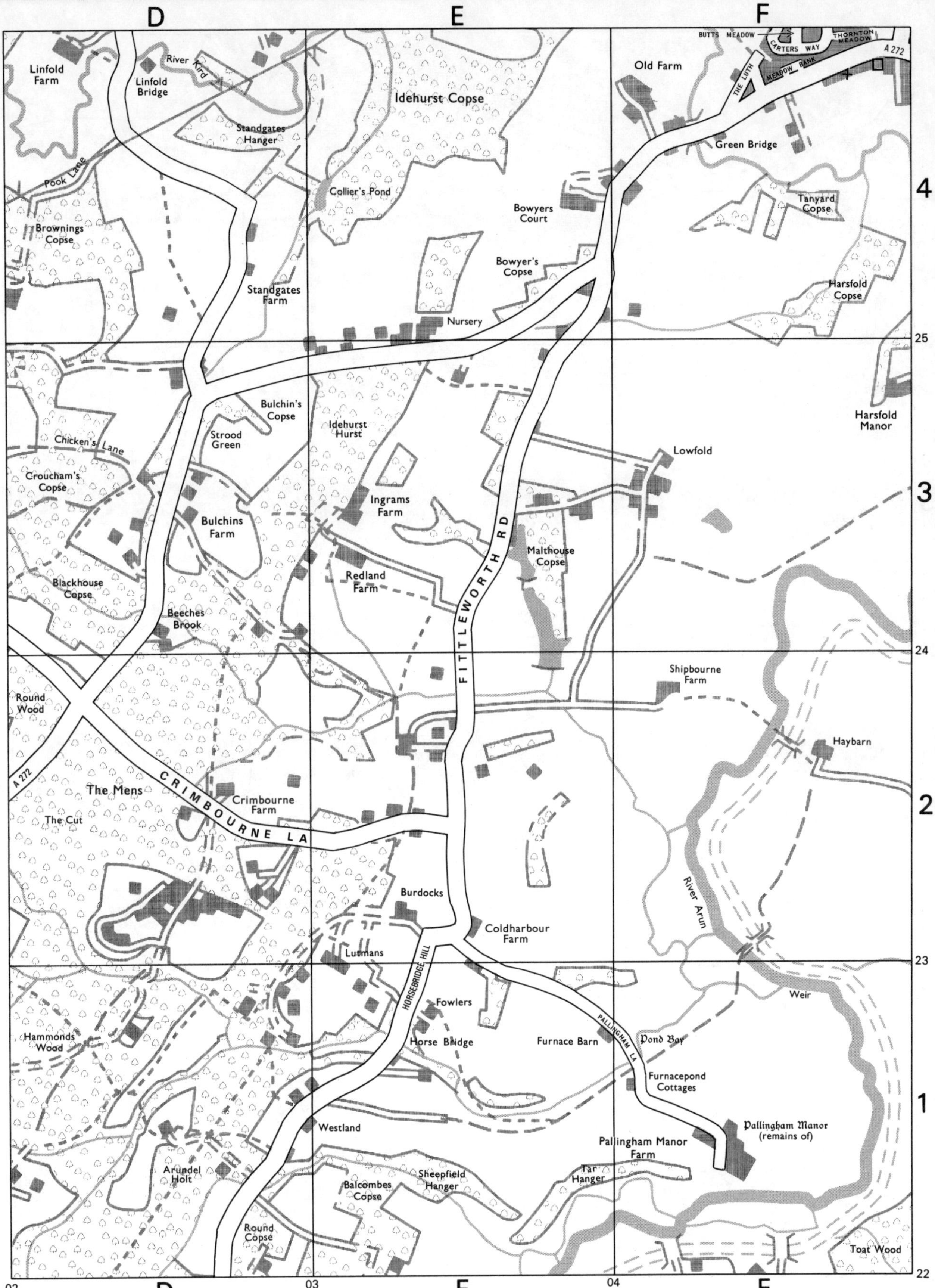
D
E
F
BUTTS MEADOW
CARTERS WAY
THORNTON MEADOW
A 272
THE LUTH
MEADOW BANK
Linfold Farm
River Kird
Linfold Bridge
Idehurst Copse
Old Farm
Green Bridge
Standgates Hanger
Pook Lane
Collier's Pond
Bowyers Court
Tanyard Copse
Brownings Copse
Bowyer's Copse
Standgates Farm
Harsfold Copse
Nursery
Harsfold Manor
Bulchin's Copse
Idehurst Hurst
Strood Green
Chicken's Lane
Lowfold
Croucham's Copse
Ingrams Farm
Bulchins Farm
FITTLEWORTH RD
Malthouse Copse
Redland Farm
Blackhouse Copse
Beeches Brook
Shipbourne Farm
Round Wood
Haybarn
A 272
The Mens
CRIMBOURNE LA
Crimbourne Farm
The Cut
River Arun
Burdocks
Coldharbour Farm
Lutmans
HORSEBRIDGE HILL
Weir
Fowlers
Hammonds Wood
Horse Bridge
Furnace Barn
PALLINGHAM LA
Pond Bay
Furnacepond Cottages
Westland
Pallingham Manor (remains of)
Pallingham Manor Farm
Arundel Holt
Tar Hanger
Sheepfield Hanger
Balcombes Copse
Round Copse
Toat Wood
4
25
3
24
2
23
1
22
02
03
04
D
E
F

74

95

52

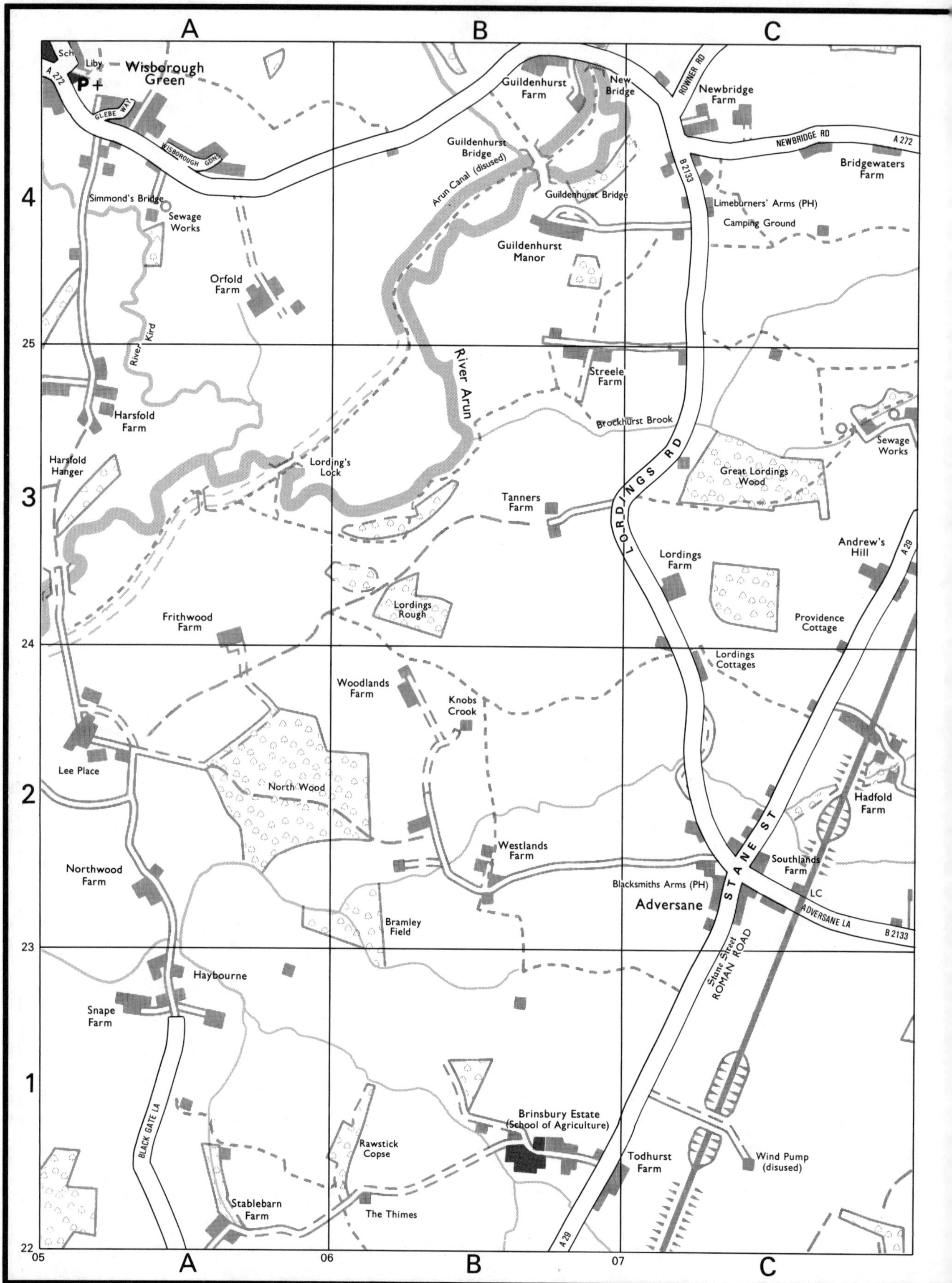
A
B
C
Sch
Liby
A 272
Wisborough Green
GLEBE WAY
WISBOROUGH GDNS
Guildenhurst Farm
New Bridge
ROWNER RD
Newbridge Farm
NEWBRIDGE RD
A 272
Guildenhurst Bridge
Arun Canal (disused)
B 2133
Bridgewaters Farm
4
Simmond's Bridge
Sewage Works
Guildenhurst Bridge
Limeburners' Arms (PH)
Camping Ground
Guildenhurst Manor
Orfold Farm
River Kird
25
River Arun
Streele Farm
Harsfold Farm
Brockhurst Brook
Sewage Works
Harsfold Hanger
Lording's Lock
LORDINGS RD
Great Lordings Wood
3
Tanners Farm
Andrew's Hill
A29
Lordings Farm
Lordings Rough
Frithwood Farm
Providence Cottage
24
Lordings Cottages
Woodlands Farm
Knobs Crook
Lee Place
2
North Wood
Hadfold Farm
STANE ST
Westlands Farm
Southlands Farm
Northwood Farm
Blacksmiths Arms (PH)
LC
Adversane
ADVERSANE LA
B 2133
Bramley Field
23
Stane Street ROMAN ROAD
Haybourne
Snape Farm
1
BLACK GATE LA
Brinsbury Estate (School of Agriculture)
Rawstick Copse
Todhurst Farm
Wind Pump (disused)
Stablebarn Farm
The Thimes
A29
22
05
06
07
A
B
C

73

96

53

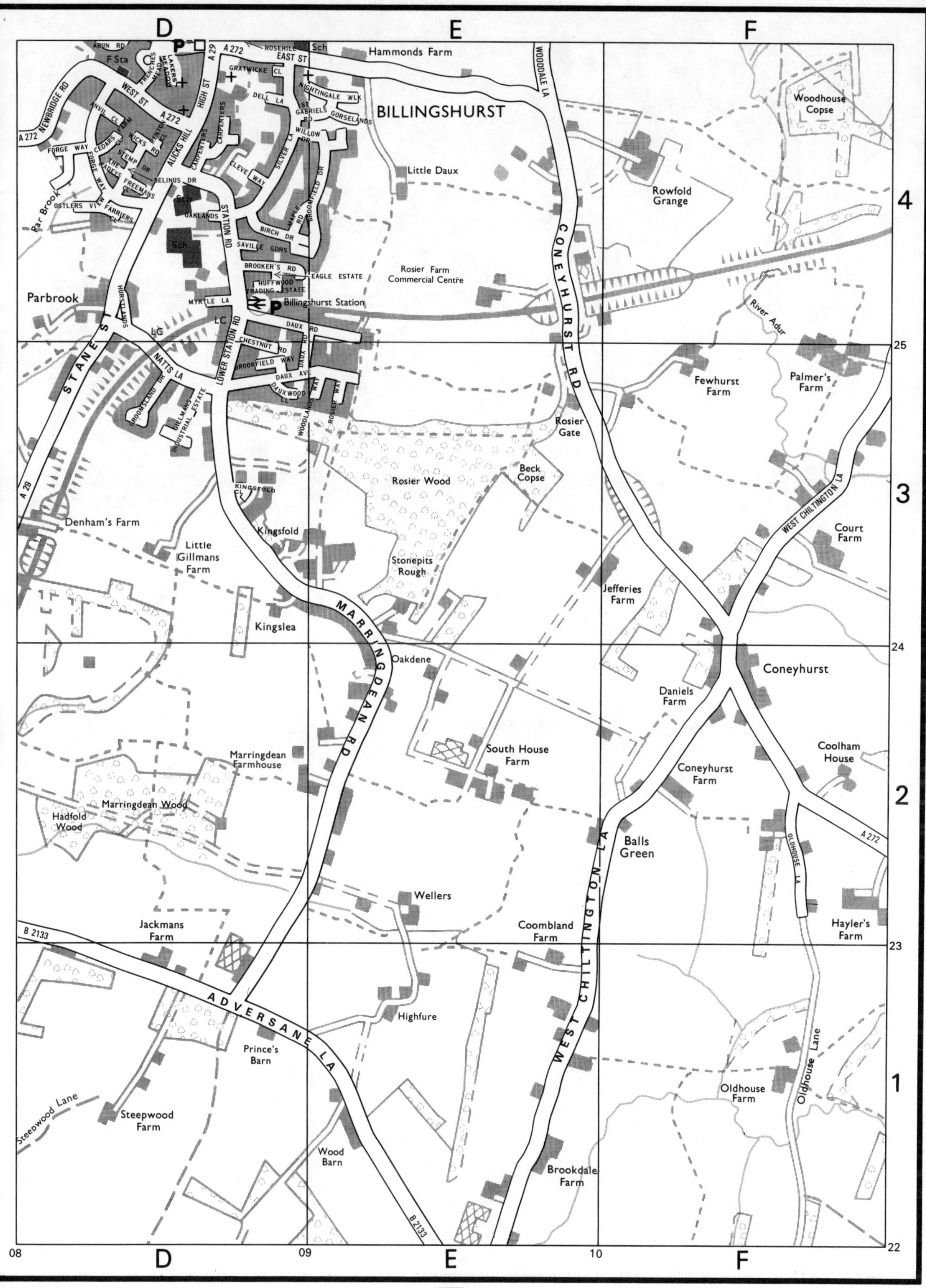
D
E
F
4
3
2
1
25
24
23
22
08
09
10
BILLINGSHURST
Hammonds Farm
Woodhouse Copse
Little Daux
Rowfold Grange
Rosier Farm Commercial Centre
Billingshurst Station
EAGLE ESTATE
HUFFWOOD TRADING ESTATE
River Adur
Parbrook
Par Brook
Fewhurst Farm
Palmer's Farm
Rosier Gate
Rosier Wood
Beck Copse
Denham's Farm
Little Gillmans Farm
Kingsfold
Stonepits Rough
Court Farm
Jefferies Farm
Kingslea
Oakdene
Coneyhurst
Daniels Farm
Marringdean Farmhouse
South House Farm
Coolham House
Coneyhurst Farm
Hadfold Wood
Marringdean Wood
Balls Green
Wellers
Jackmans Farm
Coombland Farm
Hayler's Farm
Highfure
Prince's Barn
Oldhouse Farm
Oldhouse Lane
Steepwood Lane
Steepwood Farm
Wood Barn
Brookdale Farm
A 272
A 29
B 2133
STANE ST
CONEYHURST RD
MARRINGDEAN RD
ADVERSANE LA
WEST CHILTINGTON LA
WEST CHILTINGTON LA
OLDHOUSE LA
WOODDALE LA
NEWBRIDGE RD
WEST ST
EAST ST
HIGH ST
ALICKS HILL
STATION RD
LOWER STATION RD
NATTS LA
DAUX RD
DAUX AVE
DAUX WAY
CHESTNUT RD
BROOKFIELD WAY
MYRTLE LA
BROOKER'S RD
SAVILLE GDNS
BIRCH DR
MAPLE RD
BROOMFIELD DR
SILVER LA
CLEVE WAY
CARPENTERS
BELINUS DR
OAKLANDS
FORGE WAY
CEDARS FARM
OSTLERS VIEW
FARRIERS CL
HURSTLANDS
GROOMSLAND DR
GILLMANS INDUSTRIAL ESTATE
WOODLANDS WAY
ROSIER WAY
DAUXWOOD CL
KINGSFOLD CL
GRATWICKE CL
DELL LA
NIGHTINGALE WLK
ST GABRIELS RD
GORSELANDS
WILLOW DR
ROSEHILL
ARUN RD
F Sta
Sch
LC

76

97

54

75

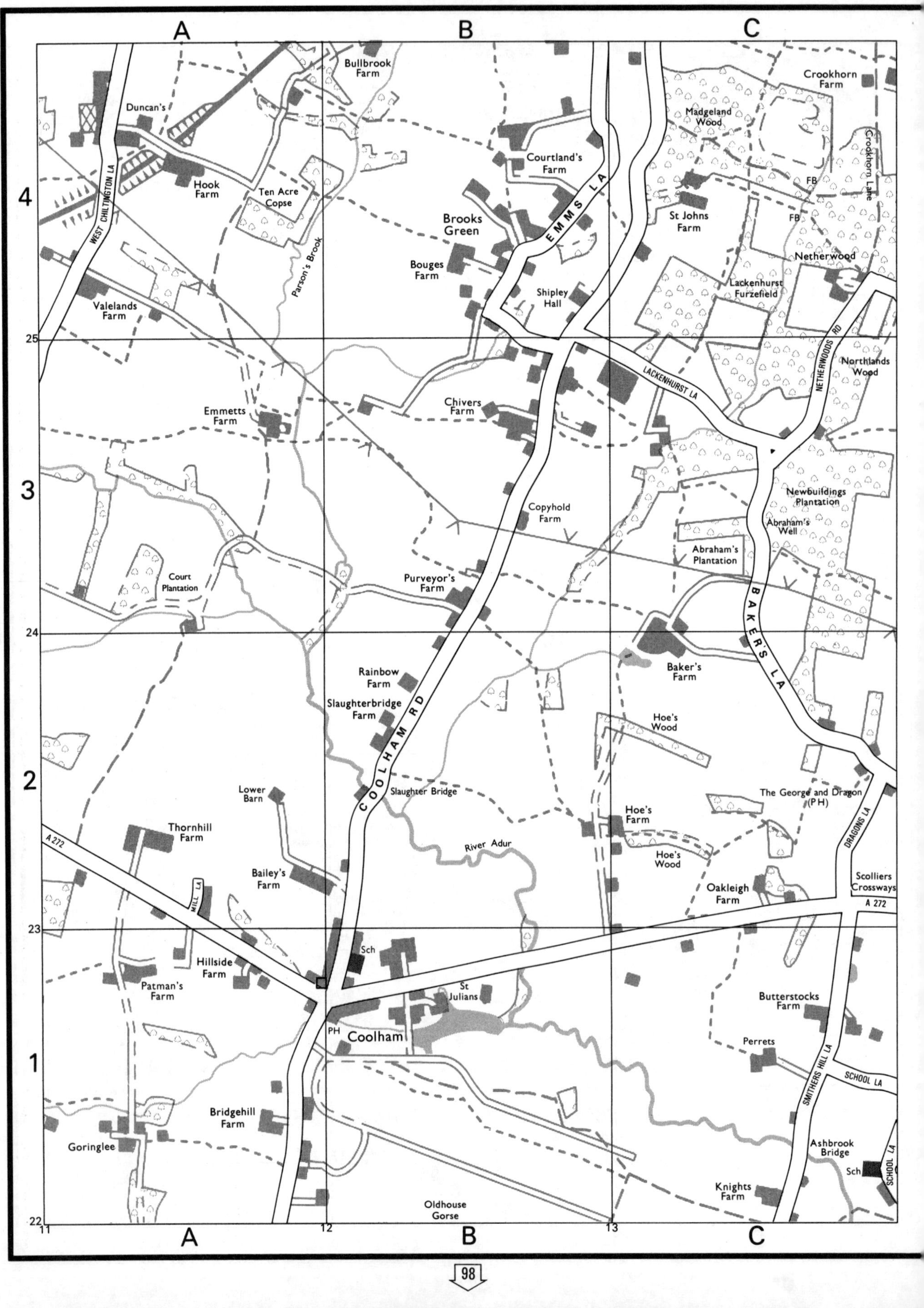
A
B
C
4
3
2
1
25
24
23
22
11
12
13
Bullbrook Farm
Duncan's
Hook Farm
Ten Acre Copse
WEST CHILTINGTON LA
Valelands Farm
Parson's Brook
Courtland's Farm
Brooks Green
EMMS LA
Bouges Farm
Shipley Hall
Crookhorn Farm
Madgeland Wood
Crookhorn Lane
FB
St Johns Farm
Netherwood
Lackenhurst Furzefield
NETHERWOODS RD
Northlands Wood
LACKENHURST LA
Emmetts Farm
Chivers Farm
Copyhold Farm
Newbuildings Plantation
Abraham's Well
Abraham's Plantation
Court Plantation
Purveyor's Farm
BAKER'S LA
Baker's Farm
Rainbow Farm
Slaughterbridge Farm
COOLHAM RD
Hoe's Wood
Lower Barn
Slaughter Bridge
The George and Dragon (PH)
Hoe's Farm
Thornhill Farm
A 272
River Adur
DRAGONS LA
Hoe's Wood
Bailey's Farm
Oakleigh Farm
Scolliers Crossways
MILL LA
Sch
Hillside Farm
Patman's Farm
St Julians
Butterstocks Farm
PH
Coolham
Perrets
SMITHERS HILL LA
SCHOOL LA
Bridgehill Farm
Goringlee
Ashbrook Bridge
Sch
SCHOOL LA
Knights Farm
Oldhouse Gorse

98

55

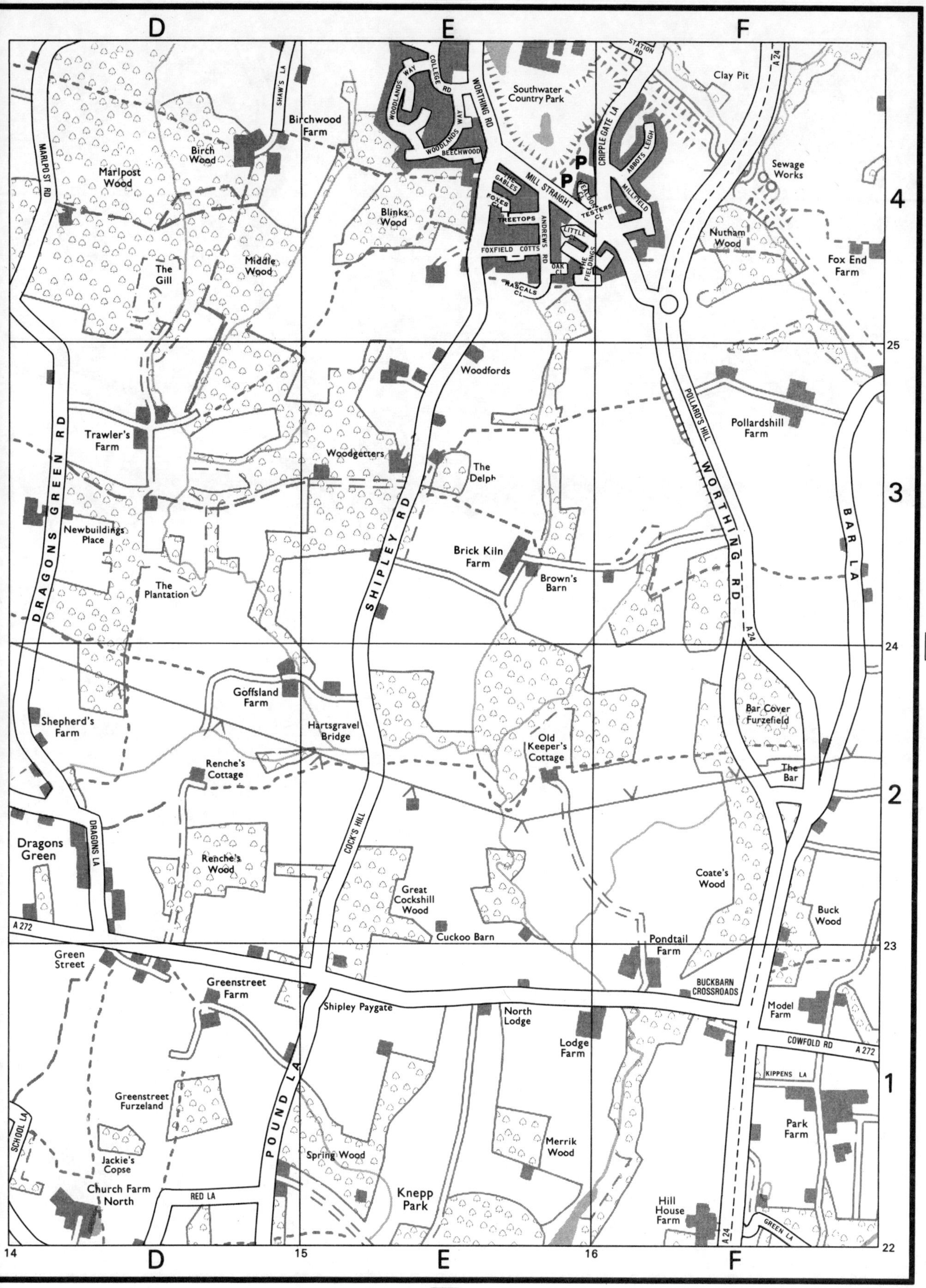

D
E
F
Southwater Country Park
Clay Pit
Sewage Works
Birchwood Farm
Birch Wood
Marlpost Wood
MARLPOST RD
SHAW'S LA
WOODLANDS WAY
COLLEGE RD
WORTHING RD
BEECHWOOD
MILL STRAIGHT
THE GABLES
FOXES CL
TREETOPS
ANDREWS RD
FOXFIELD COTTS
RASCALS CL
OAK CL
LITTLE
THE FIELDINGS
TESTERS CL
CRIPPLE GATE LA
ABBOTS LEIGH
MILLFIELD
STATION RD
A24
P
Blinks Wood
Middle Wood
The Gill
Nutham Wood
Fox End Farm
4
25
Woodfords
Trawler's Farm
Woodgetters
The Delph
Pollardshill Farm
POLLARD'S HILL
WORTHING RD
DRAGONS GREEN RD
Newbuildings Place
The Plantation
Brick Kiln Farm
Brown's Barn
SHIPLEY RD
BAR LA
3
24
Goffsland Farm
Shepherd's Farm
Hartsgravel Bridge
Bar Cover Furzefield
Old Keeper's Cottage
Renche's Cottage
The Bar
2
Dragons Green
DRAGONS LA
Renche's Wood
COCK'S HILL
Great Cockshill Wood
Coate's Wood
Buck Wood
Cuckoo Barn
A 272
Pondtail Farm
23
Green Street
Greenstreet Farm
Shipley Paygate
North Lodge
BUCKBARN CROSSROADS
Model Farm
Lodge Farm
COWFOLD RD
A 272
KIPPENS LA
1
Greenstreet Furzeland
POUND LA
Park Farm
Merrik Wood
SCHOOL LA
Jackie's Copse
Spring Wood
Church Farm North
RED LA
Knepp Park
Hill House Farm
GREEN LA
14
15
16
22

78

99

56

77

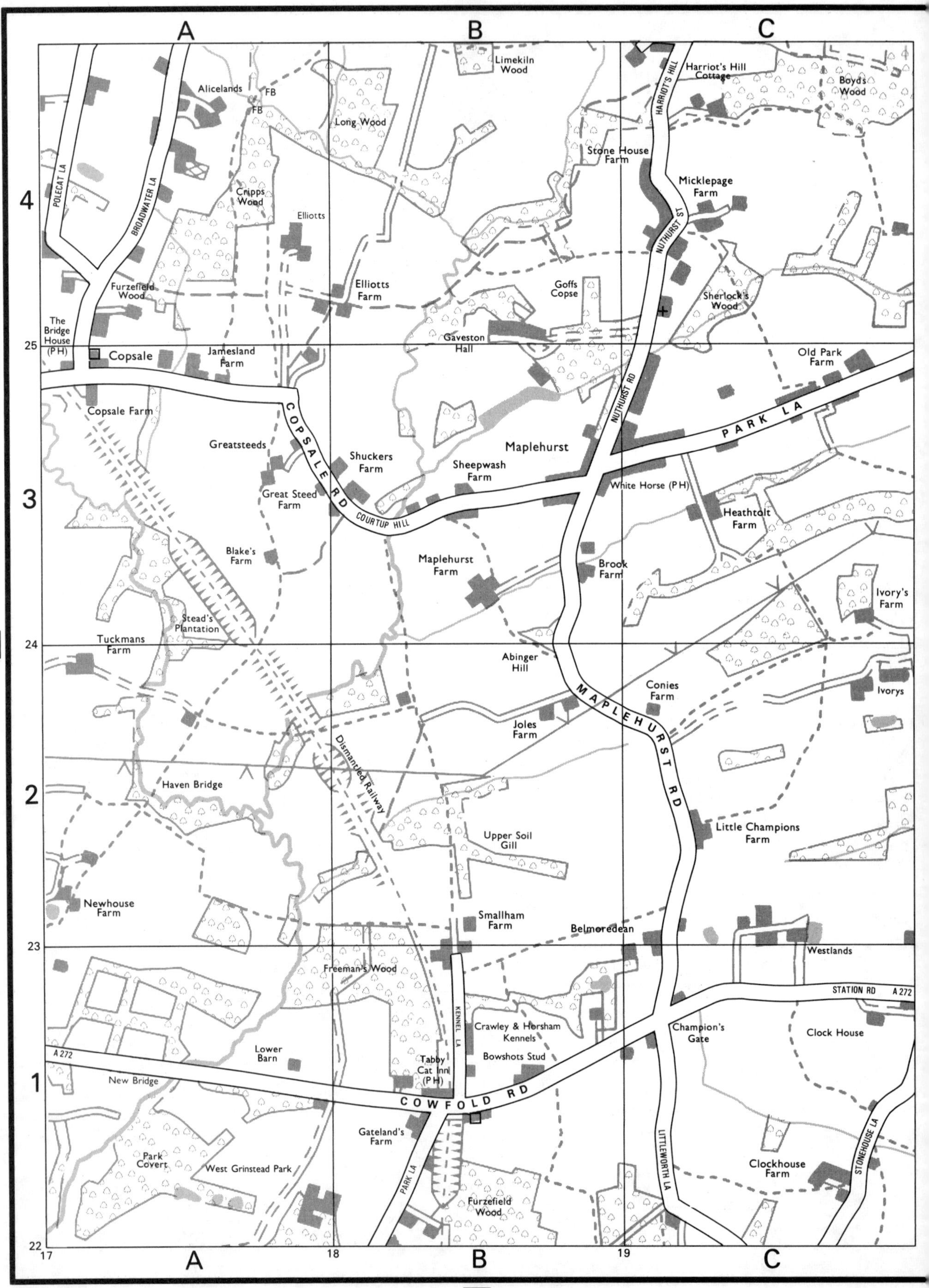
A
B
C
4
3
2
1
25
24
23
22
17
18
19
Limekiln Wood
Harriot's Hill Cottage
HARRIOT'S HILL
Boyds Wood
Alicelands
FB
Long Wood
Stone House Farm
POLECAT LA
BROADWATER LA
Cripps Wood
Elliotts
Micklepage Farm
NUTHURST ST
Furzefield Wood
Elliotts Farm
Goffs Copse
Sherlock's Wood
The Bridge House (PH)
Copsale
Jamesland Farm
Gaveston Hall
Old Park Farm
NUTHURST RD
Copsale Farm
COPSALE RD
PARK LA
Greatsteeds
Shuckers Farm
Maplehurst
Sheepwash Farm
White Horse (PH)
Great Steed Farm
COURTUP HILL
Heathtolt Farm
Blake's Farm
Maplehurst Farm
Brook Farm
Ivory's Farm
Stead's Plantation
Tuckmans Farm
Abinger Hill
Conies Farm
Ivorys
MAPLEHURST RD
Joles Farm
Dismantled Railway
Haven Bridge
Little Champions Farm
Upper Soil Gill
Newhouse Farm
Smallham Farm
Belmoredean
Westlands
Freeman's Wood
STATION RD
A 272
KENNEL LA
Crawley & Horsham Kennels
Champion's Gate
Clock House
Lower Barn
Bowshots Stud
Tabby Cat Inn (PH)
New Bridge
COWFOLD RD
Gateland's Farm
LITTLEWORTH LA
STONEHOUSE LA
Park Covert
West Grinstead Park
PARK LA
Clockhouse Farm
Furzefield Wood

100

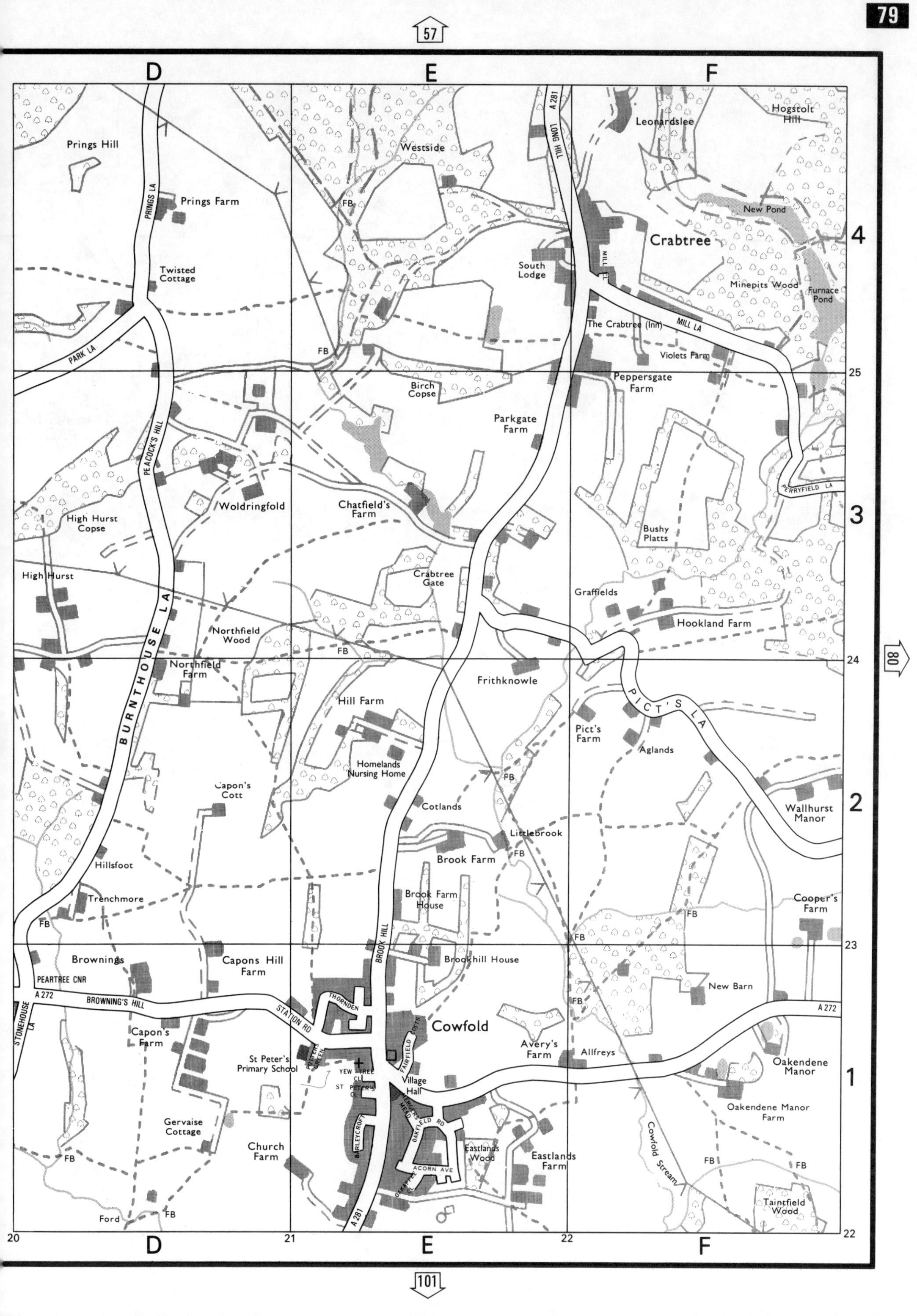

57
D
E
F
Prings Hill
Prings Farm
PRINGS LA
Twisted Cottage
PARK LA
Westside
FB
A 281
LONG HILL
Leonardslee
Hogstolt Hill
New Pond
Crabtree
South Lodge
MILL LA
Minepits Wood
Furnace Pond
The Crabtree (Inn)
Violets Farm
Peppersgate Farm
Birch Copse
Parkgate Farm
PEACOCK'S HILL
Woldringfold
Chatfield's Farm
High Hurst Copse
High Hurst
PERRYFIELD LA
Bushy Platts
Crabtree Gate
Graffields
Hookland Farm
Northfield Wood
Northfield Farm
BURNTHOUSE LA
Frithknowle
PICT'S LA
Hill Farm
Pict's Farm
Aglands
Homelands Nursing Home
Capon's Cott
Cotlands
Wallhurst Manor
Littlebrook
Brook Farm
Hillsfoot
Trenchmore
Brook Farm House
Cooper's Farm
BROOK HILL
Brownings
Capons Hill Farm
Brookhill House
New Barn
PEARTREE CNR
A 272
BROWNING'S HILL
STATION RD
THORNDEN
STONEHOUSE LA
Cowfold
Capon's Farm
St Peter's Primary School
YEW TREE CL
ST PETER'S CL
FAIRFIELD COTTS
Village Hall
Avery's Farm
Allfreys
Oakendene Manor
Oakendene Manor Farm
Gervaise Cottage
BARLEYCROFT
OAKFIELD RD
Eastlands Wood
ACORN AVE
Church Farm
Eastlands Farm
Cowfold Stream
Taintfield Wood
Ford
20
21
22
22
23
24
25
1
2
3
4
80
101

58

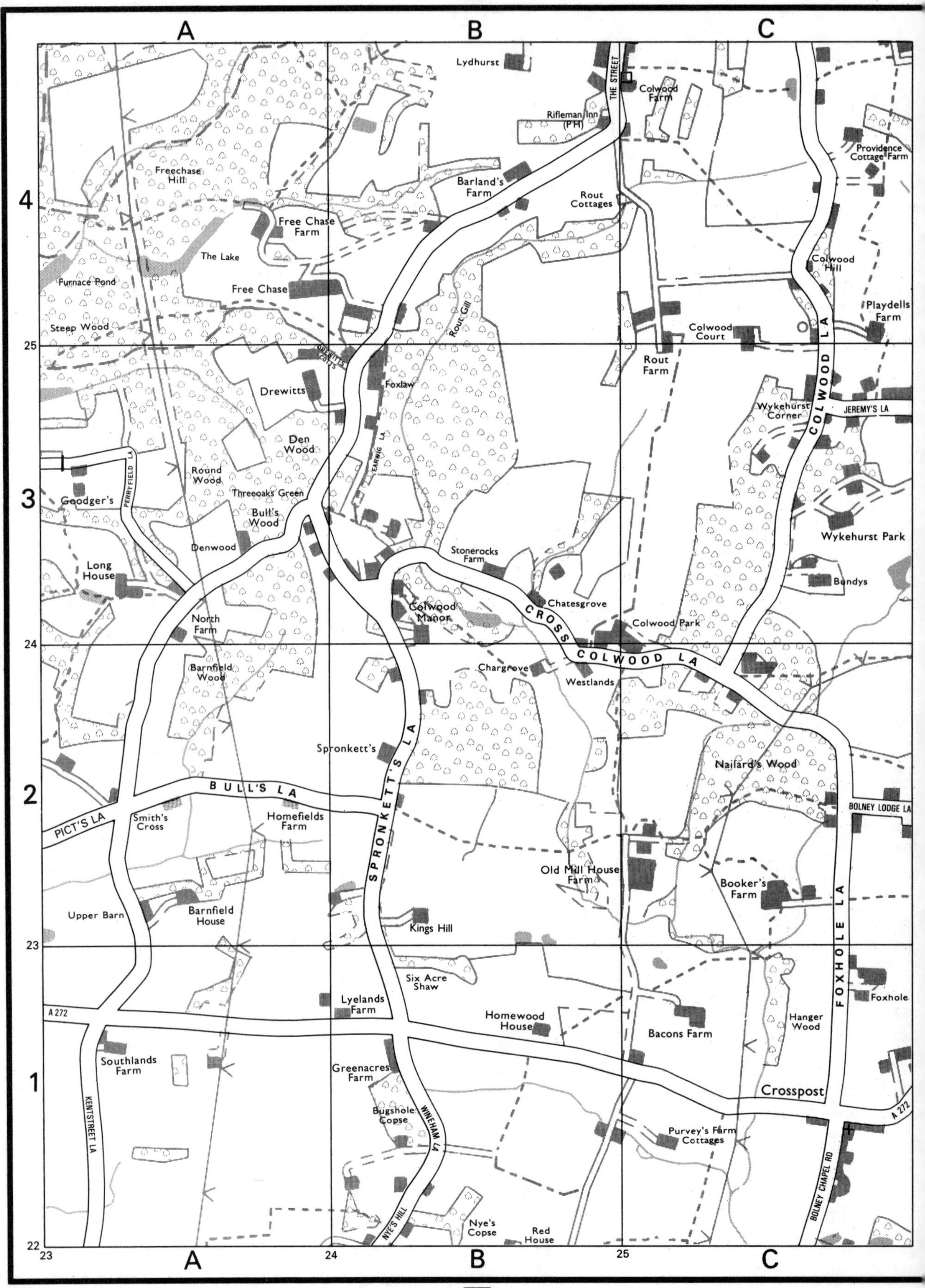

A
B
C
Lydhurst
THE STREET
Colwood Farm
Rifleman Inn (PH)
Providence Cottage Farm
Freechase Hill
Barland's Farm
Rout Cottages
4
Free Chase Farm
The Lake
Colwood Hill
Furnace Pond
Free Chase
Playdells Farm
Steep Wood
Rout Gill
Colwood Court
25
DREWITTS COTTS
Rout Farm
Foxlaw
Drewitts
Wykehurst Corner
JEREMY'S LA
COLWOOD LA
Den Wood
EARWIG LA
PERRYFIELD LA
Round Wood
Threeoaks Green
3
Goodger's
Bull's Wood
Wykehurst Park
Denwood
Stonerocks Farm
Long House
Bundys
Chatesgrove
North Farm
Colwood Manor
CROSS
Colwood Park
24
COLWOOD LA
Barnfield Wood
Chargrove
Westlands
Spronkett's
Nailard's Wood
2
BULL'S LA
BOLNEY LODGE LA
PICT'S LA
Smith's Cross
Homefields Farm
SPRONKETT'S LA
Old Mill House Farm
Booker's Farm
Upper Barn
Barnfield House
Kings Hill
23
FOXHOLE LA
Six Acre Shaw
Foxhole
Lyelands Farm
A 272
Homewood House
Hanger Wood
Bacons Farm
Southlands Farm
1
Greenacres Farm
KENTSTREET LA
Crosspost
A 272
Bugshole Copse
WINEHAM LA
Purvey's Farm Cottages
BOLNEY CHAPEL RD
NYE'S HILL
Nye's Copse
Red House
22
23
24
25

79

102

59

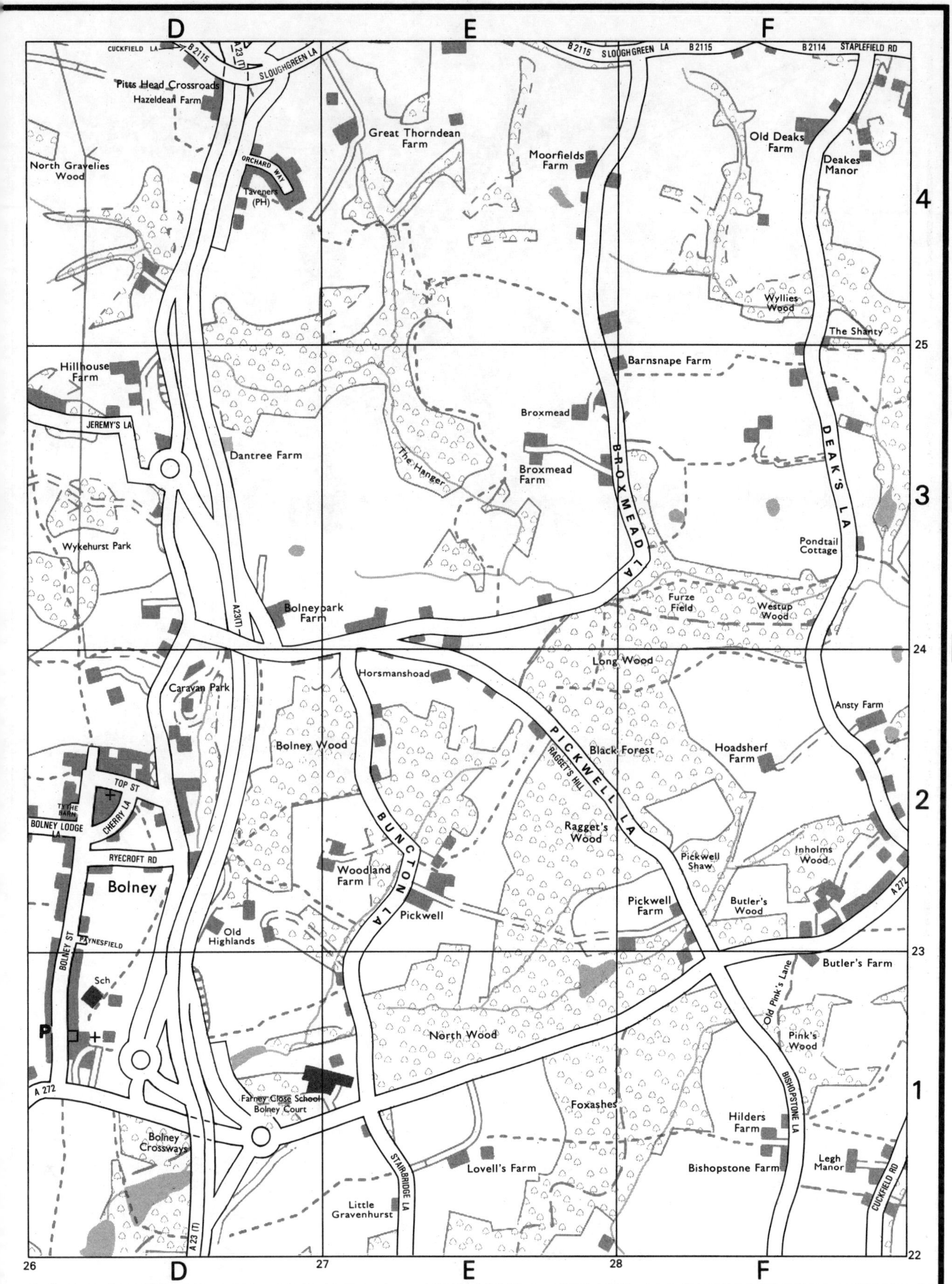
D
E
F
CUCKFIELD LA
B 2115
A 23 (T)
SLOUGHGREEN LA
B 2115
SLOUGHGREEN LA
B 2115
B 2114
STAPLEFIELD RD
Pitts Head Crossroads
Hazeldean Farm
Great Thorndean Farm
Moorfields Farm
Old Deaks Farm
Deakes Manor
North Gravelies Wood
ORCHARD WAY
Taveners (PH)
4
Wyllies Wood
The Shanty
25
Hillhouse Farm
Barnsnape Farm
JEREMY'S LA
Broxmead
Dantree Farm
The Hanger
Broxmead Farm
BROXMEAD LA
DEAK'S LA
3
Wykehurst Park
Pondtail Cottage
A23(T)
Bolneypark Farm
Furze Field
Westup Wood
24
Long Wood
Horsmanshoad
Caravan Park
Ansty Farm
PICKWELL LA
Bolney Wood
Black Forest
Hoadsherf Farm
RAGGET'S HILL
TOP ST
TYTHE BARN
CHERRY LA
BOLNEY LODGE LA
BUNCTON LA
2
Ragget's Wood
RYECROFT RD
Inholms Wood
Pickwell Shaw
Bolney
Woodland Farm
Pickwell Farm
Butler's Wood
A 272
Pickwell
Old Highlands
PAYNESFIELD
BOLNEY ST
23
Butler's Farm
Sch
Old Pink's Lane
P
North Wood
Pink's Wood
A 272
1
Farney Close School Bolney Court
Foxashes
Hilders Farm
BISHOPSTONE LA
Bolney Crossways
STAIRBRIDGE LA
Lovell's Farm
Bishopstone Farm
Legh Manor
CUCKFIELD RD
Little Gravenhurst
A 23 (T)
22
26
27
28
D
E
F

82

103

60

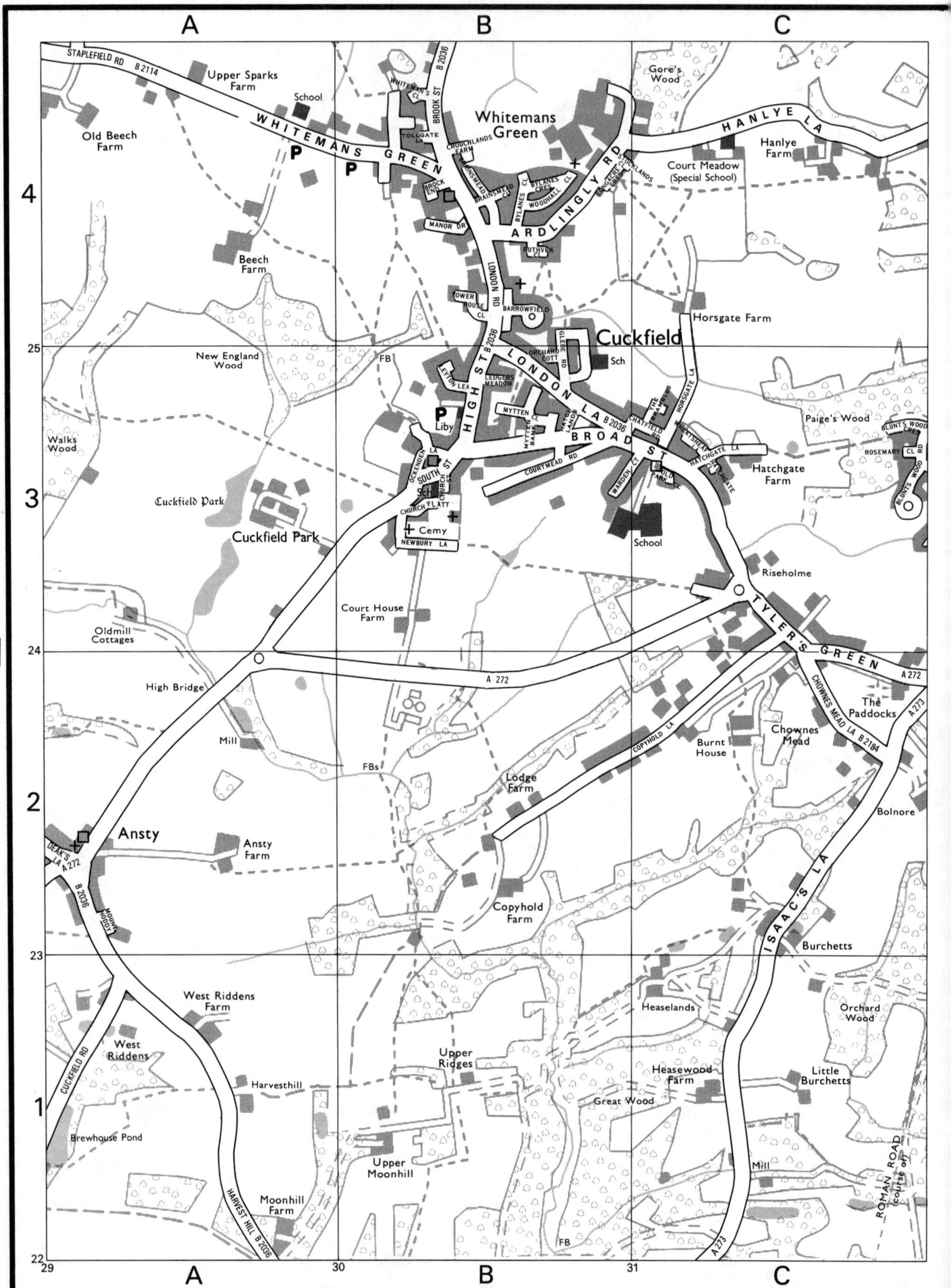

A
B
C
STAPLEFIELD RD B2114
Upper Sparks Farm
School
WHITEMANS GREEN
Old Beech Farm
Whitemans Green
Gore's Wood
HANLYE LA
Hanlye Farm
Court Meadow (Special School)
ARDLINGLY RD
BROOK ST
B2036
Beech Farm
LONDON RD
Horsgate Farm
Cuckfield
Sch
New England Wood
FB
HIGH ST B2036
LONDON LA B2036
BROAD ST
Liby
Walks Wood
Paige's Wood
Hatchgate Farm
Cuckfield Park
Cemy
NEWBURY LA
School
Riseholme
Court House Farm
Oldmill Cottages
TYLER'S GREEN
A 272
High Bridge
The Paddocks
Mill
COPYHOLD LA
Burnt House
Chownes Mead
CHOWNES MEAD LA B2184
A 273
FBs
Lodge Farm
Ansty
Ansty Farm
Bolnore
ISAAC'S LA
Copyhold Farm
Burchetts
West Riddens Farm
Heaselands
Orchard Wood
West Riddens
CUCKFIELD RD
Upper Ridges
Harvesthill
Heasewood Farm
Little Burchetts
Great Wood
Brewhouse Pond
Upper Moonhill
Mill
Moonhill Farm
ROMAN ROAD (course of)
HARVEST HILL B2036
FB
A 273
4
3
2
1
25
24
23
22
29
30
31

81

104

61

D
E
F
HAYWARDS HEATH
HANLYE LA
BALCOMBE RD
Penland Farm
School
Sunte House
FB
BIRCHEN LA
BROOK LA
GATESMEAD
ROUNDWOOD LA
PORTSMOUTH LA
SUNTE AVE
BROOKWAY
HICKMAN'S LA
DENMAN'S LA
HIGH ST
B2028
B2111 LEWES RD
FRANCIS RD
DUKES RD
NEWTON RD
BLACK HILL
WEST COMM
COLLEGE RD
SUMMERHILL LA
GANDER HILL
GANDER GREEN
OLD WICKHAM LA
WICKHAM WAY
CHESTNUTS
SUMMERHILL DR
OAK BANK
BRIDGE RD
Amb Sta
SYDNEY RD
GORDON RD
QUEENS RD
MILL GREEN RD
F Sta
Oathall School
Sch
BECKWORTH LA
APPLEDORE GDNS
PELHAM RD
MEADOW LA
WEST VIEW
HARLANDS RD
QUARRY HILL
BLUNTS WOOD RD
PASTURE HILL RD
THE GROVE WAY
LUCASTES AVE
LUCASTES LA
Leisure Centre
Haywards Heath Station
Mag Crt
BOLTRO RD
MILTON RD
THE BROADWAY B2028
PERRYMOUNT RD
CLAIR RD
OATHALL RD
OATHALL AVE
B2112
PENN CRES
WASHINGTON RD
WILMINGTON WAY
HAYLIND RD
WESTLANDS RD
GRAVELYE LA
AMERICA LA
BENTSWOOD CRES
FARLINGTON AVE
School
Liby
Hospital
MUSTER GREEN N
MUSTER GREEN S
BUTLER'S GREEN RD
A 272
Mag Ct
Parkfield
Convent
Recn Gd
SOUTH RD
HAZELGROVE RD
NEW ENGLAND RD
WOODLANDS RD
NORTH RD
WESTERN RD
Cemy
LYOTH LA
NORTHLANDS AVE
HOBLANDS
GRAVELYE LA
REED POND WLK
Franklands Village
FRANKLYNN RD
SUSSEX RD
PARK RD
HAYWARDS RD
GOWER RD
WOOD RIDE
SUNNYWOOD DR
FRANKTON AVE
LEWES RD
A 272
COLWELL RD
COLWELL LA
Ashenground Br
Catt's Wood
Pierce's Wood
ASHENGROUND RD
VALE RD
SANDROCKS WAY
WIVELSFIELD RD
ST JOHN'S RD
The Princess Royal Hospital
Rookhurst House
Asylum Wood
GREENHILL WAY
HURSTWOOD LA
Hospital Farm
Oldhouse Farm
High Bridge
ROCKY LA
Rookery Fm
Sandrocks
PINEWOOD WAY
FOX HILL
B2112
Hurst Wood
Bankey Wood
Hurstwood House
COLWELL LA
32
33
34
22
23
24
25
1
2
3
4

84

105

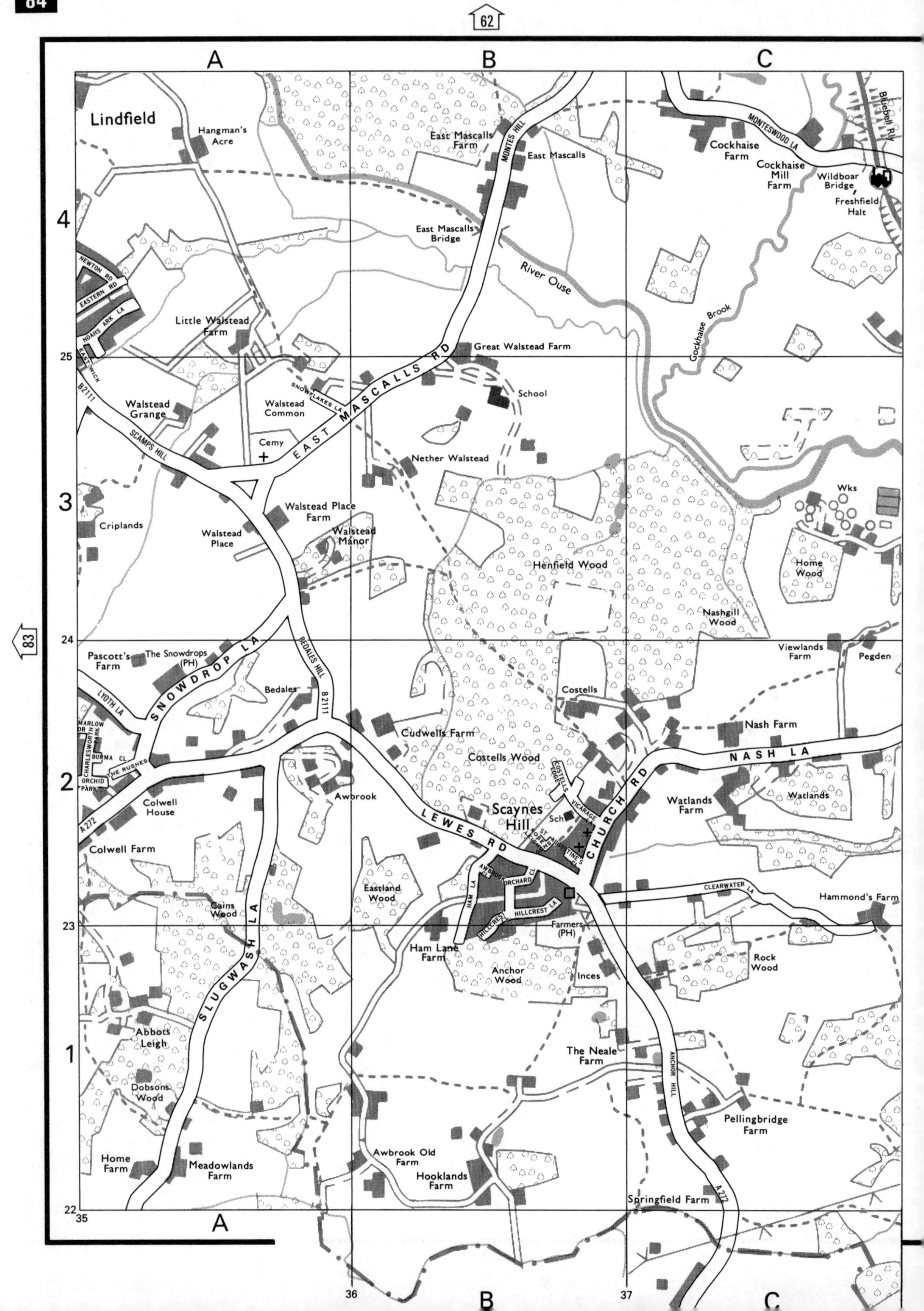
62
A
B
C
Lindfield
Hangman's Acre
East Mascalls Farm
MONTES HILL
East Mascalls
MONTESWOOD LA
Cockhaise Farm
Cockhaise Mill Farm
Wildboar Bridge
Freshfield Halt
Bluebell Rly
East Mascalls Bridge
River Ouse
Cockhaise Brook
NEWTON RD
EASTERN RD
NOAHS ARK LA
EASTWICK
Little Walstead Farm
Great Walstead Farm
EAST MASCALLS RD
SNOWFLAKES LA
School
B2111
Walstead Grange
Walstead Common
SCAMPS HILL
Cemy
Nether Walstead
Wks
Criplands
Walstead Place Farm
Walstead Manor
Walstead Place
Henfield Wood
Home Wood
Nashgill Wood
83
Pascott's Farm
The Snowdrops (PH)
SNOWDROP LA
BEDALES HILL
Viewlands Farm
Pegden
LYOTH LA
Bedales
Costells
MARLOW DR
CHARLESWORTH PARK
BURMA CL
THE RUSHES
ORCHID PARK
Cudwells Farm
Nash Farm
Costells Wood
NASH LA
Colwell House
Awbrook
COSTELLS EDGE
Scaynes Hill
Watlands Farm
Watlands
A 272
LEWES RD
Sch
VICARAGE
ST AUGUSTINE'S CL
CHURCH RD
Colwell Farm
AWBROOK CL
ORCHARD CL
CLEARWATER LA
Hammond's Farm
Eastland Wood
HAM LA
HILLCREST LA
HILLCREST CL
Cains Wood
Farmers (PH)
Ham Lane Farm
Rock Wood
Anchor Wood
Inces
SLUGWASH LA
Abbots Leigh
The Neale Farm
ANCHOR HILL
Dobsons Wood
Pellingbridge Farm
Home Farm
Meadowlands Farm
Awbrook Old Farm
Hooklands Farm
Springfield Farm
A272
4
3
2
1
25
24
23
22
35
36
37

63

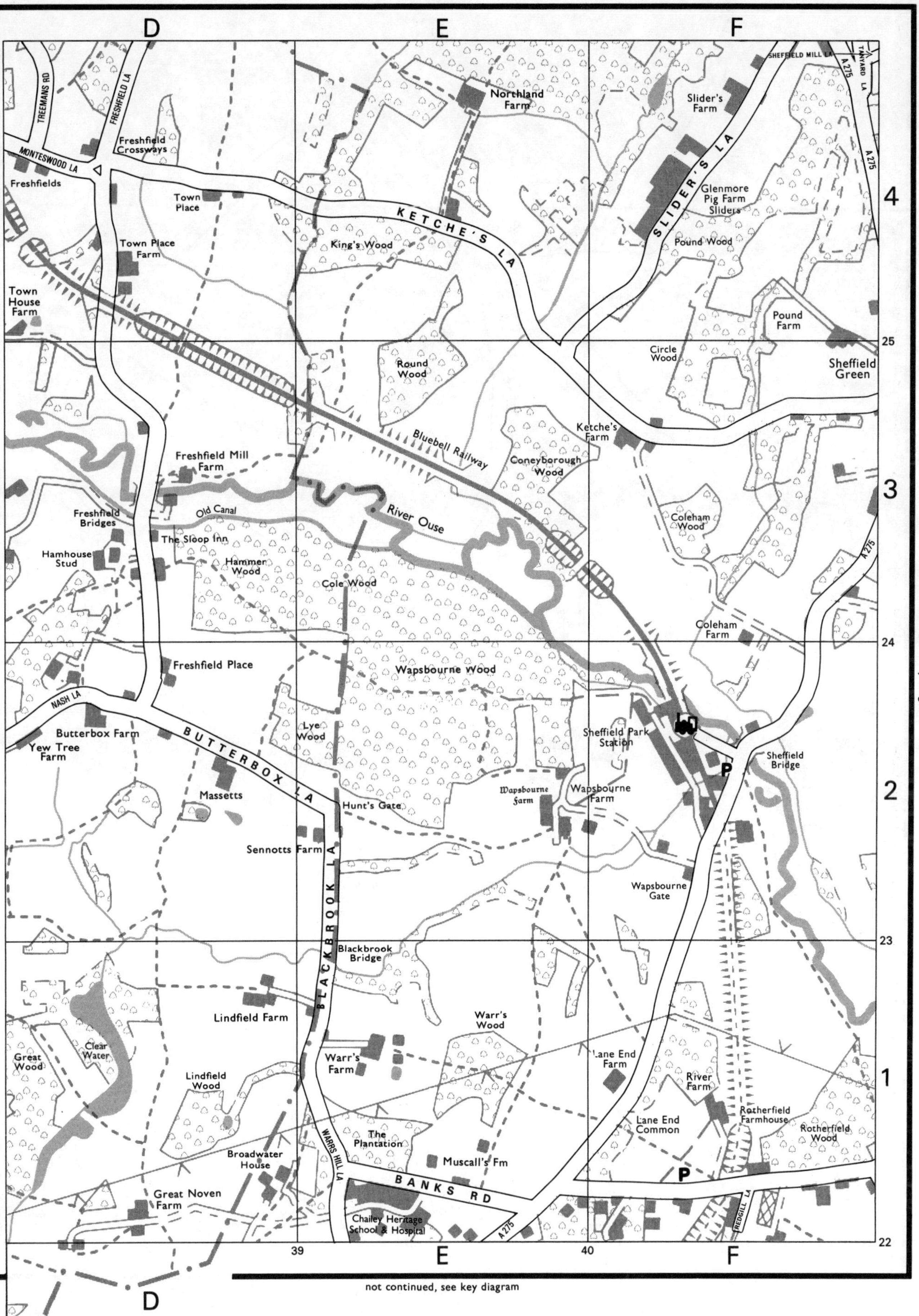

not continued, see key diagram

not continued, see key diagram

64

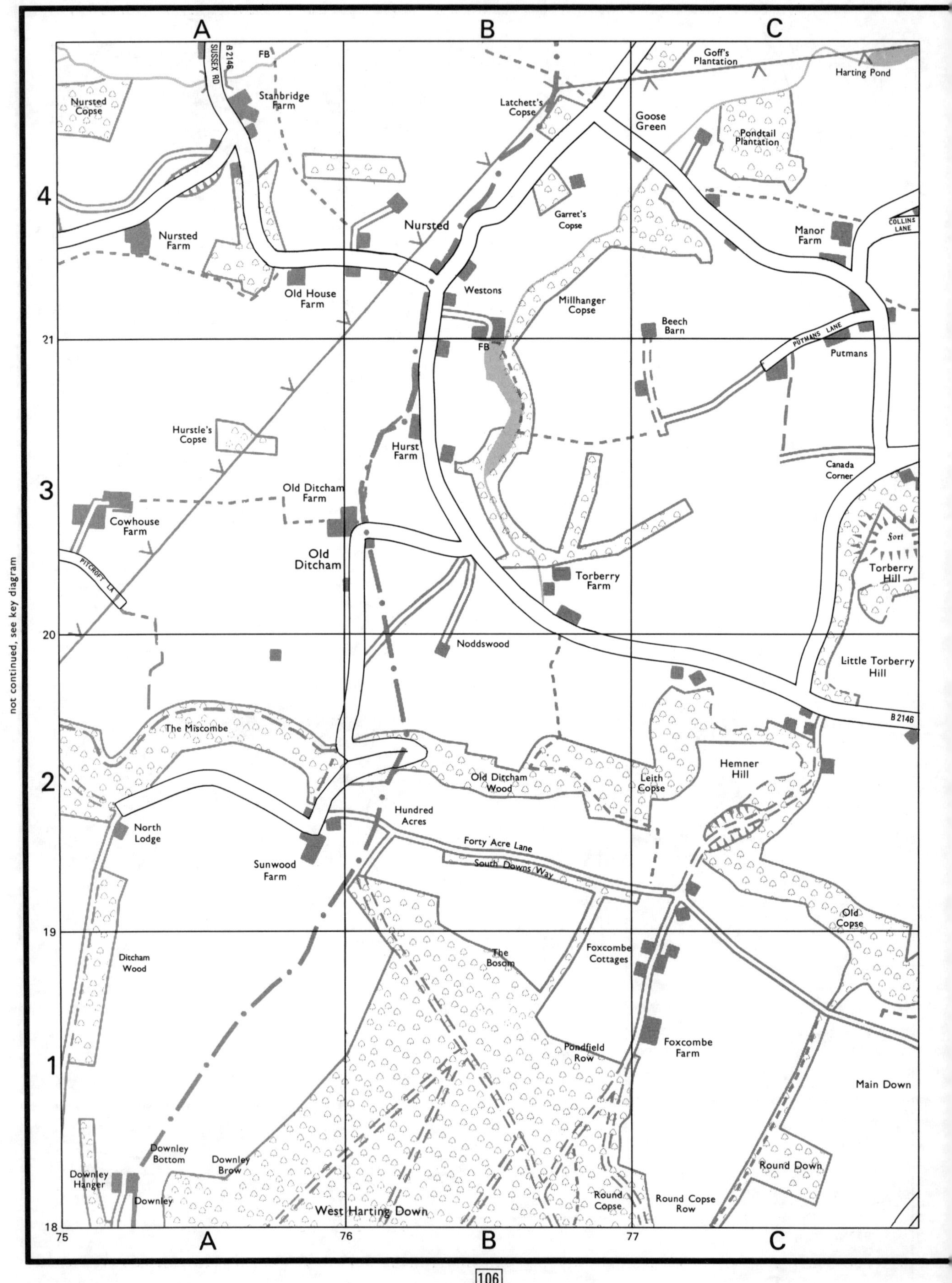
A
B
C
FB
B 2146
SUSSEX RD
Stanbridge Farm
Nursted Copse
Latchett's Copse
Goff's Plantation
Harting Pond
Goose Green
Pondtail Plantation
Garret's Copse
Nursted
Nursted Farm
Old House Farm
Manor Farm
COLLINS LANE
Westons
Millhanger Copse
Beech Barn
PUTMANS LANE
Putmans
FB
Hurstle's Copse
Hurst Farm
Old Ditcham Farm
Canada Corner
Cowhouse Farm
Fort
Torberry Hill
Old Ditcham
PITCROFT LA
Torberry Farm
Noddswood
Little Torberry Hill
B 2146
The Miscombe
Hemner Hill
Old Ditcham Wood
Leith Copse
North Lodge
Hundred Acres
Forty Acre Lane
South Downs Way
Sunwood Farm
Old Copse
Ditcham Wood
The Bosom
Foxcombe Cottages
Pondfield Row
Foxcombe Farm
Main Down
Downley Bottom
Downley Brow
Round Down
Downley Hanger
Downley
Round Copse
Round Copse Row
West Harting Down
4
3
2
1
21
20
19
18
75
76
77
not continued, see key diagram

106

65

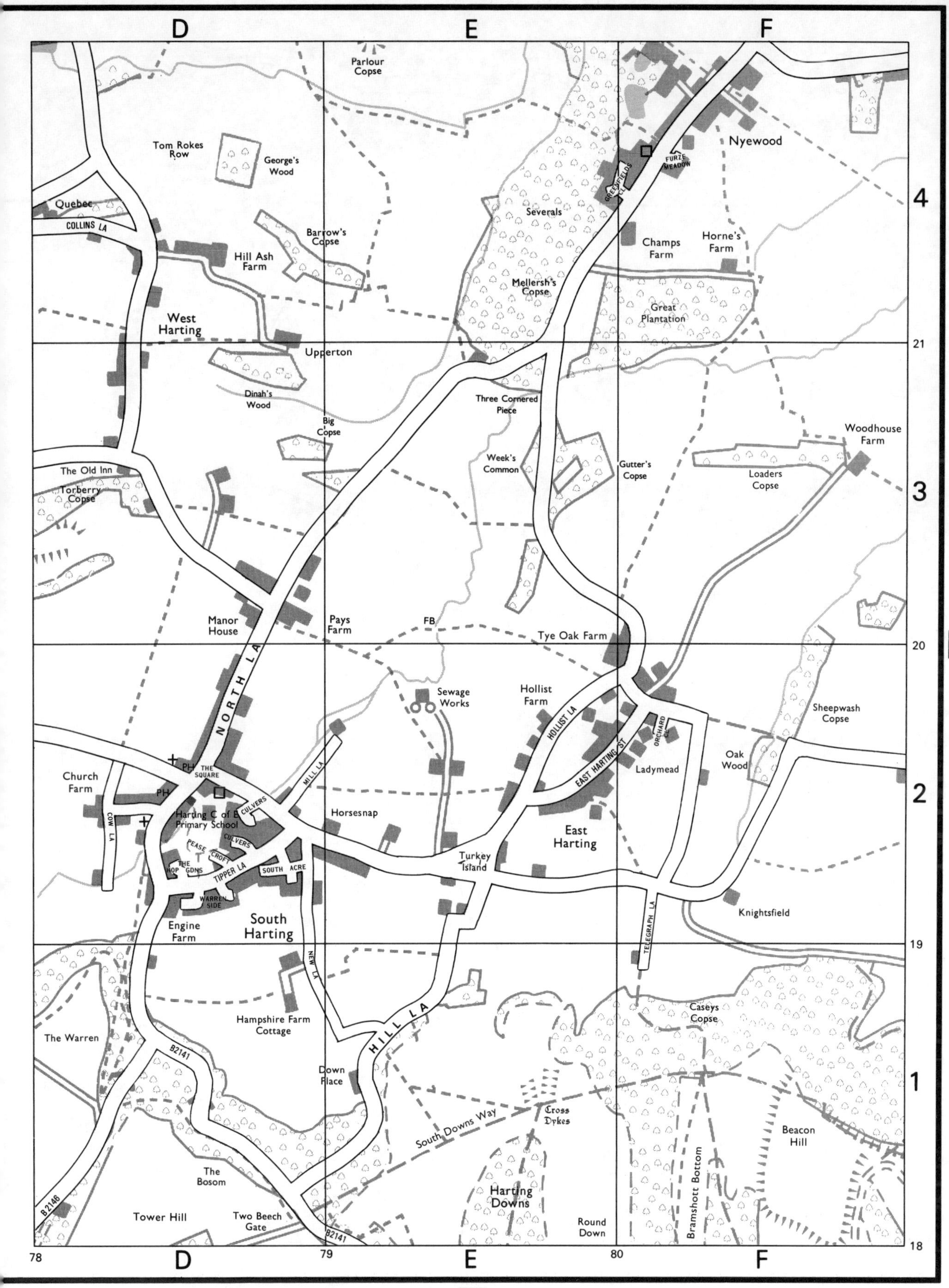
D
E
F
Parlour Copse
Tom Rokes Row
George's Wood
Nyewood
GREENFIELDS CL
FURZE MEADOW
Quebec
COLLINS LA
Barrow's Copse
Severals
Champs Farm
Horne's Farm
Hill Ash Farm
Mellersh's Copse
Great Plantation
West Harting
Upperton
Dinah's Wood
Three Cornered Piece
Big Copse
Woodhouse Farm
The Old Inn
Torberry Copse
Week's Common
Gutter's Copse
Loaders Copse
Manor House
Pays Farm
FB
Tye Oak Farm
Sewage Works
Hollist Farm
HOLLIST LA
NORTH LA
Sheepwash Copse
ORCHARD CL
Church Farm
PH
THE SQUARE
MILL LA
EAST HARTING ST
Ladymead
Oak Wood
COW LA
Harting C of E Primary School
CULVERS
Horsesnap
PEASE CROFT
THE HOP GDNS
TIPPER LA
SOUTH ACRE
East Harting
Turkey Island
WARREN SIDE
Engine Farm
South Harting
TELEGRAPH LA
Knightsfield
NEW LA
Hampshire Farm Cottage
HILL LA
Caseys Copse
The Warren
B2141
Down Place
Cross Dykes
South Downs Way
Beacon Hill
The Bosom
Harting Downs
Bramshott Bottom
Tower Hill
Two Beech Gate
Round Down
B2146
4
21
3
20
2
19
1
18
78
79
80
88

107

66

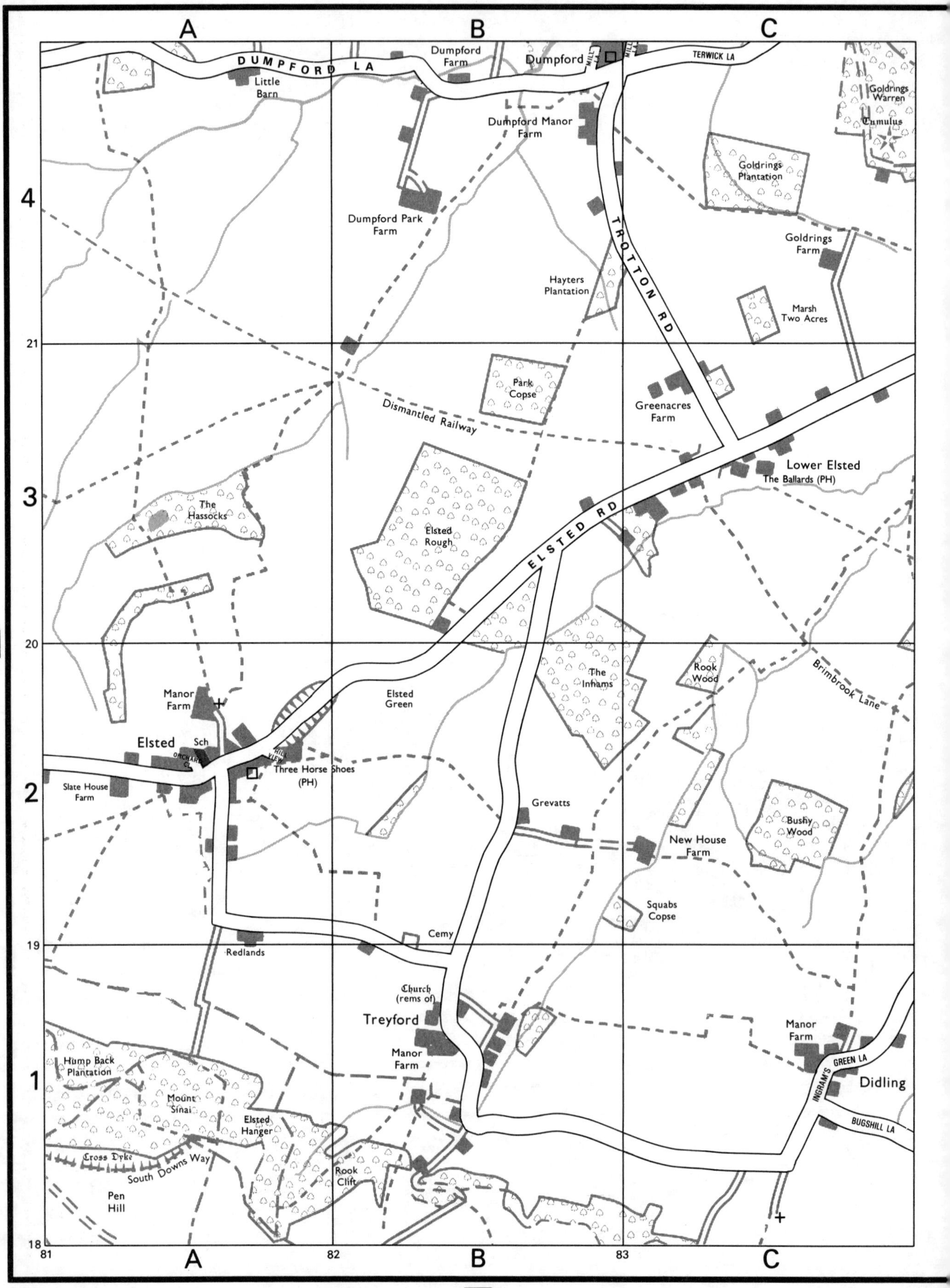

A
B
C
4
3
2
1
21
20
19
18
81
82
83
DUMPFORD LA
Little Barn
Dumpford Farm
Dumpford
MILL LA
TERWICK LA
Goldrings Warren
Tumulus
Dumpford Manor Farm
Goldrings Plantation
Dumpford Park Farm
TROTTON RD
Goldrings Farm
Hayters Plantation
Marsh Two Acres
Park Copse
Greenacres Farm
Dismantled Railway
Lower Elsted
The Ballards (PH)
The Hassocks
Elsted Rough
ELSTED RD
The Inhams
Rook Wood
Brimbrook Lane
Manor Farm
Elsted Green
Elsted
Sch
ORCHARD CL
HILL VIEW
Three Horse Shoes (PH)
Slate House Farm
Grevatts
New House Farm
Bushy Wood
Squabs Copse
Cemy
Redlands
Church (rems of)
Treyford
Manor Farm
Manor Farm
GREEN LA
INGRAM'S
Didling
BUGSHILL LA
Hump Back Plantation
Mount Sinai
Elsted Hanger
Cross Dyke
South Downs Way
Rook Clift
Pen Hill

87

108

67

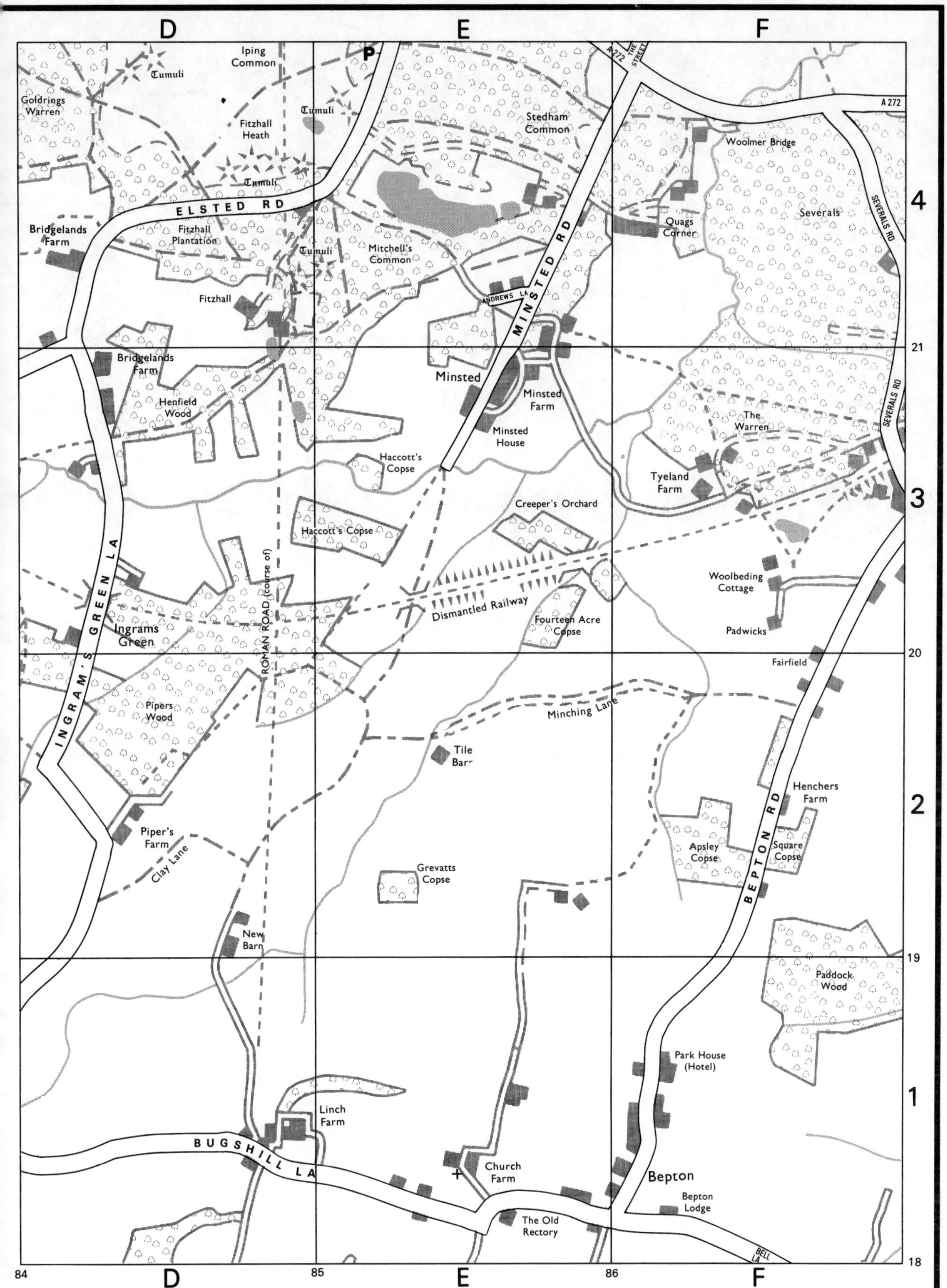
D
E
F
Iping Common
Cumuli
Goldrings Warren
Tumuli
Fitzhall Heath
Tumuli
Stedham Common
A 272
THE STREET
Woolmer Bridge
ELSTED RD
Bridgelands Farm
Fitzhall Plantation
Tumuli
Mitchell's Common
MINSTED RD
Quags Corner
Severals
SEVERALS RD
4
Fitzhall
ANDREWS LA
21
Bridgelands Farm
Minsted
Minsted Farm
Henfield Wood
Minsted House
The Warren
SEVERALS RD
Haccott's Copse
Tyeland Farm
3
Creeper's Orchard
Haccott's Copse
ROMAN ROAD (course of)
Woolbeding Cottage
INGRAM'S GREEN LA
Dismantled Railway
Fourteen Acre Copse
Ingrams Green
Padwicks
20
Fairfield
Minching Lane
Pipers Wood
Tile Barn
Henchers Farm
2
Piper's Farm
BEPTON RD
Clay Lane
Apsley Copse
Square Copse
Grevatts Copse
New Barn
19
Paddock Wood
Park House (Hotel)
1
Linch Farm
BUGSHILL LA
Church Farm
Bepton
Bepton Lodge
The Old Rectory
BELL LA
18
84
85
86
D
E
F

90

109

68

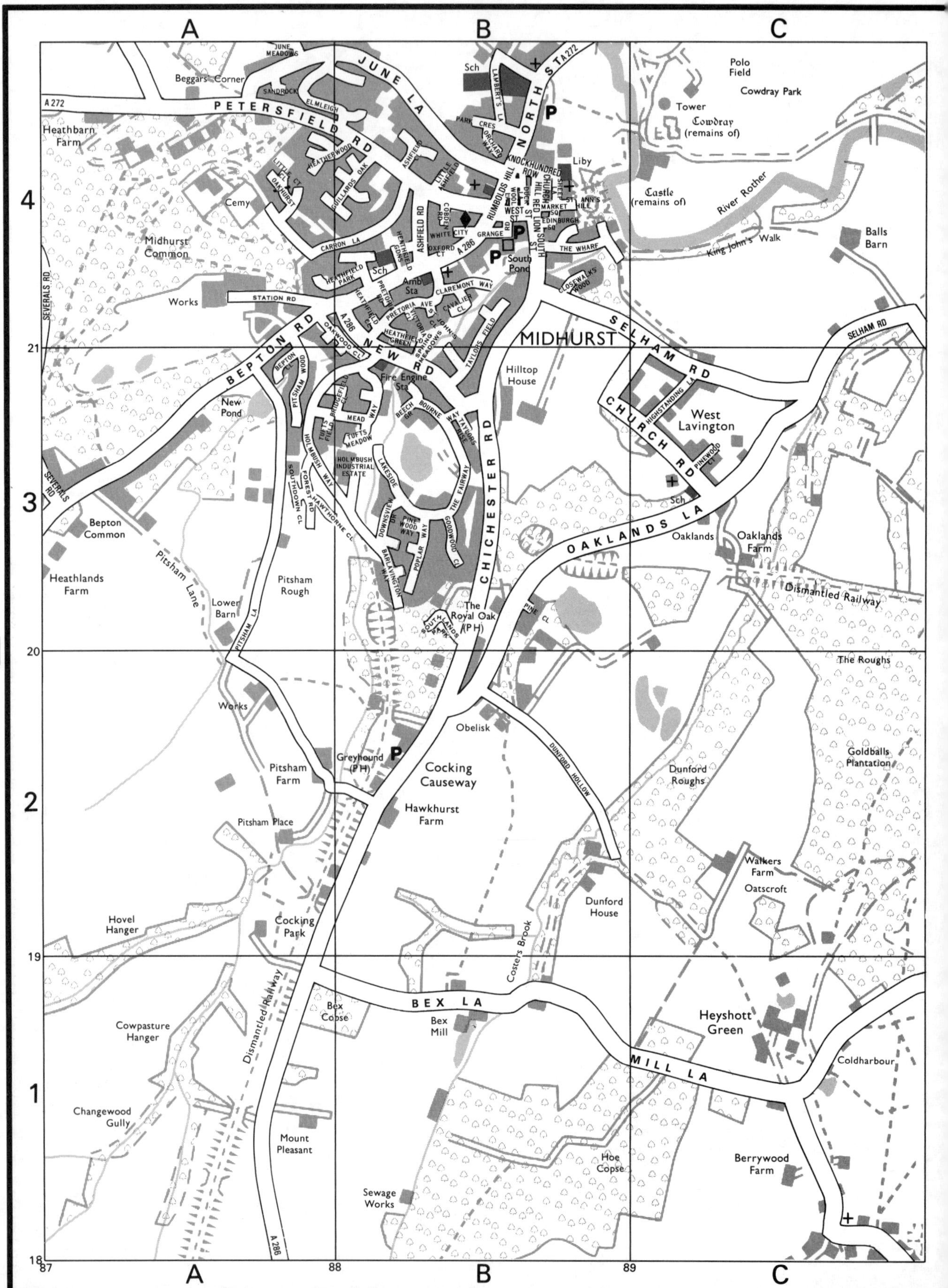
A
B
C
4
3
2
1
21
20
19
18
87
88
89
Beggars Corner
Heathbarn Farm
Cemy
Midhurst Common
Works
PETERSFIELD RD
JUNE LA
JUNE MEADOWS
SANDROCK
ELMLEIGH
A 272
NORTH ST
A 272
Sch
Polo Field
Cowdray Park
Tower
Cowdray (remains of)
Castle (remains of)
River Rother
King John's Walk
Balls Barn
Liby
KNOCKHUNDRED ROW
RUMBOLDS HILL
WEST ST
MARKET SQ
EDINBURGH SQ
CHURCH HILL
RED LION ST
SOUTH ST
ST ANN'S HILL
THE WHARF
South Pond
CLOSEWALKS WOOD
GRANGE
A 286
CITY
WHITE
OXFORD CT
COBDEN RD
ASHFIELD RD
LITTLE ASHFIELD
ASHFIELD
HEATHERWOOD
GUILLARDS OAK
LITTLE CL
OAKHURST
CARRON LA
HEATHFIELD GDNS
HEATHFIELD PARK
Sch
Amb Sta
CLAREMONT WAY
STATION RD
PRETORIA AVE
VICTORIA CL
ST JOHN'S CL
CAVALIER CL
TAYLORS FIELD
SPRING MEADOWS
HEATHFIELD GREEN
HEATHFIELD CL
MIDHURST
SELHAM RD
BEPTON RD
OAKWOOD CL
NEW RD
BEPTON CL
PITSHAM WOOD
Fire Engine Sta
Hilltop House
SELHAM RD
HIGHSTANDING LA
CHURCH RD
West Lavington
PINEWOOD CT
Sch
New Pond
BRIDGEFIELD CL
MEAD WAY
TUFTS FIELD
TUFTS MEADOW
BEECH GR
BOURNE WAY
TAYLORS RISE
CHICHESTER RD
HOLMBUSH WAY
HOLMBUSH INDUSTRIAL ESTATE
LAKESIDE
THE FAIRWAY
SOUTHDOWN CL
FOREST RD
HAWTHORNE CL
DOWNSVIEW DR
PINE WOOD WAY
POPLAR WAY
GOODWOOD CL
BARLAVINGTON WAY
SEVERALS RD
SEVERALS RD
Bepton Common
Heathlands Farm
Pitsham Lane
Lower Barn
PITSHAM LA
Pitsham Rough
OAKLANDS LA
Oaklands
Oaklands Farm
Dismantled Railway
PINE CL
The Royal Oak (PH)
SOUTHLANDS PARK
The Roughs
Works
Obelisk
DUNFORD HOLLOW
Goldballs Plantation
Greyhound (PH)
Cocking Causeway
Pitsham Farm
Dunford Roughs
Hawkhurst Farm
Pitsham Place
Walkers Farm
Oatscroft
Dunford House
Hovel Hanger
Cocking Park
Costers Brook
BEX LA
Bex Copse
Bex Mill
Heyshott Green
Cowpasture Hanger
Dismantled Railway
MILL LA
Coldharbour
Changewood Gully
Mount Pleasant
Hoe Copse
Berrywood Farm
Sewage Works
A 286
P

89

110

69

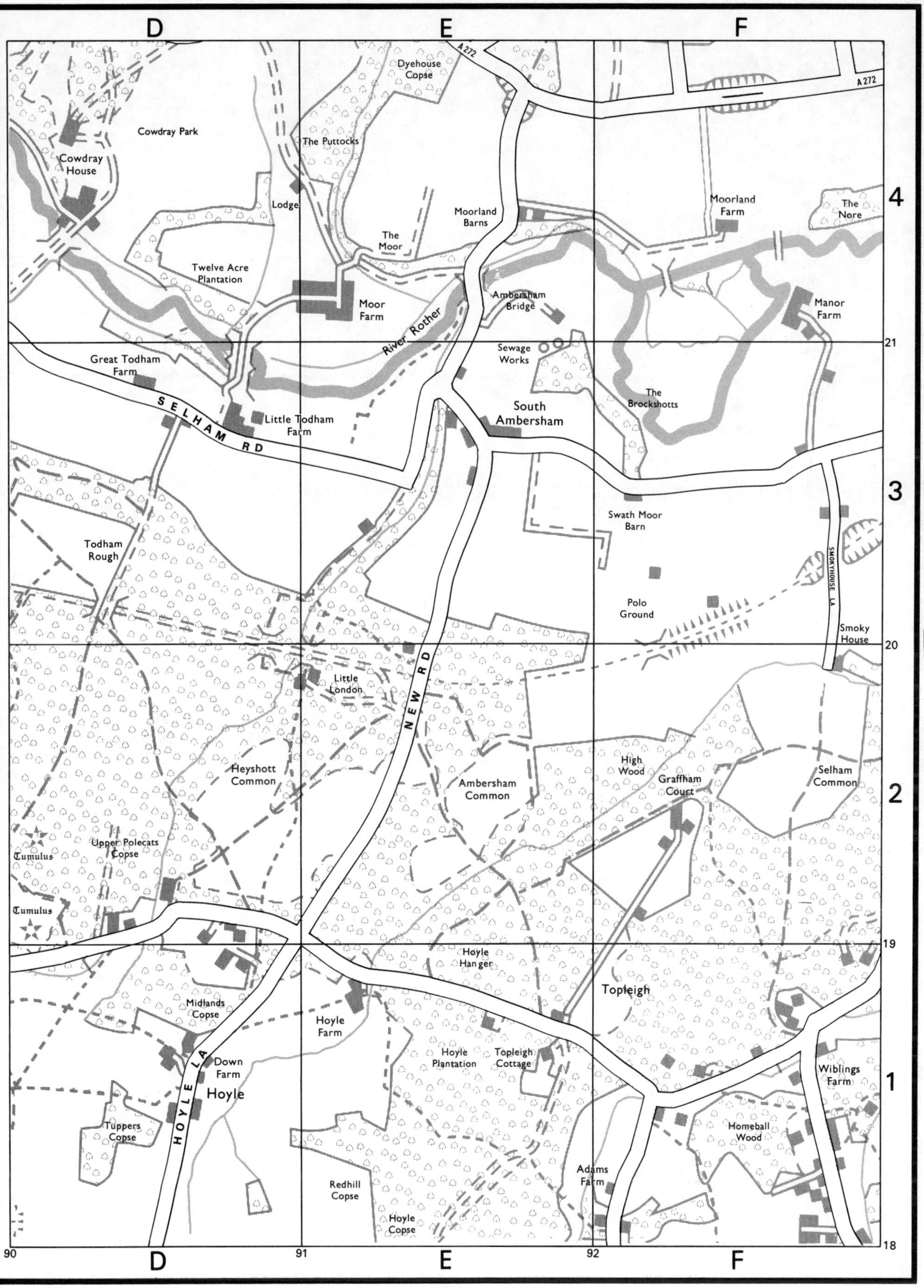

D
E
F
A272
A272
Dyehouse Copse
Cowdray Park
The Puttocks
Cowdray House
Lodge
Moorland Barns
Moorland Farm
The Nore
4
The Moor
Twelve Acre Plantation
Moor Farm
River Rother
Ambersham Bridge
Manor Farm
Great Todham Farm
Sewage Works
21
The Brockshotts
SELHAM RD
Little Todham Farm
South Ambersham
3
Swath Moor Barn
Todham Rough
SMOKYHOUSE LA
Polo Ground
Smoky House
20
Little London
NEW RD
High Wood
Graffham Court
Selham Common
Heyshott Common
Ambersham Common
2
Tumulus
Upper Polecats Copse
Tumulus
19
Hoyle Hanger
Topleigh
Midlands Copse
Hoyle Farm
Hoyle Plantation
Topleigh Cottage
Down Farm
Wiblings Farm
1
Hoyle
HOYLE LA
Tuppers Copse
Homeball Wood
Adams Farm
Redhill Copse
Hoyle Copse
90
91
92
18

92

111

70

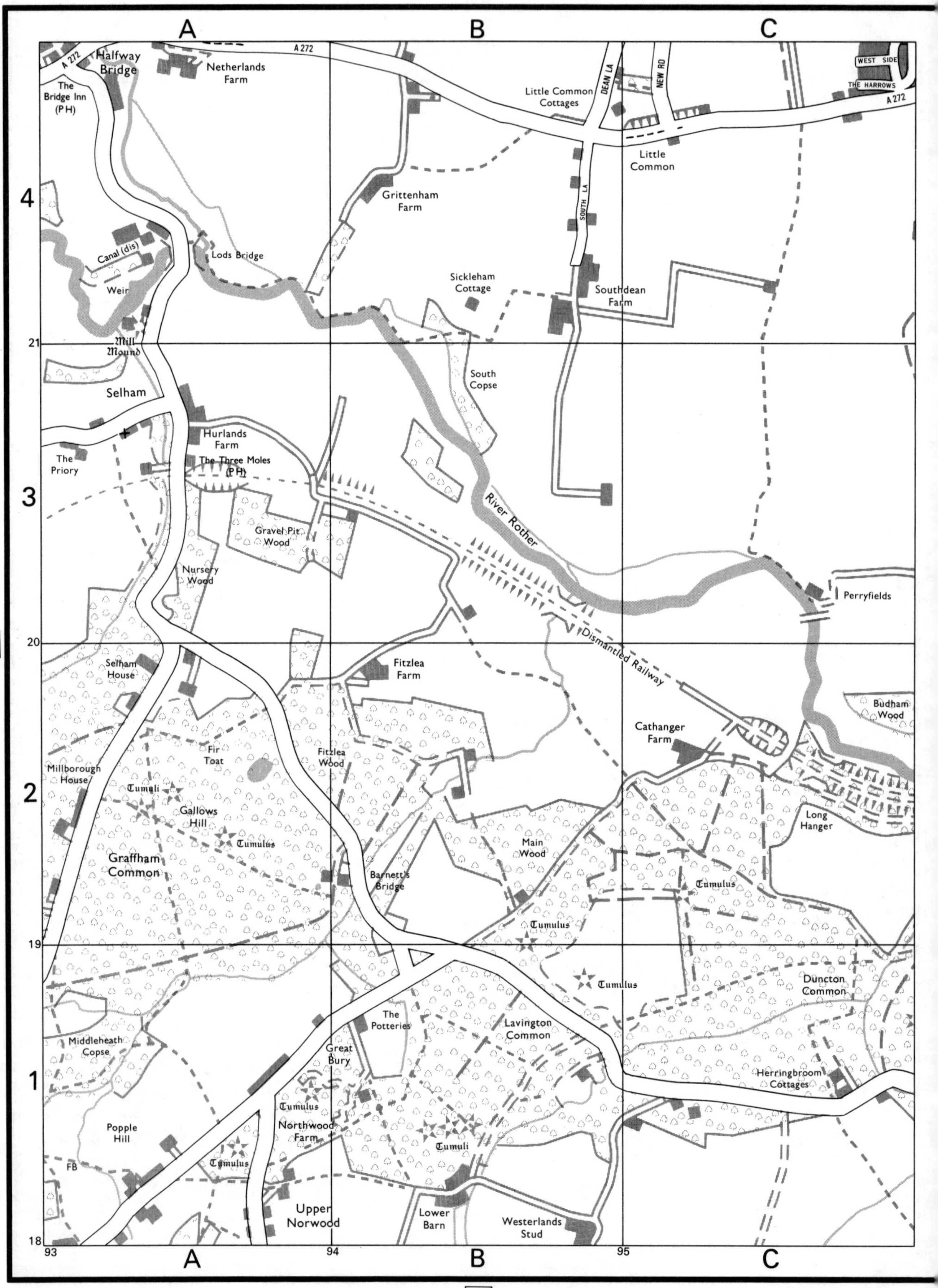
A
B
C
4
3
2
1
21
20
19
18
93
94
95
A 272
Halfway Bridge
The Bridge Inn (PH)
Netherlands Farm
Little Common Cottages
DEAN LA
NEW RD
WEST SIDE
THE HARROWS
Little Common
Grittenham Farm
SOUTH LA
Canal (dis)
Lods Bridge
Weir
Sickleham Cottage
Southdean Farm
Mill Mound
South Copse
Selham
Hurlands Farm
The Three Moles (PH)
The Priory
River Rother
Gravel Pit Wood
Nursery Wood
Perryfields
Dismantled Railway
Selham House
Fitzlea Farm
Budham Wood
Cathanger Farm
Fir Toat
Fitzlea Wood
Millborough House
Tumuli
Gallows Hill
Tumulus
Long Hanger
Main Wood
Graffham Common
Barnett's Bridge
Duncton Common
The Potteries
Lavington Common
Middleheath Copse
Great Bury
Herringbroom Cottages
Popple Hill
Northwood Farm
FB
Upper Norwood
Lower Barn
Westerlands Stud

91

112

71

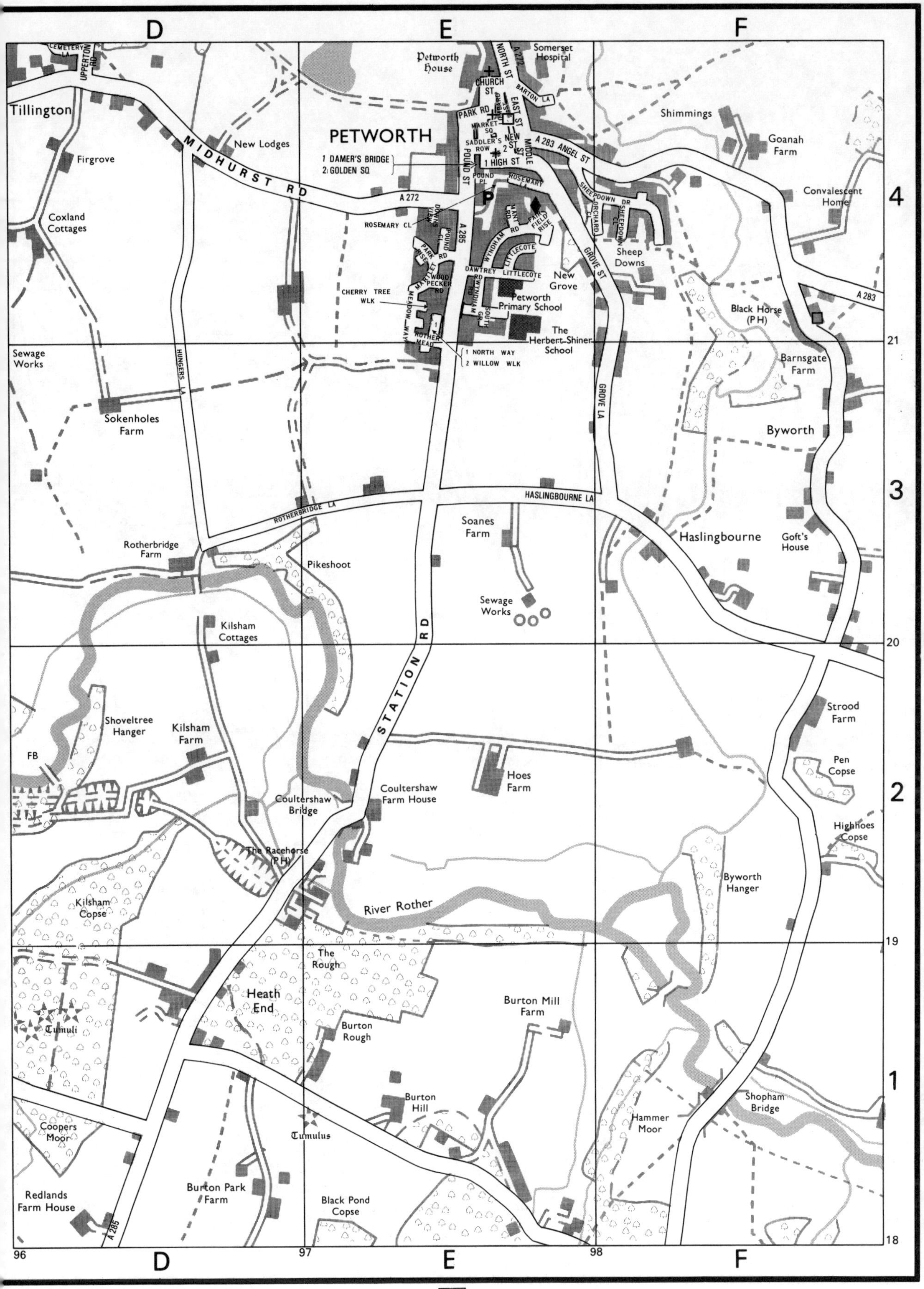
D
E
F
Tillington
PETWORTH
Petworth House
Somerset Hospital
CEMETERY LA
UPPERTON RD
MIDHURST RD
New Lodges
Firgrove
Coxland Cottages
1 DAMER'S BRIDGE
2 GOLDEN SQ
NORTH ST
CHURCH ST
EAST ST
BARTON LA
PARK RD
MARKET SQ
NEW ST
SADDLER'S ROW
HIGH ST
MIDDLE ST
POUND ST
POUND PL
ROSEMARY LA
A 283 ANGEL ST
A 272
ROSEMARY CL
DOWNS VIEW
A 285
POUND CL
PARK RISE
PARK RD
MANT RD
FAIRFIELD RISE
WYNDHAM RD
LITTLECOTE
DAWTREY RD
WOODPECKER RD
MEADOW WAY
CHERRY TREE WLK
ROTHER MEAD
SOUTH GR
1 NORTH WAY
2 WILLOW WLK
Petworth Primary School
The Herbert Shiner School
New Grove
SHEEPDOWN DR
SHEEPDOWN CL
ORCHARD CL
Sheep Downs
GROVE ST
GROVE LA
Shimmings
Goanah Farm
Convalescent Home
Black Horse (PH)
A 283
Barnsgate Farm
Byworth
Sewage Works
HUNGERS LA
Sokenholes Farm
HASLINGBOURNE LA
ROTHERBRIDGE LA
Soanes Farm
Haslingbourne
Goft's House
Rotherbridge Farm
Pikeshoot
Sewage Works
Kilsham Cottages
STATION RD
Shoveltree Hanger
Kilsham Farm
FB
Strood Farm
Pen Copse
Hoes Farm
Coultershaw Farm House
Coultershaw Bridge
The Racehorse (PH)
Highhoes Copse
Byworth Hanger
Kilsham Copse
River Rother
The Rough
Heath End
Tumuli
Burton Mill Farm
Burton Rough
Burton Hill
Shopham Bridge
Hammer Moor
Coopers Moor
Tumulus
Redlands Farm House
A 285
Burton Park Farm
Black Pond Copse
96
97
98
18
19
20
21
1
2
3
4

94

113

72

93

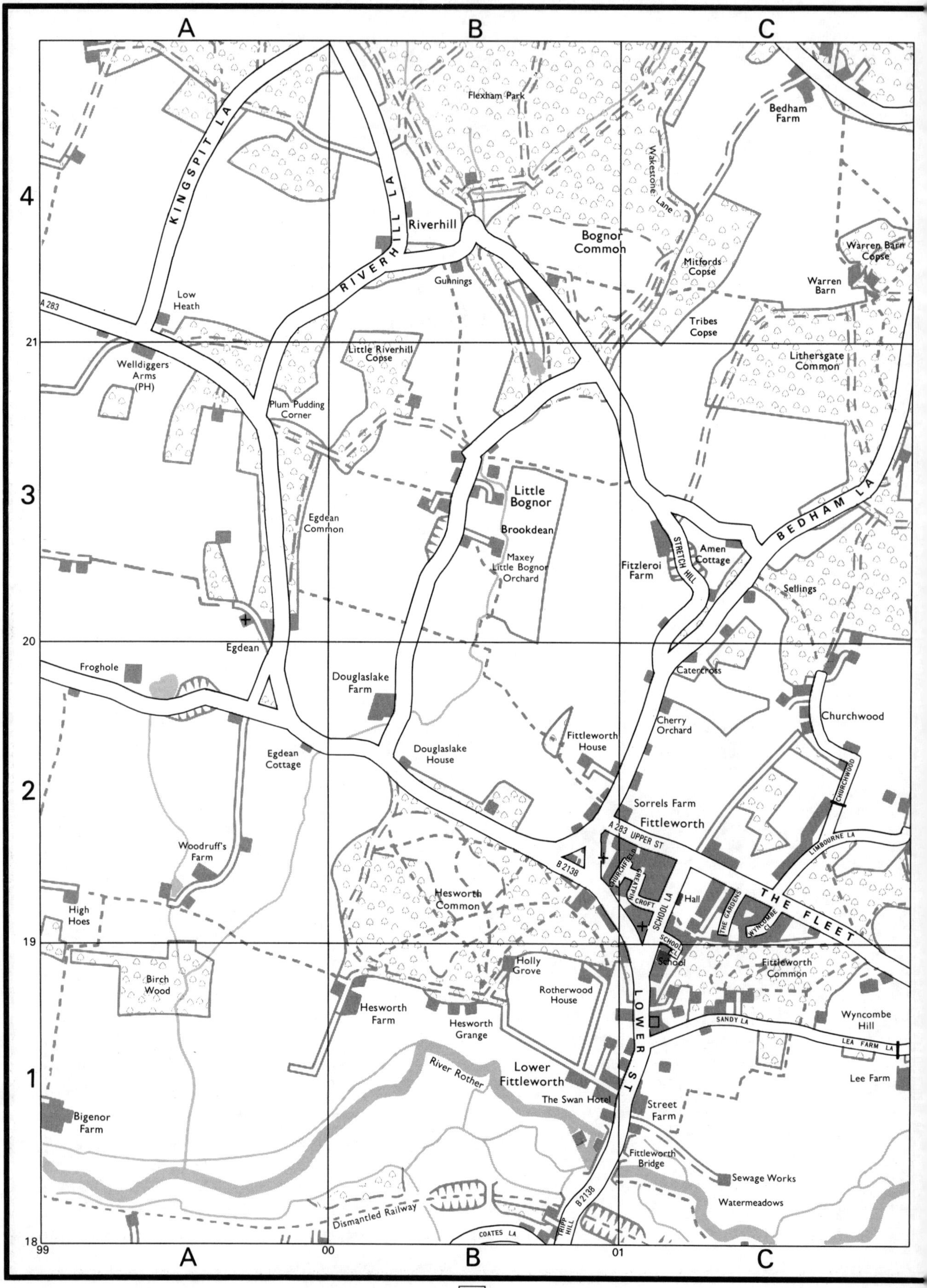
A
B
C
4
3
2
1
21
20
19
18
99
00
01
Flexham Park
Bedham Farm
KINGSPIT LA
RIVERHILL LA
Riverhill
Wakestone Lane
Bognor Common
Mitfords Copse
Warren Barn Copse
Warren Barn
Gunnings
Low Heath
A 283
Tribes Copse
Little Riverhill Copse
Lithersgate Common
Welldiggers Arms (PH)
Plum Pudding Corner
Little Bognor
Brookdean
Egdean Common
Maxey Little Bognor Orchard
Fitzleroi Farm
STRETCH HILL
Amen Cottage
BEDHAM LA
Sellings
Egdean
Froghole
Douglaslake Farm
Catercross
Churchwood
Cherry Orchard
Fittleworth House
Egdean Cottage
Douglaslake House
CHURCHWOOD
Sorrels Farm
Fittleworth
A 283 UPPER ST
LIMBOURNE LA
Woodruff's Farm
B 2138
CHURCHFIELD
GREATPIN CROFT
SCHOOL LA
Hall
THE GARDENS
WYNCOMBE CL
THE FLEET
Hesworth Common
High Hoes
SCHOOL
School
Holly Grove
Fittleworth Common
Birch Wood
Rotherwood House
Hesworth Farm
Hesworth Grange
LOWER ST
SANDY LA
Wyncombe Hill
LEA FARM LA
River Rother
Lower Fittleworth
Lee Farm
The Swan Hotel
Street Farm
Bigenor Farm
Fittleworth Bridge
Sewage Works
Watermeadows
Dismantled Railway
B 2138
TRIPP HILL
COATES LA

114

73

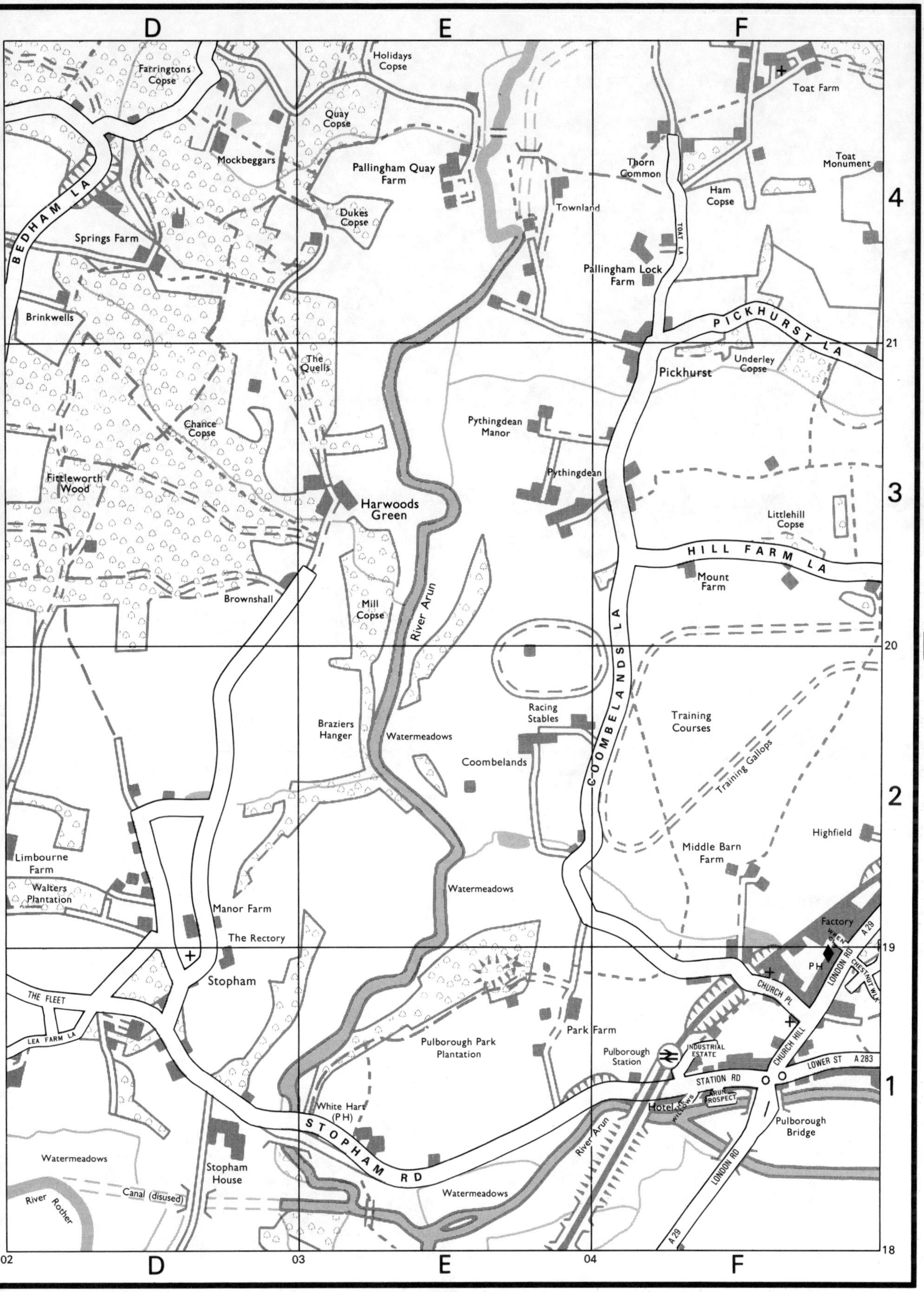
D
E
F
Holidays Copse
Farringtons Copse
Toat Farm
Quay Copse
Mockbeggars
Pallingham Quay Farm
Thorn Common
Toat Monument
BEDHAM LA
Ham Copse
Townland
Dukes Copse
Springs Farm
TOAT LA
Pallingham Lock Farm
Brinkwells
PICKHURST LA
The Quells
Underley Copse
Pickhurst
Pythingdean Manor
Chance Copse
Pythingdean
Fittleworth Wood
Harwoods Green
Littlehill Copse
HILL FARM LA
Mount Farm
Brownshall
Mill Copse
River Arun
COOMBELANDS LA
Racing Stables
Training Courses
Braziers Hanger
Watermeadows
Coombelands
Training Gallops
Highfield
Limbourne Farm
Middle Barn Farm
Walters Plantation
Watermeadows
Manor Farm
Factory
The Rectory
PH
LONDON RD
CHESTNUT WLK
A 29
Stopham
THE FLEET
CHURCH PL
LEA FARM LA
Park Farm
Pulborough Park Plantation
Pulborough Station
INDUSTRIAL ESTATE
CHURCH HILL
LOWER ST
A 283
STATION RD
White Hart (PH)
Hotel
ARUN PROSPECT
Pulborough Bridge
STOPHAM RD
River Arun
Watermeadows
Stopham House
LONDON RD
Canal (disused)
River Rother
Watermeadows
A 29
02
03
04
18
19
20
21
1
2
3
4

96

115

74

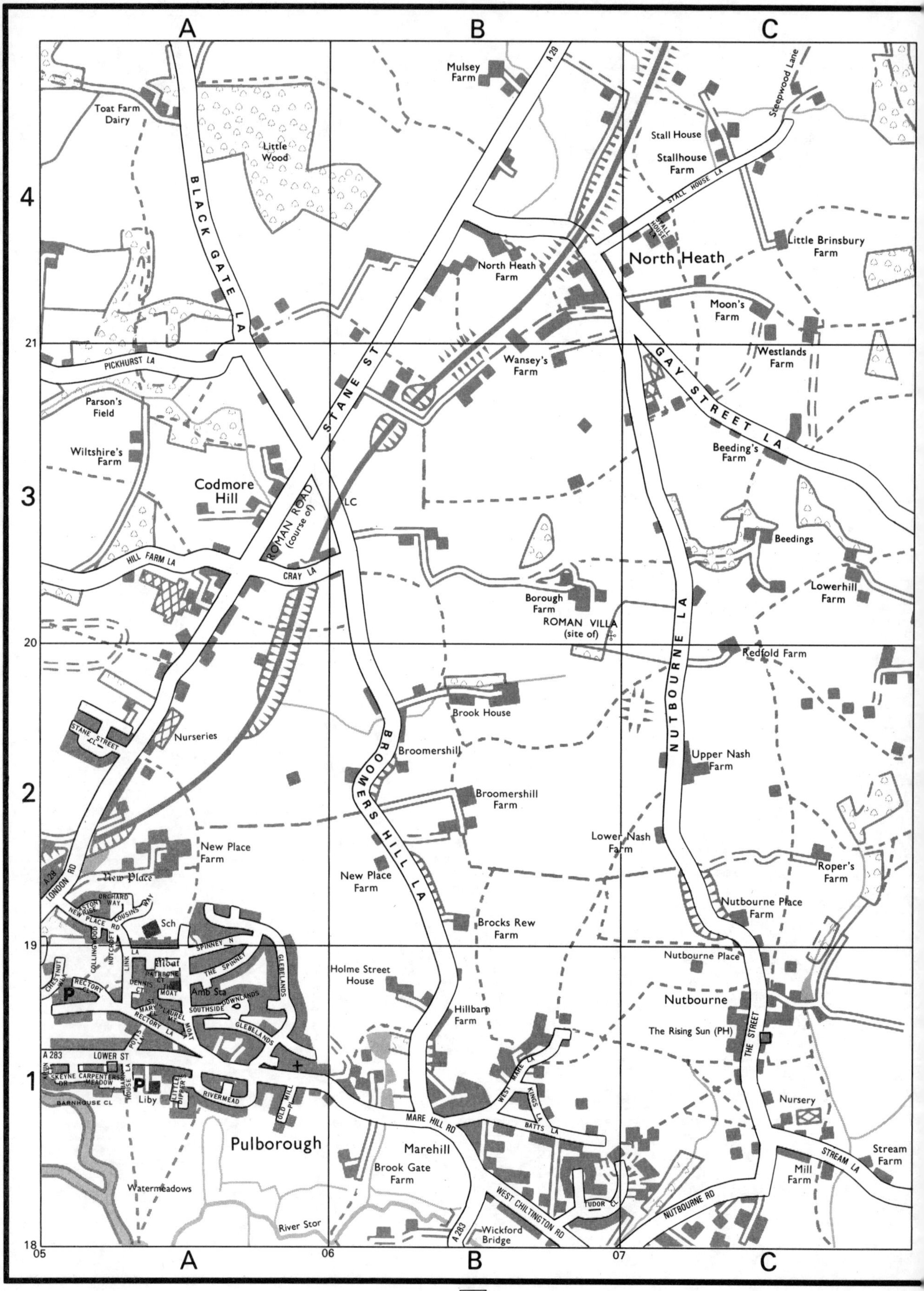
A
B
C
4
3
2
1
21
20
19
18
05
06
07
Toat Farm Dairy
Little Wood
Mulsey Farm
Steepwood Lane
Stall House
Stallhouse Farm
STALL HOUSE LA
Little Brinsbury Farm
North Heath
North Heath Farm
Moon's Farm
Westlands Farm
BLACK GATE LA
STANE ST
A 29
PICKHURST LA
Parson's Field
Wansey's Farm
GAY STREET LA
Beeding's Farm
Wiltshire's Farm
Codmore Hill
ROMAN ROAD (course of)
LC
Beedings
HILL FARM LA
CRAY LA
Borough Farm
Lowerhill Farm
ROMAN VILLA (site of)
Redfold Farm
Brook House
STANE STREET CL
Nurseries
Broomershill
BROOMERS HILL LA
NUTBOURNE LA
Upper Nash Farm
Broomershill Farm
Lower Nash Farm
New Place Farm
New Place
New Place Farm
Roper's Farm
Nutbourne Place Farm
Brocks Rew Farm
A 29
LONDON RD
ORCHARD WAY
COUSINS WAY
Sch
SPINNEY N
THE SPINNEY
GLEBELANDS
Nutbourne Place
Holme Street House
Nutbourne
The Rising Sun (PH)
THE STREET
CHESTNUT WALK
RECTORY CL
COLLINGWOOD
NUTCROFT
LINK LA
RATHBONE CT
DENNIS CT
THE MOAT
Amb Sta
DOWNLANDS
SOUTHSIDE
GLEBELANDS
ST MARY'S CL
LAUREL MS
MOAT
RECTORY LA
POTTS LA
Hillbarn Farm
A 283
LOWER ST
SKEYNE DR
CARPENTERS MEADOW
BARNHOUSE LA
LITTLE DIPPERS
RIVERMEAD
OLD MILL PL
Liby
BARNHOUSE CL
MARE HILL RD
WEST MARE LA
KINGS LA
BATTS LA
Nursery
Pulborough
Marehill
Brook Gate Farm
STREAM LA
Stream Farm
Mill Farm
Watermeadows
WEST CHILTINGTON RD
TUDOR CL
NUTBOURNE RD
River Stor
A 283
Wickford Bridge

95

116

75

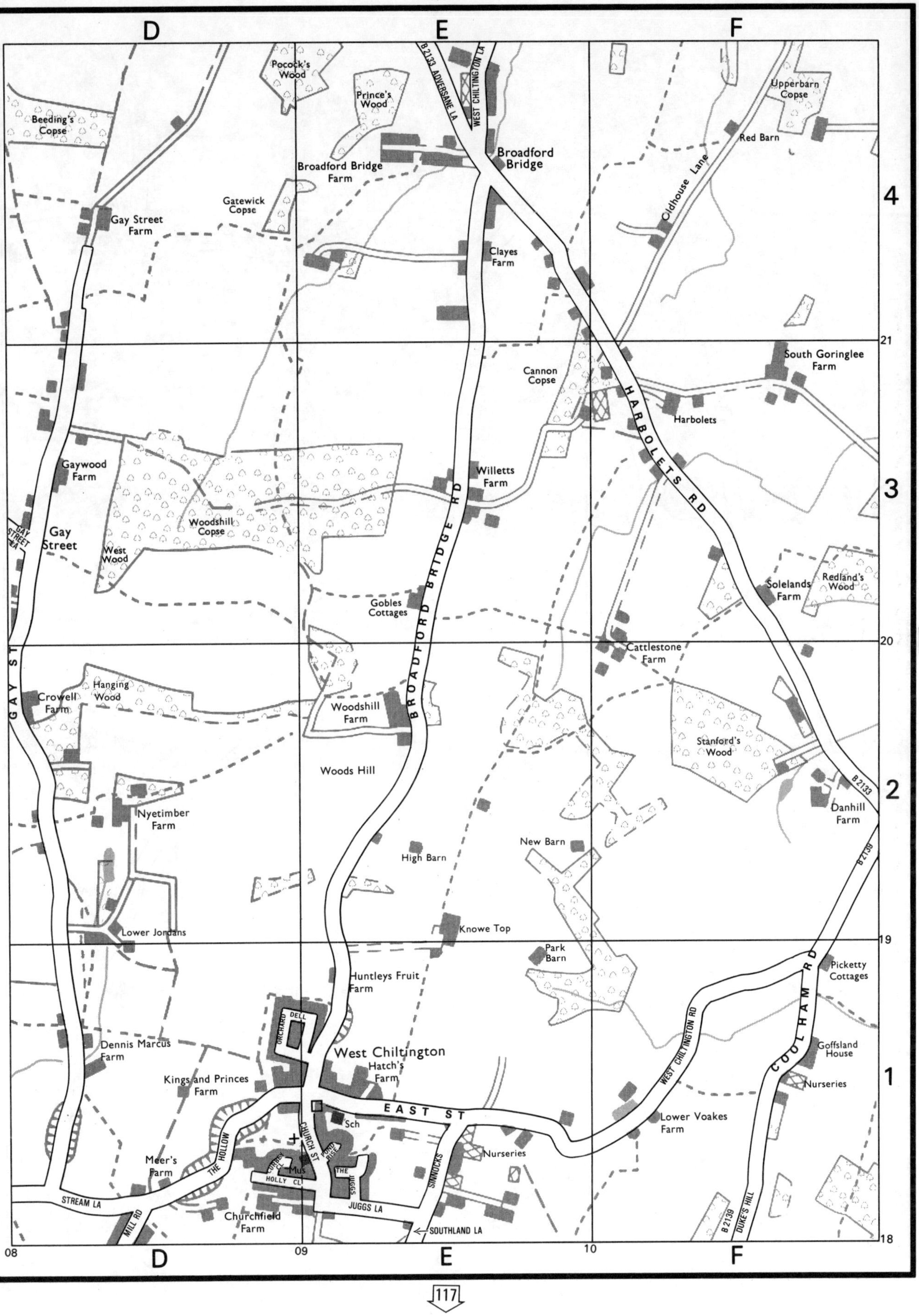
D
E
F
D
E
F
4
3
2
1
21
20
19
18
08
09
10
Pocock's Wood
Prince's Wood
Beeding's Copse
B2133 ADVERSANE LA
WEST CHILTINGTON LA
Upperbarn Copse
Red Barn
Broadford Bridge
Broadford Bridge Farm
Gatewick Copse
Gay Street Farm
Oldhouse Lane
Clayes Farm
South Goringlee Farm
Cannon Copse
Harbolets
HARBOLETS RD
Gaywood Farm
Willetts Farm
Woodshill Copse
Gay Street
GAY STREET LA
West Wood
BROADFORD BRIDGE RD
Solelands Farm
Redland's Wood
Gobles Cottages
Cattlestone Farm
GAY ST
Hanging Wood
Crowell Farm
Woodshill Farm
Stanford's Wood
Woods Hill
B2133
Danhill Farm
Nyetimber Farm
New Barn
High Barn
B2139
Lower Jordans
Knowe Top
Park Barn
Huntleys Fruit Farm
Picketty Cottages
COOLHAM RD
ORCHARD DELL
Dennis Marcus Farm
West Chiltington
Hatch's Farm
WEST CHILTINGTON RD
Goffsland House
Kings and Princes Farm
Nurseries
EAST ST
Sch
Lower Voakes Farm
THE HOLLOW
CHURCH ST
Nurseries
Meer's Farm
Mus
HOLLY CL
THE JUGGS
SINNOCKS
STREAM LA
JUGGS LA
MILL RD
Churchfield Farm
SOUTHLAND LA
B2139
DUKE'S HILL

86

117

76

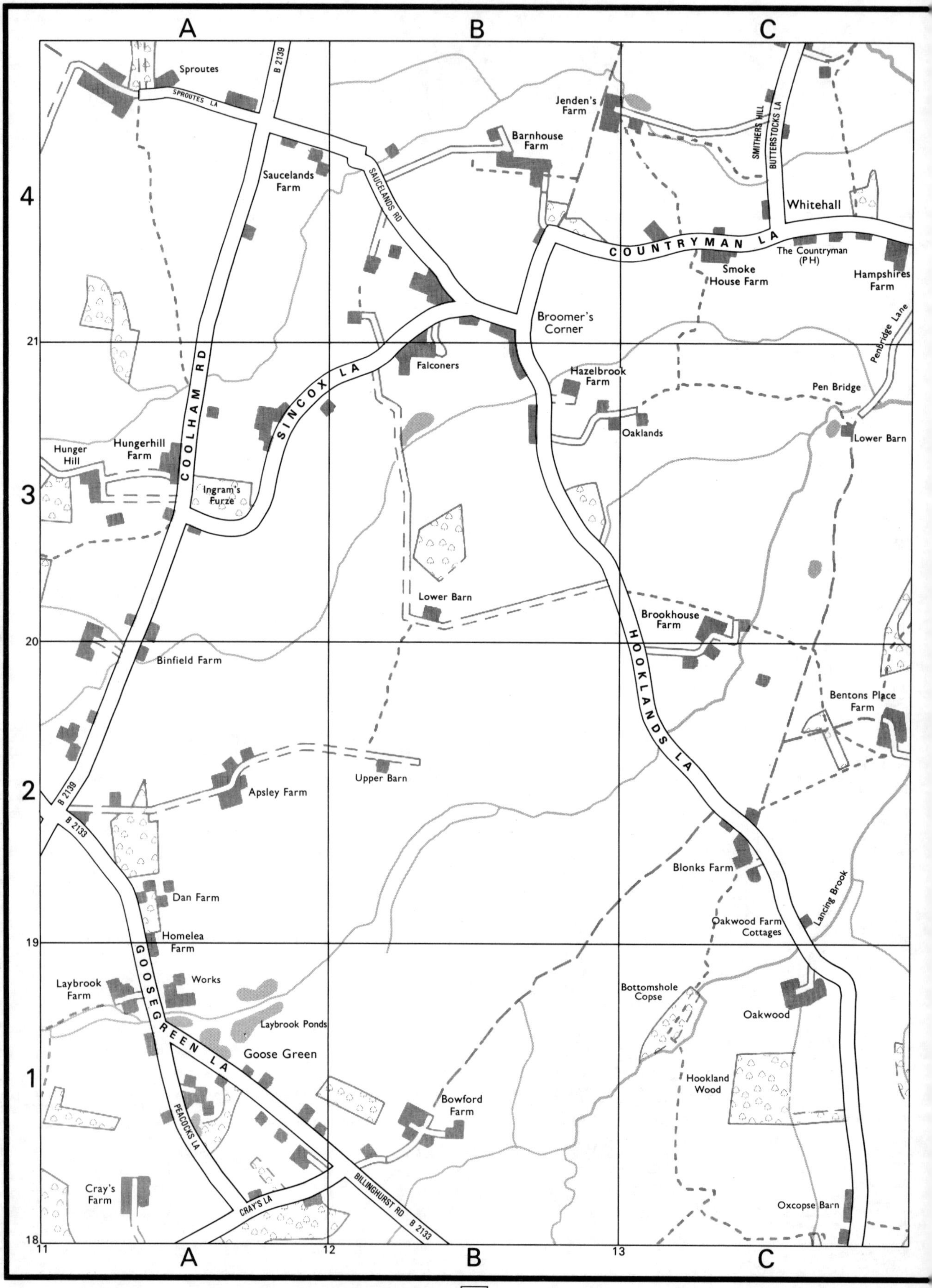
A
B
C
4
3
2
1
21
20
19
18
11
12
13
Sproutes
SPROUTES LA
B 2139
Jenden's Farm
Barnhouse Farm
SMITHERS HILL
BUTTERSTOCKS LA
Saucelands Farm
SAUCELANDS RD
Whitehall
COUNTRYMAN LA
The Countryman (PH)
Smoke House Farm
Hampshires Farm
Broomer's Corner
Penbridge Lane
Falconers
SINCOX LA
Hazelbrook Farm
Pen Bridge
COOLHAM RD
Oaklands
Lower Barn
Hunger Hill
Hungerhill Farm
Ingram's Furze
Lower Barn
Brookhouse Farm
Binfield Farm
HOOKLANDS LA
Bentons Place Farm
Upper Barn
Apsley Farm
B 2139
B 2133
Blonks Farm
Dan Farm
Lancing Brook
Oakwood Farm Cottages
Homelea Farm
GOOSEGREEN LA
Laybrook Farm
Works
Bottomshole Copse
Laybrook Ponds
Oakwood
Goose Green
Hookland Wood
Bowford Farm
PEACOCKS LA
Cray's Farm
CRAY'S LA
BILLINGHURST RD
B 2133
Oxcopse Barn

97

118

77

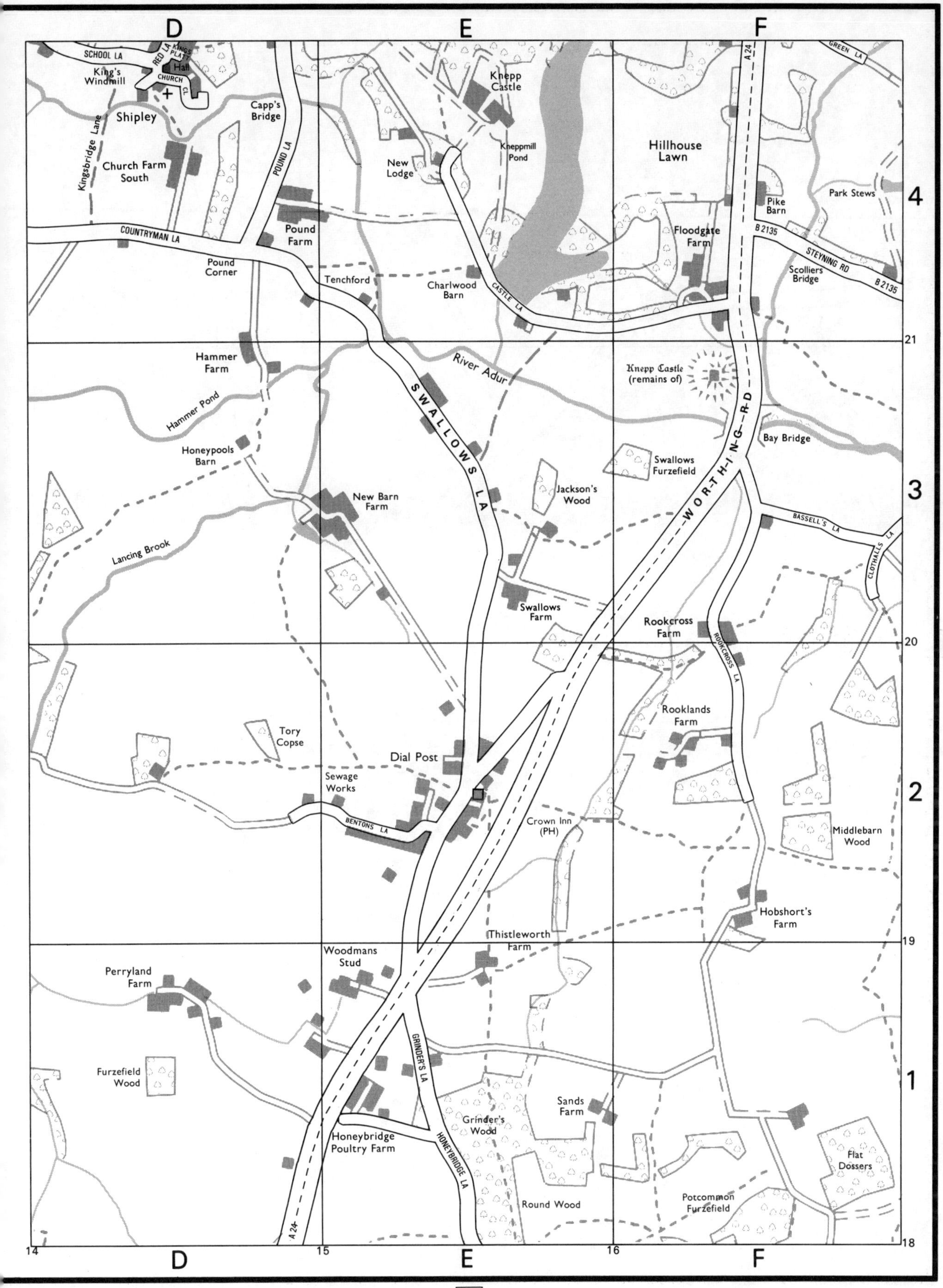
D
E
F
SCHOOL LA
RED LA
KINGS PLATT
King's Windmill
Hall
CHURCH CL
Shipley
Kingsbridge Lane
Church Farm South
Capp's Bridge
POUND LA
Knepp Castle
Kneppmill Pond
New Lodge
Hillhouse Lawn
A 24
GREEN LA
Pike Barn
Park Stews
COUNTRYMAN LA
Pound Farm
Pound Corner
Tenchford
Charlwood Barn
CASTLE LA
Floodgate Farm
B 2135
STEYNING RD
Scolliers Bridge
Hammer Farm
River Adur
Knepp Castle (remains of)
Hammer Pond
SWALLOWS LA
WORTHING RD
Bay Bridge
Honeypools Barn
Swallows Furzefield
Jackson's Wood
New Barn Farm
BASSELL'S LA
Lancing Brook
CLOTHALLS LA
Swallows Farm
Rookcross Farm
ROOKCROSS LA
Rooklands Farm
Tory Copse
Dial Post
Sewage Works
BENTONS LA
Crown Inn (PH)
Middlebarn Wood
Hobshort's Farm
Thistleworth Farm
Woodmans Stud
Perryland Farm
GRINDER'S LA
Furzefield Wood
Sands Farm
Grinder's Wood
HONEYBRIDGE LA
Honeybridge Poultry Farm
Flat Dossers
Round Wood
Potcommon Furzefield
4
3
2
1
21
20
19
18
14
15
16

100

119

78

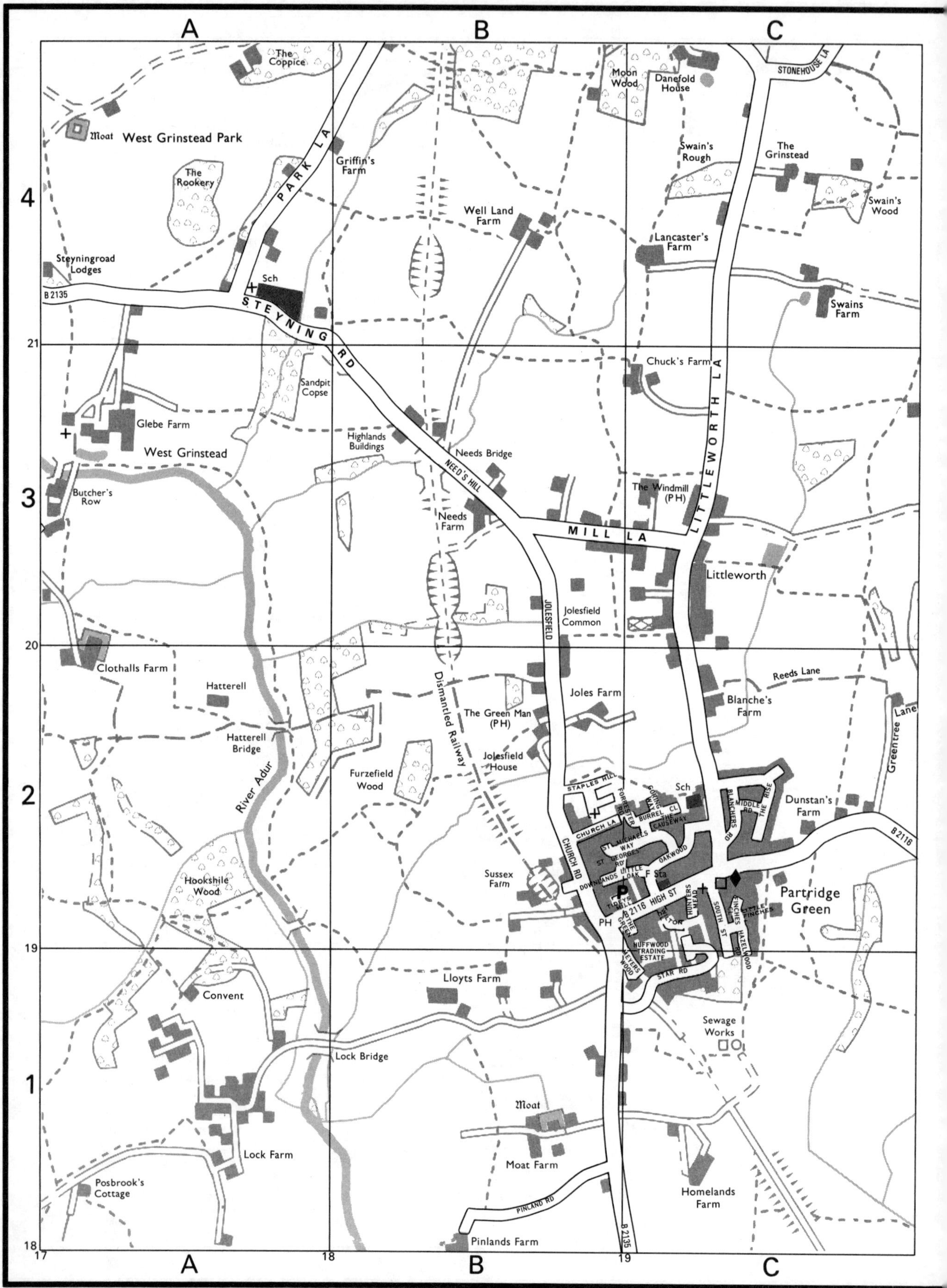

A
B
C
The Coppice
Moon Wood
Danefold House
STONEHOUSE LA
Moat
West Grinstead Park
The Rookery
PARK LA
Griffin's Farm
Swain's Rough
The Grinstead
Swain's Wood
4
Well Land Farm
Lancaster's Farm
Steyningroad Lodges
Sch
B 2135
STEYNING RD
Swains Farm
21
Chuck's Farm
Sandpit Copse
LITTLEWORTH LA
Glebe Farm
Highlands Buildings
West Grinstead
Needs Bridge
NEED'S HILL
Butcher's Row
The Windmill (PH)
3
Needs Farm
MILL LA
Littleworth
JOLESFIELD
Jolesfield Common
20
Clothalls Farm
Reeds Lane
Hatterell
Joles Farm
Blanche's Farm
Dismantled Railway
The Green Man (PH)
Greentree Lane
Hatterell Bridge
Jolesfield House
Furzefield Wood
2
River Adur
STAPLES HILL
Sch
Dunstan's Farm
CHURCH LA
BURREL CL
THE CAUSEWAY
BLANCHERS RD
MIDDLE RD
THE RISE
B 2116
CHURCH RD
OAKWOOD
Sussex Farm
Hookshile Wood
DOWNLANDS
LITTLE OAK
F Sta
P
Partridge Green
B 2116 HIGH ST
HUNTERS MEAD
SOUTH ST
FINCHES
LITTLE FINCHES
PH
HAZELWOOD
HUFFWOOD TRADING ESTATE
19
STAR RD
Lloyts Farm
Convent
Sewage Works
Lock Bridge
1
Moat
Lock Farm
Moat Farm
Posbrook's Cottage
PINLAND RD
Homelands Farm
B 2135
Pinlands Farm
18
17
18
19
A
B
C

99

120

79

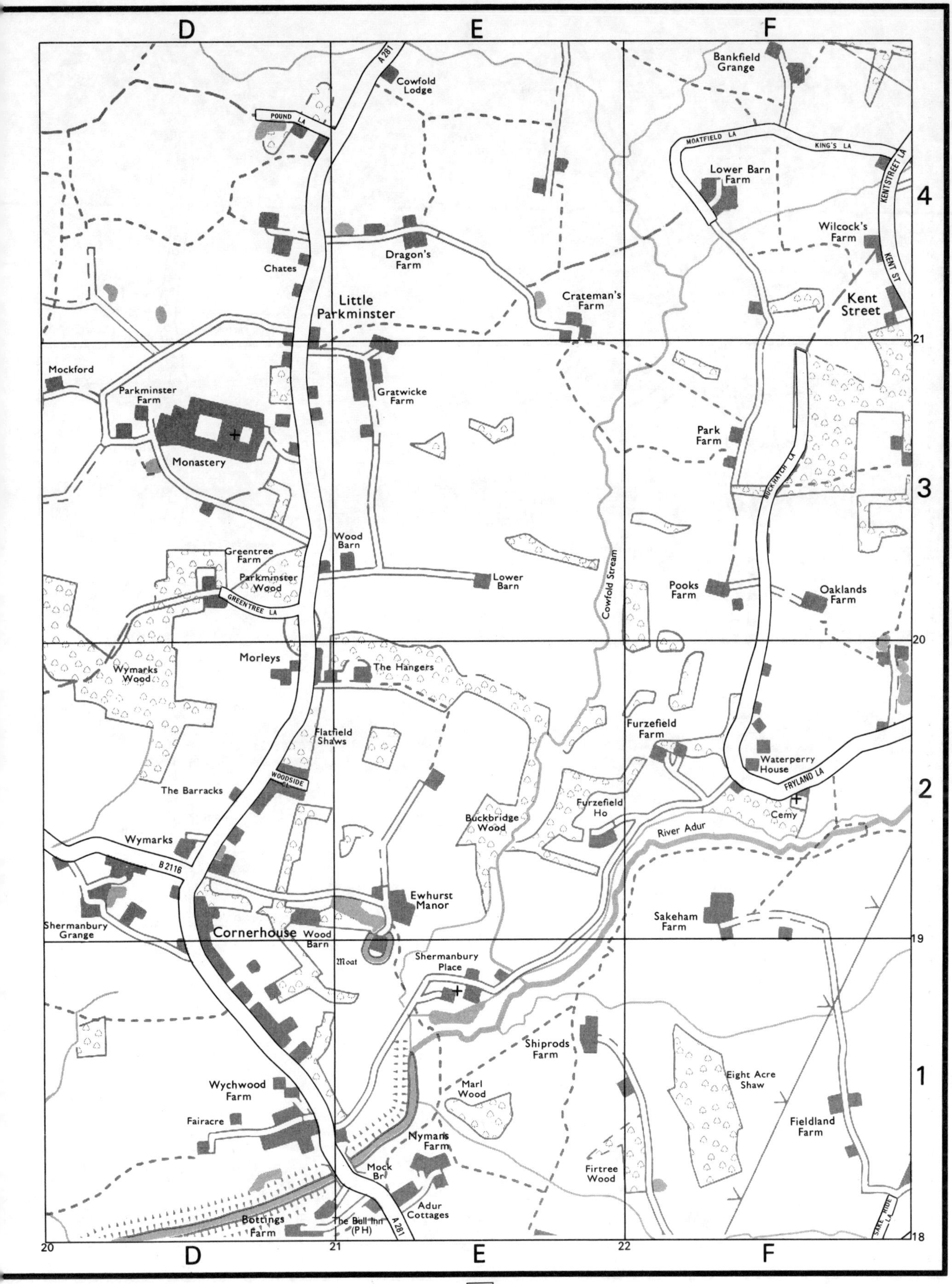
D
E
F
Bankfield Grange
Cowfold Lodge
A 281
POUND LA
MOATFIELD LA
KING'S LA
KENTSTREET LA
Lower Barn Farm
4
Wilcock's Farm
KENT ST
Dragon's Farm
Chates
Little Parkminster
Crateman's Farm
Kent Street
21
Mockford
Parkminster Farm
Gratwicke Farm
Monastery
Park Farm
BUCKHATCH LA
3
Wood Barn
Greentree Farm
Parkminster Wood
Lower Barn
Cowfold Stream
Pooks Farm
Oaklands Farm
GREENTREE LA
20
Morleys
The Hangers
Wymarks Wood
Flatfield Shaws
Furzefield Farm
Waterperry House
FRYLAND LA
WOODSIDE CL
The Barracks
Furzefield Ho
Buckbridge Wood
Cemy
2
River Adur
Wymarks
B 2116
Ewhurst Manor
Sakeham Farm
Shermanbury Grange
Cornerhouse
Wood Barn
Moat
19
Shermanbury Place
Shiprods Farm
1
Marl Wood
Eight Acre Shaw
Wychwood Farm
Fieldland Farm
Fairacre
Nymans Farm
Mock Br
Firtree Wood
Adur Cottages
Bottings Farm
The Bull Inn (PH)
SAKE RIDE LA
18
20
21
22

102

121

80
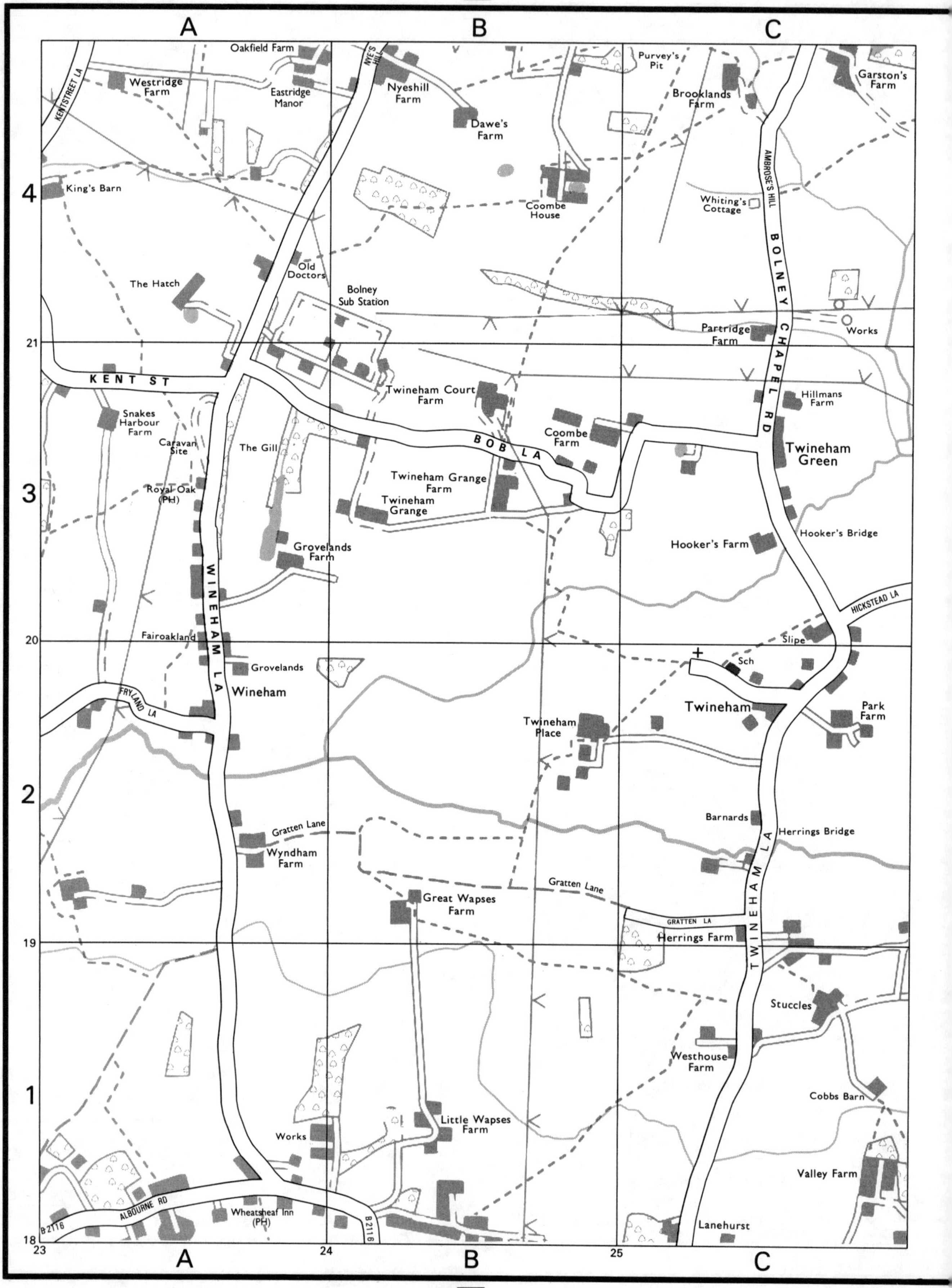
A
B
C
Oakfield Farm
Westridge Farm
Eastridge Manor
NYE'S HILL
Nyeshill Farm
Dawe's Farm
Purvey's Pit
Brooklands Farm
Garston's Farm
KENTSTREET LA
King's Barn
Coombe House
Whiting's Cottage
AMBROSE'S HILL
BOLNEY CHAPEL RD
4
The Hatch
Old Doctors
Bolney Sub Station
Partridge Farm
Works
21
KENT ST
Twineham Court Farm
Hillmans Farm
Snakes Harbour Farm
Caravan Site
The Gill
BOB LA
Coombe Farm
Twineham Green
Royal Oak (PH)
Twineham Grange Farm
Twineham Grange
3
Hooker's Farm
Hooker's Bridge
Grovelands Farm
WINEHAM LA
HICKSTEAD LA
Fairoakland
Slipe
20
Grovelands
Sch
Wineham
FRYLAND LA
Twineham
Park Farm
Twineham Place
2
Barnards
Herrings Bridge
Gratten Lane
Wyndham Farm
Gratten Lane
TWINEHAM LA
Great Wapses Farm
GRATTEN LA
Herrings Farm
19
Stuccles
Westhouse Farm
1
Cobbs Barn
Little Wapses Farm
Works
Valley Farm
ALBOURNE RD
B2116
Wheatsheaf Inn (PH)
B2116
Lanehurst
18
23
24
25
A
B
C
101
122

81

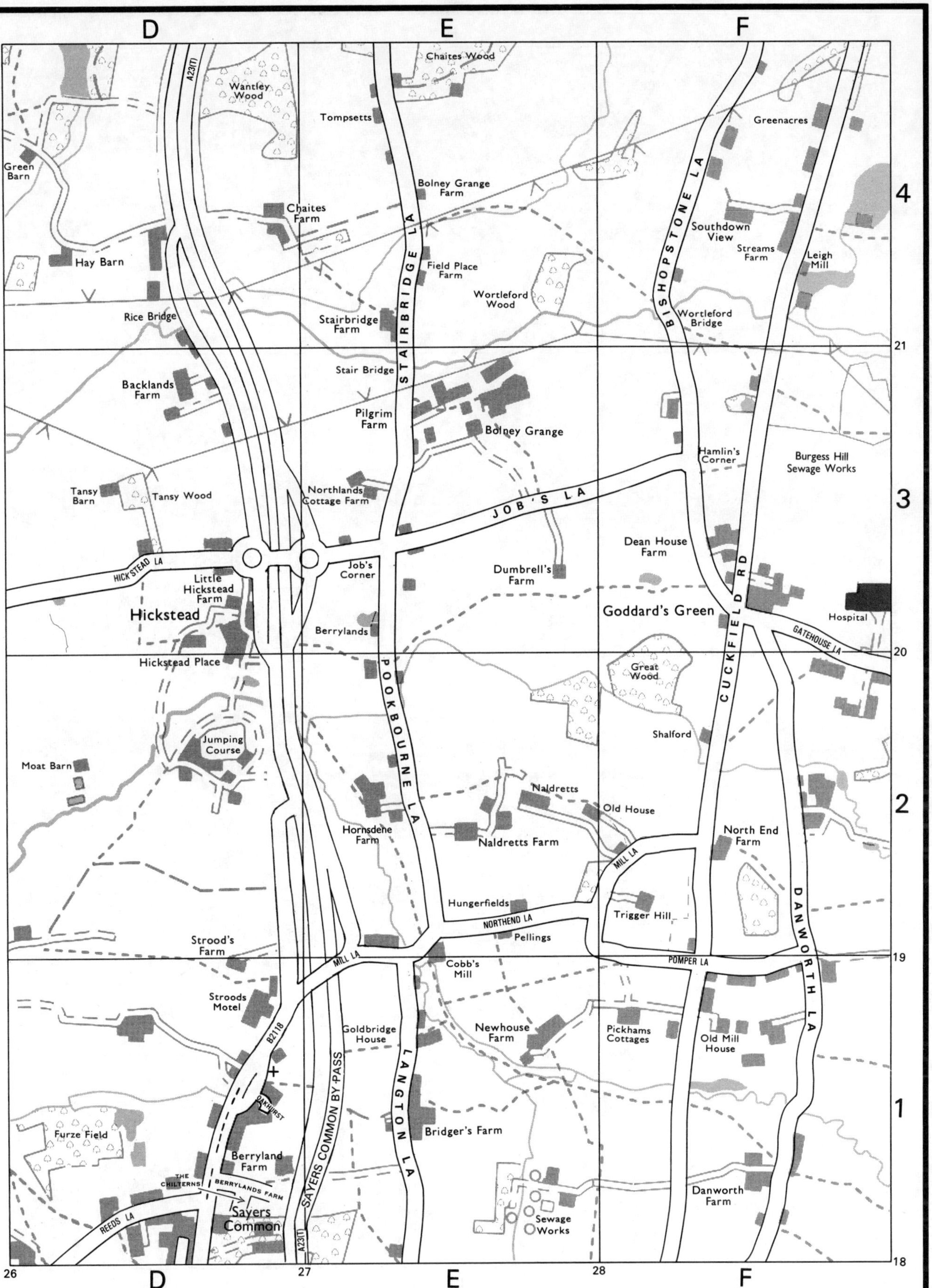
D
E
F
Chaites Wood
Wantley Wood
A23(T)
Tompsetts
Green Barn
Greenacres
Bolney Grange Farm
Chaites Farm
BISHOPSTONE LA
Southdown View
Streams Farm
Leigh Mill
Hay Barn
Field Place Farm
STAIRBRIDGE LA
Wortleford Wood
Wortleford Bridge
Rice Bridge
Stairbridge Farm
4
21
Stair Bridge
Backlands Farm
Pilgrim Farm
Bolney Grange
Hamlin's Corner
Burgess Hill Sewage Works
Tansy Barn
Tansy Wood
Northlands Cottage Farm
JOB'S LA
3
Dean House Farm
HICKSTEAD LA
Job's Corner
Dumbrell's Farm
Little Hickstead Farm
CUCKFIELD RD
Hickstead
Goddard's Green
Hospital
Berrylands
GATEHOUSE LA
20
Hickstead Place
POOKBOURNE LA
Great Wood
Jumping Course
Shalford
Moat Barn
Naldretts
2
Old House
Hornsdene Farm
North End Farm
Naldretts Farm
MILL LA
DANWORTH LA
Hungerfields
Trigger Hill
NORTHEND LA
Pellings
Strood's Farm
19
MILL LA
POMPER LA
Cobb's Mill
Stroods Motel
Goldbridge House
Newhouse Farm
Pickhams Cottages
Old Mill House
B2118
SAYERS COMMON BY-PASS
LANGTON LA
OAKHURST
1
Furze Field
Bridger's Farm
Berryland Farm
THE CHILTERNS
BERRYLANDS FARM
Danworth Farm
REEDS LA
Sayers Common
A23(T)
Sewage Works
18
26
27
28
D
E
F

104

123

82

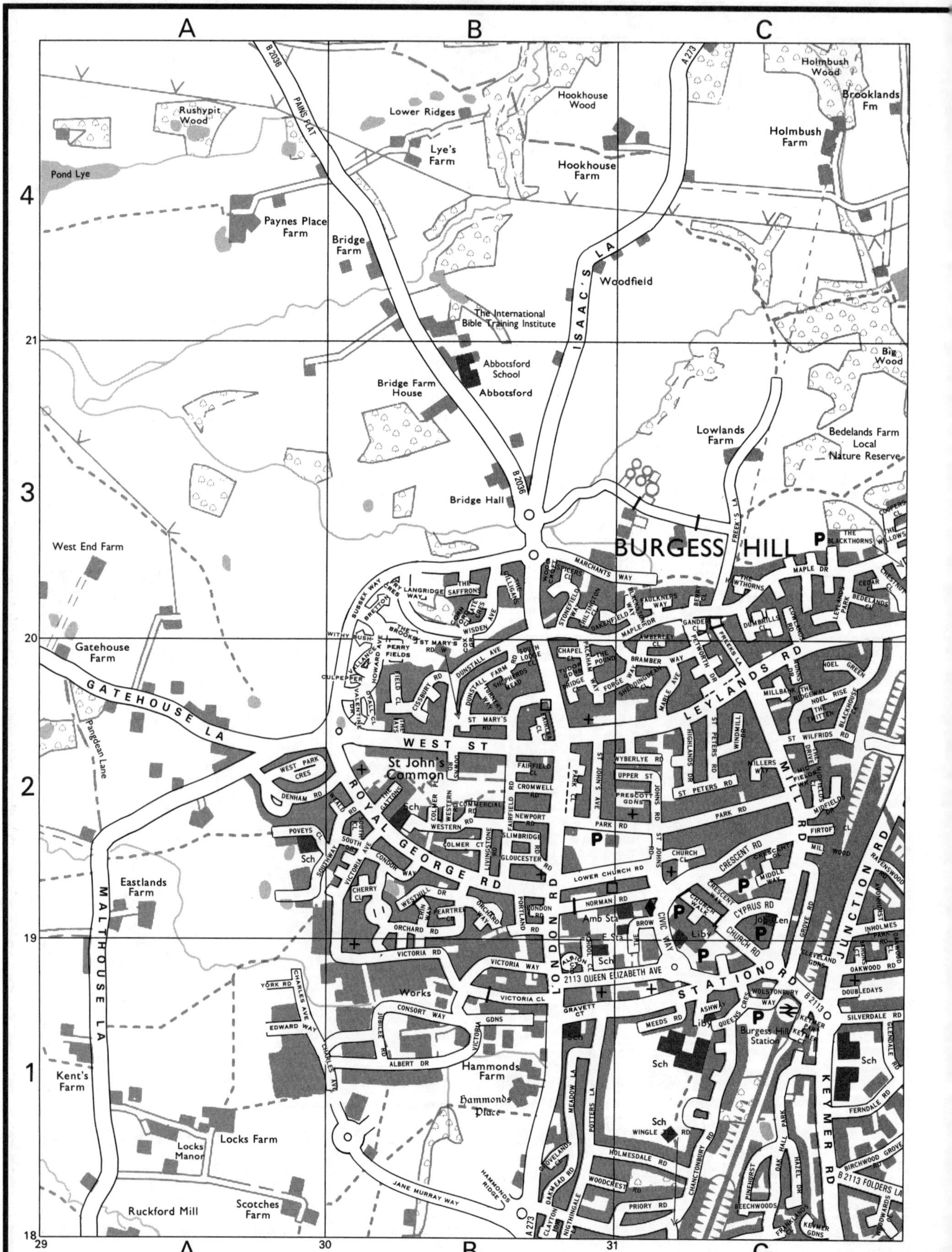
A
B
C
4
3
2
1
21
20
19
18
29
30
31
Rushypit Wood
Pond Lye
Lower Ridges
Lye's Farm
Hookhouse Wood
Hookhouse Farm
Holmbush Wood
Brooklands Fm
Holmbush Farm
Paynes Place Farm
Bridge Farm
Woodfield
The International Bible Training Institute
ISAAC'S LA
PAINS FLAT
B 2036
A 273
Abbotsford School
Abbotsford
Bridge Farm House
Lowlands Farm
Big Wood
Bedelands Farm Local Nature Reserve
Bridge Hall
West End Farm
BURGESS HILL
Gatehouse Farm
GATEHOUSE LA
Pangdean Lane
WEST ST
St John's Common
ROYAL GEORGE RD
LEYLANDS RD
MILL RD
JUNCTION RD
LONDON RD
STATION RD
CIVIC WAY
2113 QUEEN ELIZABETH AVE
Eastlands Farm
MALTHOUSE LA
Works
Hammonds Farm
Hammonds Place
Burgess Hill Station
Kent's Farm
Locks Manor
Locks Farm
Ruckford Mill
Scotches Farm
JANE MURRAY WAY
KEYMER RD
B 2113 FOLDERS LA
Sch
Liby
Amb Sta
F Sta
Job Cen
P

103

124

83

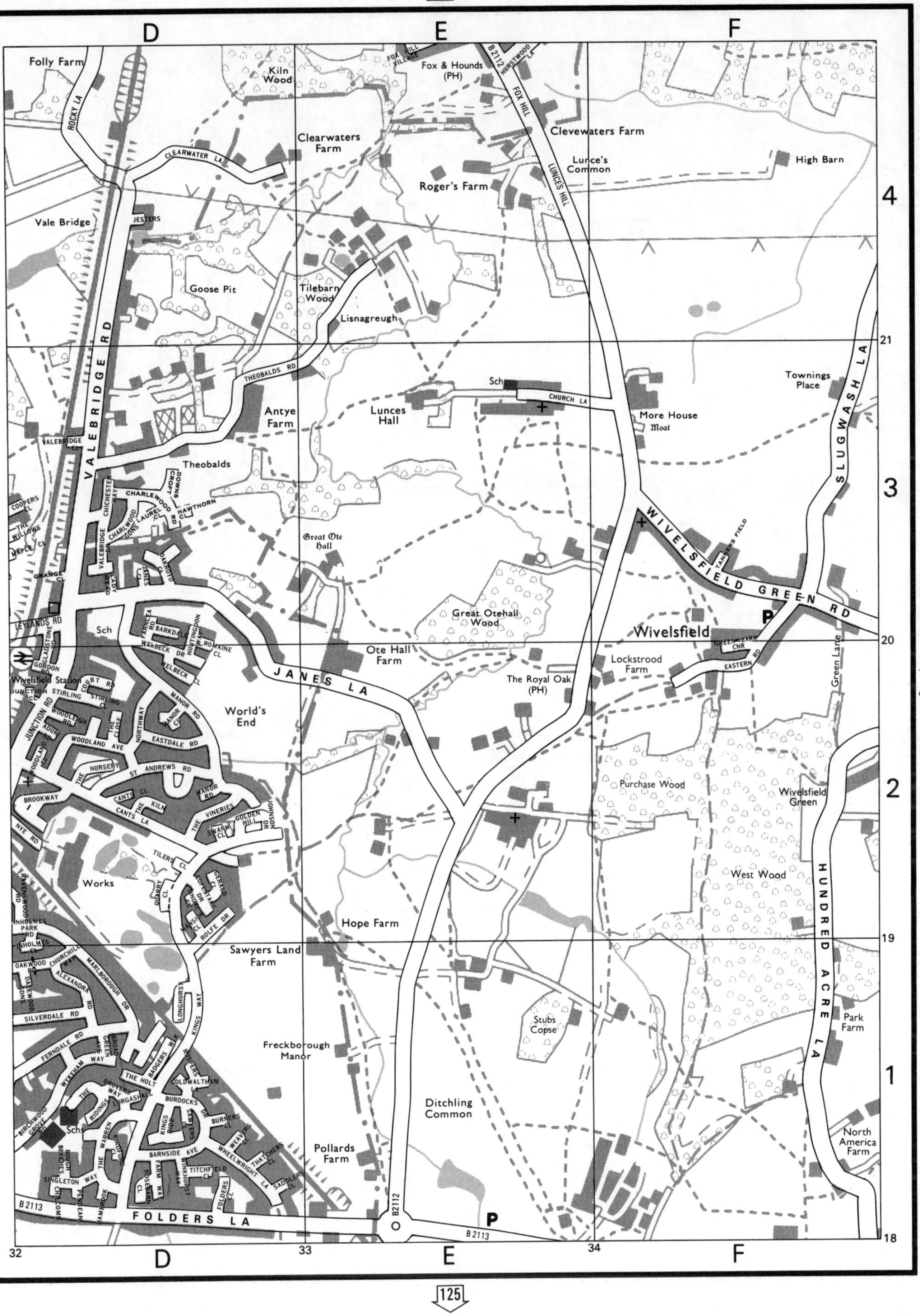

not continued, see key diagram

125

86

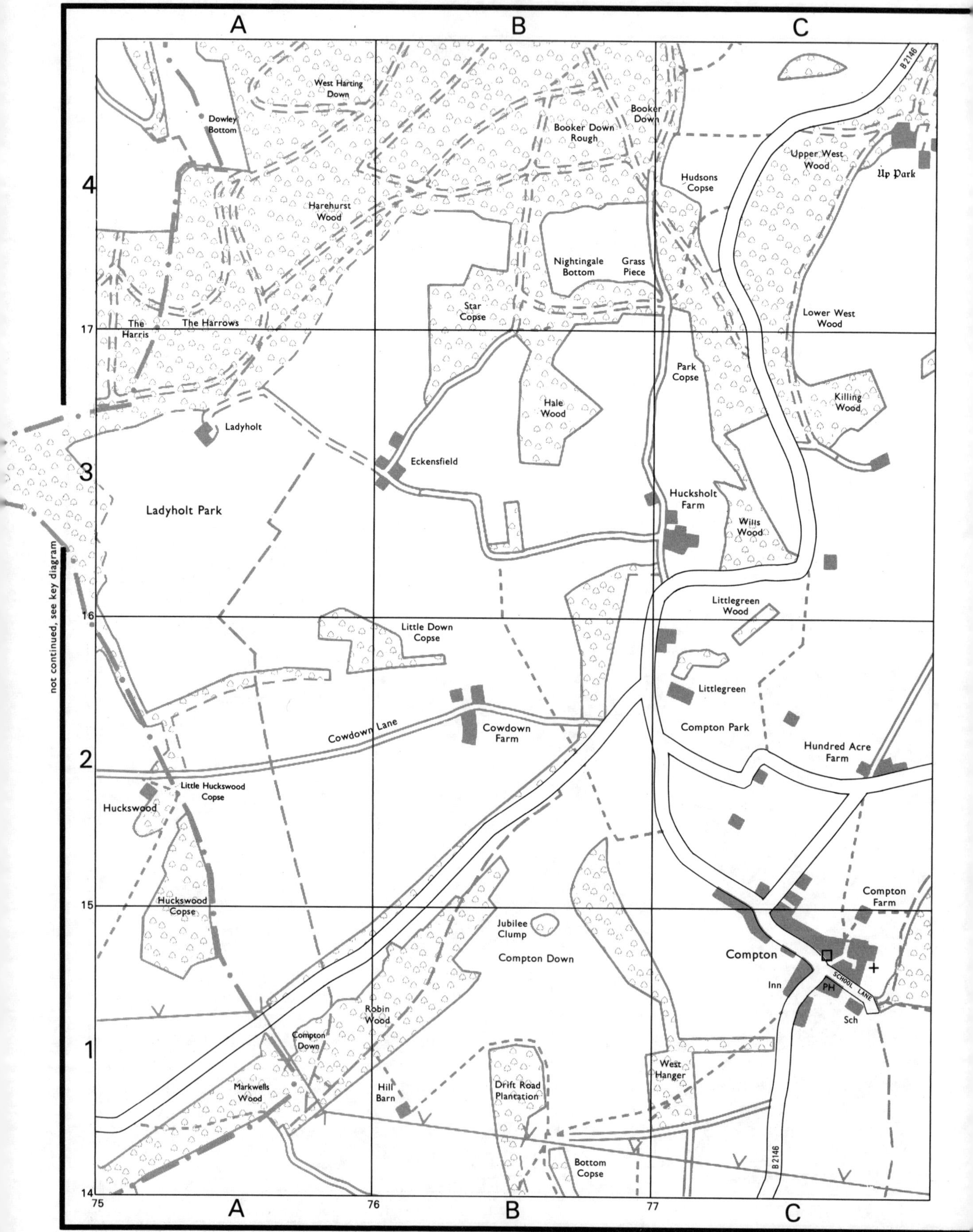
A
B
C
4
3
2
1
17
16
15
14
75
76
77
West Harting Down
Dowley Bottom
Booker Down Rough
Booker Down
B 2146
Upper West Wood
Up Park
Hudsons Copse
Harehurst Wood
Nightingale Bottom
Grass Piece
Star Copse
Lower West Wood
The Harris
The Harrows
Park Copse
Hale Wood
Killing Wood
Ladyholt
Eckensfield
Hucksholt Farm
Ladyholt Park
Wills Wood
Littlegreen Wood
Little Down Copse
Littlegreen
Cowdown Lane
Cowdown Farm
Compton Park
Hundred Acre Farm
Little Huckswood Copse
Huckswood
Huckswood Copse
Compton Farm
Jubilee Clump
Compton Down
Compton
Inn
PH
School Lane
Sch
Robin Wood
Compton Down
Markwells Wood
Hill Barn
Drift Road Plantation
West Hanger
Bottom Copse
B 2146
not continued, see key diagram

127

87

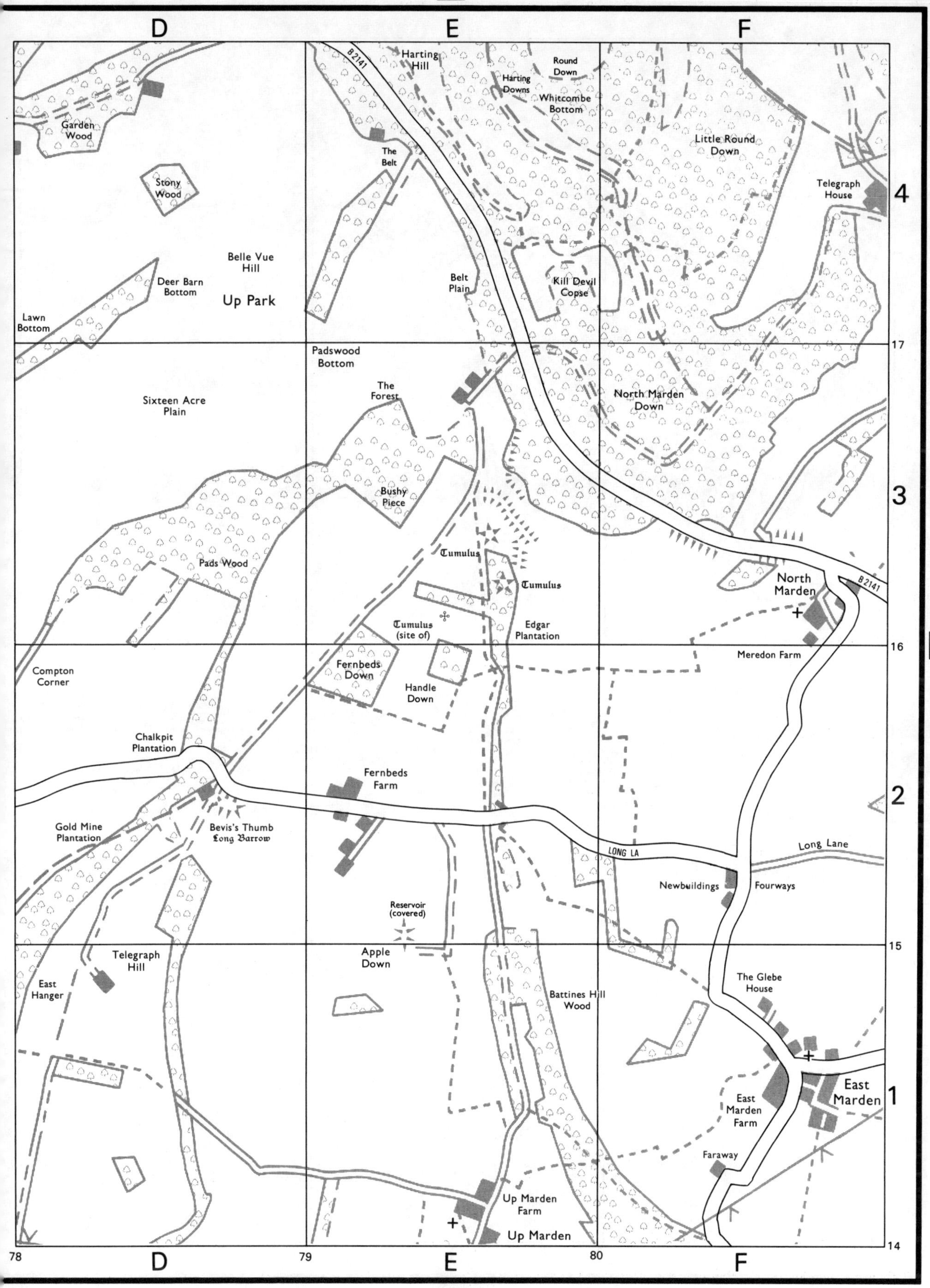

D
E
F
B2141
Harting Hill
Round Down
Harting Downs
Whitcombe Bottom
Garden Wood
The Belt
Little Round Down
Stony Wood
Telegraph House
4
Belle Vue Hill
Deer Barn Bottom
Belt Plain
Kill Devil Copse
Up Park
Lawn Bottom
17
Padswood Bottom
The Forest
Sixteen Acre Plain
North Marden Down
Bushy Piece
3
Cumulus
Pads Wood
Cumulus
North Marden
B2141
Cumulus (site of)
Edgar Plantation
16
Meredon Farm
Compton Corner
Fernbeds Down
Handle Down
Chalkpit Plantation
Fernbeds Farm
2
Gold Mine Plantation
Bevis's Thumb
Long Barrow
LONG LA
Long Lane
Newbuildings
Fourways
Reservoir (covered)
15
Telegraph Hill
Apple Down
The Glebe House
East Hanger
Battines Hill Wood
East Marden
1
East Marden Farm
Faraway
Up Marden Farm
Up Marden
14
78
79
80
D
E
F

108

128

88

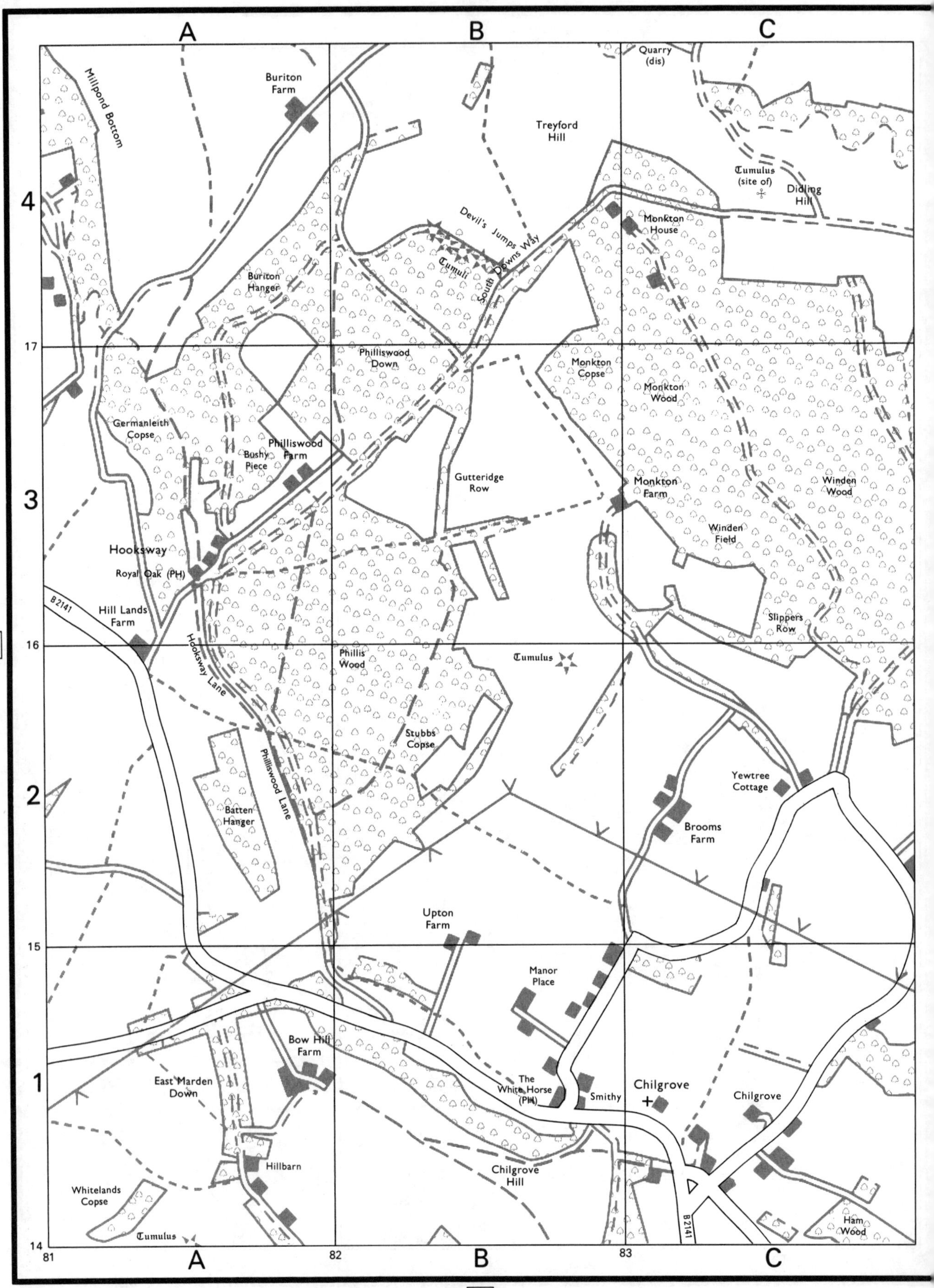

A
B
C
Millpond Bottom
Buriton Farm
Treyford Hill
Quarry (dis)
Cumulus (site of)
Didling Hill
Devil's Jumps
Tumuli
South Downs Way
Monkton House
Buriton Hanger
4
17
Philliswood Down
Monkton Copse
Monkton Wood
Germanleith Copse
Philliswood Farm
Bushy Piece
Gutteridge Row
Monkton Farm
Winden Wood
3
Hooksway
Winden Field
Royal Oak (PH)
B2141
Hill Lands Farm
Slippers Row
16
Phillis Wood
Tumulus
Hooksway Lane
Stubbs Copse
Philliswood Lane
Yewtree Cottage
2
Batten Hanger
Brooms Farm
Upton Farm
15
Manor Place
Bow Hill Farm
1
East Marden Down
The White Horse (PH)
Smithy
Chilgrove
Chilgrove
Hillbarn
Chilgrove Hill
Whitelands Copse
B2141
Ham Wood
Tumulus
14
81
82
83
A
B
C

107

129

89

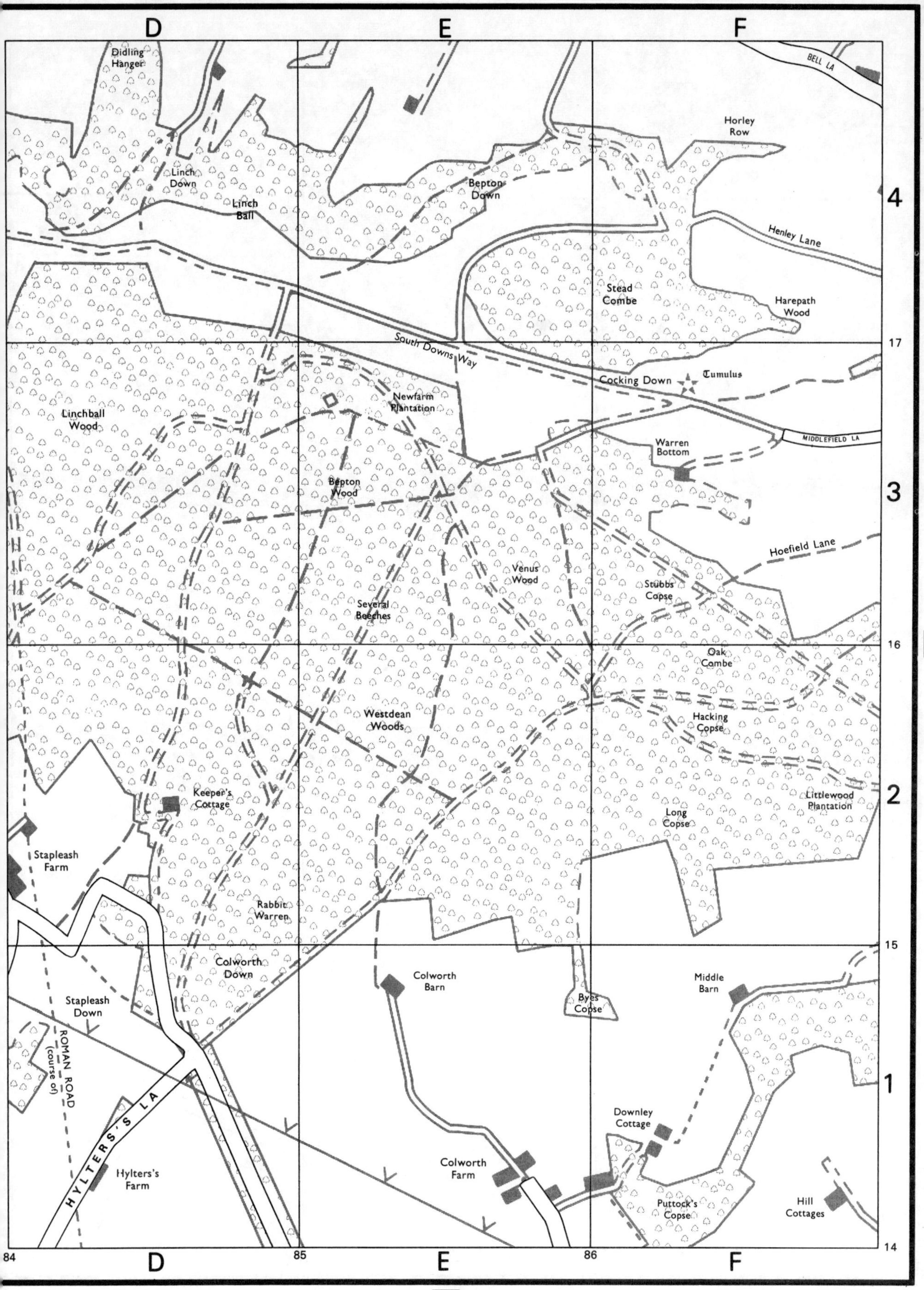

D
E
F
Didling Hanger
Linch Down
Linch Ball
Bepton Down
Horley Row
BELL LA
4
Henley Lane
Stead Combe
Harepath Wood
17
South Downs Way
Cocking Down
Tumulus
Linchball Wood
Newfarm Plantation
Warren Bottom
MIDDLEFIELD LA
Bepton Wood
3
Hoefield Lane
Venus Wood
Stubbs Copse
Several Beeches
16
Oak Combe
Westdean Woods
Hacking Copse
2
Keeper's Cottage
Littlewood Plantation
Long Copse
Stapleash Farm
Rabbit Warren
15
Colworth Down
Colworth Barn
Middle Barn
Stapleash Down
Byes Copse
ROMAN ROAD (course of)
1
Downley Cottage
HYLTERS'S LA
Hylters's Farm
Colworth Farm
Puttock's Copse
Hill Cottages
14
84
85
86
D
E
F

110

130

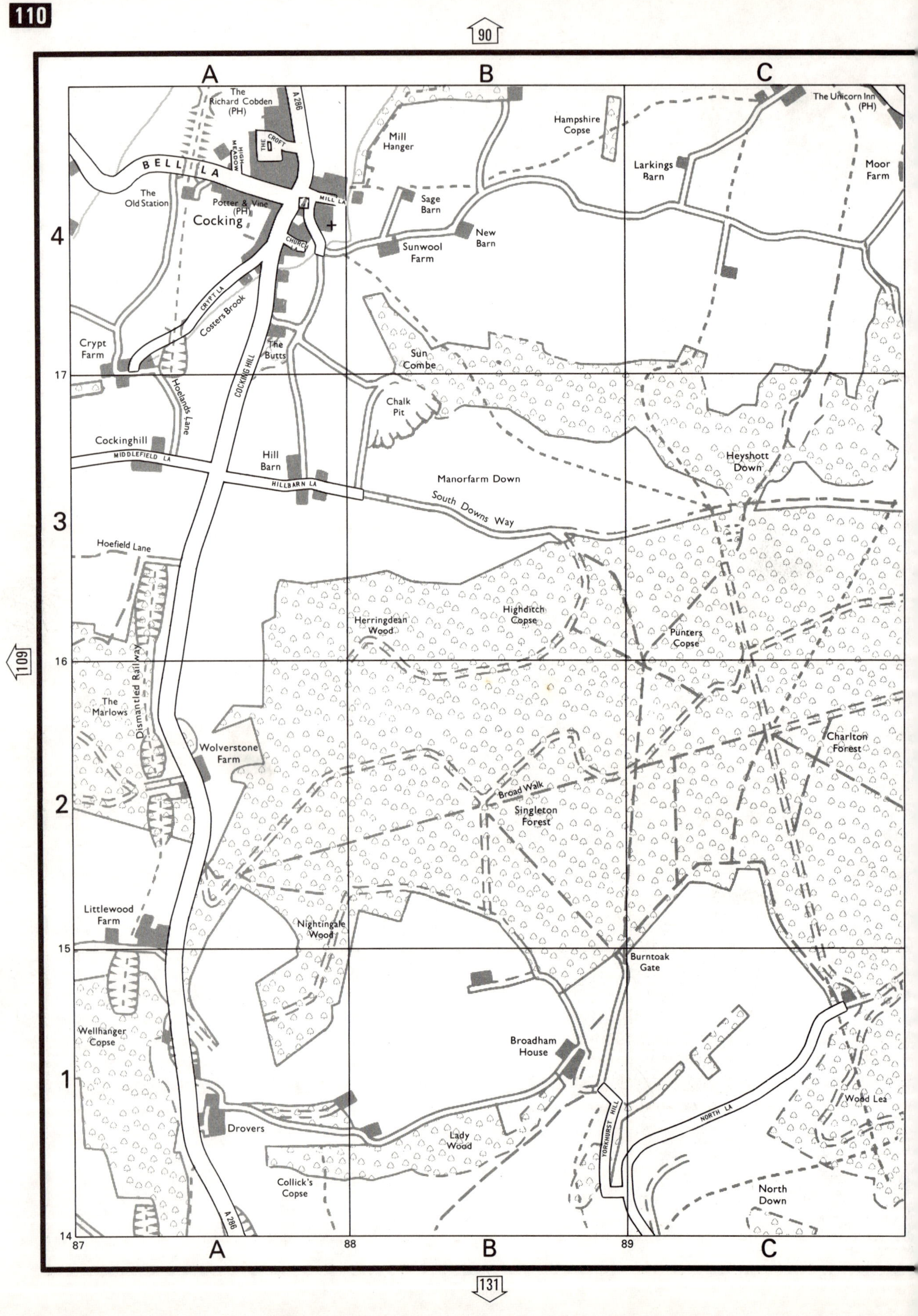
90
A
B
C
The Richard Cobden (PH)
A 286
THE CROFT
HIGH MEADOW
BELL LA
Mill Hanger
Hampshire Copse
The Unicorn Inn (PH)
Larkings Barn
Moor Farm
The Old Station
Potter & Vine (PH)
MILL LA
Cocking
CHURCH
Sage Barn
New Barn
Sunwool Farm
4
CRYPT LA
Costers Brook
Crypt Farm
The Butts
Sun Combe
17
COCKING HILL
Hoelands Lane
Chalk Pit
Cockinghill
MIDDLEFIELD LA
Hill Barn
HILLBARN LA
Manorfarm Down
Heyshott Down
South Downs Way
3
Hoefield Lane
Herringdean Wood
Highditch Copse
Punters Copse
16
Dismantled Railway
The Marlows
Wolverstone Farm
Charlton Forest
Broad Walk
Singleton Forest
2
Littlewood Farm
Nightingale Wood
15
Burntoak Gate
Wellhanger Copse
Broadham House
1
Drovers
Lady Wood
YORKHURST HILL
NORTH LA
Wood Lea
Collick's Copse
North Down
A 286
14
87
88
89
109
131

91

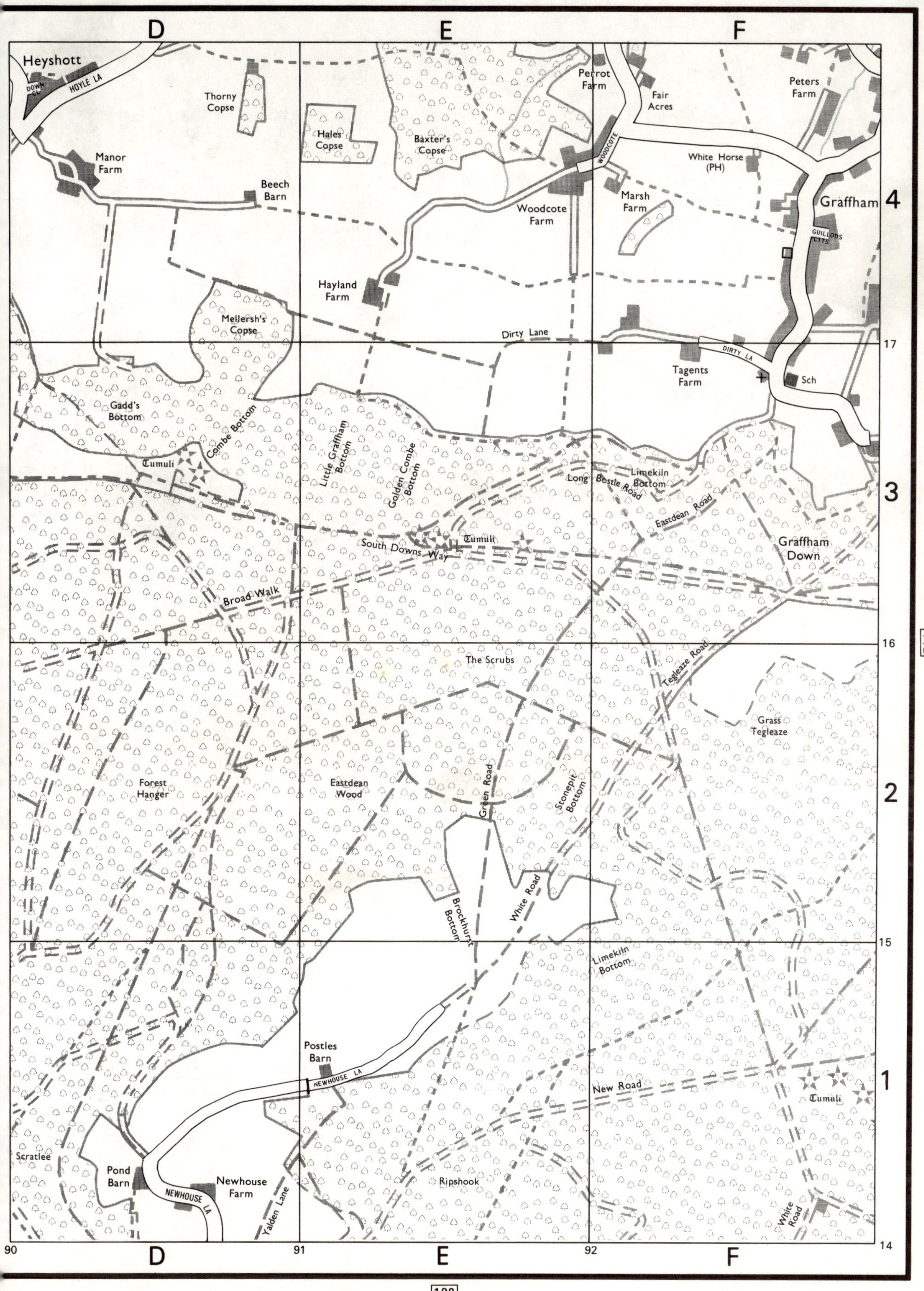
D
E
F
Heyshott
DOWN CL
HOYLE LA
Thorny Copse
Hales Copse
Baxter's Copse
Perrot Farm
Fair Acres
Peters Farm
Manor Farm
Beech Barn
WOODCOTE
White Horse (PH)
Marsh Farm
Woodcote Farm
Graffham
GUILLODS CTTS
4
Hayland Farm
Mellersh's Copse
Dirty Lane
DIRTY LA
Tagents Farm
Sch
17
Gadd's Bottom
Combe Bottom
Little Graffham Bottom
Golden Combe Bottom
Tumuli
Long Bostle Road
Limekiln Bottom
Eastdean Road
3
Graffham Down
South Downs Way
Broad Walk
16
The Scrubs
Tegleaze Road
Grass Tegleaze
Forest Hanger
Eastdean Wood
Green Road
Stonepit Bottom
2
White Road
Brockhurst Bottom
15
Limekiln Bottom
Postles Barn
NEWHOUSE LA
New Road
1
Scratlee
Pond Barn
Newhouse Farm
Yalden Lane
Ripshook
White Road
14
90
91
92
D
E
F

112

132

92

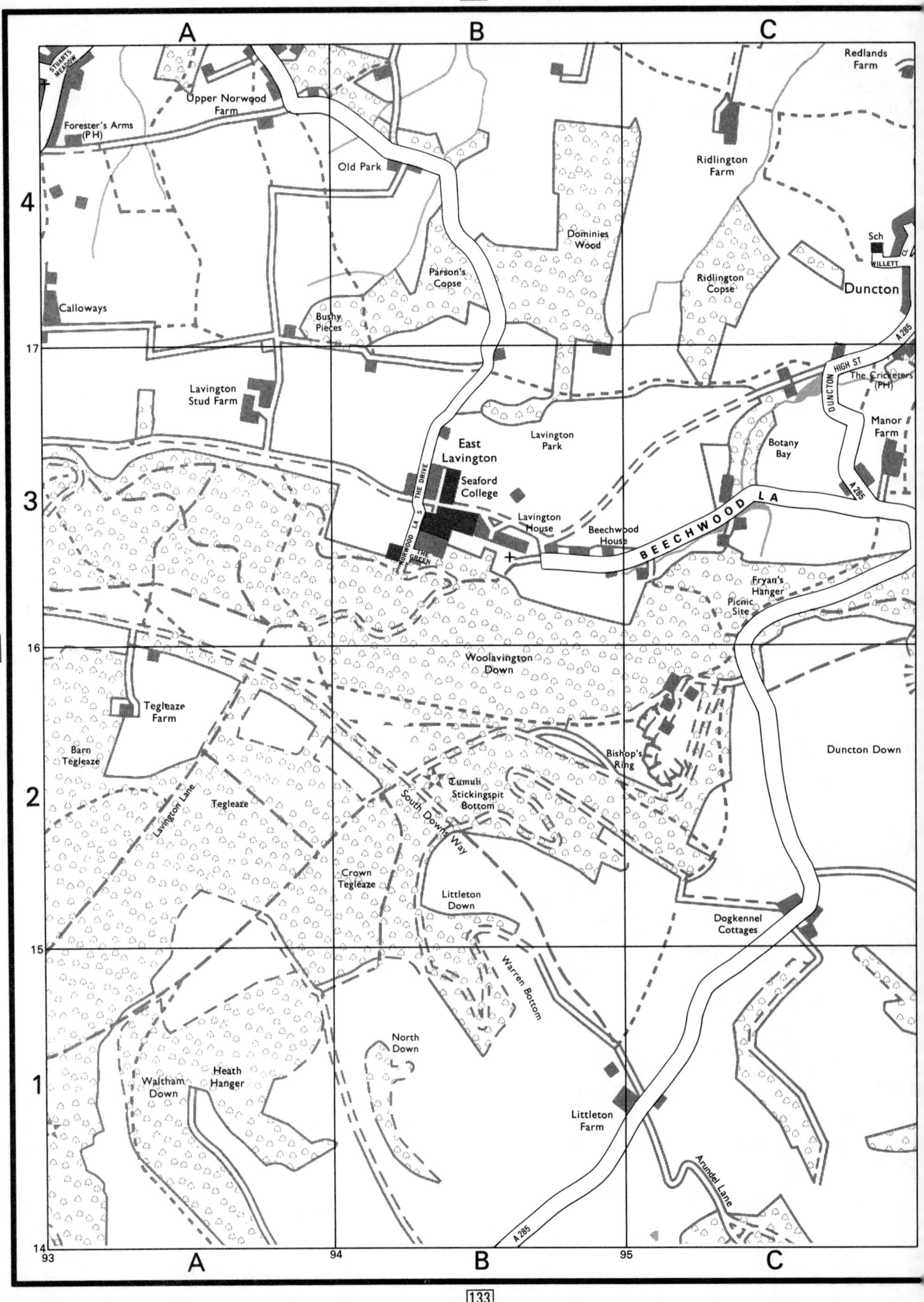
A
B
C
Redlands Farm
Upper Norwood Farm
Forester's Arms (PH)
Old Park
Ridlington Farm
Dominies Wood
Sch
WILLETT CL
Ridlington Copse
Duncton
Parson's Copse
Calloways
Bushy Pieces
A 285
DUNCTON HIGH ST
The Cricketers (PH)
Lavington Stud Farm
Lavington Park
Manor Farm
Botany Bay
East Lavington
Seaford College
THE DRIVE
NORWOOD LA
THE GREEN
Lavington House
Beechwood House
BEECHWOOD LA
Fryan's Hanger
Picnic Site
Woolavington Down
Tegleaze Farm
Barn Tegleaze
Bishop's Ring
Duncton Down
Tumuli
Stickingspit Bottom
Tegleaze
Lavington Lane
South Downs Way
Crown Tegleaze
Littleton Down
Dogkennel Cottages
Warren Bottom
North Down
Heath Hanger
Waltham Down
Littleton Farm
Arundel Lane
4
3
2
1
17
16
15
14
93
94
95

111

133

93

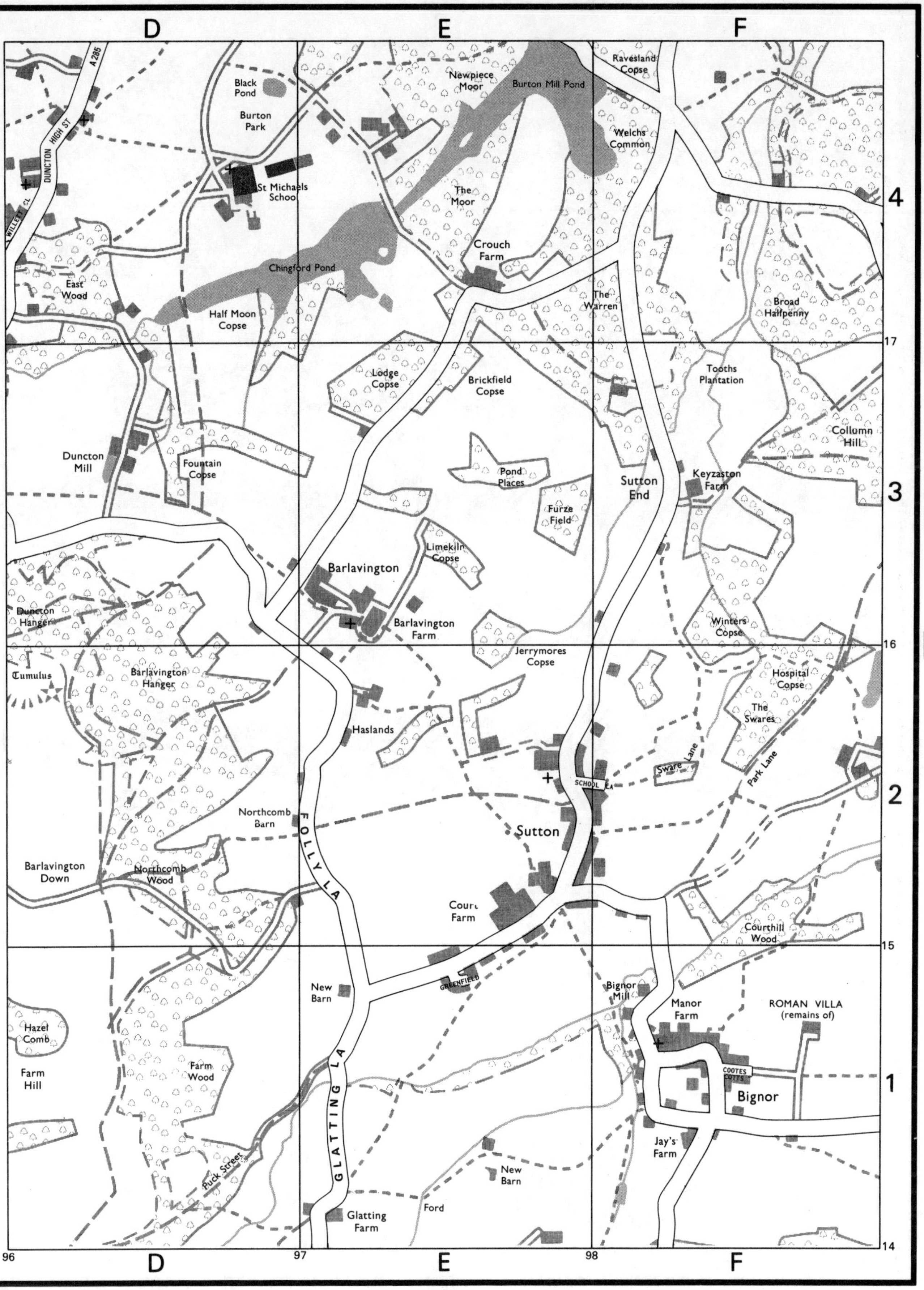

D
E
F
Ravesland Copse
Black Pond
Newpiece Moor
Burton Mill Pond
A285
Burton Park
DUNCTON HIGH ST
Welchs Common
St Michaels School
The Moor
WILLETT CL
4
Crouch Farm
Chingford Pond
East Wood
The Warren
Broad Halfpenny
Half Moon Copse
17
Lodge Copse
Tooths Plantation
Brickfield Copse
Collumn Hill
Duncton Mill
Fountain Copse
Pond Places
Sutton End
Keyzaston Farm
3
Furze Field
Limekiln Copse
Barlavington
Duncton Hanger
Barlavington Farm
Winters Copse
Jerrymores Copse
16
Tumulus
Barlavington Hanger
Hospital Copse
The Swares
Haslands
Sware Lane
Park Lane
SCHOOL LA
2
Northcomb Barn
FOLLY LA
Sutton
Barlavington Down
Northcomb Wood
Court Farm
Courthill Wood
15
New Barn
GREENFIELD
Bignor Mill
Manor Farm
ROMAN VILLA (remains of)
Hazel Comb
Farm Hill
Farm Wood
GLATTING LA
COOTES COTTS
1
Bignor
Jay's Farm
Puck Street
New Barn
Ford
Glatting Farm
96
97
98
14

114

134

94

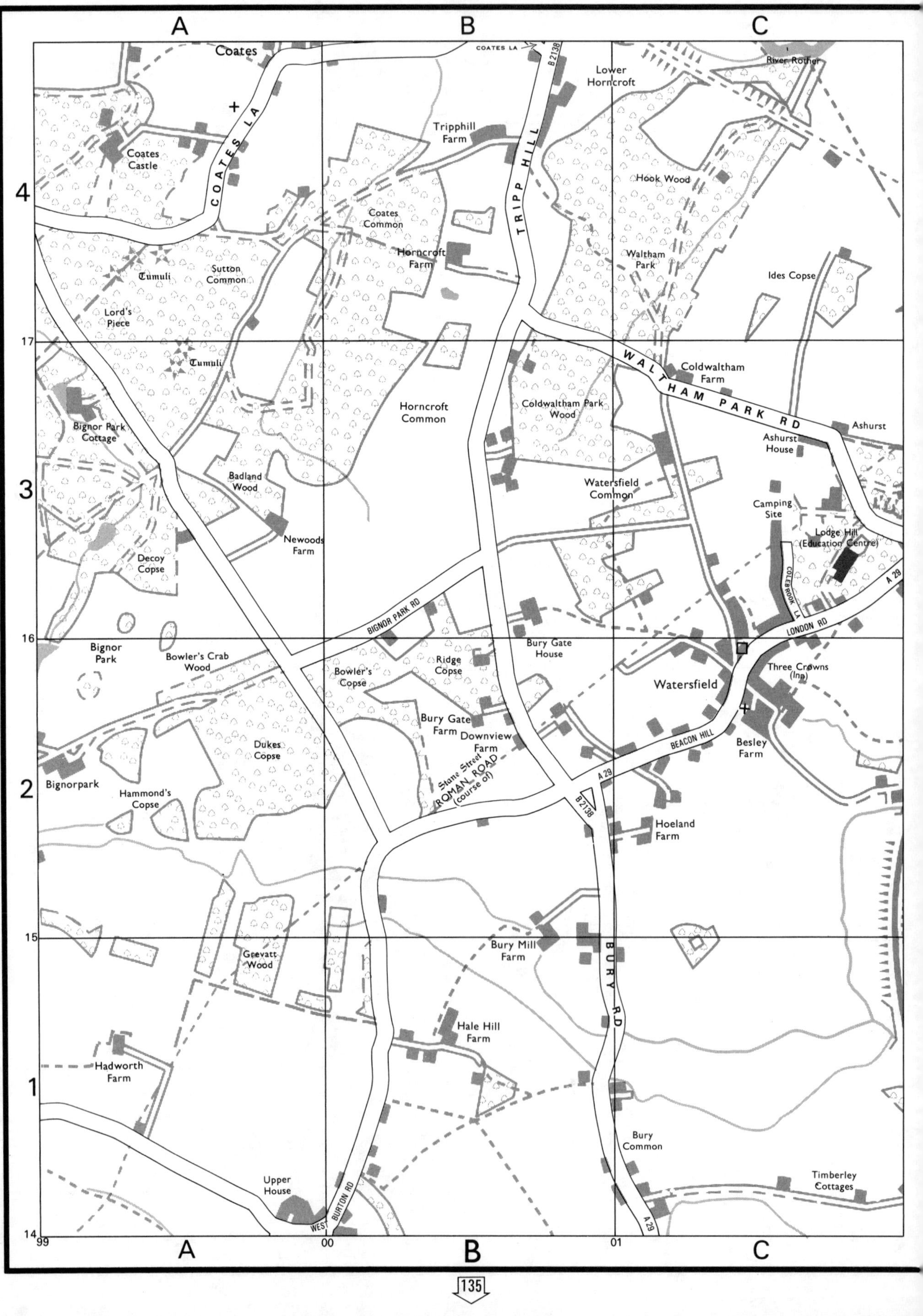

A
B
C
4
3
2
1
17
16
15
14
99
00
01
Coates
COATES LA
B 2138
Lower Horncroft
River Rother
COATES LA
Coates Castle
Tripphill Farm
TRIPP HILL
Hook Wood
Coates Common
Horncroft Farm
Waltham Park
Ides Copse
Tumuli
Sutton Common
Lord's Piece
Tumuli
WALTHAM PARK RD
Coldwaltham Farm
Horncroft Common
Coldwaltham Park Wood
Ashurst
Ashurst House
Bignor Park Cottage
Badland Wood
Watersfield Common
Camping Site
Newoods Farm
Lodge Hill (Education Centre)
Decoy Copse
COLEBROOK LA
A 29
BIGNOR PARK RD
LONDON RD
Bignor Park
Bowler's Crab Wood
Bury Gate House
Bowler's Copse
Ridge Copse
Three Crowns (Inn)
Watersfield
Bury Gate Farm
Downview Farm
Dukes Copse
BEACON HILL
Besley Farm
Stane Street
ROMAN ROAD (course of)
A 29
Bignorpark
Hammond's Copse
B 2138
Hoeland Farm
Bury Mill Farm
Grevatt Wood
BURY RD
Hale Hill Farm
Hadworth Farm
Bury Common
Upper House
Timberley Cottages
WEST BURTON RD
A 29

113

135

95

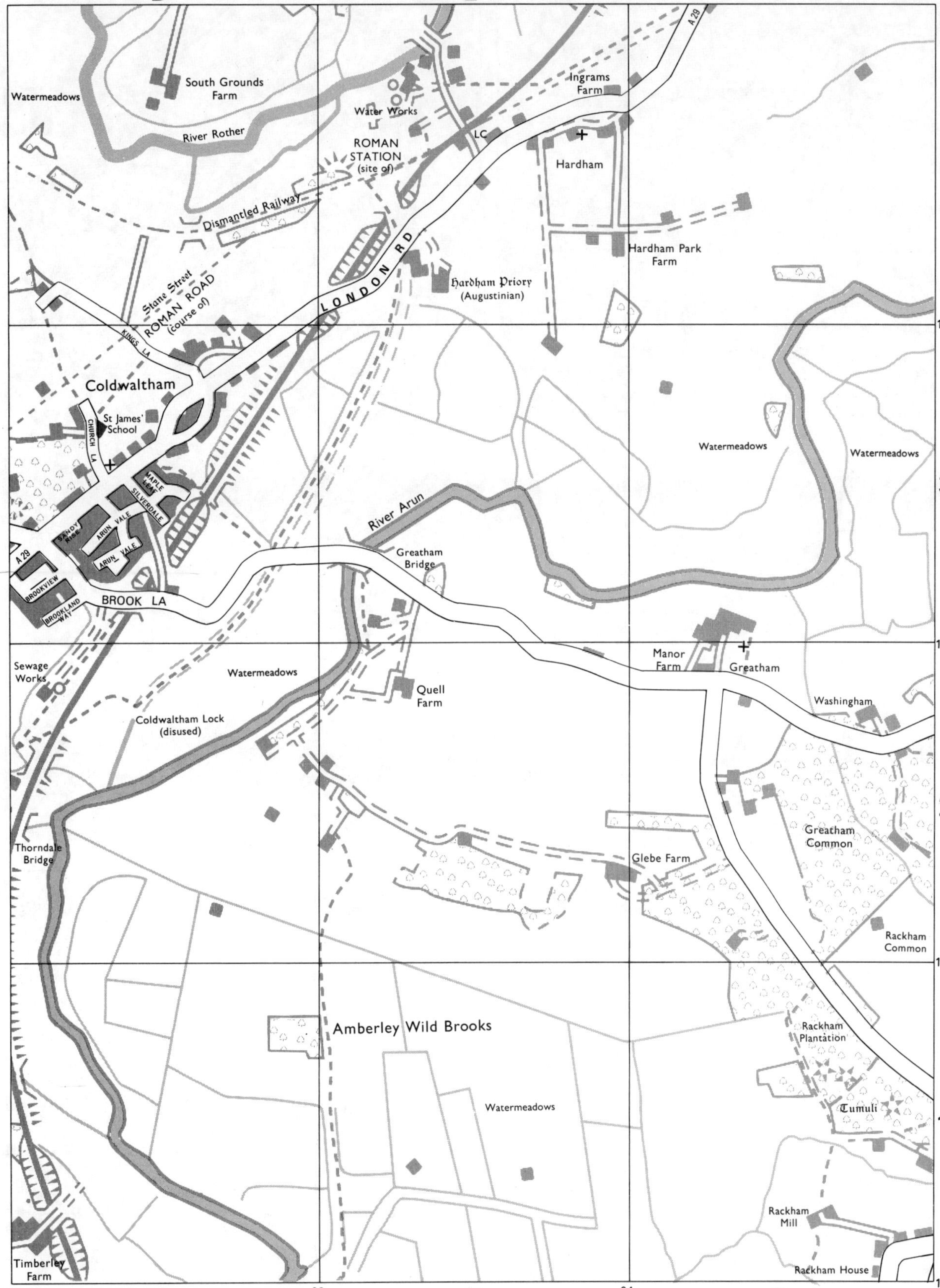
D
E
F
Watermeadows
South Grounds Farm
River Rother
Water Works
ROMAN STATION (site of)
Ingrams Farm
LC
Hardham
Dismantled Railway
Hardham Park Farm
Stane Street
ROMAN ROAD (course of)
LONDON RD
Hardham Priory (Augustinian)
A 29
KINGS LA
Coldwaltham
St James' School
CHURCH LA
MAPLE WAY
SILVERDALE
ARUN VALE
SANDY RISE
A 29
BROOKVIEW
BROOKLAND WAY
BROOK LA
River Arun
Greatham Bridge
Watermeadows
Watermeadows
Sewage Works
Watermeadows
Coldwaltham Lock (disused)
Quell Farm
Manor Farm
Greatham
Washingham
Greatham Common
Thorndale Bridge
Glebe Farm
Rackham Common
Amberley Wild Brooks
Rackham Plantation
Watermeadows
Tumuli
Rackham Mill
Rackham House
Timberley Farm
4
3
2
1
17
16
15
14
02
03
04

116

136

96

115

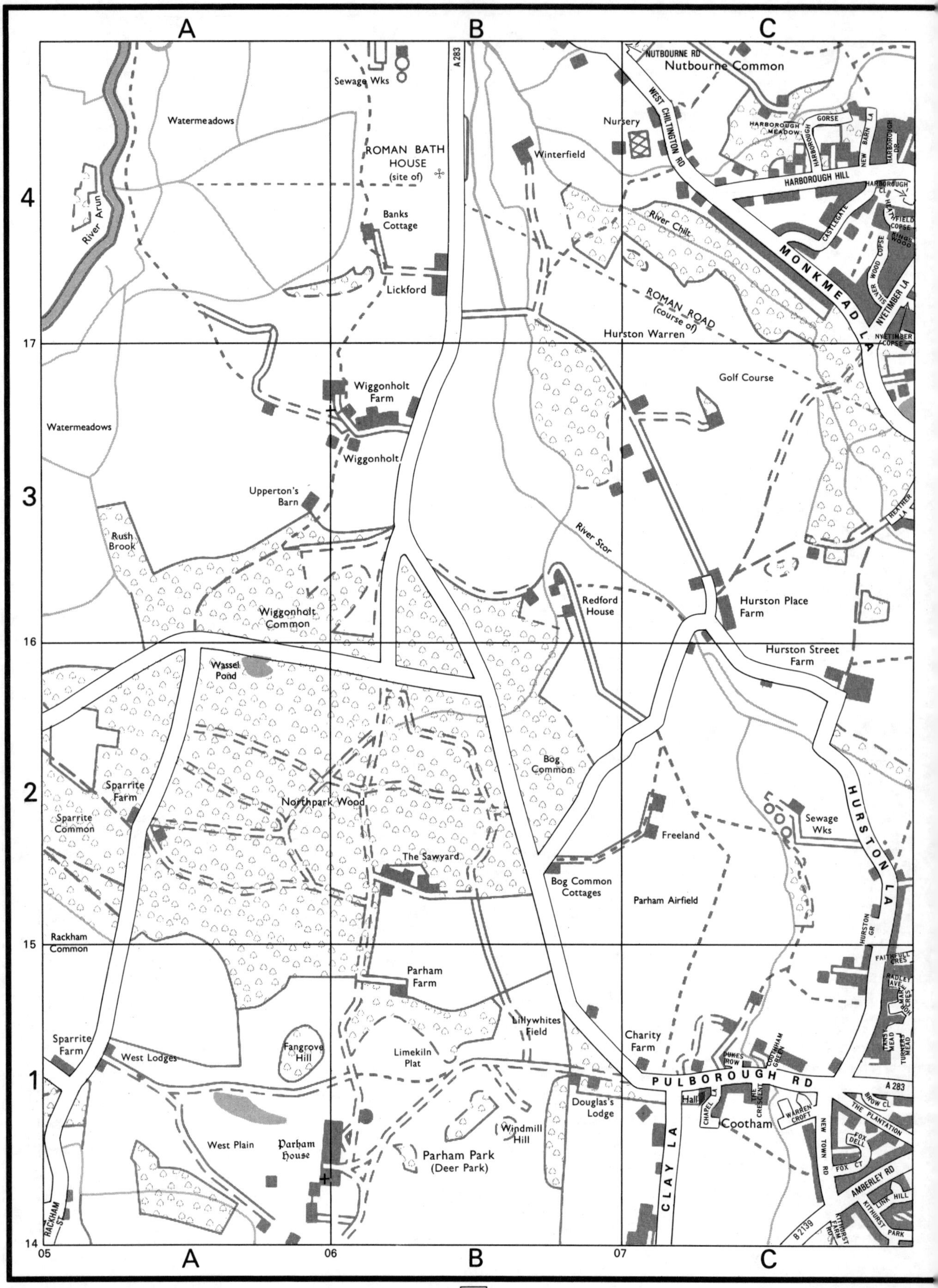

A
B
C
4
3
2
1
17
16
15
14
05
06
07
Sewage Wks
A 283
NUTBOURNE RD
Nutbourne Common
Watermeadows
WEST CHILTINGTON RD
Nursery
HARBOROUGH MEADOW
GORSE
HARBOROUGH
NEW BARN LA
HARBOROUGH DR
ROMAN BATH HOUSE (site of)
Winterfield
HARBOROUGH HILL
HARBOROUGH CL
River Arun
Banks Cottage
River Chilt
CASTLEGATE
HEATHFIELD COPSE
KINGS WOOD
SILVER WOOD COPSE
MONKMEAD LA
NYETIMBER LA
ROMAN ROAD (course of)
Lickford
Hurston Warren
NYETIMBER COPSE
Golf Course
Wiggonholt Farm
Watermeadows
Wiggonholt
Upperton's Barn
HEATHER
Rush Brook
River Stor
Hurston Place Farm
Redford House
Wiggonholt Common
Hurston Street Farm
Wassel Pond
Bog Common
Sparrite Farm
Northpark Wood
HURSTON LA
Sewage Wks
Sparrite Common
Freeland
The Sawyard
Bog Common Cottages
Parham Airfield
Rackham Common
HURSTON GR
FAITHFULL CRES
BADLEY AVE
Parham Farm
Lillywhites Field
Charity Farm
TANSY MEAD
TURNERS MEAD
Sparrite Farm
Fangrove Hill
Limekiln Plat
DUKES ROW
COOTHAM GREEN
West Lodges
PULBOROUGH RD
A 283
THE CRESCENT
Hall
CHAPEL LA
WARREN CROFT
BROW CL
THE PLANTATION
Douglas's Lodge
Cootham
Windmill Hill
NEW TOWN RD
FOX DELL
West Plain
Parham House
Parham Park (Deer Park)
FOX CT
AMBERLEY RD
CLAY LA
LINK HILL
KITHURST LA
KITHURST PARK
KITHURST FARM RD
B 2139
RACKHAM ST

137

97

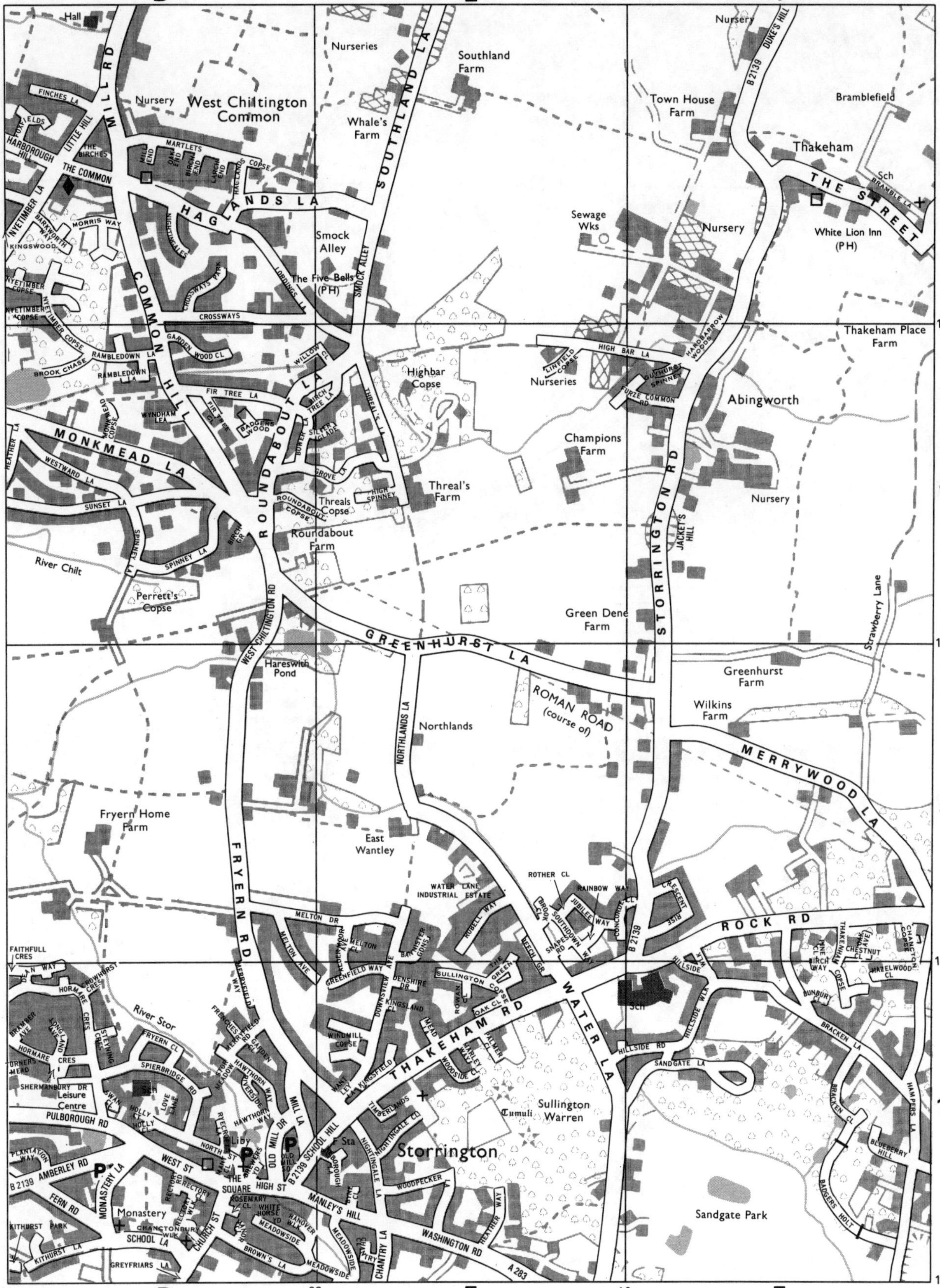

D
E
F
4
3
2
1
17
16
15
14
08
09
10
Hall
Nurseries
Southland Farm
Nursery
West Chiltington Common
Whale's Farm
SOUTHLAND LA
Town House Farm
Bramblefield
Thakeham
B2139 DUKE'S HILL
THE STREET
Sch
White Lion Inn (PH)
FINCHES LA
LITTLE HILL
MILL RD
HARBOROUGH HILL
THE BIRCHES
THE COMMON
MARTLETS
HAGLANDS COPSE
HAGLANDS LA
NYETIMBER LA
MORRIS WAY
BARKWORTH WAY
KINGSWOOD
COMMON HILL
NIGHTINGALES
CROSSWAYS PARK
CROSSWAYS
Smock Alley
SMOCK ALLEY
The Five Bells (PH)
LORDINGS LA
Sewage Wks
Nursery
NYETIMBER COPSE
Thakeham Place Farm
GARDEN WOOD CL
RAMBLEDOWN LA
BROOK CHASE
WILLOW CL
HIGH BAR LA
LINFIELD COPSE
HARDBARROW WOODS
GUYHURST SPINNEY
FURZE COMMON RD
Highbar Copse
Nurseries
Abingworth
FIR TREE LA
WYNDHAM LEA
MONKMEAD COPSE
BADGERS WOOD
BIRCH TREE LA
SILVER GLADE
BOWER LA
TIDEBALLS LA
MONKMEAD LA
WESTWARD LA
HEATHER LA
Champions Farm
STORRINGTON RD
ROUNDABOUT LA
GROVE LA
HIGH SPINNEY
Threal's Farm
Threals Copse
ROUNDABOUT COPSE
SUNSET LA
Roundabout Farm
Nursery
JACKET'S HILL
SPINNEY LA
SPINNEY LA
BIRCH GR
River Chilt
Perrett's Copse
WEST CHILTINGTON RD
Green Dene Farm
Strawberry Lane
GREENHURST LA
Hareswith Pond
Greenhurst Farm
ROMAN ROAD (course of)
Wilkins Farm
NORTHLANDS LA
Northlands
MERRYWOOD LA
Fryern Home Farm
East Wantley
FRYERN RD
WATER LANE INDUSTRIAL ESTATE
ROTHER CL
RAINBOW WAY
CRESCENT RISE
JUBILEE WAY
SOUTHDOWN RD
CONCORDE CL
MELTON DR
MELTON AVE
MELTON CL
BANNISTER GDNS
HUBELL WAY
BEECH GR
SNAPE RD
B 2139
ROCK RD
HILLSIDE
THAKEHAM COPSE
CHESTNUT CL
CHANCTONBURY COPSE
BIRCH WAY
HAZELWOOD CL
BUNBURY CL
FAITHFULL CRES
GREENFIELD WAY
DENSHIRE DR
KINGSLAND CL
SULLINGTON COPSE
THE GREEN
OAK CL
WATER LA
Sch
HILLSIDE WLK
River Stor
BRAMBER AVE
LONGLAND AVE
HORMARE CRES
STEYNING CRES
FRYERN CL
SPIERBRIDGE RD
WINDMILL COPSE
THAKEHAM RD
PALMER CL
HILLSIDE RD
SANDGATE LA
BRACKEN LA
TURNERS MEAD
SHERMANBURY DR
Leisure Centre
HOLLY CL
LOVE LANE
HAWTHORN WAY
KINGSFIELD
TIMBERLANDS
NIGHTINGALE CL
Sullington Warren
Cumuli
HAMPERS LA
BRACKEN CL
BLUEBERRY HILL
PULBOROUGH RD
PLANTATION WAY
AMBERLEY RD
MONASTERY LA
WEST ST
NORTH ST
Liby
OLD MILL DR
MILL LA
SCHOOL HILL
F Sta
Storrington
B 2139
RECTORY RD
RECTORY WLK
THE SQUARE
HIGH ST
ROSEMARY CL
WHITE HORSE RD
MANLEY'S HILL
WOODPECKER
HEATHER WAY
Sandgate Park
BADGERS HOLT
FERN RD
Monastery
CHANCTONBURY WLK
KITHURST PARK
KITHURST LA
SCHOOL LA
CHURCH ST
MEADOWSIDE
HANOVER WLK
BROWN'S LA
MEADOWSIDE
CHANTRY LA
WASHINGTON RD
A 283
GREYFRIARS LA

118

138

98

117

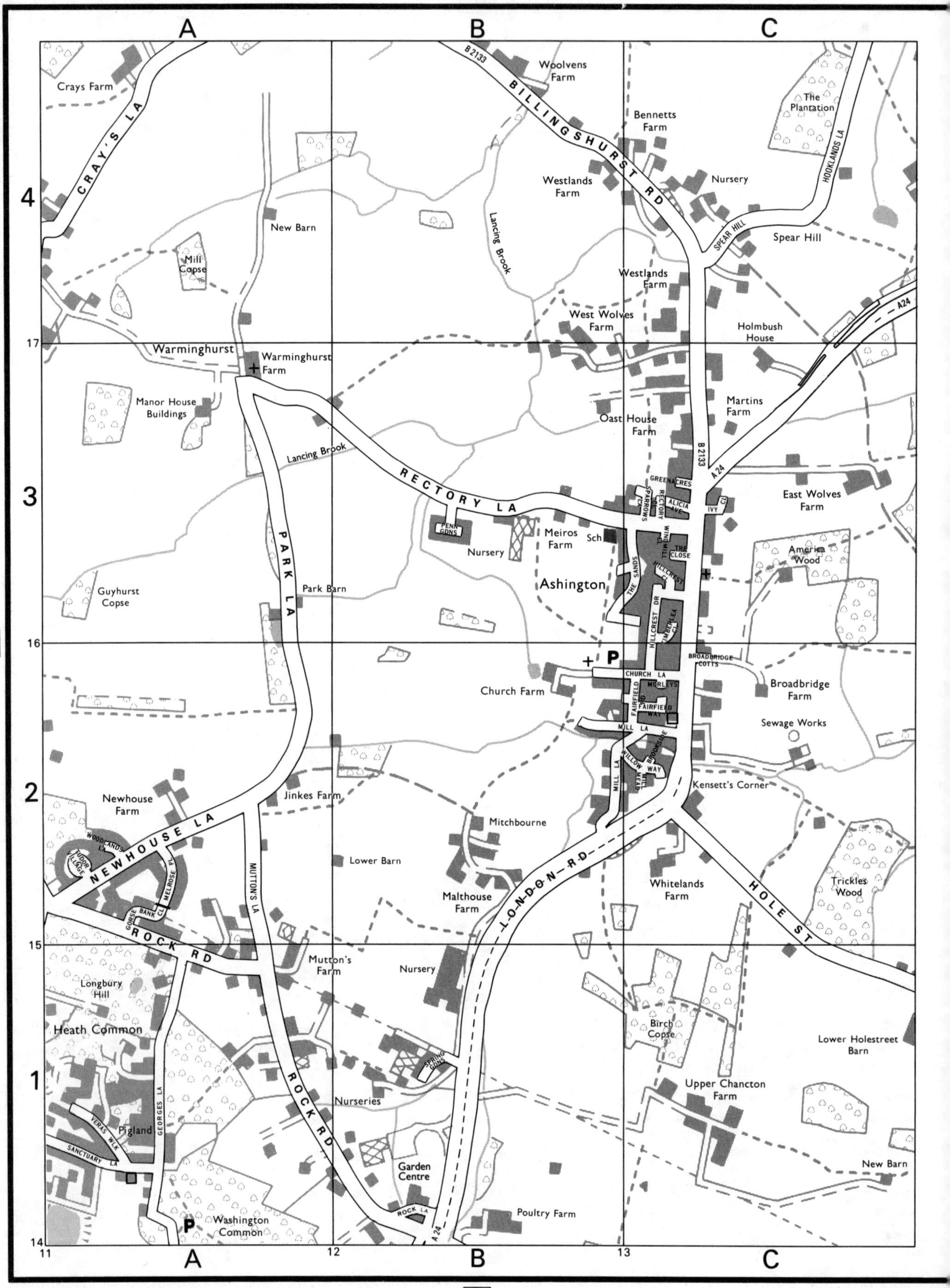
A
B
C
4
3
2
1
17
16
15
14
11
12
13
Crays Farm
CRAY'S LA
B2133
BILLINGSHURST RD
Woolvens Farm
Bennetts Farm
The Plantation
HOOKLANDS LA
Westlands Farm
Nursery
New Barn
Lancing Brook
SPEAR HILL
Spear Hill
Mill Copse
Westlands Farm
West Wolves Farm
Holmbush House
A24
Warminghurst
Warminghurst Farm
Manor House Buildings
Martins Farm
Oast House Farm
Lancing Brook
RECTORY LA
B2133
A 24
GREENACRES
SPARROWS CL
RECTORY CL
ALICIA AVE
IVY CL
East Wolves Farm
PENN GDNS
Nursery
Meiros Farm
Sch
WINDMILL CL
THE CLOSE
HILLCREST CL
America Wood
PARK LA
Guyhurst Copse
Park Barn
Ashington
THE SANDS
HILLCREST DR
TIMBERLEA CL
BROADBRIDGE COTTS
P
Church Farm
CHURCH LA
MORLEYS
FAIRFIELD RD
FAIRFIELD WAY
Broadbridge Farm
Sewage Works
MILL LA
BROOKSIDE
WILLOW WAY
MILL MEAD
MILL LA
Kensett's Corner
Newhouse Farm
Jinkes Farm
Mitchbourne
NEWHOUSE LA
WOODLANDS LA
TUDOR VILLAGE
MELROSE PL
BANK CL
GORSE
MUTTON'S LA
Lower Barn
LONDON RD
Whitelands Farm
HOLE ST
Trickles Wood
Malthouse Farm
ROCK RD
Mutton's Farm
Nursery
Longbury Hill
Heath Common
Birch Copse
Lower Holestreet Barn
SPRING GDNS
ROCK RD
Nurseries
Upper Chancton Farm
GEORGES LA
VERAS WLK
Pigland
SANCTUARY LA
Garden Centre
New Barn
ROCK LA
A 24
Poultry Farm
Washington Common

139

99

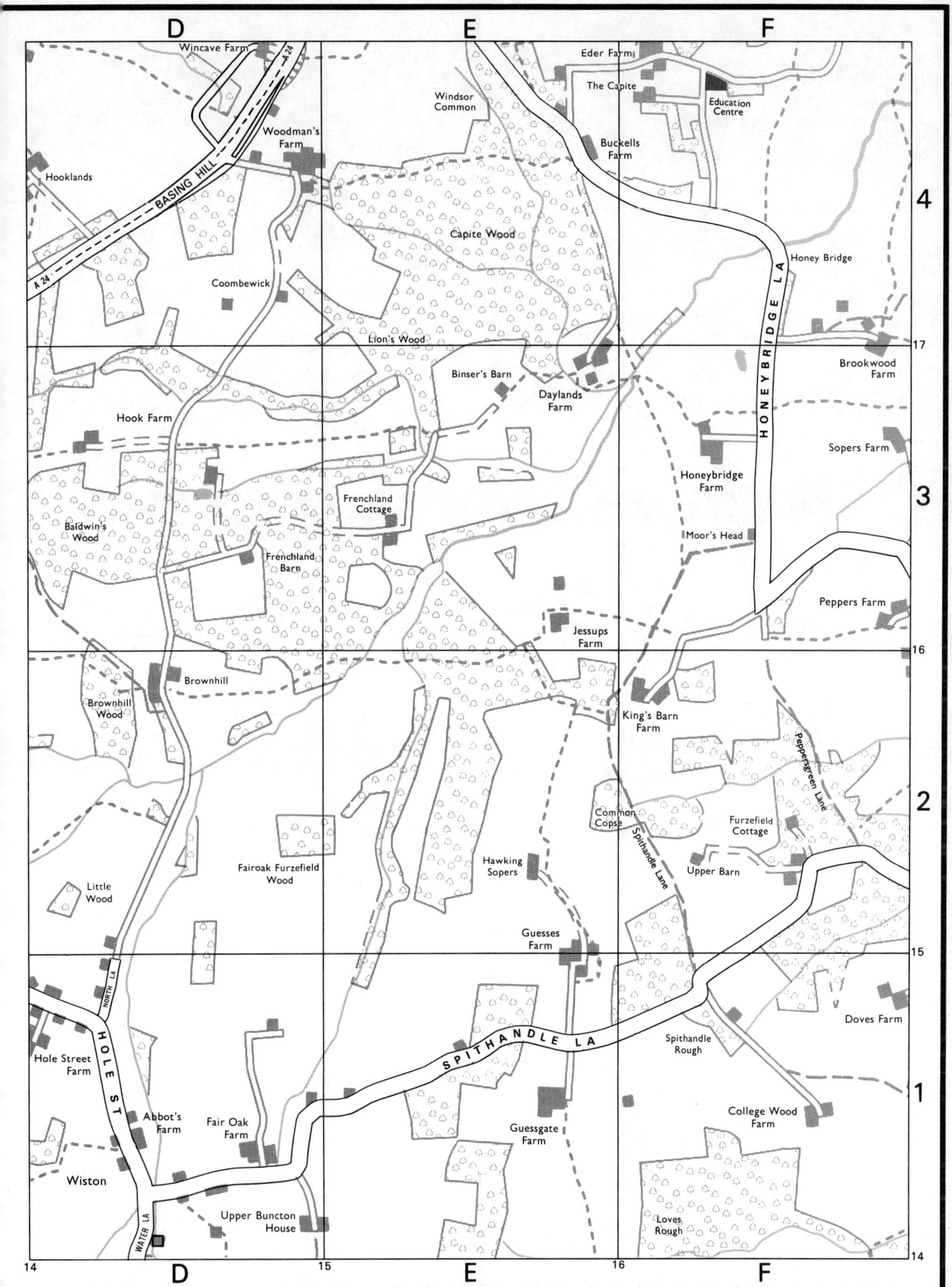
D
E
F
Wincave Farm
A 24
Eder Farm
The Capite
Education Centre
Windsor Common
Woodman's Farm
Buckells Farm
Hooklands
BASING HILL
4
Capite Wood
Honey Bridge
A 24
Coombewick
HONEYBRIDGE LA
Lion's Wood
17
Brookwood Farm
Binser's Barn
Daylands Farm
Hook Farm
Sopers Farm
Honeybridge Farm
3
Frenchland Cottage
Baldwin's Wood
Moor's Head
Frenchland Barn
Peppers Farm
Jessups Farm
16
Brownhill
Brownhill Wood
King's Barn Farm
Peppersgreen Lane
2
Common Copse
Furzefield Cottage
Spithandle Lane
Fairoak Furzefield Wood
Hawking Sopers
Upper Barn
Little Wood
Guesses Farm
15
NORTH LA
Doves Farm
HOLE ST
SPITHANDLE LA
Spithandle Rough
Hole Street Farm
1
College Wood Farm
Abbot's Farm
Fair Oak Farm
Guessgate Farm
Wiston
Upper Buncton House
WATER LA
Loves Rough
14
14
15
16
D
E
F

120

140

100

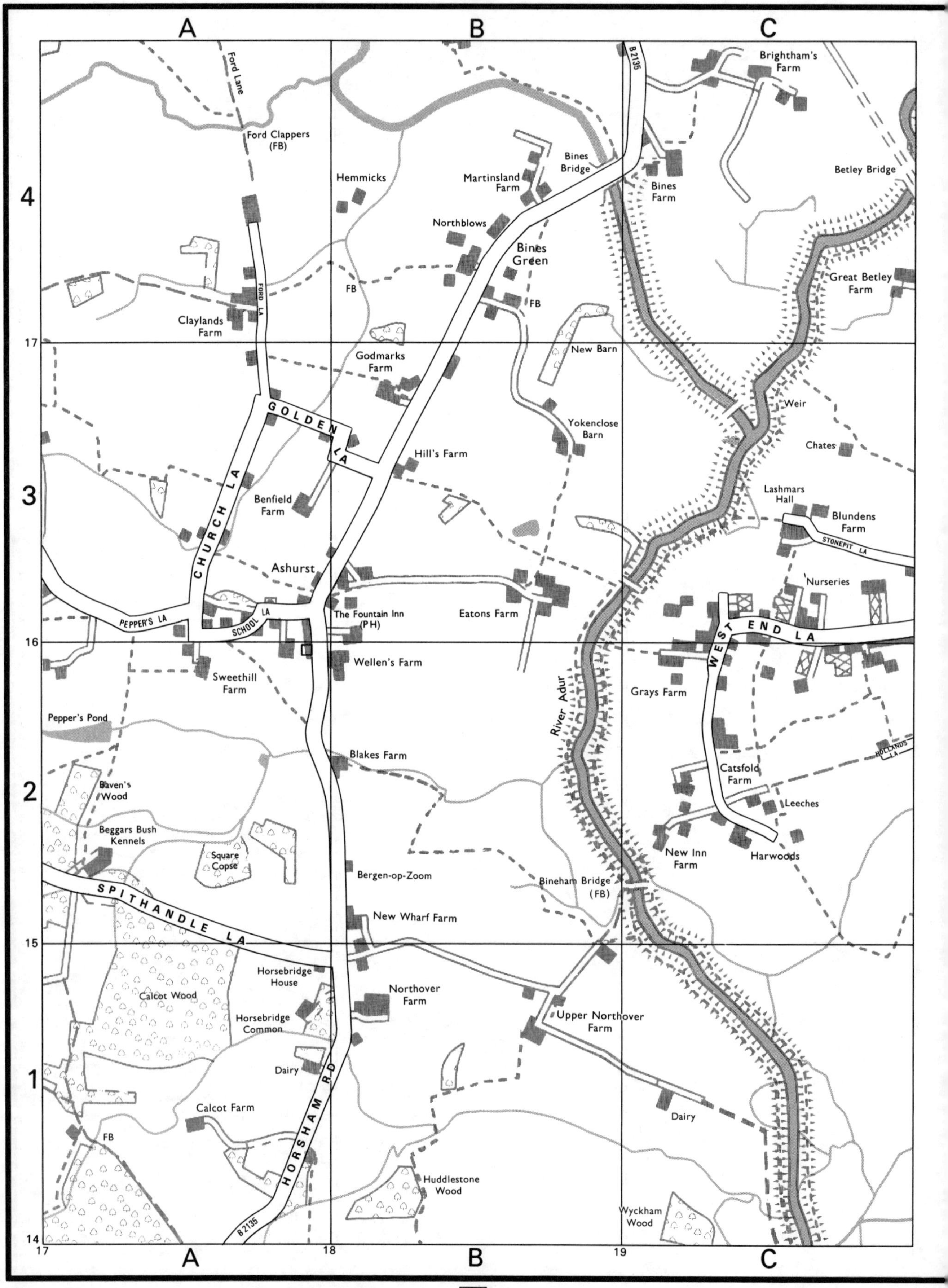
A
B
C
4
3
2
1
17
16
15
14
18
19
Ford Lane
Ford Clappers (FB)
Hemmicks
Martinsland Farm
Bines Bridge
Bines Farm
Brightham's Farm
Betley Bridge
B2135
Northblows
Bines Green
FB
Great Betley Farm
Claylands Farm
FORD LA
New Barn
Godmarks Farm
Weir
GOLDEN LA
Yokenclose Barn
Chates
Hill's Farm
CHURCH LA
Benfield Farm
Lashmars Hall
Blundens Farm
STONEPIT LA
Ashurst
Nurseries
PEPPER'S LA
SCHOOL LA
The Fountain Inn (PH)
Eatons Farm
WEST END LA
Wellen's Farm
Sweethill Farm
Grays Farm
River Adur
Pepper's Pond
Blakes Farm
HOLLANDS LA
Catsfold Farm
Baven's Wood
Leeches
Beggars Bush Kennels
New Inn Farm
Harwoods
Square Copse
Bergen-op-Zoom
Bineham Bridge (FB)
SPITHANDLE LA
New Wharf Farm
Horsebridge House
Northover Farm
Calcot Wood
Horsebridge Common
Upper Northover Farm
Dairy
HORSHAM RD
Calcot Farm
Dairy
FB
Huddlestone Wood
Wyckham Wood
B2135

119

141

101

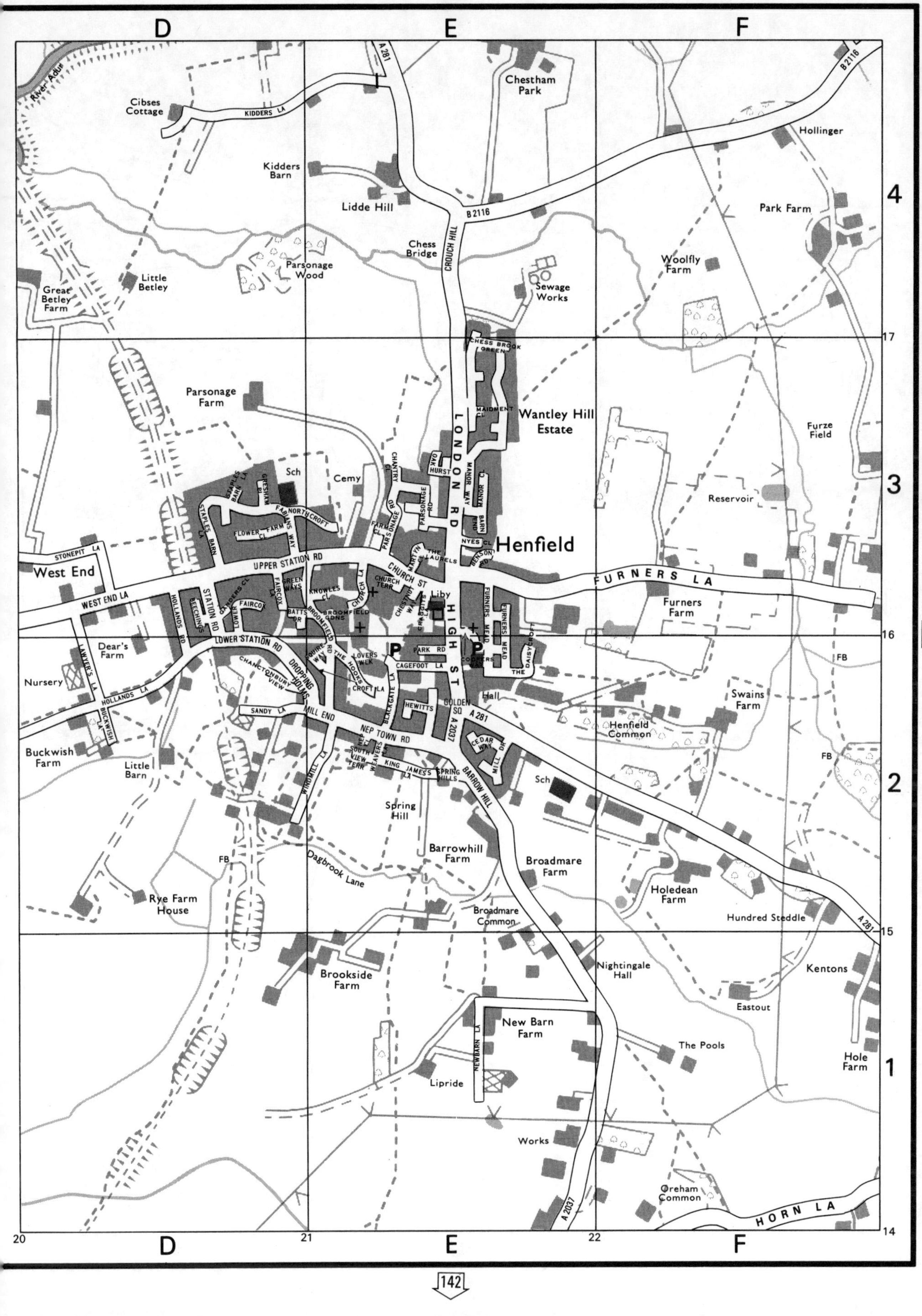
D
E
F
River Adur
Cibses Cottage
KIDDERS LA
A 281
Chestham Park
B 2116
Hollinger
Kidders Barn
Lidde Hill
B 2116
CROUCH HILL
4
Park Farm
Chess Bridge
Parsonage Wood
Little Betley
Great Betley Farm
Sewage Works
Woolfly Farm
17
CHESS BROOK GREEN
Parsonage Farm
MAIDMENT CL
LONDON RD
Wantley Hill Estate
Furze Field
Sch
Cemy
3
Reservoir
Henfield
STONEPIT LA
West End
UPPER STATION RD
CHURCH ST
FURNERS LA
WEST END LA
HIGH ST
Liby
Furners Farm
16
Dear's Farm
LOWER STATION RD
FB
Nursery
Swains Farm
HOLLANDS LA
BUCKWISH LA
SANDY LA
MILL END
NEP TOWN RD
A 281
A 2037
Henfield Common
Buckwish Farm
Little Barn
KING JAMES'S LA
BARROW HILL
Sch
FB
2
Spring Hill
Barrowhill Farm
Broadmare Farm
FB
Dagbrook Lane
Holedean Farm
Rye Farm House
Hundred Steddle
Broadmare Common
A 281
15
Nightingale Hall
Kentons
Brookside Farm
Eastout
New Barn Farm
NEWBARN LA
The Pools
Hole Farm
1
Lipride
Works
Oreham Common
A 2037
HORN LA
20
21
22
14
D
E
F

122

142

102

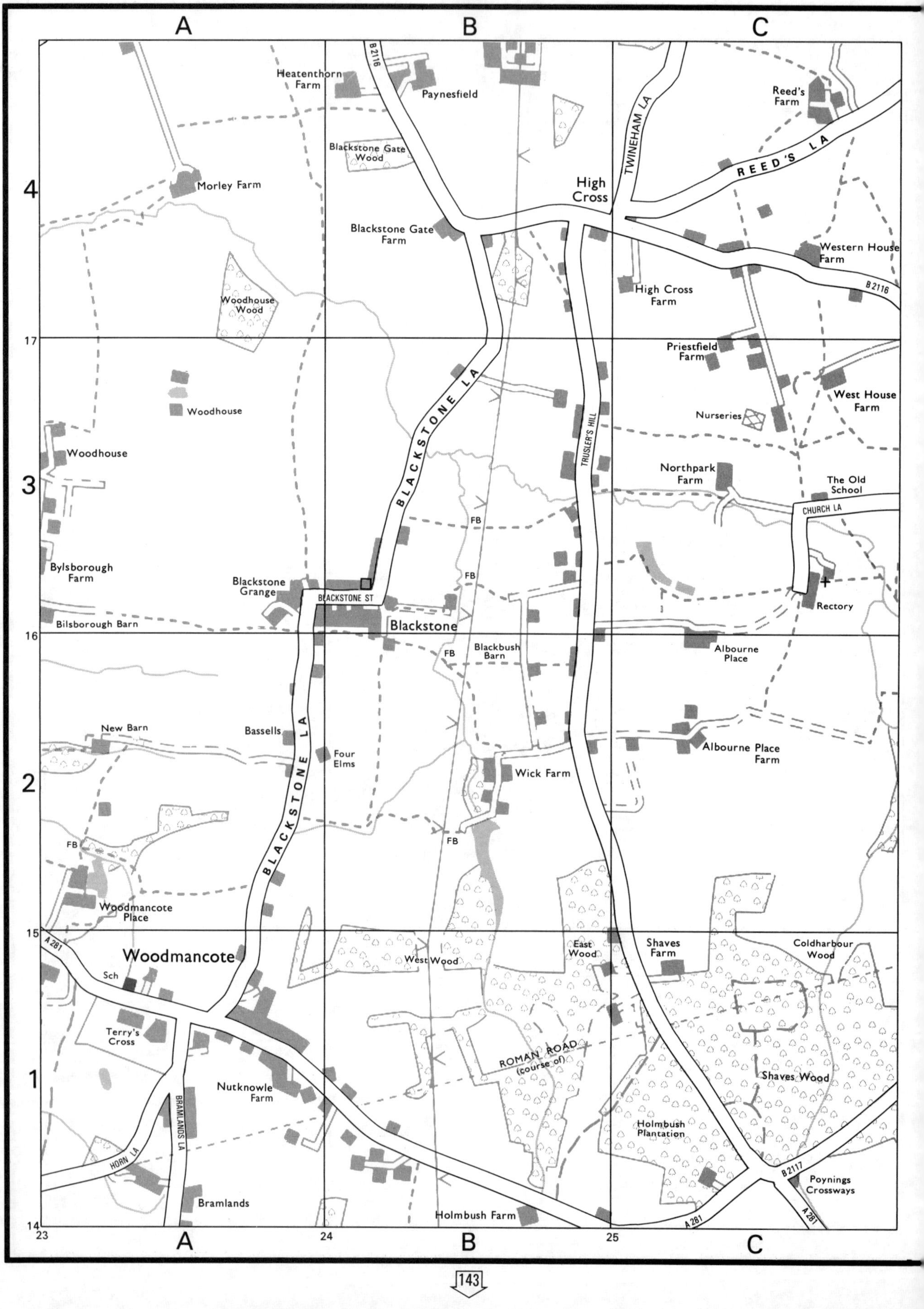

A
B
C
4
3
2
1
17
16
15
14
23
24
25
Heatenthorn Farm
Paynesfield
B2116
Blackstone Gate Wood
Morley Farm
High Cross
TWINEHAM LA
Reed's Farm
REED'S LA
Blackstone Gate Farm
Western House Farm
B2116
High Cross Farm
Woodhouse Wood
Priestfield Farm
West House Farm
Woodhouse
Nurseries
BLACKSTONE LA
TRUSLER'S HILL
Woodhouse
Northpark Farm
The Old School
CHURCH LA
FB
FB
Bylsborough Farm
Blackstone Grange
BLACKSTONE ST
Rectory
Bilsborough Barn
Blackstone
Blackbush Barn
FB
Albourne Place
New Barn
Bassells
BLACKSTONE LA
Four Elms
Albourne Place Farm
Wick Farm
FB
FB
Woodmancote Place
A 281
Woodmancote
Sch
West Wood
East Wood
Shaves Farm
Coldharbour Wood
Terry's Cross
ROMAN ROAD (course of)
Shaves Wood
Nutknowle Farm
BRAMLANDS LA
Holmbush Plantation
HORN LA
B2117
Poynings Crossways
Bramlands
Holmbush Farm
A 281
A 281

121

143

103

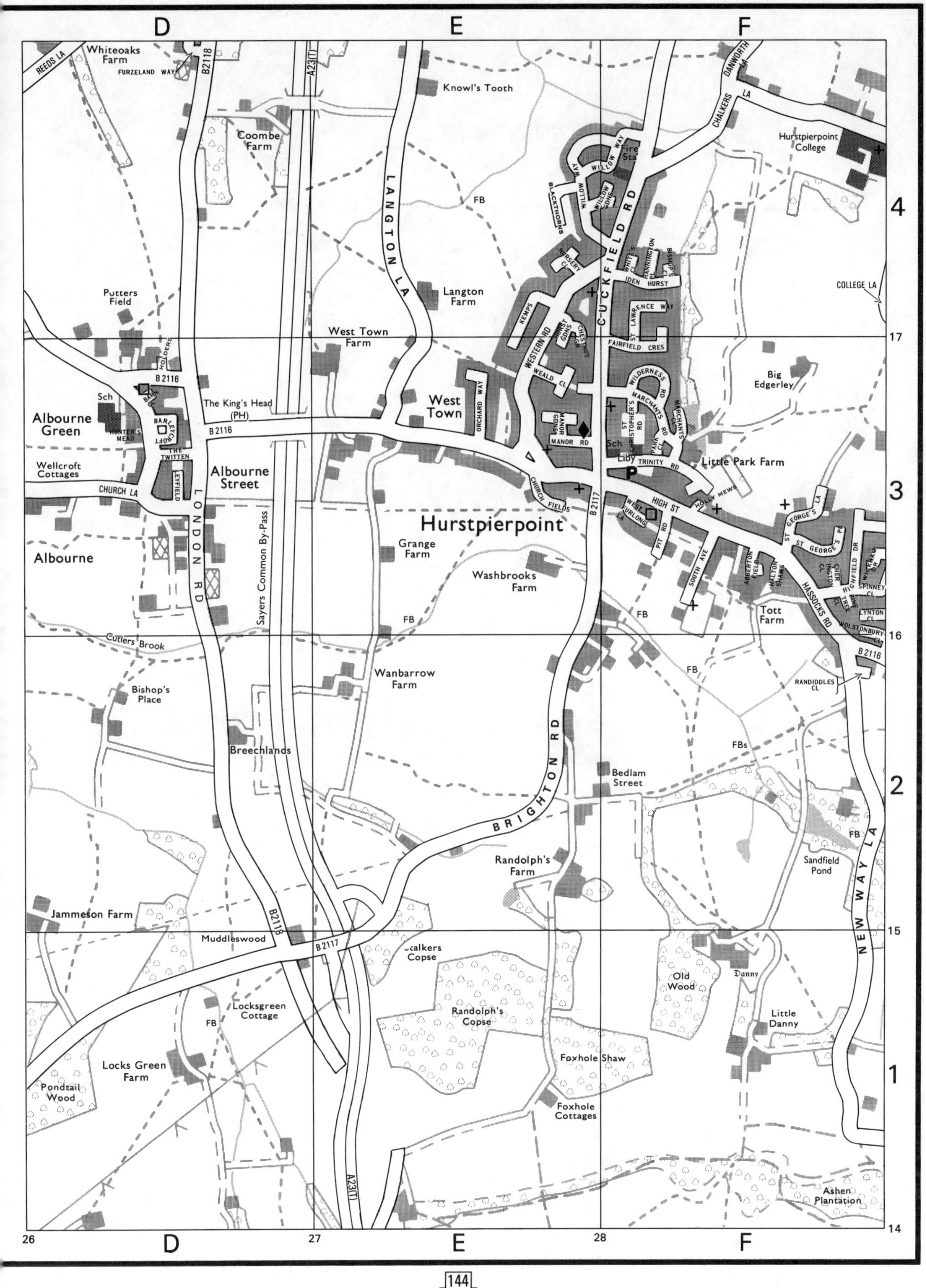
D
E
F
Whiteoaks Farm
REEDS LA
FURZELAND WAY
B2118
A23(T)
Knowl's Tooth
DANWORTH LA
CHALKERS LA
Coombe Farm
Hurstpierpoint College
Fire Sta
WILLOW WAY
WILLOW GDNS
BLACKTHORNS
CUCKFIELD RD
LANGTON LA
FB
4
NURSERY CL
WHITE'S CL
HANNINGTON PL
BISHOPS CL
IDEN HURST
Putters Field
Langton Farm
COLLEGE LA
KEMPS
LAWRENCE WAY
West Town Farm
WESTERN RD
HURST GDNS
CHESTNUT GR
FAIRFIELD CRES
17
HOLDERS
B2116
WEALD CL
WILDERNESS RD
Big Edgerley
Sch
ORCHARD WAY
West Town
MARCHANTS RD
MARCHANTS CL
The King's Head (PH)
Albourne Green
BARN CL
BARLEYCROFT
HUNTER'S MEAD
B2116
MANOR GDNS
MANOR RD
ST CHRISTOPHER'S RD
PARK CL
Sch
Liby
TRINITY RD
Little Park Farm
THE TWITTEN
Wellcroft Cottages
Albourne Street
LEYFIELD
CHURCH LA
CHURCH FIELDS
B2117
HIGH ST
HOLLY MEWS
3
WEST FURLONG LA
ST GEORGE'S LA
Hurstpierpoint
LONDON RD
Sayers Common By-Pass
Grange Farm
PIT RD
SOUTH AVE
ABBERTON FIELD
HALTON SHAWS
ST GEORGE'S PL
WICKHAM DR
HIGHFIELD DR
Albourne
Washbrooks Farm
HASSOCKS RD
SPINNEY CL
LYNTON CL
FB
FB
Tott Farm
WOLSTONBURY CL
Cutlers Brook
16
B2116
FB
Wanbarrow Farm
RANDIDDLES CL
Bishop's Place
BRIGHTON RD
FBs
Breechlands
Bedlam Street
2
FB
Sandfield Pond
Randolph's Farm
Jammeson Farm
B2118
15
Muddleswood
B2117
Stalkers Copse
NEW WAY LA
Old Wood
Danny
Locksgreen Cottage
FB
Randolph's Copse
Little Danny
Locks Green Farm
Foxhole Shaw
1
Pondtail Wood
Foxhole Cottages
A23(T)
Ashen Plantation
14
26
27
28
D
E
F

124

144

104

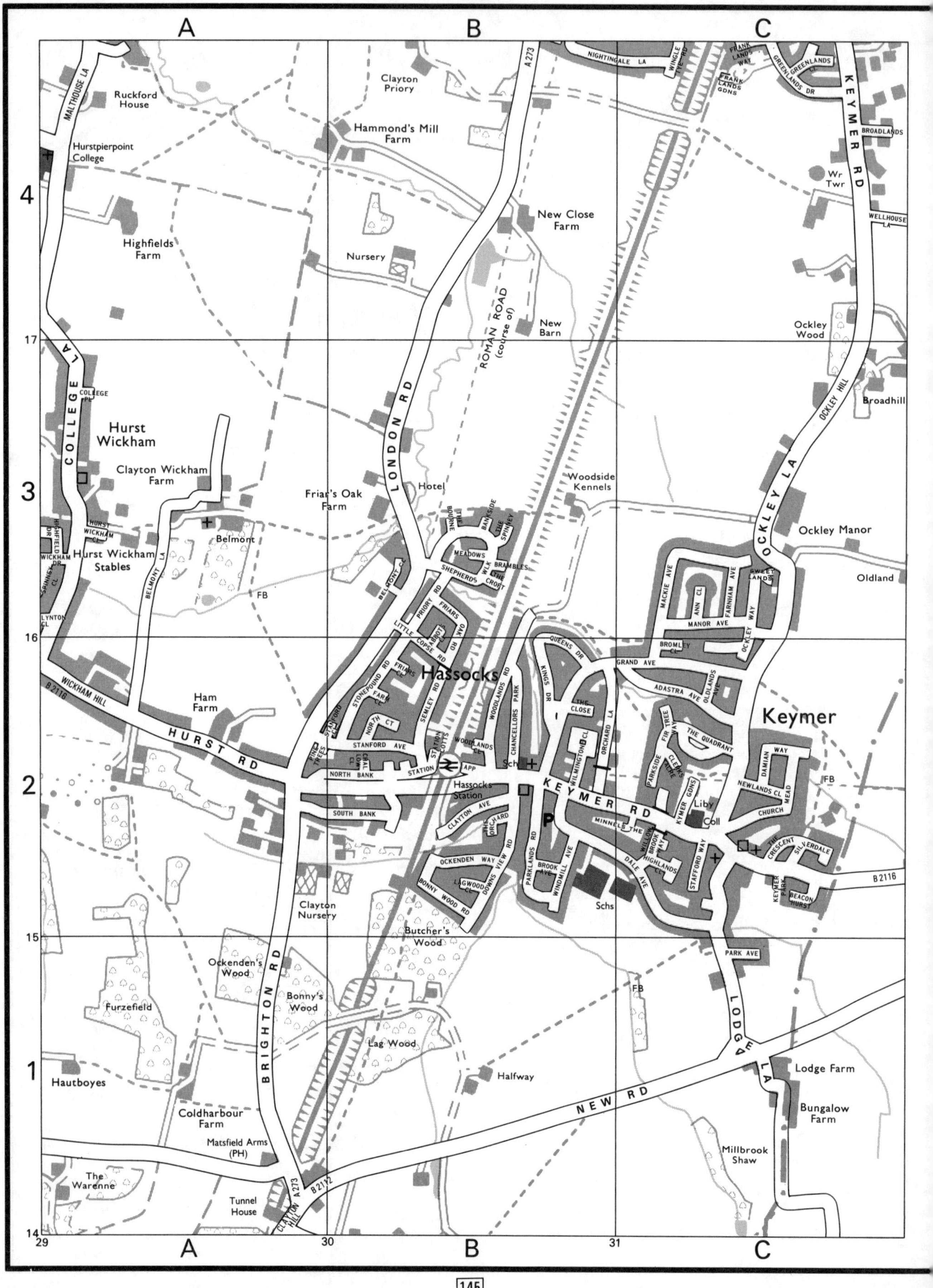
A
B
C
4
3
2
1
17
16
15
14
29
30
31
Ruckford House
Clayton Priory
Hammond's Mill Farm
Hurstpierpoint College
Highfields Farm
Nursery
New Close Farm
New Barn
ROMAN ROAD (course of)
Ockley Wood
Broadhill
Wr Twr
Hurst Wickham
Clayton Wickham Farm
Friar's Oak Farm
Hotel
Woodside Kennels
Belmont
Hurst Wickham Stables
Ockley Manor
Oldland
FB
Ham Farm
Hassocks
Keymer
Hassocks Station
Sch
Schs
Liby
Coll
Clayton Nursery
Butcher's Wood
Ockenden's Wood
Bonny's Wood
Furzefield
Lag Wood
Halfway
Hautboyes
Coldharbour Farm
Matsfield Arms (PH)
The Warenne
Tunnel House
Millbrook Shaw
Lodge Farm
Bungalow Farm
MALTHOUSE LA
NIGHTINGALE LA
WINGLE TYE RD
FRANKLANDS WAY
FRANKLANDS GDNS
GREENLANDS DR
GREENLANDS CL
KEYMER RD
BROADLANDS
WELLHOUSE LA
LONDON RD
OCKLEY HILL
OCKLEY LA
COLLEGE LA
COLLEGE PL
HIGHFIELD DR
HURST WICKHAM CL
WICKHAM DR
SPINNEY CL
LYNTON CL
BELMONT LA
BELMONT CL
WICKHAM HILL
B2116
HURST RD
BOURNE THE
BANKSIDE
THE SPINNEY
MEADOWS
SHEPHERDS WLK
BRAMBLES
THE CROFT
PRIORY RD
FRIARS OAK RD
LITTLE COPSE RD
ABBOTS CL
STONEPOUND RD
FRIARS CL
FARM CL
NORTH CT
SEMLEY RD
STANFORD CL
STANFORD AVE
PINE TREES
CHALLOW CL
NORTH BANK
STATION
SOUTH BANK
STATION APP
WOODLANDS RD
WOODLANDS CL
CHANCELLORS PARK
QUEENS DR
KINGS DR
THE CLOSE
ORCHARD LA
WILMINGTON CL
CLAYTON AVE
THE ORCHARD
OCKENDEN WAY
DOWNS VIEW RD
LAGWOOD CL
BONNY WOOD RD
PARKLANDS RD
BROOK AVE
WINDMILL AVE
MINNELS THE
WILLOWBROOK WAY
HIGHLANDS
DALE AVE
STAFFORD WAY
KEYMER GDNS
PARKSIDE
FIR TREE WAY
CLEARS
THE QUADRANT
OLDLANDS AVE
ADASTRA AVE
GRAND AVE
BROMLEY CL
MANOR AVE
MACKIE AVE
ANN CL
FARNHAM AVE
OCKLEY WAY
SWEETLANDS
DAMIAN WAY
NEWLANDS CL
MEAD
CHURCH
THE CRESCENT
SILVERDALE
KEYMER PARK
BEACON HURST
PARK AVE
LODGE LA
NEW RD
BRIGHTON RD
A273
B2112
CLAYTON HILL

123

145

105

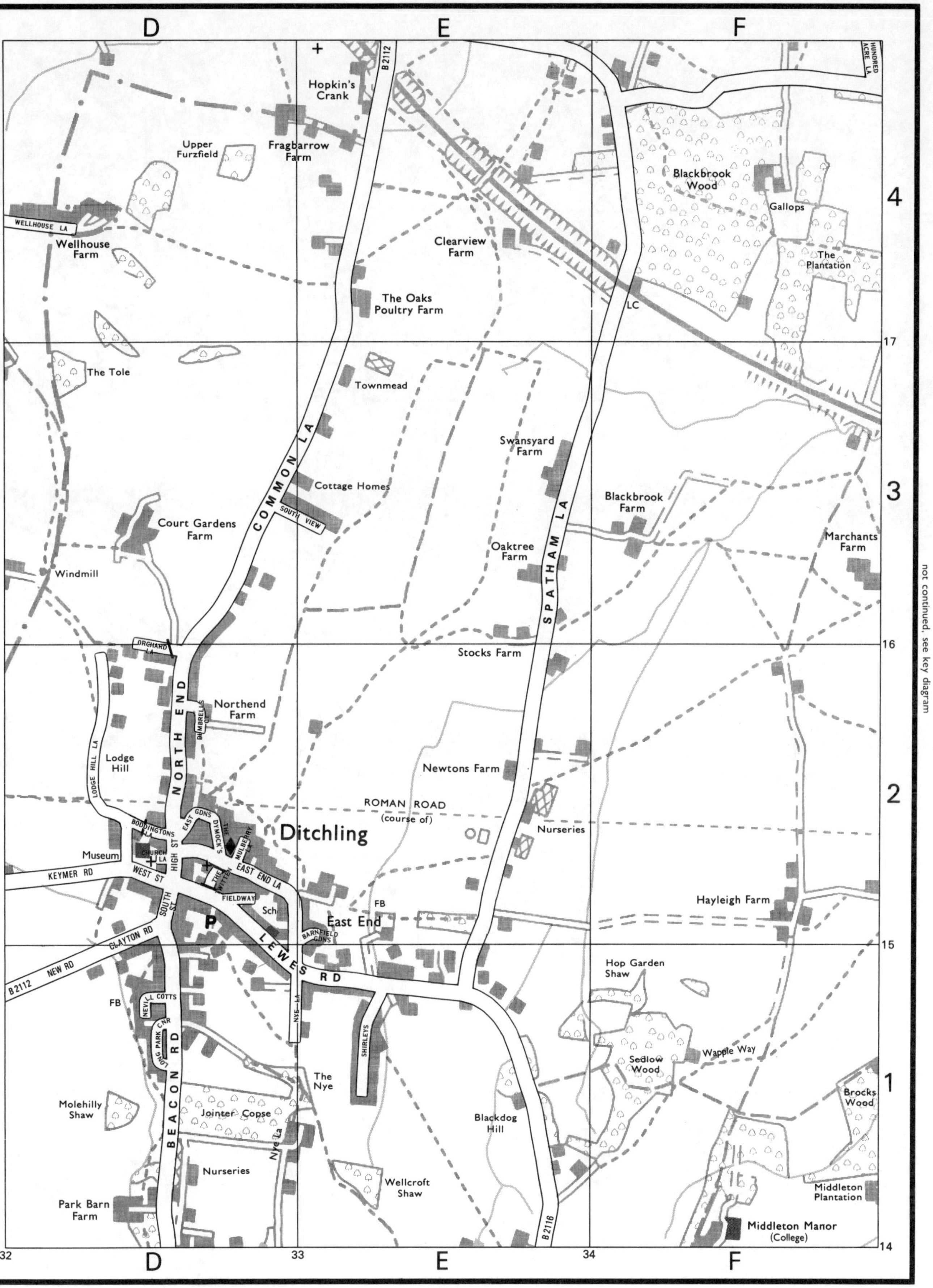

not continued, see key diagram

146

not continued, see key diagram

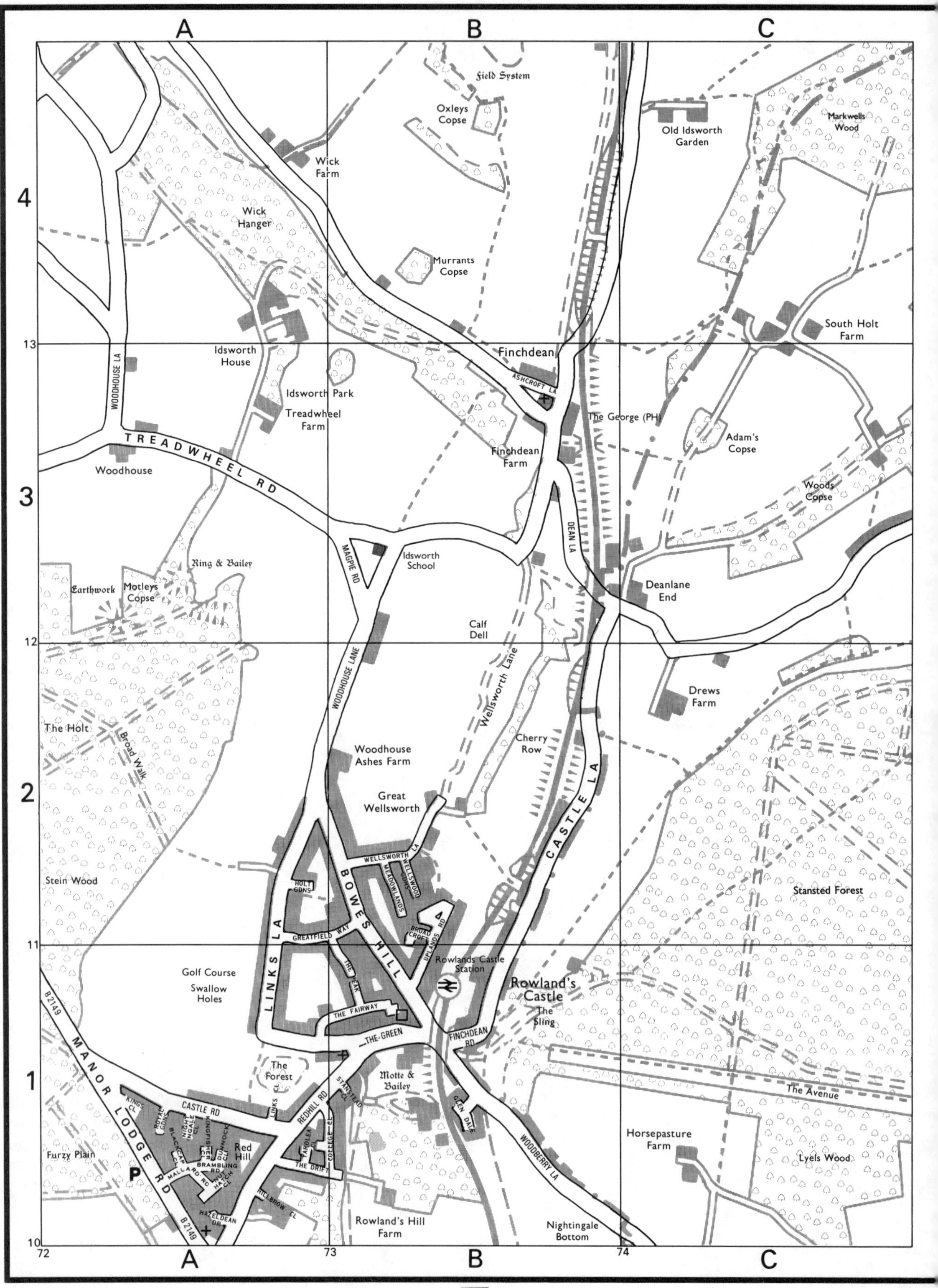

not continued, see key diagram

106

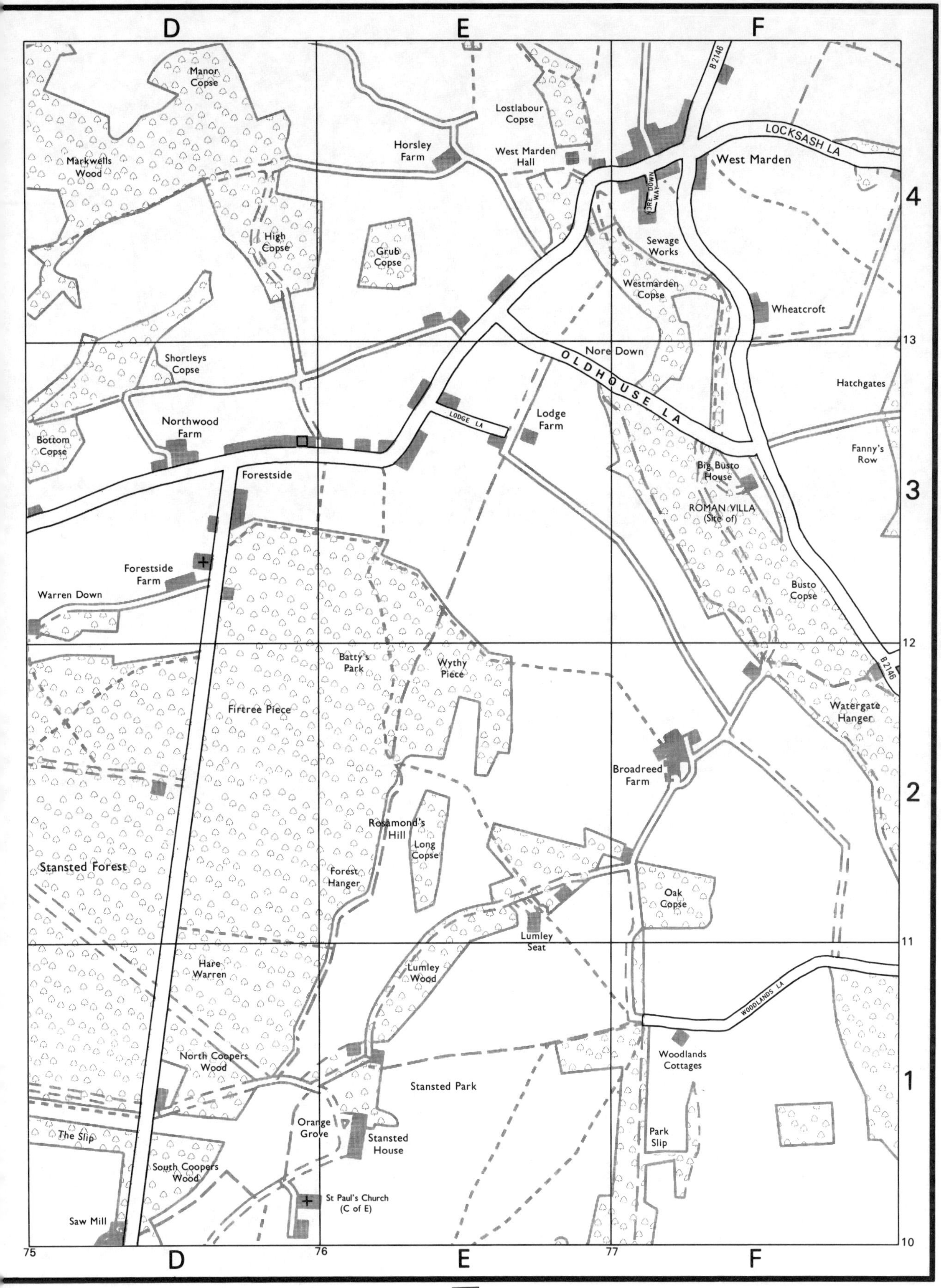
D
E
F
Manor Copse
Markwells Wood
Lostlabour Copse
Horsley Farm
West Marden Hall
LOCKSASH LA
West Marden
B2146
NORE DOWN WAY
High Copse
Grub Copse
Sewage Works
Westmarden Copse
Wheatcroft
Nore Down
OLDHOUSE LA
Shortleys Copse
Hatchgates
Northwood Farm
LODGE LA
Lodge Farm
Bottom Copse
Fanny's Row
Forestside
Big Busto House
ROMAN VILLA (Site of)
Forestside Farm
Warren Down
Busto Copse
Batty's Park
Wythy Piece
Firtree Piece
Watergate Hanger
Broadreed Farm
Rosamond's Hill
Long Copse
Stansted Forest
Forest Hanger
Oak Copse
Lumley Seat
Hare Warren
Lumley Wood
WOODLANDS LA
Woodlands Cottages
North Coopers Wood
Stansted Park
The Slip
Orange Grove
Stansted House
Park Slip
South Coopers Wood
St Paul's Church (C of E)
Saw Mill
4
3
2
1
13
12
11
10
75
76
77

128

148

107

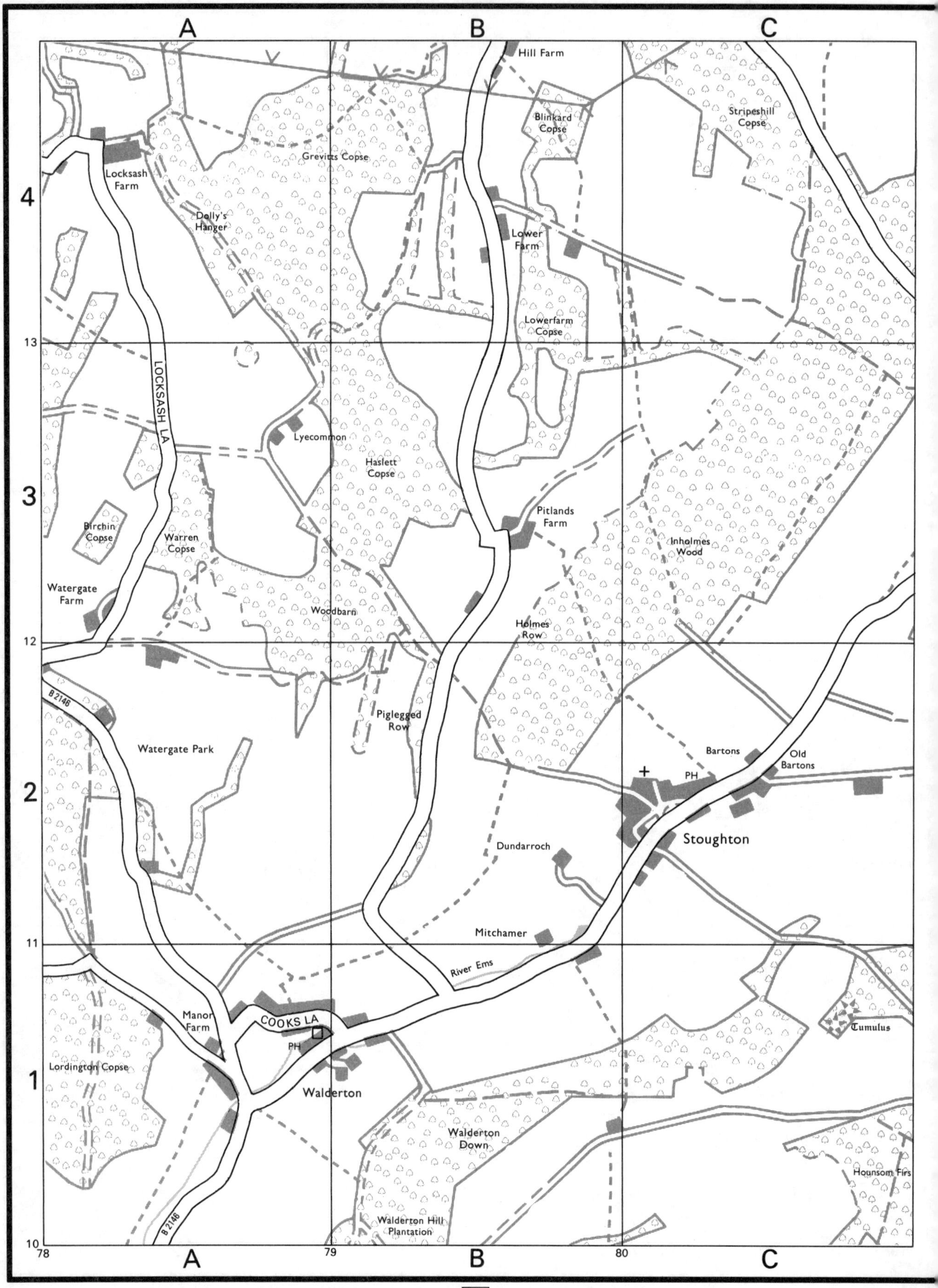
A
B
C
Hill Farm
Blinkard Copse
Stripeshill Copse
Grevitts Copse
Locksash Farm
Dolly's Hanger
Lower Farm
Lowerfarm Copse
LOCKSASH LA
Lyecommon
Haslett Copse
Pitlands Farm
Inholmes Wood
Birchin Copse
Warren Copse
Watergate Farm
Woodbarn
Holmes Row
B 2146
Piglegged Row
Watergate Park
Bartons
Old Bartons
PH
Stoughton
Dundarroch
Mitchamer
River Ems
Manor Farm
COOKS LA
PH
Tumulus
Lordington Copse
Walderton
Walderton Down
Hounsom Firs
Walderton Hill Plantation
B 2146
4
3
2
1
13
12
11
10
78
79
80

127

149

108

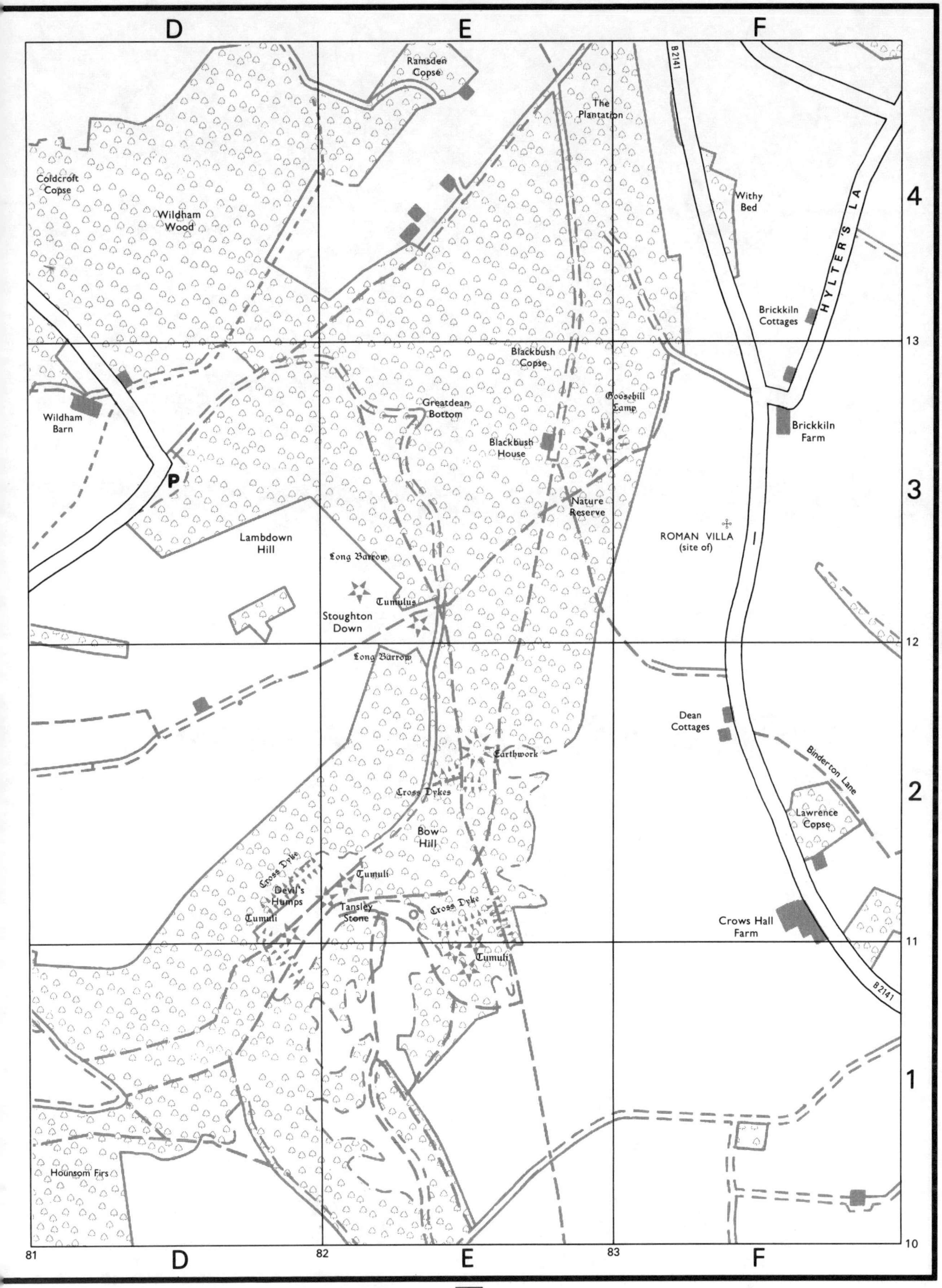
D
E
F
Ramsden Copse
The Plantation
B2141
Coldcroft Copse
Wildham Wood
Withy Bed
HYLTER'S LA
4
Brickkiln Cottages
13
Blackbush Copse
Wildham Barn
Greatdean Bottom
Goosehill Camp
Brickkiln Farm
Blackbush House
P
3
Nature Reserve
ROMAN VILLA (site of)
Lambdown Hill
Long Barrow
Tumulus
Stoughton Down
12
Long Barrow
Dean Cottages
Binderton Lane
Earthwork
2
Cross Dykes
Lawrence Copse
Bow Hill
Cross Dyke
Tumuli
Devil's Humps
Tansley Stone
Cross Dyke
Tumuli
Crows Hall Farm
11
Tumuli
B2141
1
Hounsom Firs
81
82
83
10
D
E
F

130

150

109

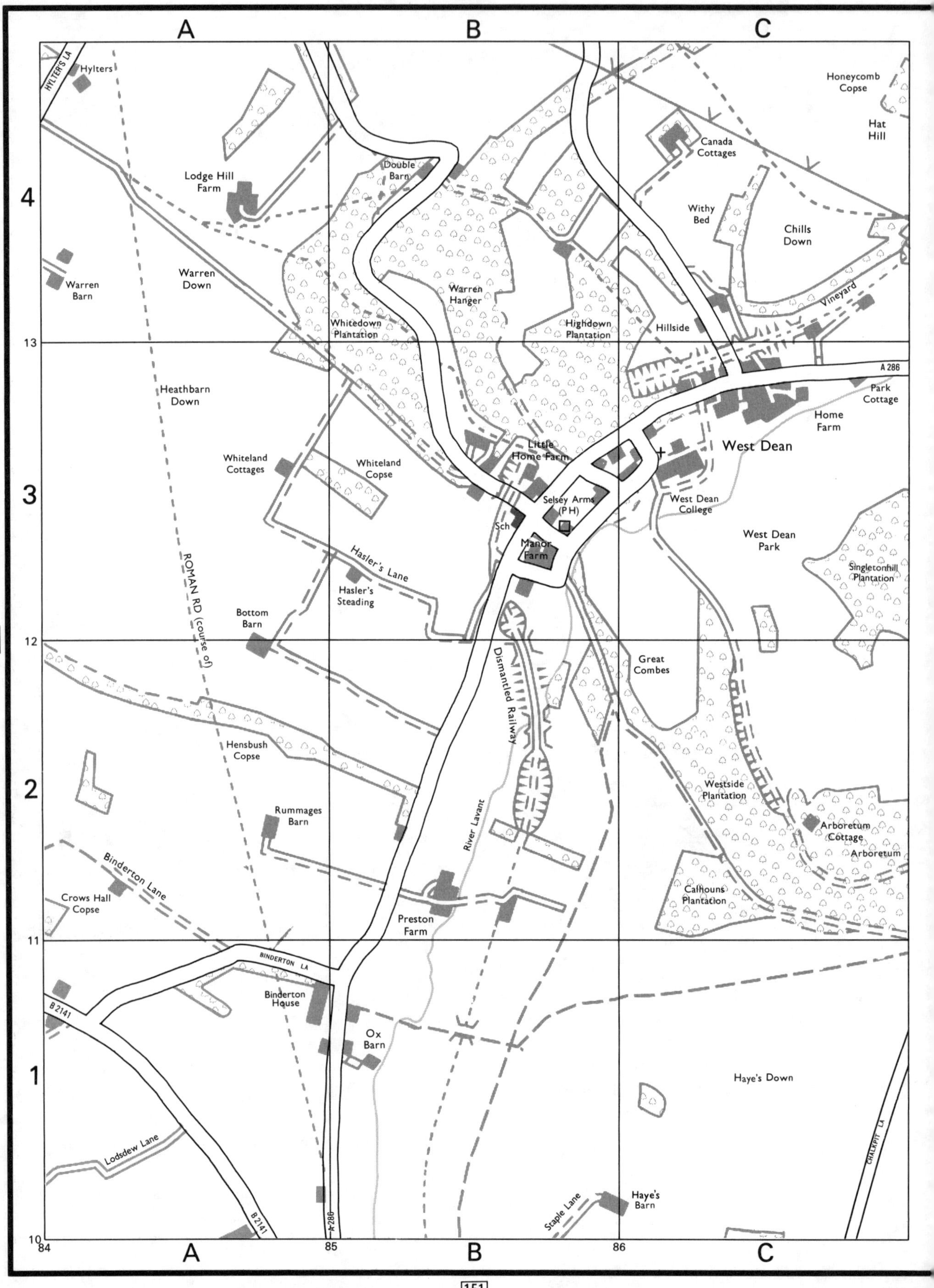
A
B
C
4
3
2
1
13
12
11
10
84
85
86
HYLTER'S LA
Hylters
Lodge Hill Farm
Double Barn
Canada Cottages
Honeycomb Copse
Hat Hill
Withy Bed
Chills Down
Warren Barn
Warren Down
Warren Hanger
Whitedown Plantation
Highdown Plantation
Hillside
Vineyard
A 286
Park Cottage
Home Farm
West Dean
Heathbarn Down
Little Home Farm
Whiteland Cottages
Whiteland Copse
Selsey Arms (PH)
Sch
West Dean College
West Dean Park
Manor Farm
Singletonhill Plantation
Hasler's Lane
Hasler's Steading
Bottom Barn
ROMAN RD (course of)
Dismantled Railway
Great Combes
Hensbush Copse
Westside Plantation
Rummages Barn
River Lavant
Arboretum Cottage
Arboretum
Binderton Lane
Crows Hall Copse
Preston Farm
Calhouns Plantation
BINDERTON LA
Binderton House
B 2141
Ox Barn
Haye's Down
Lodsdew Lane
CHALKPIT LA
Scaple Lane
Haye's Barn
A 286
B 2141

129

151

110

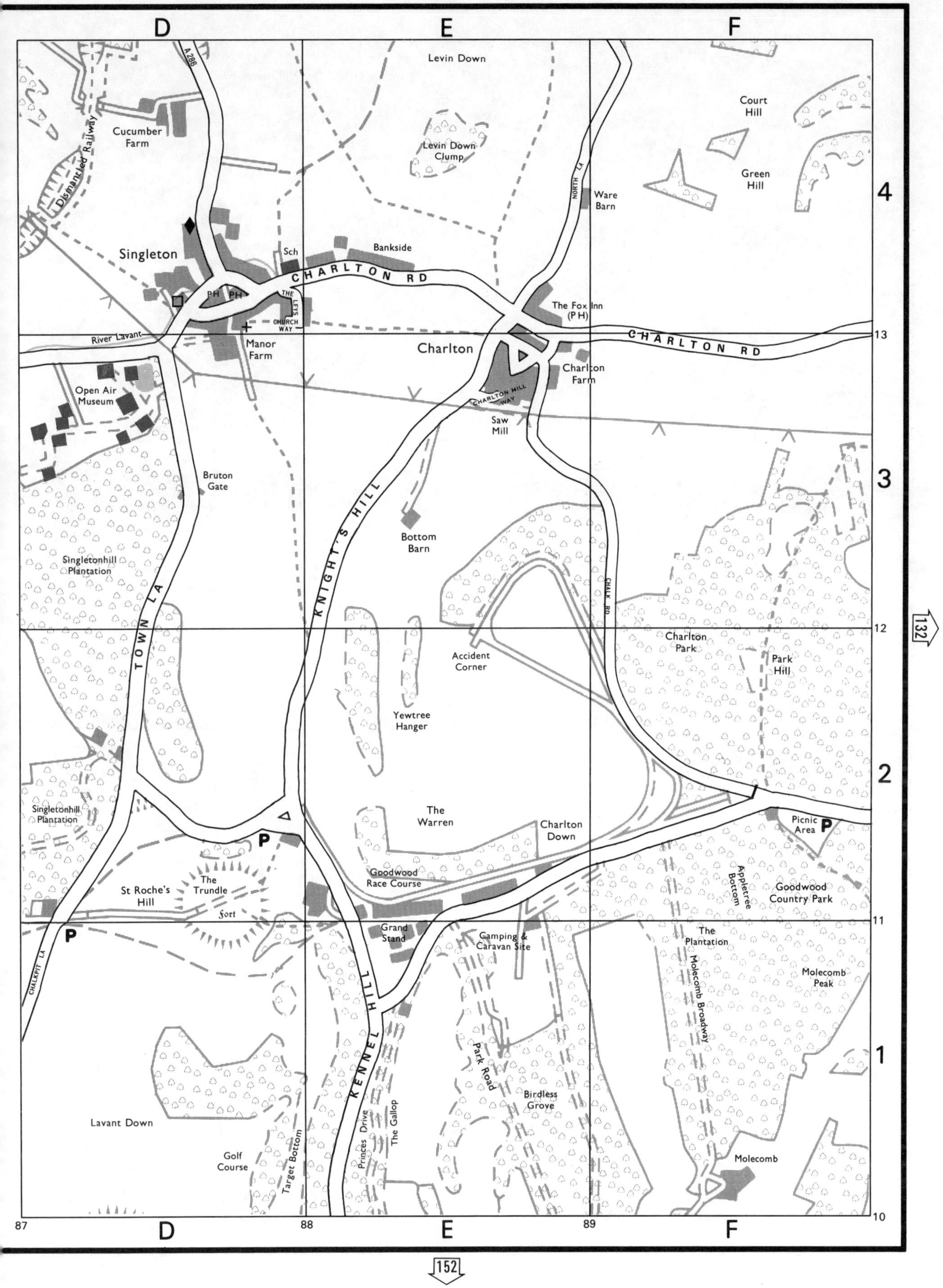
D
E
F
Levin Down
Court Hill
Cucumber Farm
Dismantled Railway
A 286
Levin Down Clump
Green Hill
NORTH LA
Ware Barn
4
Singleton
Sch
Bankside
CHARLTON RD
PH
PH
THE LEYS
CHURCH WAY
The Fox Inn (PH)
River Lavant
Manor Farm
Charlton
CHARLTON RD
13
Charlton Farm
Open Air Museum
CHARLTON HILL WAY
Saw Mill
Bruton Gate
3
KNIGHT'S HILL
Bottom Barn
Singletonhill Plantation
CHALK RD
TOWN LA
12
Charlton Park
Accident Corner
Park Hill
Yewtree Hanger
2
Singletonhill Plantation
The Warren
Charlton Down
Picnic Area
P
P
Goodwood Race Course
Appletree Bottom
Goodwood Country Park
St Roche's Hill
The Trundle
Fort
Grand Stand
Camping & Caravan Site
The Plantation
11
P
CHALKPIT LA
Molecomb Broadway
Molecomb Peak
KENNEL HILL
1
Park Road
Birdless Grove
Lavant Down
Princes Drive
The Gallop
Golf Course
Target Bottom
Molecomb
87
88
89
10
D
E
F

132

152

111

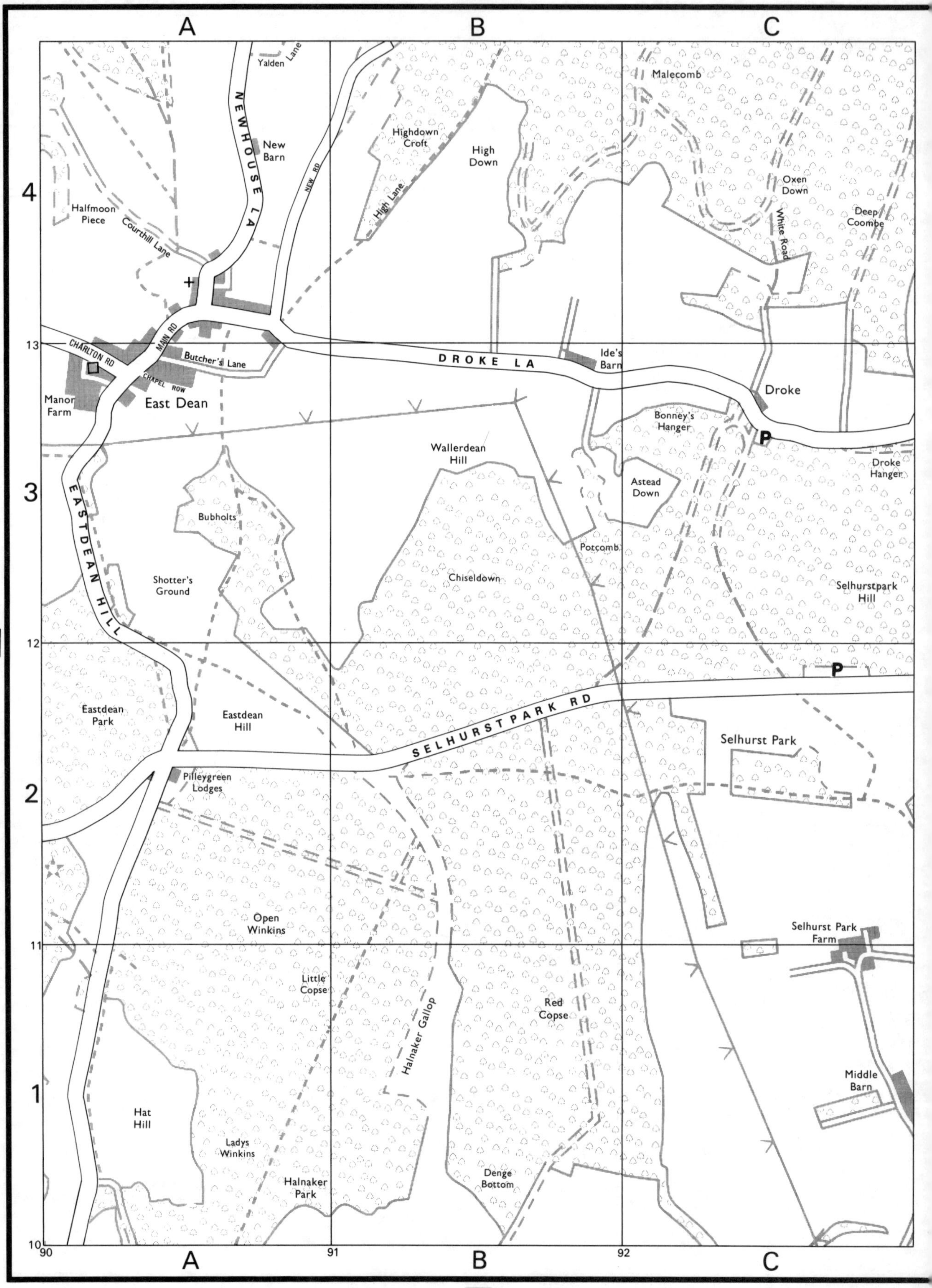
A
B
C
4
13
3
12
2
11
1
10
90
91
92
Yalden Lane
NEWHOUSE LA
New Barn
NEW RD
Highdown Croft
High Lane
High Down
Malecomb
Oxen Down
White Road
Deep Coombe
Halfmoon Piece
Courthill Lane
CHARLTON RD
MAIN RD
Butcher's Lane
CHAPEL ROW
DROKE LA
Ide's Barn
Droke
Manor Farm
East Dean
Bonney's Hanger
P
Wallerdean Hill
Droke Hanger
EASTDEAN HILL
Bubholts
Astead Down
Potcomb
Chiseldown
Shotter's Ground
Selhurstpark Hill
Eastdean Park
Eastdean Hill
SELHURSTPARK RD
Selhurst Park
Pilleygreen Lodges
Open Winkins
Selhurst Park Farm
Little Copse
Halnaker Gallop
Red Copse
Middle Barn
Hat Hill
Ladys Winkins
Halnaker Park
Denge Bottom

131
153

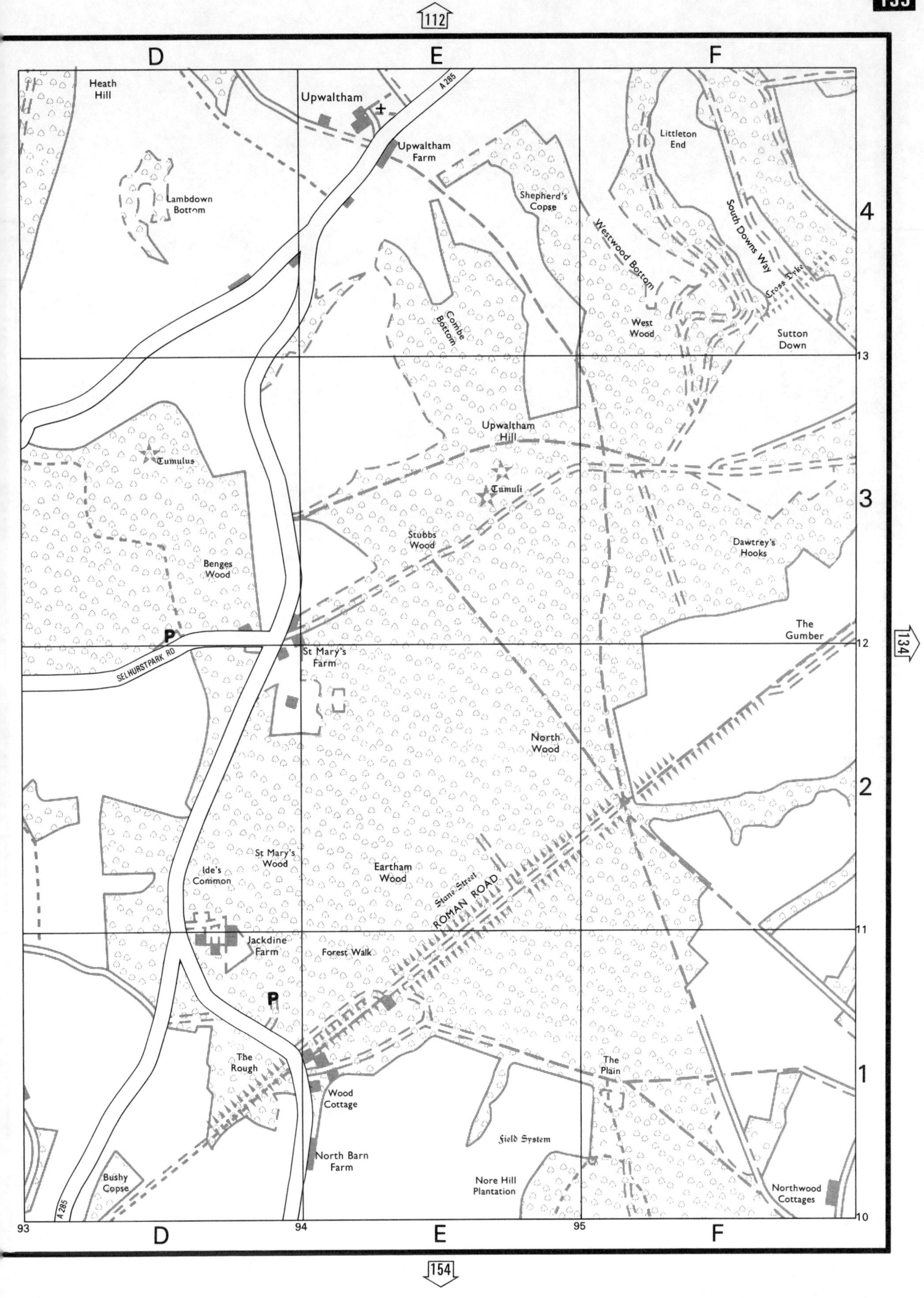
112
D
E
F
Heath Hill
Upwaltham
A 285
Upwaltham Farm
Lambdown Bottom
Shepherd's Copse
Littleton End
Westwood Bottom
South Downs Way
Cross Dyke
West Wood
Sutton Down
Combe Bottom
4
13
Upwaltham Hill
Tumulus
Tumuli
3
Stubbs Wood
Benges Wood
Dawtrey's Hooks
The Gumber
P
SELHURSTPARK RD
St Mary's Farm
12
134
North Wood
2
St Mary's Wood
Ide's Common
Eartham Wood
Stane Street
ROMAN ROAD
11
Jackdine Farm
Forest Walk
P
The Rough
The Plain
1
Wood Cottage
Field System
North Barn Farm
Bushy Copse
Nore Hill Plantation
Northwood Cottages
A 285
10
93
94
95
D
E
F
154

113

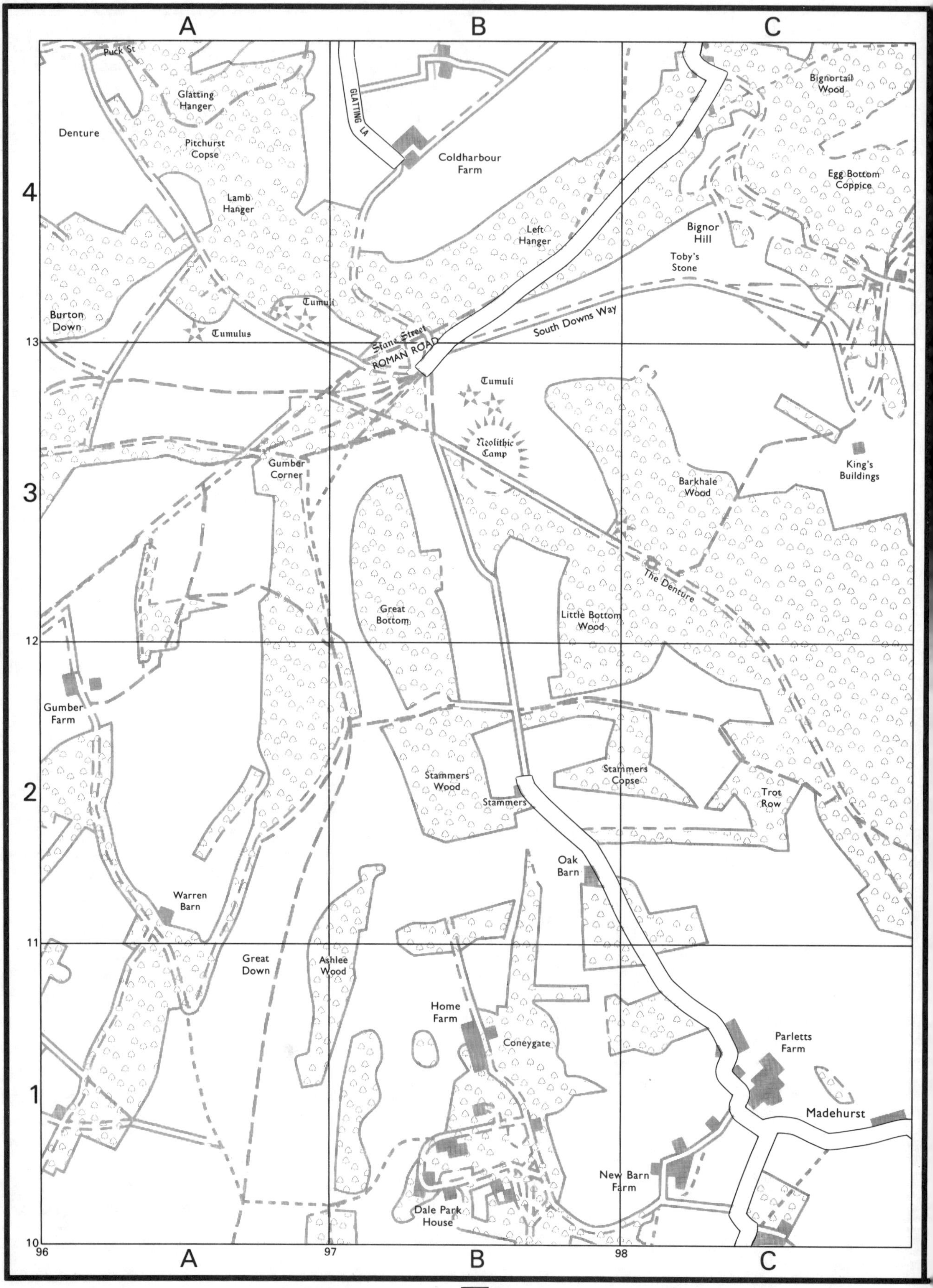
A
B
C
Puck St
Glatting Hanger
Denture
Pitchurst Copse
Lamb Hanger
GLATTING LA
Coldharbour Farm
Left Hanger
Bignortail Wood
Egg Bottom Coppice
Bignor Hill
Toby's Stone
Burton Down
Cumuli
Cumulus
Stane Street
ROMAN ROAD
South Downs Way
Neolithic Camp
Gumber Corner
Barkhale Wood
King's Buildings
The Denture
Great Bottom
Little Bottom Wood
Gumber Farm
Stammers Wood
Stammers
Stammers Copse
Trot Row
Oak Barn
Warren Barn
Great Down
Ashlee Wood
Home Farm
Coneygate
Parletts Farm
Madehurst
New Barn Farm
Dale Park House
4
3
2
1
13
12
11
10
96
97
98

133

155

114

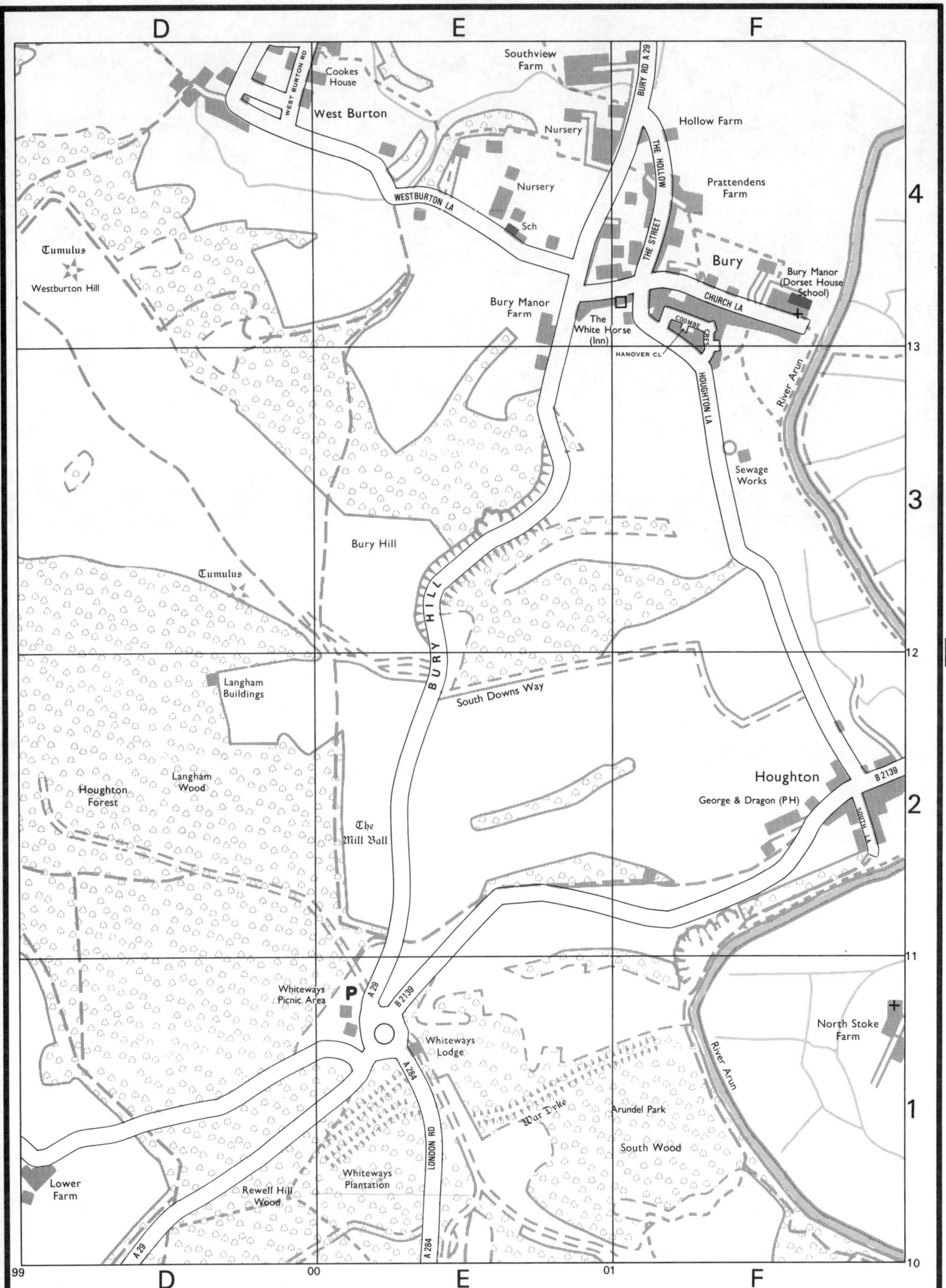
D
E
F
Southview
Farm
Cookes
House
WEST BURTON RD
West Burton
BURY RD A 29
Hollow Farm
Nursery
THE HOLLOW
Nursery
Prattendens
Farm
WESTBURTON LA
Sch
THE STREET
Bury
Bury Manor
(Dorset House
School)
Tumulus
Westburton Hill
Bury Manor
Farm
CHURCH LA
The
White Horse
(Inn)
COOMBE CRES
HANOVER CL
HOUGHTON LA
River Arun
Sewage
Works
Bury Hill
Tumulus
BURY HILL
Langham
Buildings
South Downs Way
Houghton
B 2139
Langham
Wood
Houghton
Forest
George & Dragon (PH)
SOUTH LA
The
Mill Ball
Whiteways
Picnic Area
P
A 29
B 2139
North Stoke
Farm
Whiteways
Lodge
A 284
River Arun
War Dyke
Arundel Park
South Wood
LONDON RD
Whiteways
Plantation
Lower
Farm
Rewell Hill
Wood
A 29
A 284
4
3
2
1
13
12
11
10
99
00
01

136

156

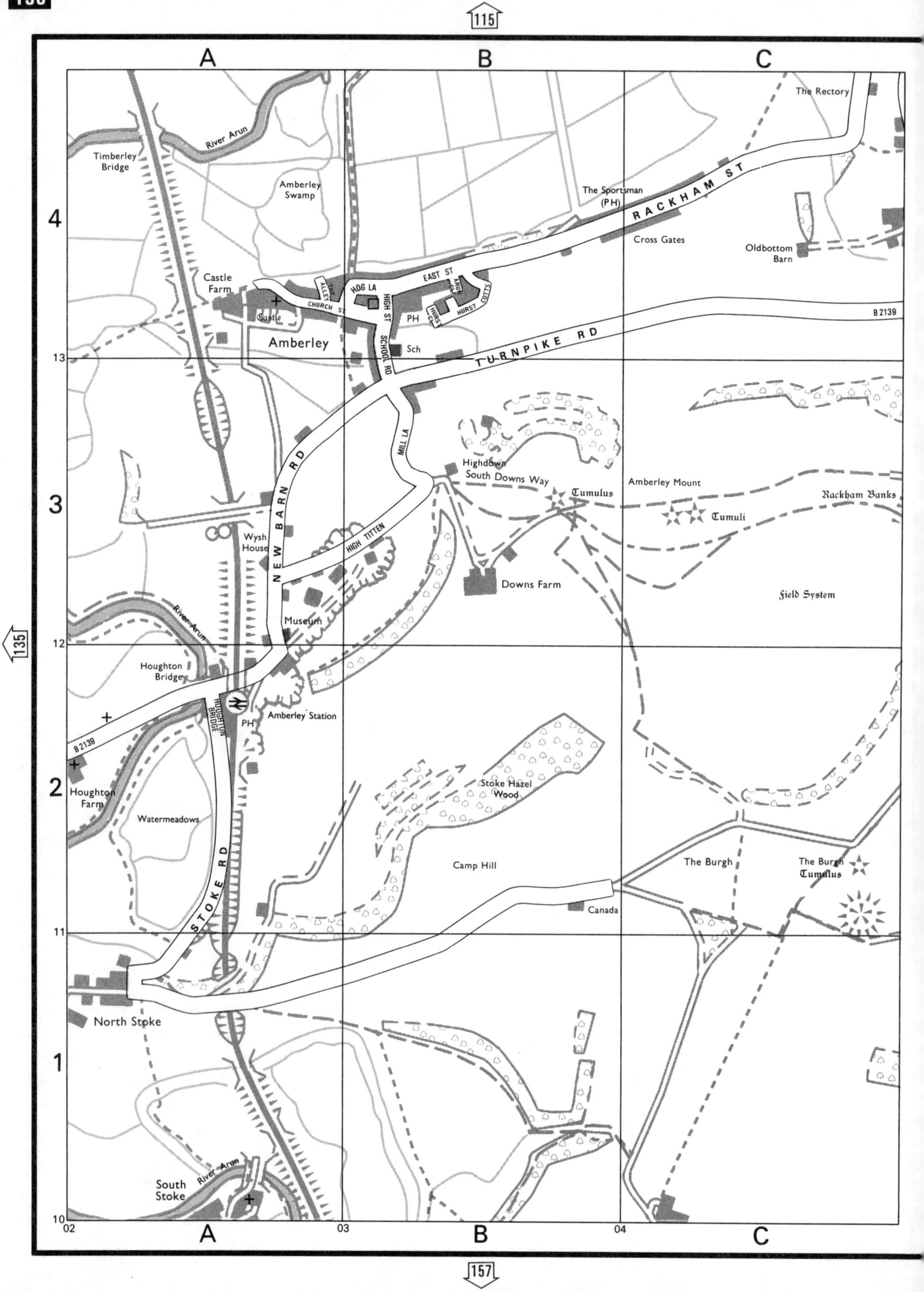
115
A
B
C
4
3
2
1
135
157
River Arun
Timberley Bridge
Amberley Swamp
The Rectory
The Sportsman (PH)
RACKHAM ST
Cross Gates
Oldbottom Barn
Castle Farm
Castle
Amberley
THE ALLEY
CHURCH ST
HOG LA
HIGH ST
EAST ST
HURST COTTS
PH
Sch
SCHOOL RD
TURNPIKE RD
B 2139
MILL LA
NEW BARN RD
HIGH TITTEN
Highdown
South Downs Way
Tumulus
Amberley Mount
Tumuli
Rackham Banks
Wysh House
Downs Farm
Field System
Museum
Houghton Bridge
HOUGHTON BRIDGE
Amberley Station
Houghton Farm
Watermeadows
Stoke Hazel Wood
Camp Hill
The Burgh
The Burgh Tumulus
Canada
STOKE RD
North Stoke
South Stoke
13
12
11
10
02
03
04

116

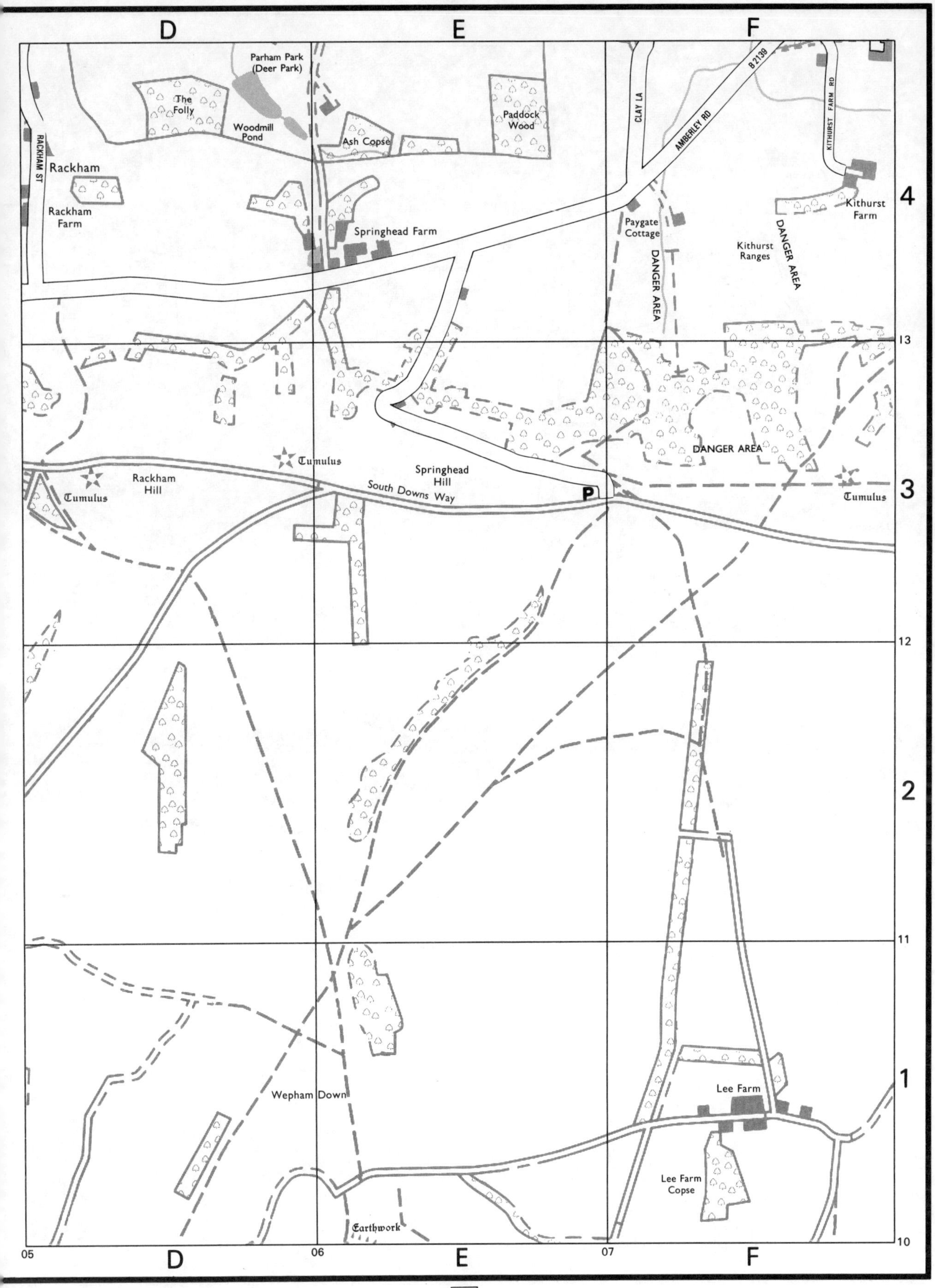
D
E
F
Parham Park
(Deer Park)
The
Folly
Woodmill
Pond
Ash Copse
Paddock
Wood
CLAY LA
AMBERLEY RD
B 2139
KITHURST FARM RD
RACKHAM ST
Rackham
Rackham
Farm
Springhead Farm
Paygate
Cottage
DANGER AREA
Kithurst
Ranges
DANGER AREA
Kithurst
Farm
4
13
DANGER AREA
Tumulus
Springhead
Hill
Rackham
Hill
Tumulus
South Downs Way
P
Tumulus
3
12
2
11
1
Wepham Down
Lee Farm
Lee Farm
Copse
Earthwork
10
05
06
07
D
E
F

138

158

117

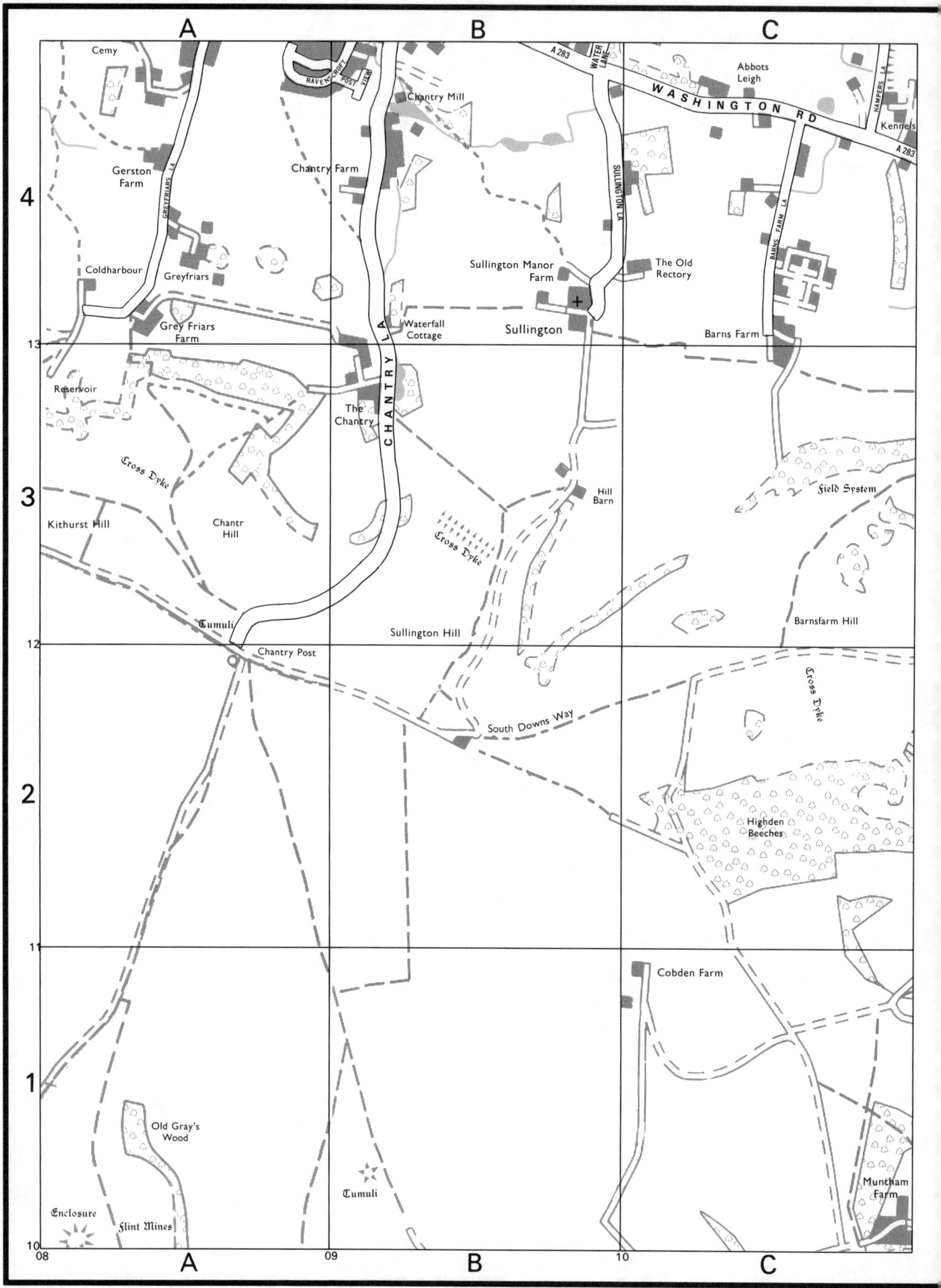
A
B
C
4
3
2
1
13
12
11
10
08
09
10
Cemy
Gerston Farm
GREYFRIARS LA
Coldharbour
Greyfriars
Grey Friars Farm
Reservoir
RAVENSCROFT
POST VIEW
Chantry Mill
Chantry Farm
CHANTRY LA
Waterfall Cottage
The Chantry
A 283
WATER LANE
SULLINGTON LA
Sullington Manor Farm
Sullington
Abbots Leigh
WASHINGTON RD
HAMPERS LA
Kennels
A 283
BARNS FARM LA
The Old Rectory
Barns Farm
Cross Dyke
Kithurst Hill
Chantr Hill
Cross Dyke
Hill Barn
Field System
Barnsfarm Hill
Tumuli
Sullington Hill
Chantry Post
South Downs Way
Cross Dyke
Highden Beeches
Cobden Farm
Old Gray's Wood
Tumuli
Enclosure
Flint Mines
Muntham Farm

137

159

118

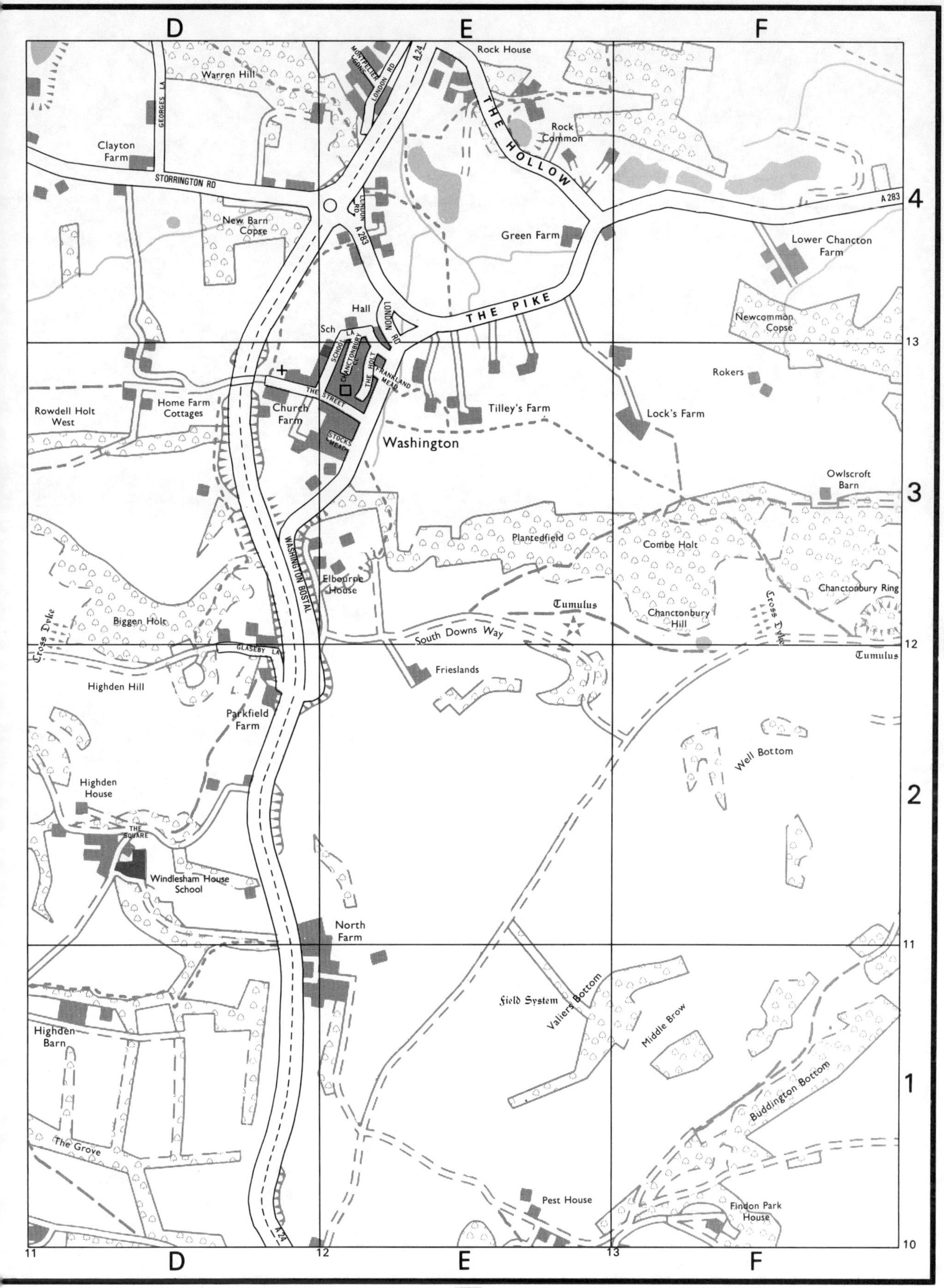
D
E
F
Rock House
Warren Hill
GEORGES LA
MONTPELIER GDNS
LONDON RD
A24
THE HOLLOW
Rock Common
Clayton Farm
STORRINGTON RD
A 283
4
New Barn Copse
LONDON RD
A 283
Green Farm
Lower Chancton Farm
THE PIKE
Hall
LONDON RD
Newcommon Copse
Sch
SCHOOL LA
CHANCTONBURY CL
THE HOLT
FRANKLAND MEAD
13
Rokers
THE STREET
Home Farm Cottages
Rowdell Holt West
Church Farm
Tilley's Farm
Lock's Farm
STOCKS MEAD
Washington
Owlscroft Barn
3
Plantedfield
Combe Holt
WASHINGTON BOSTAL
Elbourne House
Chanctonbury Ring
Tumulus
Cross Dyke
Biggen Holt
Chanctonbury Hill
Cross Dyke
South Downs Way
12
Tumulus
GLASEBY LA
Frieslands
Highden Hill
Parkfield Farm
Well Bottom
Highden House
2
THE SQUARE
Windlesham House School
North Farm
11
Field System
Valiers Bottom
Middle Brow
Highden Barn
1
Buddington Bottom
The Grove
Pest House
Findon Park House
A24
10
11
12
13
D
E
F

140

160

119

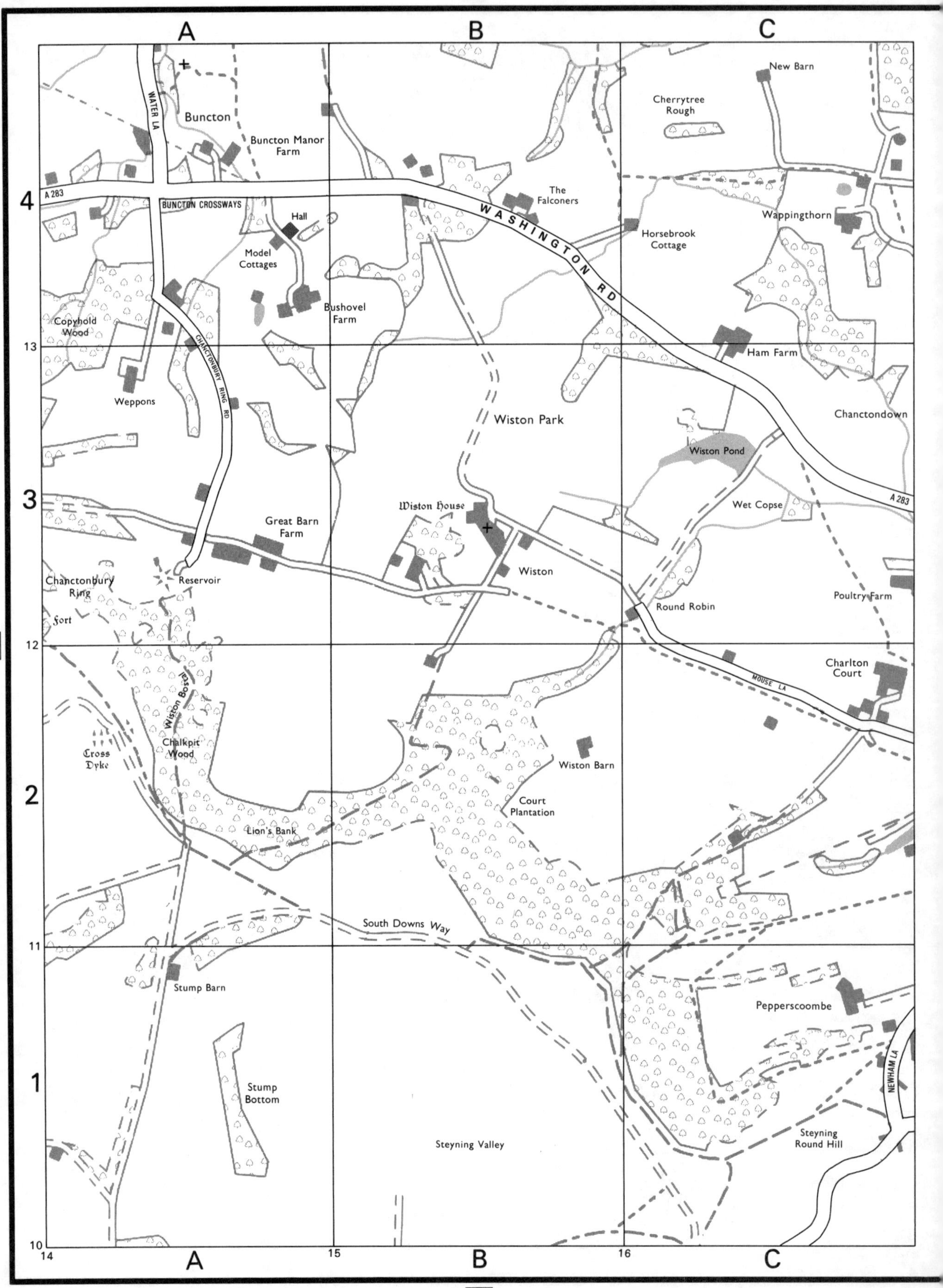
A
B
C
Buncton
Bungton Manor Farm
WATER LA
New Barn
Cherrytree Rough
A 283
BUNCTON CROSSWAYS
Hall
The Falconers
WASHINGTON RD
Horsebrook Cottage
Wappingthorn
Model Cottages
Bushovel Farm
Copyhold Wood
CHANCTONBURY RING RD
Ham Farm
Weppons
Wiston Park
Chanctondown
Wiston Pond
Wiston House
Great Barn Farm
Wet Copse
A 283
Wiston
Chanctonbury Ring
Reservoir
Fort
Round Robin
Poultry Farm
MOUSE LA
Charlton Court
Wiston Bostal
Chalkpit Wood
Cross Dyke
Wiston Barn
Court Plantation
Lion's Bank
South Downs Way
Stump Barn
Pepperscoombe
NEWHAM LA
Stump Bottom
Steyning Valley
Steyning Round Hill
4
3
2
1
13
12
11
10
14
15
16

139

161

120

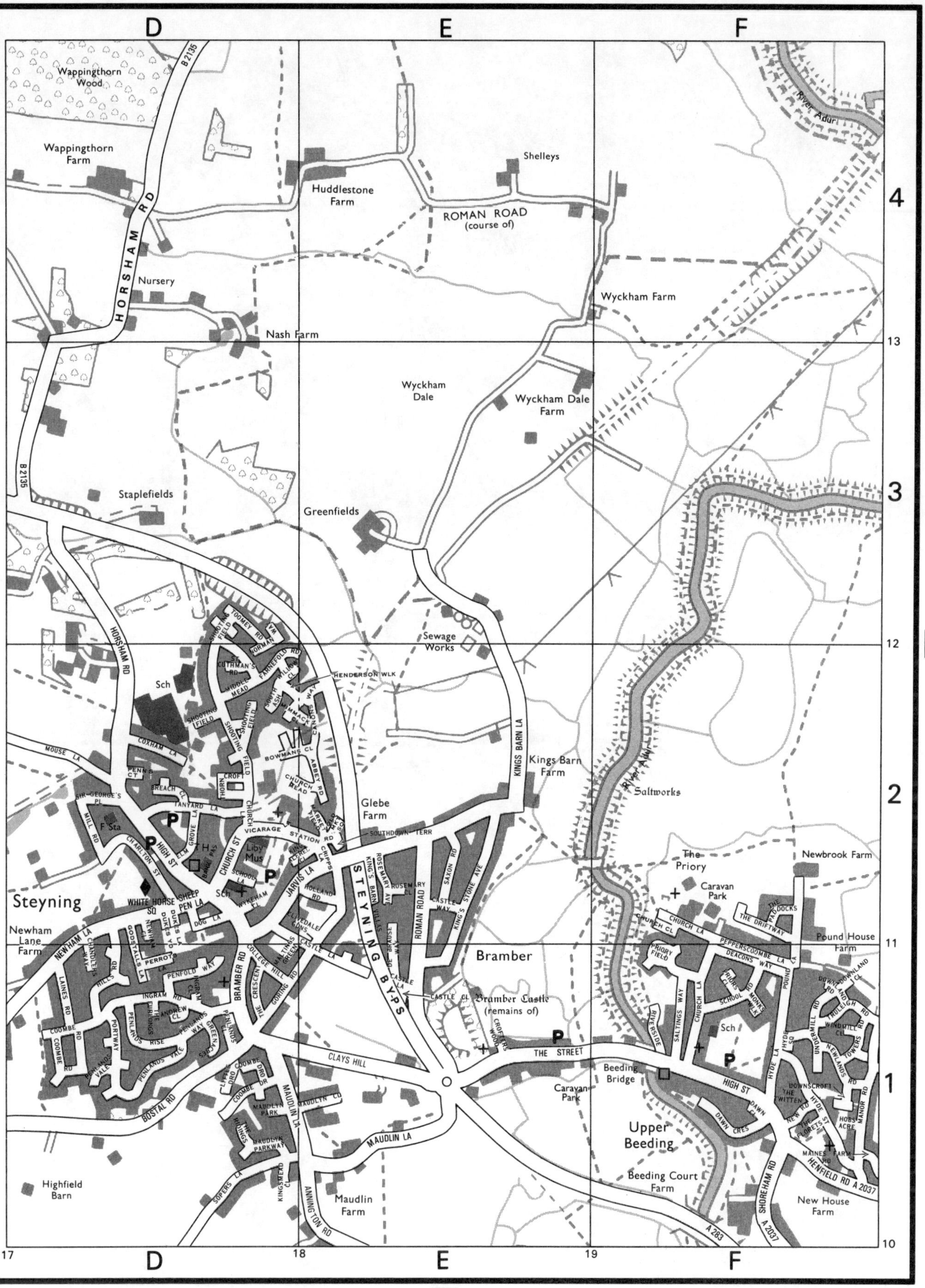
D
E
F
Wappingthorn Wood
Wappingthorn Farm
B2135
Shelleys
Huddlestone Farm
ROMAN ROAD
(course of)
HORSHAM RD
River Adur
Nursery
Nash Farm
Wyckham Farm
Wyckham Dale
Wyckham Dale Farm
Staplefields
Greenfields
Sewage Works
Sch
HORSHAM RD
HENDERSON WLK
KINGS BARN LA
MOUSE LA
COXHAM LA
BOWMANS CL
Kings Barn Farm
River Adur
Saltworks
Glebe Farm
SOUTHDOWN TERR
VICARAGE
STATION RD
TANYARD LA
MILL RD
F Sta
HIGH ST
CHURCH ST
Liby Mus
JARVIS LA
STEYNING BY-PS
ROMAN ROAD
SAXON RD
KING'S STONE AVE
The Priory
Newbrook Farm
Caravan Park
Steyning
WHITE HORSE SQ
SHEEP PEN LA
DOG LA
Newham Lane Farm
NEWHAM LA
CHURCH CL
CHURCH LA
THE DRIFTWAY
PEPPERSCOMBE LA
DEACONS WAY
Pound House Farm
Bramber
BRAMBER RD
CASTLE LA
CASTLE CL
Bramber Castle
(remains of)
CROFTERS WOOD
THE STREET
LAINES RD
COOMBE RD
PENLANDS RISE
PENLANDS VALE
PENLANDS WAY
CLAYS HILL
Beeding Bridge
Caravan Park
HIGH ST
SALTINGS WAY
RIVERSIDE
HYDE LA
Sch
BOSTAL RD
MAUDLIN LA
MAUDLIN LA
Upper Beeding
DAWN CRES
HENFIELD RD A 2037
Highfield Barn
SOPERS LA
ANNINGTON RD
Maudlin Farm
Beeding Court Farm
SHOREHAM RD
A 2037
A 283
New House Farm
4
3
2
1
13
12
11
10
17
18
19

142

162

121

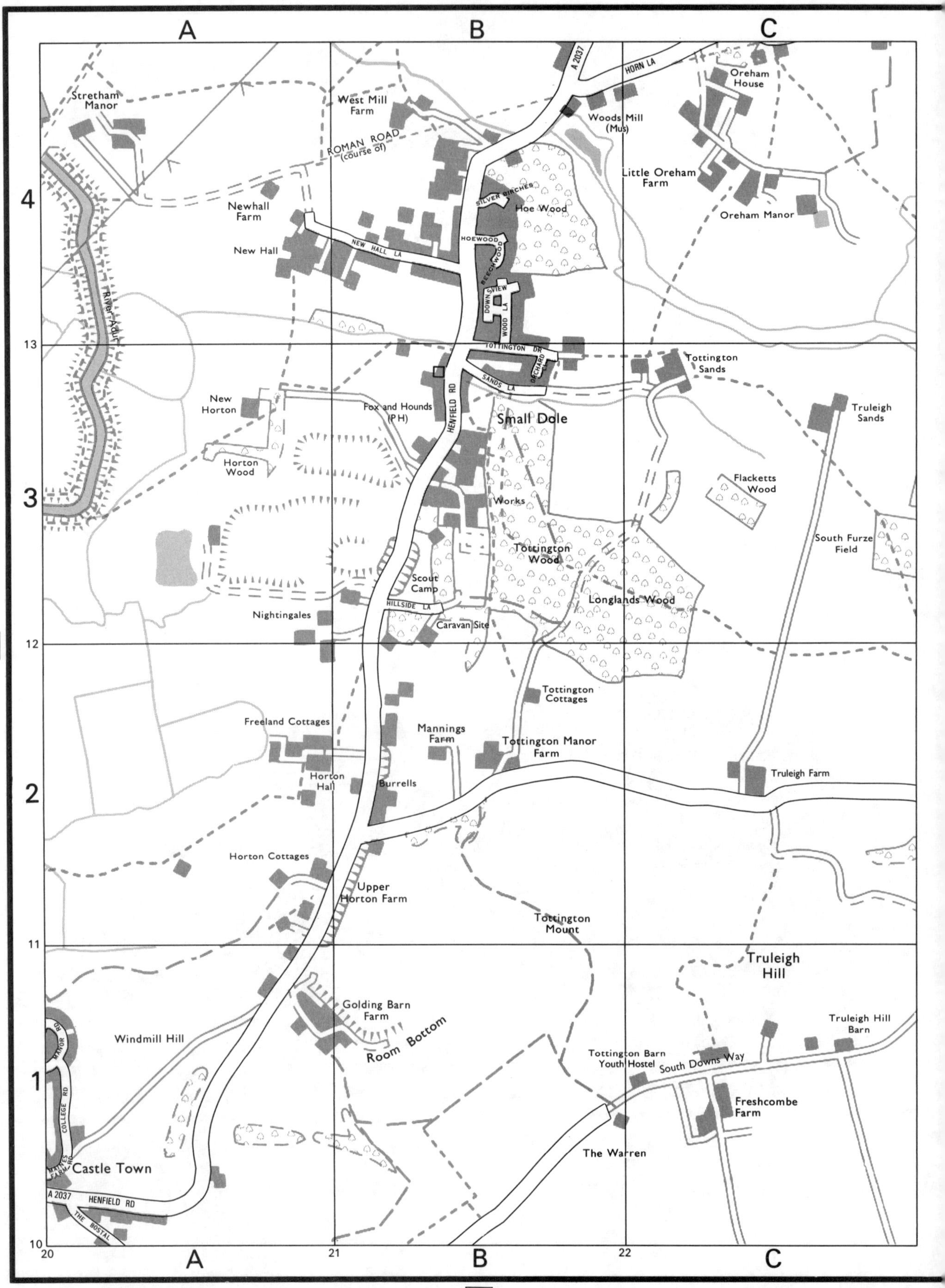

A
B
C
Stretham Manor
West Mill Farm
A 2037
HORN LA
Oreham House
Woods Mill (Mus)
ROMAN ROAD (course of)
Little Oreham Farm
Oreham Manor
SILVER BIRCHES
Hoe Wood
Newhall Farm
New Hall
NEW HALL LA
HOEWOOD
BEECHWOOD
DOWNSVIEW
WOOD LA
River Adur
TOTTINGTON DR
ORCHARD
SANDS LA
Tottington Sands
New Horton
Fox and Hounds (PH)
HENFIELD RD
Small Dole
Truleigh Sands
Horton Wood
Flacketts Wood
Works
South Furze Field
Tottington Wood
Scout Camp
HILLSIDE LA
Longlands Wood
Nightingales
Caravan Site
Tottington Cottages
Freeland Cottages
Mannings Farm
Tottington Manor Farm
Horton Hall
Burrells
Truleigh Farm
Horton Cottages
Upper Horton Farm
Tottington Mount
Truleigh Hill
Golding Barn Farm
Room Bottom
Windmill Hill
MANOR RD
COLLEGE RD
Tottington Barn Youth Hostel
South Downs Way
Truleigh Hill Barn
Freshcombe Farm
Castle Town
The Warren
A 2037
HENFIELD RD
THE BOSTAL
4
3
2
1
13
12
11
10
20
21
22

141

122

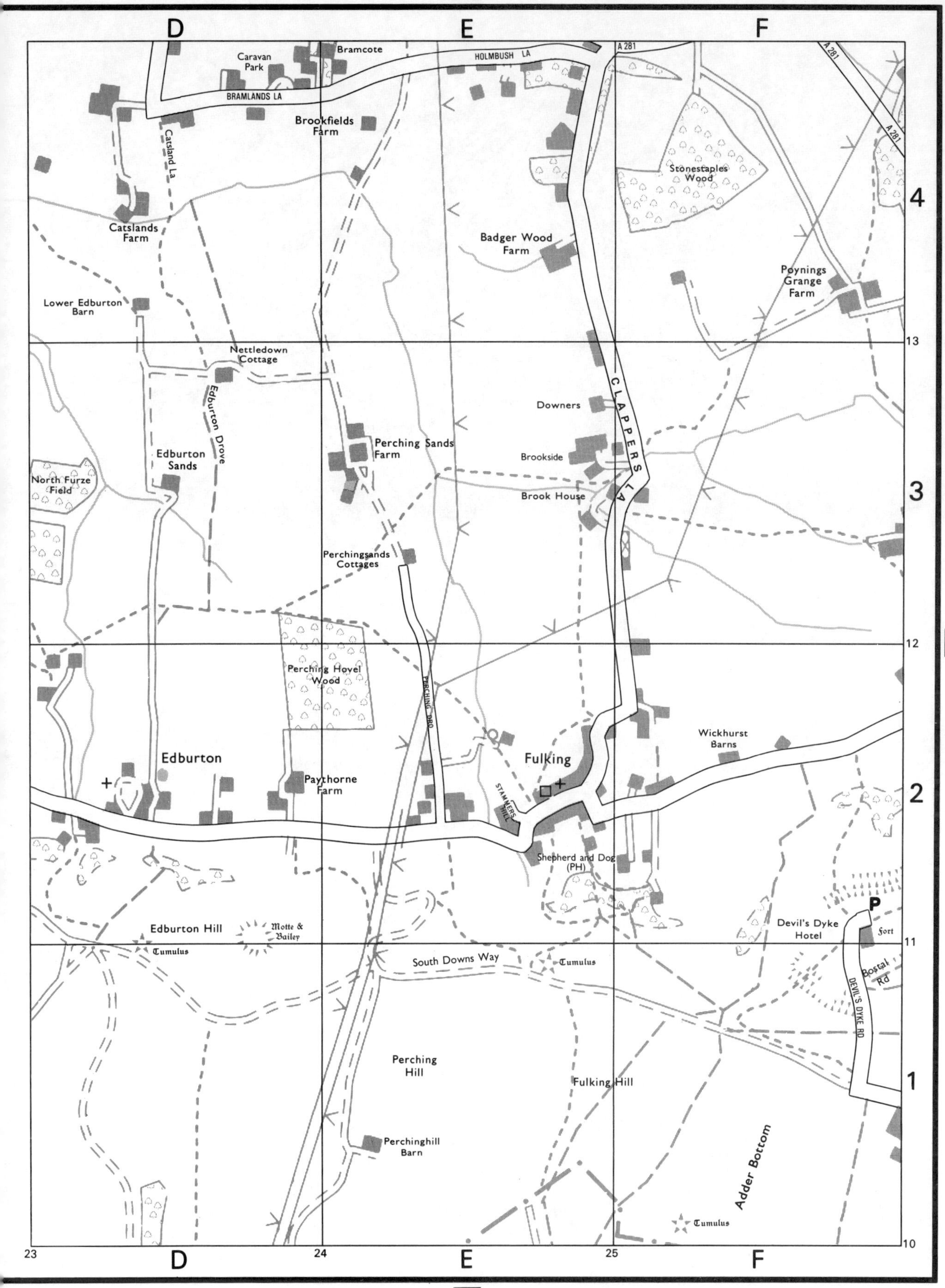
D
E
F
Caravan Park
Bramcote
HOLMBUSH LA
A 281
BRAMLANDS LA
Brookfields Farm
Catsland La
Stonestaples Wood
Catslands Farm
Badger Wood Farm
Poynings Grange Farm
Lower Edburton Barn
Nettledown Cottage
Edburton Drove
Downers
CLAPPERS LA
Brookside
Perching Sands Farm
Edburton Sands
North Furze Field
Brook House
Perchingsands Cottages
Perching Hovel Wood
PERCHING DRO
Wickhurst Barns
Edburton
Fulking
Paythorne Farm
STAMMERS HILL
Shepherd and Dog (PH)
Devil's Dyke Hotel
Fort
Edburton Hill
Motte & Bailey
Tumulus
South Downs Way
Tumulus
Bostal Rd
DEVIL'S DYKE RD
Perching Hill
Fulking Hill
Perchinghill Barn
Adder Bottom
Tumulus
4
3
2
1
13
12
11
10
23
24
25

144

164

123

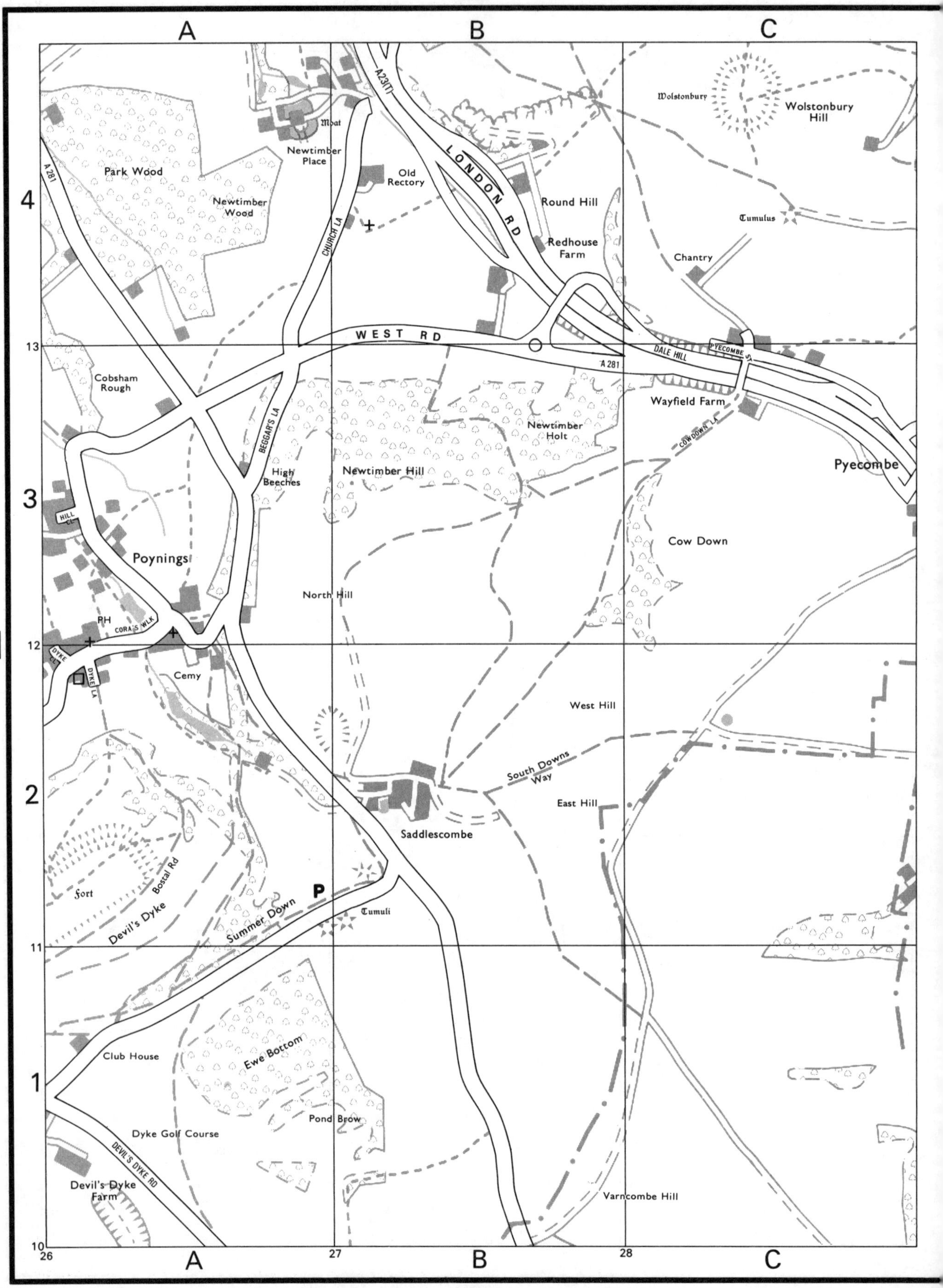
A
B
C
4
3
2
1
13
12
11
10
26
27
28
Park Wood
Newtimber Wood
Moat
Newtimber Place
Old Rectory
CHURCH LA
A 281
A23(T)
LONDON RD
Round Hill
Redhouse Farm
Wolstonbury
Wolstonbury Hill
Cumulus
Chantry
WEST RD
A 281
DALE HILL
PYECOMBE ST
Wayfield Farm
COWDOWN LA
Pyecombe
Cobsham Rough
BEGGAR'S LA
High Beeches
Newtimber Hill
Newtimber Holt
HILL CL
Poynings
Cow Down
North Hill
PH
CORA'S WLK
DYKE CL
DYKE LA
Cemy
West Hill
South Downs Way
East Hill
Saddlescombe
Fort
Bostal Rd
Devil's Dyke
P
Summer Down
Tumuli
Club House
Ewe Bottom
Pond Brow
Dyke Golf Course
DEVIL'S DYKE RD
Devil's Dyke Farm
Varncombe Hill

143

165

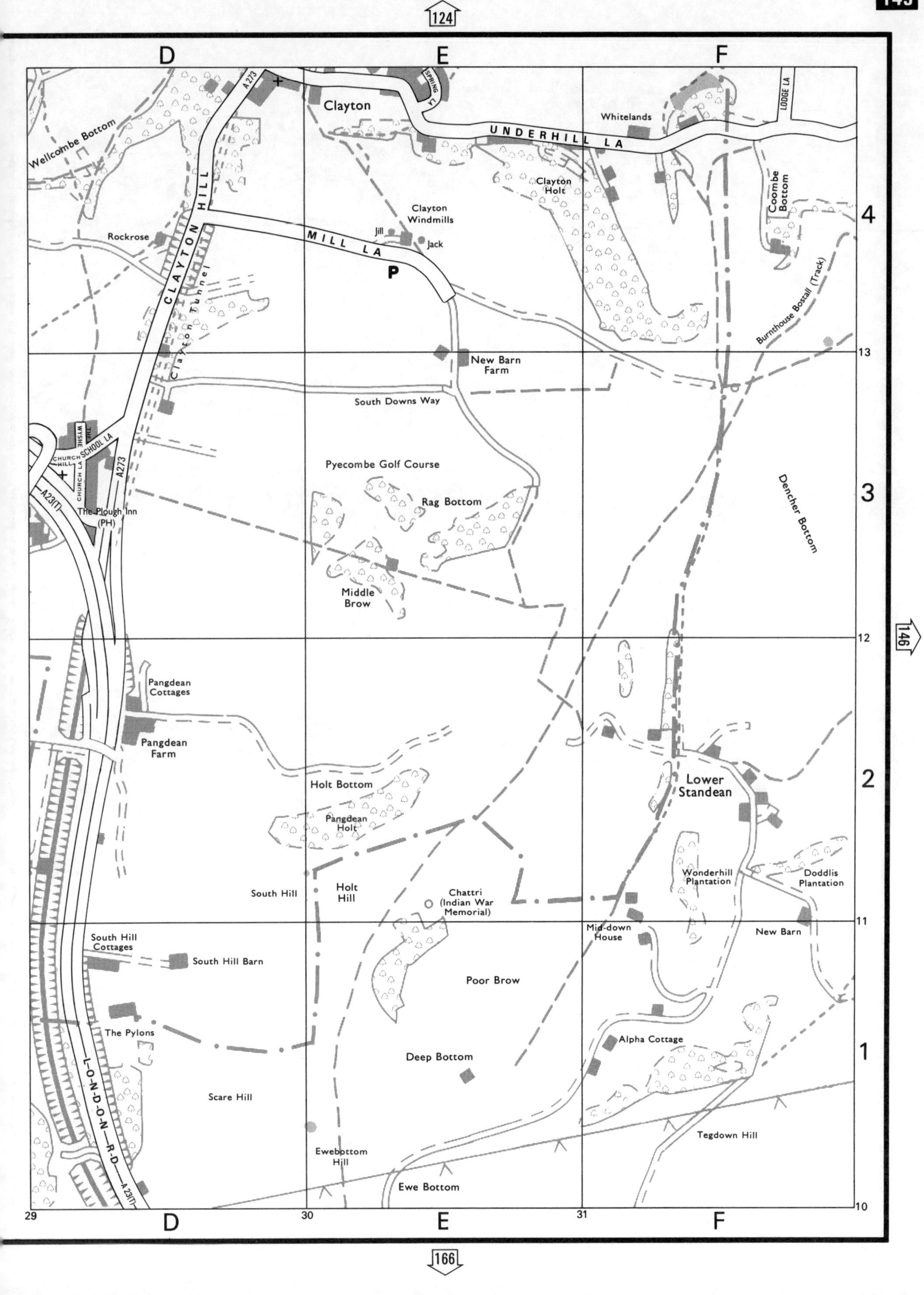
124
D
E
F
Clayton
SPRING LA
LODGE LA
Whitelands
UNDERHILL LA
A273
Wellcombe Bottom
Clayton Holt
Coombe Bottom
Clayton Windmills
Jill
Jack
MILL LA
Rockrose
CLAYTON HILL
P
Clayton Tunnel
Burnthouse Bostall (Track)
New Barn Farm
South Downs Way
THE WYSHE
SCHOOL LA
CHURCH HILL
CHURCH LA
A273
Pyecombe Golf Course
A23(T)
The Plough Inn (PH)
Rag Bottom
Dencher Bottom
Middle Brow
Pangdean Cottages
Pangdean Farm
Holt Bottom
Lower Standean
Pangdean Holt
South Hill
Holt Hill
Wonderhill Plantation
Doddlis Plantation
Chattri (Indian War Memorial)
South Hill Cottages
Mid-down House
New Barn
South Hill Barn
Poor Brow
The Pylons
Alpha Cottage
Deep Bottom
LONDON RD
Scare Hill
Tegdown Hill
Ewebottom Hill
Ewe Bottom
A23(T)
4
3
2
1
13
12
11
10
29
30
31
146
166

125

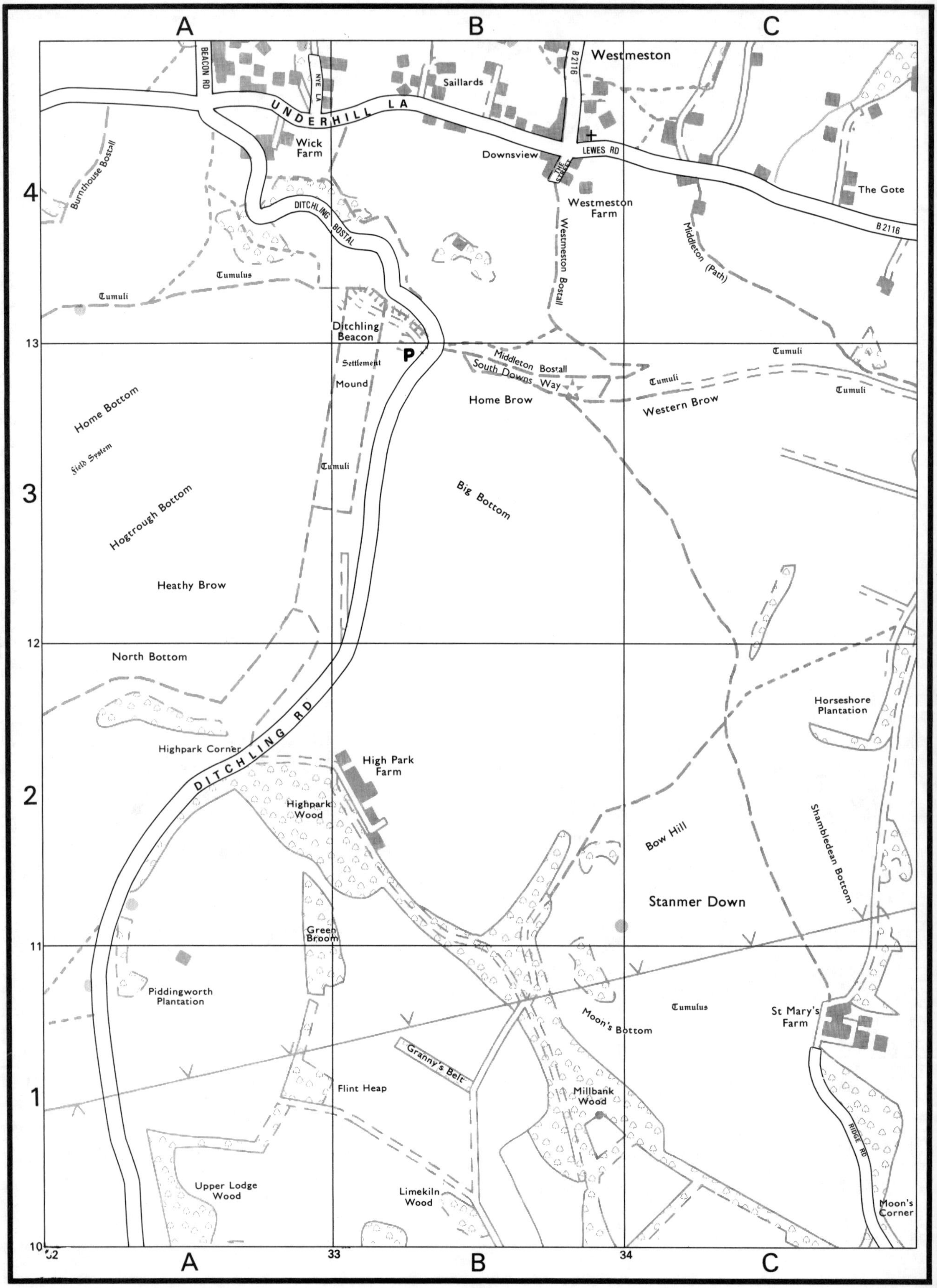
A
B
C
Westmeston
Saillards
BEACON RD
NYE LA
B2116
UNDERHILL LA
Wick Farm
Downsview
LEWES RD
THE STREET
Westmeston Farm
The Gote
B 2116
Burnthouse Bostall
DITCHLING BOSTAL
Westmeston Bostall
Middleton (Path)
Tumulus
Tumuli
Ditchling Beacon
P
Settlement
Mound
Middleton Bostall
South Downs Way
Home Brow
Western Brow
Home Bottom
Field System
Big Bottom
Hogtrough Bottom
Heathy Brow
North Bottom
Horseshore Plantation
Highpark Corner
DITCHLING RD
High Park Farm
Highpark Wood
Bow Hill
Shambledean Bottom
Stanmer Down
Green Broom
Piddingworth Plantation
Moon's Bottom
St Mary's Farm
Granny's Belt
Flint Heap
Millbank Wood
RIDGE RD
Upper Lodge Wood
Limekiln Wood
Moon's Corner
4
3
2
1
13
12
11
10
32
33
34

145

167

126

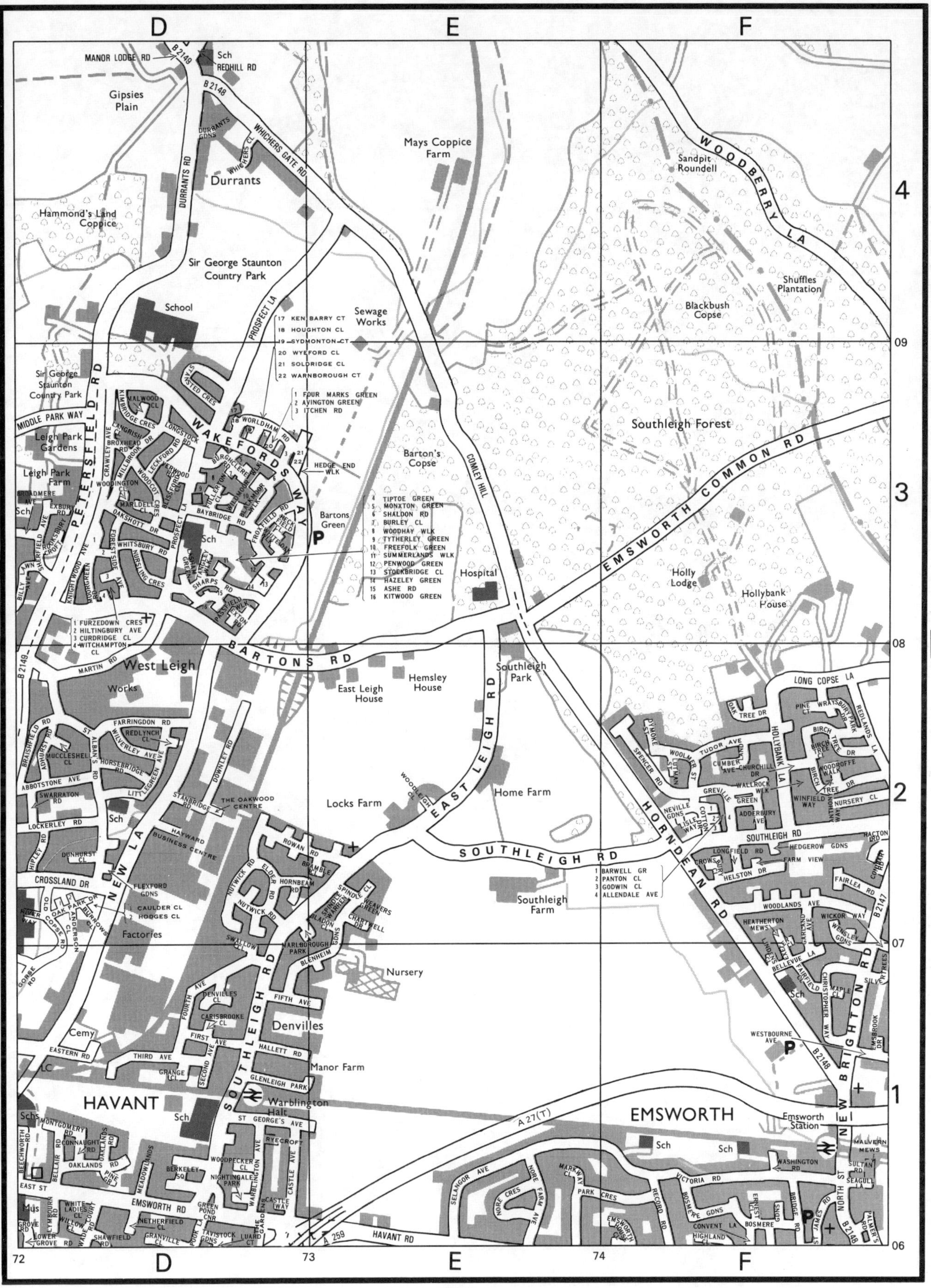
D
E
F
4
3
2
1
09
08
07
06
72
73
74
MANOR LODGE RD
B 2149
Sch
REDHILL RD
B 2148
Gipsies Plain
DURRANTS GDNS
WHICHERS CL
WHICHERS GATE RD
DURRANTS RD
Durrants
Mays Coppice Farm
WOODBERRY LA
Sandpit Roundell
Hammond's Land Coppice
Sir George Staunton Country Park
School
PROSPECT LA
17 KEN BARRY CT
18 HOUGHTON CL
19 SYDMONTON CT
20 WYEFORD CL
21 SOLDRIDGE CL
22 WARNBOROUGH CT
Sewage Works
Shuffles Plantation
Blackbush Copse
1 FOUR MARKS GREEN
2 AVINGTON GREEN
3 ITCHEN RD
Sir George Staunton Country Park
MIDDLE PARK WAY
PETERSFIELD RD
MALWOOD CL
KIMBRIDGE CRES
LANGRISH
BROXHEAD RD
MILLBROOK DR
CRAWLEY AVE
LONGSTOCK RD
LECKFORD RD
WORLDHAM RD
STAUNTON CRES
WAKEFORDS WAY
Leigh Park Gardens
Leigh Park Farm
HEDGE END WLK
Barton's Copse
COMLEY HILL
Southleigh Forest
EMSWORTH COMMON RD
BROADMERE AVE
EXBURY RD
WOODINGTON CL
MARLDELL CL
OAKSHOTT DR
BAYBRIDGE RD
FULLERTON
BURGHCLERE RD
WHITSBURY RD
FORESTSIDE AVE
NURSLING CRES
Sch
Barton's Green
P
4 TIPTOE GREEN
5 MONXTON GREEN
6 SHALDON RD
7 BURLEY CL
8 WOODHAY WLK
9 TYTHERLEY GREEN
10 FREEFOLK GREEN
11 SUMMERLANDS WLK
12 PENWOOD GREEN
13 STOCKBRIDGE CL
14 HAZELEY GREEN
15 ASHE RD
16 KITWOOD GREEN
Hospital
Holly Lodge
Hollybank House
KNIGHTWOOD AVE
WOODGREEN AVE
BILLY LAWN AVE
SHARPS RD
PASSFIELD WLK
1 FURZEDOWN CRES
2 HILTINGBURY AVE
3 CURDRIDGE CL
4 WITCHAMPTON CL
BARTONS RD
MARTIN RD
West Leigh
Works
B 2149
Southleigh Park
Hemsley House
East Leigh House
LONG COPSE LA
EAST LEIGH RD
OAK TREE DR
PINE CT
WRAYSBURY PARK DR
REDLANDS LA
FARRINGDON RD
REDLYNCH CL
WILVERLEY AVE
HORSEBRIDGE RD
BRAISHFIELD RD
ADHURST RD
HUCCLESHELL CL
ST ALBAN'S RD
ABBOTSTONE AVE
LITTLEGREEN AVE
DOWNLEY RD
DYMOKE ST
SPENCER RD
WOOLMER ST
TUDOR AVE
CUMBER AVE
CHURCHILL DR
HOLLYBANK LA
BIRCH TREE DR
WOODROFFE WALK
LUTMAN ST
SWARRATON RD
LOCKERLEY RD
Sch
STANBRIDGE RD
THE OAKWOOD CENTRE
Locks Farm
WOODLEIGH CL
Home Farm
HORNDEAN RD
NEVILLE GDNS
GREVILLE GREEN
WALLROCK WLK
WINFIELD WAY
NURSERY CL
ADDERBURY AVE
SOUTHLEIGH RD
RACTON RD
HAYWARD BUSINESS CENTRE
ROWAN RD
BRAMBLE
HEDGEROW GDNS
LONGFIELD RD
FARM VIEW
DUNHURST CL
HIPLEY RD
SOUTHLEIGH RD
CROWSBURY CL
HELSTON DR
CROSSLAND DR
NEW LA
FLEXFORD GDNS
NUTWICK RD
ELDER RD
HORNBEAM RD
SPINDLE CL
WEAVERS GREEN
1 BARWELL GR
2 PANTON CL
3 GODWIN CL
4 ALLENDALE AVE
FAIRLEA RD
OAK PARK DR
BURROWS CL
1 CAULDER CL
2 HODGES CL
SPINDLE WARREN
BLADON
CHARTWELL DR
Southleigh Farm
WOODLANDS AVE
WICKOR WAY
B 2147
HEATHERTON MEWS
WENSLEY GDNS
GORSE RD
Factories
SWALLOW
MARLBOROUGH PARK
BLENHEIM GDNS
Nursery
BELLEVUE LA
FAIRFIELD
CHRISTOPHER WAY
MAPLE CL
BRIGHTON RD
Sch
FOURTH AVE
DENVILLES CL
SOUTHLEIGH RD
FIFTH AVE
CARISBROOKE CL
Denvilles
Cemy
FIRST AVE
HALLETT RD
WESTBOURNE AVE
P
B 2148
EASTERN RD
THIRD AVE
SECOND AVE
Manor Farm
LC
GRANGE CL
GLENLEIGH PARK
HAVANT
Sch
Warblington Halt
A 27(T)
EMSWORTH
Emsworth Station
Schs
MONTGOMERY RD
CONNAUGHT RD
OAKLANDS
ST GEORGE'S AVE
RYECROFT
Sch
Sch
MALVERN MEWS
BEECHWORTH RD
BELLAIR RD
OAKLANDS RD
PINE GR
MEADOWLANDS
BERKELEY SQ
WOODPECKER CL
NIGHTINGALE PARK
WARBLINGTON AVE
CASTLE AVE
WASHINGTON RD
SULTAN RD
SEAGULL LA
EAST ST
SELANGOR AVE
NORE CRES
NORE FARM AVE
MARKWAY CL
PARK CRES
VICTORIA RD
RECORD RD
BOSMERE GDNS
ERNEST CL
BRIDGE RD
NORTH ST
Mus
WHITE LADIES CL
EMSWORTH RD
NETHERFIELD CL
GREEN POND CNR
CASTLE WAY
EMSWORTH HOUSE CL
CONVENT LA
BOSMERE
P
B 2148
PALMER'S RD
GROVE RD
LOWER GROVE RD
WILLOW CL
SHAWFIELD RD
GRANVILLE CL
TAVISTOCK GDNS
LUARD CT
THE GARDENS
A 259
HAVANT RD
HIGHLAND RD
ST JAMES RD

148

168

127

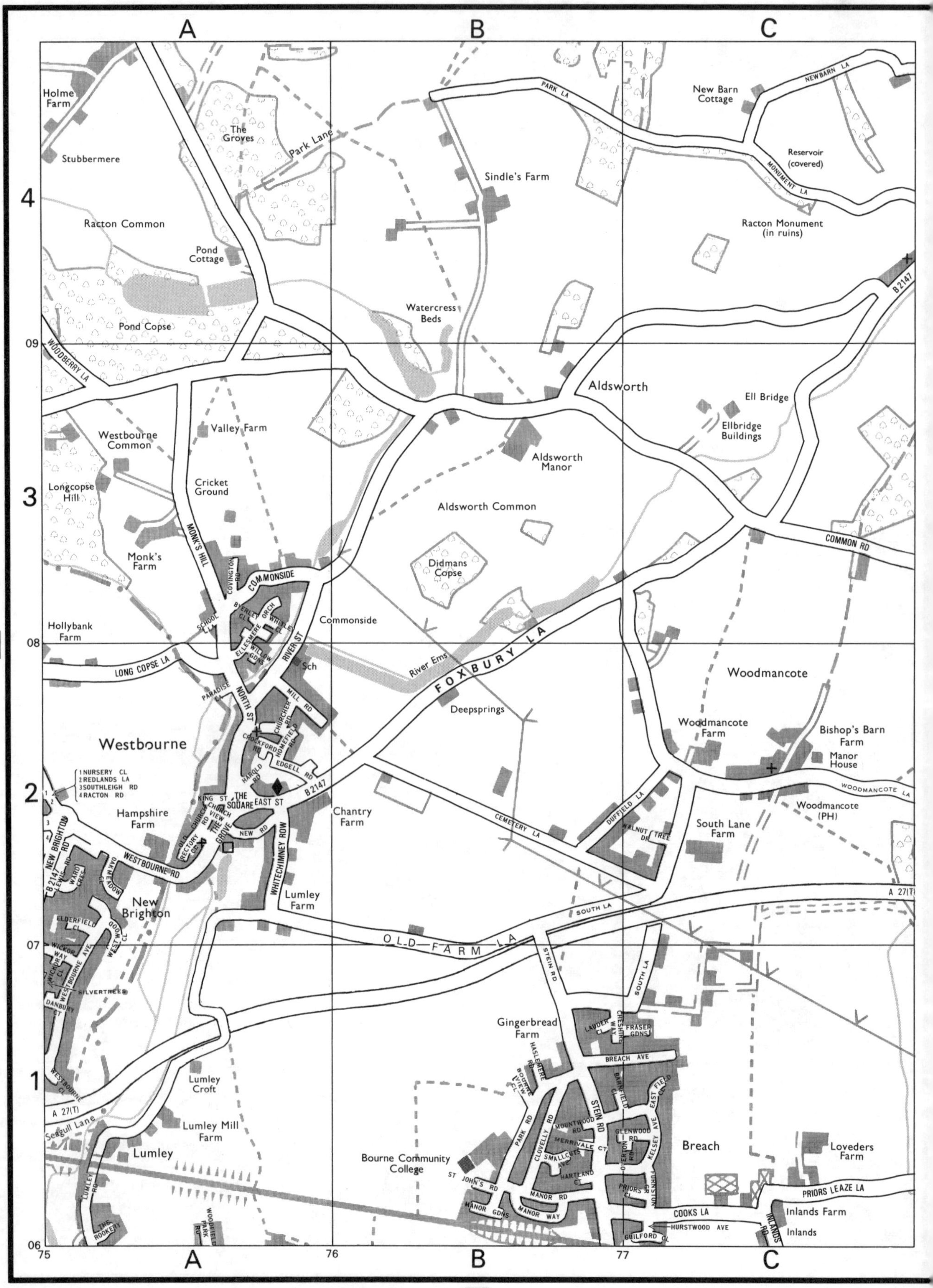
A
B
C
4
3
2
1
09
08
07
06
75
76
77
Holme Farm
Stubbermere
The Groves
Park Lane
Park La
New Barn Cottage
Newbarn La
Reservoir (covered)
Monument La
Sindle's Farm
Racton Common
Racton Monument (in ruins)
Pond Cottage
Pond Copse
Watercress Beds
B 2147
Woodberry La
Aldsworth
Ell Bridge
Ellbridge Buildings
Westbourne Common
Valley Farm
Aldsworth Manor
Longcopse Hill
Cricket Ground
Aldsworth Common
Common Rd
Monk's Hill
Monk's Farm
Didmans Copse
Covington Rd
Commonside
Hollybank Farm
School La
Byerley Cl
Orchard
Whitley Cl
Ellesmere
Willow Gdns
River St
Sch
River Ems
Foxbury La
Long Copse La
Paradise La
North St
Mill Rd
Woodmancote
Deepsprings
Churcher Rd
Homefield Rd
Crockford Rd
Woodmancote Farm
Bishop's Barn Farm
Manor House
Westbourne
Edgell Rd
Harold Rd
1 Nursery Cl
2 Redlands La
3 Southleigh Rd
4 Racton Rd
King St
The Square
East St
B 2147
Chantry Farm
Duffield La
Woodmancote La
Woodmancote (PH)
Hampshire Farm
Church View
Old Rectory Cl
The Grove
New Rd
Whitechimney Row
Cemetery La
Walnut Tree Dr
South Lane Farm
New Brighton Rd
Lewis Rd
Ward Cres
Oakmeadow Cl
Westbourne Rd
B 2147
New Brighton
Lumley Farm
A 27(T)
South La
Elderfield Cl
Godwin Cl
West Cl
Wickor Way
Meadow Cl
Westbourne Ave
Old Farm La
Stein Rd
South La
Silvertrees
Danbury Ct
Gingerbread Farm
Lauder Cl
Cheshire Way
Fraser Gdns
Breach Ave
Haslemere Rd
Bourne View Cl
Barnfield Cl
East Field Cl
Westbourne Cl
Lumley Croft
A 27(T)
Seagull Lane
Lumley Mill Farm
Park Rd
Clovelly Rd
Mountwood Rd
Merrivale Ct
Smallcuts Ave
Hartland Ct
Stein Rd
Glenwood Rd
Overton Rd
Kelsey Ave
Breach
Lumley
Bourne Community College
Loveders Farm
St John's Rd
Manor Rd
Priors Cl
Furniston Gr
Priors Leaze La
Manor Gdns
Manor Way
Cooks La
Hurstwood Ave
Guilford Cl
Inlands Rd
Inlands Farm
Inlands
Lumley Rd
The Rookery
Woodfield Park Rd

147

169

128

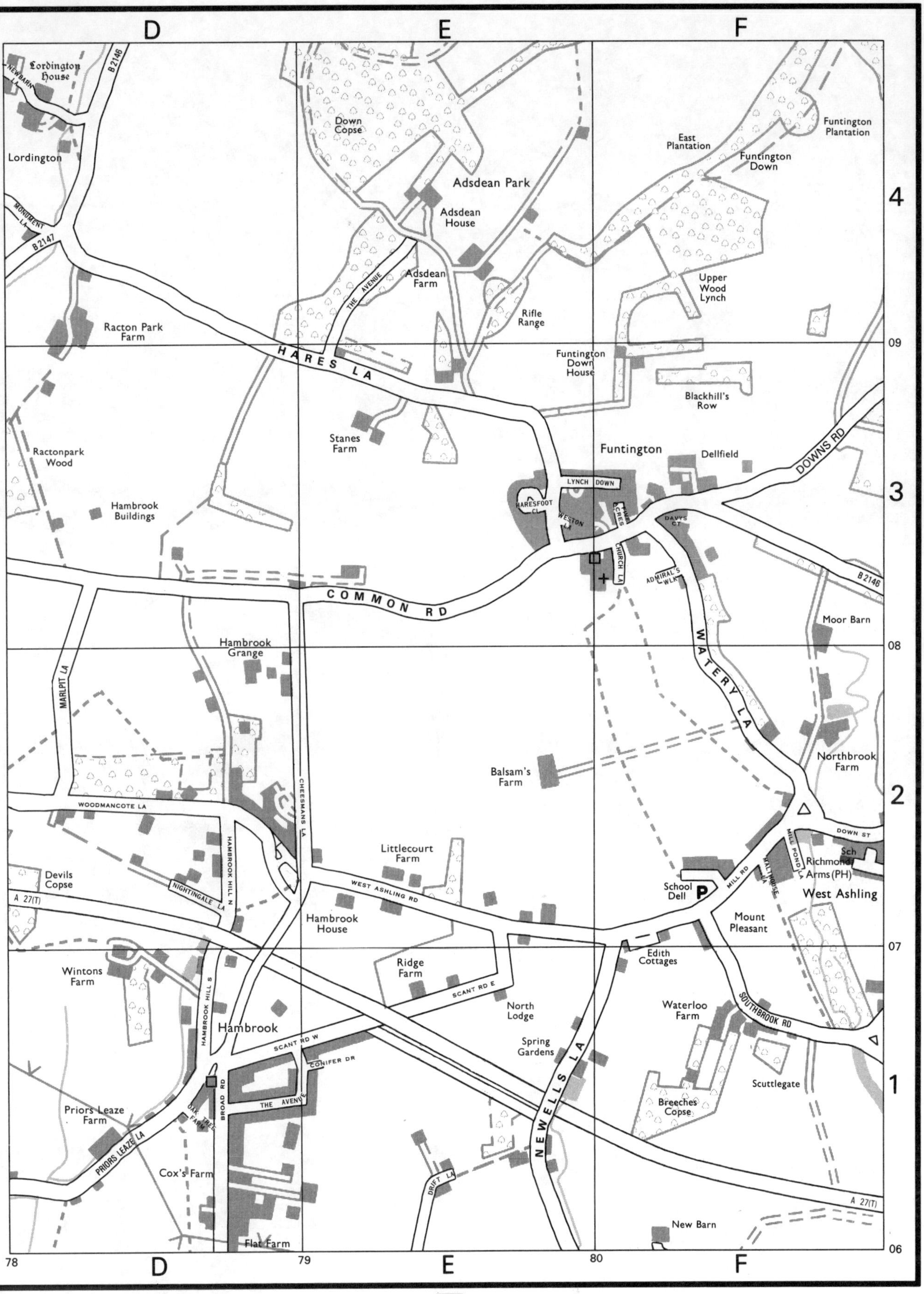

D
E
F
4
3
2
1
09
08
07
06
78
79
80
Lordington House
NEWBARN LA
B2146
Lordington
MONUMENT LA
B2147
Down Copse
Adsdean Park
Adsdean House
Adsdean Farm
THE AVENUE
Rifle Range
East Plantation
Funtington Down
Funtington Plantation
Upper Wood Lynch
Racton Park Farm
HARES LA
Funtington Down House
Blackhill's Row
Stanes Farm
Ractonpark Wood
Funtington
Dellfield
DOWNS RD
LYNCH DOWN
HARESFOOT CL
WESTON LA
FIVE ACRES
CHURCH LA
DAVYS CT
ADMIRAL'S WLK
B2146
Hambrook Buildings
COMMON RD
Moor Barn
WATERY LA
Hambrook Grange
MARLPIT LA
Balsam's Farm
Northbrook Farm
CHEESMANS LA
WOODMANCOTE LA
HAMBROOK HILL N
DOWN ST
MILL POND LA
Sch
Richmond Arms (PH)
MALTHOUSE LA
MILL RD
Littlecourt Farm
Devils Copse
NIGHTINGALE LA
WEST ASHLING RD
School Dell
P
West Ashling
Mount Pleasant
A 27(T)
Hambrook House
Edith Cottages
Wintons Farm
Ridge Farm
SCANT RD E
North Lodge
Waterloo Farm
SOUTHBROOK RD
HAMBROOK HILL S
Hambrook
Spring Gardens
NEWELLS LA
SCANT RD W
CONIFER DR
Scuttlegate
BROAD RD
THE AVENUE
Breeches Copse
Priors Leaze Farm
OAK TREE FARM
PRIORS LEAZE LA
Cox's Farm
DRIFT LA
A 27(T)
New Barn
Flat Farm

150

170

129

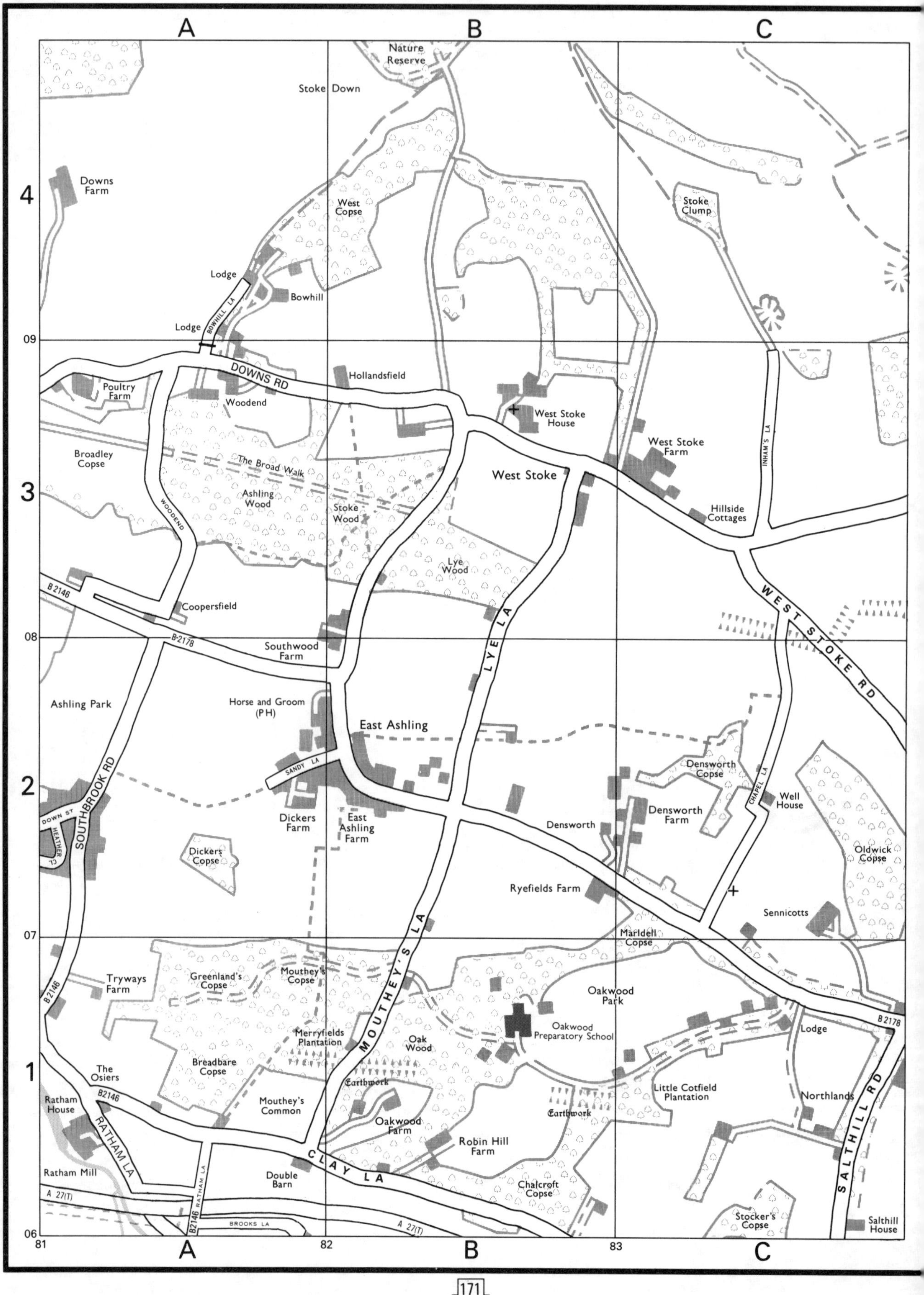

A
B
C
Nature Reserve
Stoke Down
Downs Farm
West Copse
Stoke Clump
Lodge
Bowhill
BOWHILL LA
Lodge
09
DOWNS RD
Hollandsfield
Poultry Farm
Woodend
West Stoke House
Broadley Copse
The Broad Walk
West Stoke Farm
West Stoke
INHAM'S LA
Ashling Wood
WOODEND
Stoke Wood
Hillside Cottages
Lye Wood
B 2146
Coopersfield
WEST STOKE RD
08
B 2178
Southwood Farm
LYE LA
Ashling Park
Horse and Groom (PH)
East Ashling
SOUTHBROOK RD
Densworth Copse
SANDY LA
CHAPEL LA
Well House
Densworth Farm
DOWN ST
Dickers Farm
East Ashling Farm
Densworth
HEATHER CL
Dickers Copse
Oldwick Copse
Ryefields Farm
Sennicotts
07
Marldell Copse
Mouthey's Copse
Tryways Farm
Greenland's Copse
MOUTHEY'S LA
Oakwood Park
B 2146
Oakwood Preparatory School
B 2178
Lodge
Merryfields Plantation
Oak Wood
Breadbare Copse
Earthwork
Little Cotfield Plantation
The Osiers
Northlands
Ratham House
B2146
Mouthey's Common
Earthwork
Oakwood Farm
RATHAM LA
Robin Hill Farm
SALTHILL RD
Ratham Mill
CLAY LA
Double Barn
Chalcroft Copse
A 27(T)
RATHAM LA
B2146
Stocker's Copse
BROOKS LA
A 27(T)
Salthill House
06
81
82
83

149

171

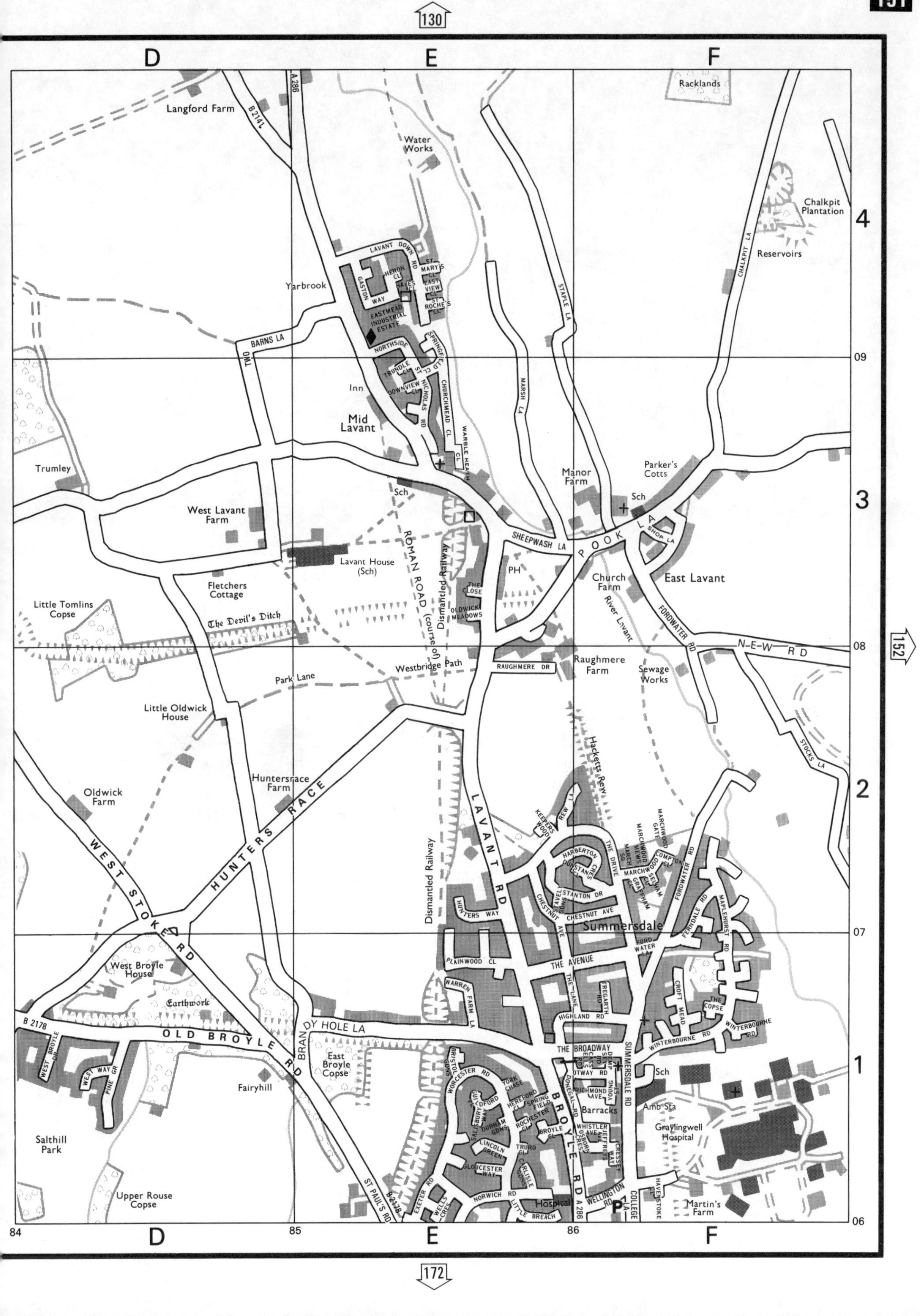
130
D
E
F
Racklands
Langford Farm
Water Works
Chalkpit Plantation
Reservoirs
Yarbrook
Mid Lavant
Inn
Trumley
West Lavant Farm
Manor Farm
Parker's Cotts
Sch
East Lavant
Church Farm
Lavant House (Sch)
Fletchers Cottage
Little Tomlins Copse
The Devil's Ditch
ROMAN ROAD (course of)
Dismantled Railway
Westbridge Path
Park Lane
Raughmere Farm
Sewage Works
Little Oldwick House
Hackets Row
Oldwick Farm
Huntersrace Farm
HUNTERS RACE
WEST STOKE RD
LAVANT RD
Summersdale
West Broyle House
Earthwork
OLD BROYLE RD
BRANDY HOLE LA
East Broyle Copse
Fairyhill
Salthill Park
Upper Rouse Copse
Barracks
Amb Sta
Graylingwell Hospital
Hospital
Martin's Farm
SHEEPWASH LA
POOK LA
NEW RD
FORDWATER RD
STOCKS LA
CHALKPIT LA
STAPLE LA
MARSH LA
BARNS LA
THE AVENUE
THE BROADWAY
SUMMERSDALE RD
BROYLE RD
ST PAUL'S RD
B 2178
A 286
B 2141
RAUGHMERE DR
84
85
86
09
08
07
06
4
3
2
1
152
172

131

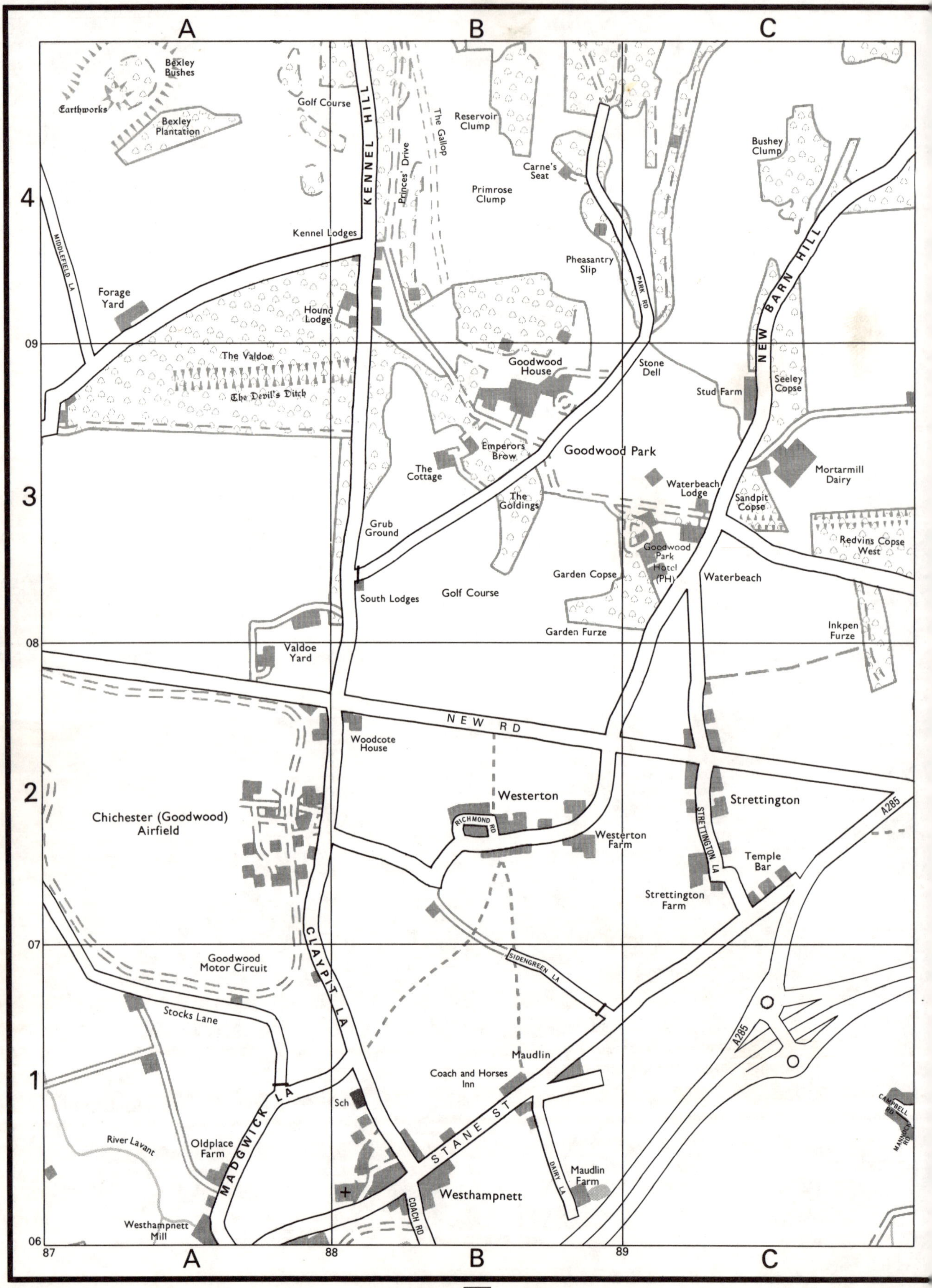
A
B
C
Bexley Bushes
Earthworks
Bexley Plantation
Golf Course
KENNEL HILL
Princes' Drive
The Gallop
Reservoir Clump
Carne's Seat
Primrose Clump
Bushey Clump
4
MIDDLEFIELD LA
Kennel Lodges
Pheasantry Slip
PARK RD
NEW BARN HILL
Forage Yard
Hound Lodge
09
The Valdoe
The Devil's Ditch
Goodwood House
Stone Dell
Stud Farm
Seeley Copse
Emperors Brow
Goodwood Park
The Cottage
Waterbeach Lodge
Mortarmill Dairy
3
The Goldings
Sandpit Copse
Grub Ground
Goodwood Park Hotel (PH)
Redvins Copse West
Garden Copse
Waterbeach
South Lodges
Golf Course
Garden Furze
Inkpen Furze
08
Valdoe Yard
NEW RD
Woodcote House
2
Chichester (Goodwood) Airfield
Westerton
Strettington
RICHMOND RD
Westerton Farm
STRETTINGTON LA
A285
Temple Bar
Strettington Farm
07
SIDENGREEN LA
Goodwood Motor Circuit
CLAYPIT LA
Stocks Lane
Maudlin
1
Coach and Horses Inn
MADGWICK LA
Sch
STANE ST
A285
CAMPBELL RD
MANNOCK RD
River Lavant
Oldplace Farm
DAIRY LA
Maudlin Farm
COACH RD
Westhampnett
Westhampnett Mill
06
87
88
89
A
B
C

151

173

132

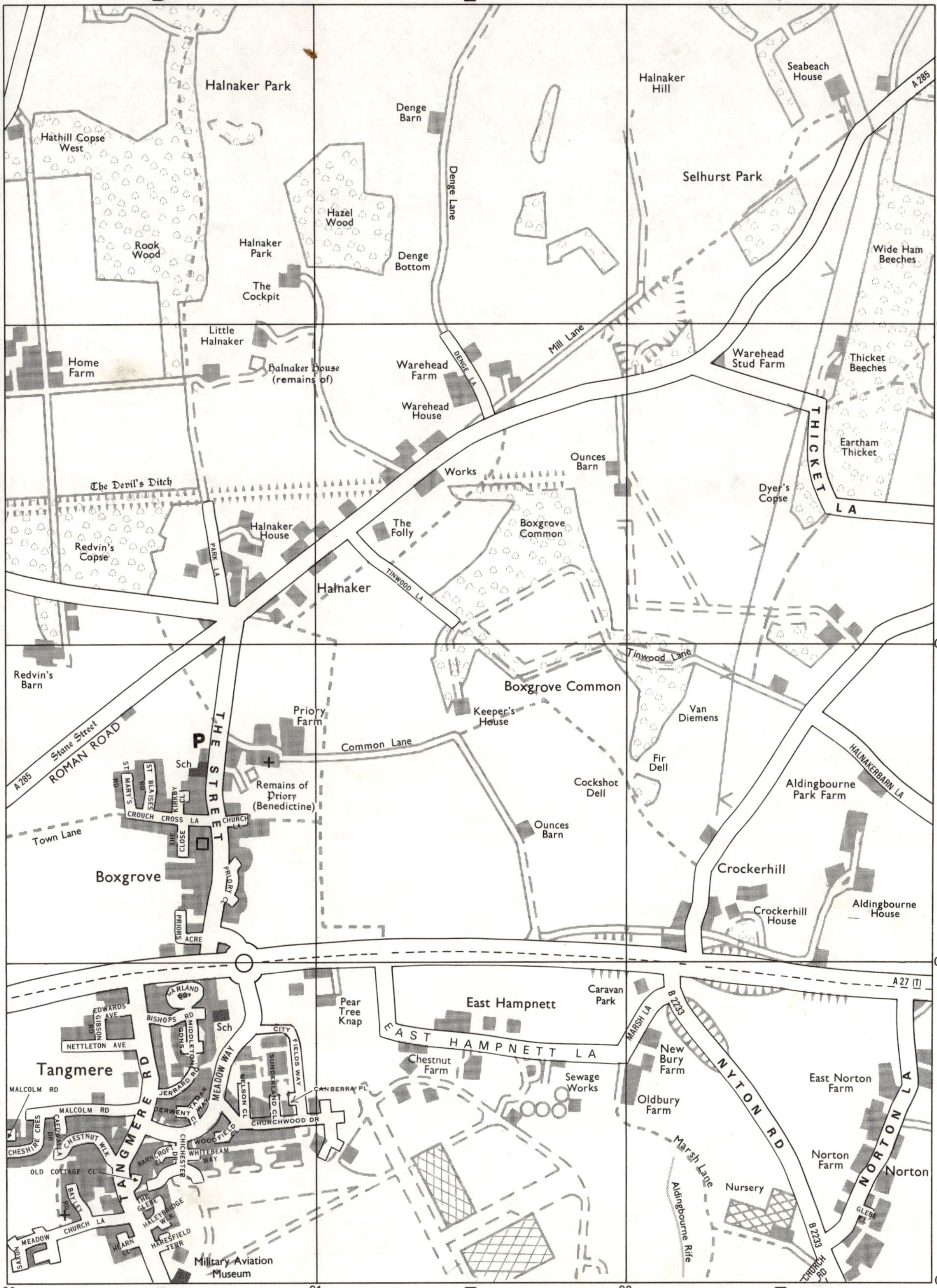
D
E
F
Halnaker Park
Hathill Copse West
Rook Wood
Halnaker Park
Hazel Wood
Denge Barn
Denge Lane
Denge Bottom
The Cockpit
Halnaker Hill
Seabeach House
A 285
Selhurst Park
Wide Ham Beeches
4
09
Little Halnaker
Home Farm
Halnaker House (remains of)
Warehead Farm
DENGE LA
Mill Lane
Warehead House
Warehead Stud Farm
Thicket Beeches
THICKET LA
Eartham Thicket
Ounces Barn
Works
The Devil's Ditch
Dyer's Copse
3
Halnaker House
The Folly
Boxgrove Common
Redvin's Copse
PARK LA
Halnaker
TINWOOD LA
Tinwood Lane
08
154
Redvin's Barn
Boxgrove Common
Van Diemens
Keeper's House
Priory Farm
THE STREET
Stane Street
ROMAN ROAD
A 285
P
Common Lane
Sch
Fir Dell
HALNAKERBARN LA
ST MARY'S RD
ST BLAISES RD
KIRKBY CL
Remains of Priory (Benedictine)
Cockshot Dell
Aldingbourne Park Farm
2
CROUCH CROSS LA
CHURCH LA
Town Lane
THE CLOSE
Ounces Barn
Boxgrove
PRIORY CL
Crockerhill
Crockerhill House
Aldingbourne House
PRIORS ACRE
07
A 27 (T)
GARLAND SQ
EDWARDS AVE
GIBSON RD
BISHOPS RD
MIDDLETON GDNS
Sch
Pear Tree Knap
East Hampnett
Caravan Park
MARSH LA
B 2233
NETTLETON AVE
CITY FIELDS WAY
EAST HAMPNETT LA
New Bury Farm
Tangmere
MEADOW WAY
SUNDERLAND CL
Chestnut Farm
Sewage Works
East Norton Farm
MALCOLM RD
JERRARD RD
TAMAR WAY
NELSON CL
CANBERRA PL
NYTON RD
NORTON LA
MALCOLM RD
DERWENT
Oldbury Farm
1
TANGMERE RD
CHURCHWOOD DR
WOODFIELD
CHESHIRE CRES
CADWALLA DR
CHESTNUT WLK
CHICHESTER DR
WHITEBEAM WAY
BARNCROFT CL
Marsh Lane
Norton Farm
Norton
OLD COTTAGE CL
Aldingbourne Rife
Nursery
BAYLEY RD
THE GLEBE
HALEYBRIDGE WLK
GLEBE CL
CHURCH LA
B 2233
SAXON MEADOW
HEARN CL
HARESFIELD TERR
Military Aviation Museum
CHURCH RD
06
90
91
92
D
E
F

174

133

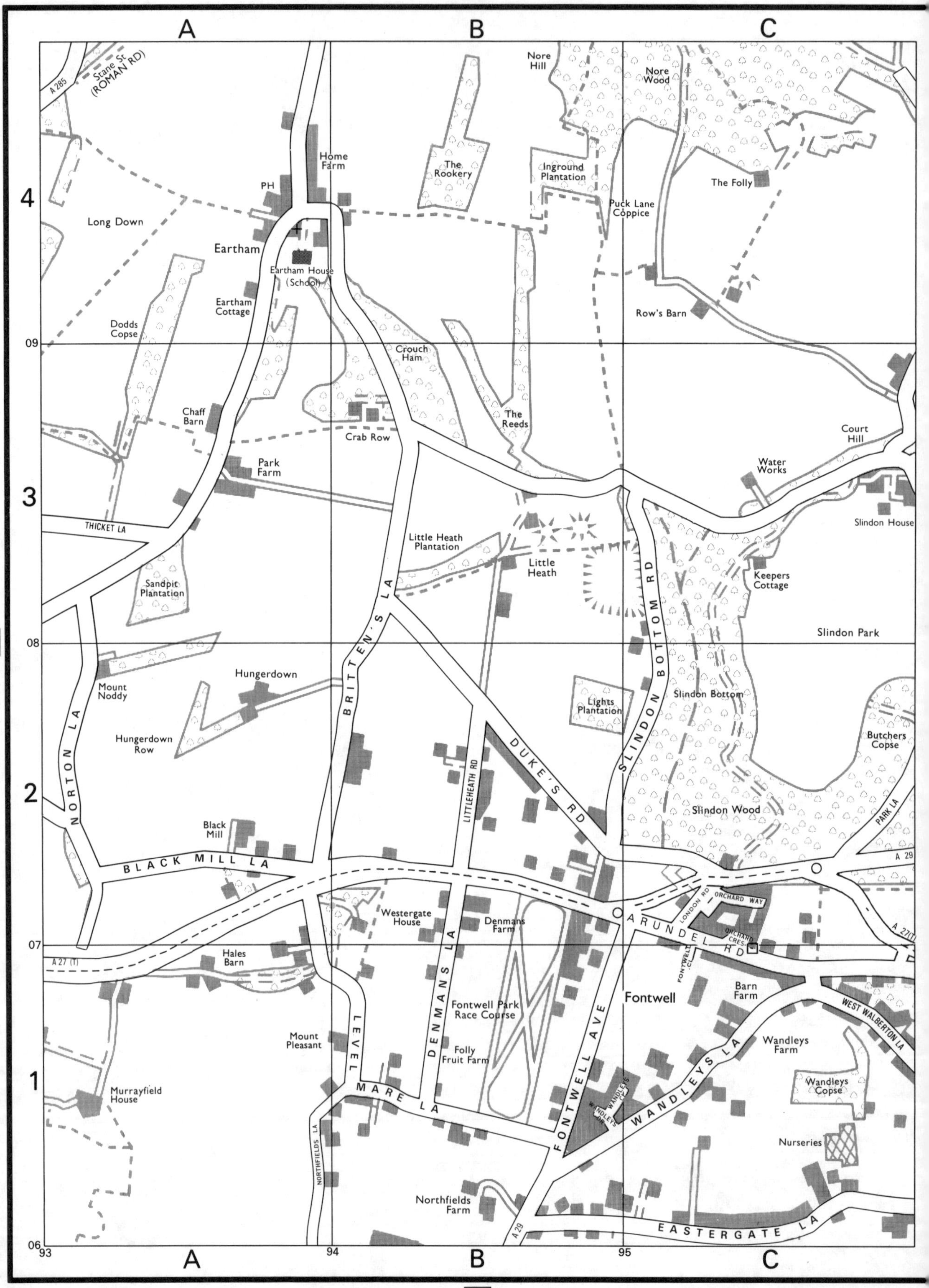
A
B
C
4
3
2
1
09
08
07
06
93
94
95
A 285
Stane St. (ROMAN RD)
Nore Hill
Nore Wood
Home Farm
PH
The Rookery
Inground Plantation
The Folly
Puck Lane Coppice
Long Down
Eartham
Eartham House (School)
Eartham Cottage
Row's Barn
Dodds Copse
Crouch Ham
Chaff Barn
The Reeds
Court Hill
Crab Row
Park Farm
Water Works
THICKET LA
Slindon House
Little Heath Plantation
Little Heath
Keepers Cottage
Sandpit Plantation
Slindon Park
Hungerdown
Mount Noddy
Slindon Bottom
Lights Plantation
Butchers Copse
Hungerdown Row
BRITTEN'S LA
SLINDON BOTTOM RD
DUKE'S RD
NORTON LA
LITTLEHEATH RD
Slindon Wood
PARK LA
Black Mill
BLACK MILL LA
A 29
Westergate House
Denmans Farm
ARUNDEL RD
LONDON RD
ORCHARD WAY
ORCHARD CRES.
FONTWELL CL
A 27(T)
Hales Barn
Barn Farm
Fontwell
WEST WALBERTON LA
Fontwell Park Race Course
Mount Pleasant
LEVEL
DENMANS LA
FONTWELL AVE
Wandleys Farm
Folly Fruit Farm
WANDLEYS LA
Murrayfield House
MARE LA
WANDLEYS CL
WANDLEYS DR
Wandleys Copse
Nurseries
NORTHFIELDS LA
Northfields Farm
EASTERGATE LA
A 29

153

175

134

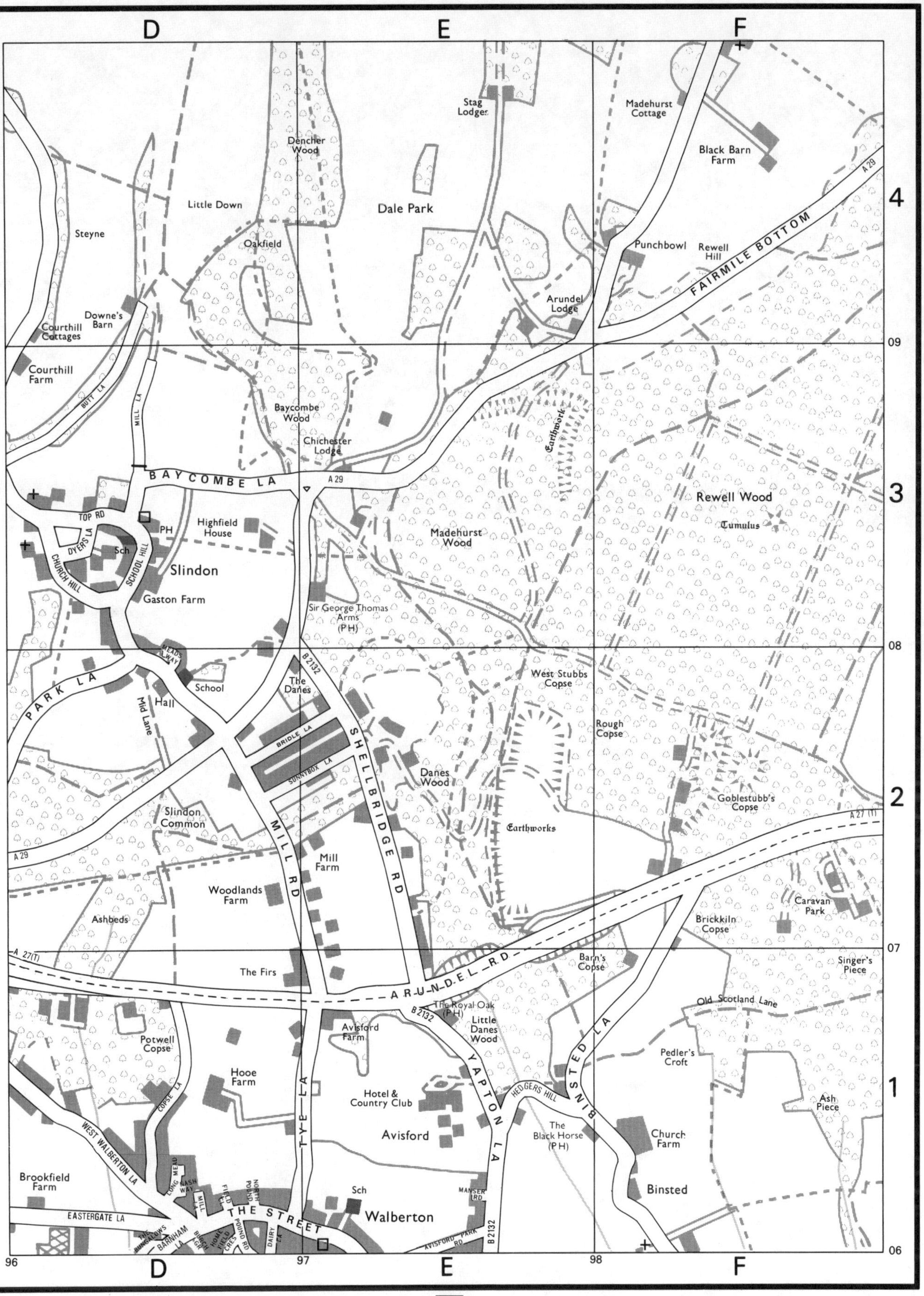
D
E
F
Stag Lodge
Madehurst Cottage
Dencher Wood
Black Barn Farm
Little Down
Dale Park
Steyne
Oakfield
Punchbowl
Rewell Hill
FAIRMILE BOTTOM
A 29
Downe's Barn
Courthill Cottages
Arundel Lodge
Courthill Farm
BUTT LA
MILL LA
Baycombe Wood
Earthwork
Chichester Lodge
BAYCOMBE LA
A 29
Rewell Wood
TOP RD
Highfield House
Madehurst Wood
Tumulus
PH
DYERS LA
Sch
SCHOOL HILL
CHURCH HILL
Slindon
Gaston Farm
Sir George Thomas Arms (PH)
MEADS WAY
B 2132
West Stubbs Copse
The Danes
School
PARK LA
Hall
Mid Lane
BRIDLE LA
SHELLBRIDGE RD
Rough Copse
SUNNYBOX LA
Danes Wood
Goblestubb's Copse
Slindon Common
Earthworks
A 27 (T)
A 29
MILL RD
Mill Farm
Woodlands Farm
Caravan Park
Ashbeds
Brickkiln Copse
A 27(T)
Barn's Copse
Singer's Piece
The Firs
ARUNDEL RD
The Royal Oak (PH)
Old Scotland Lane
B 2132
Little Danes Wood
Avisford Farm
Potwell Copse
Pedler's Croft
Hooe Farm
YAPTON LA
BINSTED LA
HEDGERS HILL
Hotel & Country Club
Ash Piece
TYE LA
COPSE LA
WEST WALBERTON LA
The Black Horse (PH)
Church Farm
Avisford
Brookfield Farm
LONG MEAD
NASH WAY
NORTH POUND
MILL
FIELD
Sch
MANSER RD
Binsted
EASTERGATE LA
THE STREET
Walberton
THE BUNGALOWS
BARNHAM LA
BIRCH GR
HOME FIELD CRES
POUND RD
DAIRY LA
AVISFORD PARK RD
B 2132
96
97
98
09
08
07
06
4
3
2
1

156

176

135

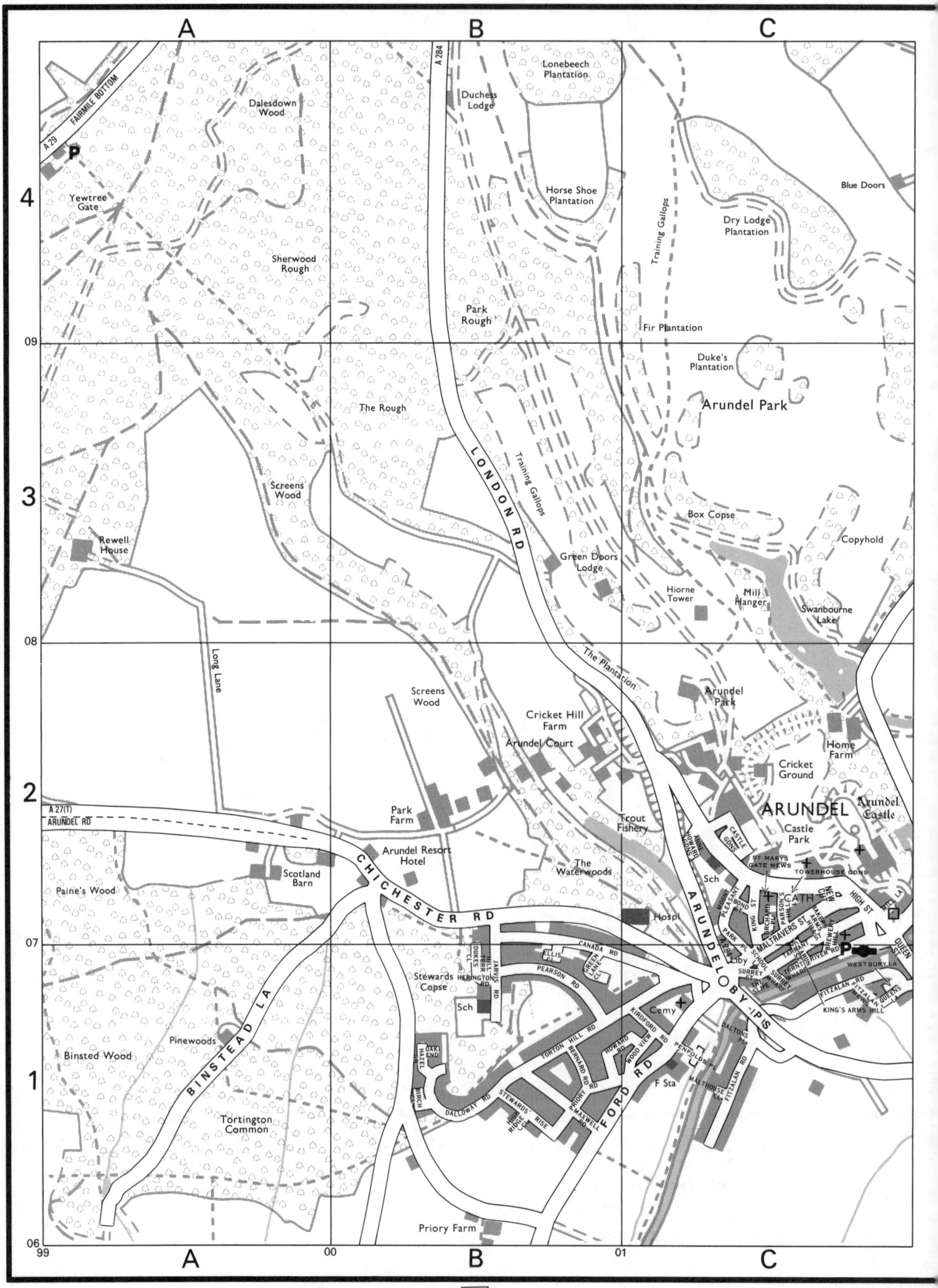
A
B
C
4
3
2
1
09
08
07
06
99
00
01
A 29
FAIRMILE BOTTOM
Dalesdown Wood
Yewtree Gate
Sherwood Rough
A 284
Lonebeech Plantation
Duchess Lodge
Horse Shoe Plantation
Park Rough
Training Gallops
Dry Lodge Plantation
Blue Doors
Fir Plantation
Duke's Plantation
Arundel Park
The Rough
LONDON RD
Training Gallops
Screens Wood
Rewell House
Box Copse
Copyhold
Green Doors Lodge
Hiorne Tower
Mill Hanger
Swanbourne Lake
Long Lane
The Plantation
Screens Wood
Cricket Hill Farm
Arundel Park
Arundel Court
Home Farm
Cricket Ground
ARUNDEL
Arundel Castle
A 27(T)
ARUNDEL RD
Park Farm
Trout Fishery
Castle Park
Arundel Resort Hotel
Scotland Barn
Paine's Wood
The Waterwoods
CHICHESTER RD
ARUNDEL BY-PASS
Sch
ST MARYS GATE MEWS
TOWERHOUSE GDNS
CATH
HIGH ST
Hospl
MALTRAVERS ST
CANADA RD
ELLIS CL
PEARSON RD
Stewards Copse
Sch
Cemy
Liby
WESTBURY LA
FITZALAN RD
KING'S ARMS HILL
KIRKFORD RD
PENFOLDS PL
Pinewoods
Binsted Wood
BINSTEAD LA
TORTON HILL RD
BERNARD RD
FORD RD
F Sta
DALLOWAY RD
STEWARDS' RISE
MAXWELL RD
MALTHOUSE CL
FITZALAN RD
Tortington Common
Priory Farm

155

177

136

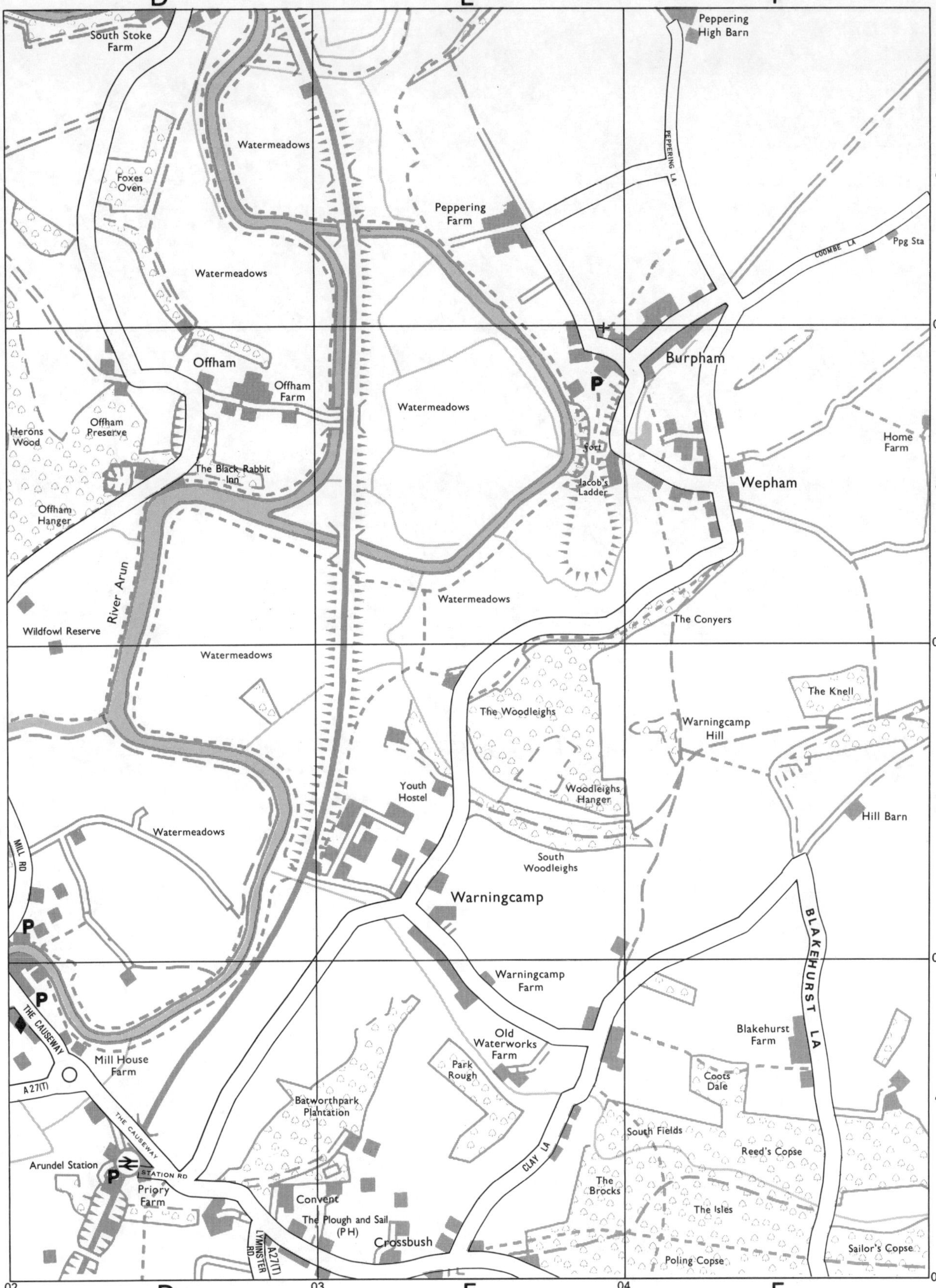
D
E
F
South Stoke Farm
Peppering High Barn
Watermeadows
Foxes Oven
Peppering Farm
PEPPERING LA
COOMBE LA
Ppg Sta
Watermeadows
Offham
Offham Farm
Burpham
Watermeadows
Herons Wood
Offham Preserve
Fort
Home Farm
The Black Rabbit Inn
Jacob's Ladder
Wepham
Offham Hanger
River Arun
Watermeadows
Wildfowl Reserve
The Conyers
Watermeadows
The Knell
The Woodleighs
Warningcamp Hill
Youth Hostel
Woodleighs Hanger
Hill Barn
Watermeadows
MILL RD
South Woodleighs
Warningcamp
BLAKEHURST LA
Warningcamp Farm
THE CAUSEWAY
Old Waterworks Farm
Blakehurst Farm
Mill House Farm
Park Rough
Coots Dale
A27(T)
Batworthpark Plantation
THE CAUSEWAY
CLAY LA
South Fields
Arundel Station
Reed's Copse
STATION RD
The Brocks
Priory Farm
Convent
The Isles
The Plough and Sail (PH)
LYMINSTER RD
A27(T)
Crossbush
Sailor's Copse
Poling Copse
02
03
04
06
07
08
09
1
2
3
4
D
E
F

158

178

137

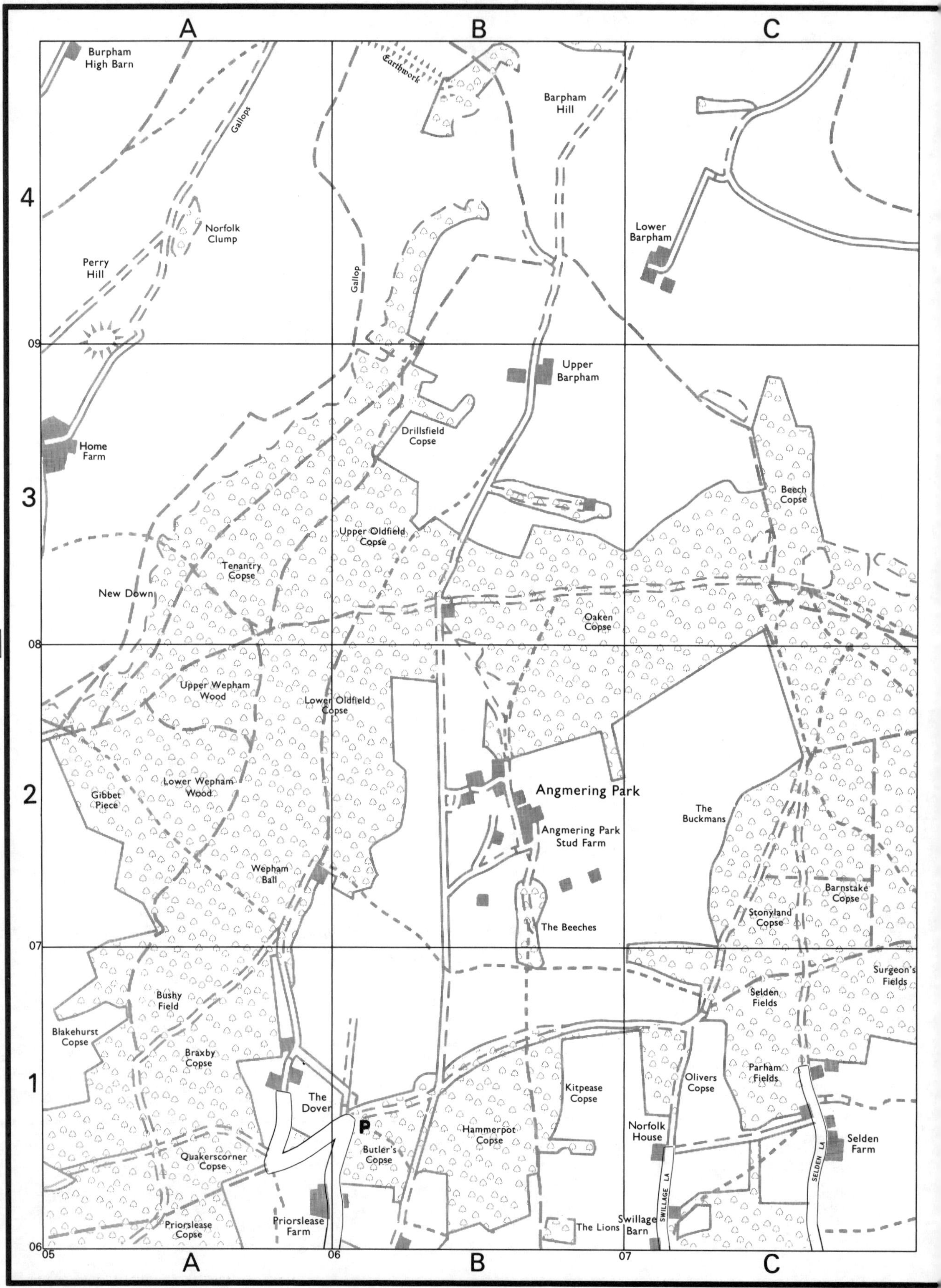
A
B
C
4
3
2
1
09
08
07
06
05
06
07
Burpham High Barn
Gallops
Earthwork
Barpham Hill
Lower Barpham
Norfolk Clump
Perry Hill
Gallop
Upper Barpham
Home Farm
Drillsfield Copse
Beech Copse
Upper Oldfield Copse
Tenantry Copse
New Down
Oaken Copse
Upper Wepham Wood
Lower Oldfield Copse
Angmering Park
Gibbet Piece
Lower Wepham Wood
The Buckmans
Angmering Park Stud Farm
Wepham Ball
Barnstake Copse
Stonyland Copse
The Beeches
Surgeon's Fields
Selden Fields
Bushy Field
Blakehurst Copse
Braxby Copse
Parham Fields
Olivers Copse
Kitpease Copse
The Dover
P
Hammerpot Copse
Norfolk House
Selden Farm
Butler's Copse
Quakerscorner Copse
SWILLAGE LA
SELDEN LA
Priorslease Farm
Priorslease Copse
The Lions
Swillage Barn

157

179

138

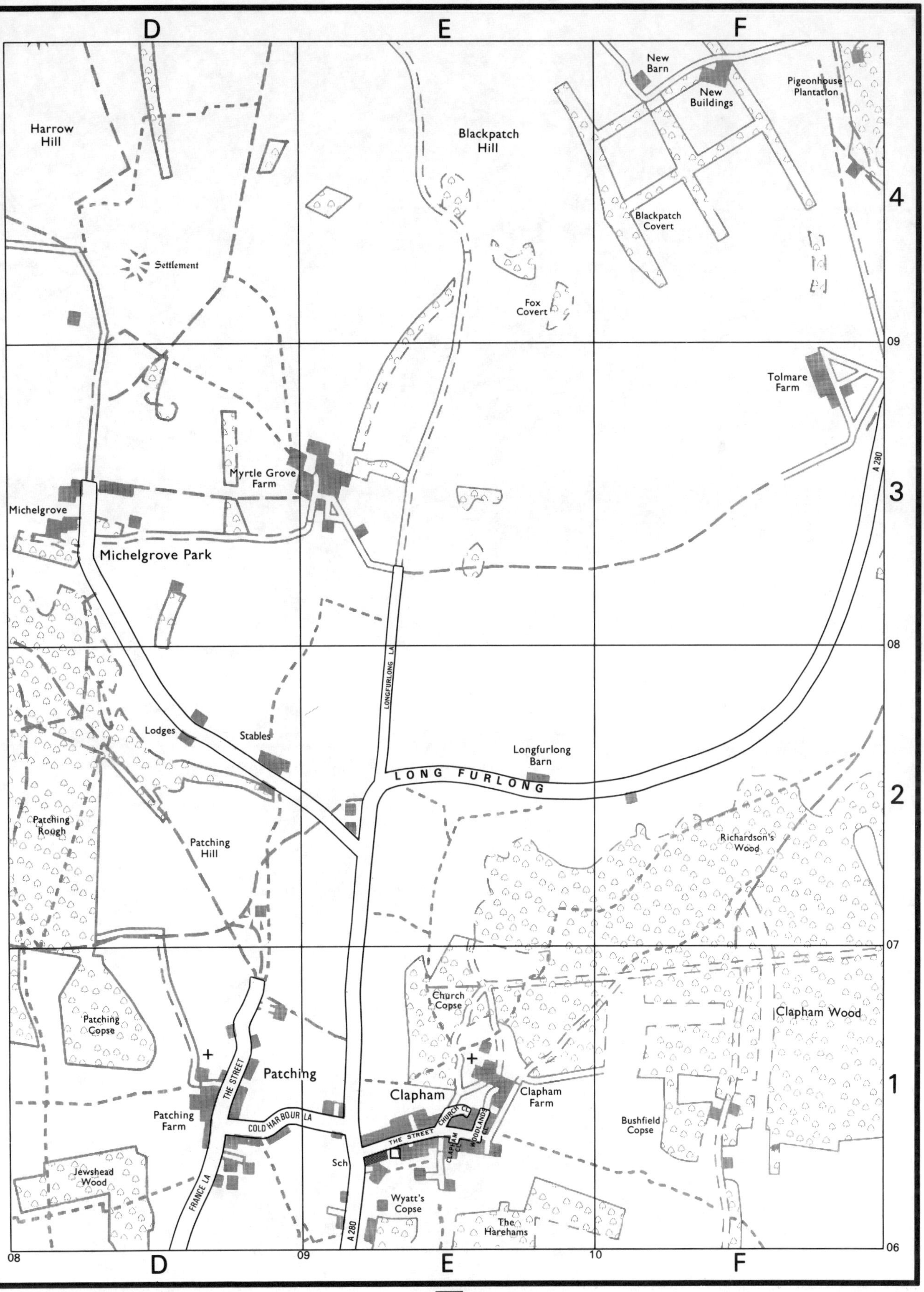

D
E
F
Harrow Hill
Settlement
Blackpatch Hill
New Barn
New Buildings
Pigeonhouse Plantation
Blackpatch Covert
Fox Covert
4
09
Tolmare Farm
A 280
Myrtle Grove Farm
Michelgrove
Michelgrove Park
3
08
LONGFURLONG LA
Lodges
Stables
Longfurlong Barn
LONG FURLONG
2
Patching Rough
Patching Hill
Richardson's Wood
07
Church Copse
Clapham Wood
Patching Copse
Patching
Clapham
Clapham Farm
1
THE STREET
Patching Farm
COLD HARBOUR LA
THE STREET
CHURCH CL
WOODLANDS CL
CLAPHAM CL
Bushfield Copse
Sch
Jewshead Wood
FRANCE LA
Wyatt's Copse
A 280
The Harehams
08
09
10
06
D
E
F

160

180

139

159

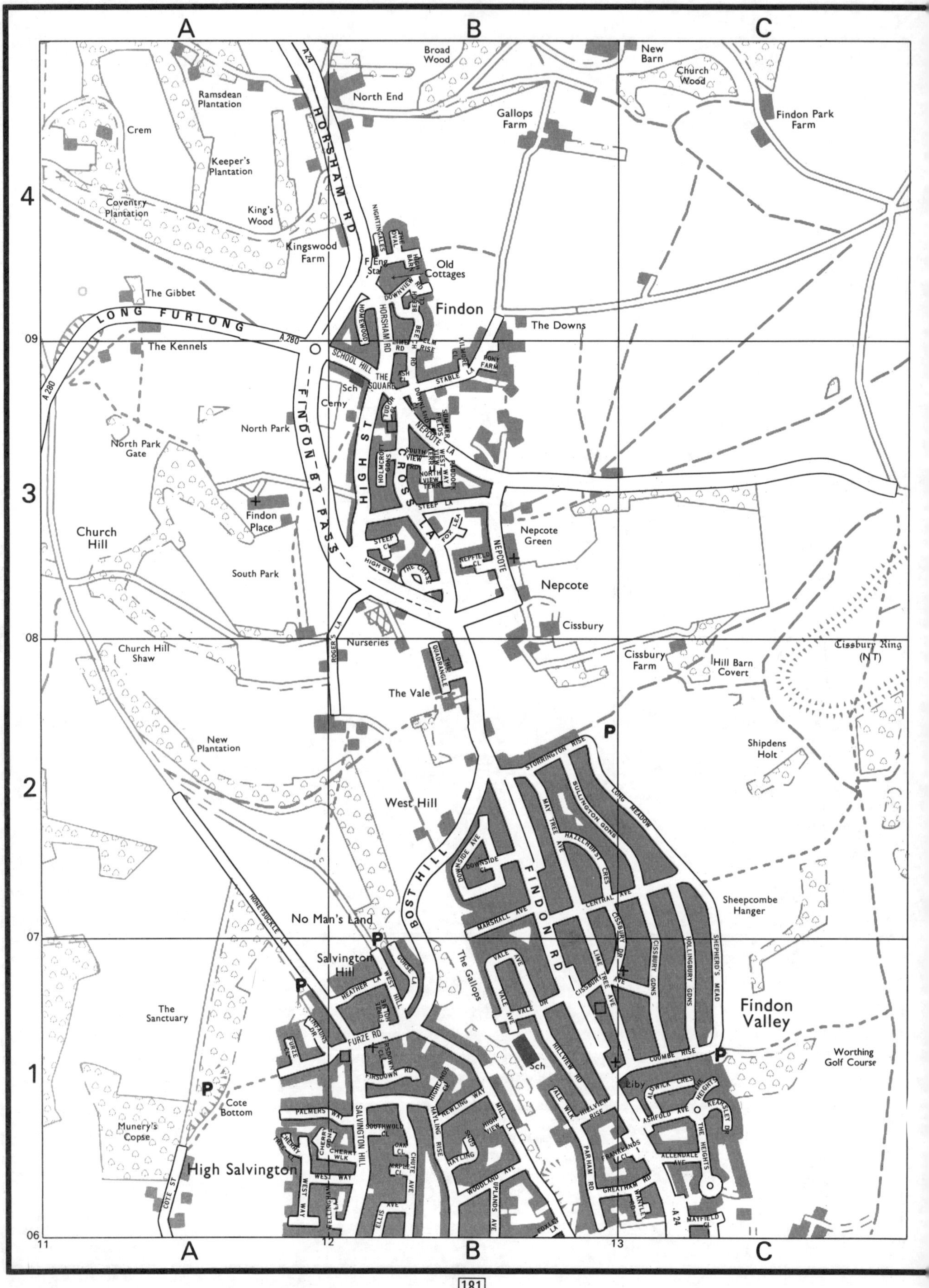
A
B
C
4
3
2
1
09
08
07
06
11
12
13
Broad Wood
New Barn
Church Wood
Ramsdean Plantation
North End
Findon Park Farm
Gallops Farm
Crem
Keeper's Plantation
Coventry Plantation
King's Wood
HORSHAM RD
A24
Kingswood Farm
F Eng Sta
Old Cottages
The Gibbet
Findon
The Downs
LONG FURLONG
A 280
The Kennels
SCHOOL HILL
THE SQUARE
Sch
STABLE LA
PONY FARM
Cemy
FINDON BY-PASS
HIGH ST
CROSS LA
North Park
North Park Gate
NEPCOTE LA
STEEP LA
Church Hill
Findon Place
South Park
Nepcote Green
NEPCOTE
REPFIELD CL
FOX LEA
THE CHASE
Nepcote
Cissbury
ROGER'S LA
Nurseries
Church Hill Shaw
THE QUADRANGLE
Cissbury Farm
Hill Barn Covert
Cissbury Ring (NT)
The Vale
New Plantation
P
Shipdens Holt
STORRINGTON RISE
SULLINGTON GDNS
LONG MEADOW
MAY TREE AVE
HAZELHURST CRES
West Hill
BOST HILL
DOWNSIDE AVE
DOWNSIDE CL
FINDON RD
CENTRAL AVE
Sheepcombe Hanger
HONEYSUCKLE LA
No Man's Land
MARSHALL AVE
CISSBURY DR
LIME TREE AVE
CISSBURY GDNS
HOLLINGBURY GDNS
SHEPHERD'S MEAD
Salvington Hill
GORSE LA
The Gallops
VALE AVE
VALE DR
HEATHER LA
WEST HILL
The Sanctuary
Findon Valley
FURZE RD
FIRSDOWN CL
FIRSDOWN RD
COOMBE RISE
Worthing Golf Course
Sch
HILLVIEW RD
Liby
ALDWICK CRES
THE HEIGHTS
KEARSLEY DR
Cote Bottom
PALMERS WAY
SALVINGTON HILL
SOUTHWOLD CL
HAYLING RISE
NEWLING WAY
HIGHLANDS CL
HIGH VIEW
MILL LA
VALE WLK
HILLVIEW RISE
ASHFOLD AVE
Munery's Copse
CHERRY WLK
OAK CL
CHUTE AVE
HAYLING
FRANKLANDS CL
ALLENDALE AVE
THE HEIGHTS
High Salvington
WEST WAY
MAPLE CL
WOODLAND AVE
UPLANDS AVE
PARHAM RD
GREATHAM RD
WANTLEY RD
COTE ST
WELLINGHAM
ELLIS AVE
FOXLEY LA
A24
MATFIELD CL

181

140

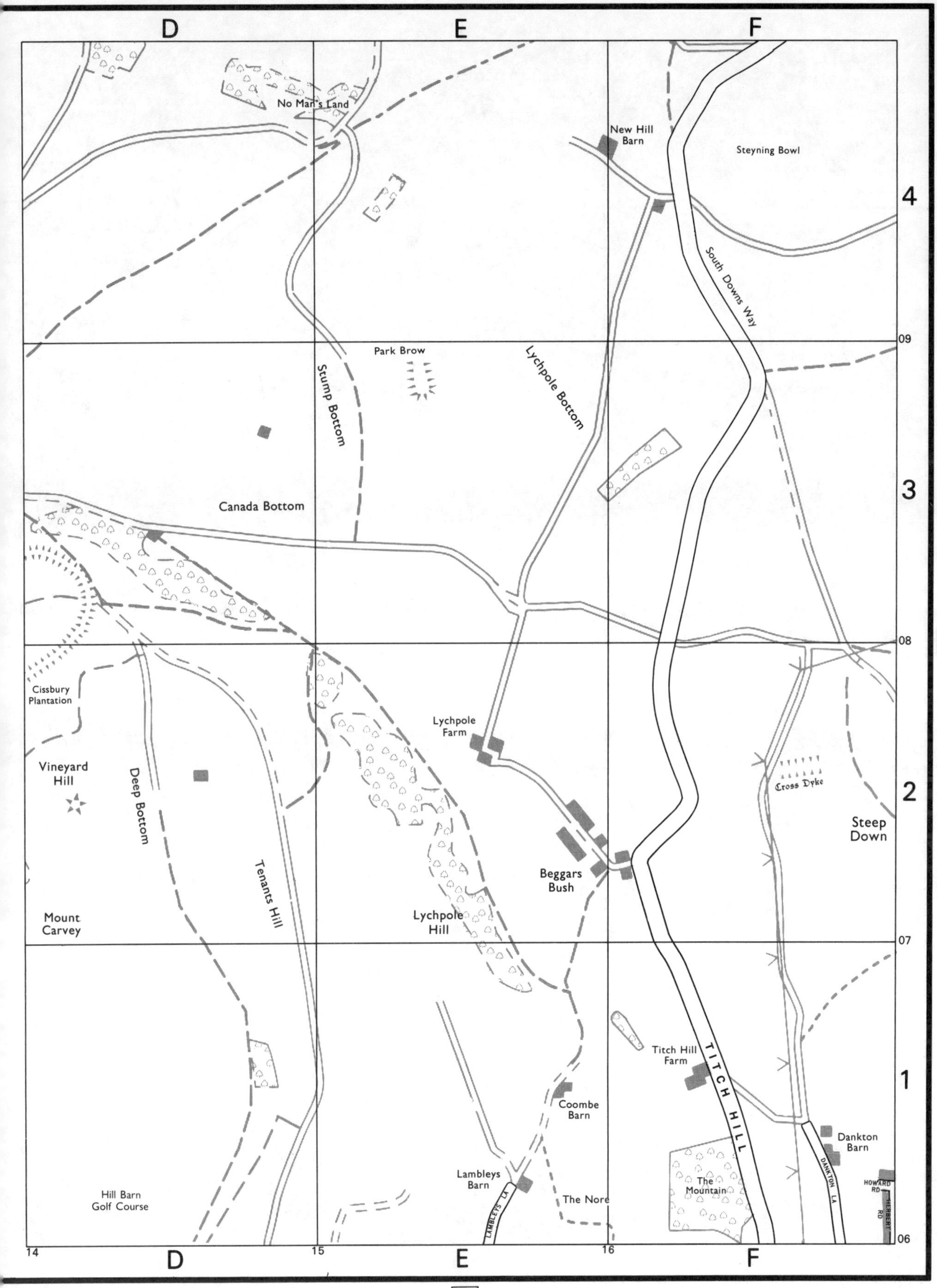
D
E
F
No Man's Land
New Hill Barn
Steyning Bowl
4
South Downs Way
09
Park Brow
Stump Bottom
Lychpole Bottom
3
Canada Bottom
08
Cissbury Plantation
Lychpole Farm
Vineyard Hill
Deep Bottom
Cross Dyke
2
Steep Down
Beggars Bush
Tenants Hill
Mount Carvey
Lychpole Hill
07
Titch Hill Farm
TITCH HILL
1
Coombe Barn
Dankton Barn
DANKTON LA
Lambleys Barn
LAMBLEYS LA
HOWARD RD
HERBERT RD
Hill Barn Golf Course
The Nore
The Mountain
06
14
15
16
D
E
F

162

182

141

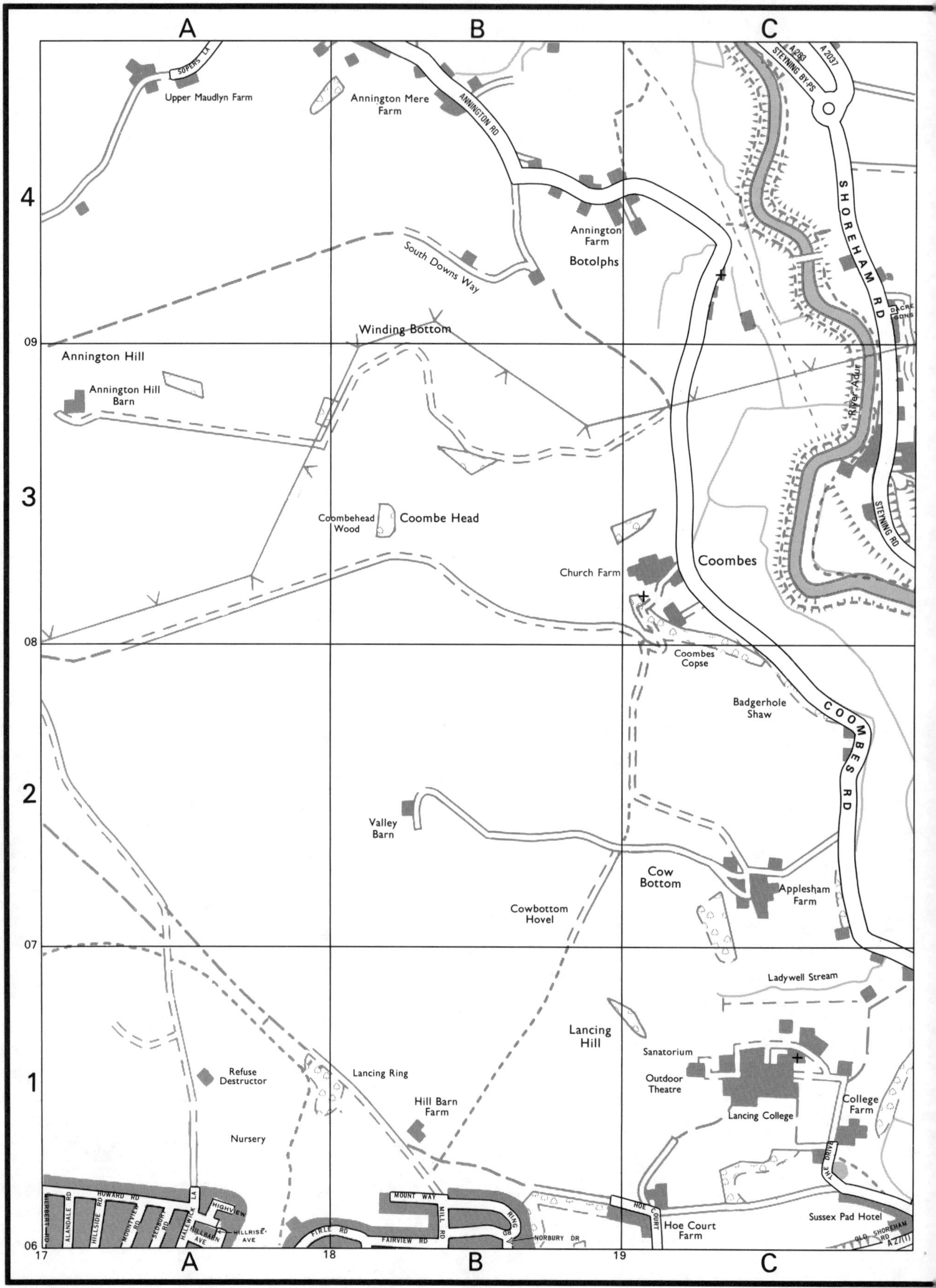

A
B
C
4
3
2
1
09
08
07
06
17
18
19
Upper Maudlyn Farm
SOPERS LA
Annington Mere Farm
ANNINGTON RD
Annington Farm
Botolphs
South Downs Way
A283
A 2037
STEYNING BY-PS
SHOREHAM RD
DACRE GDNS
River Adur
STEYNING RD
Winding Bottom
Annington Hill
Annington Hill Barn
Coombehead Wood
Coombe Head
Church Farm
Coombes
Coombes Copse
Badgerhole Shaw
COOMBES RD
Valley Barn
Cow Bottom
Applesham Farm
Cowbottom Hovel
Ladywell Stream
Lancing Hill
Sanatorium
Outdoor Theatre
Lancing College
College Farm
Refuse Destructor
Lancing Ring
Hill Barn Farm
Nursery
THE DRIVE
Sussex Pad Hotel
OLD SHOREHAM RD
A 27(T)
HOE COURT
Hoe Court Farm
NORBURY DR
RING RD
MILL RD
MOUNT WAY
FAIRVIEW RD
FIRLE RD
HOWARD RD
HIGHVIEW
HILLRISE AVE
HILLBARN AVE
HALEWICK LA
SEDBURY RD
MOUNTVIEW RD
HILLSIDE RD
ALANDALE RD
HERBERT RD

161

183

142

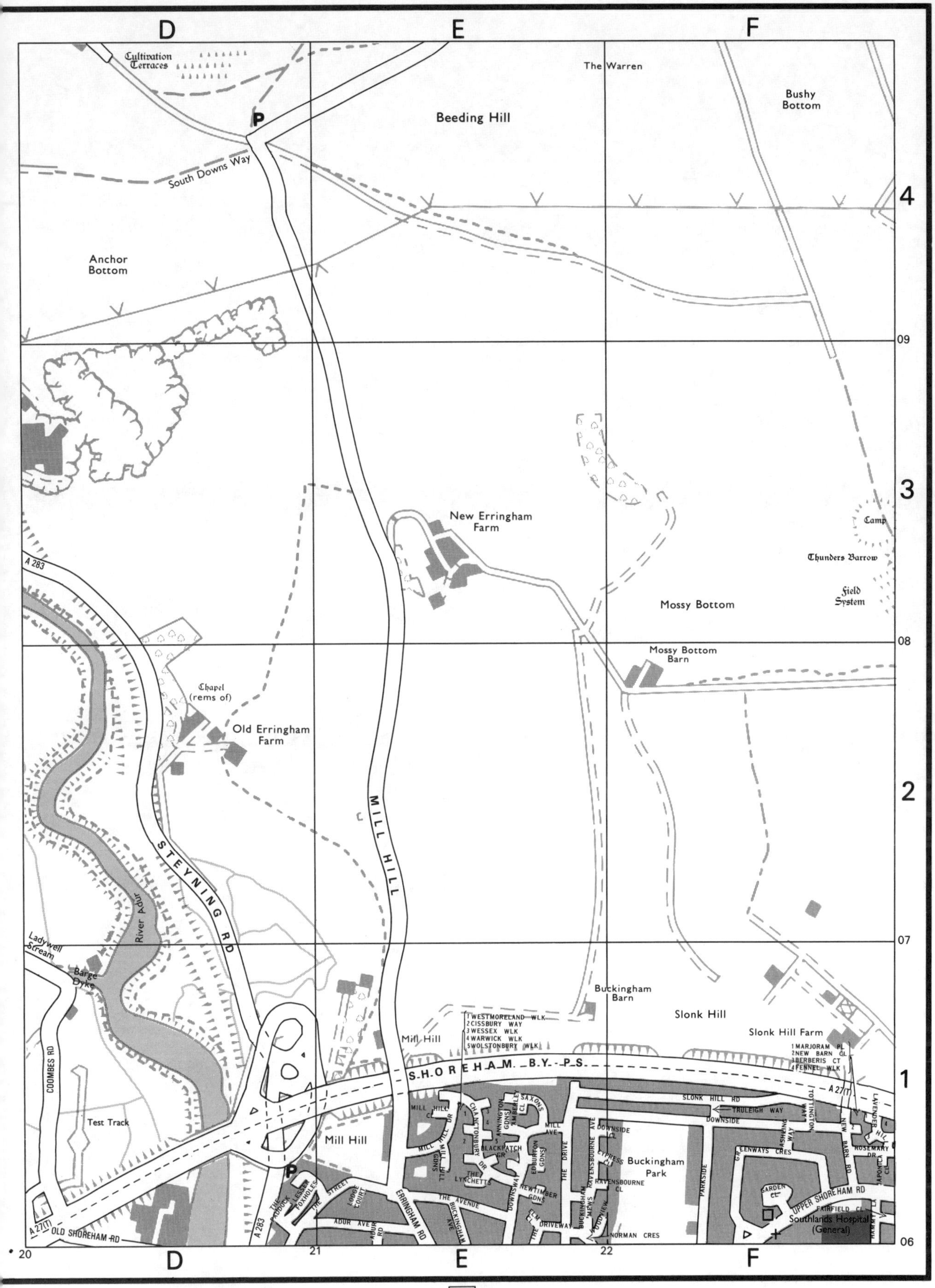
D
E
F
Cultivation Terraces
The Warren
Bushy Bottom
Beeding Hill
South Downs Way
Anchor Bottom
4
09
3
New Erringham Farm
Camp
Thunders Barrow
Field System
Mossy Bottom
A 283
08
Mossy Bottom Barn
Chapel (rems of)
Old Erringham Farm
2
MILL HILL
STEYNING RD
River Adur
Ladywell Stream
Barge Dyke
07
Buckingham Barn
Slonk Hill
Slonk Hill Farm
Mill Hill
1 WESTMORELAND WLK
2 CISSBURY WAY
3 WESSEX WLK
4 WARWICK WLK
5 WOLSTONBURY WLK
1 MARJORAM PL
2 NEW BARN CL
3 BERBERIS CT
4 FENNEL WLK
SHOREHAM BY-PS
1
A 27(T)
COOMBES RD
Test Track
Mill Hill
SLONK HILL RD
TRULEIGH WAY
DOWNSIDE
TOTTINGTON WAY
LAVENDER HILL
ROSEMARY DR
NEW BARN RD
JAPONICA CL
WASHINGTON WAY
GREENWAYS CRES
MILL HILL CL
MILL HILL DR
MILL HILL GDNS
CHANCTONBURY DR
ANNINGTON GDNS
AMBERLEY CL
SAXONS
BLACKPATCH GR
EDBURTON GDNS
MILL AVE
THE DRIVE
RAVENSBOURNE AVE
DOWNSIDE CL
CYPRESS CL
Buckingham Park
PARKSIDE
RAVENSBOURNE CL
THE LYNCHETTS
DOWNSWAY
NEWTIMBER GDNS
THE AVENUE
BUCKINGHAM AVE
BUCKINGHAM MEWS
ELM DRIVEWAY
WOODVIEW
NORMAN CRES
ERRINGHAM RD
LODGE COURT
THE STREET
FOXHOLES
LESSER
THE PADDOCK
ADUR AVE
ADUR RD
A 283
A 27(T)
OLD SHOREHAM RD
UPPER SHOREHAM RD
GARDEN CL
FAIRFIELD CL
Southlands Hospital (General)
06
20
21
22

164

184

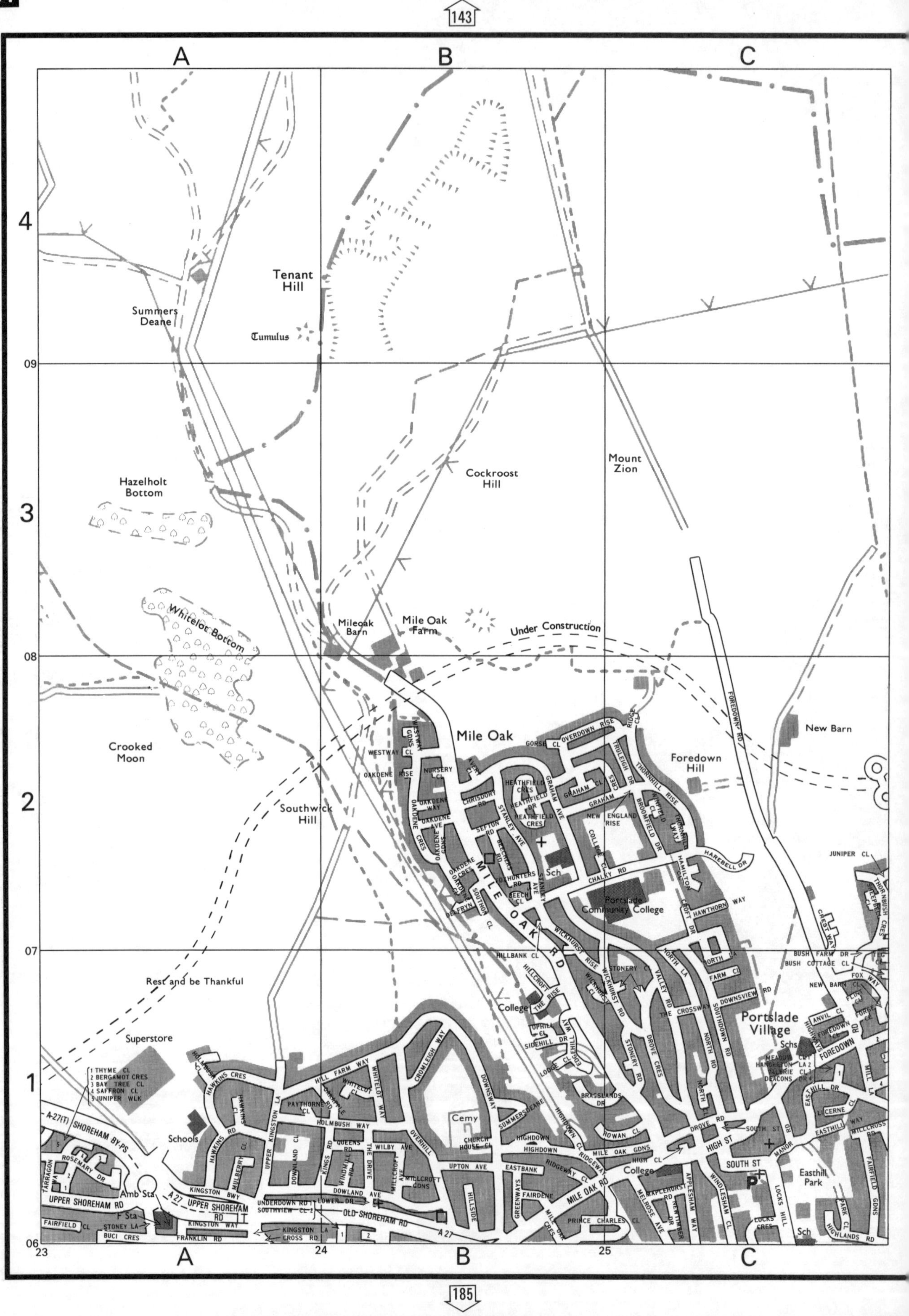
143
A
B
C
4
3
2
1
09
08
07
06
23
24
25
163
Tenant Hill
Summers Deane
Tumulus
Hazelholt Bottom
Whitelot Bottom
Crooked Moon
Southwick Hill
Cockroost Hill
Mount Zion
Mileoak Barn
Mile Oak Farm
Under Construction
Mile Oak
Foredown Hill
New Barn
Rest and be Thankful
Superstore
Portslade Community College
Portslade Village
Easthill Park
Schools
Cemy
College
Sch
Schs
Amb Sta
F Sta
MILE OAK RD
FOREDOWN RD
HIGH ST
SOUTH ST
UPPER SHOREHAM RD
OLD SHOREHAM RD
A 27
A 27(T) SHOREHAM BY-PS
1 THYME CL
2 BERGAMOT CRES
3 BAY TREE CL
4 SAFFRON CL
5 JUNIPER WLK
185

144

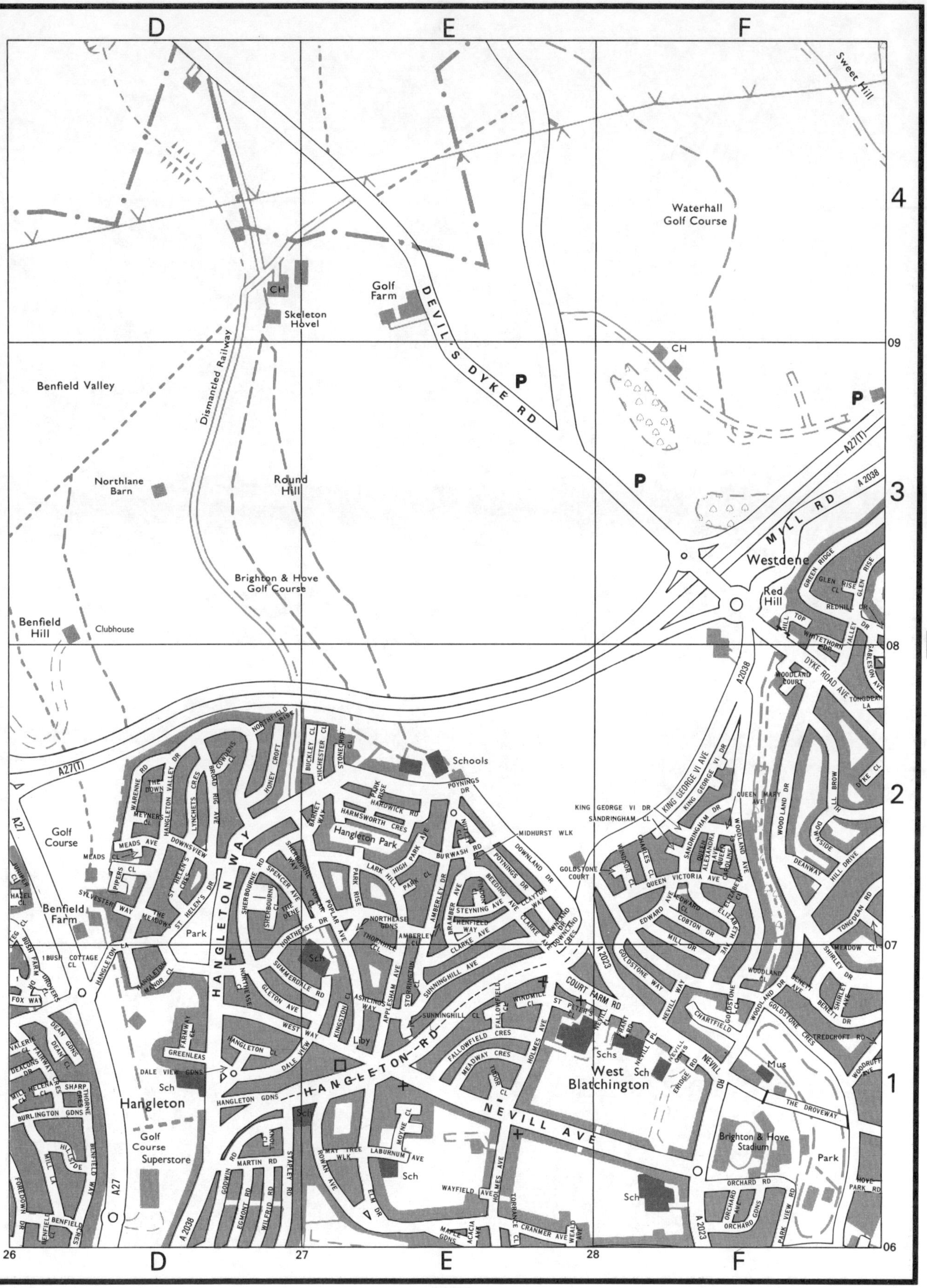

D
E
F
4
3
2
1
09
08
07
06
26
27
28
Sweet Hill
Waterhall Golf Course
Golf Farm
CH
Skeleton Hovel
DEVIL'S DYKE RD
Dismantled Railway
Benfield Valley
Northlane Barn
Round Hill
Brighton & Hove Golf Course
Benfield Hill
Clubhouse
A27(T)
A2038
MILL RD
Westdene
Red Hill
GREEN RIDGE
GLEN RISE
REDHILL DR
VALLEY DR
WHITETHORN DR
DYKE ROAD AVE
WOODLAND COURT
TONGDEAN LA
WOODLAND DR
DEANWAY
HILL DRIVE
TONGDEAN RD
MEADOW CL
SHIRLEY DR
BENETT AVE
BENETT DR
TREDCROFT RD
WOODRUFF AVE
Schools
POYNINGS DR
KING GEORGE VI AVE
KING GEORGE VI DR
SANDRINGHAM CL
SANDRINGHAM DR
QUEEN MARY AVE
WOODLAND AVE
MIDHURST WLK
GOLDSTONE COURT
QUEEN VICTORIA AVE
EDWARD AVE
COBTON DR
MILL DR
GOLDSTONE WAY
NEVILL WAY
CHARTFIELD
GOLDSTONE CRES
Golf Course
Benfield Farm
Hangleton Park
Park
HANGLETON WAY
HANGLETON VALLEY DR
DOWNSVIEW
ST HELEN'S DR
THE MEADOWS
SYLVESTER WAY
MEADS AVE
NORTHFIELD RISE
HONEY CROFT
BROAD RIG AVE
LYNCHETS CRES
WARENNE RD
BUCKLEY CL
CHICHESTER CL
STONECROFT CL
PARK RISE
HARDWICK RD
HARMSWORTH CRES
BURWASH RD
DOWNLAND DR
NORTHEASE DR
POPLAR AVE
SUMMERDALE RD
GLETON AVE
STEYNING AVE
CLARKE AVE
SUNNINGHILL AVE
COURT FARM RD
A 2023
HANGLETON RD
NEVILL AVE
NEVILL RD
WEST WAY
DALE VIEW
Liby
Sch
Schs
West Blatchington
Mus
THE DROVEWAY
Brighton & Hove Stadium
Park
HOVE PARK RD
ORCHARD RD
PARK VIEW RD
Hangleton
Golf Course Superstore
A27
BENFIELD WAY
MILL LA
BURLINGTON GDNS
GREENLEAS
HANGLETON GDNS
MARTIN RD
STAPLEY RD
GODWIN RD
EGMONT RD
WILFRID RD
ROWAN AVE
LABURNUM AVE
WAYFIELD AVE
HOLMES AVE
TORRANCE CL
CRANMER AVE
WEALD AVE
FALLOWFIELD CRES
MEADWAY CRES
ELM DR

166

186

145

165

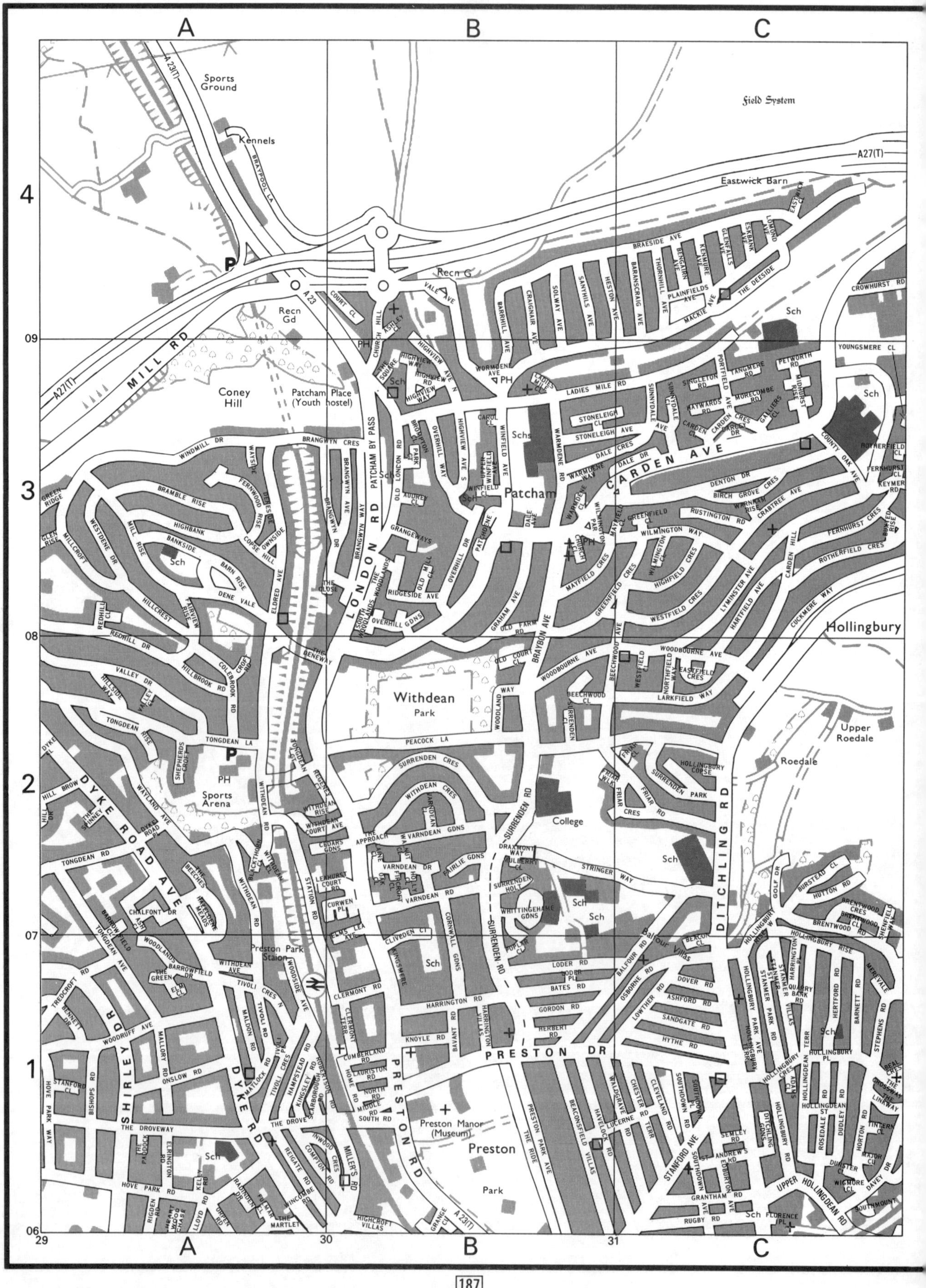
A
B
C
4
3
2
1
09
08
07
06
29
30
31
Sports Ground
Kennels
BRAYPOOL LA
A 23(T)
A27(T)
Field System
Eastwick Barn
BRAESIDE AVE
THORNHILL AVE
BENGAIRN AVE
KENMURE AVE
GLENFALLS AVE
ESKBANK AVE
LOMOND AVE
EASTWICK CL
PLAINFIELDS AVE
MACKIE AVE
THE DEESIDE
CROWHURST RD
Sch
Recn G
VALE AVE
A 23
Recn Gd
COURT CL
CHURCH HILL
ASHLEY CL
PH
BARRHILL AVE
CRAIGNAIR AVE
SOLWAY AVE
SANYHILLS AVE
HESTON AVE
BARANSCRAIG AVE
MILL RD
A27(T)
Coney Hill
Patcham Place (Youth hostel)
THE SQUARE
HIGHVIEW WAY
HIGHVIEW AVE N
WORMDENE AVE
LADIES MILE CL
LADIES MILE RD
SUNNYDALE AVE
SINGLETON RD
TANGMERE RD
PETWORTH RD
YOUNGSMERE CL
MAYWARDS RD
MORECOMBE RD
MIDHURST RISE
GALLIERS CL
STONELEIGH CL
STONELEIGH AVE
DALE CRES
DALE DR
WARMDENE RD
CARDEN AVE
COUNTY OAK AVE
ROTHERFIELD CL
FERNHURST CL
KEYMER RD
WINDMILL DR
BRANGWYN CRES
PATCHAM BY PASS
LONDON RD
OLD LONDON RD
BROUGHTON PARK
OVERHILL WAY
HIGHVIEW AVE S
CAROL CL
WINFIELD AVE
UPPER WINFIELD AVE
Schs
Patcham
DENTON DR
BIRCH GROVE CRES
CRABTREE AVE
RUSTINGTON RD
GREENFIELD CRES
WILMINGTON WAY
FERNHURST CRES
ROTHERFIELD CRES
BUNKER RD
GREEN RIDGE
BRAMBLE RISE
FERNWOOD RISE
WAYSIDE
DENES SIDE
COPSE HILL
OWNSIDE
HIGHBANK
BANKSIDE
MILL RISE
WESTDENE DR
MILLCROFT
GLEN RISE
Sch
BARN RISE
DENE VALE
HILLCREST
FAIRVIEW RISE
REDHILL CL
REDHILL DR
ELDRED AVE
BRANGWYN AVE
BRANGWYN DR
BRANGWYN WAY
GRANGEWAYS
AUDREY CL
OVERHILL DR
PATCHDENE
DALE AVE
CHURCH HILL
MAYFIELD CRES
HIGHFIELD CRES
WILMINGTON PAR
LYMINSTER AVE
CARDEN HILL
CUCKMERE WAY
HARTFIELD AVE
WESTFIELD CRES
GREENFIELD CRES
RIDGESIDE AVE
OVERHILL GDNS
THE CLOSE
THE WOODLANDS
SOUTH WOODLANDS
GRAHAM AVE
OLD FARM RD
BRAYBON AVE
Hollingbury
THE DENEWAY
VALLEY DR
HILLSIDE WAY
HILLBROOK RD
COLEBROOK RD
CROFT RD
Withdean
Park
OLD COURT CL
WOODBOURNE AVE
BEECHWOOD AVE
WESTFIELD AVE
NORTHFIELD WAY
EASTFIELD CRES
LARKFIELD WAY
BEECHWOOD CL
SURRENDEN CL
WOODLAND WAY
Upper Roedale
Roedale
TONGDEAN RISE
TONGDEAN LA
PEACOCK LA
SHEPHERDS CROFT
PH
Sports Arena
WAYLAND AVE
DYKE ROAD AVE
HILL BROW
THE SPINNEY
SURRENDEN CRES
WITHDEAN CRES
VARNDEAN GDNS
FRIAR CL
FRIAR WLK
FRIAR CRES
FRIAR RD
HOLLINGBURY COPSE
SURRENDEN PARK
College
DITCHLING RD
Sch
TONGDEAN RD
THE BEECHES
WITHDEAN RD
WITHDEAN RISE
WITHDEAN COURT AVE
CEDARS GDNS
THE APPROACH
VARNDEAN DR
FAIRLIE GDNS
DRAXMONT WAY
MULBERRY CL
STRINGER WAY
SURRENDEN HOLT
STATION RD
CURWEN PL
VARNDEAN RD
WHITTINGEHAME GDNS
Sch
Sch
GOLF DR
BURSTEAD CL
HUTTON RD
BRENTWOOD CRES
BRENTWOOD RD
SHENFIELD WAY
CHALFONT DR
BARROWFIELD
WOODLANDS
THE GREEN
BARROWFIELD DR
WITHDEAN AVE
Preston Park Station
TIVOLI CRES
TIVOLI CRES N
CLIVEDEN CT
KINGSMERE
CORNWALL GDNS
Sch
SURRENDEN RD
Balfour Villas
BALFOUR RD
LODER RD
BATES RD
BEACON CL
HOLLINGBURY RISE
HARRINGTON RD
STANMER VILLAS
QUARRY BANK RD
MEREVALE
TREDCROFT RD
BENNETT DR
SHIRLEY DR
WOODRUFF AVE
MALLORY RD
MALDON RD
TIVOLI RD
WOODSIDE AVE
CLERMONT RD
CLERMONT TERR
HARRINGTON RD
HARRINGTON VILLAS
BAVANT RD
GORDON RD
HERBERT RD
OSBORNE RD
LOWTHER RD
DOVER RD
ASHFORD RD
SANDGATE RD
HYTHE RD
HOLLINGBURY PARK AVE
STANMER PARK RD
HERTFORD RD
BARNETT RD
STEPHENS RD
KNOYLE RD
PRESTON DR
CUMBERLAND RD
LAURISTON RD
NORTH RD
SOUTH RD
ONSLOW RD
DYKE RD
MATLOCK RD
HAMPSTEAD RD
KINGSLEY RD
SCARBOROUGH RD
ROBERTSON RD
PRESTON RD
HOME RD
HOVE PARK WAY
BISHOPS RD
STANFORD CL
THE DROVEWAY
THE DROVE
Preston Manor (Museum)
Preston
Park
THE RIDE
PRESTON PARK AVE
BEACONSFIELD VILLAS
HAVELOCK RD
WALDEGRAVE RD
CHESTER TERR
CLEVELAND RD
LUCERNE RD
SOUTHDOWN RD
SOUTHDOWN PL
DITCHLING GDNS
HOLLINGBURY RD
HOLLINGBURY PL
HOLLINGDEAN TERR
HOLLINGDEAN ST
ROSEDALE CL
DUDLEY RD
HORTON RD
LINKWAY
SEMLEY RD
ST ANDREWS RD
STANFORD AVE
EDBURTON AVE
GRANTHAM RD
RUGBY RD
Sch
FLORENCE PL
UPPER HOLLINGDEAN RD
DUNSTER CL
WIGMORE CL
DAVEY DR
SOUTHMOUNT
Sch
ELRINGTON RD
KELLY RD
THE PADDOCK
HOVE PARK RD
RIGDEN RD
LLOYD RD
RADINDEN DR
REIGATE RD
COMPTON RD
INWOOD CRES
MILLER'S RD
WINCOMBE RD
THE MARTLET
HIGHCROFT VILLAS
GRANGE CL
A 23(T)

187

146

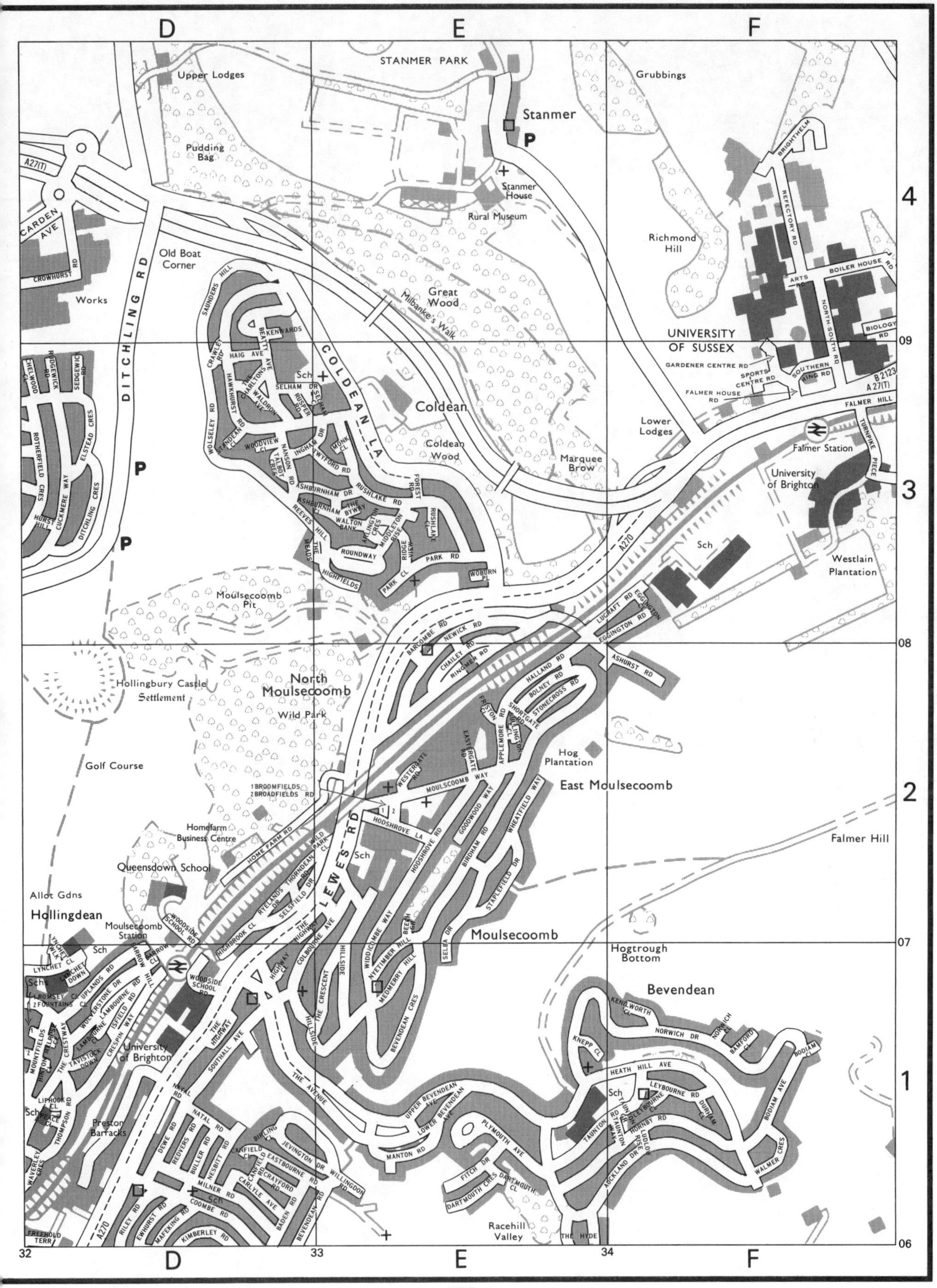

not continued, see key diagram

188

147

not continued, see key diagram

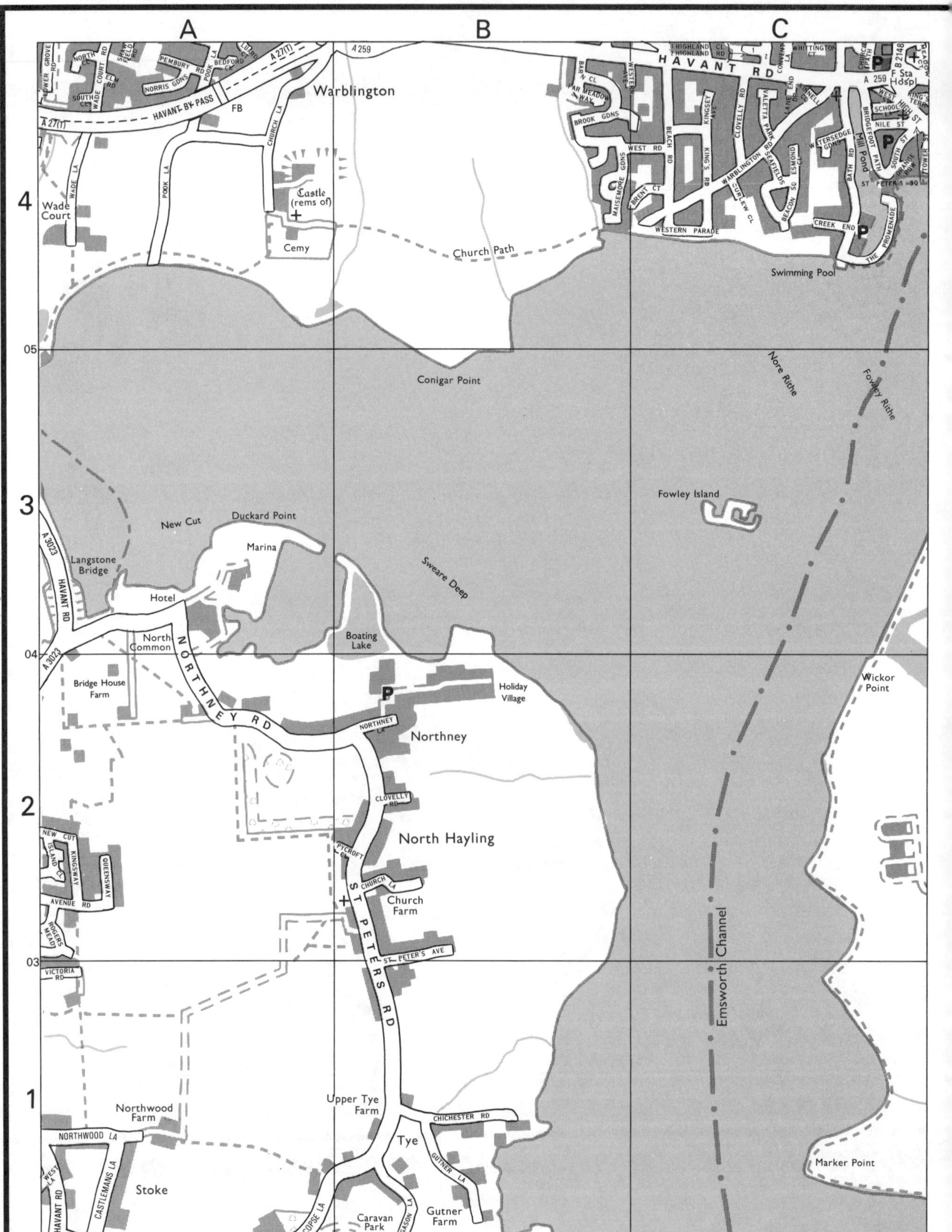

189

148

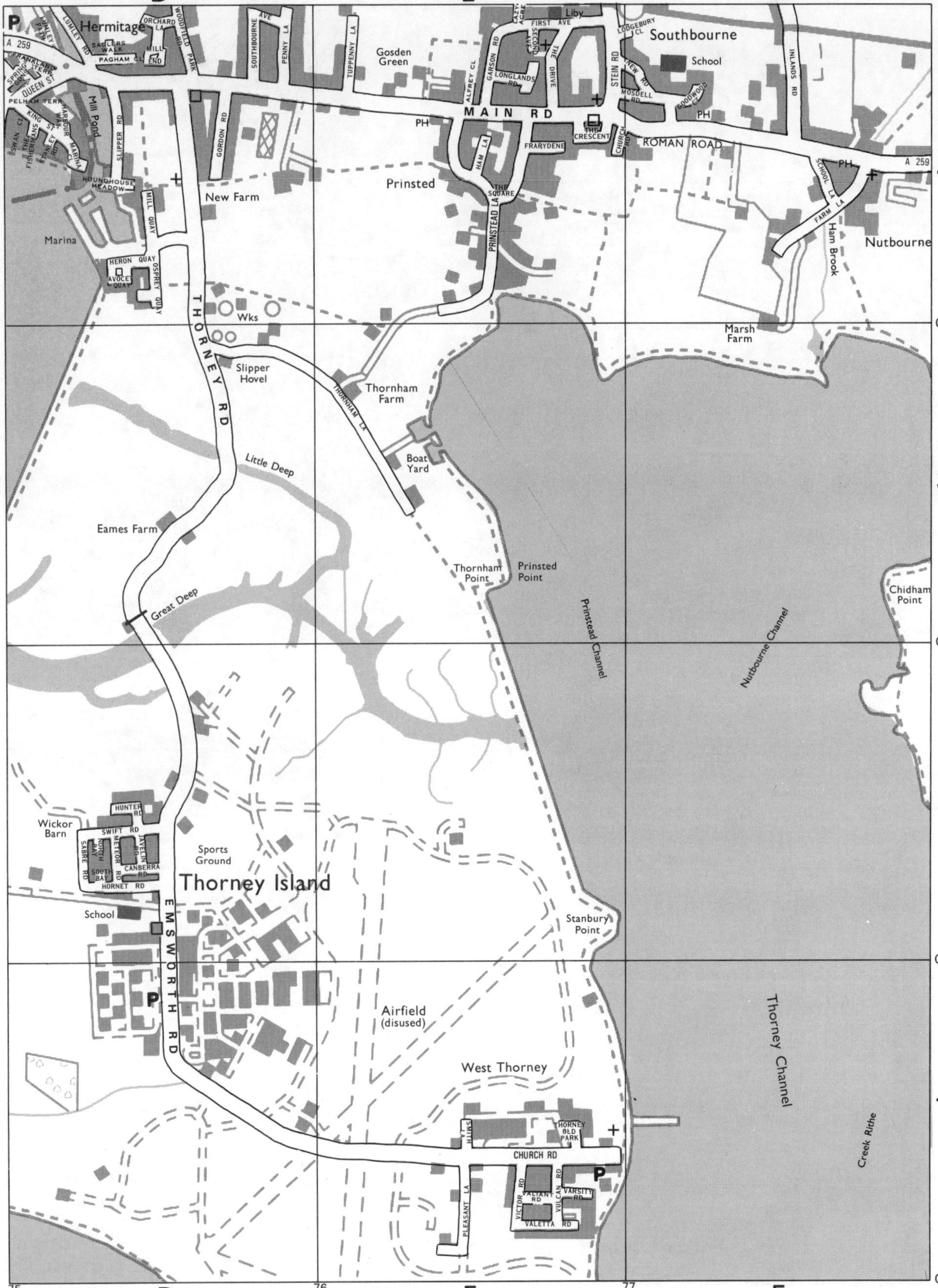
Hermitage
Southbourne
School
Gosden Green
MAIN RD
ROMAN ROAD
A 259
PH
Prinsted
New Farm
Marina
Mill Pond
Nutbourne
Ham Brook
Marsh Farm
Wks
Slipper Hovel
Thornham Farm
Boat Yard
THORNEY RD
Little Deep
Eames Farm
Great Deep
Thornham Point
Prinsted Point
Prinsted Channel
Nutbourne Channel
Chidham Point
Wickor Barn
Sports Ground
Thorney Island
EMSWORTH RD
Stanbury Point
Airfield (disused)
West Thorney
CHURCH RD
Thorney Channel
Creek Rithe
D
E
F
4
3
2
1
05
04
03
02
75
76
77

170

190

149

169

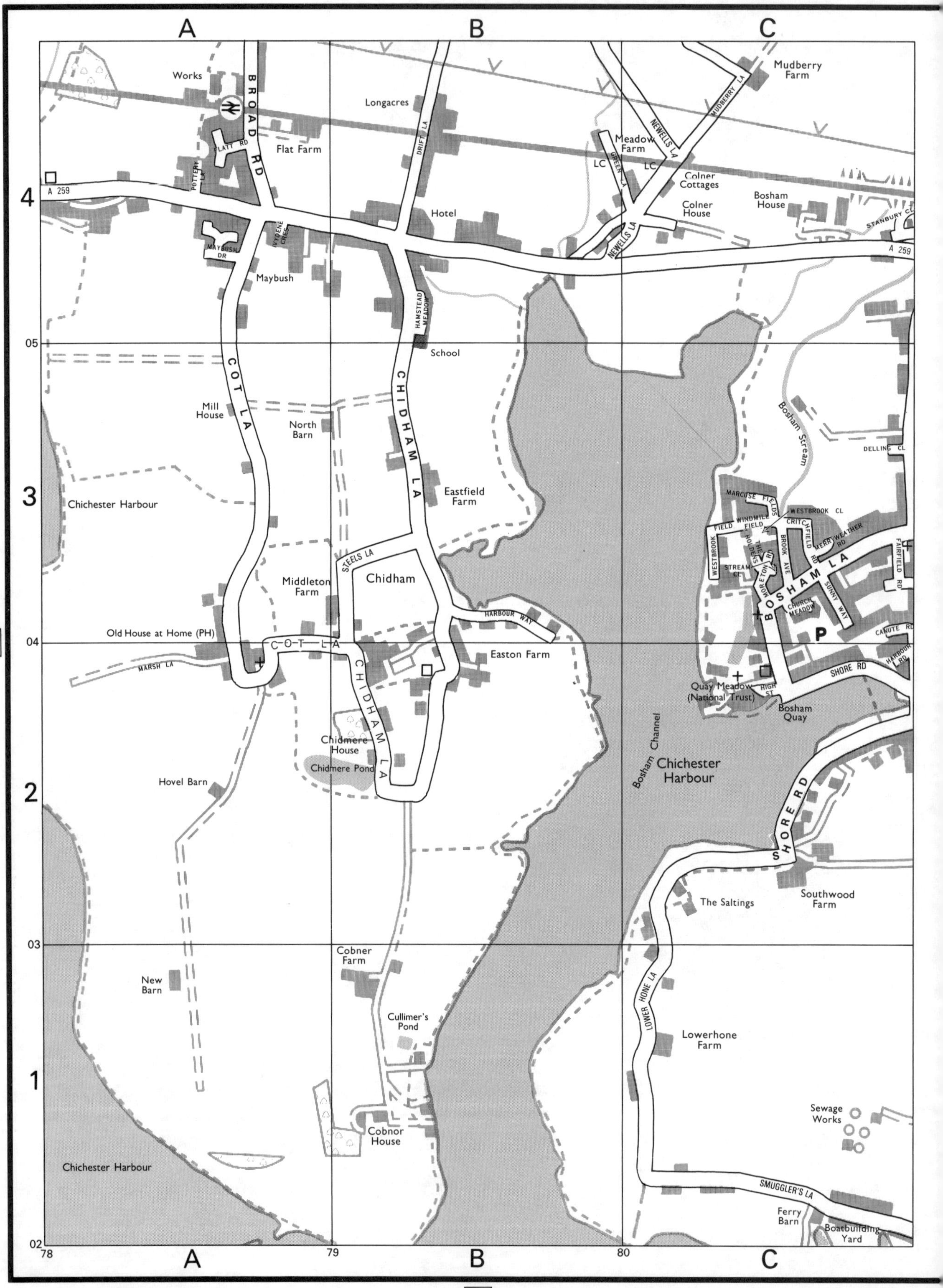
A
B
C
Works
BROAD RD
FLATT RD
POTTERY LA
Flat Farm
Longacres
DRIFT LA
Meadow Farm
GREEN LA
LC
LC
NEWELLS LA
Mudberry Farm
MUDBERRY LA
Colner Cottages
Colner House
Bosham House
STANBURY CL
A 259
Hotel
IVYDENE CRES
MAYBUSH DR
Maybush
HAMSTEAD MEADOW
School
05
COT LA
CHIDHAM LA
Mill House
North Barn
Bosham Stream
DELLING CL
Eastfield Farm
Chichester Harbour
MARCUSE FIELDS
WESTBROOK CL
WINDMILL FIELD
FIELD
CRITCHFIELD RD
MERRYWEATHER RD
FAIRFIELD RD
WESTBROOK
BROOK AVE
MORETON RD
STREAM CL
BOSHAM LA
SUNNY WAY
CHURCH MEADOW
STEELS LA
Chidham
Middleton Farm
HARBOUR WAY
CANUTE RD
HARBOUR RD
P
Old House at Home (PH)
04
COT LA
MARSH LA
Easton Farm
SHORE RD
HIGH ST
Quay Meadow (National Trust)
Bosham Quay
CHIDHAM LA
Chidmere House
Chidmere Pond
Bosham Channel
Chichester Harbour
Hovel Barn
SHORE RD
The Saltings
Southwood Farm
03
Cobner Farm
New Barn
LOWER HONE LA
Cullimer's Pond
Lowerhone Farm
Sewage Works
Cobnor House
Chichester Harbour
SMUGGLER'S LA
Ferry Barn
Boatbuilding Yard
02
78
79
80
A
B
C
4
3
2
1

191

150

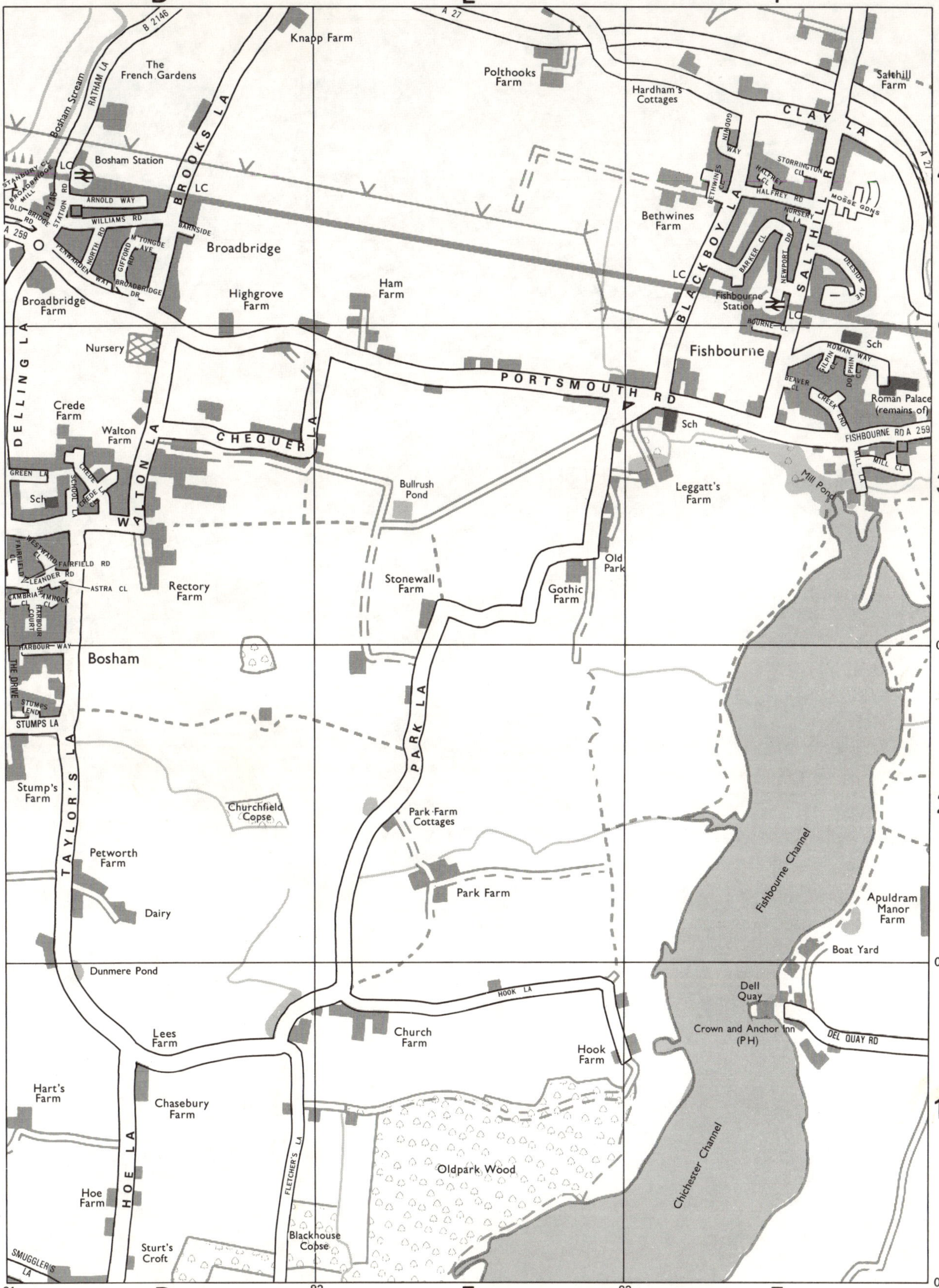

D
E
F
Knapp Farm
A 27
B 2146
The French Gardens
Polthooks Farm
Hardham's Cottages
Salthill Farm
RATHAM LA
Bosham Stream
BROOKS LA
CLAY LA
Bosham Station
LC
GODWIN WAY
STORRINGTON CL
HALFREY CL
HALFREY RD
MOSSE GDNS
A 27
STANBURY CL
BROADBRIDGE MILL
OLD BRIDGE RD
B 2146
STATION RD
ARNOLD WAY
WILLIAMS RD
BARNSIDE
BETHWINES CL
Bethwines Farm
NURSERY LA
A 259
PENWARDEN WAY
NORTH RD
GIFFORD RD
M'TONGUE AVE
BROADBRIDGE DR
Broadbridge
BARKER CL
NEWPORT DR
DEESIDE AVE
Broadbridge Farm
Highgrove Farm
Ham Farm
BLACKBOY LA
SALTHILL RD
Fishbourne Station
BOURNE CL
05
Nursery
Fishbourne
Sch
ROMAN WAY
GILPIN CL
DOLPHIN CL
BEAVER CL
CREEK END
DELLING LA
PORTSMOUTH RD
Roman Palace (remains of)
Crede Farm
Walton Farm
CHEQUER LA
Sch
FISHBOURNE RD A 259
MILL LA
MILL CL
GREEN LA
CREDE CL
SCHOOL LA
Sch
WALTON LA
Bullrush Pond
Leggatt's Farm
Mill Pond
3
WESTWARD CL
FAIRFIELD CL
FAIRFIELD RD
LEANDER RD
ASTRA CL
CAMBRIA CL
SHAMROCK CL
HARBOUR COURT
Rectory Farm
Stonewall Farm
Gothic Farm
Old Park
HARBOUR WAY
Bosham
04
172
THE DRIVE
STUMPS END
STUMPS LA
PARK LA
Stump's Farm
TAYLOR'S LA
Churchfield Copse
2
Park Farm Cottages
Petworth Farm
Fishbourne Channel
Park Farm
Dairy
Apuldram Manor Farm
Boat Yard
Dunmere Pond
03
HOOK LA
Dell Quay
Crown and Anchor Inn (PH)
DEL QUAY RD
Lees Farm
Church Farm
Hook Farm
Hart's Farm
Chasebury Farm
1
Chichester Channel
FLETCHER'S LA
Oldpark Wood
HOE LA
Hoe Farm
Blackhouse Copse
Sturt's Croft
SMUGGLER'S LA
02
81
82
83
D
E
F

192

151

171

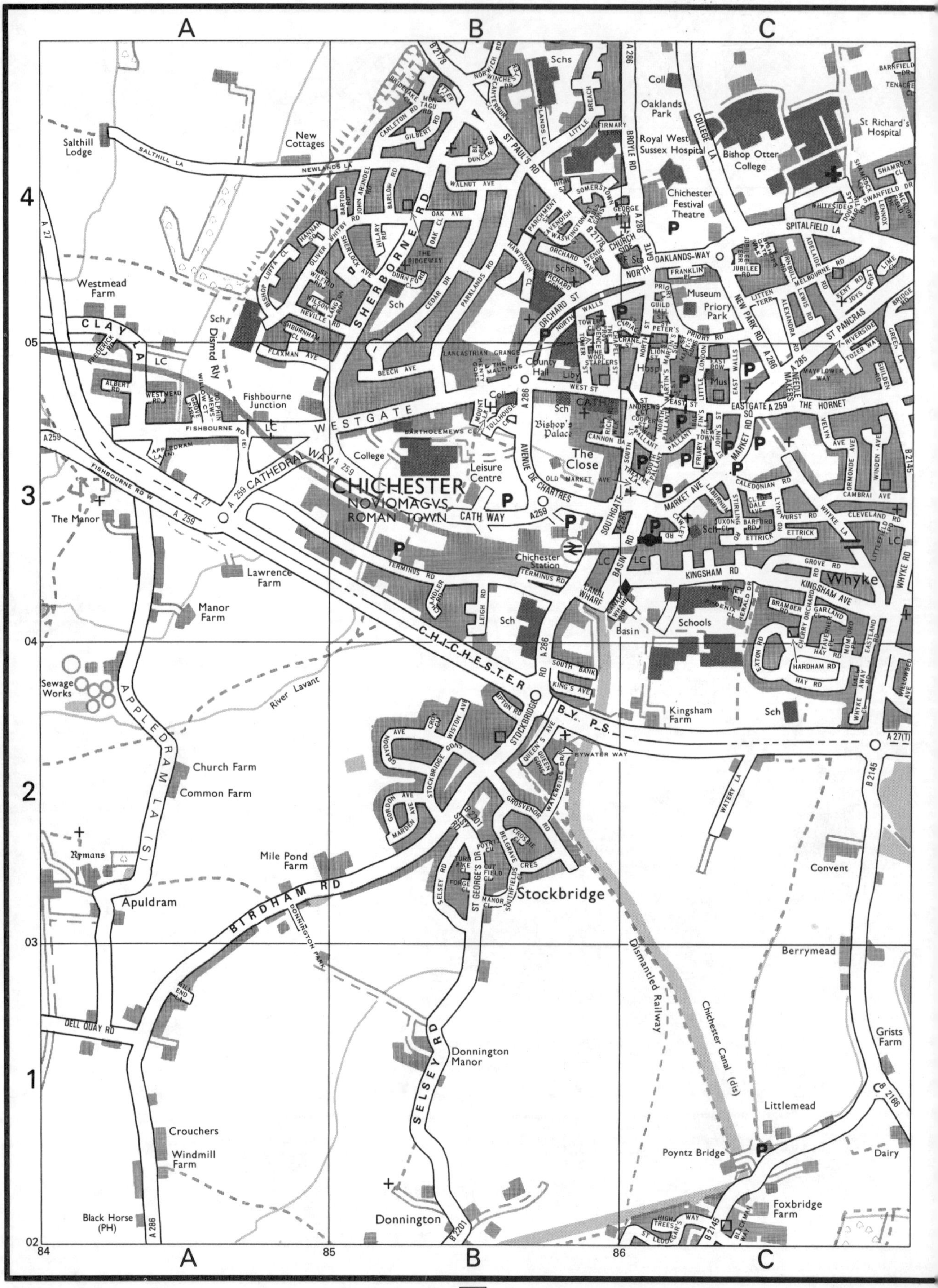
A
B
C
4
3
2
1
05
04
03
02
84
85
86
CHICHESTER
NOVIOMAGVS
ROMAN TOWN
Salthill Lodge
SALTHILL LA
NEWLANDS LA
New Cottages
Westmead Farm
CLAY LA
Dismtd Rly
Fishbourne Junction
WESTGATE
CATHEDRAL WAY
FISHBOURNE RD W
The Manor
Lawrence Farm
Manor Farm
Sewage Works
River Lavant
APPLEDRAM LA (S)
Church Farm
Common Farm
Rymans
Mile Pond Farm
Apuldram
BIRDHAM RD
DONNINGTON PARK
DELL QUAY RD
Crouchers
Windmill Farm
Black Horse (PH)
A 286
A 27
A 259
SHERBORNE RD
Sch
Schs
Coll
Oaklands Park
Royal West Sussex Hospital
Chichester Festival Theatre
Bishop Otter College
St Richard's Hospital
SPITALFIELD LA
OAKLANDS WAY
NORTH GATE
Museum
Priory Park
County Hall
Liby
CATH
Bishop's Palace
The Close
Leisure Centre
College
AVENUE DE CHARTRES
CATH WAY
Chichester Station
TERMINUS RD
EASTGATE SQ
THE HORNET
ST PANCRAS
Hospl
Mus
MARKET AVE
KINGSHAM RD
KINGSHAM AVE
Whyke
Schools
Basin
CANAL WHARF
CHICHESTER BY PS
Kingsham Farm
STOCKBRIDGE RD
Stockbridge
SELSEY RD
Donnington Manor
Donnington
Dismantled Railway
Chichester Canal (dis)
Convent
Berrymead
Grists Farm
Littlemead
Poyntz Bridge
Dairy
Foxbridge Farm
B 2145
B 2201
B 2166
A 27(T)

193

152

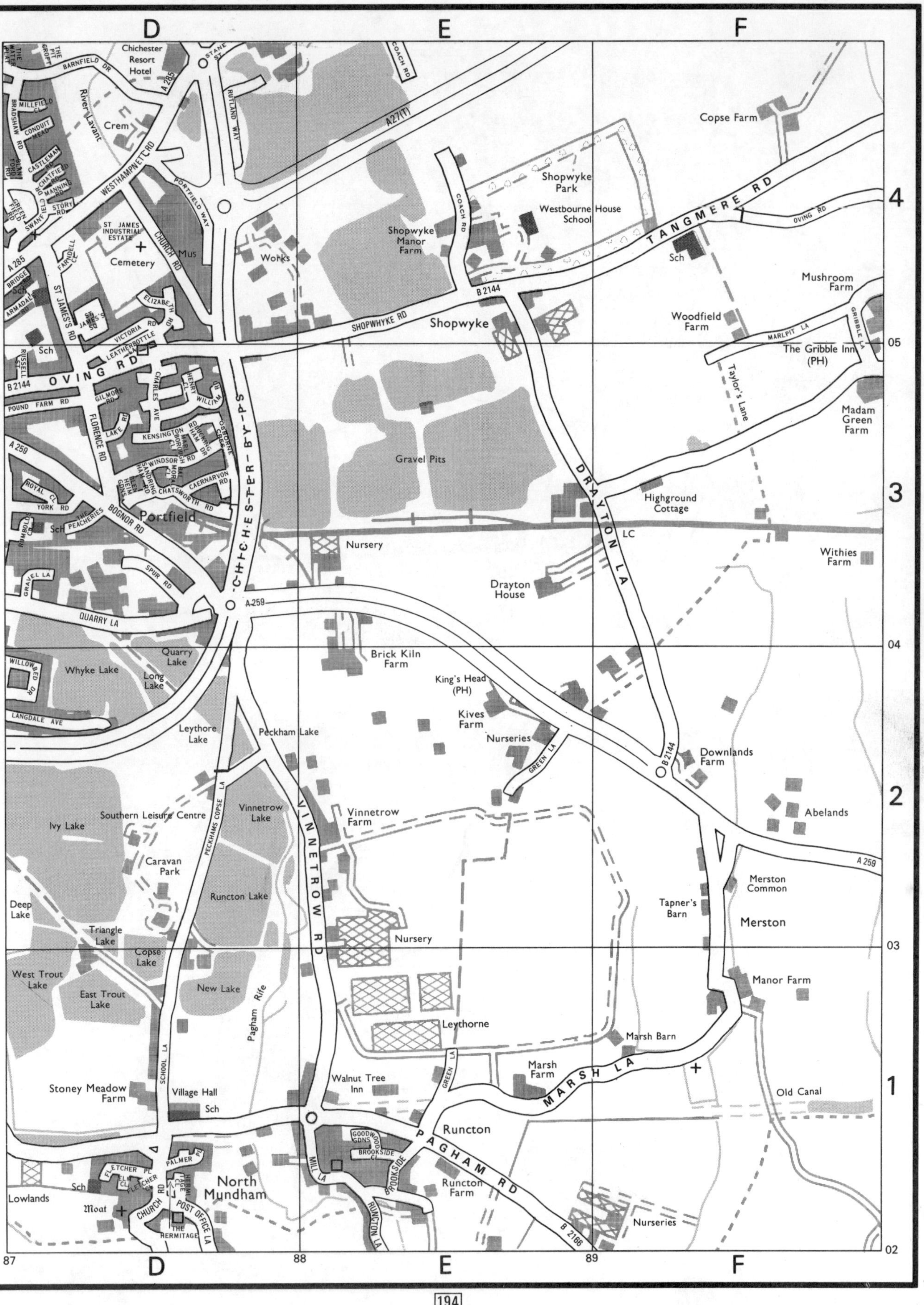

D
E
F
Chichester Resort Hotel
Crem
River Lavant
Cemetery
Mus
Works
Shopwyke Manor Farm
Shopwyke Park
Westbourne House School
Copse Farm
Sch
Mushroom Farm
Woodfield Farm
The Gribble Inn (PH)
Madam Green Farm
Shopwyke
Gravel Pits
Highground Cottage
Portfield
Nursery
Withies Farm
Drayton House
LC
Brick Kiln Farm
King's Head (PH)
Kives Farm
Nurseries
Downlands Farm
Whyke Lake
Quarry Lake
Long Lake
Leythore Lake
Peckham Lake
Ivy Lake
Southern Leisure Centre
Vinnetrow Lake
Vinnetrow Farm
Abelands
Caravan Park
Runcton Lake
Merston Common
Tapner's Barn
Merston
Deep Lake
Triangle Lake
Nursery
Copse Lake
West Trout Lake
East Trout Lake
New Lake
Pagham Rife
Manor Farm
Leythorne
Marsh Barn
Marsh Farm
Stoney Meadow Farm
Village Hall
Sch
Walnut Tree Inn
Runcton
Old Canal
North Mundham
Lowlands
Moat
Runcton Farm
Nurseries
THE HERMITAGE
A27(T)
A 285
A 259
B 2144
B 2166
TANGMERE RD
OVING RD
SHOPWHYKE RD
COACH RD
RUTLAND WAY
STANE ST
PORTFIELD WAY
CHURCH RD
WESTHAMPNETT RD
ST JAMES INDUSTRIAL ESTATE
ST JAMES'S RD
CHICHESTER BY-PS
DRAYTON LA
MARLPIT LA
GRIBBLE LA
Taylor's Lane
OVING RD
QUARRY LA
SPUR RD
GRAVEL LA
BOGNOR RD
FLORENCE RD
POUND FARM RD
GREEN LA
VINNETROW RD
PECKHAMS COPSE LA
SCHOOL LA
MARSH LA
PAGHAM RD
MILL LA
RUNCTON LA
BROOKSIDE
POST OFFICE LA
CHURCH RD
FLETCHER PL
PALMER PL
LANGDALE AVE
WILLOWBED DR
BARNFIELD DR
MILLFIELD CL
BRADSHAW RD
CONDUIT MEAD
CASTLEMAN RD
CHATFIELD RD
STORY RD
SWANFIELD DR
FARNDELL CL
ARMADALE RD
BRIDGE RD
ELIZABETH RD
VICTORIA RD
LEATHERBOTTLE LA
RUSSELL ST
GILMORE RD
CHARLES AVE
HENRY CL
WILLIAM RD
KENSINGTON RD
LAKE RD
WINDSOR RD
CHATSWORTH RD
CAERNARVON RD
OSBORNE CRES
ROYAL CL
YORK RD
THE PEACHERIES
GOODWOOD GDNS
BROOKSIDE CL
4
3
2
1
05
04
03
02
87
88
89

174

194

153

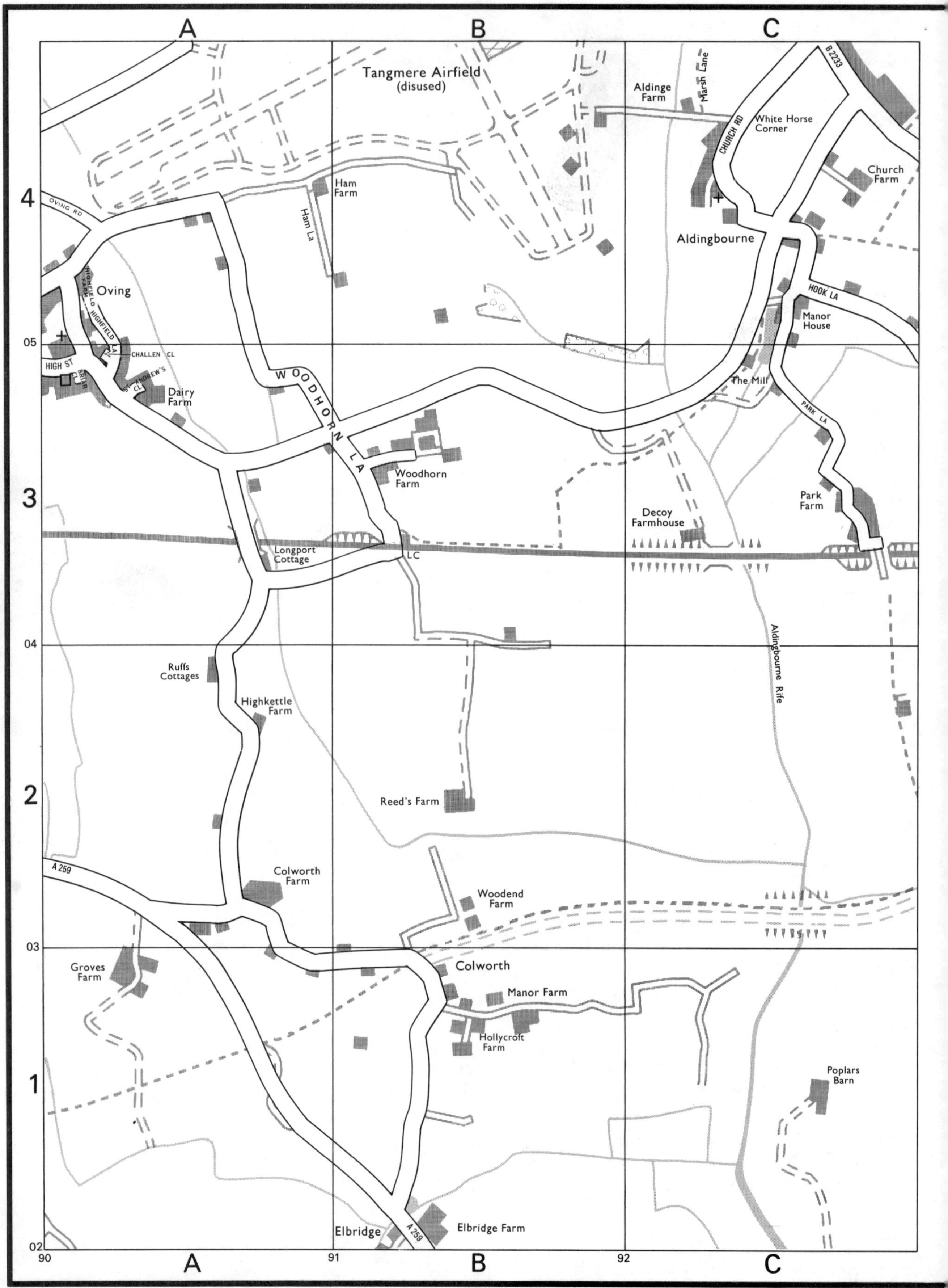
A
B
C
Tangmere Airfield
(disused)
Aldinge Farm
Marsh Lane
B 2233
CHURCH RD
White Horse Corner
Church Farm
Ham Farm
Ham La
Aldingbourne
4
OVING RD
HIGHFIELD FARM
HIGHFIELD LA
Oving
HOOK LA
Manor House
05
CHALLEN CL
HIGH ST
BRIAR CL
ST ANDREW'S CL
Dairy Farm
WOODHORN LA
The Mill
PARK LA
Woodhorn Farm
3
Park Farm
Decoy Farmhouse
Longport Cottage
LC
04
Aldingbourne Rife
Ruffs Cottages
Highkettle Farm
2
Reed's Farm
A 259
Colworth Farm
Woodend Farm
03
Groves Farm
Colworth
Manor Farm
Hollycroft Farm
1
Poplars Barn
Elbridge
A 259
Elbridge Farm
02
90
91
92

173

195

154

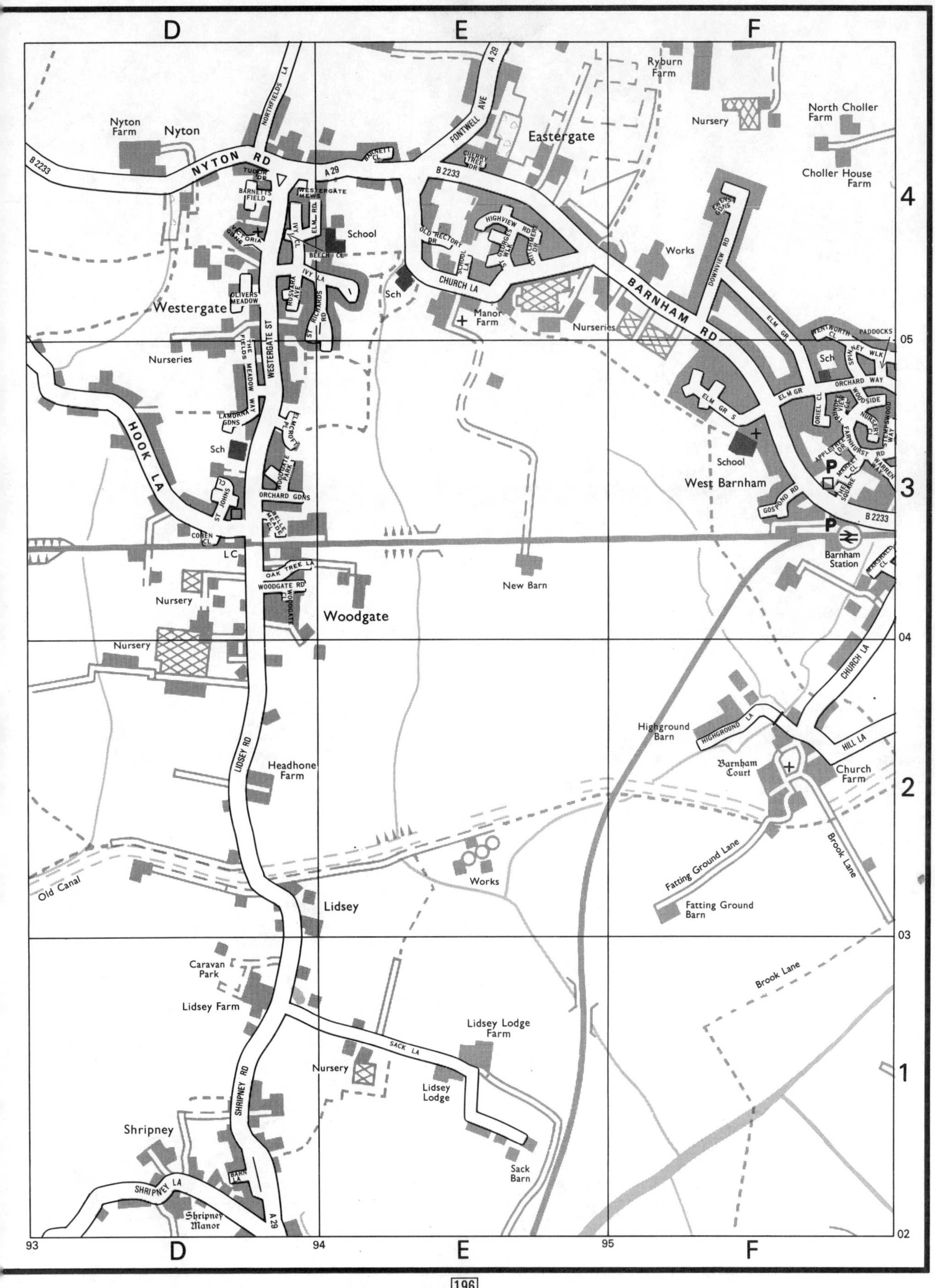
D
E
F
Ryburn Farm
North Choller Farm
Nyton Farm
Nyton
Nursery
Eastergate
Choller House Farm
NYTON RD
B 2233
A 29
NORTHFIELDS LA
FONTWELL AVE
BARNETT CL
CHERRY TREE DR
TUDOR DR
BARNETTS FIELD
WESTERGATE MEWS
School
Works
HIGHVIEW RD
OLD RECTORY DR
VICTORIA GDNS
IVY CL
ELM RD
BEECH CL
IVY LA
SCHOOL LA
ST GEORGES WLK
CRITCHMERE DR
CHURCH LA
BARNHAM RD
DOWNVIEW RD
OWENS GDNS
Sch
Westergate
OLIVERS MEADOW
ROSVARA AVE
ST RICHARDS RD
Manor Farm
Nurseries
ELM GR
WENTWORTH CL
PADDOCKS
SPINNEY WLK
Nurseries
THE FIELDS
WESTERGATE ST
MEADOW WAY
ORCHARD WAY
ELM GR S
ORIEL CL
WOODSIDE
NURSERY CL
LAMORNA GDNS
ELMCROFT PL
HOOK LA
Sch
School
APPLETREE DR
FARNHURST RD
STEMPSWOOD WAY
WARREN WAY
MARKET CL
THE SQUARE
West Barnham
ST JOHNS CL
WOODGATE PARK
ORCHARD GDNS
GOSPORT RD
P
B 2233
BELLE MEADE CL
COBEN CL
LC
Barnham Station
MARSHALL CL
OAK TREE LA
WOODGATE RD
WOODGATE CL
Nursery
New Barn
Woodgate
Nursery
CHURCH LA
Highground Barn
HIGHGROUND LA
HILL LA
LIDSEY RD
Headhone Farm
Barnham Court
Church Farm
Brook Lane
Old Canal
Fatting Ground Lane
Works
Lidsey
Fatting Ground Barn
Caravan Park
Brook Lane
Lidsey Farm
Lidsey Lodge Farm
SACK LA
Nursery
SHRIPNEY RD
Lidsey Lodge
Shripney
Sack Barn
BARN LA
SHRIPNEY LA
Shripney Manor
A 29
4
3
2
1
05
04
03
02
93
94
95

176

196

155

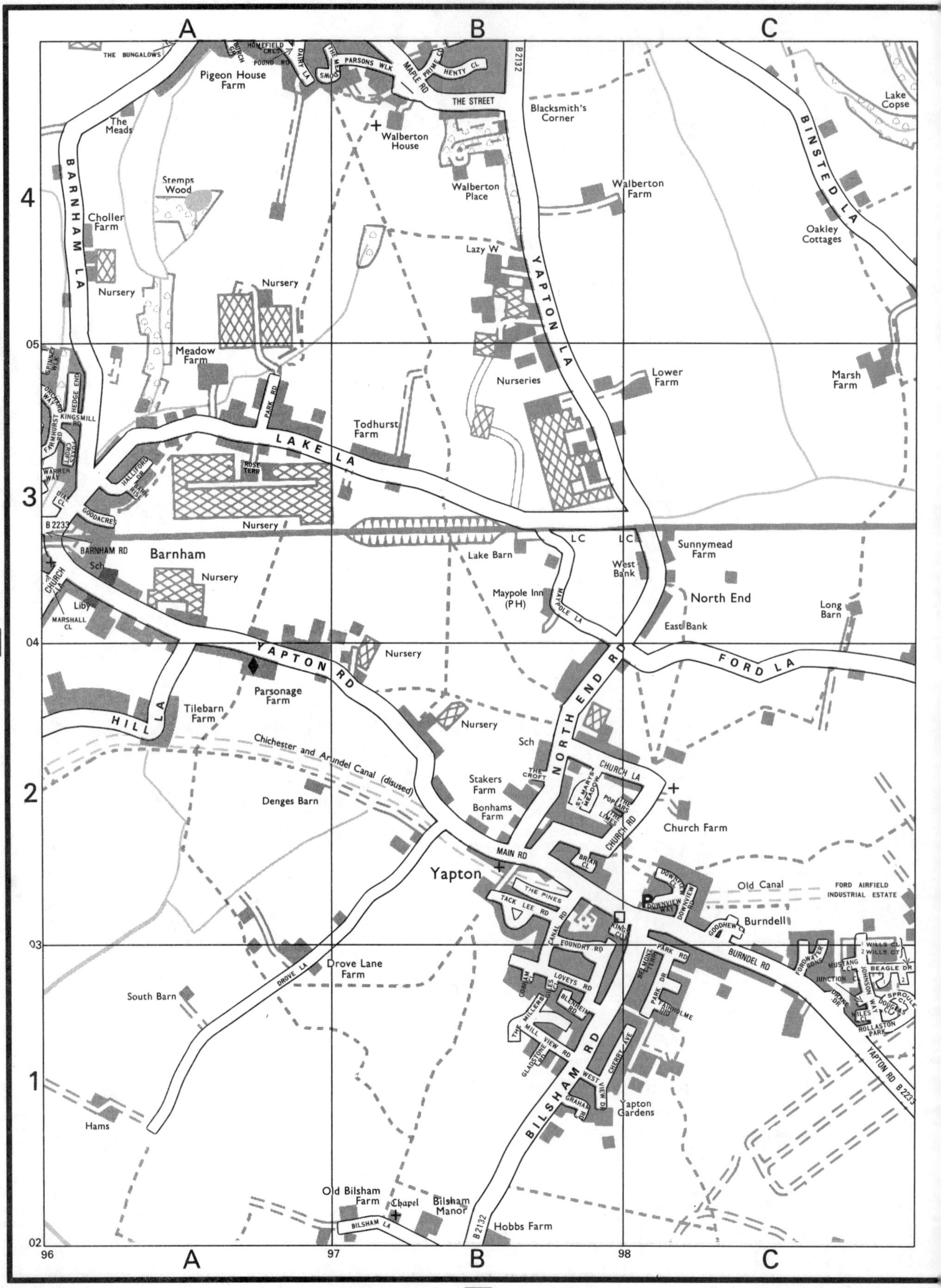
A
B
C
THE BUNGALOWS
HOMEFIELD CRES
POUND RD
DAIRY LA
PARSONS WLK
MAPLE RD
PRIME CL
HENTY CL
B2132
THE STREET
Pigeon House Farm
Walberton House
Blacksmith's Corner
Lake Copse
BINSTED LA
The Meads
BARNHAM LA
Stemps Wood
Walberton Place
Walberton Farm
Oakley Cottages
Choller Farm
Lazy W
YAPTON LA
Nursery
Nursery
Meadow Farm
PARK RD
Nurseries
Lower Farm
Marsh Farm
SPINNEY WLK
ORCHARD WAY
HEDGE END
KINGSMILL RD
FARMHURST RD
WARREN WAY
LAKE LA
Todhurst Farm
ROSE TERR
HALLIFORD DR
GOODACRES
B 2233
Nursery
LC
Lake Barn
West Bank
Sunnymead Farm
BARNHAM RD
Barnham
Sch
Nursery
CHURCH LA
Liby
MARSHALL CL
Maypole Inn (PH)
MAYPOLE LA
North End
East Bank
Long Barn
YAPTON RD
Nursery
NORTH END RD
FORD LA
Parsonage Farm
Tilebarn Farm
HILL LA
Nursery
Sch
Chichester and Arundel Canal (disused)
THE CROFT
CHURCH LA
ST MARYS MEADOW
POPLARS
THE LIMES
CHURCH RD
Stakers Farm
Bonhams Farm
Denges Barn
Church Farm
MAIN RD
BRIAR CL
Yapton
DOWNVIEW CL
Old Canal
FORD AIRFIELD INDUSTRIAL ESTATE
THE PINES
TACK LEE RD
CANAL RD
KINGS CL
DOWNVIEW WAY
DOWNVIEW RD
GOODHEW CL
Burndell
FOUNDRY RD
PARK RD
BURNDEL RD
WILLS CL
WILLS CT
BEAGLE DR
MUSTANG CL
FORDWATER GDNS
JUNCTION
JOHNSON WAY
DRAKE DR
Drove Lane Farm
DROVE LA
COBHAM
LOVEYS RD
BELMONT TERR
MILLERS
BLENHEIM RD
PARK DR
FAIRHOLME
SPROULE CL
DOUGLAS
MILES CL
ROLLASTON PARK
South Barn
THE MILL
MILL VIEW RD
GLADSTONE RD
BILSHAM RD
CHERRY AVE
WEST VIEW DR
GRAHAM RD
Yapton Gardens
YAPTON RD
B 2233
Hams
Old Bilsham Farm
Chapel
Bilsham Manor
BILSHAM LA
B2132
Hobbs Farm
4
3
2
1
05
04
03
02
96
97
98

175

197

156

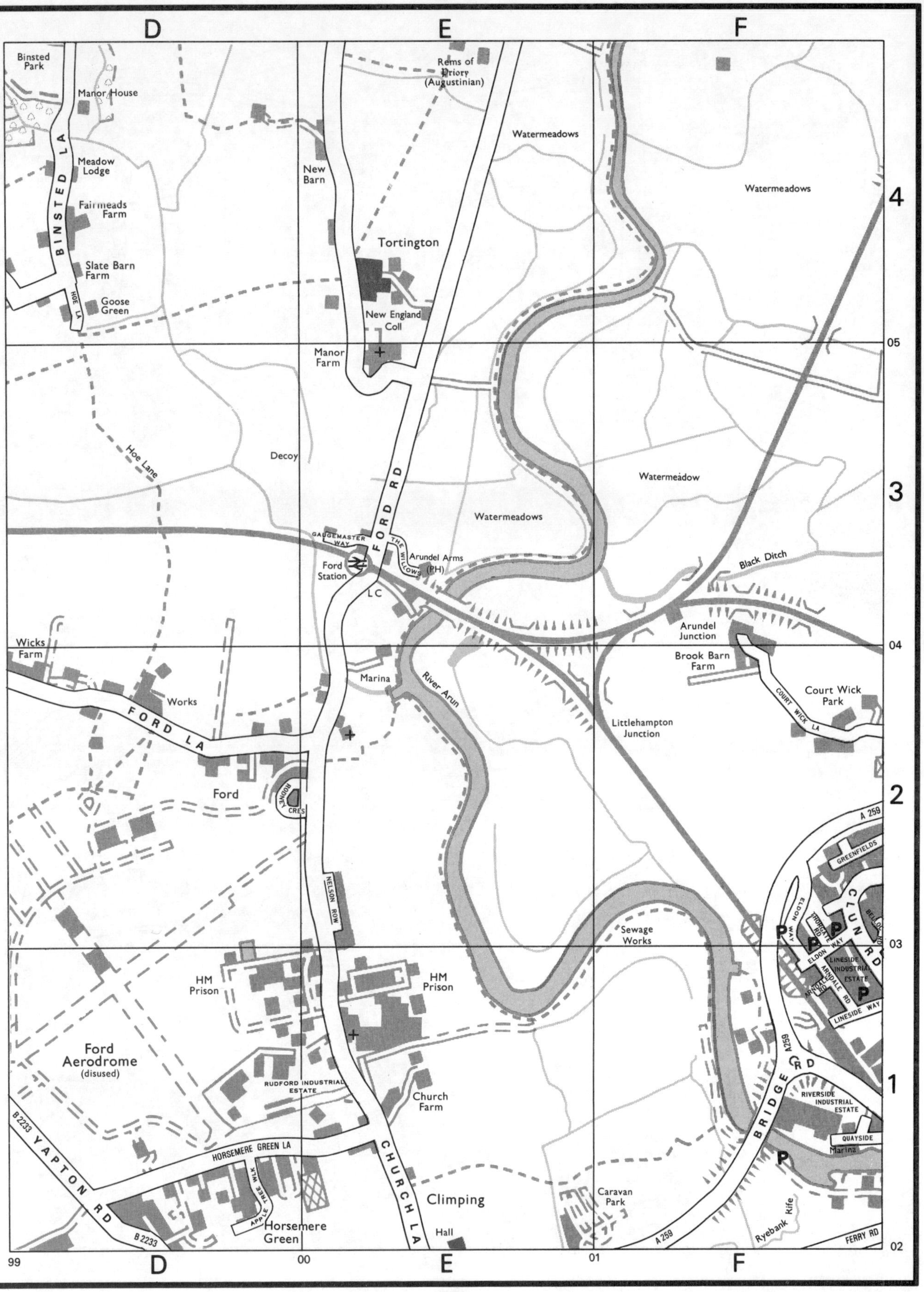
D
E
F
Binsted Park
Manor House
Meadow Lodge
BINSTED LA
Fairmeads Farm
Slate Barn Farm
HOE LA
Goose Green
Rems of Priory (Augustinian)
New Barn
Tortington
New England Coll
Manor Farm
Watermeadows
Watermeadows
Watermeadow
Watermeadows
Hoe Lane
Decoy
FORD RD
GAUGEMASTER WAY
THE WILLOWS
Arundel Arms (PH)
Ford Station
L C
Black Ditch
Arundel Junction
Brook Barn Farm
Court Wick Park
COURT WICK LA
Wicks Farm
Works
FORD LA
Marina
River Arun
Littlehampton Junction
Ford
RODNEY CRES
NELSON ROW
A 259
GREENFIELDS
CLUN RD
ELDON WAY
THORGATE RD
BELLOC RD
LINESIDE INDUSTRIAL ESTATE
ARNDALE RD
LINESIDE WAY
Sewage Works
HM Prison
HM Prison
Ford Aerodrome (disused)
RUDFORD INDUSTRIAL ESTATE
Church Farm
A259
BRIDGE RD
RIVERSIDE INDUSTRIAL ESTATE
QUAYSIDE
Marina
B 2233
YAPTON RD
HORSEMERE GREEN LA
APPLE TREE WLK
Horsemere Green
CHURCH LA
Climping
Hall
Caravan Park
A 259
Ryebank Rife
FERRY RD
4
3
2
1
05
04
03
02
99
00
01

178

198

157

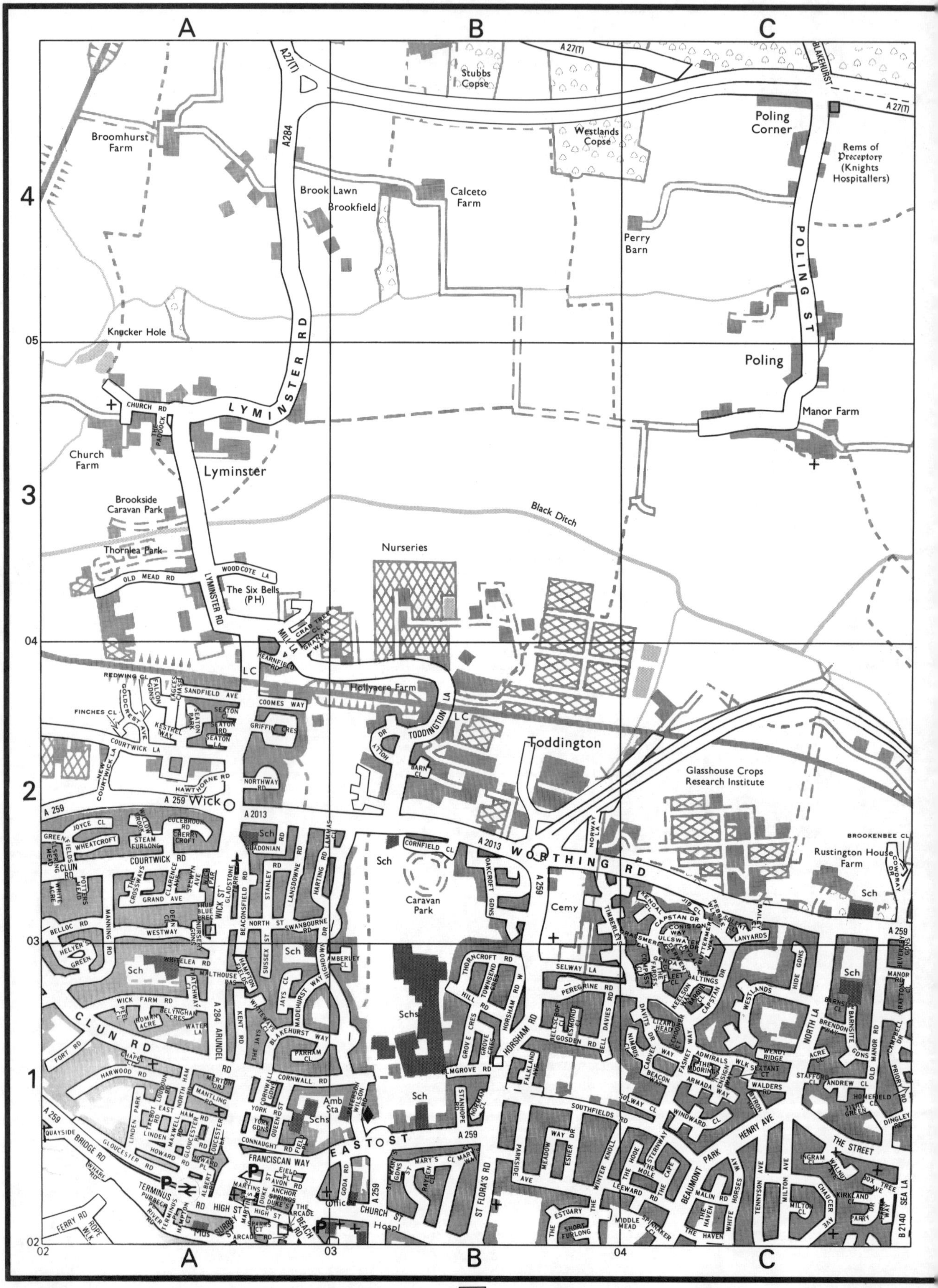
A
B
C
4
3
2
1
05
04
03
02
A27(T)
A284
Stubbs Copse
Westlands Copse
Poling Corner
Rems of Preceptory (Knights Hospitallers)
Broomhurst Farm
Brook Lawn
Brookfield
Calceto Farm
Perry Barn
BLAKEHURST LA
POLING ST
Knucker Hole
Poling
Manor Farm
LYMINSTER RD
CHURCH RD
THE PADDOCK
Church Farm
Lyminster
Brookside Caravan Park
Black Ditch
Thornlea Park
Nurseries
OLD MEAD RD
WOODCOTE LA
The Six Bells (PH)
MILL LA
CRAB TREE CL
GRATTAN WAY
HEARNFIELD RD
LC
Hollyacre Farm
REDWING CL
SANDFIELD AVE
FINCHES CL
COOMES WAY
GRIFFIN CRES
TODDINGTON LA
HOLLY DR
Toddington
COURTWICK LA
NEW COURTWICK LA
KESTREL WAY
SEATON CL
SEATON RD
HAWTHORNE RD
NORTHWAY RD
BARN CL
Glasshouse Crops Research Institute
A 259
Wick
A 2013
JOYCE CL
COLEBROOK RD
CHERRY CROFT
WHEATCROFT
STEAM FURLONG
Sch
GUADONIAN
CORNFIELD CL
WORTHING RD
NORWAY LA
BROOKENBEE CL
Rustington House Farm
COWDRAY DR
COURTWICK RD
CLUN RD
STANLEY RD
LANSDOWNE RD
HARTING RD
OAKCROFT GDNS
Caravan Park
Cemy
JIB CL
CAPSTAN DR
CONISTON WAY
ULLSWATER
LANYARDS
GRAND AVE
BEACONSFIELD RD
NORTH ST
SWANBOURNE RD
BELLOC RD
WESTWAY
MANNING RD
HELYER'S GREEN
WHITELEA RD
MALTHOUSE PAS
SUSSEX ST
AMBERLEY CL
THORNCROFT RD
TOWNSEND CRES
SELWAY LA
PEREGRINE RD
THE SALTINGS
WESTLANDS
HIDE GDNS
MANOR RD
WICK FARM RD
BELYNGHAM CRES
A 284 ARUNDEL
KENT RD
JAYS CL
MADEHURST WAY
BLAKEHURST WAY
HILL RD
GROVE CRES
HORSHAM RD
BELL DAVIES RD
DAVITS DR
SCHOONER WAY
ADMIRALS WLK
NORTH LA
BRENDON WAY
OLD MANOR RD
FORT RD
HARWOOD RD
PARHAM CL
CORNWALL RD
Schs
ELMGROVE RD
FALKLAND AVE
BEACON WAY
ARMADA WAY
SEXTANT CT
WALDERS RD
STAFFORD CL
ANDREW CL
PRIORY RD
Amb Sta
STANHOPE RD
SOUTHFIELDS RD
SOLWAY CL
WINDWARD CL
HENRY AVE
HOMEFIELD AVE
TITHE GREEN
DINGLEY RD
QUAYSIDE
BRIDGE RD
GLOUCESTER RD
HOWARD RD
CONNAUGHT RD
FIELD RD
EAST ST
FRANCISCAN WAY
MARY'S CL
ST FLORA'S RD
PARKSIDE AVE
MEADOW WAY
ESHER DR
WINTER KNOLL
THE HOBE
STERNWAY
THE MOLE
THE CAPE
BEAUMONT PARK
WHITE HORSES WAY
TENNYSON AVE
MILTON AVE
THE STREET
INGRAM CL
CHAUCER AVE
BOX TREE AVE
KIRKLAND CL
TERMINUS RD
WHARF RD
ALBERT RD
HIGH ST
DUKE ST
ANCHOR SPRINGS
THE ARCADE
BEACH RD
Office
CHURCH ST
Hospl
A 259
GODA RD
RAYDEN CL
LEEWARD RD
MIDDLE MEAD
SPINNAKER CL
THE HAVEN
MALIN RD
THE ESTUARY
SHORT FURLONG
FERRY RD
ROPE WLK
Mus
SURREY ST
ARCADE RD
B 2140 SEA LA
02
03
04

177

199

158
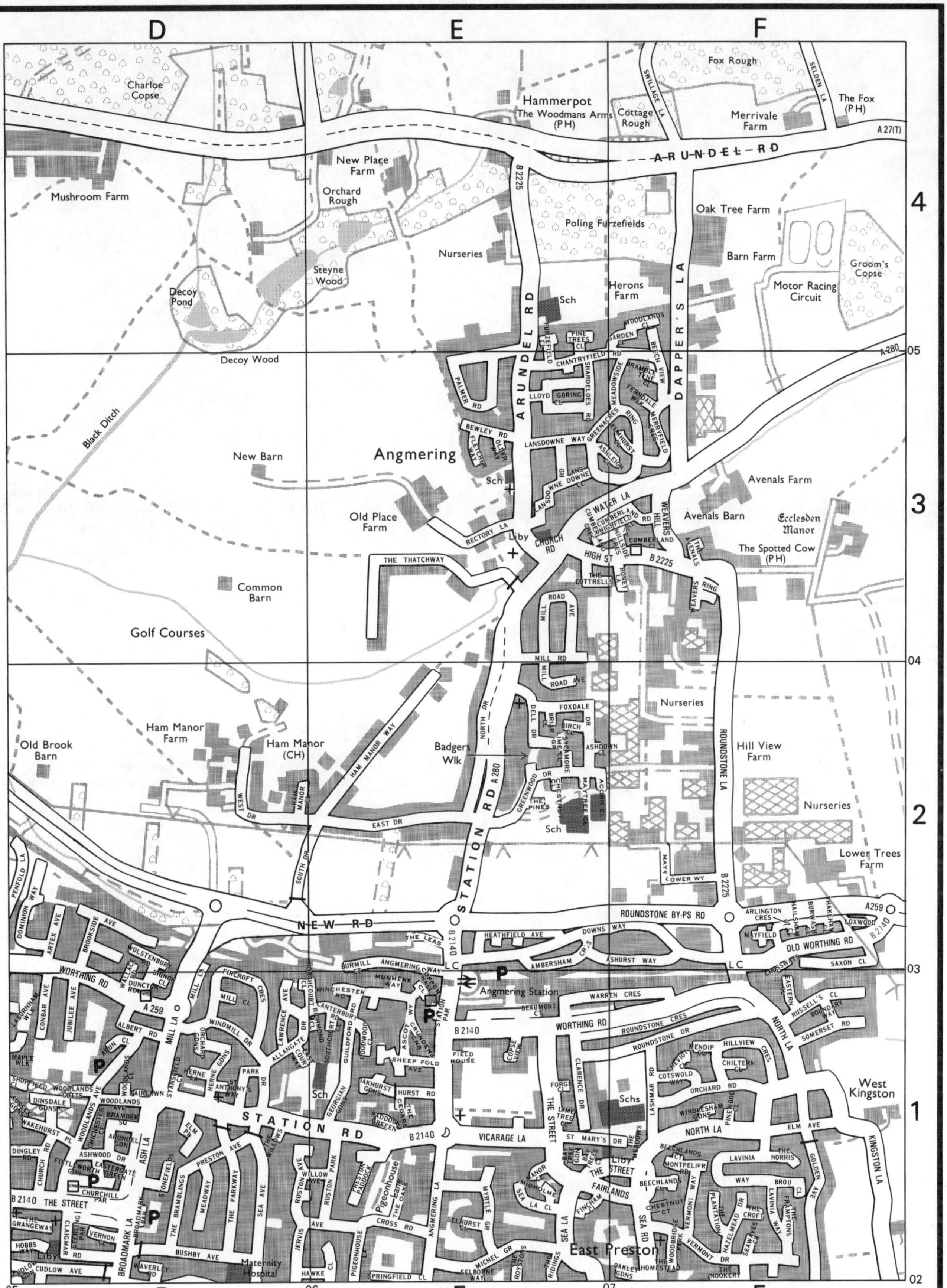
D
E
F
Charloe Copse
Hammerpot
The Woodmans Arms (PH)
Cottage Rough
Fox Rough
Merrivale Farm
The Fox (PH)
SWILLAGE LA
SELDEN LA
A 27(T)
ARUNDEL RD
New Place Farm
Orchard Rough
Mushroom Farm
B 2225
Poling Furzefields
Oak Tree Farm
Barn Farm
Nurseries
Steyne Wood
Decoy Pond
Herons Farm
Motor Racing Circuit
Groom's Copse
Sch
DAPPER'S LA
Decoy Wood
A 280
05
PALMER RD
ARUNDEL RD
Black Ditch
BEWLEY RD
LANSDOWNE WAY
New Barn
Angmering
Avenals Farm
Sch
WATER LA
WEAVERS HILL
Avenals Barn
Ecclesden Manor
Old Place Farm
RECTORY LA
Liby
CHURCH RD
HIGH ST
CUMBERLAND CT
The Spotted Cow (PH)
THE THATCHWAY
THE COTTRELLS
Common Barn
WEAVERS RING
MILL ROAD AVE
Golf Courses
MILL RD
04
FOXDALE
NORTH DR
Nurseries
Ham Manor Farm
HAM MANOR WAY
Old Brook Barn
Ham Manor (CH)
Badgers Wlk
ROUNDSTONE LA
Hill View Farm
DELL DR
ASHDOWN CL
A 280
WEST DR
HAM MANOR CL
GREENWOOD DR
THE PINES
ACORN CL
Nurseries
EAST DR
Sch
STATION RD
Lower Trees Farm
PENFOLD LA
SOUTH DR
LOWER WAY
B 2225
DOMINION WAY
NEW RD
ROUNDSTONE BY-PS RD
ARLINGTON CRES
LOXWOOD
A 259
ARTEX AVE
BROOKSIDE AVE
HEATHFIELD AVE
DOWNS WAY
THE LEAS
B 2140
MAYFIELD
OLD WORTHING RD
B 2140
WOLSTENBURY
WORTHING RD
AMBERSHAM
ASHURST WAY
LC
SAXON CL
03
DUNCTON RD
FIRCROFT CRES
BURMILL
ANGMERING WAY
LC
Angmering Station
WARREN CRES
LABURNHAM WLK
CONBAR AVE
JUBILEE AVE
A 259
MILL LA
MILL CL
WINCHESTER
CANTERBURY RD
BEAUMONT CT
EASTERN CL
RUSSELL'S CL
BOUNDARY WAY
ALBERT RD
WINDMILL DR
LAWRENCE AVE
ALLANGATE DR
GUILDFORD RD
WORTHING RD
ROUNDSTONE CRES
NORTH LA
SOMERSET RD
ARUN CL
ORCHARD GDNS
ASCOT WAY
B 2140
ROUNDSTONE DR
MAPLE WLK
HERNE GDNS
PARK DR
SHEEP FOLD AVE
FIELD HOUSE
COPSE VIEW
MENDIP CL
HILLVIEW CRES
CHILTERN CL
SHOPFIELD
WOODLANDS
FAIRLAWN
STANSFIELD
ST ANTHONY'S WAY
OAKHURST GDNS
HURST RD
COTSWOLD WAY
West Kingston
DINSDALE GDNS
Sch
CLARENCE DR
LASHMAR RD
ORCHARD RD
BRAMBER
FORGE
Schs
WAKEHURST PL
STATION RD
WINDLESHAM GDNS
PINEWOOD
ARUNDEL GDN
THE WILLOWS
B 2140
VICARAGE LA
THE STREET
NORTH LA
ELM AVE
DINGLEY RD
ASHWOOD DR
ASH LA
ELM PK
PRESTON AVE
ST MARY'S DR
THE MEADOWS
BEECHLANDS
KINGSTON LA
MONTPELIER RD
LAVINIA
THE NORRIS
CHURCH RD
FITTLEWORTH GDNS
EASTERGATE GREEN
STONEFIELDS
RUSTON AVE
WILLOW AVE
RUSTON PARK
PRESTON PADDOCK
Pigeonhouse Lane
THE OAKS
Liby
THE STREET
FAIRLANDS
BEECHLANDS CL
WAY
GOLDEN AVE
CHURCHILL PAR
THE BRAMBLINGS
MEADOWAY
THE PARKWAY
SEA AVE
ANGMERING LA
MYRTLE GR
MIDHOLME
SEA LA CL
FINCHAM CL
SEA RD
CHESTNUT CT
VERMONT WAY
THE PLANTATION
HAZELMEAD DR
THE CROFT
THE FRAMPTONS
B 2140
THE STREET
THE GRANGEWAY
CLAIGMAR RD
VERNON CL
BROADMARK LA
CROSS RD
SELHURST CL
SEA LA
LAVINIA WAY
SEAWAVES CL
HOBBS WAY
Liby
JERVIS AVE
PIGEONHOUSE LA
MICHEL GR
THE ROYSTONS
THE RIDINGS
East Preston
VERMONT DR
BUSHBY AVE
Maternity Hospital
THE WOODBRIDGE
CUDLOW AVE
WAVERLEY RD
HAWKE CL
SPRINGFIELD CL
SELBORNE WAY
OAKLEY GDNS
THE HOMESTEAD
THE NOOKERY
05
06
07
02
D
E
F
4
3
2
1
04
03
180
200

159

179

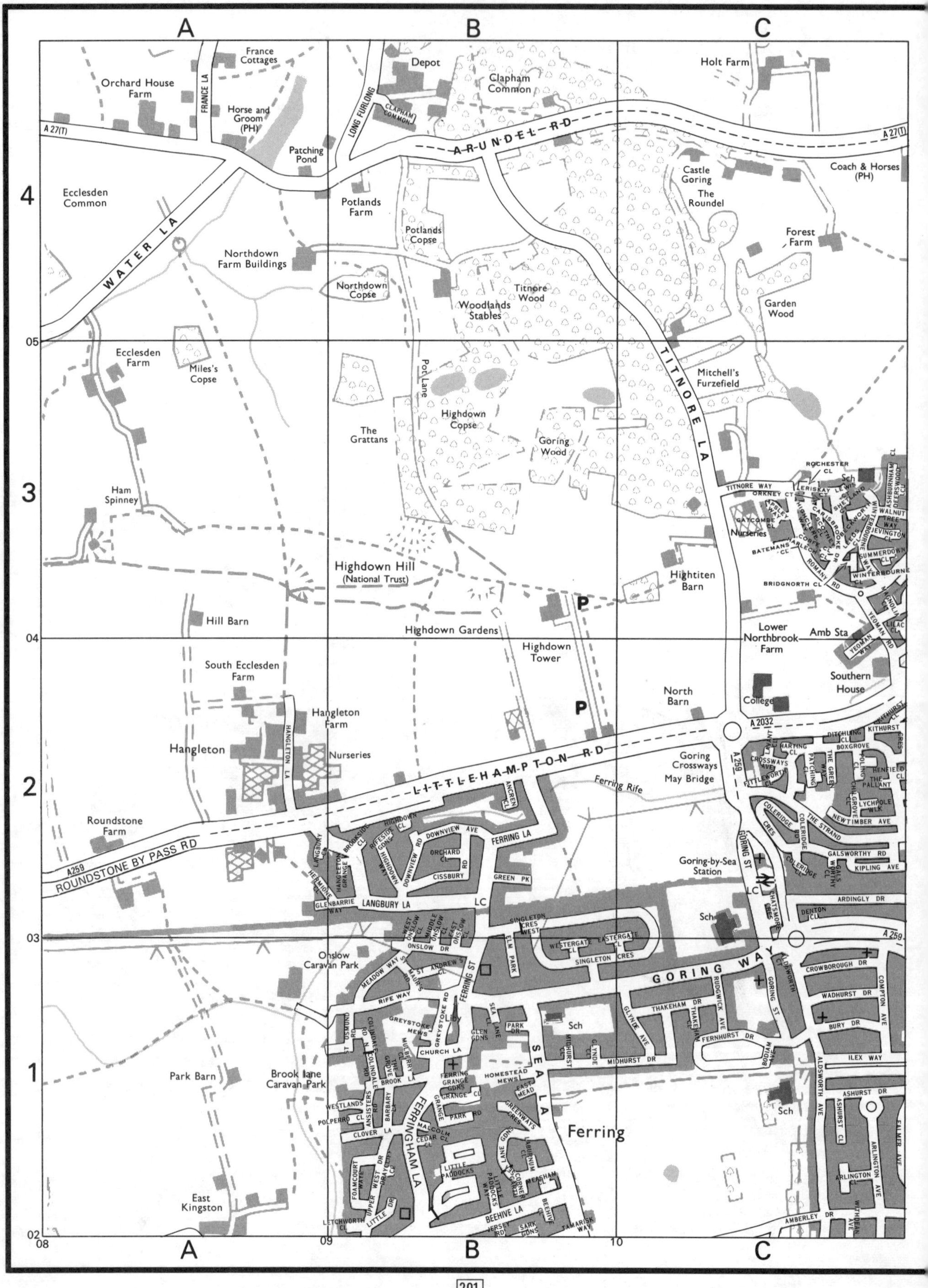
A
B
C
France Cottages
Orchard House Farm
FRANCE LA
Horse and Groom (PH)
Depot
LONG FURLONG
CLAPHAM COMMON
Clapham Common
Holt Farm
A 27(T)
ARUNDEL RD
Patching Pond
Coach & Horses (PH)
Castle Goring
The Roundel
4
Ecclesden Common
Potlands Farm
Potlands Copse
Forest Farm
WATER LA
Northdown Farm Buildings
Northdown Copse
Titnore Wood
Woodlands Stables
Garden Wood
05
Ecclesden Farm
Miles's Copse
Pot Lane
TITNORE LA
Mitchell's Furzefield
Highdown Copse
The Grattans
Goring Wood
3
Ham Spinney
ROCHESTER CL
TITNORE WAY
ORKNEY CT
Sch
Nurseries
BATEMANS CL
BRIDGNORTH CL
Highdown Hill
(National Trust)
Hightiten Barn
P
Hill Barn
Highdown Gardens
Lower Northbrook Farm
Amb Sta
04
Highdown Tower
South Ecclesden Farm
North Barn
Southern House
College
P
Hangleton Farm
HANGLETON LA
A 2032
Hangleton
Nurseries
LITTLEHAMPTON RD
Goring Crossways
May Bridge
A 259
Ferring Rife
2
Roundstone Farm
ROUNDSTONE BY PASS RD
A259
FERRING LA
DOWNVIEW AVE
ORCHARD CL
CISSBURY RD
GREEN PK
NEWTIMBER AVE
GALSWORTHY RD
KIPLING AVE
GORING ST
Goring-by-Sea Station
LANGBURY LA
LC
ARDINGLY DR
SINGLETON CRES WEST
Sch
DENTON CL
A 259
03
Onslow Caravan Park
ONSLOW DR
FERRING ST
ELM PARK
WESTERGATE CL
EASTERGATE CL
SINGLETON CRES
GORING WAY
CROWBOROUGH DR
RIFE WAY
THAKEHAM DR
RUDGWICK AVE
WADHURST DR
COMPTON AVE
GREYSTOKE RD
Liby
Sch
MIDHURST
BURY DR
GLYNDE AVE
FERNHURST DR
CHURCH LA
SEA LANE
MIDHURST DR
ILEX WAY
1
Park Barn
Brook lane Caravan Park
BROOK LA
HOMESTEAD MEWS
ALDSWORTH AVE
ASHURST DR
WESTLANDS
ASHURST CL
PARK RD
Sch
Ferring
CLOVER LA
FERRINGHAM LA
GREENWAYS CRES
ARLINGTON AVE
FALMER AVE
LITTLE PADDOCKS
ARLINGTON CL
East Kingston
BEEHIVE LA
AMBERLEY DR
TAMARISK WAY
02
08
09
10
A
B
C

201

160

D
E
F
Cote
Swandean Hospl
Cemy
Mill Plantation
ARUNDEL RD
SALVINGTON HILL
DURRINGTON HILL
CROCKHURST HILL A 27(T)
OFFINGTON CNR
WARREN RD
HALF MOON LA
FINDON RD
4
Durrington
Salvington
SALVINGTON RD
Recn Gd
Schs
Liby
05
Shopping Centre
DURRINGTON LA
COLUMBIA DR
LITTLEHAMPTON RD
POULTER'S CNR
POULTER'S LA
A 2032
3
Longcroft Park
Palatine Park
PALATINE RD
TERRINGES AVE
RECTORY RD
04
West Tarring
SOUTH ST
THE BOULEVARD
Sch
Offices
2
College
Durrington-on-Sea Station
West Worthing Sta
TARRING RD
A 2031
SHAFTESBURY AVE
Recn Gd
REIGATE RD
03
GORING RD
Goring-by-Sea
A 259
COWPER RD
HEENE RD
MILL RD
GRAND AVE
GEORGE V AVE
ALINORA AVE
SEA LA
Hospl
1
MARINE CRES
WEST PAR
ESPLANADE
MARINE PAR
02
WORTHING
12
13
D
E
F

182

161

181

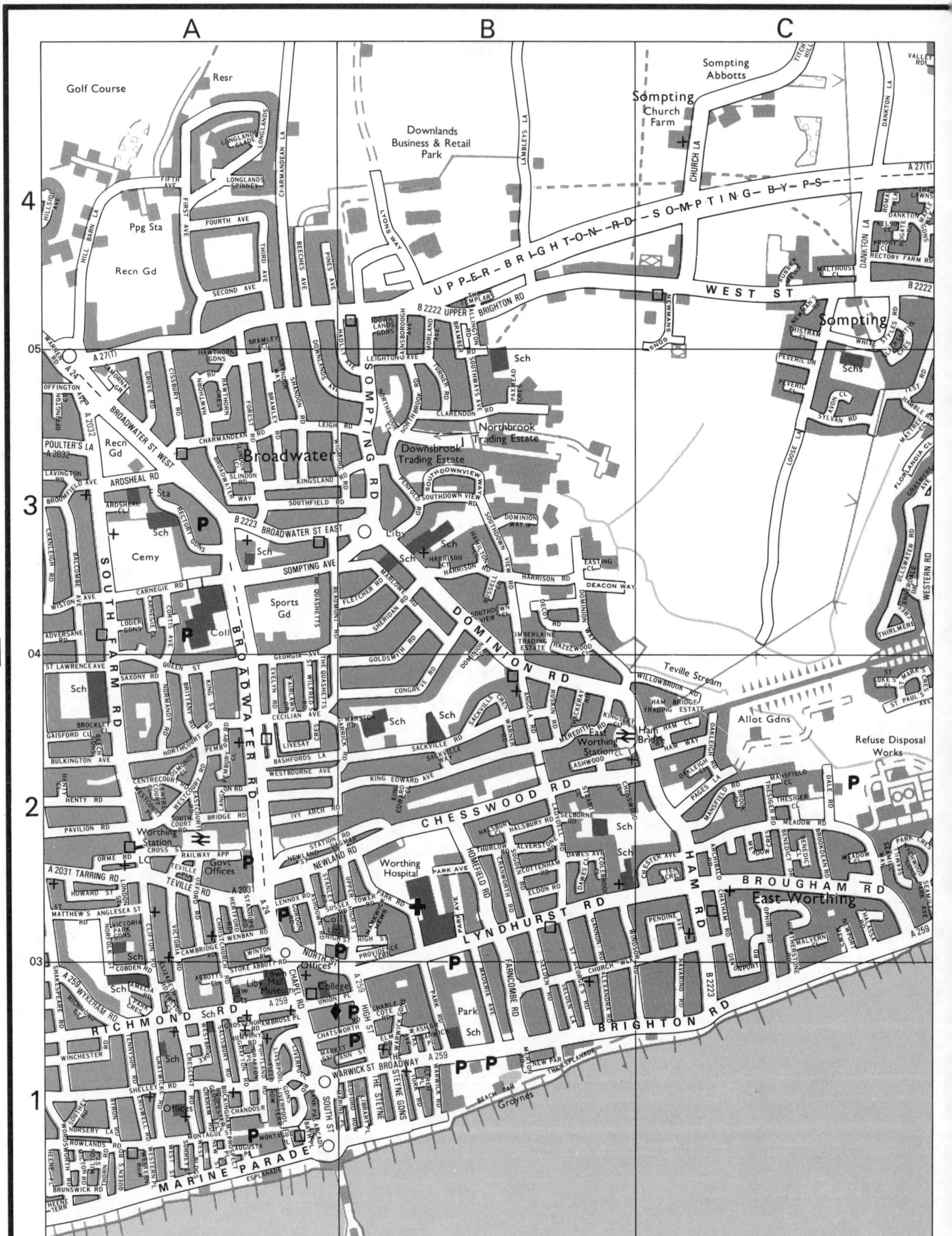
A
B
C
4
3
2
1
05
04
03
02
14
15
16
Golf Course
Resr
Ppg Sta
Recn Gd
Downlands
Business & Retail
Park
Sompting
Abbotts
Sompting
Church
Farm
UPPER BRIGHTON RD
SOMPTING BY-PS
A 27(T)
WEST ST
B 2222
Sompting
Schs
Sch
Northbrook
Trading Estate
Downsbrook
Trading Estate
Broadwater
Recn
Gd
BROADWATER ST WEST
BROADWATER ST EAST
B 2223
A 2032
A 24
SOMPTING RD
Cemy
Sports
Gd
SOUTH FARM RD
BROADWATER RD
Coll
Liby
DOMINION RD
Teville Stream
Allot Gdns
Refuse Disposal
Works
HAM BRIDGE
TRADING ESTATE
Ham
Bridge
East
Worthing
Station
CHESSWOOD RD
KING EDWARD AVE
SACKVILLE RD
Worthing
Station
Govt
Offices
Worthing
Hospital
LYNDHURST RD
HAM RD
BROUGHAM RD
East Worthing
A 2031 TARRING RD
TEVILLE RD
RICHMOND RD
Town
Hall
Museum
Law
Cts
College
Offices
Park
A 259
BRIGHTON RD
MARINE PARADE
ESPLANADE
THE ESPLANADE
Groynes
Pier
SOUTH ST
HIGH ST
CHAPEL RD
WARWICK ST
BROADWAY
THE STEYNE
STEYNE GDNS

162

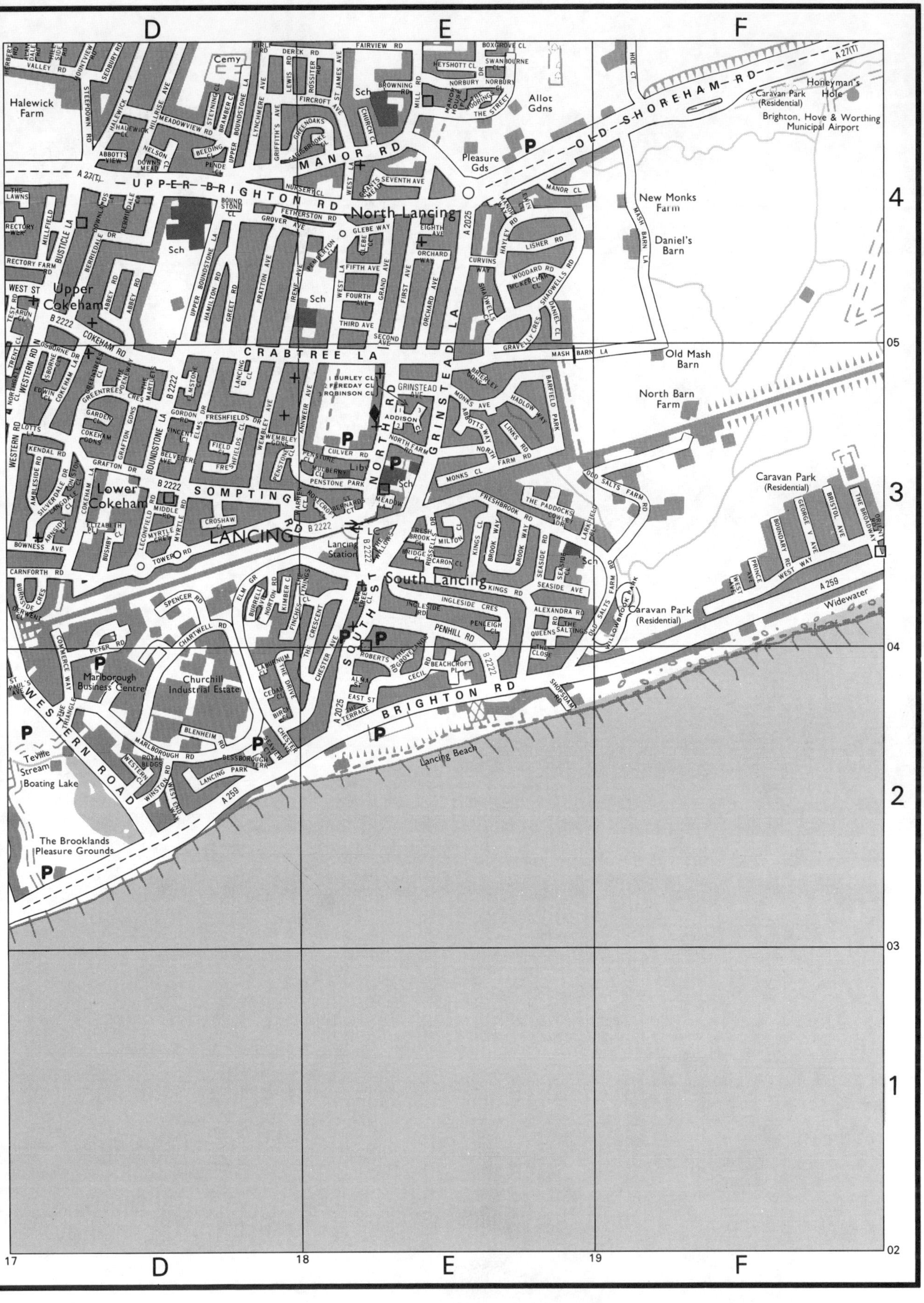
D
E
F
4
3
2
1
05
04
03
02
17
18
19
Halewick Farm
Cemy
Sch
Allot Gdns
Pleasure Gds
OLD SHOREHAM RD
A 27(T)
Caravan Park (Residential)
Honeyman's Hole
Brighton, Hove & Worthing Municipal Airport
MANOR RD
UPPER BRIGHTON RD
North Lancing
New Monks Farm
Daniel's Barn
MASH BARN LA
Upper Cokeham
CRABTREE LA
Old Mash Barn
North Barn Farm
GRINSTEAD LA
NORTH RD
SOMPTING RD
Lower Cokeham
LANCING
Lancing Station
South Lancing
Caravan Park (Residential)
A 259
Widewater
Caravan Park (Residential)
Marlborough Business Centre
Churchill Industrial Estate
BRIGHTON RD
WESTERN ROAD
Lancing Beach
Teville Stream
Boating Lake
The Brooklands Pleasure Grounds
FAIRVIEW RD
DEREK RD
BOXGROVE CL
HEYSHOTT CL
SWANBOURNE CL
NORBURY
BROWNING RD
HOE CT
STEEPDOWN RD
SEDBURY RD
HALEWICK LA
HILLRISE AVE
MEADOWVIEW RD
STEYNING CL
BRAMBER CL
UPPER BOUNDSTONE LA
LYNCHMERE AVE
GRIFFITH'S AVE
LEWIS RD
ROSSITER RD
ST JAMES AVE
FIRCROFT AVE
CHURCH CL
MILL RD
THE STREET
GREENOAKS
CARISBROOKE CL
SEVENTH AVE
NURSERY CL
MANOR CL
FETHERSTON RD
GROVER AVE
GLEBE WAY
EIGHTH AVE
ORCHARD WAY
CURVINS WAY
HAYLEY RD
LISHER RD
WOODARD RD
MCKERCHAR CL
SHADWELLS RD
DANIEL CL
GRAVELLY CRES
RECTORY FARM RD
MILLFIELD
BUSTICLE LA
BERRIEDALE DR
WEST ST
ABBEY RD
BOUNDSTONE LA
HAMILTON RD
GREET RD
PRATTON AVE
IRENE AVE
PENDERTON CL
WEST LA
FIFTH AVE
FOURTH AVE
THIRD AVE
SECOND AVE
GRAND AVE
FIRST AVE
ORCHARD AVE
B 2222
COKEHAM RD
COKEHAM LA
WESTERN RD
EDWIN CL
GREENTREES CRES
THE MARTLETS
GORDON RD
FRESHFIELDS DR
WEMBLEY AVE
ANNWEIR AVE
1 BURLEY CL
2 FEREDAY CL
3 ROBINSON CL
GRINSTEAD AVE
ADDISON CL
NORTH FARM RD
MONKS AVE
ABBOTTS WAY
HADLOW WAY
LINKS RD
BARFIELD PARK
MONKS CL
OLD SALTS FARM RD
KENDAL RD
GARDEN CL
GRAFTON GDNS
GRAFTON DR
COKEHAM GDNS
ELMS DR
FIELD CL
WEMBLEY GDNS
PENSTONE CT
CULVER RD
PENSTONE PARK
Liby
MEADOW CL
FRESHBROOK RD
THE PADDOCKS
COWLEY DR
LARKFIELD WAY
ELIZABETH PL
BUSHBY CL
LECONFIELD RD
MYRTLE CRES
MIDDLE RD
CROSHAW CL
TOWER RD
BOWNESS AVE
CARNFORTH RD
RUSSELLS DR
MILTON CT
KINGS CL
BROOK WAY
SEASIDE RD
SEASIDE AVE
KINGS RD
INGLESIDE CRES
INGLESIDE RD
ALEXANDRA RD
PENLEIGH CL
PENHILL RD
THE SALTINGS
WILLOWBROOK PARK
BOUNDARY RD
GEORGE V AVE
BRISTOL AVE
THE BROADWAY
PRINCE AVE
WEST WAY
WEST AVE
SPENCER RD
ELM GR
BURRELL
NORTON RD
KIMBER CL
FINCHES CL
THE CRESCENT
CHESTER AVE
SOUTH ST
ROBERTS RD
THE GROVE
CECIL RD
BEACHCROFT PL
THE CLOSE
SHOPSDAM RD
CHARTWELL RD
PETER RD
COMMERCE WAY
THE TRIANGLE
THE DRIVE
LABURNUM
CEDAR CL
BIRCH CL
ALMA ST
EAST ST
THE TERRACE
BLENHEIM RD
MARLBOROUGH RD
ROYAL BLDGS
WESTERN CL
WINSTON RD
WEST END WAY
BESSBOROUGH TERR
LANCING PARK
ST PAUL'S AVE
A 2025

184

163

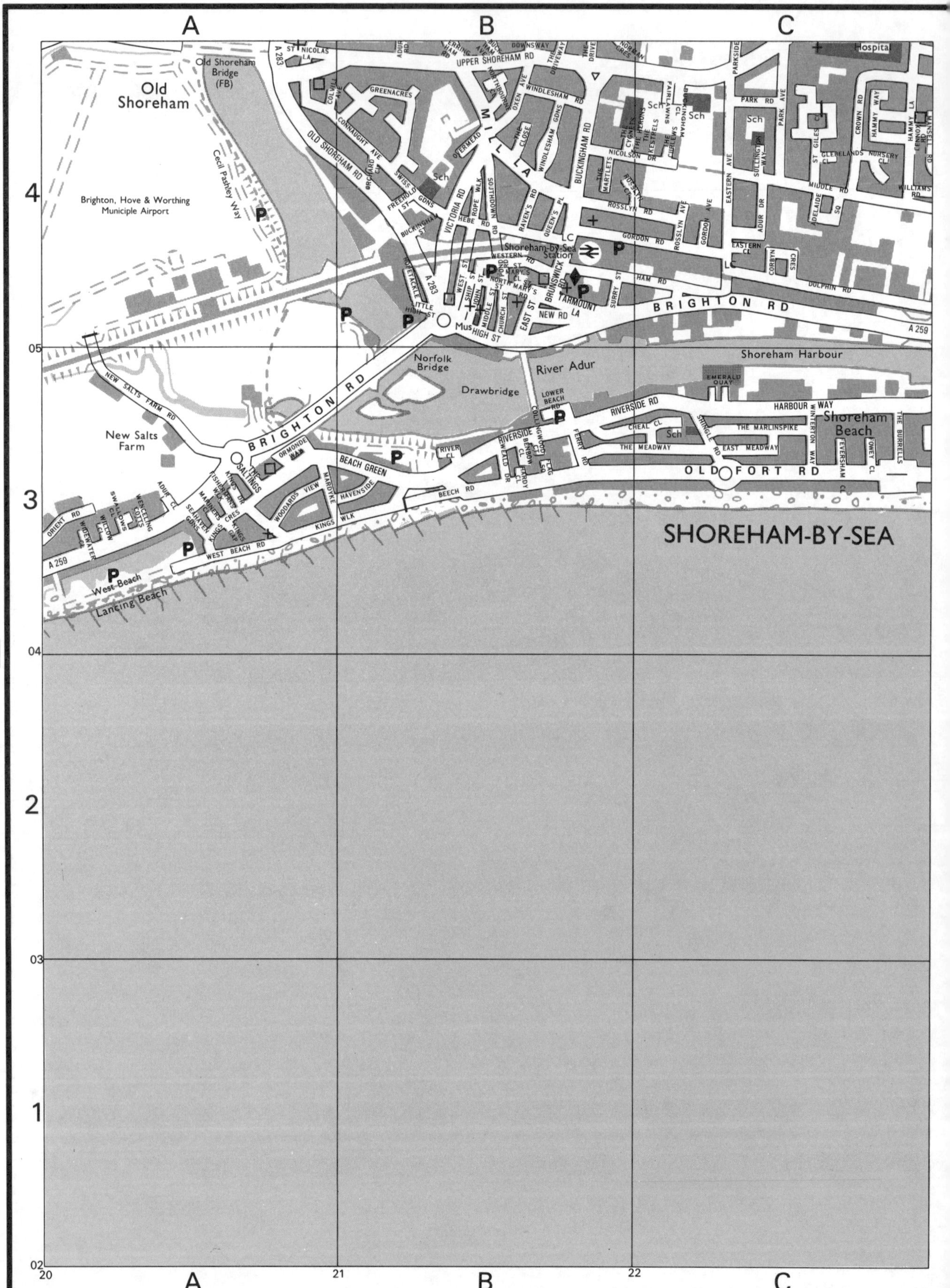

A
B
C
4
3
2
1
Old Shoreham
Old Shoreham Bridge (FB)
Cecil Pashley Way
Brighton, Hove & Worthing Municiple Airport
UPPER SHOREHAM RD
MILL LA
OLD SHOREHAM RD
GREENACRES
CONNAUGHT AVE
SWISS GDNS
FREEHOLD ST
BUCKINGHAM ST
VICTORIA RD
ROPE WLK
HEBE RD
SOUTHDOWN RD
WINDLESHAM RD
WINDLESHAM GDNS
RAVEN'S RD
QUEEN'S PL
BUCKINGHAM RD
ROSSLYN RD
ROSSLYN AVE
GORDON RD
GORDON AVE
NICOLSON DR
THE MARTLETS
PARK RD
PARK AVE
EASTERN AVE
EASTERN CL
ADUR DR
ADELAIDE SQ
MIDDLE RD
ST GILES CL
CROWN RD
GLEBELANDS
NURSERY CL
CORBYN CRES
HAM RD
DOLPHIN RD
Hospital
Sch
Shoreham-by-Sea Station
LC
WESTERN RD
WEST ST
SHIP ST
JOHN ST
MIDDLE ST
CHURCH ST
EAST ST
BRUNSWICK RD
NEW RD
YARMOUNT LA
SURRY ST
ROPETACKLE
LITTLE HIGH ST
HIGH ST
Mus
BRIGHTON RD
A 283
A 259
Shoreham Harbour
River Adur
Norfolk Bridge
Drawbridge
EMERALD QUAY
LOWER BEACH RD
RIVERSIDE RD
HARBOUR WAY
THE MARLINSPIKE
CHEAL CL
THE MEADWAY
EAST MEADWAY
SHINGLE RD
WINTERTON WAY
FEVERSHAM CL
FOWEY CL
THE BURRELLS
Shoreham Beach
OLD FORT RD
FERRY RD
COLLINGWOOD CL
WEALD DR
RIVER CL
BEACH RD
BEACH GREEN
ORMONDE WAY
HAVENSIDE
MARDYKE
WOODARDS VIEW
KINGS WLK
WEST BEACH RD
THE SALTINGS
KINGS DR
FISHERSGATE
SEAHAVEN GDNS
MARINERS CL
KINGS GAP
KINGS CRES
NEW SALTS FARM RD
New Salts Farm
ADUR CL
SWALLOWS CL
WENCELING COTTS
WILLOW CL
WIDEWATER CL
ORIENT RD
West Beach
Lancing Beach
SHOREHAM-BY-SEA
P
05
04
03
02
20
21
22

183

164
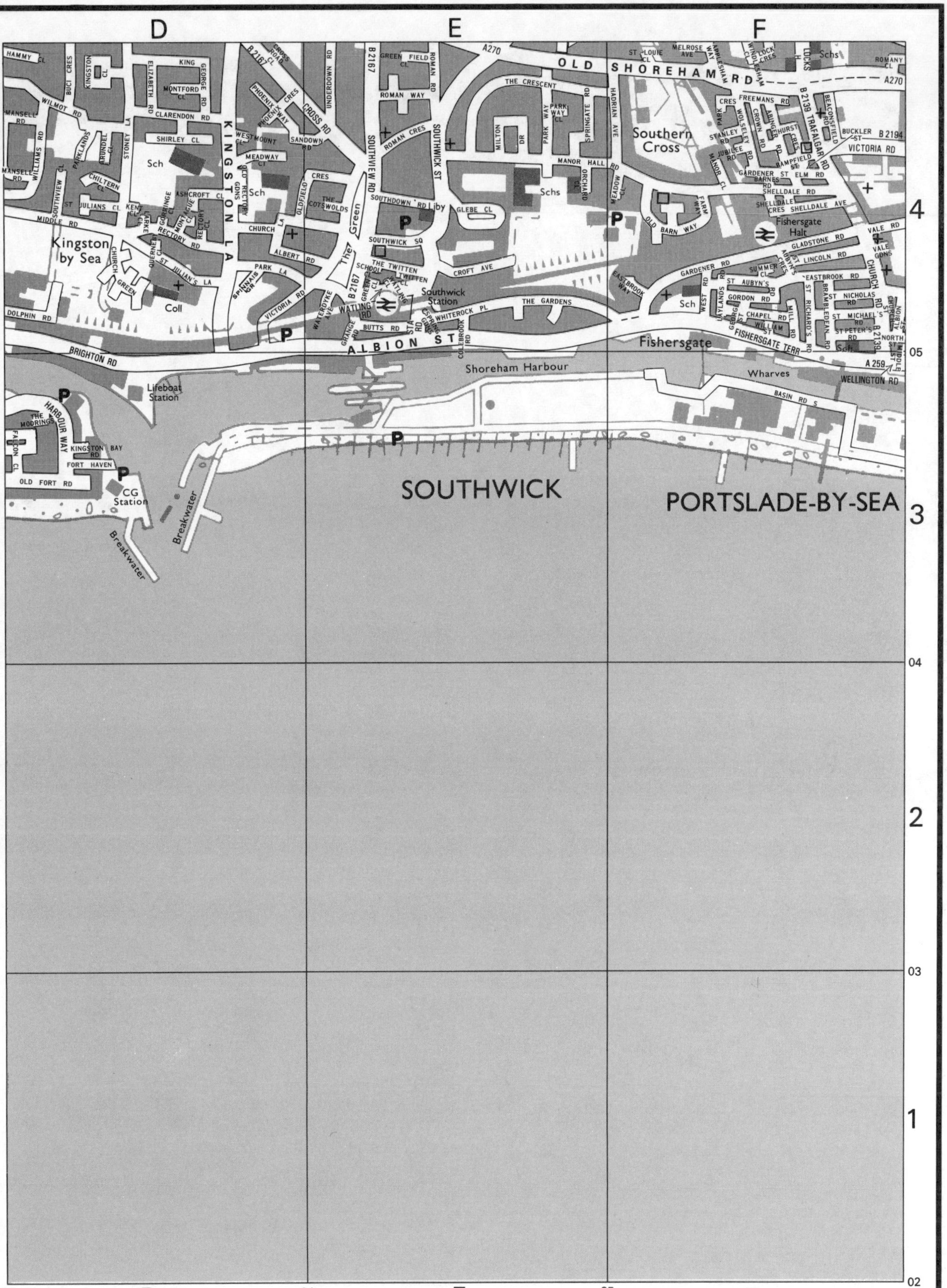
D
E
F
SOUTHWICK
PORTSLADE-BY-SEA
Kingston by Sea
Southern Cross
Fishersgate
Fishersgate Halt
Southwick Station
Shoreham Harbour
Wharves
Lifeboat Station
CG Station
Breakwater
Breakwater
OLD SHOREHAM RD
A270
ALBION ST
BRIGHTON RD
A 259
KINGSTON LA
SOUTHWICK ST
FISHERSGATE TERR
WELLINGTON RD
BASIN RD S
HARBOUR WAY
OLD FORT RD
THE GARDENS
The Green
Sch
Schs
Coll
Liby
23
24
25
05
04
03
02
4
3
2
1
186

165

185

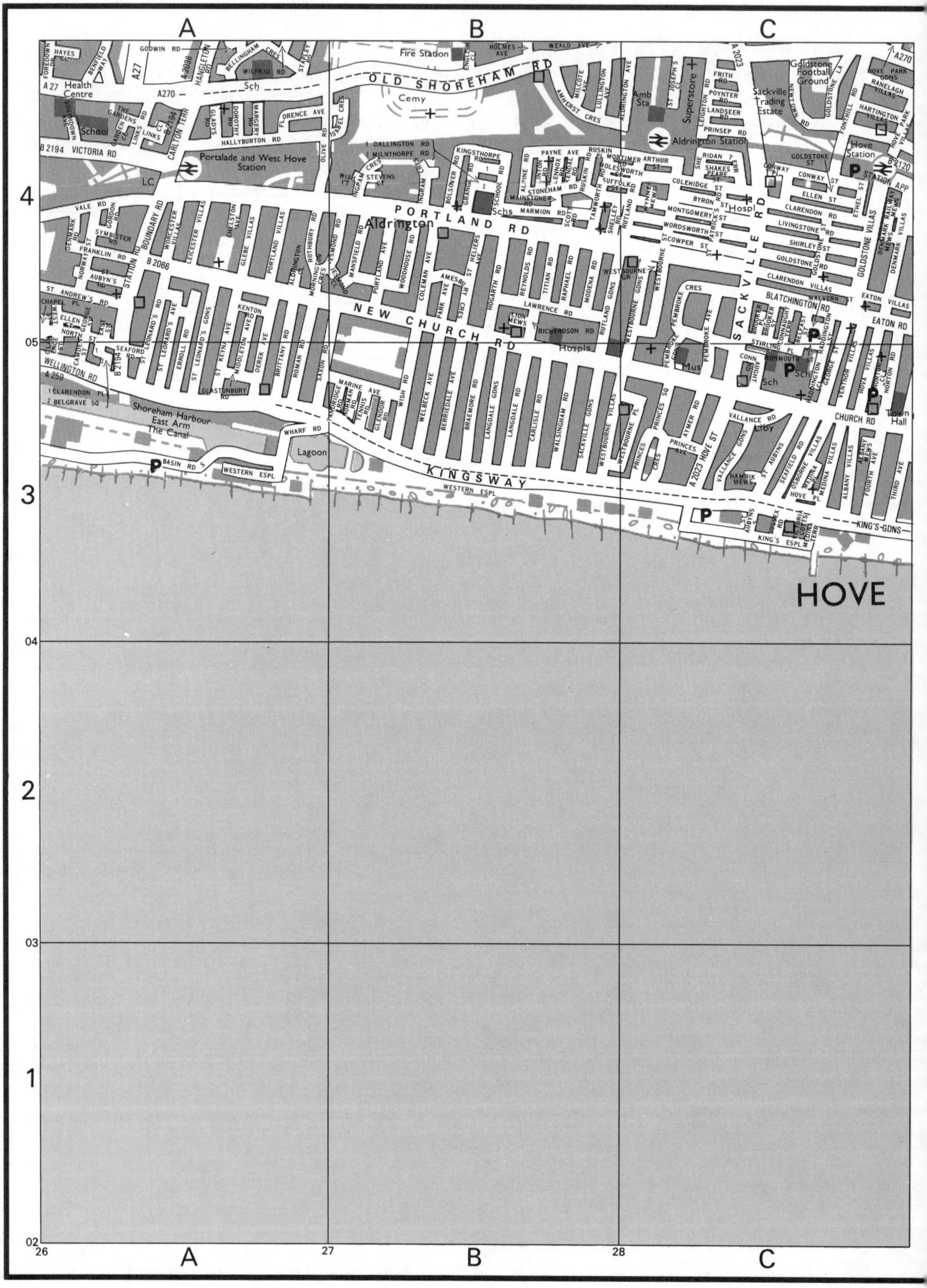
A
B
C
4
3
2
1
05
04
03
02
26
27
28
HOVE
OLD SHOREHAM RD
PORTLAND RD
NEW CHURCH RD
KINGSWAY
WESTERN ESPL
KING'S ESPL
KING'S GDNS
SACKVILLE RD
CHURCH RD
Aldrington
Aldrington Station
Portslade and West Hove Station
Hove Station
Fire Station
Cemy
Health Centre
School
Schs
Hospl
Hospls
Mus
Liby
Town Hall
Superstore
Amb Sta
Goldstone Football Ground
Sackville Trading Estate
Shoreham Harbour East Arm The Canal
Lagoon
BASIN RD S
WHARF RD
VICTORIA RD
BOUNDARY RD
STATION RD
WELLINGTON RD
A 259
A 270
A 27
A 2023
B 2194
B 2066
B 2120
GODWIN RD
HALLYBURTON RD
VALE RD
BLATCHINGTON RD
EATON RD
GOLDSTONE VILLAS
CLARENDON VILLAS
WESTBOURNE VILLAS
HOVE ST

166

D
E
F
4
3
2
1
05
04
03
02
29
30
31
OLD SHOREHAM RD
DYKE RD
DYKE ROAD DR
NEW ENGLAND RD
PRESTON PARK
STANFORD AVE
LONDON RD
DITCHLING RD
VIADUCT RD
HOLLINGDEAN RD
Round Hill
London Road Station
Brighton Station
TERMINUS RD
QUEEN'S RD
WEST ST
NORTH ST
CHURCH RD
WESTERN RD
LANSDOWNE RD
CROMWELL RD
EATON RD
THE DRIVE
County Cricket Ground
Magistrates Court
Gdns
Hospital
School
College
Sch
Mus
Coll
Seven Dials
Churchill Square
Dome
Library & Museum
Royal Pavilion
Aquarium
KINGSWAY
Kings Lawns
Brunswick Lawns
HOVE SEA WALL
KING'S RD
ESPLANADE
GRAND JUNCTION RD
MARINE PAR
MADEIRA DR
West Pier
Palace Pier
BRIGHTON
1 NORFOLK ST
2 NORFOLK MEWS
3 NORFOLK BLDGS
4 NORFOLK PL
5 LITTLE WESTERN ST
1 SHIP ST CT
2 BRIGHTON SQ
3 BRIGHTON PL
4 BLACK LION ST
5 BARTHOLOMEWS
6 LITTLE EAST ST
7 BRILLS LA

188

167

187

A
B
C
4
3
2
1
05
04
03
02
32
33
34
BEAR RD
WARREN RD
Cemy
Cemeteries
Race Hill
Race Course
Woodingdean
Burial Ground
TENANTRY DOWN RD
LADYSMITH RD
HOLLINGDEAN RD
UPPER LEWES RD
A270 LEWES RD
NEWMARKET RD
NEWMARKET TERR
GLADSTONE PL
1 INVERNESS RD
2 ABERDEEN RD
SHANKLIN RD
HARTINGTON RD
ELM GR
Schs
Amb Sta
Brighton General Hospital
CLAYTON RD
PANKHURST AVE
FIRLE RD
QUEEN'S PARK RD
FRESHFIELD RD
QUEENSWAY
TILGATE CL
THE CAUSEWAY
MONUMENT VIEW
Whitehawk Camp
MANOR HILL
WHITEHAWK HILL RD
WHITEHAWK CRES
WHITEHAWK ROAD
HORSHAM CL
ALBOURNE CL
SWANBOROUGH PL
SWANBOROUGH DR
VINES CROSS RD
WILSON AVE
Whitehawk
Sheepcote Valley
Golf Course
Sch
Newhouse Farm
P
Blackrock Valley
Red Hill
Park
Sports Ground
Golf Course
Roedean Bottom
Liby
WADHURST RISE
Schs
Park
WEST DR
PARK HILL
SOUTH AVE
FRESHFIELD PL
Schs
Sch
Coll
ESSEX COTTS
COALBROOK
TELEGRAPH ST
Sch
Hospl
EASTERN RD
BRISTOL GATE
BRISTOL GDNS
CHURCH PL
Sch
Bell Tower Industrial Estate
F Sta
ROEDEAN RD
ROEDEAN CRES
ROEDEAN WAY
ROEDEAN VALE
Roedean
Roedean School
BRISTOL RD
B 2118
A 259
MARINE PAR
UPPER ST JAMES'S ST
SEYMOUR ST
SEYMOUR SQ
Electric Railway
1 EASTERN TERR MEWS
2 EASTERN ST
KING'S CLIFF
Kemp Town
ARUNDEL RD B 2137
Black Rock
MARINE DR
B 2118
Brighton Marina Village
Undercliff Wlk
THE STRAND
Marina
A 259
DROVE RD
DOWNLAND RD
CHANNEL VIEW RD
SEAVIEW RD

168

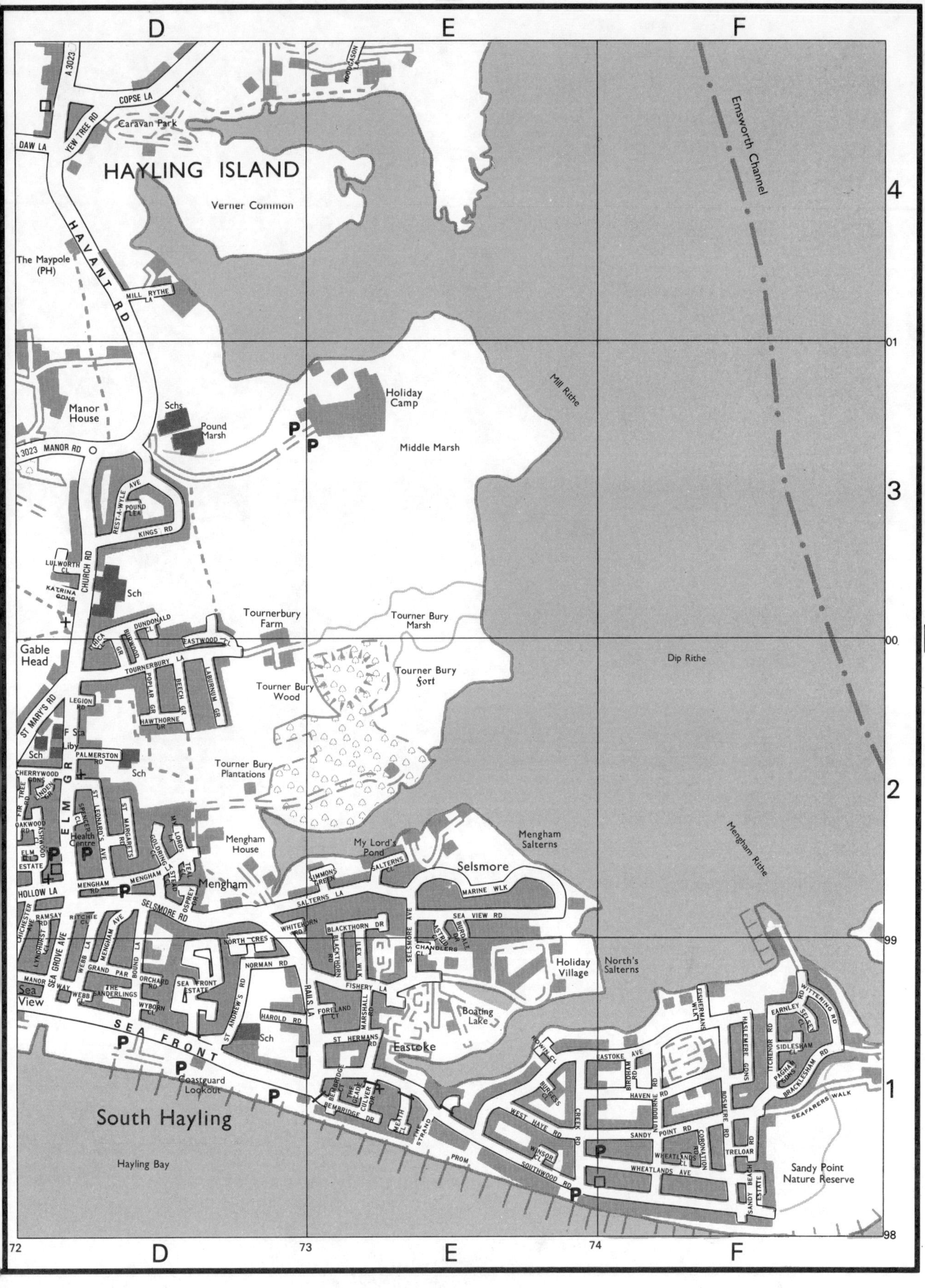
D
E
F
HAYLING ISLAND
Verner Common
Caravan Park
COPSE LA
YEW TREE RD
DAW LA
A 3023
HAVANT RD
The Maypole (PH)
MILL RYTHE LA
Ensworth Channel
Manor House
Schs
Pound Marsh
Holiday Camp
Middle Marsh
Mill Rithe
A 3023 MANOR RD
REST-A-WYLE AVE
POUND LEA
KINGS RD
LULWORTH CL
KATRINA GDNS
CHURCH RD
Sch
Tournerbury Farm
Tourner Bury Marsh
DUNDONALD CL
EASTWOOD CL
Gable Head
TOURNERBURY LA
POPLAR GR
BEECH GR
LABURNUM GR
HAWTHORNE GR
LEGION RD
ST MARY'S RD
Tourner Bury Wood
Tourner Bury Fort
Dip Rithe
F Sta
Liby
PALMERSTON RD
Sch
Tourner Bury Plantations
CHERRYWOOD GDNS
ELM GR
FIR TREE RD
OAKWOOD RD
ST LEONARD'S AVE
ST MARGARETS RD
Health Centre
MY LORDS LA
GOLDRING CL
Mengham House
My Lord's Pond
Mengham Salterns
Mengham Rithe
Selsmore
ELM GR ESTATE
HOLLOW LA
MENGHAM RD
MENGHAM LA
Mengham
SIMMONS GREEN
SALTERNS CL
SALTERNS LA
MARINE WLK
SEA VIEW RD
SELSMORE RD
RITCHIE CT
RAMSAY RD
CHICHESTER AVE
MENGHAM AVE
WHITETHORN RD
BLACKTHORN DR
SELSMORE AVE
BURDALE DR
CHANDLERS CL
NORTH CRES
LYNDHURST CL
SEA GROVE AVE
WEBB LA
GRAND PAR
BOUND LA
ORCHARD RD
NORMAN RD
BLACKTHORN RD
ILEX WLK
Holiday Village
North's Salterns
MANOR WAY
Sea View
WEBB CL
THE SANDERLINGS
WYBORN CL
SEA FRONT ESTATE
ST ANDREW'S RD
RAILS LA
FISHERY LA
FORELAND CT
MARSHALL RD
Boating Lake
FISHERMANS WLK
HASLEMERE GDNS
EARNLEY RD
SELSEY CL
WITTERING RD
SEA FRONT
HAROLD RD
Sch
ST HERMANS RD
Eastoke
ROWIN CL
EASTOKE AVE
BIRDHAM RD
ITCHENOR RD
SIDLESHAM CL
BRACKLESHAM RD
PAGHAM GDNS
Coastguard Lookout
BEMBRIDGE CT
THE GLADE
CULVER RD
BEMBRIDGE DR
MEATH CL
THE STRAND
HAVEN RD
NUTBOURNE RD
BOSMERE RD
SEAFARERS WALK
South Hayling
WEST HAYE RD
BURGESS CL
CREEK RD
SANDY POINT RD
CORONATION RD
TRELOAR RD
WINSOR CL
WHEATLANDS CL
WHEATLANDS AVE
SANDY BEACH ESTATE
PROM
SOUTHWOOD RD
Sandy Point Nature Reserve
Hayling Bay
4
3
2
1
01
00
99
98
72
73
74
D
E
F

190

169

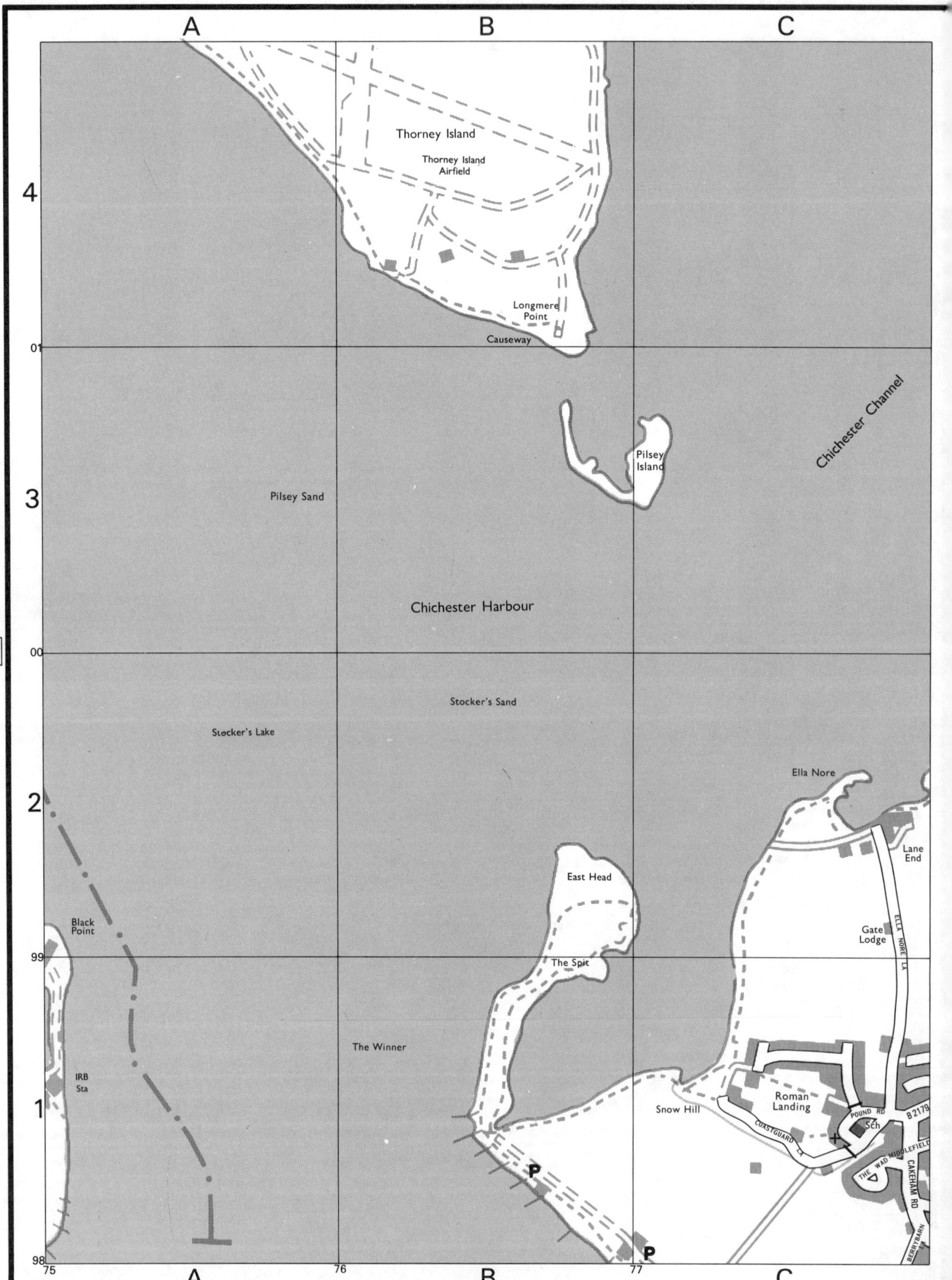
A
B
C
4
3
2
1
01
00
99
98
75
76
77
Thorney Island
Thorney Island Airfield
Longmere Point
Causeway
Pilsey Island
Chichester Channel
Pilsey Sand
Chichester Harbour
Stocker's Sand
Stocker's Lake
Ella Nore
Lane End
East Head
Black Point
Gate Lodge
ELLA NORE LA
The Spit
The Winner
IRB Sta
Roman Landing
Snow Hill
POUND RD
B2179
Sch
COASTGUARD LA
THE WAD
MIDDLEFIELD
CAKEHAM RD
BERRYBARN
P
P

189

202

170

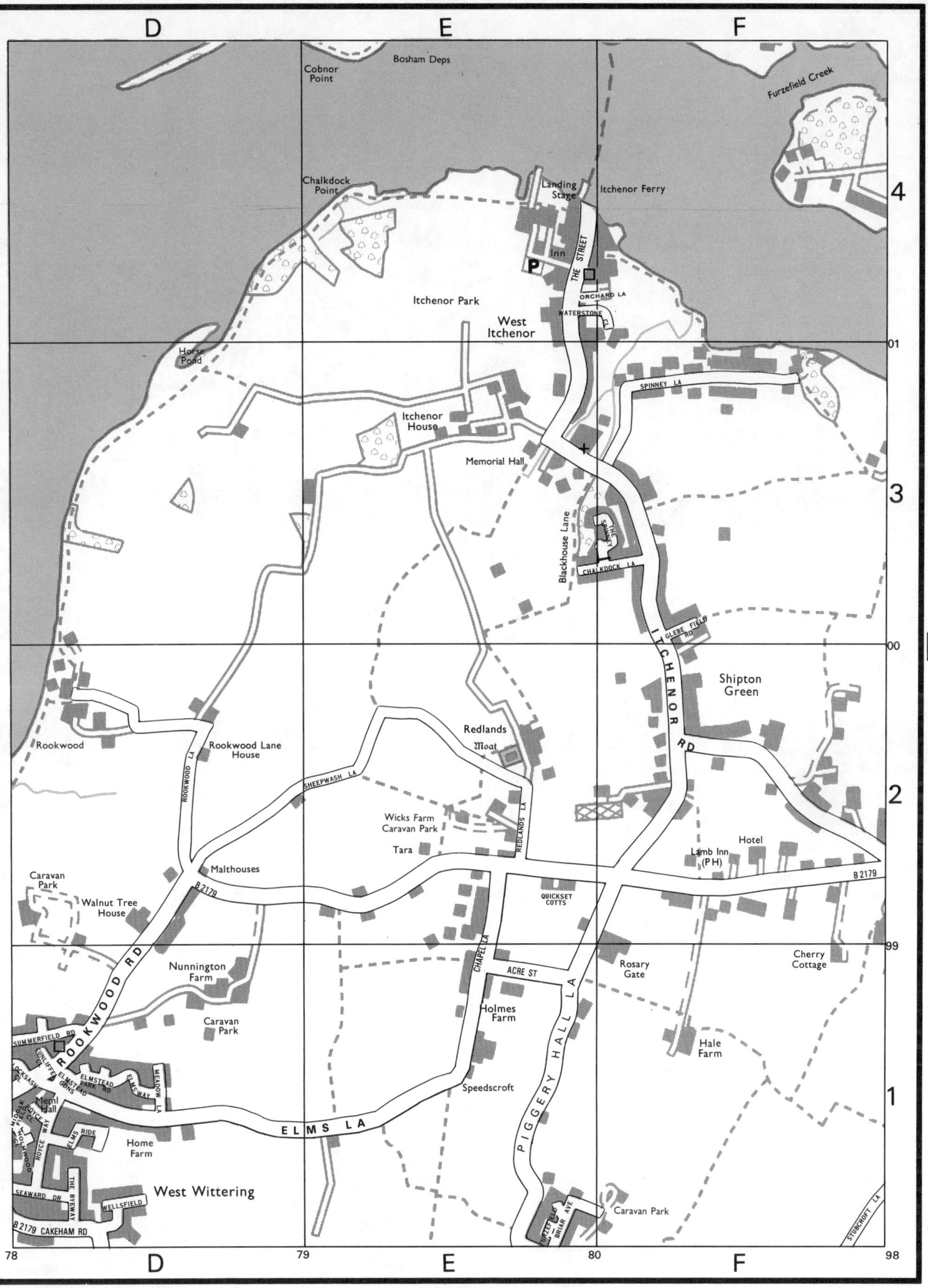
D
E
F
Cobnor Point
Bosham Deps
Furzefield Creek
Chalkdock Point
Landing Stage
Itchenor Ferry
Inn
P
THE STREET
ORCHARD LA
WATERSTONE CL
Itchenor Park
West Itchenor
Horse Pond
SPINNEY LA
Itchenor House
Memorial Hall
Blackhouse Lane
THE SPINNEY
CHALKDOCK LA
GLEBE FIELD RD
ITCHENOR RD
Shipton Green
Redlands
Moat
Rookwood
Rookwood Lane House
ROOKWOOD LA
SHEEPWASH LA
Wicks Farm Caravan Park
REDLANDS LA
Tara
Hotel
Lamb Inn (PH)
B 2179
Malthouses
Caravan Park
Walnut Tree House
QUICKSET COTTS
Nunnington Farm
CHAPEL LA
ACRE ST
Rosary Gate
Cherry Cottage
ROOKWOOD RD
Holmes Farm
PIGGERY HALL LA
Hale Farm
Caravan Park
SUMMERFIELD RD
CUNLIFFE
ELMSTEAD GDNS
ELMSTEAD PARK RD
ELMS WAY
MEADOW LA
LOCKSASH CL
Meml Hall
ROYCE CL
MIDDLE FIELD
Speedscroft
ELMS LA
HOLLYWOOD
ROYCE WAY
ELMS RIDE
Home Farm
West Wittering
THE BYEWAY
SEAWARD DR
WELLSFIELD
B 2179 CAKEHAM RD
FURZEFIELD
BRIAR AVE
Caravan Park
STUBCROFT LA
4
01
3
00
2
99
1
78
79
80
98

192

202

171

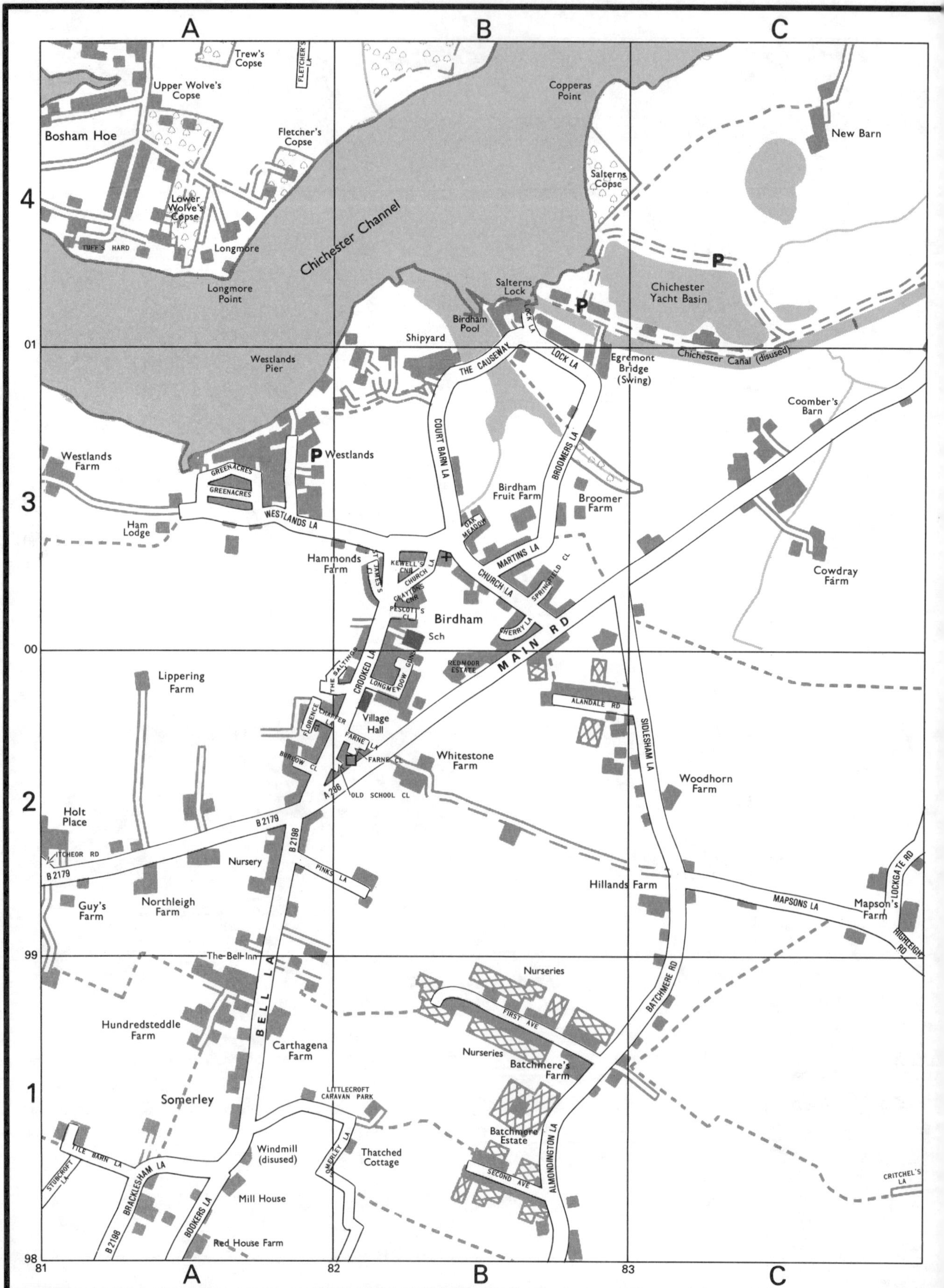
A
B
C
Trew's Copse
FLETCHER'S LA
Upper Wolve's Copse
Copperas Point
New Barn
Bosham Hoe
Fletcher's Copse
Salterns Copse
4
Lower Wolve's Copse
Chichester Channel
TUFF'S HARD
Longmore
P
Chichester Yacht Basin
Longmore Point
Salterns Lock
LOCK LA
P
Birdham Pool
Shipyard
01
Westlands Pier
THE CAUSEWAY
LOCK LA
Egremont Bridge (Swing)
Chichester Canal (disused)
Coomber's Barn
COURT BARN LA
BROOMERS LA
Westlands Farm
P Westlands
GREENACRES
GREENACRES
Birdham Fruit Farm
Broomer Farm
3
WESTLANDS LA
Ham Lodge
OAK MEADOW
MARTINS LA
Hammonds Farm
KEWELL'S CNR
CHURCH LA
ST JAMES'S CL
CLAYTONS CNR
SPRINGFIELD CL
Cowdray Farm
CHURCH LA
PESCOTT'S CL
Birdham
Sch
CHERRY LA
MAIN RD
00
REDMOOR ESTATE
Lippering Farm
THE SALTINGS
CROOKED LA
LONGMEADOW GDNS
ALANDALE RD
FLORENCE CL
CHAFFER LA
Village Hall
SIDLESHAM LA
FARNE LA
FARNE CL
Whitestone Farm
BURLOW CL
A 286
OLD SCHOOL CL
Woodhorn Farm
2
Holt Place
B 2179
B 2198
ITCHEOR RD
Nursery
B 2179
PINKS LA
Hillands Farm
LOCKGATE RD
Guy's Farm
Northleigh Farm
MAPSONS LA
Mapson's Farm
HIGHLEIGH RD
99
The Bell Inn
Nurseries
BELL LA
FIRST AVE
BATCHMERE RD
Hundredsteddle Farm
Carthagena Farm
Nurseries
Batchmere's Farm
1
LITTLECROFT CARAVAN PARK
Somerley
Batchmere Estate
Windmill (disused)
SOMERLEY LA
Thatched Cottage
TILE BARN LA
BRACKLESHAM LA
SECOND AVE
ALMONDINGTON LA
CRITCHEL'S LA
STUBCROFT LA
Mill House
B 2198
BOOKERS LA
Red House Farm
98
81
82
83
A
B
C

191

203

172

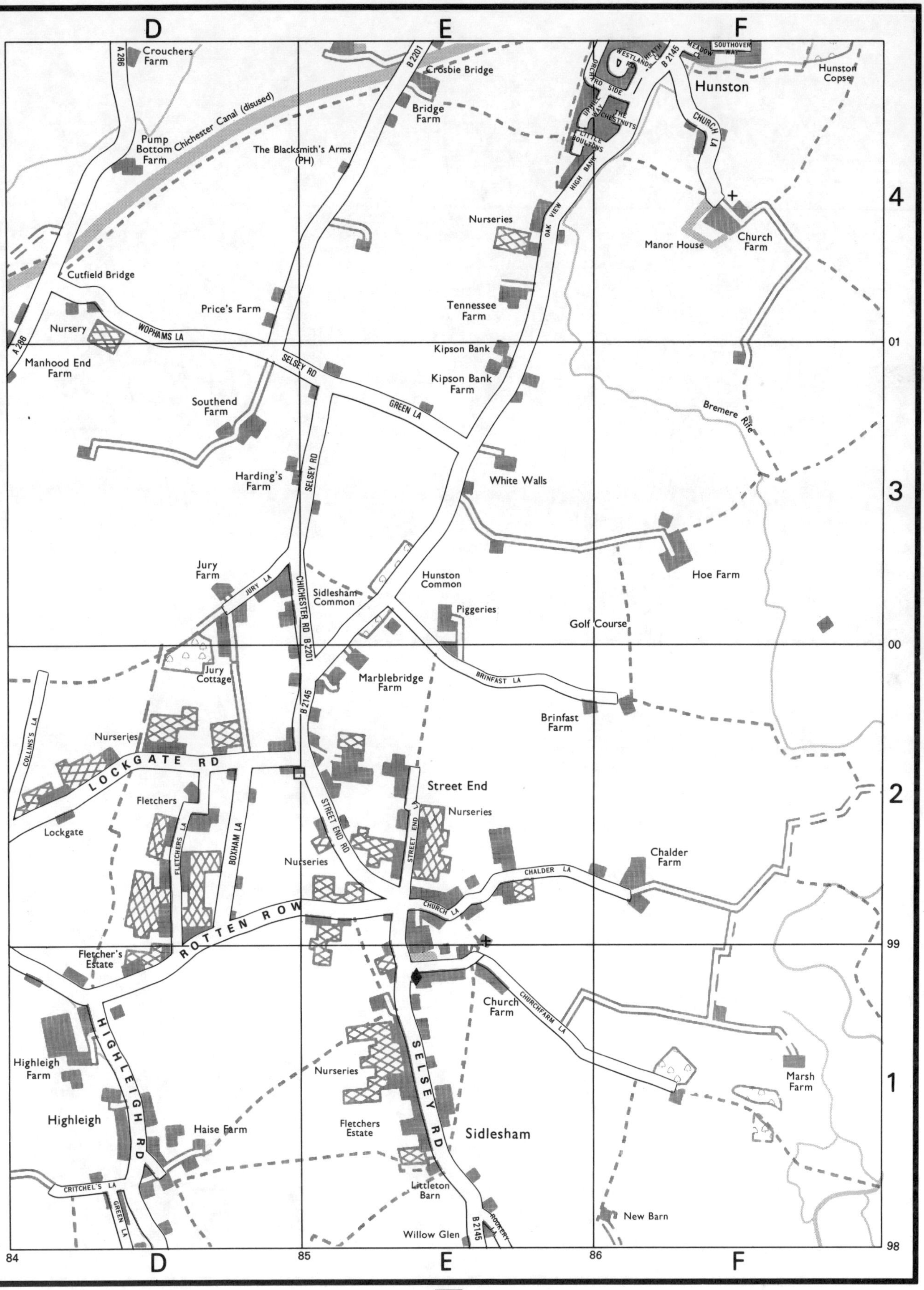
D
E
F
Crouchers Farm
A 286
B 2201
Crosbie Bridge
Chichester Canal (disused)
Bridge Farm
Pump Bottom Farm
The Blacksmith's Arms (PH)
WESTLANDS
HEATH
B 2145
MEADOW
SOUTHOVER WAY
ORCHARD SIDE
THE CHESTNUTS
LITTLE BOULTONS
Hunston
Hunston Copse
CHURCH LA
HIGH BANK
OAK VIEW
Nurseries
Manor House
Church Farm
Cutfield Bridge
Tennessee Farm
Price's Farm
Nursery
WOPHAMS LA
Manhood End Farm
Kipson Bank
Kipson Bank Farm
SELSEY RD
GREEN LA
Southend Farm
Bremere Rife
Harding's Farm
SELSEY RD
White Walls
Jury Farm
JURY LA
CHICHESTER RD B2201
Sidlesham Common
Hunston Common
Hoe Farm
Piggeries
Golf Course
Jury Cottage
Marblebridge Farm
BRINFAST LA
Brinfast Farm
B 2145
COLLINS'S LA
Nurseries
LOCKGATE RD
Street End
Fletchers
STREET END LA
Nurseries
Lockgate
STREET END RD
FLETCHERS LA
BOXHAM LA
Nurseries
Chalder Farm
CHALDER LA
ROTTEN ROW
CHURCH LA
Fletcher's Estate
Church Farm
CHURCHFARM LA
HIGHLEIGH RD
Highleigh Farm
Nurseries
SELSEY RD
Marsh Farm
Highleigh
Haise Farm
Fletchers Estate
Sidlesham
CRITCHEL'S LA
GREEN LA
Littleton Barn
ROOKERY LA
B 2145
Willow Glen
New Barn
4
3
2
1
01
00
99
98
84
85
86

194

204

173

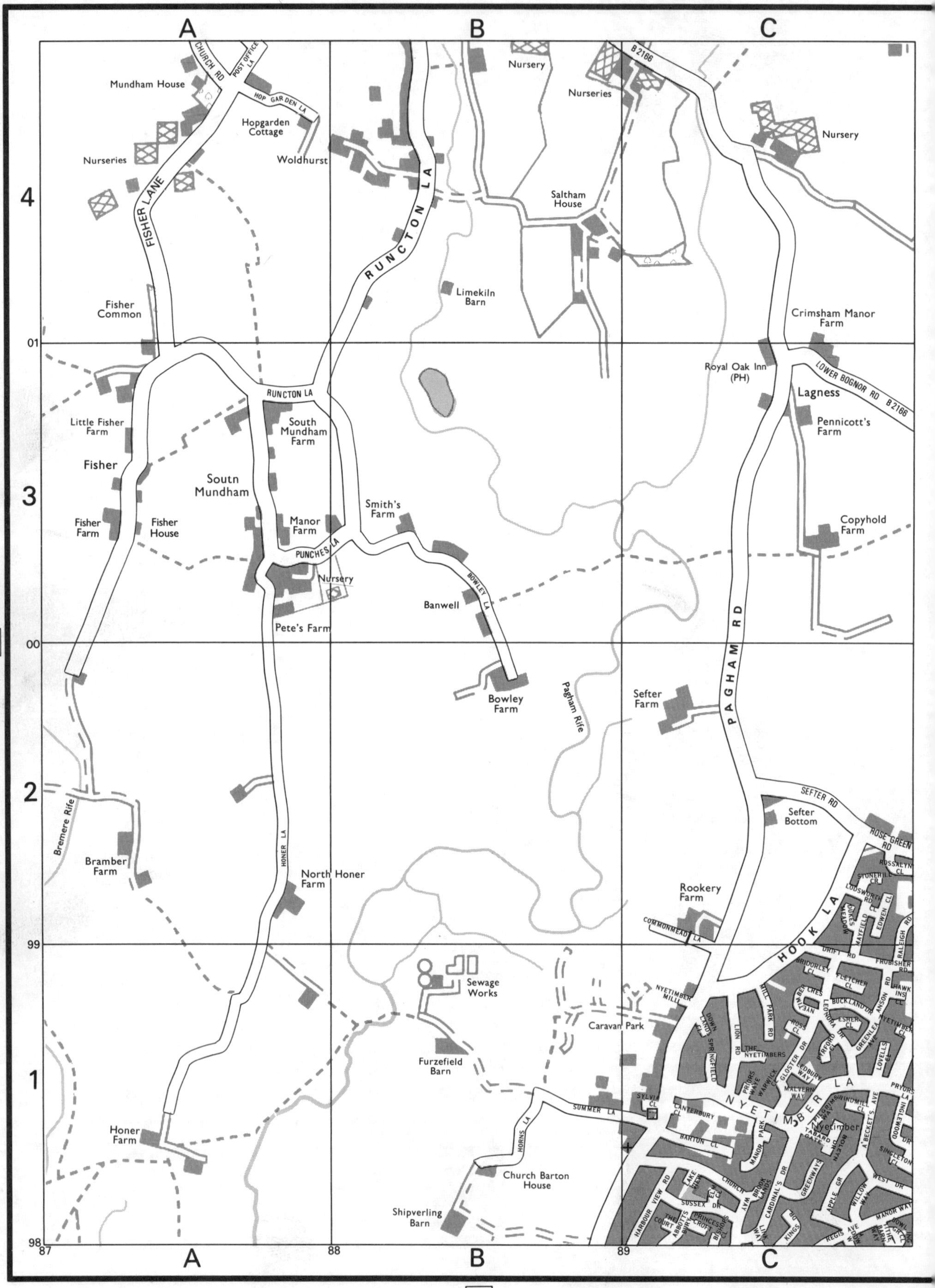

A
B
C
4
3
2
1
01
00
99
98
87
88
89
CHURCH RD
POST OFFICE LA
HOP GARDEN LA
Mundham House
Hopgarden Cottage
Nurseries
Woldhurst
FISHER LANE
RUNCTON LA
Nursery
Nurseries
B 2166
Nursery
Saltham House
Limekiln Barn
Fisher Common
Crimsham Manor Farm
RUNCTON LA
Royal Oak Inn (PH)
LOWER BOGNOR RD B 2166
Lagness
Pennicott's Farm
Little Fisher Farm
South Mundham Farm
Fisher
Soutn Mundham
Smith's Farm
Fisher Farm
Fisher House
Manor Farm
Copyhold Farm
PUNCHES LA
Nursery
BOWLEY LA
Banwell
Pete's Farm
PAGHAM RD
Bowley Farm
Pagham Rife
Sefter Farm
SEFTER RD
Sefter Bottom
ROSE GREEN RD
Bremere Rife
Bramber Farm
HONER LA
North Honer Farm
Rookery Farm
HOOK LA
COMMONMEAD LA
Sewage Works
NYETIMBER MILL
Caravan Park
Furzefield Barn
NYETIMBER LA
SUMMER LA
Honer Farm
HORNS LA
Nyetimber
Church Barton House
Shipverling Barn
HARBOUR VIEW RD

193

174

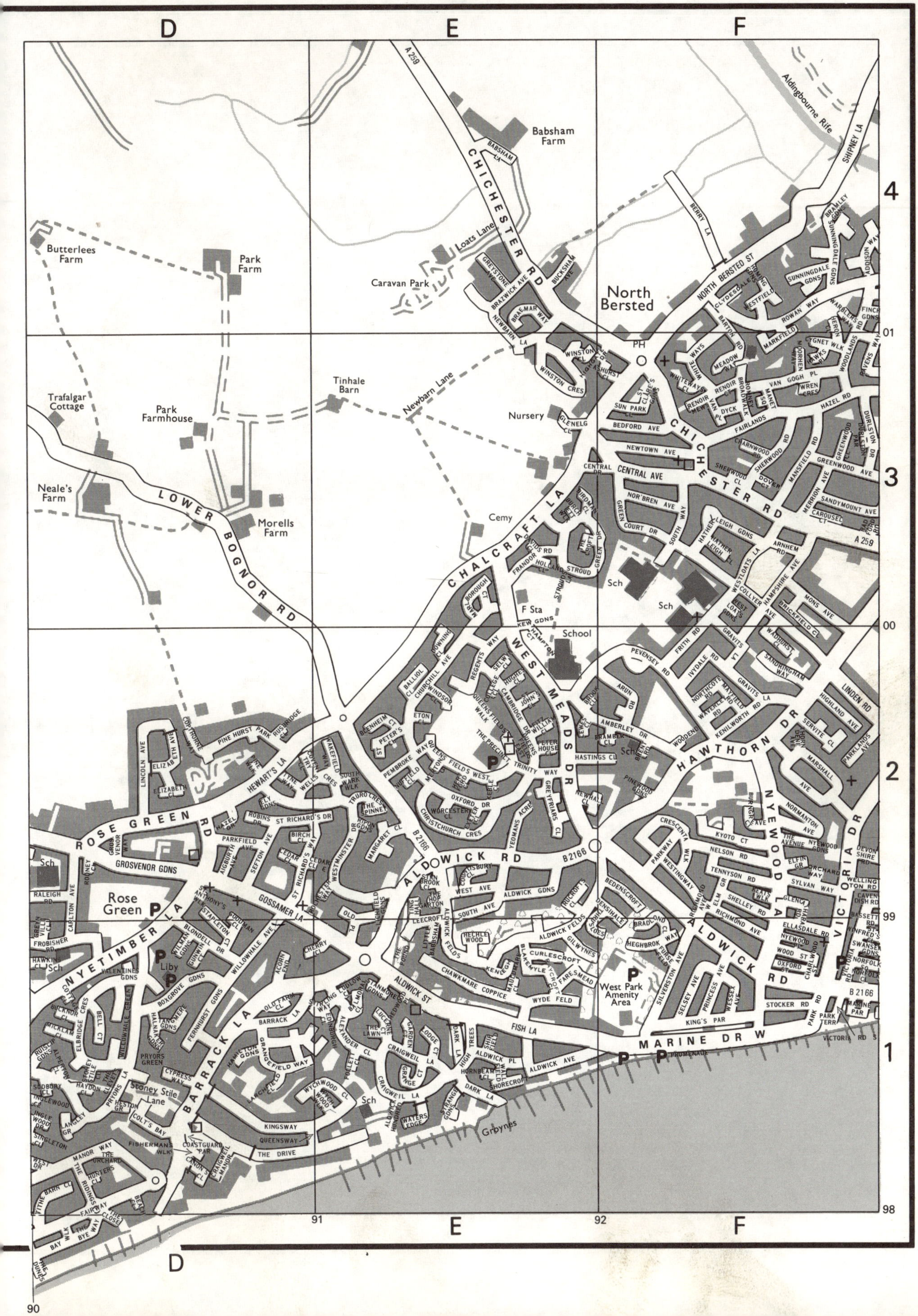
D
E
F
4
3
2
1
01
00
99
98
90
91
92
A 259
Babsham Farm
BABSHAM LA
CHICHESTER RD
Loats Lane
BUCKSHAM AVE
Aldingbourne Rife
SHIPNEY LA
BERRY LA
Butterlees Farm
Park Farm
Caravan Park
North Bersted
NORTH BERSTED ST
GREYSTONE AVE
BRAZWICK AVE
BRAEMAR WAY
NEWBARN LA
WINSTON CRES
PH
SUNNINGDALE GDNS
ROWAN WAY
WESTFIELD
CLYDESDALE
BARTON RD
MARKFIELD
CYGNET WLK
WOODLANDS
HAZEL RD
Trafalgar Cottage
Tinhale Barn
Newbarn Lane
Park Farmhouse
Nursery
SUN PARK CL
BEDFORD AVE
FAIRLANDS
VAN GOGH PL
NEWTOWN AVE
CENTRAL AVE
CHICHESTER RD
SHERWOOD RD
MANSFIELD RD
GREENWOOD AVE
SANDYMOUNT AVE
CAROUSEL CT
A 259
Neale's Farm
LOWER BOGNOR RD
Morells Farm
Cemy
CHALCRAFT LA
NOR'BREN AVE
COURT DR
SOUTH WAY
LEIGH GDNS
ARNHEM RD
HAMPSHIRE AVE
MONS AVE
BRICKFIELD CL
Sch
F Sta
School
KEW GDNS
WEST MEADS DR
PEVENSEY RD
FRITH RD
GRAVITS LA
SANDRINGHAM WAY
LINDEN RD
HIGHLAND AVE
PINE HURST PARK
RUSBRIDGE
HEWART'S LA
LINCOLN AVE
ELIZABETH AVE
BALLIOL
CHURCHILL AVE
REGENTS WAY
QUEENSFIELDS WEST
TRINITY WAY
HASTINGS CL
AMBERLEY DR
HAWTHORN DR
NYEWOOD LA
KENILWORTH RD
SERVITE CL
PARKLANDS AVE
MARSHALL AVE
ROSE GREEN RD
ST RICHARD'S DR
PARKFIELD AVE
WESTMINSTER DR
TRURO CRES
OXFORD DR
CHRISTCHURCH CRES
YEOMANS ACRE
GREYFRIARS CL
PINEWOOD GDNS
CRESCENTA WLK
KYOTO CT
NELSON RD
TENNYSON RD
SYLVAN WAY
VICTORIA DR
GROSVENOR GDNS
Sch
Rose Green
ALDWICK RD
B2166
WEST AVE
SOUTH AVE
ALDWICK GDNS
BEDENSCROFT
SHELLEY RD
RICHMOND AVE
ELLASDALE RD
GOSSAMER LA
NYETIMBER LA
RALEIGH RD
CARLTON AVE
FROBISHER
Liby
Sch
BARRACK LA
ACORN END
CHERRY
ALDWICK FIELDS
CHAWKMARE COPPICE
CURLESCROFT
WYDE FELD
West Park Amenity Area
ALDWICK RD
STOCKER RD
KING'S PAR
SILVERSTON AVE
SELSEY AVE
PRINCESS AVE
WESSEX AVE
B 2166
PARK TERR
MARINE PAR
ALDWICK ST
FISH LA
MARINE DR W
PROMENADE
VICTORIA RD S
ALDWICK AVE
BOXGROVE GDNS
FERNHURST GDNS
BELL CT
Pryors Green
Stoney Stile Lane
CRAIGWEIL LA
Sch
KINGSWAY
QUEENSWAY
THE DRIVE
COASTGUARD PAR
FISHERMANS WLK
COLT'S BAY
MANOR WAY
THE RIDINGS
FAIRWAY
THE CLOSE
BAY WLK
THE BYE WAY
Groynes
E
F
D

196

175

195

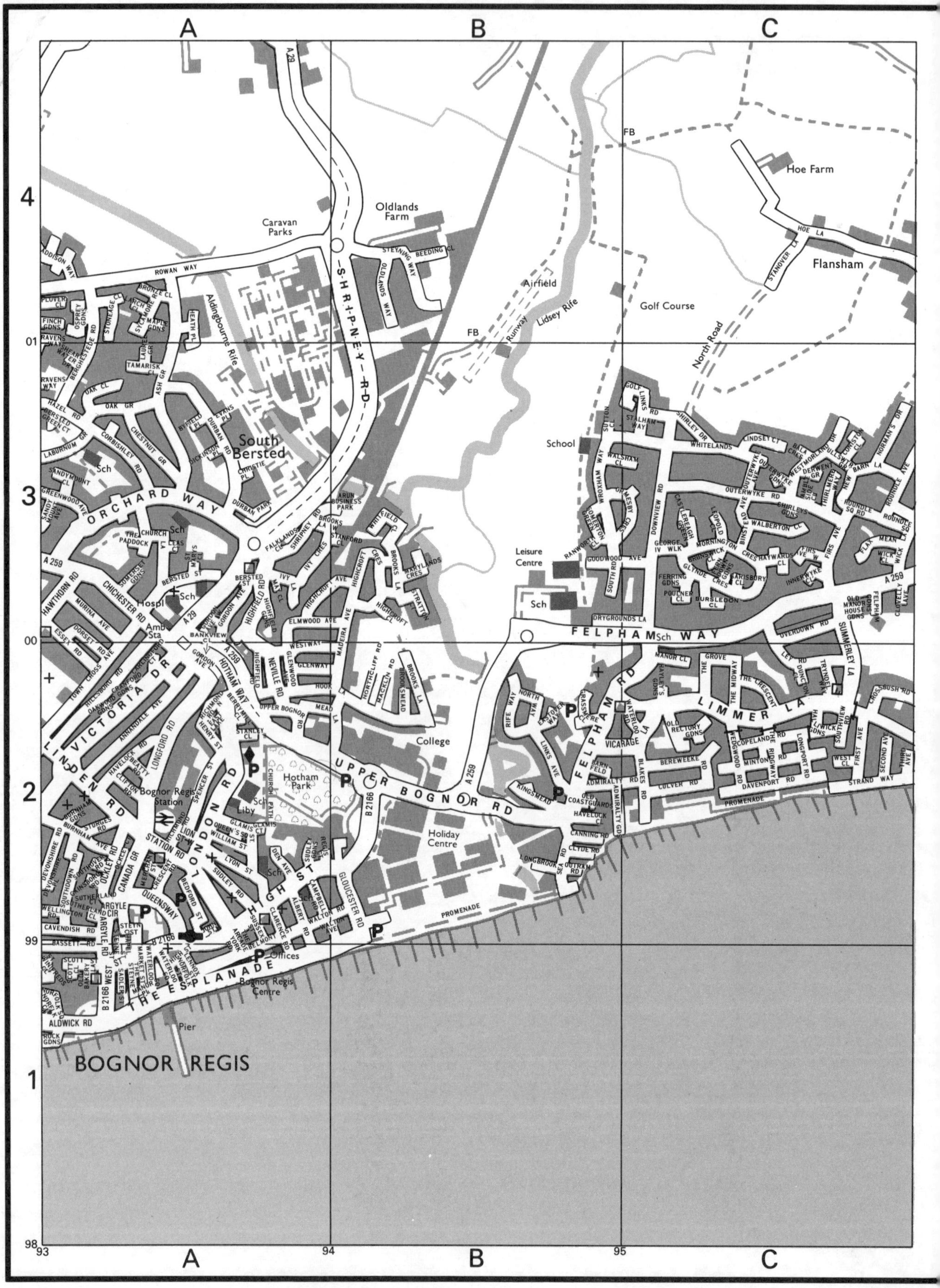
A
B
C
4
3
2
1
01
00
99
98
93
94
95
A 29
Caravan Parks
Oldlands Farm
Hoe Farm
HOE LA
STANOVER LA
Flansham
FB
Airfield
Runway
Lidsey Rife
Golf Course
North Road
ROWAN WAY
STEYNING WAY
BEEDING CL
OLDLANDS WAY
Aldingbourne Rife
S·H·R·I·P·N·E·Y RD
South Bersted
ORCHARD WAY
A 259
School
Leisure Centre
Sch
FELPHAM WAY
ARUN BUSINESS PARK
FALKLANDS
SHRIPNEY
HIGHCROFT AVE
ELMWOOD AVE
BANKVIEW
Hospl
Amb Sta
HAWTHORN RD
CHICHESTER RD
VICTORIA DR
LINDEN RD
LONGFORD RD
HOTHAM WAY
UPPER BOGNOR RD
College
Hotham Park
Bognor Regis Station
Liby
STATION RD
LONDON RD
HIGH ST
GLOUCESTER RD
B 2166
Holiday Centre
PROMENADE
QUEENSWAY
Offices
THE ESPLANADE
Bognor Regis Centre
ALDWICK RD
Pier
BOGNOR REGIS
FELPHAM RD
LIMMER LA
VICARAGE
SUMMERLEY LA
STRAND WAY
COASTGUARDS
GOLF LINKS RD
SHIRLEY DR
WHITELANDS
DOWNVIEW RD
GOODWOOD AVE
DRYGROUNDS LA
MANOR CL
ADMIRALTY RD
BLAKES RD
ROWAN WAY

176

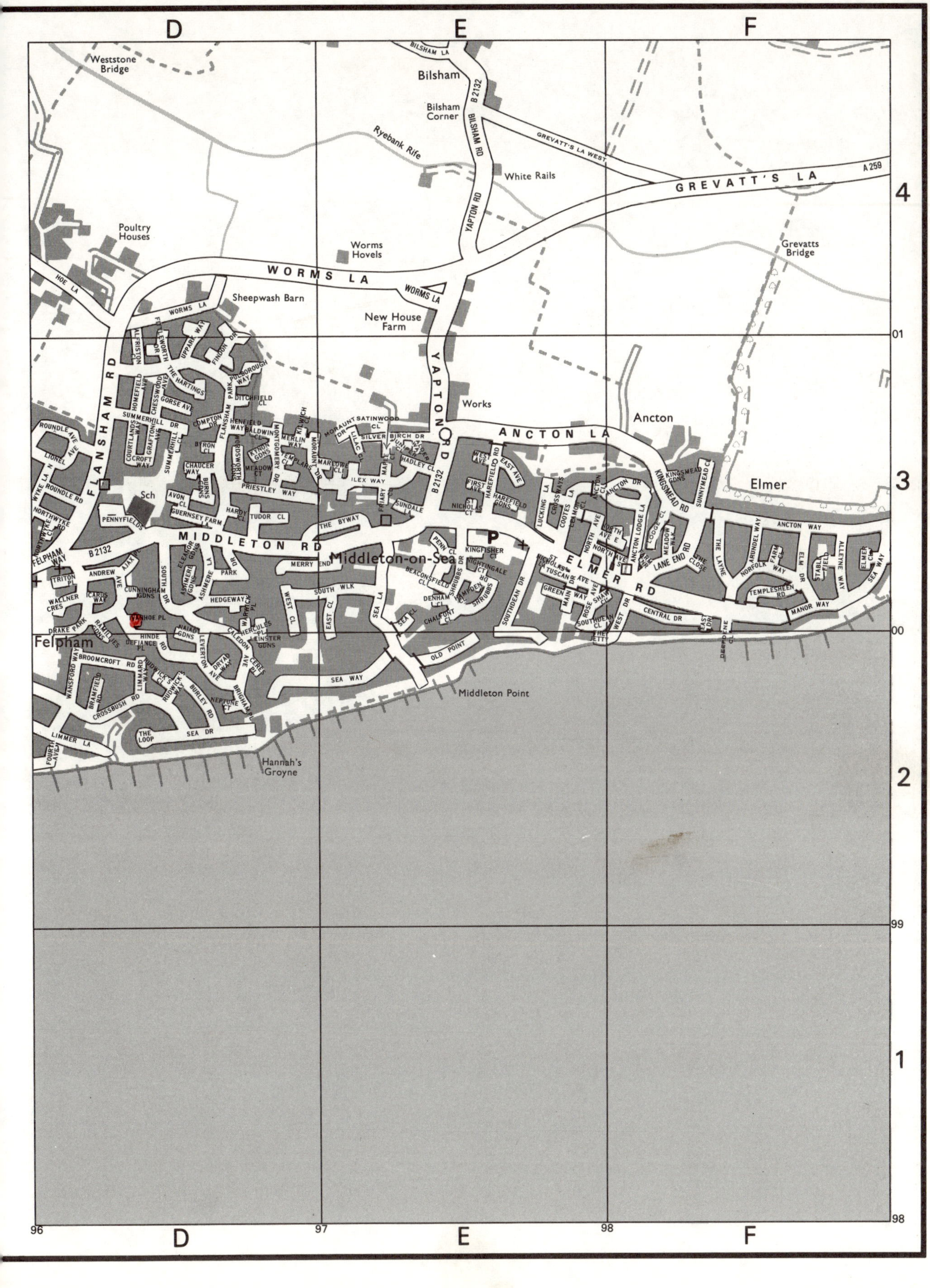
D
E
F
Weststone Bridge
Bilsham
Bilsham Corner
BILSHAM LA
B 2132
BILSHAM RD
Ryebank Rife
GREVATT'S LA WEST
White Rails
GREVATT'S LA
A 259
Poultry Houses
Worms Hovels
YAPTON RD
Grevatts Bridge
WORMS LA
HOE LA
Sheepwash Barn
New House Farm
Works
Ancton
ANCTON LA
YAPTON RD
FLANSHAM RD
Elmer
Sch
MIDDLETON RD
B2132
Middleton-on-Sea
ELMER RD
Felpham
SEA WAY
OLD POINT
Middleton Point
Hannah's Groyne
SEA DR
THE LOOP
LIMMER LA
ANCTON WAY
MANOR WAY
CENTRAL DR
LANE END RD
KINGSMEAD RD
SOUTHDEAN DR
WEST DR
SEA LA
SOUTH WLK
MERRY END
THE BYWAY
4
3
2
1
01
00
99
98
96
97
98

198

177

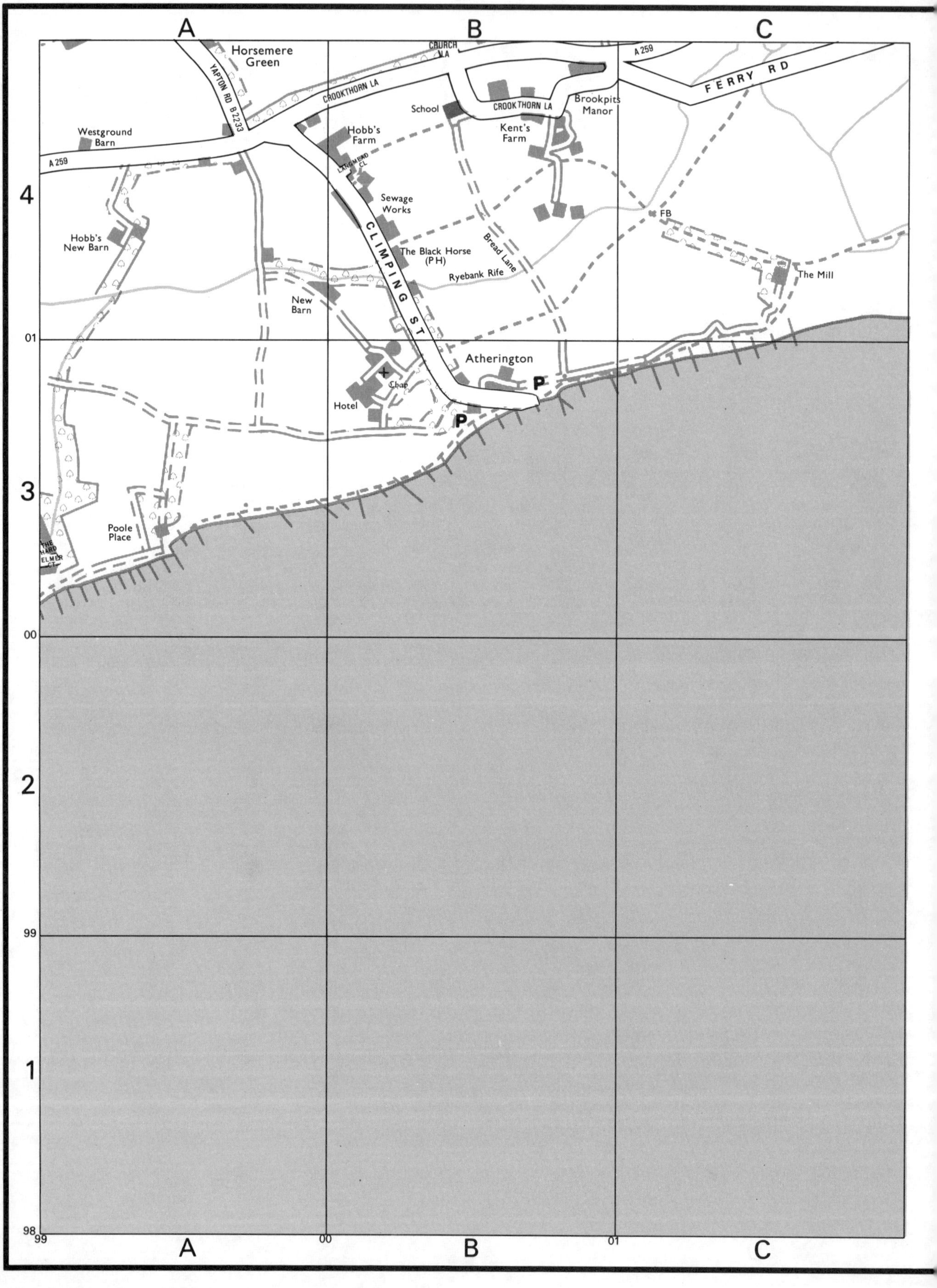
A
B
C
Horsemere Green
CHURCH LA
A 259
FERRY RD
YAPTON RD B2233
CROOKTHORN LA
School
CROOKTHORN LA
Brookpits Manor
Westground Barn
Hobb's Farm
Kent's Farm
A 259
LANGMEAD CL
4
Sewage Works
FB
Hobb's New Barn
CLIMPING ST
Bread Lane
The Black Horse (PH)
The Mill
Ryebank Rife
New Barn
01
Atherington
Chap
P
Hotel
P
3
Poole Place
THE HARD
ELMER CT
00
2
99
1
98
99
00
01

197

178

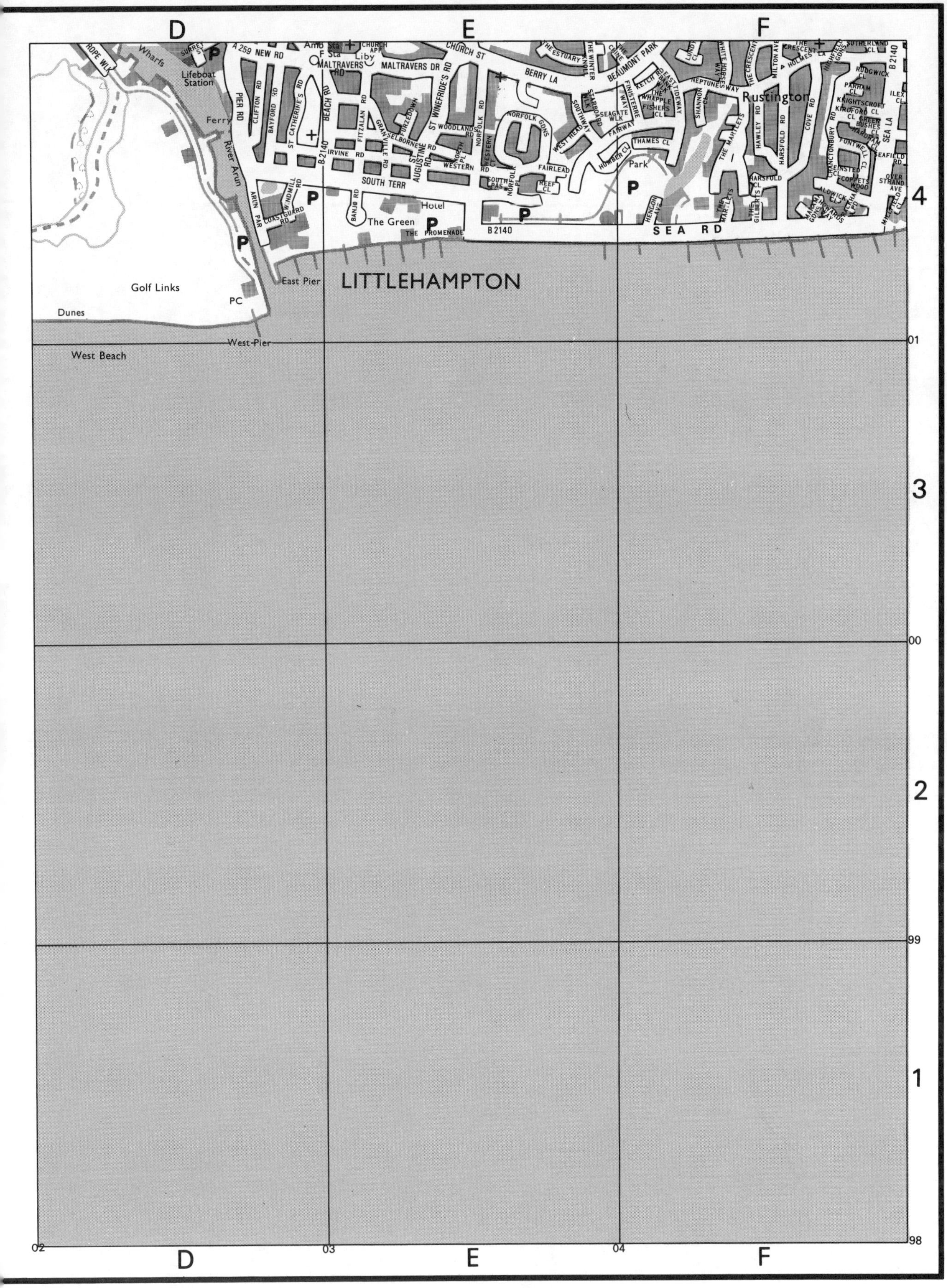
D
E
F
LITTLEHAMPTON
Rustington
Golf Links
Dunes
West Beach
West Pier
East Pier
PC
River Arun
Ferry
Lifeboat Station
Wharfs
HOPE WLK
A 259 NEW RD
Amb Sta
F Sta
Liby
CHURCH ST
MALTRAVERS DR
MALTRAVERS RD
PIER RD
CLIFTON RD
BAYFORD RD
ST CATHERINE'S RD
BEACH RD
B 2140
IRVINE RD
FITZALAN RD
GRANVILLE RD
SELBORNE RD
FURZEDOWN
AUGUSTINE RD
ST WINEFRIDE'S RD
WOODLANDS RD
NORFOLK RD
WESTERN RD
BERRY LA
NORFOLK GDNS
SOUTH TERR
ARUN PAR
WINDMILL RD
COASTGUARD RD
BANJO RD
The Green
Hotel
THE PROMENADE
B 2140
FAIRLEAD
REEF CL
THE ESTUARY
THE WINTER KNOLL
BEAUMONT PARK
SOUTHWAY
STARBOARD WLK
WEST REEF
FINISTERRE WAY
SEAGATE WLK
FAIRWAY
THE WHAPPLE
FISHERS CL
EAST TIDEWAY
THAMES CL
HUMBER CL
Park
HENGOAN AVE
SEA RD
SHANNON CL
NEPTUNES WAY
WHITE HORSES WAY
THE CRESCENT
MILTON AVE
HOLMES LA
THE MARTLETS
HAWLEY RD
HARSFOLD RD
HARSFOLD CL
THE GILBERTS
COVE RD
CHANCTONBURY RD
SUTHERLAND CL
RUDGWICK CL
PARHAM CL
KNIGHTSCROFT CL
KIRDFORD CL
FONTWELL CL
SEAFIELD RD
EINSTED CL
COPPETS WOOD
ALDWICK CL
OVER STRAND AVE
SEA LA
ILEX CL
B 2140
4
3
2
1
01
00
99
98
02
03
04

200

179

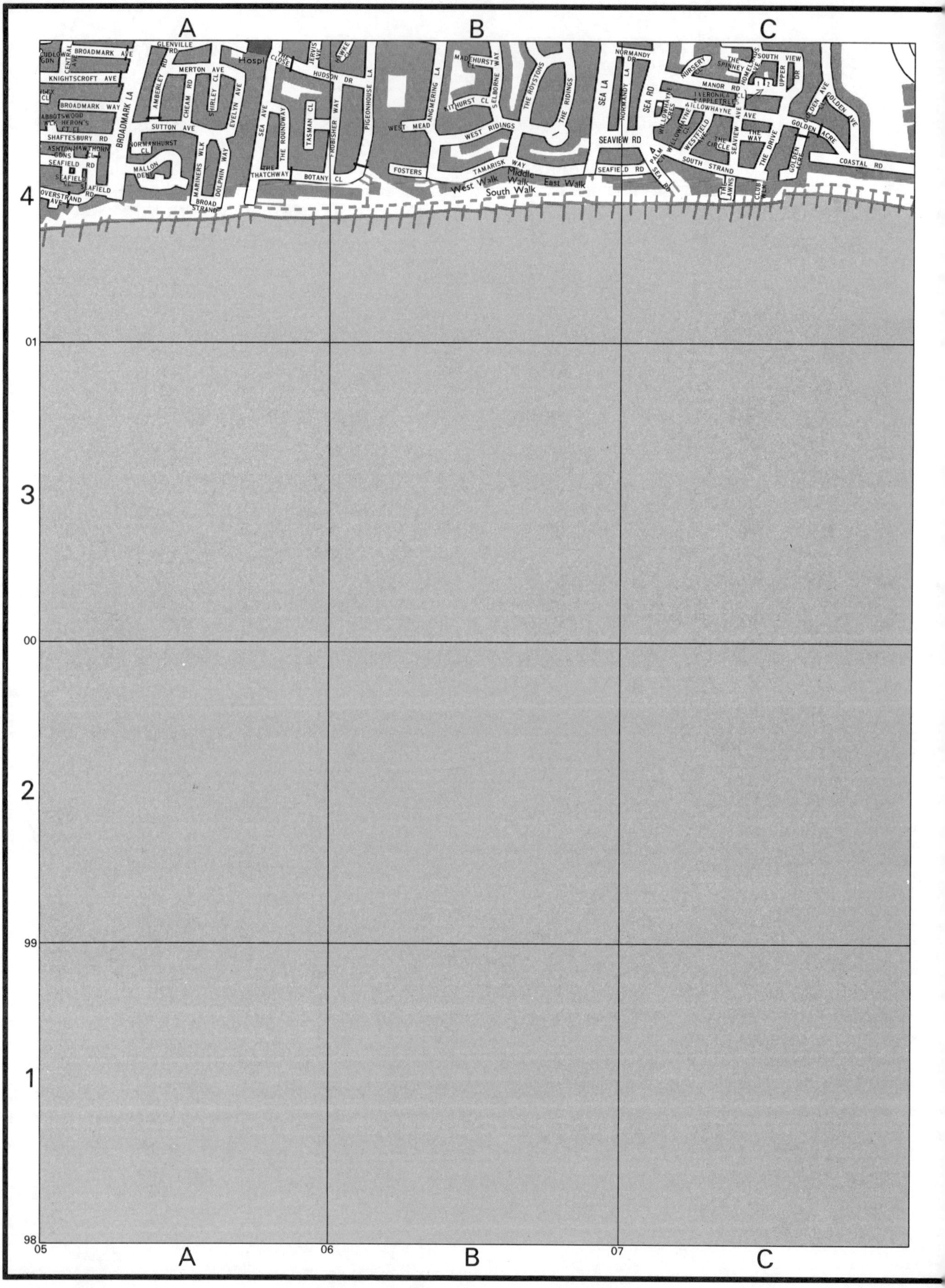
A
B
C
CUDLOW GDN
CENTRAL AVE
BROADMARK AVE
GLENVILLE RD
KNIGHTSCROFT AVE
CL
BROADMARK WAY
ABBOTSWOOD WLK
HERON'S CT CL
SHAFTESBURY RD
ASHTON GDNS
HAWTHORN CL
SEAFIELD RD
SEAFIELD CL
SEAFIELD RD
OVERSTRAND AVE
BROADMARK LA
AMBERLEY RD
MERTON AVE
CHEAM RD
SHIRLEY CL
EVELYN AVE
SUTTON AVE
NORMANHURST CL
MALLON DENE
MARINERS WLK
DOLPHIN WAY
BROAD STRAND
Hospl
THE CLOSE
JERVIS AVE
HAWKE CL
HUDSON DR
SEA AVE
THE ROUNDWAY
TASMAN CL
FROBISHER WAY
PIGEONHOUSE LA
THE THATCHWAY
BOTANY CL
MADEHURST CL
SELBORNE WAY
KITHURST CL
ANGMERING LA
WEST MEAD
WEST RIDINGS
THE ROYSTONS
THE RIDINGS
FOSTERS
TAMARISK WAY
West Walk
Middle Walk
East Walk
South Walk
SEA LA
NORMANDY DR
NORMANDY LA
SEAVIEW RD
SEAFIELD RD
SEA RD
PALM CT
SEA RD
WILLOWHAYNE CRES
WILLOWHAYNE CL
NURSERY CL
THE SPINNEY
HOMELANDS AVE
SOUTH VIEW
UPPER DR
MANOR RD
1 VERONICA CL
2 APPLETREES
WILLOWHAYNE AVE
WESTFIELD AVE
THE CIRCLE
SEAVIEW AVE
THE WAY
THE DRIVE
SOUTH STRAND
THE LAWNS
CLUB WLK
GOLDEN AVE
GOLDEN CL
GOLDEN AVE
GOLDEN ACRE
GOLDEN ACRE
COASTAL RD
4
01
3
00
2
99
1
98
05
06
07

199

180

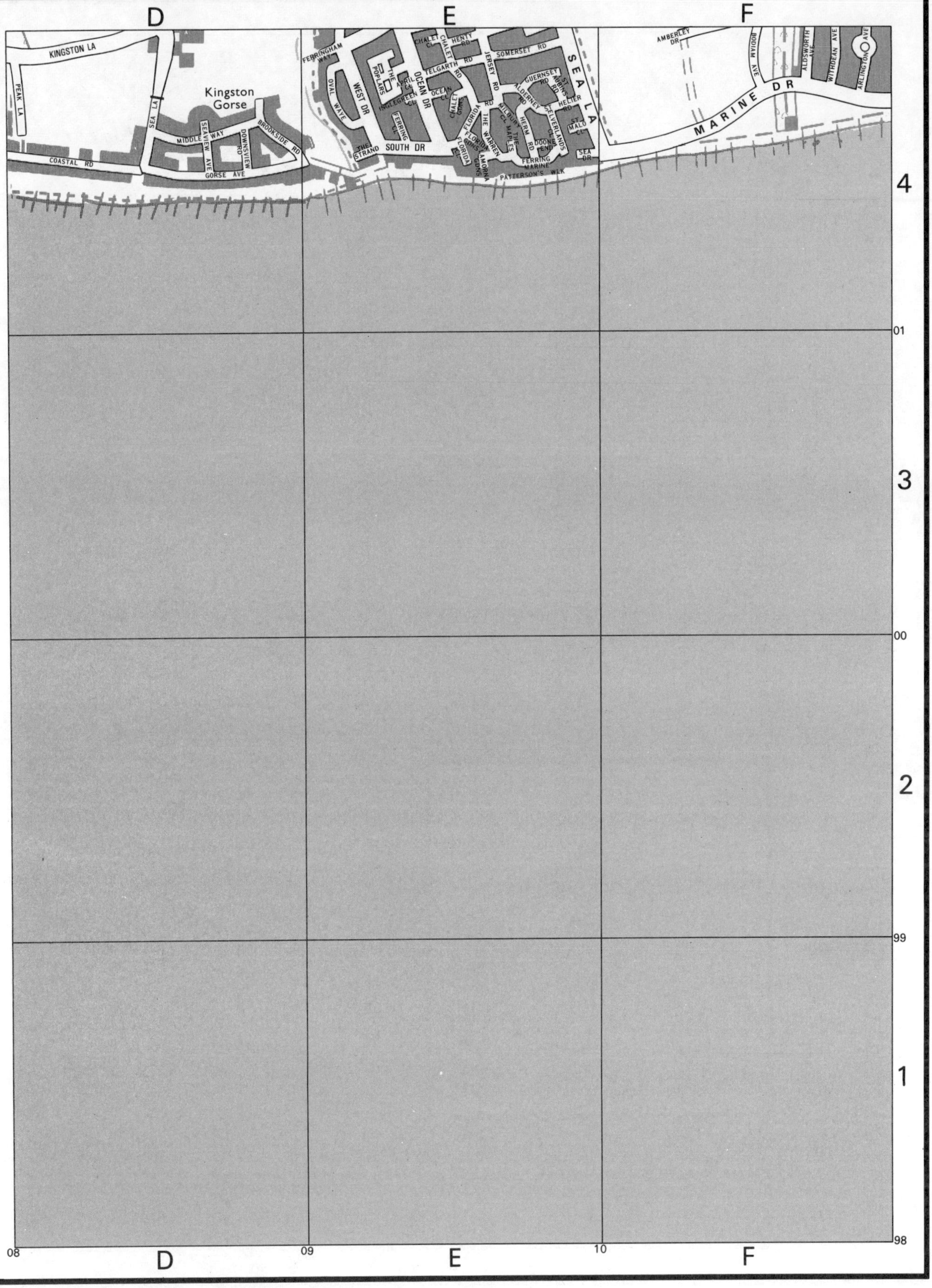
D
E
F
KINGSTON LA
PEAK LA
SEA LA
Kingston Gorse
MIDDLE WAY
SEAVIEW AVE
DOWNSVIEW RD
BROOKSIDE RD
COASTAL RD
GORSE AVE
FERRINGHAM WAY
OVAL WAYE
WEST DR
THE POPLARS
INGLEGREEN CL
OCEAN DR
FERRING CL
THE STRAND
SOUTH DR
CHALET CL
CHALET RD
HENTY RD
TELGARTH RD
OCEAN CL
CHALET GDNS
FLORIDA RD
FLORIDA CL
FLORIDA GDNS
THE WARREN
JERSEY RD
SOMERSET RD
SEA LA
GUERNSEY RD
ALDERNEY RD
ST AUBINS RD
HELIER RD
HERM RD
THE MAPLES
CLEVERLANDS
ST MALO CL
DOONE END
FERRING MARINE
PATTERSON'S WLK
SEA DR
AMBERLEY DR
BODIAM AVE
ALDSWORTH AVE
WITHDEAN AVE
ARLINGTON AVE
MARINE DR
4
3
2
1
01
00
99
98
08
09
10

181

191

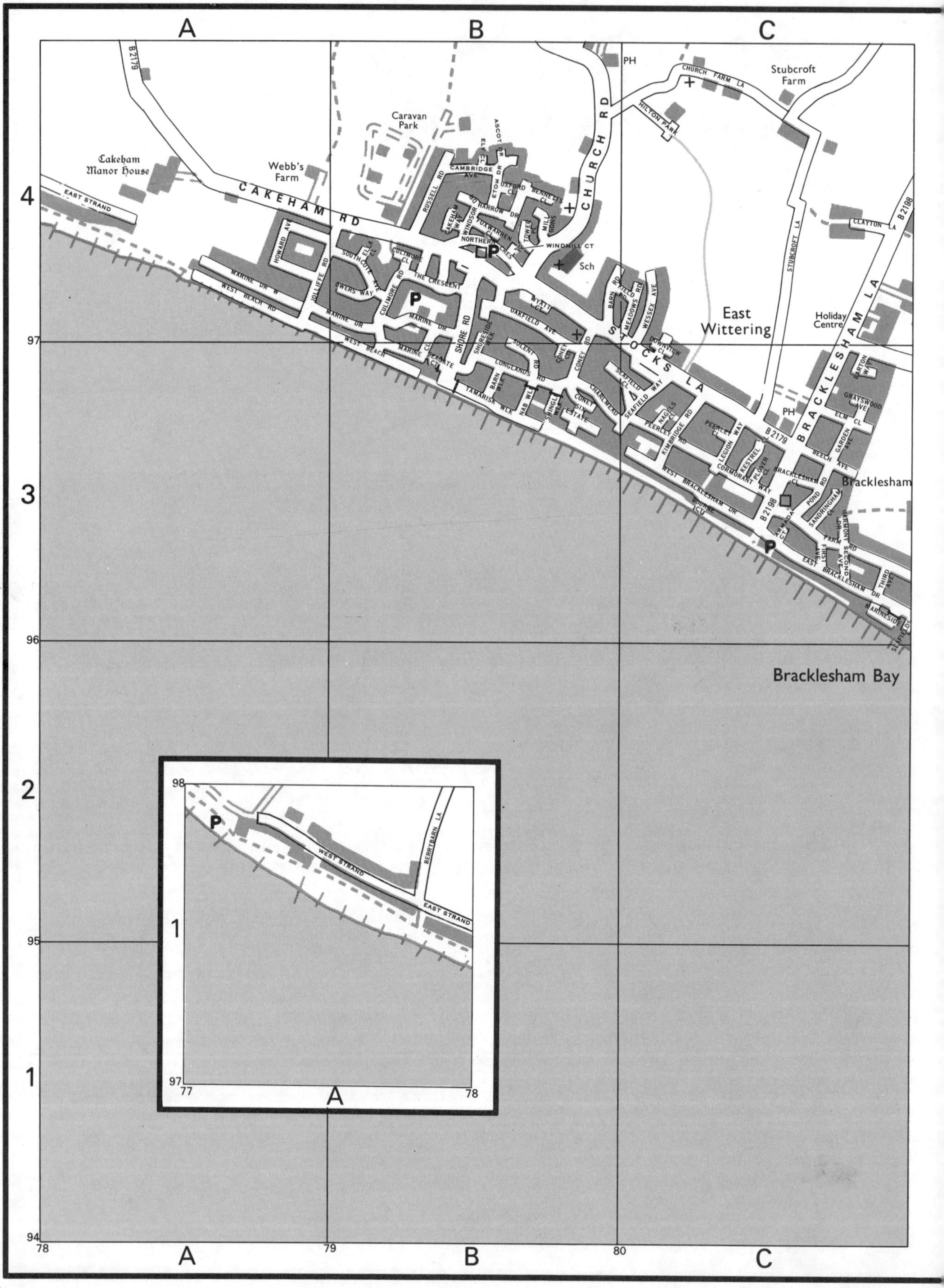
A
B
C
4
3
2
1
97
96
95
94
78
79
80
B2179
Caravan Park
Cakeham Manor House
Webb's Farm
EAST STRAND
CAKEHAM RD
CHURCH RD
PH
CHURCH FARM LA
HILTON PARK
Stubcroft Farm
STUBCROFT LA
CLAYTON LA
B2198
Sch
WINDMILL CT
East Wittering
Holiday Centre
BRACKLESHAM LA
STOCKS LA
MARINE DR W
WEST BEACH RD
JOLLIFFE RD
CULIMORE RD
THE CRESCENT
SHORE RD
MARINE DR
OAKFIELD AVE
SOLENT RD
LONGLANDS RD
TAMARISK WLK
NAB WLK
CONEY RD
SEAFIELD WAY
B2179
LEGION WAY
KIMBRIDGE RD
WEST BRACKLESHAM DR
CORMORANT WAY
BEECH AVE
ELM CL
POND RD
SANDRINGHAM CL
EAST BRACKLESHAM DR
Bracklesham
Bracklesham Bay
98
97
77
A
78
1
P
WEST STRAND
BERRYBARN LA
EAST STRAND

192

D
E
F
B2198
BRACKLESHAM LA
Cherry Tree Farm
BOOKERS LA
SOMERLEY LA
THIRD AVE
ALMODINGTON LA
Almodington
Somerley Farm
EARNLEY RD
Oldhouse Farm Cottages
OLDHOUSE LA
Earnley Grange
Holden's Farm Caravan Park
EARNLEY MANOR CL
Manor Farm
Grange Farm
Easton Cottages
Easton Farm
EASTON LA
CLAPPERS LA
Earnley
Adult Education Centre
Grange Rife
Marsh Barn
DROVE LA
Earnley Rife
Easton Rife
FARM RD
EAST BRACKLESHAM DR
SILVER WAY
Marsh Farm
STONEY LA
Holiday Camp
Greenwood Farm
Broad Rife
Ham Farm
HAM RD
Marsh Barn
Caravan Park
4
3
2
1
97
96
95
94
81
82
83

204

193

203

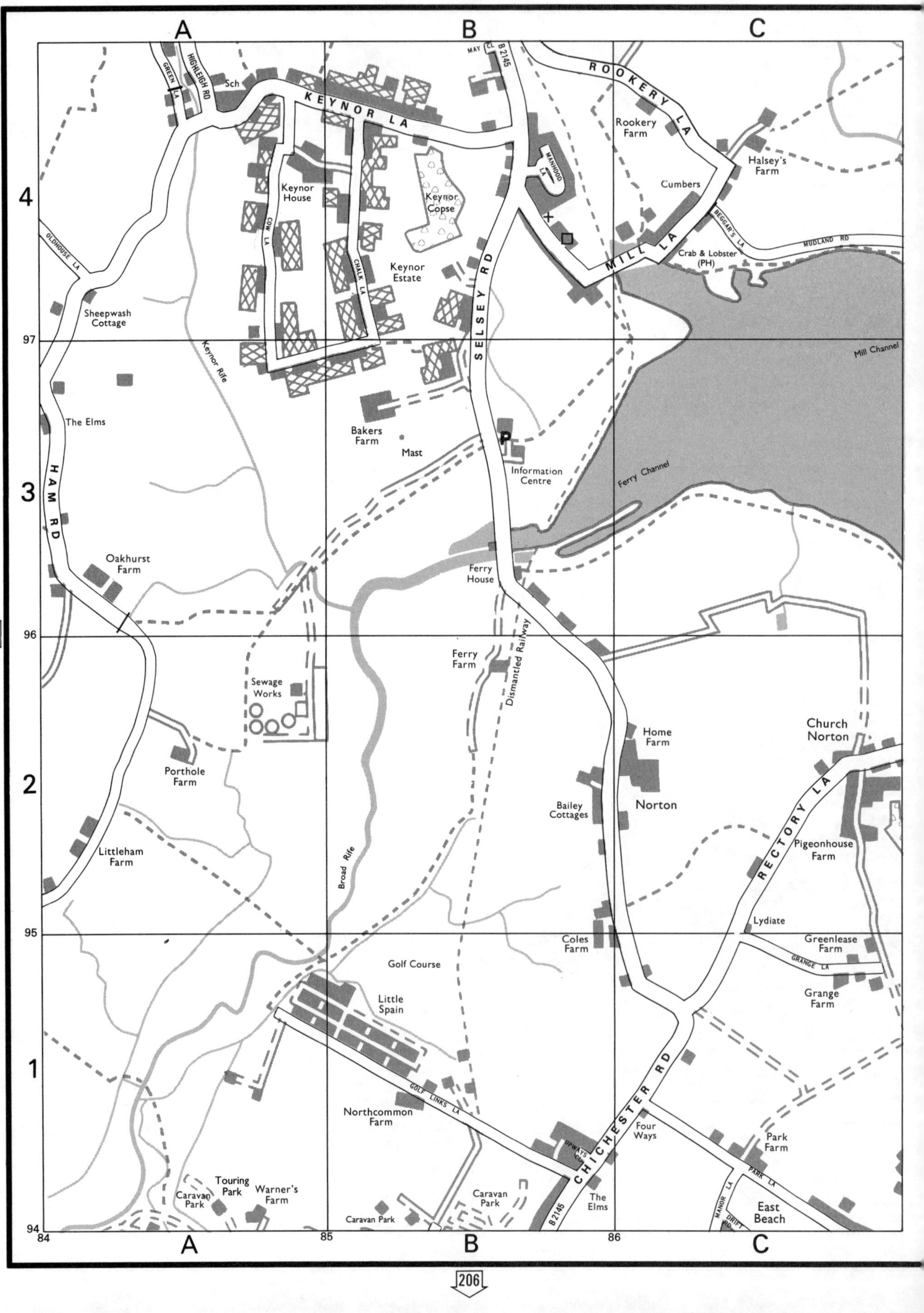
A
B
C
A
B
C
4
3
2
1
97
96
95
94
84
85
86
GREEN LA
HIGHLEIGH RD
Sch
KEYNOR LA
MAY CL
B2145
ROOKERY LA
Rookery Farm
Halsey's Farm
Cumbers
MANHOOD LA
Keynor House
Keynor Copse
COW LA
CHALK LA
Keynor Estate
OLDHOUSE LA
Sheepwash Cottage
SELSEY RD
MILL LA
BEGGAR'S LA
MUDLAND RD
Crab & Lobster (PH)
Mill Channel
Keynor Rife
The Elms
Bakers Farm
Mast
P
Information Centre
Ferry Channel
HAM RD
Oakhurst Farm
Ferry House
Dismantled Railway
Ferry Farm
Sewage Works
Home Farm
Church Norton
Porthole Farm
Bailey Cottages
Norton
RECTORY LA
Littleham Farm
Pigeonhouse Farm
Broad Rife
Lydiate
Greenlease Farm
Coles Farm
GRANGE LA
Golf Course
Little Spain
Grange Farm
CHICHESTER RD
GOLF LINKS LA
Northcommon Farm
Four Ways
Park Farm
UPWAYS CL
PARK LA
Touring Park
Warner's Farm
Caravan Park
Caravan Park
Caravan Park
The Elms
B2145
MANOR LA
DRIFT RD
East Beach

206

194

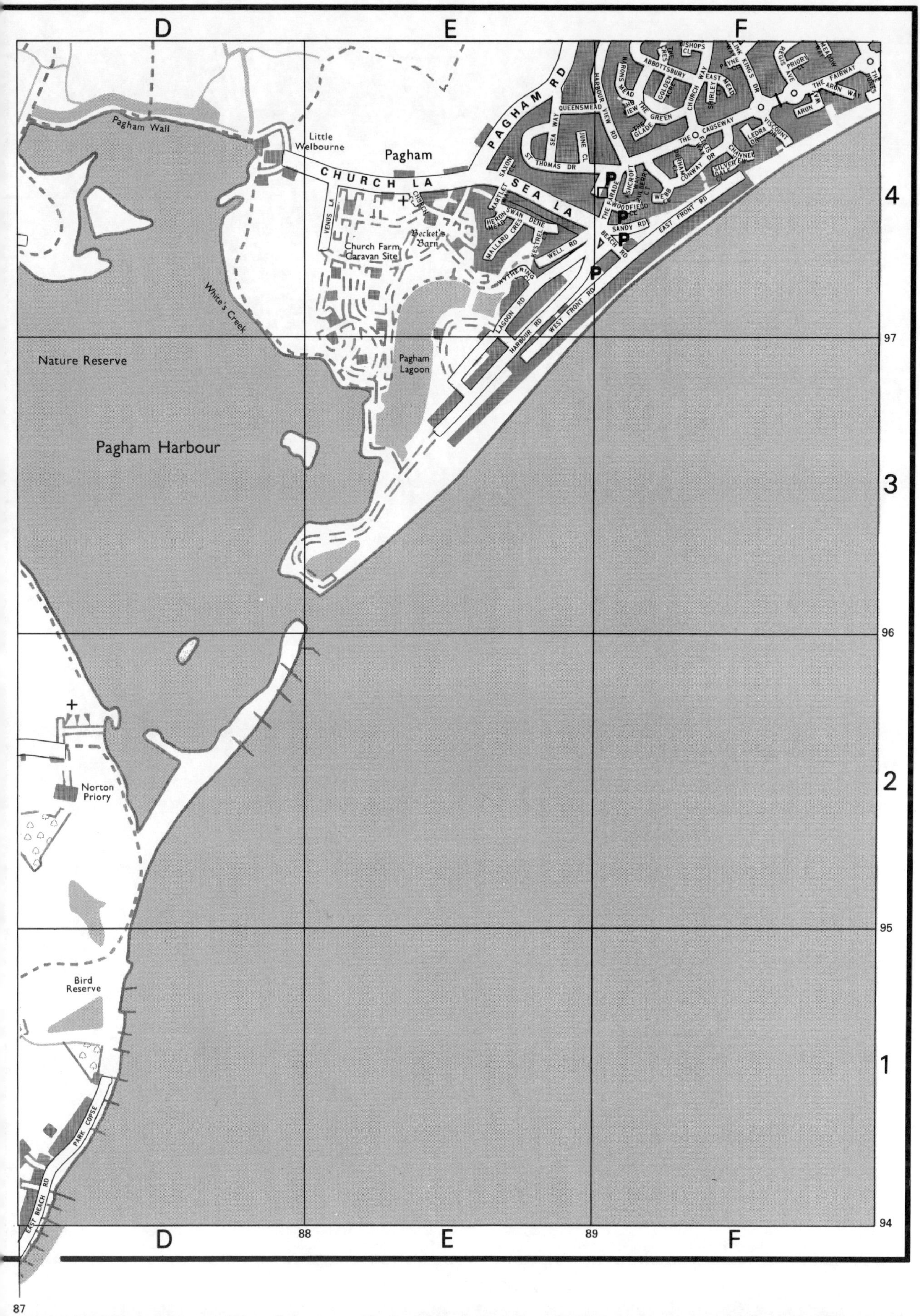
D
E
F
4
3
2
1
97
96
95
94
88
89
87
Pagham Wall
Little Welbourne
Pagham
CHURCH LA
SEA LA
PAGHAM RD
VENUS LA
Church Farm Caravan Site
Becket's Barn
White's Creek
Nature Reserve
Pagham Lagoon
Pagham Harbour
LAGOON RD
HARBOUR RD
WEST FRONT RD
EAST FRONT RD
BEACH RD
SANDY RD
WOODFIELD
THE PARADE
WYTHERING
MALLARD CRES
HERON MEAD
SWAN
DENE
KESTREL CT
WELL RD
MARTLET
SAXON CL
ST THOMAS DR
SEA WAY
QUEENSMEAD
JUNE CL
HARBOUR VIEW RD
BARONS MEAD
ABBOTTSBURY
BISHOPS CL
GOLDEN ACRE
THE GREEN
THE GLADE
CHURCH WAY
EAST MEAD
SHIRLEY CL
THE CAUSEWAY
CONWAY DR
ASHCROFT
WEBB CL
SILVER DALE CL
CHANNEL VW
LEDRA DR
VISCOUNT
KINGS DR
PAYNE CL
REGIS AVE
PRIORY CL
MEADOW WAY
THE FAIRWAY
ARUN WAY
ARUN
THE DUNES
Norton Priory
Bird Reserve
PARK COPSE
EAST BEACH RD

204

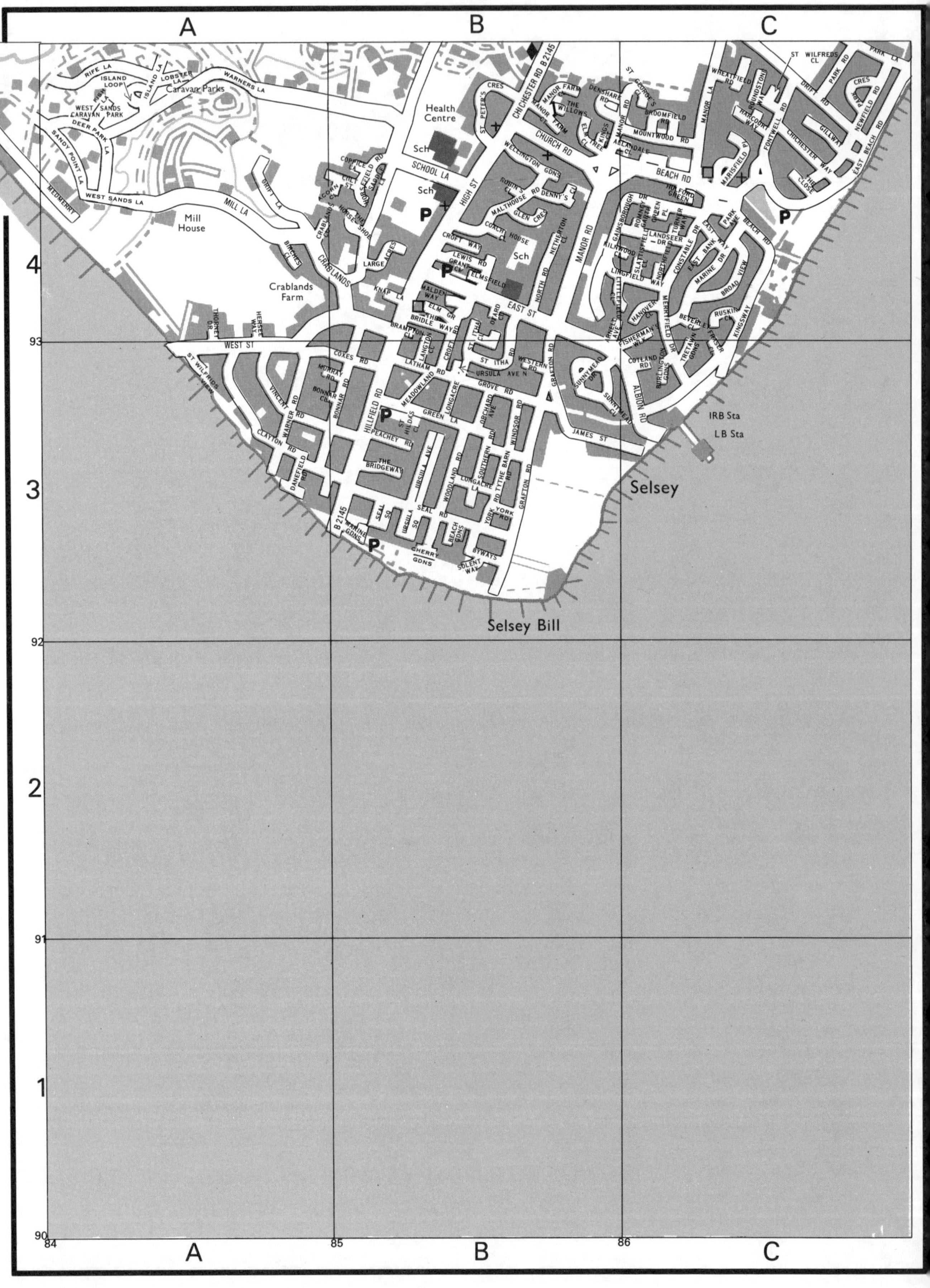
A
B
C
4
3
2
1
93
92
91
90
84
85
86
Caravan Parks
West Sands Caravan Park
Health Centre
Sch
Mill House
Crablands Farm
IRB Sta
LB Sta
Selsey
Selsey Bill
RIFE LA
ISLAND LOOP
LOBSTER LA
ISLAND LA
WARNERS LA
DEER PARK LA
SANDY POINT LA
MEDMERRY
WEST SANDS LA
MILL LA
DRIFT LA
BIRCHES CL
CRABLANDS
SCHOOL LA
HIGH ST
CHICHESTER RD B 2145
CHURCH RD
WELLINGTON GDNS
MANOR RD
MOUNTWOOD RD
BROOMFIELD RD
BEACH RD
MANOR LA
WHEATFIELD RD
ST WILFREDS CL
PARK LA
PARK RD
NEWFIELD RD
GILLWAY
CHICHESTER WAY
EAST BEACH RD
FONTWELL RD
HARCOURT WAY
THE CLOSE
MALTHOUSE RD
GLEN CRES
COACH HOUSE CL
CROFT WAY
LEWIS RD
ELMSFIELD
EAST ST
NORTH RD
NETHERTON CL
LARGE ACRES
KNAP LA
MALDEN WAY
ELM GR
THE BRIDLE WAY
BRAMPTON CL
LANGTON CL
WEST ST
ST WILFRIDS VIEW
THORNEY DR
HERSEE WAY
COXES RD
MURRAY RD
BONNAR RD
VINCENT RD
WARNER RD
CLAYTON RD
DANEFIELD RD
HILLFIELD RD
LATHAM RD
MEADOWLAND RD
GREEN LA
LONGACRE
GROVE RD
ORCHARD AVE
WINDSOR RD
URSULA AVE N
ST ITHA RD
WESTERN RD
GRAFTON RD
SUNNYMEAD DR
SUNNYMEAD CL
JAMES ST
ALBION RD
COTLAND RD
BURLINGTON GDNS
TRETAWN GDNS
FISHERMAN'S WLK
HANOVER
MERRYFIELD DR
KINGSWAY
RUSKIN CL
BROAD VIEW
MARINE DR
EAST BANK WAY
CONSTABLE DR
LANDSEER DR
GAINSBOROUGH DR
KILNWOOD CL
LINGFIELD CL
PEACHEY RD
THE BRIDGEWAY
URSULA AVE
WOODLAND RD
SOUTHERN RD
TYTHE BARN RD
LONGACRE LA
YORK RD
SEAL RD
SEAL SQ
URSULA SQ
BEACH GDNS
CHERRY GDNS
SOLENT WAY
BYWAYS
MARINE GDNS
B 2145
P

USER'S NOTES

EXPLANATION OF THE STREET INDEX REFERENCE SYSTEM

Street names are listed alphabetically and show the locality, the page number and a reference to the square in which the name falls on the map page.

Example:	Sydney Rd. Hay H..83 E3
Sydney Rd	This is the full street name, which may have been abbreviated on the map.
Hay H	This is the abbreviation for the town, village or locality in which the street falls.
83	This is the page number of the map on which the street name appears.
E3	The letter and figure indicate the square on the map in which the centre of the street falls. The square can be found at the junction of the vertical column carrying the appropriate letter and the horizontal row carrying the appropriate figure.

ABBREVIATIONS USED IN THE INDEX

Road Names

Approach..........App
Avenue..........Ave
Boulevard..........Bvd
Broadway..........Bwy
By-Pass..........By-Ps
Causeway..........Cswy
Common..........Comm
Corner..........Cnr
Cottages..........Cotts
Court..........Ct
Crescent..........Cres
Drive..........Dri
Drove..........Dro
East..........E
Gardens..........Gdns
Grove..........Gr
Heights..........Hts
Lane..........La
North..........N
Orchard..........Orch
Parade..........Par
Passage..........Pas
Place..........Pl
Pleasant..........Plea
Precinct..........Prec
Promenade..........Prom
Road..........Rd
South..........S
Square..........Sq
Street,Saint..........St
Terrace..........Terr
Walk..........Wlk
West..........W
Yard..........Yd

Key to abbreviations of Town, Village and Rural locality names used in the index of street names

Albourne	Alb	123	D3
Aldingbourne	Ald	174	C4
Alfold	Alf	30	B4
Amberley	Amb	136	A4
Angmering	Ang	179	E3
Ansty	Ans	82	A2
Apuldram	Apu	172	A2
Ardingly	Ard	61	F4
Arundel	Aru	156	C2
Ashington	Ash	118	B3
Ashurst (Henfield)	Asht H	120	A3
Ashurst Wood	Ash W	22	B3
Balcombe	Bal	39	F1
Balls Cross	Bal C	49	F1
Barlavington	Barl	113	E3
Barnham	Barn	176	A3
Barns Green	Bar G	54	B1
Bepton	Bep	89	F1
Bignor	Big	113	F1
Billingshurst	Bil	75	E4
Birdham	Bir	192	B2
Blackstone	Bla	122	B3
Bognor Regis	Bog R	196	A1
Bolney	Bol	81	D2
Bosham	Bos	171	D2
Bosham Hoe	Bos H	192	A4
Botolphs	Bot	162	C4
Boxgrove	Box	153	D2
Bramber	Bra	141	E1
Bramshott	Bram	24	A4
Brighton	Bri	187	F2
Broadbridge	Bro	171	D4
Broadbridge Heath	Bro H	34	B2
Broomer's Corner	Bro C	98	B4
Bucks Green	Buc G	31	F3
Burgess Hill	Bur H	104	C3
Burpham	Burp	157	F3
Burstow	Burs	5	F4
Bury	Bury	135	F4
Byworth	Byw	93	F3
Charlton	Cha	131	E3
Charlwood	Char	3	E4
Chichester	Chic	172	B3
Chidham	Chid	170	B3
Chilgrove	Chil	108	C1
Chithurst	Chit	67	D2
Church Norton	Chu N	204	C2
Clapham	Cla	159	E1
Clayton	Clay	145	E4
Climping	Cli	177	E1
Cocking	Coc	110	A4
Coldwaltham	Cold	115	D3
Colgate	Colg	37	D3
Colworth	Colw	174	B1
Compton	Com	106	C1
Coneyhurst	Con	75	F2
Conford	Conf	23	E4
Coolham	Cool	76	B1
Coombes	Coom	162	C3
Copsale	Cops	78	A3
Copthorne	Copt	5	F2
Cowfold	Cow	79	E1
Cox Green	Cox G	11	E1
Crabtree	Crab	79	F4
Cranleigh	Cran	10	B4
Crawley	Cra	17	E3
Crawley Down	Cra D	19	F4
Crossbush	Cros	157	E1
Crosspost	Cross	80	C1
Cuckfield	Cuc	82	B3
Cudworth	Cud	2	B4
Danehill	Dan	63	F2
Dial Post	Dia P	99	E2
Ditchling	Dit	125	E2
Domewood	Dom	6	C3
Donnington	Don	172	B1
Dormans Park	Dor P	8	B3
Dormansland	Dor	8	C4
Duncton	Dun	112	C4
Earnley	Earn	203	D3
Eartham	Eart	154	A4
Easebourne	E	68	C1
East Ashling	E Ash	150	B2
East Dean	E Dean	132	A4
East Grinstead	E Gri	8	B1
East Harting	E Har	87	E2
East Kingston	E King	180	A1
East Lavant	E Lav	151	F3
East Lavington	E Lavn	112	B3
East Marden	E Mar	107	F1
East Preston	E Pre	179	F1
East Wittering	E Wit	202	C4
Eastergate	Eas	175	E4
Ebernoe	Eber	49	E2
Edburton	Edb	143	D2
Ellen's Green	Ell G	11	F2
Elstead	Els	88	A2
Emsworth	Ems	147	F1
Faygate	Fay	15	E1
Felbridge	Fel	7	F2
Fernhurst	Fer	46	C3
Ferring	Ferr	180	B1
Finchdean	Finc	126	B3
Findon	Find	160	B4
Fishbourne	Fise	171	F3
Fisherstreet	Fist	27	E2
Fittleworth	Fit	94	C2
Five Oaks	Five O	53	E3
Fontwell	Fon	154	C1
Ford	F	177	D2
Forest Row	For R	22	C1
Forestside	For	127	D3
Fulking	Ful	143	E2
Funtington	Fun	149	F3
Gay Street	Gay S	97	D3
Goddard's Green	God G	103	F3
Graffham	Gra	111	F4
Greatham	Gre	115	F2
Halnaker	Hal	153	E3
Hambrook	Hamb	149	D1
Hammerwood	Hamm	9	F2
Handcross	Han	59	D4
Hardham	Har	115	E4
Haslemere	Hasl	26	A3
Hassocks	Hass	124	B2
Havant	Hav	147	D1
Haywards Heath	Hay H	83	E3
Henfield	Hen	121	E3
Henley	Henl	68	C4
Hermitage	Her	169	D4
Heyshott	Hey	111	D4
Hickstead	Hic	103	D3
Highbrook	High	41	E1
Highleigh	High	193	D1
Hill Brow	Hill B	43	D1
Hookwood	Hoo	1	A1
Horley	Horl	1	B2
Horsemere Green	Hor G	177	D1
Horsham	Hors	35	D1
Horsted Keynes	Hor K	63	D2
Houghton	Hou	135	F2
Hove	Hove	186	C3
Hunston	Hun	193	F4
Hurstpierpoint	Hur	123	E3
Ifold	Ifo	30	A2
Iping	Ipi	67	E1
Itchingfield	Itc	54	C3
Keymer	Key	124	C2
Kingsfold	Kin	13	F3
Kingsley Green	Kin G	25	F1
Kingston Gorse	K Gor	201	D4
Kirdford	Kir	50	C1
Lambs Green	Lam G	15	E3
Lancing	Lan	183	D3
Lickfold	Lic	69	F4
Linchmere	Lin	24	C1
Liphook	Lip	23	F2
Liss	Liss	43	D2
Liss Forest	Liss F	43	D3
Littlehampton	Lit	199	E4
Lodsworth	Lod	69	F2
Lower Beeding	Low B	57	F2
Loxwood	Lox	30	B2
Lurgashall	Lur	48	A2
Lyminster	Lym	178	A3
Madehurst	Mad	134	C1
Manningsheath	Man H	57	D3
Maplehurst	Map	78	B3
Marley Heights	Mar H	25	F1
Merston	Mer	173	F2
Mid Lavant	M Lav	151	E3
Middleton-on-Sea	M Sea	197	E3
Midhurst	Mid	90	B4
Milland	Mil	44	C1
Newdigate	Newd	2	A4
Newpound Common	New C	52	A2
North End	N End	160	B4
North Hayling	N Hay	168	B2
North Heath	N Hea	96	C4
North Marden	N Mar	107	F3
North Mundham	N Mun	173	D1
North Stoke	N Sto	136	A1
Northchapel	N	48	C4
Norton	Nor	153	F1
Nursted	Nur	86	B4
Nutbourne	Nutb	96	C1
Nuthurst	Nuth	56	C1
Nyewood	Nye	87	F4
Nyton	Nyt	175	D4
Oakwoodhill	Oak	12	B4
Oving	Ovi	174	A4
Pagham	Pag	205	E4
Partridge Green	Par G	100	C2
Passfield	Pass	23	E4
Patching	Pat	159	D1
Pease Pottage	Pea P	38	A3
Petersfield	Pete	64	A2
Petworth	Petw	93	E4
Plaistow	Pla	29	E1
Poling	Pol	178	C3
Portslade-by-Sea	Por S	185	F3
Poynings	Poy	144	A3
Pulborough	Pul	96	A1
Pyecombe	Pye	144	C3
Rackham	Rac	137	D4
Rake	Rake	43	F2
Rogate	Rog	65	F2
Roundstreet Common	Rou C	52	A3
Rowhook	Row	12	B1
Rowland's Castle	Row C	126	B1
Rudgwick	Rud	32	A4
Runcton	Run	173	E1
Rusper	Rusp	15	D4
Rustington	Rust	199	F4
Salfords	Sal	1	C4
Sayers Common	Say C	103	D1
Scayne's Hill	Sca H	84	B2
Selham	Sel	92	A3
Selsey	Sels	206	C4
Selsfield Common	Sel C	19	F1
Sharpthorne	Sha	41	F3
Sheet	She	64	A3
Shipley	Shi	99	D4
Shipton Green	Shi G	191	F2
Shoreham-by-Sea	S Sea	184	C3
Shripney	Shr	175	D1
Sidlesham	Sid	193	E1
Singleton	Sin	131	D4
Slaugham	Sla	58	C3
Slindon	Sli	155	D3
Slinfold	Slin	33	D2
Small Dole	Sma D	142	B3
Somerley	Som	192	A1
Sompting	Somp	182	C4
South Ambersham	Sou	191	E3
South Harting	S Har	87	D2
South Hayling	S Hay	189	D1
South Mundham	S Mun	194	A3
South Stoke	S Sto	136	A1
Southbourne	Sou	169	F4
Southwater	Sour	55	E1
Southwick	Sock	185	E3
Staplefield	Sta	59	E3
Stedham	Ste	67	F1
Steyning	Stey	141	D2
Stoke	Sto	168	A1
Stopham	Stop	95	D1
Storrington	Stor	117	E1
Stoughton	Stou	128	C2
Street End	S End	193	E2
Strettington	Str	152	C2
Sullington	Sul	138	B4
Sutton	Sut	113	E2
Tangmere	Tan	153	D1
Thakeham	Tha	117	F4
Thorney Island	Tho I	169	D2
Tilgate Forest Row	T Row	38	A3
Tillington	Til	93	D4
Toddington	Tod	178	B2
Tortington	Tor	177	E4
Treyford	Tre	88	B1
Trotton	Tro	66	C1
Turners Hill	Tur H	19	F2
Twineham	Twi	102	C2
Upper Beeding	Upp B	141	F1
Upperton	Upp	70	C1
Upwaltham	Upw	133	E4
Walberton	Walb	155	E1
Walderton	Wal	128	A1
Walliswood	Wall	12	A4
Warnham	Warm	34	B4
Warningcamp	Warp	157	E2
Warninglid	Ward	58	B1
Washington	Was	139	E3
Watersfield	Wat	114	C2
West Ashling	W Ash	149	D2
West Burton	W Bur	135	E4
West Chiltington	W Chi	97	E1
West Chiltington Common	W Chi C	117	D4
West Dean	W Dean	130	C3
West Grinstead	W Gri	100	A3
West Harting	W Har	87	D4
West Hoathly	W Hoa	41	E3
West Itchenor	W Itch	191	E4
West Kingston	W King	179	F1
West Lavington	W Lav	90	C3
West Marden	W Mar	127	F4
West Stoke	W Sto	150	B3
West Thorney	W Tho	169	E1
West Wittering	W Wit	191	D1
Westbourne	Wbou	148	A2
Westergate	Wgate	175	D4
Westhampnett	Wham	152	B1
Westmeston	Wmes	146	C4
Wheatsheaf Inclosure	Whe I	44	C4
Whitemans Green	Whi G	82	B4
Wick	Wick	178	A2
Wiggonholt	Wig	116	B3
Wineham	Win	102	A2
Wisborough Green	Wis G	74	A4
Wiston	Wist	119	D1
Wivelsfield	Wiv	105	F3
Wivelsfield Green	Wiv G	105	F2
Woodgate	Woo	175	E3
Woodingdean	Wood	188	C4
Woodmancote (Henfield)	Wcote H	122	A1
Woodmancote (Southbourne)	Wcote S	148	C2
Woolbeding	Wool	68	A1
Worth	Wor	18	B3
Worthing	Wing	181	F1
Yapton	Yap	176	B2

A'Becket Gdns. Wing 181 E3
A'Becket's Ave. Bog R 194 C1
Abberton Field. Hur 123 F3
Abbey Rd. Bri 188 A2
Abbey Rd. Lan 183 D4
Abbey Rd. Wing 181 F1
Abbots Cl. Hass 124 B2
Abbots Leigh. Sour 77 F4
Abbotsbury Ct. Hors 35 E2
Abbotsfield Rd. Cra 16 A2
Abbotstone Ave. Hav 147 D2
Abbotswood Wlk. Rust 200 A4
Abbotts Cl. Wing 182 A1
Abbotts View. Lan 183 D4
Abbotts Way. Lan 183 E3
Abbottsbury. Bog R 205 F4
Aberdeen Rd. Bri 188 A4
Abingdon Wlk. Wing 181 D3
Abinger Rd. Por S 185 F4
Abrahams Rd. Cra 16 C1
Acacia Ave. Hove 165 E1
Acacia Ave. Wing 181 E4
Acorn Ave. Cow 79 E1
Acorn Cl. Ang 179 E2
Acorn Cl. E Gri 21 E4
Acorn Cl. Sels 206 A4
Acorn End. Bog R 195 D1
Acorns The. Cra 16 C1
Acorns. Hors 35 F2
Acre Cl. Hay H 83 D1
Acre Cl. Rust 178 C1
Acre Cl. The 181 F1
Acre St. Shi G 191 E1
Adams Cl. Bri 166 C1
Adastra Ave. Key 124 C2
Adderbury Ave. Ems 147 F2
Addison Cl. Lan 183 E3
Addison Dr. SE12 .... 16 B3
Addison Rd. Hove 187 E4
Addison Sq. Lan 183 E3
Addison Way. Bog R 195 F4
Adelaide Cl. Cra 4 A1
Adelaide Cl. Hors 35 E2
Adelaide Cl. Wing 181 D4
Adelaide Cres. Hove 187 D3
Adelaide Rd. Chic 172 C4
Adelaide Sq. S Sea 184 C4
Adelphi Cl. Cra 18 A2
Adhurst Rd. Hav 147 D2
Admers Cres. Lip 24 A1
Admiral Rd. Cra 16 C2
Admiral's Bridge La. E Gri 21 D1
Admiral's Wlk. Fun 149 F3
Admirals Wlk. Gree 22 B3
Admirals Wlk. Lit 178 C1
Admiralty Gds. Bog R 196 B2
Admiralty Rd. Bog R 196 B2
Adrian Ct. Cra 16 C1
Adstock Rd. Grays 8 A3
Adur Ave. S Sea 163 E1
Adur Ave. Wing 181 D4
Adur Cl. Lan 184 A3
Adur Dr. S Sea 184 C4
Adur Rd. Bur H 105 D2
Adversane La. Bil 75 D2
Adversane La. W Chi 97 E4
Adversane Rd. Wing 181 F3
Agate La. Hors 35 E3
Aglaia Rd. Wing 181 E1
Agnes St. Bri 188 A4
Aigburth Ave. Bog R 195 D2
Ailsa Cl. Cra 16 C2
Ainsdale Cl. Wing 181 D3
Ainsdale Rd. Wing 181 D3
Aintree Rd. Cra 17 F2
Air St. Bri 187 E3
Airport Way. Cra 4 C4
Ajax Pl. Bog R 197 D3
Akehurst Cl. Copt 5 F2
Alan Way. Bri 188 B3
Alandale Rd. Bir 192 B2
Alandale Rd. Lan 162 A1
Albany Cl. Wing 181 F1
Albany Mews. Hove 186 C3
Albany Rd. Cra 17 D3
Albany Villas. Hove 186 C3
Albert Cl. Hay H 83 F2
Albert Crane Ct. Cra 16 C4
Albert Dr. Bur H 104 B1
Albert Mews. Hove 187 D3
Albert Rd. Bog R 196 A2
Albert Rd. Bri 187 E3
Albert Rd. Chic 172 A3
Albert Rd. Horl 1 C2
Albert Rd. Lit 178 A1
Albert Rd. Rust 179 D1
Albert Rd. Sock 185 D4
Alberta Rd. Wing 181 D3
Alberta Wlk. Wing 181 D3
Albery Cl. Hors 34 C2
Albion Cl. Cra 18 A3
Albion Ct. Bur H 104 B1
Albion Hill. Bri 187 F3
Albion Pl. Bri 187 F3
Albion Rd. Bex 19 D4
Albion Rd. Sels 206 C3
Albion St. Bri 187 F3
Albion St. Sock 185 E4
Albion Way. Hors 35 D1
Albourne Cl. Bri 188 B4
Albury Keep. Horl 1 C2
Alder Cl. Cra D 19 F4
Alder Cl. Wing 181 D3
Alder Copse. Hors 34 C1
Alder Way. M Sea 197 E3
Aldermoor Ave. Stor 117 E2
Alderney Rd. Ferr 201 E4
Alders Ave. E Gri 8 B2
Alders View Dr. E Gri 8 B2
Aldingbourne Cl. Cra 16 B4
Aldrich Cl. Bri 188 B3
Aldrington Ave. Hove 186 C4
Aldrington Cl. Hove 186 A4
Aldsworth Ave. Wing 201 F4
Aldsworth Ct. Wing 180 C1
Aldwick Ave. Bog R 195 E1
Aldwick Cl. Rust 199 F4
Aldwick Cres. Wing 160 C1
Aldwick Felds. Bog R 195 E1
Aldwick Gdns. Bog R 195 E2
Aldwick Hundred. Bog R 195 E1
Aldwick Pl. Bog R 195 E1
Aldwick Rd. Bog R 195 F1
Aldwick St. Bog R 195 E1
Aldwych Cl. Cra 18 A2
Alexander Cl. Bog R 195 E1
Alexandra Ct. Cra 17 D3
Alexandra Ct. Wing 181 D2
Alexandra Rd. Bur H 105 D1
Alexandra Rd. Chic 172 C4
Alexandra Rd. Lan 183 E3
Alexandra Rd. Wing 182 B1
Alexandra Villas. Bri 187 E3
Alford Cl. Wing 181 F4
Alfred Cl. Cra 18 B3
Alfred Pl. Wing 182 B1
Alfred Rd. Bri 187 E3
Alfrey Cl. Sou 169 E4
Alfriston Cl. Bog R 197 D3
Alfriston Cl. Bri 188 B3
Alfriston Cl. Wing 181 F3
Alfriston Rd. Wing 181 F3
Alice St. Hove 187 D3
Alicia Ave. Ash 118 C3
Alicia Ave. Cra 18 A3
Alicks Hill. Bil 75 D4
Alinora Ave. Wing 181 D1
Alinora Cl. Wing 181 D1
Alinora Cres. Wing 181 D1
Alinora Dr. Wing 181 D1
Allandale Cl. Sels 206 C4
Allangate Dr. Rust 179 D1
Allcard Cl. Hors 35 D2
Allcot Cl. Cra 16 B2
Allee Dr. Lip 23 F3
Allen Rd. Hay H 83 F3
Allen's Cl. Ash W 22 A3
Allendale Ave. Ems 147 F2
Allendale Ave. Wing 160 C1
Allendale. Sour 55 E2
Alley The. Amb 136 A4
Alley The. Ste 67 F1
Alleyne Way. M Sea 197 F3
Allingham Gdns. Hors 35 F3
Allington Rd. Wing 182 B4
Allyington Way. Cra 18 A3
Alma Rd. Hay H 83 F4
Alma St. Lan 183 E2
Almodington La. Earn 203 E4
Almond Cl. Cra 16 C3
Almondington La. Bir 192 B1
Alperton Cl. Bog R 195 D1
Alpha Rd. Cra 17 D3
Alpine Rd. Hove 186 B4
Alston Way. Wing 181 D3
Alverstone Rd. Wing 182 B2
Amber Glade. Sour 55 E1
Amberley Cl. Bur H 104 C2
Amberley Cl. Cra 18 A3
Amberley Cl. Hay H 83 D2
Amberley Cl. Hors 35 F3
Amberley Cl. Hove 165 E2
Amberley Cl. Lit 178 B1
Amberley Cl. S Sea 163 E1
Amberley Ct. Cra 4 A2
Amberley Dr. Bog R 195 F2
Amberley Dr. Hove 165 E2
Amberley Dr. Wing 180 C1
Amberley Rd. Hors 35 F3
Amberley Rd. Rust 200 A4
Amberley Rd. Stor 116 C1
Ambersham Cres. E Pre 179 E2
Ambleside Cl. Bog R 196 C3
Ambleside Cl. Cra 16 A3
Ambleside Rd. Lan 183 D3
Ambrose Pl. Wing 182 A1
Ambrose's Hill. Twi 102 C4
Amelia Rd. Wing 182 A1
America La. Hay H 83 F3
Amesbury Cres. Hove 186 B4
Amherst Cres. Hove 186 B4
Amundsen Rd. Hors 35 D3
Anchor Hill. Sca H 84 C1
Anchor Springs. Lit 178 A1
Ancren Cl. Ferr 180 B2
Ancton Cl. M Sea 197 E3
Ancton Dr. M Sea 197 F3
Ancton La. Bog R 197 E3
Ancton Lodge La. M Sea 197 F3
Ancton Way. M Sea 197 F3
Anderson Cl. Hav 147 D2
Andrew Ave. Bog R 197 D3
Andrew Broughton Way.
Haid 106 B4
Andrew Cl. Rust 178 C1
Andrew Cl. Stey 141 D1
Andrew's La. Sour 55 E1
Andrews La. Ste 89 E4
Andrews Rd. Sour 77 E4
Andromeda Cl. Cra 16 B2
Angel St. Petw 93 E4
Anglesea St. Wing 182 A2
Anglesey Cl. Cra 17 D1
Angmering La. E Pre 179 E1
Angmering Way. Rust 179 E2
Angola Rd. Wing 182 B2
Angus Cl. Hors 35 D2
Angus Rd. Wing 181 E1
Ann Cl. Key 124 C3
Ann St. Bri 187 F4
Ann St. Wing 182 B1
Annandale Ave. Bog R 196 A2
Anne Howard Gdns. Aru 156 C2
Annington Gdns. S Sea 163 E1
Annington Rd. Bot 162 B4
Annington Rd. Stey 141 E1
Annweir Ave. Lan 183 E3
Anscombe Cl. Wing 181 E1
Anscombe Rd. Wing 181 E1
Ansisters Rd. Ferr 180 B1
Anson Ct. Wing 181 D2
Anson Rd. Bog R 194 C1
Anson Rd. Wing 181 D2
Ansty Cl. Bri 188 B3
Anthony Way. Ems 147 F2
Antlands La W. Bur 5 E3
Antlands La. Burs 5 E3
Antlands La. Cra 5 D4
Anvil Cl. Bil 75 D4
Anvil Cl. Por S 164 C1
Anvil Cl. Sour 55 E1
Apple Gr. Bog R 194 C1
Apple Tree Wlk. Hor G 177 D1
Appledore Gdns. Hay H 83 F3
Appledore Rd. Bri 167 E2
Appledram La (N). Chic 172 A3
Appledram La (S). Apu 172 A2
Appledram La N. Chic 172 A3
Appledramfulafus. Chic 172 A2
Applefield. Cra 17 E4
Applesham Ave. Hove 165 E1
Applesham Way. Por S 164 C1
Appletree Dr. Barn 175 F3
Appletrees. E Pre 200 C4
Approach The. Bri 166 B2
Approach The. Dor P 8 B3
April Cl. Ferr 201 E4
April Cl. Hors 35 D2
Apsley Ct. Cra 16 B2
Apsley Way. Wing 180 C3
Aquarius Ct. Cra 16 B2
Arbor Ct. Hay H 83 E3
Arcade Rd. Lit 178 A1
Arcade The. Bog R 196 A2
Arcade The. Lit 178 A1
Arcade. Wing 182 A1
Archibald Rd. Wing 182 C2
Arcturus Rd. Cra 16 B2
Ardale Cl. Wing 181 E1
Arden Rd. Cra 17 E2
Ardingly Cl. Cra 16 C4
Ardingly Dr. Wing 180 C2
Ardingly St. Bri 187 F3
Ardings Cl. Ard 61 F4
Ardlingly Rd. Cuc 82 B4
Ardsheal Cl. Wing 182 A3
Ardsheal Rd. Wing 182 A3
Argent St. Grays 8 A2
Argles Cl. Stone 22 A3
Argus Wlk. Cra 16 C2
Argyle Cir. Bog R 196 A2
Argyle Rd. Bog R 196 A2
Argyle Rd. Bri 187 E4
Ariadne Rd. Wing 181 F1
Ark Ave. Grays 8 A4
Arlington Ave. Wing 201 F4
Arlington Cl. Wing 180 C1
Arlington Cres. Bri 167 E3
Arlington Cres. E Pre 179 F2
Armada Ct. E Wit 202 C3
Armada Way. Lit 178 C1
Armour Rd. Pur 6 C3
Arnadale Rd. Chic 173 D4
Arndale Rd. Wick 177 F1
Arne Cl. Cra 16 B2
Arne Gr. Horl 1 B3
Arnell Ave. Sels 206 B4
Arnfield Cl. Cra 16 B3
Arnhem Rd. Bog R 195 F3
Arnold Cl. Roc 45 D1
Arnold St. Bri 188 A4
Arnold Way. Bos 171 D4
Arnsberg Way. Bex 19 E4
Arnside Cl. Lan 183 D3
Arran Cl. Cra 16 C2
Artel Croft. Cra 17 F3
Artex Ave. Rust 179 D2
Arthur D. Hors 35 D1
Arthur Rd. Cra 16 B3
Arthur St. Hove 186 C4
Arts Rd. Bri 167 F4
Arun Business Park. Bog R .. 196 B3
Arun Cl. Amb 136 B4
Arun Cl. Lan 183 D4
Arun Cl. Rust 179 D1
Arun Cl. Wing 181 D4
Arun Cres. Wing 181 D4
Arun Ct. Pul 96 A1
Arun Par. Lit 199 D4
Arun Prospect. Pul 95 F1
Arun Rd. Bil 53 D1
Arun Rd. Bog R 195 F2
Arun St. Aru 156 C1
Arun Vale. Cold 115 D3
Arun Way. Bog R 205 F4
Arun Way. Hors 35 E1
Arundel By-ps. Aru 156 C1
Arundel Cl. Cra 18 A3
Arundel Cl. S Sea 185 D4
Arundel Cl. Sour 55 F1
Arundel Gdn. Rust 179 D1
Arundel Mews. Bri 188 B2
Arundel Pl. Bri 188 B2
Arundel Rd. Ang 179 E3
Arundel Rd. Ang 179 F4
Arundel Rd. Aru 155 F2
Arundel Rd. Bri 188 B2
Arundel Rd. Chic 180 B4
Arundel Rd. Dart 20 C4
Arundel Rd. Lit 178 A1
Arundel Rd. Nor 154 B2
Arundel Rd. Walb 155 D1
Arundel Rd. Wing 181 D4
Arundel St. Bri 188 B2
Arundel Terr. Bri 188 B2
Arundel Way. M Sea 197 F3
Arunside. Hors 34 C1
Ascot Cl. E Wit 202 B4
Ascot Dr. E Wit 202 B4
Ascot Way. Rust 179 E1
Ash Cl. Cra D 20 A4
Ash Cl. Find 160 B3
Ash Cl. Hove 166 A2
Ash Gr. Bog R 196 A3
Ash Gr. Fer 46 C3
Ash Gr. Hay H 83 D1
Ash Gr. Lip 24 A2
Ash Gr. Wing 182 B1
Ash Keys. Cra 17 E3
Ash La. Rust 179 D1
Ash Rd. Cra 17 F4
Ash Rd. Sour 55 E1
Ashacre La. Wing 181 F4
Ashacre Mews. Wing 181 E4
Ashacre Way. Wing 181 F3
Ashburnham Cl. Bri 167 D3
Ashburnham Cl. Chic 172 A4
Ashburnham Cl. Wing 180 C3
Ashburnham Dr. Bri 167 D3
Ashburnham Rd. Cra 17 F2
Ashcroft Cl. S Sea 185 D4
Ashcroft La. Row C 126 B3
Ashcroft Way. Bog R 205 F4
Ashdown Cl. Ang 179 E2
Ashdown Cl. For R 22 C1
Ashdown Cl. Hay H 83 F2
Ashdown Dr. Cra 17 E1
Ashdown Rd. Bri 187 F4
Ashdown Rd. For R 22 B1
Ashdown Rd. Wing 182 A2
Ashdown View. E Gri 21 E4
Ashe Rd. Hav 147 D3
Ashenground Cl. Hay H 83 E2
Ashenground Rd. Hay H 83 E2
Ashfield Cl. Mid 90 B4
Ashfield Rd. Mid 90 B4
Ashfield Way. Cra 17 E3
Ashfield Way. Cra 17 E3
Ashfold Ave. Wing 160 C1
Ashford Rd. Bri 166 C1
Ashford Rd. Harr 109 E2
Ashleigh Cl. Ang 179 F3
Ashleigh Cl. Horl 1 B2
Ashleigh Rd. Hors 35 D2
Ashley Cl. Bri 166 B4
Ashling Way. S Sea 163 F1
Ashlings Way. Hove 165 E1
Ashmere Gdns. Bog R 197 D3
Ashmere La. Bog R 197 D3
Ashmore Rd. Cra 15 D3
Ashton Gdns. Rust 200 A4
Ashton Rise. Bri 187 F3
Ashurst Cl. Bog R 195 F3
Ashurst Cl. Hors 35 F3
Ashurst Cl. Wing 180 C1
Ashurst Dr. Cra 18 A3
Ashurst Dr. Wing 180 C1
Ashurst Rd. Bri 167 F2
Ashurst Way. E Pre 179 F2
Ashway. Bur H 104 C1
Ashwood Cl. S Hay 189 D2
Ashwood Cl. Wing 182 B2
Ashwood Dr. Rust 179 D1
Aspen Cl. Hay H 83 F2
Astley. Grays 8 A2
Aston Ct. Cra 16 C1
Aston Rise. Pul 96 A2
Astra Cl. Bos 171 D3
Astrid Cl. S Hay 189 E2
Athelstan Cl. Cra 18 B3
Athelstan Rd. Wing 181 F2
Athelstan Way. Hors 56 B4
Atlingworth St. Bri 187 F2
Attlee House. Cra 16 C1
Attree Dr. Bri 188 A3
Auckland Dr. Bri 167 F1
Audley Cl. Maid 88 B1
Audrey Cl. Bri 166 B3
Augusta Pl. Wing 182 A1
Augustines Way. Hay H 83 E2
Aukland Cl. Cra 4 A1
Aurum Cl. Horl 1 C1
Austen Cl. E Gri 7 F1
Avalon Way. Wing 181 D3
Aveling Cl. Cra 18 A2
Avenals The. Ang 179 F3
Avenue App. Chic 172 B4
Avenue Cl. Lip 23 F2
Avenue De Chartres. Chic 172 B3
Avenue Rd. N Hay 168 A2
Avenue The. Bog R 195 F2
Avenue The. Bri 167 D1
Avenue The. Chic 151 E1
Avenue The. Cra 38 B4
Avenue The. Dor 8 C3
Avenue The. Fun 149 E4
Avenue The. Hamb 149 E1
Avenue The. Hasl 25 E4
Avenue The. Hoo 1 B1
Avenue The. Lip 23 F3
Avenue The. Pea P 38 C4
Avenue The. Pete 64 A2
Avenue The. S Sea 163 E1
Avenue The. Wing 181 D2
Avery Cl. Por S 164 B2
Aviary Way. Cra D 7 D1
Avington Green. Hav 147 D3
Avisford Park Rd. Walb 155 E1
Avocet Quay. Her 169 D4
Avon Cl. Bog R 197 D3
Avon Cl. Lan 182 C3
Avon Rd. Lit 178 A1
Avon Wlk. Cra 16 B3
Avondale Cl. Horl 1 C3
Avondale Cl. Wing 181 D2
Avondale Rd. Hove 187 D4
Avonhurst. Bur H 104 C2
Avonmouth Rd. Dart 20 C3
Awbrook Cl. Sca H 84 B2
Aymer Rd. Hove 186 C3
Ayshe Ct Dr. Hors 35 E2
Azalea Dr. Hasl 25 E4

Babsham La. N Mun 195 E4
Back La. Bal 40 A4
Back La. Petw 93 E4
Back La. Pla 29 E1
Back La. Tur H 19 D1
Backwoods Cl. Hay H 83 F3
Backwoods La. Hay H 83 F3
Baden Dr. Horl 1 B2
Baden Rd. Bri 167 D1
Badger Dr. Hay H 83 D3
Badgers Cl. Hors 35 E3
Badgers Holt. Stor 117 F1
Badgers Way. Lox 30 C2
Badgers Wlk. Bur H 105 D1
Badgers Wood. W Chi C 117 D3
Baffin's La. Chic 172 C3
Bailey Cl. Hors 35 E4
Bailey Cl. Lit 178 C2
Bailey Cl. Pur 6 C3
Bailing Hill. Bro H 34 B3
Bailing Hill. Warm 34 B4
Baird Cl. Cra 4 C1
Bakehouse Barn Cl. Hors 35 E4
Bakehouse Rd. Horl 1 C3
Baker Cl. Cra 17 D2
Baker St. Bri 187 F4
Baker's La. Bar G 76 C2
Baker's La. Cool 76 C2
Bakers Arms Hill. Aru 156 C2
Bakers Mews. Low B 57 F2
Bala Cres. Bog R 196 C3
Balcombe Ave. Wing 182 A3
Balcombe La. Han 38 A1
Balcombe La. Hor K 42 B1
Balcombe La. Sha 42 A2
Balcombe Rd. Cra 5 D3
Balcombe Rd. Hay H 83 D4
Balcombe Rd. Horl 1 C2
Balcombe Rd. Wor 18 B2
Baldock Rd. Wad 178 A1
Baldwin Cl. M Sea 197 D3
Balfour Gdns. For R 22 B1
Balfour Rd. Bri 166 C1
Balliol Cl. Bog R 195 E2
Balliol Cl. Copt 5 D1
Balmoral Cl. Bog R 195 E1
Balmoral Cl. Chic 173 D3
Balmoral Ct. Cra 16 C1
Balmoral. E Gri 21 F4
Bamborough Cl. Sour 55 F1
Bamford Cl. Bri 167 F1
Bampfield St. Por S 185 F4

Bancroft Rd. Cra 18 A3
Banjo Rd. Lit 199 E4
Bank La. Cra 17 D3
Bank Pas. Stey 141 D2
Bank Pas. Wing 182 A1
Banks Rd. Cra 18 A3
Banks Rd. N Cha 85 E1
Bankside. Bri 166 A3
Bankside. Hass 124 B3
Bankview Cl. Bog R 196 A2
Bannister Gdns. Stor 117 E2
Bannister Way. Hay H 83 D3
Banstead Cl. Wing 181 D1
Bar La. Cops 77 F3
Baranscraig Ave. Bri 166 C4
Barbary La. Ferr 180 B1
Barcombe Cl. Orp 35 E1
Barcombe Rd. Bri 167 E3
Barfield Park. Lan 183 E3
Barford Rd. Chic 172 C3
Barkdale. Bur H 105 D3
Barker Cl. Fise 171 F4
Barkworth Way. W Chi C 117 D4
Barlavington Way. Mid 90 B3
Barley Cl. Cra 17 D3
Barleycroft. Alb 123 D3
Barleycroft. Cow 79 E1
Barleymead. Horl 1 C2
Barlow Rd. Chic 172 B4
Barlow Rd. Cra 16 B2
Barn Cl. Alb 123 D3
Barn Cl. Ems 168 B4
Barn Cl. Pea P 37 F4
Barn Cl. Tod 178 B2
Barn Cl. Wing 181 E4
Barn Cottage La. Hay H 83 F3
Barn End. Hen 121 E3
Barn Feld. Bog R 196 B2
Barn House La. Pul 96 A1
Barn La. Shr 175 D1
Barn Rd. E Wit 202 B4
Barn Rise. Barn 176 A3
Barn Rise. Bri 166 A3
Barn Wlk. E Wit 202 B3
Barncroft Cl. Tan 153 D1
Barnes Rd. Por S 185 F4
Barnet Way. Hove 165 E2
Barnet Way. Wing 181 D3
Barnett Cl. Wgate 175 E4
Barnett Rd. Bri 166 C1
Barnetts Field. Nyt 175 D4
Barnfield Cl. Sou 148 C1
Barnfield Dr. Chic 173 D4
Barnfield Gdns. Bri 188 A3
Barnfield Gdns. Dit 125 E2
Barnfield Rd. Cra 17 E4
Barnfield Rd. Pete 64 B2
Barnham La. Barn 176 A3
Barnham La. Walb 176 A4
Barnham Rd. Eas 175 F4
Barnhouse Cl. Pul 96 A1
Barnmead. Hay H 83 D4
Barns Farm La. Sul 138 C4
Barnsfold La. Rud 31 E3
Barnside Ave. Bur H 105 D1
Barnside. Bos 171 D4
Barnsite Cl. Rust 178 C1
Barnsite Gdns. Rust 178 C1
Barnsnap Cl. Hors 35 D3
Barnwood Cl. Cra 18 A4
Barons Ct. Bur H 104 C1
Barons Mead. Bog R 205 F4
Barque Cl. Lit 178 C1
Barrack La. Bog R 195 D1
Barrhill Ave. Bri 166 B4
Barrington Cl. Hay H 83 E4
Barrington Cl. Wing 181 D1
Barrington Rd. Cra 17 D2
Barrington Rd. Hay H 83 E4
Barrington Rd. Hors 35 E1
Barrington Rd. Wing 181 D1
Barrow Cl. Bri 167 D1
Barrow Hill. Bri 167 D1
Barrow Hill. Hen 121 E2
Barrowfield Cl. Hove 166 A2
Barrowfield Dr. Hove 166 A1
Barrowfield. Cuc 82 B4
Barry Cl. Cra 17 E2
Barry Wlk. Bri 188 A3
Bartholemews Cl. Chic 172 B3
Bartholewew Way. Hors 35 F3
Bartholomew Cl. Hasl 26 A4
Bartholomews. Bri 187 F3
Barton Cl. Bog R 194 C1
Barton Cl. Wing 181 F3
Barton Cres. E Gri 21 F4
Barton La. Petw 93 E4
Barton Rd. Bog R 195 F3
Barton Rd. Chic 172 B4
Barton Way. E Wit 202 C3
Barton Wlk. Cra 17 F2
Bartons Rd. Hav 147 D2
Barttelot Rd. Hors 35 D1
Barwell Gr. Ems 147 F2
Bashford Way. Cra 18 A4
Bashfords La. Wing 182 A2
Bashurst Hill. Five O 54 B3
Bashurst Hill. Itc 54 A2
Basildon Way. Cra 16 B1
Basin Rd S. Hove 186 A3
Basin Rd S. Por S 186 A3
Basin Rd S. Sock 185 F3
Basin Rd. Chic 172 C3
Basin Rd. Chic 172 C3
Basing Hill. Ash 119 D4
Bassell's La. Dia P 99 F3
Bassett Rd. Bog R 196 A1
Batchmere Rd. Bir 192 C1
Batemans Cl. Wing 180 C3
Batemans Ct. Cra 17 F2
Bates Rd. Bri 166 B1
Bath Pl. Wing 182 A1
Bath Rd. Ems 168 C4
Bath Rd. Wing 181 F1
Bath St. Bri 187 E4
Batts Dr. Hen 121 D3
Batts La. Pul 96 B1
Bavant Rd. Bri 166 B1
Baxter Cl. Cra 17 F2
Baxter St. Bri 188 A4
Bay Cl. Horl 1 B3
Bay Tree Cl. S Sea 164 A1
Bay Tree Gdn. E Pre 179 E1
Bay Trees Cl. E Pre 179 E1
Bay Walk. Bog R 195 D1
Baybridge Rd. Hav 147 D3
Baycombe La. Sli 155 D3
Bayfield Rd. Horl 1 B2
Bayford Rd. Lit 199 D4
Bayhams Field. Sha 41 E3
Bayley Rd. Tan 153 D1
Baylis Wlk. Cra 16 C1
Baynards Rd. Cran 10 C1
Baynham Cl. Bex 19 D3
Baytree Cl. Sid 18 A2
Beach Cl. Bog R 195 D1
Beach Gdns. Sels 206 B3
Beach Green. S Sea 184 C4
Beach Par. Wing 182 B1
Beach Rd. Bog R 205 F4
Beach Rd. Ems 168 C4
Beach Rd. Lit 178 A1
Beach Rd. Lit 199 E4
Beach Rd. S Sea 184 B3
Beach Rd. Sels 206 C4
Beachcroft Pl. Lan 183 E2
Beachside Cl. Wing 181 E1
Beachy Rd. Cra 16 C1
Beacon Cl. Bri 166 C1
Beacon Hill. Dor 8 C4
Beacon Hill. Wat 114 C2
Beacon Hurst. Key 124 C2
Beacon Rd. Dit 125 D1
Beacon Rd. Wmes 146 A4
Beacon Sq. Ems 168 C4
Beacon The. W Hoa 41 E4
Beacon Way. Lit 178 C1
Beaconsfield Cl. M Sea 197 E3
Beaconsfield Rd. Bri 187 E4
Beaconsfield Rd. Por S 185 F4
Beaconsfield Rd. Wick 178 A2
Beaconsfield Villas. Bri 166 B1
Beagle Dr. Yap 176 C1
Beal Cres. Bri 166 C1
Beale Ct. Cra 16 C2
Bear Rd. Bri 188 A4
Bearsden Way. Bro H 34 A2
Beaton Cl. Gree 22 B3
Beatty Ave. Bri 167 D3
Beatty Rd. Bog R 196 A2
Beaufort Terr. Bri 188 A3
Beaumont Cl. Cra 16 B3
Beaumont Cl. E Pre 179 E1
Beaumont Park. Lit 178 C1
Beaumont Rd. Wing 182 A3
Beautifield Cl. Sels 206 B3
Beaver Cl. Fise 171 F3
Beaver Cl. Hors 35 E3
Beaver Ind Est. Lip 24 A2
Beccles Rd. Wing 181 F1
Becket Rd. Wing 181 F2
Beckett La. Cra 4 A1
Beckett Way. E Gri 21 E4
Beckley Cl. Bri 188 B3
Beckworth Cl. Hay H 83 F3
Beckworth Cl. Wing 180 C3
Beckworth La. Hay H 83 F3
Bedale Cl. Cra 17 D2
Bedales Hill. Hay H 84 A2
Bedelands Cl. Bur H 104 C3
Bedenscroft. Bog R 195 F2
Bedford Ave. Bog R 195 F3
Bedford Cl. Hav 168 A4
Bedford Pl. Bri 187 E3
Bedford Rd. Hors 35 D1
Bedford Row. Wing 182 B1
Bedford Sq. Bri 187 E3
Bedford St. Bog R 196 A2
Bedford St. Bri 188 A2
Bedham La. Fit 94 C3
Bedham La. Fit 95 D4
Beech Ave. Chic 172 B3
Beech Ave. E Wit 202 C3
Beech Cl. Find 160 B4
Beech Cl. Por S 164 B2
Beech Cl. Wgate 175 D4
Beech Fields. E Gri 8 B2
Beech Gdns. Cra D 19 F4
Beech Gdns. Wing 182 A2
Beech Gr. Bri 167 E2
Beech Gr. Mid 90 B3
Beech Gr. S Hay 189 D2
Beech Gr. Stor 117 E2
Beech Hill. Hay H 83 F2
Beech Holme. Cra D 19 F4
Beech Hurst Cl. Hay H 83 D2
Beech Rd. Find 160 B4
Beech Rd. Hasl 26 A4
Beech Rd. Hors 36 A3
Beech Tree Cl. 17 D4
Beech View. Ang 179 F3
Beech Wood Ct. Liss F 43 D3
Beechers Rd. Por S 164 B2
Beeches Ave. Wing 182 A4
Beeches Cres. Cra 17 E2
Beeches La. Ash W 22 A3
Beeches The. Bri 166 A2
Beechey Cl. Copt 5 F2
Beechey Way. Copt 5 F2
Beeching Way. E Gri 8 B1
Beechings. Hen 121 D3
Beechlands Cl. E Pre 179 F1
Beechlands Ct. E Pre 179 F1
Beechside. Cra 17 E3
Beechwood Ave. Bri 166 B2
Beechwood Ave. Wing 181 E4
Beechwood Cl. Bri 166 B2
Beechwood La. E Lavn 112 C3
Beechwood Villa. Sal 1 C4
Beechwood. Sma D 142 B4
Beechwood. Sour 77 E4
Beechwoods. Bur H 104 C1
Beechworth Rd. Hav 147 D1
Beeding Ave. Hove 165 E2
Beeding Cl. Bog R 196 B4
Beeding Cl. Hors 35 F3
Beeding Cl. Lan 183 D4
Beedingwood Dr. Hors 36 B3
Beehive Cl. Ferr 180 B1
Beehive La. Ferr 180 B1
Beehive Ring Rd. Cra 4 C3
Beggar's La. Poy 144 A3
Beggar's La. Sid 204 C4
Belfast St. Hove 186 C4
Belfry The. E Gri 21 E4
Belgrave Cres. Chic 172 B2
Belgrave Pl. Bri 188 A2
Belgrave Sq. Por S 186 A3
Belgrave St. Bri 187 F3
Belinus Dr. Bil 75 D4
Bell Cl. Chic 172 B4
Bell Ct. Bog R 195 D1
Bell Davies Rd. Lit 178 B1
Bell Hammer. E Gri 21 E4
Bell La. Bir 192 A1
Bell La. Coc 110 A4
Bell Rd. Hasl 25 F2
Bell Rd. Kin G 25 F2
Bell Rd. Warm 34 C4
Bell Vale La. Kin G 25 F2
Bellair Rd. Hav 147 D1
Belle Meade Cl. Wgate 175 D3
Bellevue Gdns. Bri 188 A2
Bellevue La. Ems 147 F1
Bellingham Cres. Hove 186 A4
Belloc Cl. Cra 17 F4
Belloc Ct. Hors 35 F2
Belloc Rd. Wick 178 A2
Bellscroft Cl. Lit 178 B1
Bellview Rd. Wing 181 F3
Belmont Cl. Hass 124 B3
Belmont La. Hur 124 A3
Belmont St. Bog R 196 A1
Belmont St. Bri 187 F4
Belmont Terr. Yap 176 C1
Belmont Wlk. Wing 181 D3
Belmont. Bri 187 E4
Belsize Cl. Wing 181 F2
Belsize Rd. Wing 181 F1
Belton Rd. Bri 187 F4
Belvedere Ave. Lan 183 D3
Belyngham Cres. Lit 178 A1
Bembridge Ct. S Hay 189 E1
Bembridge Dr. S Hay 189 E1
Bembridge St. Bri 188 A4
Benbow Cl. S Sea 184 B3
Benchfield Cl. E Gri 8 C1
Benedict Cl. Wing 182 C2
Benedict Dr. Wing 182 C2
Benett Ave. Hove 165 F1
Benett Dr. Hove 165 F1
Benfield Cl. Por S 165 D1
Benfield Cres. Por S 165 D1
Benfield Way. Por S 165 D1
Bengairn Ave. Bri 166 C4
Benhams Cl. Horl 1 C3
Benhams Dr. Horl 1 C3
Benhenna Cl. Cra 16 B3
Benjamin Rd. Cra 18 A2
Bennett Cl. Cra 17 F1
Bennett Rd. Bri 188 B2
Bennetts Cl. E Wit 202 B4
Bennetts Rd. Hors 35 E1
Bens Acre. Hors 35 F1
Benson Rd. Hen 121 E3
Benson's La. Hors 15 D1
Bentham Rd. Bri 188 A4
Bentons La. Dia P 99 E2
Bentswood Cres. Hay H 83 F3
Bentswood Rd. Hay H 83 F3
Bepton Cl. Mid 90 A3
Bepton Down. Pete 64 A2
Bepton Rd. Bep 89 F2
Berberis Ct. S Sea 163 F1
Beresford Rd. Bri 188 A3
Bereweeke Rd. Bog R 196 C2
Bergamot Cres. S Sea 164 A1
Berghestede Rd. Bog R 196 A3
Berkeley Sq. Hav 147 D1
Berkeley Sq. Wing 181 F1
Berkley Cl. Cra 16 B1
Bernard Pl. Bri 188 A4
Bernard Rd. Aru 156 B1
Bernard Rd. Bri 188 A4
Bernard Rd. Wing 181 E1
Berriedale Ave. Hove 186 B3
Berriedale Cl. Lan 183 D4
Berriedale Dr. Lan 183 D4
Berry Cl. Bur H 104 C3
Berry La. Ard 62 A4
Berry La. Bog R 195 F4
Berry La. Lit 199 E4
Berrybarn La. E Wit 202 A1
Berrybarn La. W Wit 190 C1
Berrylands Farm. Say C 103 D1
Berrylands. Liss F 43 D4
Berrymeade Wlk. Cra 16 B3
Berrymill Cl. Bog R 196 A2
Bersted Green Ct. Bog R 196 A3
Bersted St. Bog R 196 A3
Bessborough Terr. Lan 183 D2
Betchley Cl. E Gri 8 B2
Bethune Cl. Cra 18 A3
Bethune Rd. Hors 35 E1
Bethwines Cl. Fise 171 F4
Betts Way. Cra 4 A1
Bevan Ct. Cra 16 C1
Bevendean Cres. Bri 167 E1
Bevendean Rd. Bri 167 D1
Beverley Cl. Sels 206 C4
Beverley Gdns. Rust 178 C1
Bewbush Dr. Cra 16 B1
Bewley Rd. Ang 179 E3
Bex La. Mid 90 B1
Bickley Ct. Cra 16 C2
Biggin Cl. Cra 17 D2
Bignor Cl. Hors 35 F4
Bignor Cl. Rust 179 D1
Bignor Park Rd. Wat 114 B3
Bigwood Ave. Hove 187 D4
Bilberry Cl. Cra 16 C2
Billingshurst Rd. Ash 118 B4
Billingshurst Rd. Bro H 34 A2
Billington Dr. Cra 17 F3
Billington Dr. Cra 18 A2
Billington Dr. Cra 18 A3
Billy Lawn Ave. Hav 147 D3
Bilsham La. Yap 176 B1
Bilsham Rd. Yap 197 E4
Binderton La. W Dean 130 A1
Binney Ct. Cra 5 E1
Binstead Ave. Bog R 196 C3
Binstead Cl. Cra 16 C4
Binstead La. Aru 156 A1
Binsted La. Walb 176 C4
Biology Rd. Bri 167 F4
Birch Ave. Hay H 83 F2
Birch Cl. Ang 179 E2
Birch Cl. Aru 156 B1
Birch Cl. Bog R 195 D2
Birch Cl. Cra D 20 A4
Birch Cl. Hay H 83 F2
Birch Cl. Lan 183 D2
Birch Cl. Liss 43 D2
Birch Dr. Bil 75 D4
Birch End. W Chi C 117 D4
Birch Gr. W Chi C 117 D3
Birch Grove Cres. Bri 166 C3
Birch Lea. Cra 4 C1
Birch Tree Cl. Ems 147 F2
Birch Tree Dr. Ems 147 F2
Birch Tree La. W Chi C 117 E3
Birch Way. Hay H 83 F1
Birch Way. Stor 117 F2
Birchen La. Hay H 83 E4
Birches Cl. Sels 206 A4
Birches Cl. Wing 181 D3
Birches Ind Est. E Gri 7 F2
Birches Rd. Hors 35 F3
Birches The. Cra 17 F4
Birches The. Man H 57 D4
Birches The. W Chi C 117 D4
Birchgrove La. Hor K 42 B1
Birchgrove Rd. Hor K 63 E4
Birchwood Cl. Horl 1 C2
Birchwood Grove Rd. Bur H 105 D1
Birdham Cl. Cra 16 C4
Birdham Rd. Apu 172 A2
Birdham Rd. Bri 167 E2
Birdham Rd. Chic 172 B2
Birdham Rd. S Hay 189 F1
Birdman Cl. Bog R 195 E3
Birkdale Cl. Wing 181 D3
Birkdale Dr. Cra 16 A3
Birkdale Rd. Wing 181 D3
Birling Cl. Bri 167 D1
Bishop Luffa Cl. Chic 172 A4
Bishop's Cl. Hur 123 F4
Bishopric. Hors 34 C1
Bishops Cl. Bog R 205 F4
Bishops Cl. Fer 46 C3
Bishops Cl. Wing 181 F2
Bishops Ct. Hors 35 D1
Bishops Gate Wlk. Chic 172 C4
Bishops Rd. Hove 166 A1
Bishops Rd. Tan 153 D1
Bishopsgate Wlk. Chic 172 C4
Bishopstone La. Ans 81 F1
Bishopstone La. God G 103 F4
Bishopstone Wlk. Cra 17 D1
Bitmead Cl. Cra 16 B3
Bittern Cl. Cra 16 A3
Black Dog Wlk. Cra 17 E4
Black Gate La. Pul 96 A4
Black Hill. Hay H 83 F4
Black Horse Mews. Bor G 84 B2
Black Horse Way. Hors 35 D1
Black Lion St. Bri 187 F3
Black Mill La. Nor 154 A2
Blackberry La. Dor P 8 B4
Blackberry Rd. Dor P 8 A4
Blackboy La. Fise 171 F4
Blackbridge La. Hors 34 C1
Blackbrook La. N Cha 85 E2
Blackbrook La. Sca H 85 E2
Blackcap Cl. Cra 17 D2
Blackcap Cl. Row C 126 A1
Blackcap Cl. Row C 126 A1
Blackdown Rd. Wing 181 E4
Blackehurst Way. Lit 178 A1
Blackfold Rd. Cra 17 F3
Blackgate La. Hen 121 E2
Blackheath. Cra 18 A4
Blackhouse La. Bur H 104 C2
Blackhouse La. Petw 72 A2
Blackhouse Rd. Colg 37 D3
Blacklands Cres. For R 22 B1
Blackman St. Bri 187 F3
Blackman Way. Hun 172 C1
Blackmoor Wlk. Hav 147 D3
Blackpatch Gr. S Sea 163 E1
Blacksmiths Cres. Lan 182 C4
Blackstone La. Bla 122 B3
Blackstone La. Wcote H 122 A2
Blackstone St. Bla 122 B3
Blackstone Way. Bur H 104 C3
Blackthorn Cl. Bri 166 A2
Blackthorn Cl. Cra 4 A1
Blackthorn Cl. Hors 35 F1
Blackthorn Dr. S Hay 189 E2
Blackthorn Rd. S Hay 189 E1
Blackthorns Cl. Hay H 83 F3
Blackthorns The. Bur H 104 C3
Blackthorns. Hay H 83 F4
Blackthorns. Hur 123 E4
Blackwater La. Cra 18 A3
Blackwell Farm Rd. E Gri 8 B2
Blackwell Hollow. E Gri 8 B1
Blackwell Rd. E Gri 8 B1
Bladon Cl. Hav 147 E2
Blake Cl. Cra 17 E1
Blakehurst La. Pol 178 C4
Blakehurst La. Warp 157 F1
Blakemyle. Bog R 195 E1
Blaker St. Bri 187 F3
Blakes Rd. Bog R 196 C2
Blanches Rd. Par G 100 C2
Blanford Rd. Chic 173 D4
Blann Cl. SE9 16 C3
Blatchford Cl. Hors 35 E2
Blatchford Rd. Hors 35 E2
Blatchington Rd. Hove 186 C4
Blenheim Ave. Wing 181 E3
Blenheim Cl. Cra 5 D1
Blenheim Cl. E Gri 8 C2
Blenheim Ct. Bog R 195 E2
Blenheim Gdns. Chic 173 D3
Blenheim Gdns. Hav 147 E1
Blenheim Pl. Bri 187 F3
Blenheim Rd. Hors 35 D2
Blenheim Rd. Lan 183 D2
Blenheim Rd. Yap 176 B1
Bligh Cl. Cra 17 E2
Blindley Rd. Cra 5 D1
Blissford Cl. Hav 147 D3
Blondell Dr. Bog R 195 D1
Bloomsbury Pl. Bri 188 A2
Bloomsbury St. Bri 188 A2
Bloor Cl. Hors 35 D4
Blount Ave. E Gri 8 A1
Bluebell Cl. Cra 16 C2
Bluebell Cl. E Gri 7 F1
Bluebell Cl. Hay H 83 E2
Bluebell Cl. Hors 35 E3
Blueberry Hill. Stor 117 F1
Blundell Ave. Horl 1 B2
Blunts Way. Hors 35 D2
Blunts Wood Cres. Cuc 82 C3
Blunts Wood Rd. Cuc 82 C3
Blunts Wood Rd. Hay H 83 D3
Blytons The. E Gri 7 F1
Bob La. Twi 102 B3
Bob La. Win 102 B3
Boddingtons La. Dit 125 D2
Bodiam Ave. Bri 167 F1

Bodiam Ave. Wing 180 C1
Bodiam Ave. Wing 201 F4
Bodiam Cl. Bri 167 F1
Bodiam Cl. Cra 18 A3
Bodiam Cl. Sour 55 F1
Bodmin Cl. Wing 181 D4
Bodmin Rd. Wing 181 D4
Bognor Rd. Chic 173 D3
Bognor Rd. Row 12 C1
Bognor Rd. Warm 13 D3
Boiler House Rd. Bri 167 F4
Bolding Way. Hay H 83 E3
Boleyn Dr. N Mun 194 C1
Bolney Chapel Rd. Bol 80 C1
Bolney Chapel Rd. Twi 102 C4
Bolney Ct. Cra 16 B2
Bolney Lodge La. Bol 80 C2
Bolney Rd. Bri 167 E2
Bolney St. Bol 81 D2
Bolnore Rd. Hay H 83 D2
Bolsover Rd. Hove 186 B4
Bolsover Rd. Wing 181 E2
Bolters Rd S. Horl 1 B3
Bolters Rd. Horl 1 C3
Boltro Rd. Hay H 83 D3
Bonchurch Rd. Bri 188 A4
Bond Rd. Rai (K) 76 A4
Bond St. Aru 156 C2
Bond St. Bri 187 F3
Bond Street Row. Bri 187 F3
Bonehurst Rd. Horl 1 C3
Bonehurst Rd. Sal 1 C4
Bonfire Hill. Sour 55 F2
Bonfire La. Hor K 63 D3
Bonnar Cl. Sels 206 A3
Bonnar Rd. Sels 206 B3
Bonner Wlk.. Grays 8 A4
Bonnetts La. Cra 3 F2
Bonny Wood Rd. Hass 124 B2
Bookers La. Earn 203 D4
Booth Rd. Cra 16 B2
Borage Cl. Cra 16 C2
Bordehill La. Bal 61 D3
Bordehill La. Hay H 61 D1
Borden La. Tro 66 C3
Border Chase. Copt 5 F1
Border Rd. Hasl 25 D3
Borers Arms Rd. Copt 6 A2
Borough St. Bri 187 E3
Borrowdale Cl. Cra 16 C2
Bosham La. Bos 170 C3
Bosmere Gdns. Ems 147 F1
Bosmere Rd. S Hay 189 F1
Bost Hill. Wing 160 B2
Bostal Rd. Stey 141 D1
Bostal The. Upp B 142 A1
Bostock Ave. Hors 35 F3
Boston Rd. Hay H 83 F3
Boston St. Bri 187 F4
Boswell Rd. Cra 17 E2
Botany Cl. Rust 200 B4
Bough Beeches. Bur H 105 D1
Boulevard The. Cra 17 E3
Boulevard The. Wing 181 E2
Bound La. S Hay 189 D1
Boundary Cl. Cra 17 E4
Boundary Cl. Wing 181 F1
Boundary Rd. Bal 39 F2
Boundary Rd. Bri 188 B2
Boundary Rd. Cra 17 E4
Boundary Rd. Hove 186 A4
Boundary Rd. Lan 183 F3
Boundary Rd. Wing 181 F1
Boundary Way. E Pre 179 F1
Boundstone Cl. Lan 183 D4
Boundstone La. Lan 183 D3
Bourg-de-Peage Ave. E Gri 8 C1
Bourne Cl. Fise 171 F4
Bourne Ct. E Wit 202 C3
Bourne Pk. Ton 120 A1
Bourne The. Hass 124 B3
Bourne View Cl. Sou 148 B1
Bourne Way. Mid 90 B3
Bower La. W Chi C 117 D3
Bower The. Hay H 83 D3
Bowers Pl. Cra D 19 F4
Bowes Hill. Row C 126 B2
Bowhill La. W Sto 150 A4
Bowley La. Len 129 D3
Bowley La. S Mun 194 B3
Bowling Green Cl. Bog R 194 C1
Bowling Green La. Hors 35 D2
Bowmans Cl. Stey 141 D2
Bowness Ave. Lan 183 D3
Bowness Cl. Cra 16 A3
Bowring Way. Bri 188 A3
Box Cl. Cra 17 D1
Box La. Ash W 22 B3
Box Tree Ave. Rust 178 C1
Boxes La. Hor K 63 D3
Boxgrove Cl. Lan 183 E4
Boxgrove Gdns. Bog R 195 D1
Boxgrove. Wing 180 C2
Boxham La. S End 193 D2
Boyce's St. Bri 187 E3
Bracken Cl. Copt 5 F2
Bracken Cl. Cra 17 E4
Bracken Cl. Stor 117 F1
Bracken Gr. Hors 35 F3
Bracken La. Stor 117 F1
Bracken Rd. Pete 64 B1
Brackenside. Horl 1 C2
Bracklesham Cl. E Wit 202 C3
Bracklesham La. E Wit 202 C3
Bracklesham Rd. S Hay 189 F1
Bracknell Wlk. Cra 16 B1
Bracknell Wlk. Cra 16 B2
Brading Rd. Bri 188 A4
Bradlond Cl. Bog R 195 F2
Bradshaw Rd. Chic 173 D4
Braemar Way. Bog R 195 E4
Braemore Rd. Hove 186 B3
Braeside Ave. Bri 166 C4
Braeside Cl. Hasl 25 E4
Brainsmead Cl. Cuc 82 B4
Brainsmead. Cuc 82 B4
Braishfield Rd. Hav 147 D2
Bramber Ave. Hove 165 E2
Bramber Ave. Stor 117 D1
Bramber Cl. Bog R 195 F2
Bramber Cl. Cra 17 E4
Bramber Cl. Hay H 83 D2
Bramber Cl. Hors 35 F3
Bramber Cl. Lan 183 D4
Bramber Rd. Chic 172 C3
Bramber Rd. Stey 141 D1
Bramber Rd. Wing 182 B4
Bramber Sq. Rust 179 D1
Bramber Way. Bur H 104 C2
Bramble Cl. Copt 5 F2
Bramble Cl. Hav 147 E2
Bramble Cl. Wing 181 D4
Bramble Cres. Wing 181 D4
Bramble Hill. Bal 39 E1
Bramble La. Tha 117 F4
Bramble La. Wing 181 D4
Bramble Mead. Bal 39 E1
Bramble Rd. Pete 64 B2
Bramble Rise. Bri 166 A3
Bramble The. Cuc 82 B3
Bramble Twitten. E Gri 8 C1
Bramblebye Rd. Cra 17 F3
Brambledean Rd. Por S 185 F4
Brambles. Hass 124 B3
Brambletyne Cl. Ang 179 F3
Brambling Cl. Hors 35 F1
Brambling La. Wool 67 F2
Brambling Rd. Hors 35 F1
Brambling Rd. Row C 126 A1
Brambling Rd. Row C 126 A1
Bramblings The. Rust 179 D1
Bramfield Rd. M Sea 197 D2
Bramlands La. Wcote H 143 D4
Bramley Cl. Cra 17 E3
Bramley Cl. Wing 182 A4
Bramley Gdns. Bog R 195 F4
Bramley Rd. Wing 182 A3
Brampton Cl. Sels 206 B4
Bramshott Ct. Bram 23 F4
Bramshott Vale. Bram 23 F3
Brandy Hole La. Chic 151 E1
Brangwyn Ave. Bri 166 B3
Brangwyn Cres. Bri 166 B3
Brangwyn Dr. Bri 166 B3
Brangwyn Way. Bri 166 B3
Brantridge La. Sta 38 C1
Brantridge Rd. Cra 17 E2
Brasslands Dr. Por S 164 B1
Braybon Ave. Bri 166 B2
Braypool La. Hove 166 A4
Brazwick Ave. Bog R 195 E4
Breach Ave. Sou 148 B1
Breach Cl. Stey 141 D2
Bread La. Bog R 198 B4
Bread St. Bri 187 F3
Brecon Cl. Wing 181 E4
Brede Cl. Bri 188 B3
Breezehurst Dr. Cra 16 B2
Bremner Ave. Horl 1 B2
Brendon Rd. Wing 181 E4
Brendon Way. Rust 178 C1
Brent Ct. Ems 168 C4
Brent Rd. Bog R 195 F2
Brentwood Cl. Bri 166 C2
Brentwood Cres. Bri 166 C2
Brentwood Rd. Bri 166 C2
Brettingham Cl. Cra 16 B2
Bretton. Bur H 104 B3
Bretts Orchard. Bal 39 F1
Brewells La. Rake 43 F3
Brewer Rd. Cra 17 E2
Brewer St. Bri 187 F4
Brewers Yd. Stor 117 D1
Brewery Hill. Aru 156 C1
Brewhurst La. Lox 30 C2
Breydon Wlk. Cra 17 F2
Briar Ave. Shi G 202 B3
Briar Cl. Ang 179 E2
Briar Cl. Cra 4 A1
Briar Cl. Ovi 174 A3
Briar Cl. Yap 176 B2
Briar Wood. Liss F 43 D4
Briarswood Cl. Cra 18 A4
Brick Kiln Cl. Low B 57 F2
Brickfield Cl. Bog R 195 F3
Bricklands. Cra D 19 F4
Brickyard La. Cra D 19 F4
Brideake Cl. Cra 16 C2
Brideoake Cl. Chic 172 B4
Bridge Cl. Bur H 104 B2
Bridge Cl. Lan 183 E3
Bridge Cl. Wing 181 D2
Bridge Rd. Chic 172 C4
Bridge Rd. Cli 177 F1
Bridge Rd. Ems 147 F1
Bridge Rd. Hasl 26 A4
Bridge Rd. Hay H 83 E3
Bridge Rd. Lit 177 F1
Bridge Rd. Rud 32 A4
Bridge Rd. Wing 182 A2
Bridgefield Cl. Mid 90 B3
Bridgefoot Path. Ems 168 C4
Bridgelands. Copt 5 F2
Bridgenorth Cl. Wing 180 C3
Bridgersmill. Hay H 83 D3
Bridgeway The. Sels 206 B3
Bridle La. Sli 155 D2
Bridle Way The. Sels 206 B4
Bridle Way. Cra 18 A4
Bridorley Cl. Bog R 194 C1
Brierley Gdns. Lan 183 E3
Brigden St. Bri 187 E4
Brigham Pl. M Sea 197 D2
Brighthelm. Bri 167 F4
Brighton Pl. Bri 187 F3
Brighton Rd. Alb 123 E2
Brighton Rd. Cra 17 D1
Brighton Rd. Cra 17 D2
Brighton Rd. Han 59 D4
Brighton Rd. Hass 124 A1
Brighton Rd. Horl 1 C2
Brighton Rd. Hors 56 C3
Brighton Rd. Hur 123 E2
Brighton Rd. Lan 183 E2
Brighton Rd. Low B 57 D2
Brighton Rd. Man H 57 D2
Brighton Rd. Pea P 38 A3
Brighton Rd. S Sea 184 C4
Brighton Rd. T Row 38 A2
Brighton Rd. Wing 182 B1
Brighton Sq. Bri 187 F3
Brills La. Bri 187 F2
Brimfield Rd. Pur 6 C3
Brindles Field. Ton 136 B2
Brisbane Cl. Cra 4 A1
Brisbane Cl. Wing 181 D3
Bristol Ave. Lan 183 F3
Bristol Cl. Cra 5 D1
Bristol Gate. Bri 188 A2
Bristol Gdns. Bri 188 B2
Bristol Gdns. Chic 151 E1
Bristol Mews. Bri 188 B2
Bristol Pl. Bri 188 B2
Bristol Rd. Bri 188 A2
Bristol St. Bri 188 B2
Brittany Rd. Hove 186 A3
Brittany Rd. Wing 182 A2
Britten Cl. Cra 16 B2
Britten's La. Eart 154 B3
Britten's La. Nor 154 B2
Broad Cl. Brenc 156 C2
Broad Croft. Row C 126 B2
Broad Green Ave. Bur H 105 D1
Broad Rd. Hamb 149 D1
Broad Rig Ave. Hove 165 D2
Broad St. Bri 187 F2
Broad St. Cuc 82 B3
Broad Strand. Rust 200 A4
Broad View. Sels 206 C4
Broad Wlk. Cra 17 D3
Broadbridge Cotts. Ash 118 C2
Broadbridge Dr. Bos 171 D4
Broadbridge Heath Rd. Bro H 34 A2
Broadbridge La. Burs 5 F4
Broadbridge Mill. Bos 171 D4
Broadfield Barton. Cra 16 C1
Broadfield Dr. Cra 16 C2
Broadfield Pl. Cra 16 C1
Broadfield. W Hoa 41 E4
Broadfields Rd. Bri 167 E2
Broadfields. Bri 167 E2
Broadford Bridge Rd. W Chi 105 E3
Broadlands Rd. Bur H 124 C4
Broadlands. Bur H 124 C4
Broadmark Ave. Rust 200 A4
Broadmark La. Rust 200 A4
Broadmark Par. Rust 179 D1
Broadmark Way. Rust 200 A4
Broadmere Ave. Hav 147 D3
Broadview Gdns. Wing 181 E4
Broadwater La. Cops 78 A4
Broadwater La. Nuth 56 A1
Broadwater Rd. Wing 182 A2
Broadwater St East. Wing 182 A3
Broadwater St West. Wing 182 A3
Broadwater Way. Wing 182 A3
Broadway The. Chic 151 F1
Broadway The. Cra 17 D3
Broadway The. Hay H 83 D3
Broadway The. Lan 183 F3
Broadway The. Wing 182 B1
Broadwood Cl. Hors 35 F3
Broadwood Rise. Cra 16 C1
Brock End. Cuc 82 B4
Brock Rd. Cra 3 F1
Brockhurst Cl. Hors 34 B1
Brocklebank Rd. SE7 1 B3
Brockley Cl. Wing 182 A2
Bromley Cl. Key 124 C2
Bromley High St Relief Rd. Brom 33 E1
Bromley Rd. Bri 187 F4
Bromley. Grays 8 A2
Brompton Cl. Bri 166 B3
Brontes The. E Gri 8 A1
Bronze Cl. Bog R 196 A4
Brook Ave. Bos 170 C3
Brook Ave. Key 124 B2
Brook Barn Way. Wing 181 E1
Brook Chase. W Chi C 117 D3
Brook Cl. Bog R 195 E2
Brook Cl. E Gri 8 C1
Brook Cl. Stor 117 E2
Brook Cl. Wing 182 C2
Brook Gdns. Ems 168 B4
Brook Green. Whi G 60 B1
Brook Hill. Cow 79 E2
Brook La. Cold 115 D3
Brook La. Ferr 180 B1
Brook La. Hay H 83 E4
Brook Rd. Hors 35 E3
Brook St. Whi G 60 B1
Brook The. Sour 55 F1
Brook Way. Lan 183 E3
Brookdean Rd. Wing 182 C2
Brookenbee Cl. Rust 178 C2
Brooker Pl. Hove 186 C4
Brooker St. Hove 186 C4
Brooker's Rd. Bil 75 D4
Brookfield Gdns. Hen 121 E3
Brookfield La. Lod 70 A1
Brookfield Way. Bil 75 D3
Brookhill Cl. Copt 5 F2
Brookhill Rd. Copt 5 F2
Brookland Way. Cold 115 D3
Brooklands Rd. Cra 17 D1
Brooklands Way. E Gri 8 A1
Brooklands. Bog R 194 C1
Brooklyn Ave. Wing 181 E1
Brooks La W. Bog R 196 A3
Brooks La. Bog R 196 B2
Brooks La. Bog R 196 B3
Brooks La. Bos 171 D4
Brooks La. W Ash 150 A1
Brooks The. Bur H 104 B3
Brookside Ave. Rust 179 D2
Brookside Caravan Park. Lym 178 A3
Brookside Cl. Ferr 180 B2
Brookside Cl. Run 173 E1
Brookside Rd. K Gor 201 D4
Brookside. Ash 118 C2
Brookside. Copt 5 F2
Brookside. Cra 17 E4
Brookside. Cra D 19 F4
Brookside. Run 173 E1
Brooksmead. Bog R 196 B2
Brookview. Cold 115 D3
Brookway. Bur H 105 D2
Brookway. Hay H 83 F4
Brookwood. Horl 1 C2
Broom Rd. Pete 64 B1
Broomcroft Rd. M Sea 197 D2
Broomdashers Rd. Cra 17 E4
Broome Cl. Hors 35 D3
Broomers Hill La. Pul 96 B2
Broomers La. Bir 192 B3
Broomfield Ave. Wing 181 F3
Broomfield Dr. Bil 75 E4
Broomfield Dr. Por S 164 C2
Broomfield Rd. Hen 121 E2
Broomfield Rd. Sels 206 C4
Brou Cl. E Pre 179 F1
Brougham Rd. Wing 182 C2
Brow Cl. Stor 116 C1
Brow The. Bur H 104 C2
Brown's La. Stor 117 D1
Browning Cl. Cra 18 A4
Browning Rd. Lan 183 E4
Browning Rd. Wing 181 F2
Browning's Hill. Cow 79 D1
Brownings The. E Gri 8 A1
Browns Wood. E Gri 8 B2
Broxhead Rd. Hav 147 D3
Broxmead La. Bol 81 E3
Broxmead La. Whi G 81 E3
Broyle Cl. Chic 151 E1
Broyle Rd. Chic 151 F1
Bruce Ave. Wing 181 E2
Bruce Cl. Hay H 83 E2
Bruce Way. Wing 181 E2
Bruces Wharf Rd. Grays 8 B2
Brunel Pl. Cra 17 E3
Brunswick Cl. Bog R 196 C3
Brunswick Cl. Cra 17 F2
Brunswick Mews. Hove 187 D3
Brunswick Pl. Hove 187 D3
Brunswick Rd. Hove 187 D3
Brunswick Rd. S Sea 184 B4
Brunswick Rd. Wing 182 A1
Brunswick Row. Bri 187 F4
Brunswick Sq. Hove 187 D3
Brunswick St W. Hove 187 D3
Brunswick St. Hove 187 D3
Brunswick Terr. Hove 187 D3
Brushes La. Hay H 83 F4
Brushwood Rd. Hors 35 F3
Bryce Cl. Hors 35 F3
Buchans Lawn. Cra 16 C1
Buckbarn Crossroads. W Gri 77 F1
Buckhatch La. Win 101 F3
Buckhurst Cl. E Gri 8 A2
Buckhurst Mead. E Gri 8 A2
Buckhurst Way. E Gri 8 A2
Buckingham Ave. S Sea 163 E1
Buckingham Cl. S Sea 184 C4
Buckingham Ct. Cra 16 C1
Buckingham Dr. Chic 173 D3
Buckingham Dr. E Gri 21 F4
Buckingham Gate. Cra 5 D4
Buckingham Mews. S Sea 163 E1
Buckingham Pl. Bri 187 E4
Buckingham Rd. Bri 187 E3
Buckingham Rd. S Sea 184 B4
Buckingham Rd. Wing 182 A1
Buckingham St. Bri 187 E3
Buckingham St. S Sea 184 B4
Buckland Dr. Bog R 194 C1
Buckler St. Por S 185 F4
Buckley Cl. Hove 165 E2
Buckley Pl. Cra D 19 F4
Buckmans Rd. Cra 17 D3
Bucknor Cl. Bog R 195 D1
Bucksham Ave. Bog R 195 E4
Buckshead Hill. Low B 57 E4
Buckswood Dr. Cra 16 C2
Buckwish La. Hen 121 D2
Buddington La. E 68 B2
Budgen Cl. Cra 18 A4
Buffbeards La. Hasl 25 E3
Bugshill La. Bep 89 D1
Bugshill La. Tre 88 C1
Bulkington Ave. Wing 181 F2
Bull Hill. Rake 43 F2
Bull's La. Bol 80 A2
Bull's La. Cow 80 A2
Bulldogs Bank. W Hoa 41 E3
Buller Rd. Bri 167 D1
Bullfinch Cl. Horl 1 B2
Bullfinch Cl. Hors 35 D4
Bunbury Cl. Stor 117 F1
Bunch La. Hasl 25 F4
Bunch Way. Hasl 25 F4
Buncton Crossways. Wist 140 A4
Buncton La. Bol 81 E2
Bungalows The. Walb 155 D1
Bunting Cl. Hors 35 E2
Bunyan Cl. Cra 16 B2
Burbeach Cl. Cra 16 C2
Burch Gr. Walb 155 D1
Burchett Wlk. Bog R 195 E3
Burchetts Cl. Hay H 83 D1
Burdale Dr. S Hay 189 E2
Burdett Cl. Cra 18 A3
Burdock Cl. Cra 16 C1
Burdocks Dr. Bur H 105 D1
Burford Cl. Wing 181 F4
Burford Rd. Hors 35 E1
Burgess Cl. S Hay 189 E1
Burgh Cl. Cra 5 D1
Burgh Hill Rd. Bram 23 F4
Burghclere Rd. Hav 147 D3
Burlands. Cra 3 F1
Burleigh Cl. Cra D 19 F4
Burleigh Way. Cra D 19 F4
Burley Cl. Hav 147 D3
Burley Cl. Lan 183 E3
Burley Cl. Lox 30 C2
Burley Rd. M Sea 197 D2
Burleys Rd. Cra 18 A3
Burlington Gdns. Por S 165 D1
Burlington Gdns. Sels 206 C3
Burlington Rd. Wing 181 D2
Burlington St. Bri 188 A2
Burlow Cl. Bir 192 A2
Burlow Cl. Bri 188 B3
Burma Cl. Hay H 84 A2
Burmill Ct. Rust 179 E2
Burndel Rd. Yap 176 B2
Burner Cl. Bur H 105 D1
Burney Ct. Cra 16 C2
Burngreave Ct. Bog R 195 F2
Burnham Ave. Bog R 196 A2
Burnham Gdns. Bog R 196 A2
Burnham Rd. Wing 181 E3
Burns Cl. Hors 35 E4
Burns Gdns. Bog R 197 D3
Burns Rd. Cra 18 A4
Burns Way. E Gri 8 A1
Burnside Cres. Lan 183 D3
Burnthouse La. Cow 79 D2
Burnthouse La. Crab 79 D3
Burrel Cl. Par G 100 C2
Burrel Rd. Hay H 83 D3
Burrell Ave. Lan 183 D3
Burrell Ct. Cra 16 B2
Burrell Rd. Hay H 83 D3
Burrells The. S Sea 184 C3
Burrows Cl. Hav 147 D2
Bursledon Cl. Bog R 196 C3
Burstead Cl. Bri 166 C2
Burston Gdns. E Gri 8 A2
Burstownhill La. Hig K 62 A3
Burton Cl. Horl 1 C1
Burton Villas. Hove 187 D4

Burwash Cl. E Pre 179 F2
Burwash Rd. Cra 17 F3
Burwash Rd. Hove 165 E2
Burwood Gr. S Hay 189 D2
Bury Dr. Wing 180 C1
Bury Hill. Bury 135 E3
Bury Rd. Wat 114 B1
Bury The. Wing 181 D1
Bush Cottage Cl. Por S 165 D1
Bush Farm Dr. Por S 165 D2
Bushby Ave. Rust 179 D1
Bushby Cl. Lan 183 D3
Bushfield. Pla 29 E1
Busticle La. Lan 183 D4
Bute St. Bri 188 A3
Butler's Green Rd. Hay H 83 D2
Butlers Rd. Hors 35 F2
Butser Wlk. Pete 64 A2
Butt La. Sli 155 D3
Butterbox La. Sca H 85 D2
Butterfield. E Gri 7 F2
Buttermere Cl. Hors 35 F3
Buttermere Way. Lit 178 C2
Butterstocks La. Cool 98 C4
Butts Cl. Cra 16 C4
Butts Meadow. Wis G 51 F1
Butts Rd. Sock 185 E4
Buxshalls Hill. Hay H 62 A2
Buxted Rise. Bri 166 C3
Buxton Rd. Bri 187 E4
By Sunte. Hay H 83 E4
Bycroft Way. Cra 17 F4
Bye Way The. Bog R 195 D1
Byerley Cl. Wbou 148 A3
Byerley Way. Cra 18 B4
Byeway The. W Wit 191 D1
Byfield Pl. Bog R 196 A3
Byfleets La. Bro H 34 A3
Byfleets La. Warm 34 A3
Bylanes Cl. Cuc 82 B4
Bylanes Cres. Cuc 82 B4
Byne Cl. Stor 117 E1
Byrd Rd. Cra 16 B2
Byron Cl. Bog R 197 D3
Byron Cl. Cra 17 F4
Byron Cl. Hors 35 E3
Byron Gr. E Gri 8 A1
Byron Rd. Lit 178 C1
Byron Rd. Wing 182 A1
Byron St. Hove 186 C4
Bywater Way. Chic 172 B2
Byway The. Bri 167 E3
Byway The. M Sea 197 E3
Byways. Sels 206 B3
Byworth Cl. Bri 188 B3

Caburn Heights. Cra 17 D2
Caburn Rd. Hove 187 E4
Cackstones The. Cra 18 A4
Caedwalla Dr. Tan 153 D1
Caernarvon Rd. Chic 173 D3
Caffins Cl. Cra 17 E4
Cagefoot La. Hen 121 E2
Caister's Cl. Hove 187 D4
Cakeham Rd. E Wit 202 A4
Cakeham Rd. W Wit 190 C1
Cakeham Rd. W Wit 191 D1
Cakeham Way. E Wit 202 B4
Calbourne. Hay H 83 D3
Calderdale Cl. Cra 16 C2
Caledon Ave. Bog R 197 D2
Caledonian Rd. Bri 187 F4
Caledonian Rd. Chic 172 C3
Caledonian Way. Cra 4 C4
Calkpit La. E Lav 151 F4
Callisto Cl. Cra 16 B2
Calluna Dr. Copt 5 F2
Calvecroft. Lip 24 A2
Calvin Wlk. Cra 16 B2
Cambell Rd. Cra 18 A3
Camber Cl. Bri 188 B3
Camber Cl. Cra 18 A3
Cambrai Ave. Chic 172 C3
Cambria Cl. Bos 171 D3
Cambridge Ave. E Wit 202 B4
Cambridge Dr. Bog R 195 E2
Cambridge Gr. Hove 187 D4
Cambridge Rd. Hors 35 D1
Cambridge Rd. Hove 187 D3
Cambridge Rd. Wing 182 A2
Cambridge Wlk. Bog R 195 E2
Camden Rd. Grays 8 A4
Camden St. Por S 186 A3
Camelford St. Bri 187 F2
Camelot Cl. Sour 55 F1
Camelsdale Rd. Hasl 25 E3
Campbell Cres. E Gri 7 F1
Campbell Dr. Rust 178 C1
Campbell Rd. Bog R 196 A2
Campbell Rd. Bri 187 E4
Campbell Rd. Tan 152 C1
Campion Rd. Hors 35 E3
Canada Gr. Bog R 196 A2
Canada Gr. E 68 C1
Canada Rd. Aru 156 B1
Canal Rd. Yap 176 B2
Canal Wharf Rd. Chic 172 B3
Canal Wharf. Chic 172 B3
Canberra Cl. Cra 4 A1
Canberra Pl. Hors 35 E2
Canberra Pl. Tan 153 D1
Canberra Rd. Tho I 169 D2
Canberra Rd. Wing 181 D3
Canfield Cl. Bri 167 D1
Canfield Rd. Bri 167 D1
Canhouse La. Mil 44 A2
Canning Rd. Bog R 196 B2
Canning St. Bri 188 A3
Cannon La. Chic 172 B3
Cannon Pl. Bri 187 E3
Canon's Cl. Bog R 195 D1
Canons Way. Stey 141 D2
Cansiron La. Ash W 22 B3
Cansiron La. For R 22 C3
Cantelupe Rd. E Gri 8 B1
Canter The. Cra 18 B4
Canterbury Cl. Bog R 194 C1
Canterbury Cl. Chic 172 B4
Canterbury Court. Wing 181 E2
Canterbury Dr. Bri 187 F4
Canterbury Rd. Cra 17 E1
Canterbury Rd. Rust 179 E1
Canterbury Rd. Wing 181 F2
Canterbury Way. Grays 7 D4
Cants Cl. Bur H 105 D2
Cants La. Bur H 105 D2
Canute Rd. Bos 170 C3
Canvey Cl. Cra 17 D2
Cape Copse. Rud 32 A4
Cape The. Lit 178 C1
Capel La. Cra 16 B3
Capel Rd. Rusp 14 C4
Capricorn Cl. Cra 16 B2
Capsey Rd. Cra 16 B3
Capstan Dr. Lit 178 C1
Capstan Dr. Lit 178 C2
Caravel Rd. Grays 8 A4
Caraway Cl. Cra 16 C1
Carden Ave. Bri 166 C3
Carden Cl. Bri 166 C3
Carden Cres. Bri 166 C3
Carden Hill. Bri 166 C3
Cardew Rd. Liss 43 D2
Cardinal's Dr. Bog R 194 C1
Carfax. Hors 35 D1
Cargo Forecourt Rd. Cra 4 A4
Cargo Rd. Cra 4 A4
Carisbrooke Cl. Hav 147 D1
Carisbrooke Cl. Lan 183 E4
Carisbrooke Dr. Wing 180 C3
Carisbrooke Rd. Bri 188 A4
Carleton Rd. Chic 172 B4
Carlingford Ct. Bog R 196 A2
Carlisle Gdns. Chic 151 E1
Carlisle Rd. Hove 186 B3
Carlton Ave. Bog R 195 D2
Carlton Hill. Bri 187 F3
Carlton Mews. Wing 181 F1
Carlton Pl. Bri 187 F3
Carlton Terr. Por S 186 A4
Carlyle Ave. Bri 167 D1
Carlyle St. Bri 188 A4
Carman Wlk. Cra 16 C1
Carnegie Cl. Wing 182 A3
Carnegie Rd. Wing 182 A3
Carnforth Rd. Lan 183 D3
Carol Cl. Bri 166 B3
Caroline Ct. Cra 17 D2
Caron Cl. Lan 183 E3
Carousel Ct. Bog R 195 F3
Carpenters Cl. Chath 60 A3
Carpenters Meadow. Pul 96 A1
Carpenters. Bil 75 D4
Carron La. Mid 90 B4
Cartel Cl. Pur 6 C3
Carters Way. Wis G 73 F4
Cartersland. Mil 44 C2
Carterslodge La. Low B 58 B4
Cartersmead Cl. Horl 1 C2
Carvel Way. Lit 178 C1
Casher Rd. Cra 18 A2
Cassells Rd. Chic 151 F1
Castle Ave. Hav 147 D1
Castle Cl. Bra 141 E1
Castle Cl. Wing 181 E2
Castle Gdns. Aru 156 C2
Castle La. Bra 141 E1
Castle La. Row C 126 B2
Castle La. Shi 99 E4
Castle La. Stey 141 E1
Castle La. W Gri 99 F4
Castle Rd. Bro H 34 A2
Castle Rd. Row C 126 A1
Castle Rd. Wing 181 E2
Castle Sq. Bri 187 F3
Castle St. Bri 187 E3
Castle Way. Bra 141 E2
Castle Way. Wing 181 E2
Castlegate. W Chi C 116 C4
Castleman Rd. Chic 173 D4
Castlemans La. N Hay 168 A1
Castlereagh Green. Bog R 196 C3
Castleway. Hav 147 D1
Castlewood Rd. Sour 55 F1
Caterways. Hors 34 C2
Cathedral Way. Chic 172 B3
Catkin Way. Hay H 83 F2
Causeway The. Aru 157 D1
Causeway The. Bir 192 B3
Causeway The. Bog R 205 F4
Causeway The. Bri 188 A3
Causeway The. Hors 35 D1
Causeway The. Par G 100 C2
Causeway The. Wing 181 E2
Cavalier Cl. Mid 90 B4
Cavalier Way. E Gri 21 E4
Cavell Way. Cra 18 A3
Cavell Way. Cra 18 A3
Cavell Way. Cra 18 A3
Cavendish Cl. Hors 35 D4
Cavendish Cl. Wing 181 D2
Cavendish Pl. Bri 187 E3
Cavendish Rd. Bog R 196 A2
Cavendish St. Bri 187 F3
Cavendish St. Chic 172 B4
Cawley Rd. Chic 172 C3
Cawley Rd. Chic 172 C3
Caxton Cl. Cra 17 E2
Caxton Way. Hay H 83 E2
Cecil Ave. Grays 8 A4
Cecil Pashley Way. S Sea 184 A4
Cecil Rd. Lan 183 E2
Cecilian Ave. Wing 182 A2
Cedar Ave. Wing 181 E3
Cedar Cl E. Bog R 195 E2
Cedar Cl. Bog R 195 D2
Cedar Cl. Bur H 104 C3
Cedar Cl. Cra 4 A1
Cedar Cl. Ferr 180 B1
Cedar Cl. Hors 35 D2
Cedar Cl. Lan 183 D2
Cedar Cl. Wing 181 E3
Cedar Court. Hasl 25 F3
Cedar Ct. Hasl 26 A3
Cedar Dr. Chic 172 B4
Cedar Dr. Sour 55 E1
Cedar Dr. Sour 55 F1
Cedar Way. Hay H 83 F2
Cedar Way. Hen 121 E2
Cedars Farm Cl. Bil 75 D4
Cedars Gdns. Bri 166 B2
Cedars The. Hay H 83 D4
Cedars The. Padd W 139 E2
Cedars The. Rust 179 E1
Celandine Cl. Cra 16 C1
Celedon Cl. Grays 8 A4
Cemetery La. Til 93 D4
Cemetery La. Upp 71 D1
Cemetery La. Wbou 148 B2
Cemetery La. Wcote S 148 B2
Central Ave. Bog R 195 F3
Central Ave. Rust 200 A4
Central Ave. Wing 160 B2
Central Dr. Bog R 195 F3
Central Dr. M Sea 197 F3
Centrecourt Cl. Wing 182 A2
Centrecourt Rd. Wing 182 A2
Centurion Rd. Bri 187 E3
Ceres Pl. M Sea 197 D2
Chadborn Cl. Bri 188 A3
Chadwick Cl. Cra 16 C1
Chaffer La. Bir 192 A2
Chaffinch Cl. Cra 17 D4
Chaffinch Cl. Hors 35 D4
Chaffinch Cl. Wing 181 D3
Chaffinch Way. Horl 1 B2
Chailey Cl. Cra 16 C2
Chailey Rd. Bri 167 E2
Chalcraft Cl. Lip 23 F2
Chalcraft La. Bog R 195 E3
Chalder La. S End 193 E2
Chaldon Rd. Cra 17 D1
Chalet Cl. Ferr 201 E4
Chalet Gdns. Ferr 201 E4
Chalet Rd. Ferr 201 E4
Chalfont Cl. M Sea 197 E3
Chalfont Dr. Hove 166 A2
Chalfont Way. Wing 181 D3
Chalk La. Sid 204 B4
Chalk Rd. Cha 131 F3
Chalk Rd. Ifo 30 A2
Chalkdock La. W Ich 191 F3
Chalkers La. Hur 123 F4
Chalkpit La. Sin 131 D1
Chalkpit La. W Dean 130 C1
Chalky Rd. Por S 164 B2
Challen Cl. Ovi 174 A3
Challoners. Hor K 63 D2
Challow Cl. Hass 124 B2
Chalmers Cl. Charl 3 E3
Chaloner Cl. Hay H 83 F4
Chaloner Rd. Hay H 83 F4
Chance Cl. Grays 8 A4
Chancellors Park. Hass 124 B2
Chancton Cl. Wing 181 E2
Chancton Copse. Stor 117 F2
Chancton View Rd. Wing 181 E2
Chanctonbury Cl. Was 139 E4
Chanctonbury Dr. S Sea 163 E1
Chanctonbury Rd. Bur H 104 C1
Chanctonbury Rd. Hove 187 E4
Chanctonbury Rd. Rust 199 F4
Chanctonbury Ring Rd. Wist 140 A3
Chanctonbury View. Hen 121 D2
Chanctonbury Way. Cra 17 D2
Chanctonbury Wlk. Stor 117 D1
Chandler Cl. Cra 17 D2
Chandler Rd. Chic 172 B3
Chandlers Cl. S Hay 189 E1
Chandlers Way. Stey 141 D1
Chandos Rd. Wing 182 A1
Channel View Rd. Wood 188 C4
Channel View. Bog R 205 F4
Chantlers Cl. E Gri 8 A1
Chantrey Rd. Cra 17 E2
Chantry Cl. Hen 121 E3
Chantry Cl. Horl 1 B2
Chantry Cl. Stor 117 E1
Chantry La. Stor 117 E1
Chantry La. Sul 138 B3
Chantry Rd. Wing 181 F3
Chantryfield Rd. Ang 179 F4
Chapel Cl. Bur H 104 B2
Chapel Cl. Lit 178 A1
Chapel La. Ash W 22 A3
Chapel La. Dom 6 B2
Chapel La. E Ash 150 C2
Chapel La. For R 22 B1
Chapel La. Shi G 191 E1
Chapel La. Stor 116 C1
Chapel La. W Sto 150 C2
Chapel Mews. Hove 187 D3
Chapel Pl. Por S 186 A4
Chapel Rd. Bar G 54 B1
Chapel Rd. Charl 3 E4
Chapel Rd. Sock 185 F4
Chapel Rd. Wing 182 A1
Chapel Row. E Dean 132 A3
Chapel Row. W Hoa 41 E4
Chapel St. Bog R 196 A1
Chapel St. Bri 187 F3
Chapel St. Chic 172 B4
Chapel Terr Mews. Bri 188 A2
Chapel Terr. Bri 188 A2
Chapman's La. E Gri 8 A1
Chappell Cl. Lip 24 A2
Charlecote Rd. Wing 182 B1
Charles Ave. Bur H 104 A1
Charles Ave. Chic 173 D3
Charles Cl. Hove 165 F2
Charles St. Bri 187 F2
Charlesfield Rd. Horl 1 B2
Charleston Ct. Cra 17 F2
Charlesworth Park. Hay H 84 A2
Charlewood Gdns. Bur H 105 D3
Charlmead. E Wit 202 B3
Charlock Cl. Cra 16 C1
Charlotte St. Bri 187 F2
Charlton Mill Way. Cha 131 E3
Charlton Rd. Cha 131 E4
Charlton Rd. Sin 131 D4
Charlton St. Stey 141 D2
Charltons The. Bri 167 D3
Charlwood Cl. Copt 5 F2
Charlwood La. Newd 2 C3
Charlwood Rd. Bur H 105 D3
Charlwood Rd. Cra 4 A2
Charlwood Rd. Hoo 1 A1
Charlwood Rd. Hoo 4 A4
Charlwood St. Bog R 195 F1
Charlwood Wlk. Cra 3 F1
Charlwoods Busn Cent. E Gri 8 A1
Charlwoods Pl. E Gri 8 B2
Charlwoods Rd. E Gri 8 B2
Charm Cl. Horl 1 B2
Charmandean La. Wing 182 A4
Charmandean Rd. Wing 182 A3
Charmans Cl. Hors 35 F3
Charnwood Rd. Bog R 195 F3
Charrington Way. Bro H 34 A2
Chart Way. Hors 35 D1
Chartfield. Hove 165 F1
Chartwell Dr. Hav 147 E2
Chartwell Rd. Lan 183 D3
Chase Cl. Liss 43 D2
Chase La. Hasl 26 B2
Chase Rd. Liss 43 D2
Chase The. Cra 17 F3
Chase The. Find 160 B3
Chatelet Cl. Horl 1 C2
Chatfield Rd. Chic 173 D4
Chatfield Rd. Cuc 82 C3
Chatfields. Cra 16 C2
Chatham Pl. Bri 187 E4
Chatham Rd. Wing 182 C2
Chatsmore Cres. Wing 180 C2
Chatsworth Ave. Hasl 26 A4
Chatsworth Rd. Bri 187 E4
Chatsworth Rd. Chic 173 D3
Chatsworth Rd. Wing 182 A1
Chaucer Ave. E Gri 8 A1
Chaucer Ave. Lit 178 C1
Chaucer Rd. Cra 18 A4
Chaucer Rd. Wing 181 F2
Chaucer Way. Bog R 197 D3
Chawkmare Coppice. Bog R 195 E1
Cheal Cl. S Sea 184 B3
Cheals Roundabout. Cra 16 C2
Cheam Rd. Rust 200 A4
Cheapside. Bri 187 F3
Cheeleys. Hor K 63 D3
Cheesmans La. Hamb 149 E2
Chelston Ave. Hove 186 A4
Cheltenham Pl. Bri 187 F3
Chelwood Ave. Wing 181 D1
Chelwood Cl. Bri 167 D3
Chelwood Cl. Cra 17 D2
Chennells Way. Hors 35 E3
Chepstow Cl. Cra 18 B3
Chequer Cl. For R 22 B1
Chequer La. Bos 171 D3
Chequer Rd. E Gri 8 B1
Chequers Cl. Horl 1 C2
Chequers Dr. Horl 1 C2
Cherington Cl. Hur 123 F3
Cherrimans Orchard. Hasl 25 E3
Cherry Ave. Yap 176 B1
Cherry Cl. Bog R 195 E1
Cherry Cl. Bur H 104 B2
Cherry Croft. Wick 178 A2
Cherry Ct. Hors 35 D1
Cherry Gdns. Sels 206 A4
Cherry Gdns. Wing 160 A1
Cherry La. Bal 60 B2
Cherry La. Bir 192 B3
Cherry La. Bol 81 D2
Cherry La. Cra 4 A1
Cherry Orchard Rd. Chic 172 C3
Cherry Tree Ave. Hasl 25 E4
Cherry Tree Cl. Bil 53 D1
Cherry Tree Cl. Cra 18 A4
Cherry Tree Cl. Wing 160 A1
Cherry Tree Dr. Eas 175 E4
Cherry Tree Wlk. Petw 93 E4
Cherry Wlk. Wing 160 B1
Cherrywood Gdns. S Hay 189 D2
Cherwell Rd. Wing 181 D4
Cherwell Wlk. Cra 16 B3
Chesham Cl. Wing 181 E1
Chesham Pl. Bri 188 A2
Chesham Rd. Bri 188 A2
Chesham St. Bri 188 A2
Cheshire Cres. Tan 153 D1
Cheshire Way. Sou 148 C1
Chesholt Cl. Fer 46 C3
Chesley Cl. Wing 181 D3
Chess Brook Green. Hen 121 E3
Chess Brook Green. Hen 121 E4
Chesswood Ave. Bog R 197 D3
Chesswood Cl. Wing 182 B2
Chesswood Rd. Wing 182 B2
Chester Ave. Lan 183 D2
Chester Ave. Lan 183 E2
Chester Ave. Wing 182 C2
Chester Terr. Bri 166 C1
Chesterfield Cl. Cra D 7 D2
Chesterfield Rd. Wing 181 D2
Chesters. Horl 1 B2
Chesterton Cl. E Gri 21 E4
Chestnut Ave. Chic 151 E2
Chestnut Ave. Hasl 26 A4
Chestnut Cl. Ang 179 E2
Chestnut Cl. Bur H 104 C3
Chestnut Cl. E Gri 8 C1
Chestnut Cl. Lip 24 A2
Chestnut Cl. Stor 117 F2
Chestnut Ct. E Pre 179 F1
Chestnut Gdns. Hors 35 D3
Chestnut Gr. Bog R 196 A3
Chestnut Gr. Hur 123 E4
Chestnut Rd. Bil 75 D4
Chestnut Rd. Horl 1 C3
Chestnut Way. Hen 121 E3
Chestnut Wlk. Cra 4 A1
Chestnut Wlk. Dor P 8 A4
Chestnut Wlk. Pul 95 F1
Chestnut Wlk. Tan 153 D1
Chestnut Wlk. Wing 181 D3
Chestnuts Cl. Hay H 83 F4
Chestnuts The. Hay H 83 E4
Chestnuts The. Hun 193 F4
Chestnuts The. Say C 103 D1
Chesworth Cl. Hors 56 A4
Chesworth Cres. Hors 35 D1
Chesworth Gdns. Hors 35 D1
Chesworth Gdns. Hors 35 D1
Chesworth La. Hors 35 D1
Chetnole. E Gri 8 A1
Chetwood Rd. Cra 16 A1
Chevening Cl. Cra 17 D1
Cheviot Cl. E Pre 179 F1
Cheviot Cl. Wing 181 E4
Cheviot Rd. Wing 181 E4
Cheyne Wlk. Horl 1 C1
Cheynell Wlk. Cra 16 B2
Chichester Ave. S Hay 189 D2
Chichester By-ps. Chic 172 C2
Chichester Cl. Cra 17 E1
Chichester Cl. Hove 165 E2
Chichester Ct. Rust 179 D1
Chichester Dr. Tan 153 D1
Chichester Mews. Bri 188 A2
Chichester Pl. Bri 188 A2
Chichester Rd. Aru 156 B2
Chichester Rd. Bog R 195 F3
Chichester Rd. Mid 90 B3
Chichester Rd. N Hay 168 B1
Chichester Rd. S End 193 E3
Chichester Rd. S End 193 E3
Chichester Terr. Bri 188 A2
Chichester Terr. Hors 35 D1
Chichester Way. Bur H 105 D3
Chichester Way. Sels 206 C4
Chiddingly Cl. Bri 188 B3
Chiddingly Cl. Cra 17 F3

Chidham La. Chid 170 B3
Chilcomb. Bur H 105 D1
Chilcroft La. Kin G 25 F1
Chilcroft Rd. Hasl 25 E4
Chilcrofts Rd. Kin G 25 F1
Chilgrove Cl. Wing 180 C2
Chilling St. Hor K 62 C4
Chilling St. Sha 42 A2
Chillis Wood Rd. Hay H 83 D3
Chiltern Cl. Cra 16 C3
Chiltern Cl. E Pre 179 F1
Chiltern Cl. Hasl 25 F3
Chiltern Cl. S Sea 185 D4
Chiltern Cres. Wing 181 E4
Chilterns The. Say C 103 D1
Chiltington Cl. Bur H 104 B3
Chiltlee Cl. Lip 24 A2
Chiltlee Manor. Lip 24 A2
Chiltley Way. Lip 24 A1
Chine The. Lit 199 F4
Chippendale Rd. Cra 16 C1
Chippers Cl. Wing 181 E2
Chippers Rd. Wing 181 E2
Chippers Wlk. Wing 181 E2
Chithurst La. Chit 67 D2
Chithurst La. Dom 6 B4
Chithurst La. Tro 66 C3
Chownes Mead La. Hay H 82 C2
Chrisdory Rd. Por S 164 B2
Christ's Hospital Rd. Hors 55 D3
Christ's Hospital Rd. Itc 55 D3
Christchurch Cres. Bog R 195 E2
Christchurch Rd. Wing 182 A2
Christie Pl. Bog R 196 A3
Christies. E Gri 21 D4
Christopher Rd. E Gri 8 B1
Christopher Way. Ems 147 F1
Church App. Lit 199 E4
Church Ave. Hay H 83 E3
Church Cl. Bog R 205 E4
Church Cl. Bri 166 B3
Church Cl. Bur H 104 C2
Church Cl. Cla 159 E3
Church Cl. Lan 183 E4
Church Cl. Low B 57 F2
Church Cl. Shi 99 D4
Church Cl. Upp B 141 F2
Church Farm La. E Wit 202 C4
Church Fields. Hur 123 E3
Church Green. S Sea 185 D4
Church Hill. Bri 166 B4
Church Hill. Mid 90 B4
Church Hill. Pul 95 F1
Church Hill. Pye 145 D3
Church Hill. Sli 155 D3
Church Hollow. Pur 6 B3
Church House Cl. Sock 164 B1
Church La. Alb 122 C3
Church La. Ard 61 E4
Church La. Ash 118 C2
Church La. Asht H 120 A3
Church La. Barn 176 A3
Church La. Bir 192 B3
Church La. Bog R 196 A3
Church La. Bog R 205 E4
Church La. Box 153 D2
Church La. Bram 24 A3
Church La. Bro H 34 A2
Church La. Burs 5 E4
Church La. Bury 135 F4
Church La. Cli 177 E1
Church La. Coc 110 A4
Church La. Cold 115 D3
Church La. Copt 5 F2
Church La. Dan 63 F2
Church La. Dit 125 D2
Church La. E Gri 8 B1
Church La. Eas 175 E4
Church La. Ferr 180 B1
Church La. Fun 149 F3
Church La. Hasl 26 A4
Church La. Hav 168 A4
Church La. Hen 121 E3
Church La. Hor K 63 D3
Church La. Hun 193 F4
Church La. Lan 182 C4
Church La. Low B 57 D3
Church La. N Hay 168 B2
Church La. Par G 100 B2
Church La. Poy 144 A4
Church La. Pye 145 D3
Church La. S End 193 E2
Church La. Sock 185 D4
Church La. Sour 55 E1
Church La. Stey 141 D2
Church La. Tan 153 D1
Church La. Upp B 141 F1
Church La. Upp B 141 F2
Church La. Wiv 105 E3
Church La. Yap 176 B2
Church Mead. Key 124 C2
Church Meadow. Bos 170 C3
Church Path. Ems 168 C4
Church Path. Grave 23 F3
Church Pl. Bri 188 B2
Church Pl. Pul 95 F1
Church Platt. Cuc 82 B3
Church Rd. Ald 174 C4
Church Rd. Ang 179 E3
Church Rd. Bram 24 A3
Church Rd. Bro H 34 A2
Church Rd. Bur H 104 C1
Church Rd. Burs 5 F4
Church Rd. Chic 173 D4
Church Rd. Copt 5 F2
Church Rd. Cra 4 B3
Church Rd. Cra 18 A3
Church Rd. E Wit 202 B4
Church Rd. Fer 46 C3
Church Rd. Hasl 25 E3
Church Rd. Hasl 26 A4
Church Rd. Hay H 83 E2
Church Rd. Hoo 1 B1
Church Rd. Horl 1 C2
Church Rd. Hors 35 F3
Church Rd. Hove 187 D3
Church Rd. Lym 178 A3
Church Rd. Man H 57 D3
Church Rd. N Hay 189 D3
Church Rd. Nor 153 F1
Church Rd. Par G 100 B2
Church Rd. Por S 185 F4
Church Rd. Run 173 D1
Church Rd. Rust 179 D1
Church Rd. Sca H 84 B2
Church Rd. Sels 206 B4
Church Rd. Sou 169 E4
Church Rd. Tho I 169 E1
Church Rd. Tur 19 F2
Church Rd. W Hoa 41 E3
Church Rd. W Lav 90 C3
Church Rd. Wbou 148 A2
Church Rd. Wing 181 F2
Church Rd. Wor 18 A3
Church St. Amb 136 A4
Church St. Bri 187 F3
Church St. Cra 17 D3
Church St. Cuc 82 B3
Church St. Hen 121 E3
Church St. Lit 178 B1
Church St. Petw 93 E4
Church St. Por S 185 F4
Church St. Rud 32 A4
Church St. S Sea 184 B4
Church St. Stey 141 D2
Church St. Stor 117 D1
Church St. W Chi 97 E1
Church St. Warm 34 B4
Church Terr. Hen 121 E3
Church View Cl. Horl 1 B1
Church View. Wbou 148 A2
Church Walk. Bur H 104 C2
Church Way Cl. Wing 181 F3
Church Way. Bog R 194 C1
Church Way. Sin 131 D4
Church Way. Wing 181 F3
Church Wlk. Cra 17 D3
Church Wlk. Hoo 1 B1
Church Wlk. Wing 182 B1
Churcher Rd. Wbou 148 A2
Churchfarm La. Sid 193 E1
Churchfield Rd. Pete 64 A2
Churchfield. Fit 94 C2
Churchill Ave. Bog R 195 E2
Churchill Ave. Hors 34 C2
Churchill Ct. Cra 4 C1
Churchill Dr. Ems 147 F2
Churchill Par. Rust 179 D1
Churchill Way. Bur H 105 D1
Churchmead Cl. M Lav 151 E3
Churchside. Chic 172 C4
Churchwood Dr. Tan 153 D1
Churchwood. Fit 94 C2
Chute Ave. Wing 160 B1
Chute Way. Wing 181 E4
Cidermill Rd. Newd 2 B3
Cinder Hill. Hor K 62 C4
Circle The. E Pre 200 C4
Circus St. Bri 187 F3
Cissbury Ave. Wing 160 B1
Cissbury Cl. Hors 35 F3
Cissbury Dr. Wing 160 C1
Cissbury Gdns. Wing 160 C1
Cissbury Hill. Cra 17 D2
Cissbury Rd. Bur H 104 B2
Cissbury Rd. Ferr 180 B2
Cissbury Rd. Hove 187 E4
Cissbury Rd. Wing 182 A3
Cissbury Way. S Sea 163 E1
City Fields Way. Tan 153 D1
Civic Way. Bur H 104 C1
Claigmar Rd. Rust 179 D1
Clair Ct. Hay H 83 E3
Clair Rd. Hay H 83 E3
Clapham Cl. Cla 159 E3
Clapham Comm. Cla 180 B4
Clapham St. Cla 159 E3
Clappers Gate. Cra 17 D4
Clappers La. E Wit 202 C3
Clappers La. Earn 203 D3
Clappers La. Ful 143 F3
Clappers La. Wcote H 143 F3
Clare Cl. Cra 5 D1
Clare Gdns. Pete 64 B2
Clare Wlk. Bri 188 A3
Claremont Way. Mid 90 B4
Clarence Ave. Wick 178 A2
Clarence Dr. E Pre 179 E1
Clarence Dr. Gri 21 E4
Clarence Rd. Bog R 196 A2
Clarence Rd. Hors 35 E1
Clarence Sq. Bri 187 E3
Clarence St. Por S 186 A3
Clarendon Pl. Bri 188 A2
Clarendon Pl. Por S 186 A3
Clarendon Rd. Hove 186 C4
Clarendon Rd. S Sea 185 D4
Clarendon Rd. Wing 182 B3
Clarendon Terr. Bri 188 A2
Clarendon Villas. Hove 186 C4
Clark Rd. Cra 16 C1
Clarke Ave. Hove 165 E2
Clay Hall La. Copt 6 A2
Clay La. Chic 172 A4
Clay La. Cros 157 E1
Clay La. Fise 171 F4
Clay La. Stor 137 F4
Clay La. W Ash 150 B1
Clay La. Warp 157 E1
Claygate Cross. Bor G 101 E4
Claypit La. Wham 152 B1
Clays Cl. E Gri 21 E4
Clays Hill. Stey 141 E1
Clayton Ave. Hass 124 B2
Clayton Dr. Bur H 104 B1
Clayton Hill. Cra 17 D2
Clayton Hill. Pye 145 D4
Clayton La. E Wit 202 C4
Clayton Rd. Bri 188 A4
Clayton Rd. Dit 125 D2
Clayton Rd. Sels 206 A3
Clayton Way. Hove 165 E2
Clayton Wlk. Wing 181 D3
Claytons Cnr. Bir 192 B3
Clearwater La. Sca H 84 C2
Clearwaters La. Bur H 105 D4
Cleaver La. Sta 59 F2
Cleavers La. Whi G 60 A1
Clerks Acre. Key 124 C2
Clermont Rd. Bri 166 B1
Clermont Terr. Bri 166 B1
Cleve Way. Bil 75 D4
Cleveland Cl. Wing 181 E4
Cleveland Gdns. Bur H 104 C1
Cleveland Rd. Bri 166 C1
Cleveland Rd. Chic 172 C3
Cleverland Rd. Wing 181 E4
Clevets The. Bog R 195 D1
Cliff App. Bri 188 B2
Cliff Rd. Bri 188 B2
Clifford Rd. Grays 8 A4
Clifton Hill. Bri 187 E3
Clifton Pl. Bri 187 E3
Clifton Rd. Bog R 196 A2
Clifton Rd. Bri 187 E3
Clifton Rd. Cra 18 A3
Clifton Rd. Lit 199 D4
Clifton Rd. Wing 182 A2
Clifton St. Bri 187 E3
Clifton Terr. Bri 187 E3
Climbing Cl. Hay H 83 D2
Climping Rd. Cra 16 C4
Climping St. Cli 198 B4
Clinton Hill. Dor 8 C4
Clive Ave. Wing 181 D1
Clive Way. Cra 18 A3
Clivedale Gdns. Stey 141 E2
Cliveden Ct. Bri 166 B2
Close The. Ard 61 F4
Close The. Ash 118 C3
Close The. Bog R 195 D1
Close The. Box 153 D2
Close The. Bri 166 A3
Close The. Bur H 105 D2
Close The. E Gri 21 D4
Close The. E Lav 151 E3
Close The. Key 124 B2
Close The. Lan 183 E2
Close The. Lip 24 A1
Close The. M Sea 197 F3
Close The. Rust 200 A4
Close The. S Sea 184 B4
Close The. Sels 206 C4
Closewalks Wood. Mid 90 B4
Clothalls La. Dia P 99 F3
Clovelly Ave. Bog R 196 C3
Clovelly Rd. Ems 168 C4
Clovelly Rd. N Hay 168 B2
Clovelly Rd. Sou 148 B1
Clover Bank View. Chath 60 C3
Clover La. Ferr 180 B1
Cloverlands. Cra 17 E4
Clovers End. Hors 35 F3
Clovers Way. Hors 36 A4
Club Wlk. E Pre 200 C4
Clun Rd. Lit 178 A1
Clun Rd. Wick 177 F2
Clyde Cl. Wing 181 D4
Clyde Rd. Bog R 196 B2
Clyde Rd. Bri 187 F4
Clyde Rd. Wing 181 D4
Clydesdale Ave. Chic 172 C3
Clydesdale. Bog R 195 F4
Coach House Cl. Sels 206 B4
Coach Rd. Chic 173 E4
Coach Rd. Cra 4 C4
Coach Rd. Ege 129 E1
Coachmans Dr. Cra 16 C1
Coalbrook Rd. Bri 188 A3
Coastal Rd. K Gor 201 D4
Coastal Rd. W King 201 D4
Coastguard La. W Wit 190 C1
Coastguard Par. Bog R 195 D1
Coastguard Rd. Lit 199 D4
Coates La. Fit 114 A4
Cob Cl. Cra D 20 A4
Cob La. Ard 40 C1
Cob Wlk. Cra 16 C3
Cobbett Cl. Cra 18 A4
Cobbetts Mead. Hay H 83 F2
Cobbles Cres. Cra 17 E4
Cobden La. Hasl 26 A4
Cobden Rd. Bri 188 A4
Cobden Rd. Mid 90 B4
Cobden Rd. Wing 182 A1
Cobham Cl. Yap 176 B1
Cobham Way. Cra 4 C2
Cobnor Cl. Cra 16 B2
Cobton Dr. Hove 165 F2
Cock's Hill. Shi 77 E2
Cocking Hill. Coc 110 A4
Cohen Cl. Wgate 175 D3
Cokeham Gdns. Lan 183 D3
Cokeham La. Lan 183 D3
Cokeham Rd. Lan 183 D3
Colbourne Ave. Bri 167 D3
Colbourne Rd. Hove 187 E4
Colchester Vale. For R 22 B1
Coldean La. Bri 167 E3
Coldharbour La. Pat 159 D1
Coldwaltham La. Bur H 105 D1
Cole Cl. Cra 16 C1
Colebrook Cl. Wing 182 B2
Colebrook La. Wat 114 C3
Colebrook Rd. Bri 166 A2
Colebrook Rd. Sock 185 E4
Colebrook Rd. Wick 178 A2
Coleman Ave. Hove 186 B4
Coleman St. Bri 187 F4
Coleridge Cl. Hors 35 E3
Coleridge Cl. Wing 180 C2
Coleridge Cres. Wing 180 C2
Coleridge Rd. Wing 180 C2
Coleridge St. Hove 186 C4
Colet Rd. Cra 17 D2
Colgate Cl. Bri 188 B3
Colgate Cl. Cra 16 C4
Colindale Rd N. Ferr 180 B1
Colindale Rd. Ferr 180 B1
Collards La. Hasl 26 A3
College Cl. Bog R 195 E2
College Cl. E Gri 8 B1
College Cl. Por S 164 B2
College Cl. Row C 126 B1
College Gdns. Bri 188 A2
College Gdns. Wing 181 F1
College Hill Terr. Hasl 26 A3
College Hill. Hasl 26 A3
College Hill. Stey 141 D1
College La. Chic 172 C4
College La. E Gri 8 B1
College La. Hur 124 A3
College Pl. Bri 188 A2
College Pl. Hur 124 A3
College Rd. Ard 61 F3
College Rd. Bri 188 A2
College Rd. Cra 17 E3
College Rd. Hay H 61 F3
College Rd. Hay H 83 E4
College Rd. Sour 55 E1
College Rd. Upp B 142 A1
College St. Bri 188 A2
College Terr. Bri 188 A3
Colletts Alley. Hors 35 D1
Collier Row. Cra 17 D2
Collingford La. Dan 63 F2
Collingwood Cl. E Gri 21 E4
Collingwood Cl. Horl 1 C2
Collingwood Cl. Hors 34 C2
Collingwood Ct. S Sea 184 B3
Collingwood Rd. Cra 18 A3
Collingwood Rd. Hors 34 C2
Collingwood Rd. Wing 181 D2
Collingwood. Pul 96 A2
Collins La. S Har 87 D4
Collins Rd. Cra 16 B2
Collins's La. S End 193 D2
Collyer Ave. Bog R 195 F3
Collyers Cres. Lip 24 B2
Colmer Ct. Bur H 104 B2
Colmer Pl. Bur H 104 B2
Colne Cl. Wing 181 D4
Colne Wlk. Cra 16 B2
Colonsay Rd. Cra 16 C2
Colt St. Sels 206 B4
Colt's Bay. Bog R 195 D1
Coltash Rd. Cra 17 F3
Coltsfoot Dr. Hors 35 E3
Coltstaple La. Hors 56 A2
Coltstaple La. Sour 55 F2
Columbia Dr. Wing 181 D3
Columbia Wharf Rd. Grays 8 B2
Columbia Wlk. Wing 181 D3
Colvill Ave. S Sea 184 A4
Colwell Cl. Hay H 83 E2
Colwell Gdns. Hay H 83 E2
Colwell La. Hay H 83 F1
Colwell Rd. Hay H 83 E1
Colwood La. Bol 80 C3
Colwood La. Ward 80 C3
Colwyn Cl. Cra 16 B2
Combe Rd. Hill B 43 E1
Comley Hill. Row C 147 E3
Commerce Way. Lan 183 D2
Commercial Rd. Bur H 104 B2
Common Hill. W Chi C 117 D4
Common La. Dit 125 D3
Common Rd. Fun 149 E3
Common The. W Chi C 117 D4
Common View. Ste 67 E1
Commonmead La. Bog R 194 C2
Commonside. Wbou 148 A3
Compass Cl. Lit 178 C1
Compassion Cl. Cra 16 B3
Comper Cl. Cra 16 B2
Compton Ave. Bri 187 E4
Compton Ave. Wing 180 C1
Compton Cl. Chic 151 F2
Compton Dr. Bog R 197 D3
Compton Rd. Bri 166 A1
Compton Rd. Hay H 83 F4
Comptons Brow La. Hors 35 F2
Comptons La. Hors 35 F1
Conbar Ave. Rust 179 D1
Concorde Cl. Stor 117 E2
Condor Way. Bur H 104 B2
Conduit Mead. Chic 173 D4
Coney Cl. Cra 16 C4
Coney Cl. E Wit 202 B3
Coney Croft. Hors 35 F3
Coney Rd. E Wit 202 B3
Coney Six Estate. E Wit 202 B3
Coneyhurst Rd. Bil 75 F3
Coneyhurst Rd. Con 75 F3
Congreve Rd. Wing 182 B2
Conibar Rd. Ems 147 F2
Conifer Dr. Hamb 149 E1
Conifers Cl. Hors 35 F3
Coniston Cl. Bog R 196 C3
Coniston Cl. Cra 16 A2
Coniston Cl. Hors 35 F3
Coniston Cl. Lan 183 D3
Coniston Rd. Wing 181 D2
Coniston Way. Lit 178 C2
Connaught Ave. S Sea 184 B4
Connaught Gdns. Cra 17 D4
Connaught Rd. Hav 147 D1
Connaught Rd. Hove 186 C3
Connaught Rd. Lit 178 A1
Connaught Terr. Hove 186 C4
Consort Way E. Horl 1 C1
Consort Way. Bur H 104 B1
Consort Way. Horl 1 C2
Constable Dr. Sels 206 C4
Constable Rd. Cra 17 E1
Convent La. Ems 168 C4
Conway Dr. Bog R 205 F4
Conway Pl. Hove 186 C4
Conway St. Hove 186 C4
Cook Rd. Cra 17 E2
Cook Rd. Hors 35 D3
Cook's Pond Rd. Mil 66 C4
Cooks Hill. Rud 31 F4
Cooks La. Sou 148 C1
Cooks La. Wal 128 A1
Cooks Mead. Rusp 15 D4
Cooksbridge Rd. Bri 188 B3
Coolham Dr. Bri 188 B4
Coolham Rd. Bar G 76 B2
Coolham Rd. Cool 76 B2
Coolham Rd. Tha 97 F1
Coolhurst La. Hors 35 F1
Coombe Cl. Cra 4 A1
Coombe Cl. Snod 72 B2
Coombe Cres. Bury 135 F4
Coombe Dri. Stey 141 D1
Coombe Dro. Stey 141 D1
Coombe Hill Rd. E Gri 21 D3
Coombe Hill. Bil 53 D1
Coombe La. Burp 157 F4
Coombe Rd. Bri 167 D1
Coombe Rd. Stey 141 D1
Coombe Rise. Wing 160 C1
Coombelands La. Pul 95 F2
Coombers La. Hay H 83 F3
Coombers. Bal 39 F1
Coombes Rd. Coom 162 C2
Coombes Rd. Lan 162 C1
Coomes Way. Wick 178 A2
Cooper Row. Cra 17 D2
Cooper St. Chic 172 C3
Cooper St. Chic 172 C3
Coopers Cl. Bur H 104 C3
Coopers The. Bar G 54 A2
Cooperway. Hen 121 E3
Coos La. Han 58 C4
Coos La. Sla 58 C3
Cootes Ave. Hors 34 C2
Cootes La. M Sea 197 E3
Cootham Green. Stor 116 C1
Copeland Rd. Bog R 196 C2
Copestake Dr. Bur H 105 D2
Copnall Way. Hors 35 D1
Coppedhall Rd. Bil 53 D2
Copper Hall Cl. Rust 179 E1

Copperfield Pl. Hors 34 C2
Coppets Wood. Lit 199 F4
Coppice La. Sels 206 B4
Coppice Rd. Hors 35 F3
Coppice The. Cra D 19 F4
Coppice Way. Hay H 83 D2
Coppice Wlk. Cra 17 F4
Copsale Rd. Cops 78 A3
Copsale Rd. Map 78 B3
Copse Cl. Cra D 19 F4
Copse Cl. E Gri 8 C2
Copse Cl. Hors 35 E3
Copse Cl. Liss 43 D2
Copse Cl. Pete 64 B2
Copse Cl. SE7 1 B2
Copse Cres. Cra 17 D4
Copse Hill. Bri 166 A3
Copse La. Walb 155 D1
Copse Rd. Hasl 25 D3
Copse The. Chic 151 F1
Copse The. Hay H 83 F3
Copse The. Sour 55 E1
Copse View. E Pre 179 E1
Copthorne Bank. Burs 6 A3
Copthorne Bank. Copt 5 F2
Copthorne Cl. Wing 181 F4
Copthorne Common Rd. Copt 5 F1
Copthorne Hill. Wing 181 F4
Copthorne Rd. Copt 5 E1
Copthorne Rd. Cra 18 A4
Copthorne Rd. Dom 6 C2
Copthorne Rd. Fel 7 E2
Copthorne Rd. Wor 18 B3
Copthorne Way. Bog R 195 D2
Copthorne Way. Copt 5 E1
Copyhold La. Cuc 82 C2
Copyhold La. Hay H 61 E1
Copyhold Rd. E Gri 21 D4
Corbishley Rd. Bog R 196 A3
Corby Cl. Cra 16 B2
Corbyn Cres. S Sea 184 C4
Corfe Cl. Sour 55 F1
Corfe Cl. Wing 180 C3
Cormorant Way. E Wit 202 C3
Corner Garth. Ferr 180 B1
Cornfield Cl. Lit 178 B2
Cornford Cl. Bur H 104 B3
Cornford Pk. Pem 154 C1
Cornwall Gdns. Bri 166 B1
Cornwall Gdns. E Gri 21 E4
Cornwall Gdns. Lit 178 A1
Cornwall Rd. Lit 178 A1
Coronation Rd. E Gri 21 E4
Coronation Rd. S Hay 189 F1
Coronation St. Bri 188 A4
Coronet Cl. Cra 18 B4
Corsletts Ave. Bro H 34 A2
Cortis Ave. Wing 182 A3
Corunna Dr. Hors 35 E1
Costells Edge. Sca H 84 B2
Cot La. Chid 170 A3
Cote St. Wing 160 A1
Cotland Rd. Sels 206 C3
Cotswold Cl. Cra 16 C3
Cotswold Cl. Wing 181 E4
Cotswold Ct. Hors 35 E1
Cotswold Rd. Wing 181 E4
Cotswold Way. E Pre 179 F1
Cotswolds The. Sock 185 E4
Cottage Cl. Bog R 195 D1
Cottage Cl. Hors 35 F3
Cottage Pl. Copt 6 B2
Cottenham Rd. Wing 182 B2
Cottingham Ave. Hors 35 D4
Cotton Dr. Ems 147 F2
Cotton Wlk. Cra 16 C1
Cottrells The. Ang 179 E3
Countisbury Cl. Bog R 195 E2
Countryman La. Bro C 98 C4
Countryman La. Shi 99 D4
County Oak Ave. Bri 166 C3
County Oak La. Cra 4 A1
County Oak Way. Cra 4 A1
Court Barn La. Bir 192 B3
Court Cl. Bri 166 B4
Court Cl. E Gri 8 B1
Court Cl. Lip 23 F2
Court Cres. E Gri 8 B1
Court Farm Rd. Hove 165 F1
Court Lodge Rd. Horl 1 B2
Court The. Bog R 194 C1
Court Wick La. Wick 178 A2
Courtlands Cl. Wing 181 E1
Courtlands Way. Bog R 197 D3
Courtlands Way. Wing 181 E1
Courtlands. Hay H 83 E2
Courtmead Rd. Cuc 82 B3
Courts Hill Rd. Hasl 25 F3
Courts Mount Rd. Hasl 25 F3
Courtup Hill. Map 78 B3
Courtwick La. Wick 178 A2
Courtwick Rd. Wick 178 A2
Courtyard The. Cra 17 D3
Courtyard The. E Gri 8 C1
Courtyard The. Hors 35 D1
Cousins Way. Pul 96 A2
Cove Rd. Lit 199 F4
Coventry Cl. Bog R 195 E2
Coventry St. Bri 187 E4
Covert Cl. Cra 17 E4
Covert Head. Han 58 C4
Covey The. Cra 18 B4
Covington Rd. Wbou 148 A3
Cow La. S Har 87 D2
Cow La. Sid 204 A4
Cowdens Cl. Hove 165 D2
Cowdown La. Com 106 A2
Cowdray Cl. Cra 18 A3
Cowdray Cl. Wing 181 D1
Cowdray Dr. Rust 178 C2
Cowdray Dr. Wing 181 D1
Cowdray Rd. E 68 C1
Cowfold Cl. Cra 16 B2
Cowfold Rd. Bri 188 B3
Cowfold Rd. W Gri 78 B1
Cowley Ave. Stone 22 A3
Cowley Dr. Lan 183 E3
Cowper Rd. Wing 181 F1
Cowper St. Hove 186 C4
Cox Gr. Bur H 104 B2
Cox Green Rd. Cox G 11 D1
Coxcomb Wlk. Cra 16 C2
Coxes Rd. Sels 206 B3
Coxham La. Stey 141 D2
Crab Tree Cl. Wick 178 A3
Crabbet Rd. Cra 17 F4
Crablands Cl. Sels 206 A4
Crabtree Ave. Bri 166 C3
Crabtree La. Lan 183 E3
Crabtree La. Len 129 E2
Crabtree Rd. Cra 17 D4
Cradock Pl. Wing 181 E4
Craggits La. Hen 121 E3
Cragie Wlk. Rai (K) 76 A4
Craigans. Cra 16 C3
Craignair Ave. Bri 166 B4
Craigweil La. Bog R 195 E1
Craigweil Manor. Bog R 195 D1
Cranborne Wlk. Cra 17 F2
Cranbourne Cl. Horl 1 C3
Cranbourne St. Bri 187 E3
Crane St. Chic 172 C3
Cranford Gdns. Bog R 196 A2
Cranleigh Rd. Wing 182 A3
Cranmer Ave. Hove 165 E1
Cranmer Rd. Wing 181 F2
Cranmer Wlk. Cra 18 A3
Cranston Rd. E Gri 8 B1
Cranworth Rd. Wing 182 B2
Craven Rd. Bri 188 A3
Craven Rd. Cra 17 F3
Crawford Gdns. Hors 35 E2
Crawford Way. E Gri 8 B2
Crawley Ave. Cra 4 C1
Crawley Ave. Hav 147 D3
Crawley Down Rd. Fel 7 E2
Crawley La. Bal 39 E2
Crawley La. Cra 18 A4
Crawley Rd. Bri 167 D3
Crawley Rd. Fay 16 A1
Crawley Rd. Hors 35 F2
Crawley South Western By Pass. Cra 16 B1
Crawters Cl. Cra 17 E4
Cray La. Pul 96 A3
Cray's La. Tha 118 A4
Crayford Rd. Bri 167 D1
Crede Cl. Bos 171 D3
Crede La. Bos 171 D3
Creek End. Ems 168 C4
Creek End. Fise 171 F3
Creek Rd. S Hay 189 E1
Crescent Cl. Bur H 104 C2
Crescent Pl. Bri 188 A2
Crescent Rd. Bog R 196 A2
Crescent Rd. Bri 187 F4
Crescent Rd. Bur H 104 C2
Crescent Rd. E Gri 8 A1
Crescent Rd. Wing 182 A1
Crescent Rise. Stor 117 F2
Crescent The. Bog R 196 C2
Crescent The. Bog R 205 F4
Crescent The. Bri 167 E1
Crescent The. Dor P 8 A4
Crescent The. E Wit 202 B4
Crescent The. Horl 4 C4
Crescent The. Hors 34 C1
Crescent The. Key 124 C2
Crescent The. Lan 183 E3
Crescent The. Lit 199 F4
Crescent The. Sock 185 E4
Crescent The. Sou 169 E4
Crescent The. Stey 141 D1
Crescent The. Stor 116 C1
Crescent Way. Bur H 104 C2
Crescent Way. Horl 1 C1
Crescenta Wlk. Bog R 195 F2
Crespin Way. Bri 167 D1
Cressey Way. Chic 151 F1
Crest Way. Por S 164 C2
Crestway The. Bri 167 D1
Crewdson Rd. Horl 1 C2
Cricket Cl. E Gri 8 B2
Cricket Field Rd. Hors 34 C1
Crimbourne La. Petw 73 D2
Cripland Cl. Hay H 83 F3
Cripplecrutch Hill. N 27 E3
Cripplegate La. Sour 77 F4
Cripps House. Cra 16 C1
Cripps La. Stey 141 E2
Critchel's La. High 193 D1
Critchfield Rd. Bos 170 C3
Critchmere Dr. Eas 175 E4
Critchmere Hill. Hasl 25 E4
Critchmere La. Hasl 25 E3
Critchmere Vale. Hasl 25 E3
Crockford Rd. Wbou 148 A2
Crockham Cl. Cra 17 D2
Crockhurst Hill. Wing 181 E4
Croft Ave. Sock 185 E4
Croft Dr. Por S 164 C2
Croft La. Hen 121 E2
Croft Mead. Chic 151 F1
Croft Rd. Bri 166 A2
Croft Rd. Sels 206 B4
Croft The. Bog R 195 E3
Croft The. Coc 110 A4
Croft The. Cra 16 C3
Croft The. E Pre 179 F1
Croft The. Hass 124 B3
Croft The. Lod 69 F2
Croft The. Yap 176 B2
Croft Way. Bog R 197 D3
Croft Way. Hors 34 C2
Croft Way. Sels 206 B4
Crofters Wood. Bra 141 E1
Cromleigh Way. Sock 164 B1
Crompton Way. Cra 4 B1
Cromwell Pl. E Gri 21 E4
Cromwell Rd. Bur H 104 B2
Cromwell Rd. Hove 187 D4
Cromwell St. Bri 188 A4
Crooked La. Bir 192 B2
Crookthorn La. Cli 198 B4
Crosbie Cl. Chic 172 B2
Crosbie Cl. Chic 172 B2
Crosby Cl. Wing 181 D3
Croshaw Cl. Lan 183 D3
Cross Colwood La. Bol 80 B2
Cross Keys. Cra 17 D3
Cross La. Bar G 54 C1
Cross La. Burs 6 A4
Cross La. Find 160 B3
Cross Oak La. Sal 1 C4
Cross Rd. Rust 179 E1
Cross Rd. Sock 185 D4
Cross Road Cl. Sock 185 D4
Cross St. Bri 187 F4
Cross St. Hove 187 D3
Cross St. Wing 182 A2
Crossbush Rd. Bri 188 B3
Crossbush Rd. M Sea 197 D2
Crossfield. Fer 46 C3
Crossland Dr. Hav 147 D3
Crossland Dr. Hav 147 D2
Crossman Ct. Cra 16 C1
Crosspath. Cra 17 E4
Crossway The. Bri 166 C1
Crossway The. Por S 164 C1
Crossways Ave. E Gri 8 A1
Crossways Ave. Wing 180 C2
Crossways Cl. Cra 17 E4
Crossways Park. W Chi C 117 D4
Crossways The. Wick 178 A2
Crossways. Cra 17 F4
Crossways. E 68 C1
Crossways. E Pre 179 F2
Crossways. M Sea 197 E3
Crossways. W Chi C 117 D4
Crouch Cross La. Box 153 D2
Crouch Hill. Hen 121 E4
Crouchlands Farm. Cuc 82 B4
Crowberry Cl. Cra 16 C1
Crowborough Dr. Wing 180 C1
Crowhurst Cl. Cra 18 B3
Crowhurst Keep. Cra 18 B3
Crowhurst Rd. Bri 167 D4
Crown Gdns. Bri 187 E3
Crown Rd. Por S 185 F4
Crown Rd. S Sea 184 C4
Crown St. Bri 187 E3
Crownhurst Cres. Stor 117 D1
Crowsbury Cl. Ems 147 F2
Croxton La. Hay H 83 F3
Croy Cl. Chic 172 B2
Croy Cl. Chic 172 B2
Crundens Cnr. Rust 179 E1
Crutchfield La. Sal 1 A3
Crypt La. Coc 110 A4
Cuckfield Cl. Cra 16 B2
Cuckfield Cres. Wing 181 E3
Cuckfield La. Ward 58 C2
Cuckfield Rd. God G 103 F3
Cuckfield Rd. Hur 103 F3
Cuckfield Rd. Hur 123 F4
Cuckfield Rd. Sta 59 F2
Cuckfield Rd. Whi G 59 F2
Cuckmere Cres. Cra 16 B3
Cuckmere Way. Bri 166 C3
Cudlow Ave. Rust 179 D1
Cudlow Gdn. Rust 179 D1
Cudlow Gdn. Rust 200 A4
Cudworth La. Newd 2 B4
Culimore Cl. E Wit 202 B4
Culimore Rd. E Wit 202 B4
Culpepper. Bur H 104 B2
Culross Ave. Hay H 83 D3
Culver Dr. S Hay 189 E1
Culver Rd. Bog R 196 C2
Culver Rd. Lan 183 E3
Culvers. S Har 87 D2
Cumberland Ave. Ems 147 F2
Cumberland Ave. Wing 181 D3
Cumberland Cl. Ang 179 F3
Cumberland Cres. Ang 179 E3
Cumberland Rd. Ang 179 F3
Cumberland Rd. Bri 166 B1
Cumbernauld Walk. Cra 16 B1
Cumbernauld Wlk. Cra 16 B1
Cumbrian Cl. Wing 181 E4
Cunliffe Cl. W Wit 191 D1
Cunningham Gdns. Bog R 197 D3
Curbey Cl. W Chi 97 D1
Curdridge Cl. Hav 147 D3
Curlescroft. Bog R 195 E1
Curlew Cl. Ems 168 C4
Curlews The. S Sea 184 C4
Curteys Wlk. Cra 16 C2
Curvins Way. Lan 183 E4
Curwen Pl. Bri 166 B2
Curzon Ave. Hors 34 C1
Curzon Cl. Wing 181 E3
Curzon Dr. Grays 8 C2
Cutfield Cl. Chic 172 B2
Cuthbert Rd. Bri 188 A3
Cuttinglye La. Cra D 6 C1
Cuttinglye Rd. Cra D 7 D1
Cygnet Wlk. Bog R 195 F3
Cygnets The. S Sea 184 B4
Cylinders The. Fer 46 C3
Cypress Ave. Wing 181 D3
Cypress Cl. S Sea 163 E1
Cypress Way. Bog R 195 D1
Cyprus Rd. Bur H 104 C2
D'aubigny Rd. Bri 187 F4
Dacre Gdns. Upp B 162 C4
Dagmar St. Wing 182 B2
Dairy La. Chic 173 E4
Dairy La. Walb 155 D1
Dairy La. Wham 152 B1
Dairyfields. Cra 16 C3
Daisycroft The. Hen 121 E2
Daisycroft The. Hen 121 E2
Dakins The. E Gri 21 E4
Dale Ave. Bri 166 B3
Dale Ave. Key 124 C2
Dale Cl. Hors 35 E3
Dale Cres. Bri 166 B3
Dale Dr. Bri 166 C3
Dale Hill. Pye 144 C3
Dale Rd. For R 22 B1
Dale Rd. Wing 182 C2
Dale View Gdns. Hove 165 D1
Dale View. Hasl 25 F3
Dale View. Hove 165 E1
Dalewood Gdns. Bur H 105 F1
Dalewood Gdns. Cra 17 E4
Dallaway Gdns. E Gri 8 B1
Dallaway Rd. Chic 172 C2
Dallington Rd. Hove 186 B4
Dalloway Rd. Aru 156 B1
Dalton Cl. Cra 16 C1
Daltons Pl. Aru 156 C1
Damer's Bridge. Petw 93 E4
Damian Way. Key 124 C2
Dampier Wlk. Cra 16 C1
Danbury Ct. Ems 148 A1
Danefield Rd. Sels 206 A3
Danehill La. Hor K 63 E3
Danehill Rd. Bri 188 B3
Danehurst Cres. Hors 35 E1
Daniel Cl. Grays 8 A4
Daniel Cl. Lan 183 E4
Dankton Gdns. Lan 182 C4
Dankton La. Lan 182 C4
Dankton La. Somp 161 F1
Danley La. Lin 24 C2
Danworth La. God G 103 F2
Danworth La. Hur 103 F2
Dapper's La. Ang 179 F4
Darcey Dr. Bri 166 C3
Darenth Way. Horl 1 B3
Dark Burr Rd. Grays 8 A4
Dark La. Bog R 195 E1
Darleydale. Cra 17 D2
Dart Cl. Wing 181 D4
Dartmouth Cl. Bri 167 E1
Dartmouth Cres. Bri 167 E1
Darwin Cl. Hors 35 E2
Daux Ave. Bil 75 D3
Daux Hill. Warm 34 C4
Daux Rd. Bil 75 D4
Dauxwood Cl. Bil 75 D3
Davenport Rd. Bog R 196 C2
Davey Dr. Bri 166 C1
Davids Cl. Bog R 195 E3
Davigdor Rd. Hove 187 E4
Davis Cl. Cra 16 C1
Davis Rd. Grays 8 A4
Davits Dr. Lit 178 C1
Davys Ct. Fun 149 F3
Daw Lane. N Hay 189 D4
Dawes Ave. Wing 182 B2
Dawes Cl. Wing 182 B2
Dawn Cl. Upp B 141 F1
Dawn Cres. Upp B 141 F1
Dawn Rise. Copt 5 F2
Dawson Terr. Bri 188 A3
Dawtrey Rd. Petw 93 E4
De Brause Way. Bra 141 E1
De Courcel Rd. Bri 188 B2
De La Warr Rd. E Gri 8 B1
De Monkfort Rd. Bri 188 A4
Deacon Way. Wing 182 B3
Deacons Dr. Por S 165 D1
Deacons Way. Upp B 141 F1
Deak's La. Ans 81 F3
Deak's La. Whi G 81 F3
Dean Cl. Por S 165 D1
Dean Cl. Wick 178 A2
Dean Gdns. Por S 165 D1
Dean La. Row C 126 B3
Dean La. Til 92 B4
Dean La. Upp 70 C1
Dean St. Bri 187 E3
Dean Way. Stor 117 D1
Deanland Rd. Bal 39 F1
Deanway. Hove 165 F2
Decoy Rd. Wing 182 B3
Dedisham Cl. Cra 17 F3
Deepdene Cl. M Sea 197 F3
Deepdene. Hasl 25 E3
Deepfields. Horl 1 B3
Deer Park La. Sels 206 A4
Deerswood Cl. Cra 16 C4
Deerswood Cl. Wing 180 C3
Deerswood Rd. Cra 16 C4
Deeside Ave. Fise 171 F4
Deeside The. Bri 166 C4
Defiance Pl. M Sea 197 D2
Del Quay Rd. Apu 171 F1
Delfryn. Por S 164 B2
Dell Cl. Hasl 25 F4
Dell Dr. Ang 179 E2
Dell La. Bil 75 D4
Dell The. E Gri 8 C1
Delling Cl. Bos 170 C3
Delling La. Bos 171 D3
Dellney Ave. Hay H 83 E2
Delta Dr. Horl 1 C1
Dempsey Rd. Chic 151 F1
Den Ave. Bog R 196 A2
Denbigh Rd. Hasl 26 A3
Denchers Plat. Cra 4 A1
Dene Cl. Hasl 26 A3
Dene Cl. Horl 1 B3
Dene The. Hove 165 D2
Dene The. Sour 55 F1
Dene Tye. Cra 18 A4
Dene Vale. Bri 166 A3
Deneside. Bri 166 A3
Deneway The. Bri 166 A2
Deneway The. Lan 183 D3
Denge La. Box 153 E3
Denham Cl. M Sea 197 E3
Denham Rd. Bur H 104 A2
Denman's Cl. Hay H 83 F4
Denman's La. Hay H 83 F4
Denmans La. Nor 154 B1
Denmans. Cra 18 A4
Denmark Mews. Hove 186 C4
Denmark Rd. Por S 186 A4
Denmark Terr. Bri 187 E3
Denmark Villas. Hove 186 C4
Denne Par. Hors 35 D1
Denne Rd. Cra 17 D3
Denne Rd. Hors 35 D1
Dennis Ct. Pul 96 A1
Dennis Way. Liss 43 D2
Denny's Cl. Sels 206 B4
Denshare Rd. Sels 206 B4
Denshire Dr. Stor 117 E1
Densihale. Bog R 195 F2
Denton Cl. Wing 180 C2
Denton Dr. Bri 166 C3
Denvilles Cl. Hav 147 D1
Depot Rd. Cra 4 A1
Depot Rd. Hors 35 F2
Derby Rd. Hasl 25 F4
Derek Ave. Hove 186 A3
Derek Rd. Lan 183 E4
Derwent Cl. Cra 16 B3
Derwent Cl. Hors 35 F3
Derwent Cl. Lan 183 D3
Derwent Cl. Lit 178 C2
Derwent Cl. Tan 153 D1
Derwent Dr. Wing 181 D3
Derwent Gr. Bog R 196 C3
Desmond Way. Bri 188 B3
Detling Rd. Cra 17 D1
Devereux Rd. Grays 8 A4
Devil's Dyke Rd. Hove 165 E3
Devil's Dyke Rd. Poy 144 A1
Devils La. Lip 24 B2
Devonport Rd. Wing 182 C1
Devonshire Pl. Bog R 196 A2
Devonshire Pl. Bri 187 F3
Devonshire Rd. Bog R 196 A2
Devonshire Rd. Grays 8 A4
Devonshire Rd. Hors 35 D1
Dewar Cl. Cra 16 B3
Dewe Rd. Bri 167 D1
Dexter Dr. E Gri 21 E4
Dial Cl. Barn 176 A3

Dickens Cl. E Gri 8 A1
Dickens Rd. Cra 17 E2
Dickins Way. Hors 56 B4
Dickinson Pl. Bog R 196 A3
Dingle The. Cra 16 C3
Dingley Rd. Rust 179 D1
Dinsdale Gdns. Rust 179 D1
Dione Wlk. Cra 16 B2
Dirty La. Ash W 22 B3
Dirty La. Gra 111 F3
Dirty La. Hamm 22 A3
Ditchfield Cl. Bog R 197 D3
Ditchling Bostal. Wmes 146 A4
Ditchling Cl. Wing 180 C2
Ditchling Cres. Bri 167 D3
Ditchling Gdns. Bri 166 C1
Ditchling Hill. Cra 17 D2
Ditchling Rd. Bri 166 C2
Ditchling Rd. Wmes 146 A2
Ditchling Rise. Bri 187 F4
Dobbins Pl. Cra 16 B3
Dobson Rd. Cra 4 A1
Dodsley Gr. E 68 B1
Dodsley La. E 68 C1
Dog La. Stey 141 D2
Dollis Cl. Cra 18 A3
Dolphin Cl. Fise 171 F3
Dolphin Cl. Hasl 25 E3
Dolphin Mews. Chic 172 A3
Dolphin Rd. Hay H 83 D2
Dolphin Rd. S Sea 184 C4
Dolphin Way. Rust 200 A4
Dominion Cl. Wing 182 B3
Dominion Rd. Wing 182 B3
Dominion Way W. Wing 182 B3
Dominion Way. Rust 179 D2
Dominion Way. Wing 182 B3
Donald Hall Rd. Bri 188 A3
Doncaster Wlk. Cra 17 F2
Donegal Rd. Chic 151 E1
Donkey La. Cra 5 D4
Donkey Mews. Hove 187 D3
Donne Cl. Cra 17 F4
Donnington Ct. Cra 16 B2
Donnington Park. Chic 172 A2
Doomsday Gdn. Hors 35 F1
Doone End. Ferr 201 E4
Dorchester Gdns. Wing 181 F1
Dorking Rd. Hors 34 C4
Dorking Rd. Kin 13 F2
Dorking Rd. Warn 13 F1
Dormans Cl. Dor 8 C4
Dormans Gdns. Dor P 8 B3
Dormans High St. Dor 8 C4
Dormans Park Rd. Dor P 8 B3
Dormans Park Rd. E Gri 8 A2
Dormans Station Rd. Dor 8 B4
Dormans. Cra 16 C3
Dorothy Rd. Hove 186 A4
Dorset Ave. E Gri 8 A2
Dorset Gdns. Bri 187 F3
Dorset Gdns. E Gri 8 A2
Dorset Pl. Bri 187 F3
Dorset Pl. Wing 181 F3
Dorset Rd. Bog R 196 A3
Dorset St. Bri 187 F3
Doubledays. Bur H 104 C1
Douglas Ave. Wing 181 E1
Douglas Cl. Wing 181 E1
Douglas Cl. Yap 176 C1
Douglas Martin Rd. Chic 172 C4
Dove Cl. Cra 17 D4
Dovedale Cres. Cra 17 D2
Dover Cl. Sour 55 F1
Dover Ct. Bog R 195 F3
Dover Rd. Bri 166 C1
Dover Rd. Wing 181 F1
Dowding Way. T W 154 A3
Dower Wlk. Cra 16 C3
Dowland Ave. Sock 164 B1
Dowlands La. Burs 6 A4
Down Cl. Hey 111 D4
Down St. W Ash 149 F2
Down Terr. Bri 188 A3
Down The. Hove 165 D2
Down View Rd. Wing 181 F1
Downash Cl. Bri 188 B3
Downe Cl. Horl 1 B3
Downe Wlk. Wing 181 D3
Downing Cl. Bog R 195 E2
Downland Cl. Find 160 B3
Downland Cl. Sock 164 A1
Downland Cl. Upp B 141 F1
Downland Cl. Wood 188 C4
Downland Cres. Hove 165 E2
Downland Dr. Cra 17 D2
Downland Dr. Hove 165 E2
Downland Pl. Cra 17 D2
Downland Rd. Upp B 141 F1
Downland Rd. Wood 188 C4
Downlands Ave. Wing 182 A3
Downlands Cl. Bog R 194 C1
Downlands Cl. Lan 183 D4
Downlands Gdns. Wing 182 B4
Downlands. Par G 100 B2
Downlands. Pul 96 A1
Downs Mead. Lan 183 D4
Downs Rd. Bur H 104 B2
Downs Rd. W Sto 150 A3
Downs View Rd. Hass 124 B2
Downs Way. E Pre 179 E2
Downs Way. Sock 164 B1
Downscroft. Bur H 105 D3
Downscroft. Upp B 141 F1
Downside Ave. Wing 160 B2
Downside Cl. S Sea 163 E1
Downside Cl. Wing 160 B2
Downside. Hove 165 F2
Downside. S Sea 163 F1
Downsview Ave. Stor 117 E1
Downsview Dr. Mid 90 B3
Downsview Rd. Hors 35 F3
Downsview Rd. K Gor 201 D4
Downsview Rd. Por S 164 C1
Downsview. Hove 165 D2
Downsview. Petw 93 E4
Downsview. Sma D 142 B4
Downsway. S Sea 163 E1
Downview Ave. Ferr 180 B2
Downview Cl. E Wit 202 B3
Downview Cl. M Lav 151 E3
Downview Cl. Yap 176 C2
Downview Rd. Barn 175 F4
Downview Rd. Bog R 196 C3
Downview Rd. Ferr 180 B2
Downview Rd. Find 160 B4
Downview Rd. Yap 176 C2
Downview Way. Yap 176 C2
Dragons Green Rd. Shi 77 D3
Dragons Green Rd. Sour 77 D3
Dragons La. Cool 76 C2
Dragons La. Shi 77 D2
Drake Ave. Wing 181 D2
Drake Cl. Hors 35 E3
Drake Dr. Yap 176 C1
Drake Park. Bog R 197 D3
Drake Rd. Cra 17 D2
Drake Rd. Grays 8 A4
Drakeley's Field. Mil 44 C1
Draxmont Way. Bri 166 B2
Draycliff Cl. Ferr 180 B1
Drayton La. Chic 173 E3
Drewitts Cotts. Ward 80 B3
Drift La. Hamb 170 B4
Drift La. Sels 206 A4
Drift Rd. Bog R 194 C1
Drift Rd. Sels 206 C4
Drift The. Row C 126 A1
Driftway The. Upp B 141 F2
Drive The. Bog R 195 D1
Drive The. Bos 171 D2
Drive The. Bur H 104 C2
Drive The. Chic 151 F2
Drive The. Copt 6 A2
Drive The. E Lavn 112 B3
Drive The. E Pre 200 C4
Drive The. Horl 1 C1
Drive The. Hove 187 D4
Drive The. Ifo 30 A1
Drive The. Lan 162 C1
Drive The. Lan 183 D2
Drive The. S Sea 163 E1
Drive The. Sock 164 B1
Drive The. Sou 169 E4
Drive The. Wing 181 E2
Driveway The. S Sea 163 E1
Droke La. E Dean 132 B3
Dropping Holms. Hen 121 D2
Drove Cres. Por S 164 C1
Drove La. Earn 203 D3
Drove La. Yap 176 A1
Drove Rd. Por S 164 C1
Drove Rd. Wood 188 C4
Drove The. Bri 166 A1
Drovers Cl. Por S 165 D1
Drovers Way. Bur H 105 D1
Drovers. Bol 81 D2
Droveway The. Hay H 83 D3
Droveway The. Hove 166 A1
Drummond Cl. Hay H 83 D2
Drummond Rd. Cra 16 B3
Drummond Rd. Wing 181 E1
Drungewick La. Lox 31 D1
Drungewick La. New C 52 A4
Drury Cl. Cra 18 A2
Dryad Way. M Sea 197 D2
Drygrounds La. Bog R 196 B3
Duarte Pl. Grays 8 A4
Duck La. Mid 90 B4
Duckmead La. Liss 43 D3
Dudley Cl. Grays 8 A4
Dudley Rd. Bri 166 C1
Duffield La. Wcote S 148 C2
Duke St. Bri 187 E3
Duke St. Lit 178 A1
Duke's Ct. Lit 178 A1
Duke's Hill. Tha 97 F1
Duke's Hill. Tha 117 F4
Duke's Mound. Bri 188 A2
Duke's Pas. Bri 187 E3
Duke's Rd. Newd 2 A3
Duke's Rd. Nor 154 B2
Dukes Cl. Aru 156 B1
Dukes La. Bri 187 E3
Dukes La. Stey 141 D2
Dukes Meadow. Bog R 194 C2
Dukes Rd. Hay H 83 F4
Dukes Row. Stor 116 C1
Dukes Yd. Stey 141 D2
Dumbrells Ct. Dit 125 D2
Dumbrills Cl. Bur H 104 C3
Dumpford La. Tro 88 A4
Duncan Rd. Chic 172 B4
Duncton Cl. Bog R 196 C2
Duncton Cl. Cra 16 C4
Duncton Cl. Hay H 83 D2
Duncton High St. Dun 112 C3
Duncton Rd. Rust 179 D1
Dundonald Cl. S Hay 189 D3
Dunes The. Bog R 205 F4
Dunford Hollow. Mid 90 B2
Dunhurst Cl. Hav 147 D2
Dunning's Rd. E Gri 21 E4
Dunnock Cl. Row C 126 A1
Dunsfold Cl. Cra 16 C3
Dunsfold Rd. Pla 29 D2
Dunstall Ave. Bur H 104 B2
Dunstall Farm Rd. Bur H 104 B2
Dunstan Cl. Chic 151 F2
Dunster Cl. Bri 166 C1
Durban Park. Bog R 196 A3
Durban Rd. Bog R 196 A3
Durbans Rd. Wis G 52 A2
Durfold Hill. Warn 13 F2
Durfold Rd. Hors 35 E4
Durfold Wood. Pla 29 D3
Durford Rd. Pete 64 B2
Durham Cl. Bog R 205 F4
Durham Cl. Bri 167 F1
Durham Cl. Cra 17 E1
Durham Gdns. Chic 151 E1
Durkins Rd. E Gri 8 A2
Durlston Dr. Bog R 195 F3
Durlston Parade. Bog R 195 F3
Durnford Cl. Chic 172 B4
Durrants Gdns. Row C 147 D4
Durrants Rd. Row C 147 D4
Durrell Gdns. Chath 60 C3
Durrington Gdns. Wing 181 D2
Durrington Hill. Wing 181 D4
Durrington La. Wing 181 D3
Dutchells Copse. Hors 35 E4
Dyall Cl. Bur H 104 B2
Dyers La. Sli 155 D3
Dyke Cl. Hove 165 F2
Dyke Cl. Poy 144 A2
Dyke La. Poy 144 A2
Dyke Rd. Bri 166 A1
Dyke Road Ave. Hove 166 A2
Dyke Road Dr. Bri 187 E4
Dyke Road Mews. Bri 187 E4
Dyke Road Pl. Bri 166 A2
Dymock's The. Dit 125 D2
Dymoke St. Ems 147 F2
Dyson Wlk. Cra 16 C1

E Mascalls Rd. Hay H 84 A3
Eady Cl. Hors 35 E1
Eagle Estate. Bil 75 D4
Eagle Way. Grave 23 E3
Eagles Chase. Wick 178 A2
Eagles Rd. Gree 22 B3
Earles Meadow. Hors 35 F3
Earlswood Cl. Hors 35 E2
Early Commons. Cra 17 E4
Earnley Manor Cl. Earn 203 D4
Earnley Rd. Earn 203 D4
Earnley Rd. S Hay 189 F1
Earwig La. Ward 80 B3
Easebourne La. E 68 C1
Easebourne St. E 69 D3
Easebourne St. Lic 69 D3
East Ave. M Sea 197 E3
East Ave. Wing 181 E1
East Bank Wlk. Lit 199 F4
East Bank. Sels 206 C4
East Beach Rd. Sels 206 C4
East Bracklesham Dr. E Wit 202 C3
East Cl. M Sea 197 E3
East Court Way. Rust 179 E1
East Dr. Bri 188 A3
East Dr. M Sea 197 F3
East Dr. Rust 179 E2
East End La. Dit 125 D2
East Field Cl. Sou 148 C1
East Front Rd. Bog R 205 F4
East Gdns. Dit 125 D2
East Ham Rd. Lit 178 A1
East Hampnett La. Tan 153 E1
East Harting St. E Har 87 E2
East Hill Dr. Liss 43 D2
East Hill La. Burs 6 A3
East Hill. Dor P 8 B3
East Lake. Bog R 196 A2
East Leigh Rd. Hav 147 E2
East Mead. Bog R 205 F4
East Mead. Ferr 180 B1
East Meadway. S Sea 184 C3
East Onslow Cl. Ferr 180 B2
East Pallant. Chic 172 C3
East Pallant. Chic 172 C3
East Park La. Dom 7 D4
East Park. Cra 17 D3
East Row. Chic 172 C3
East St. Amb 136 B4
East St. Bil 75 D4
East St. Bri 187 F2
East St. Chic 172 C3
East St. Hav 147 D1
East St. Hors 35 D1
East St. Lan 183 E2
East St. Lit 178 B1
East St. Petw 93 E4
East St. Por S 186 A4
East St. Rusp 15 E4
East St. S Sea 184 B4
East St. Sels 206 B4
East St. Tur H 20 A2
East St. W Bou 148 A2
East St. W Chi 97 E1
East Strand. E Wit 202 A4
East Tyne. Wing 181 D3
East View Cl. M Lav 151 E4
East Walls. Chic 172 C3
East Way. Sels 206 C4
East Wick. Hay H 84 A4
Eastbank. Sock 164 B1
Eastbourne Rd. Bri 167 D1
Eastbourne Rd. Fel 7 E4
Eastbrook Rd. Por S 185 F4
Eastbrook Way. Sock 185 F4
Eastcourt Rd. Wing 182 A2
Eastcroft Mews. Hors 34 B1
Eastdale Rd. Bur H 105 D2
Eastdean Hill. E Dean 132 A3
Easteds La. Sour 55 F1
Eastergate Cl. Wing 180 B2
Eastergate Green. Rust 179 D1
Eastergate La. Fon 154 C1
Eastergate La. Walb 155 D1
Eastergate Rd. Bri 167 E2
Eastern Ave. S Sea 184 C4
Eastern Cl. E Pre 179 F1
Eastern Cl. S Sea 184 C4
Eastern Pl. Bri 188 B2
Eastern Rd. Bri 188 A2
Eastern Rd. Hav 147 D1
Eastern Rd. Hay H 83 E2
Eastern Rd. Hay H 84 A4
Eastern Rd. Wiv 105 F2
Eastern St. Bri 188 A2
Eastern Terr Mews. Bri 188 A2
Eastern Terr. Bri 188 A2
Eastfield Cres. Bri 166 C2
Eastgate Sq. Chic 172 C3
Easthill Dr. Por S 164 C1
Easthill Way. Por S 164 C1
Easting Cl. Wing 182 B3
Eastlake Cl. Pete 64 B2
Eastland Rd. Chic 172 C3
Eastmead Ind Est. M Lav 151 E4
Eastoke Ave. S Hay 189 F1
Easton La. High 203 F3
Eastover Way. Bog R 196 B2
Eastshaw La. Wool 68 A2
Eastway E. Cra 4 C4
Eastway. Cra 4 C4
Eastwick Cl. Bri 166 C4
Eastwood Cl. S Hay 189 D3
Eastwood. Cra 17 E3
Eaton Gdns. Hove 187 D4
Eaton Gr. Hove 187 D4
Eaton Pl. Bri 188 A2
Eaton Rd. Hove 187 D3
Eaton Villas. Hove 186 C4
Edburton Ave. Bri 166 C1
Edburton Gdns. S Sea 163 E1
Eddington Hill. Cra 16 C1
Eden Rd. Cra 16 B2
Eden Vale. Dor P 8 B3
Eden Vale. E Gri 8 B3
Edgar Cl. Cra 18 B3
Edgehill Cl. Wing 181 E4
Edgehill Way. Por S 164 B1
Edgell Rd. Wbou 148 A2
Edinburgh Cl. Bog R 195 E1
Edinburgh Cl. Sour 55 F1
Edinburgh Rd. Bri 187 F4
Edinburgh Sq. Mid 90 B4
Edinburgh Way. E Gri 21 E4
Edith Cotts. W Ash 149 F2
Edmonton Rd. Wing 181 D3
Edrich Rd. Cra 16 C1
Edward Ave. Hove 165 F2
Edward Cl. Hove 165 F2
Edward Rd. Hay H 83 E1
Edward St. Bri 187 F3
Edward Way. Bur H 104 A1
Edwards Ave. Tan 153 D1
Edwen Cl. Bog R 194 C2
Edwin Cl. Lan 183 D3
Effingham La. Copt 6 B2
Effingham Rd. Burs 6 A3
Egerton Rd. Lit C 147 F3
Eggington Cl. Bri 167 F3
Eggington Rd. Bri 167 F3
Egmont Rd. E 68 C1
Egmont Rd. Hove 165 D1
Egremont Pl. Bri 187 F3
Eighth Ave. Lan 183 E4
Einsted Cl. Rust 199 F4
Eirene Ave. Wing 181 E1
Eirene Rd. Wing 181 E1
Elbridge Cres. Bog R 195 D1
Elder Pl. Bri 187 F4
Elder Rd. Hav 147 D2
Elderfield Cl. Ems 148 A2
Eldon Rd. Wing 182 B2
Eldon Way. Wick 177 F2
Eldred Ave. Bri 166 A3
Eleanor Gdns. Bog R 197 D3
Elfin Gr. Bog R 195 F2
Elfin Mews. Bog R 195 F2
Elger Way. Copt 5 F2
Elgin Cl. Hors 35 E2
Elgin Rd. Wing 181 D1
Eliot Dr. Hasl 25 E3
Elizabeth Ave. Bog R 195 D2
Elizabeth Ave. Hove 165 F2
Elizabeth Cl. Bog R 195 D2
Elizabeth Cl. Hove 165 F2
Elizabeth Cres. E Gri 8 B2
Elizabeth Ct. Horl 1 C2
Elizabeth Pl. Lan 183 D3
Elizabeth Rd. Chic 173 D4
Elizabeth Rd. S Sea 185 D4
Elizabeth Rd. Wing 182 A1
Elizabeth Smith's Ct. Di 87 D2
Elizabethan Way. Cra 18 A3
Ella Cl. E Wit 202 B4
Ella Nore La. W Wit 190 C1
Ellasdale Rd. Bog R 195 F1
Ellen St. Hove 186 C4
Ellen St. Por S 186 A4
Ellesmere Orch. Wbou 148 A3
Elliot Cl. Cra 18 A2
Elliott Cl. Cra 18 A2
Ellis Ave. Wing 181 E4
Ellis Cl. Aru 156 B1
Ellis Way. Bog R 205 F4
Ellman Rd. Cra 16 B2
Ellson Cl. Cra 18 A2
Ellson Cl. Cra 18 A2
Elm Ave. E Pre 179 F1
Elm Cl Estate. S Hay 189 D2
Elm Cl. Bog R 194 C1
Elm Cl. E Wit 202 C3
Elm Cl. Hove 166 A1
Elm Cl. Run 173 D1
Elm Cl. S Sea 163 E1
Elm Dr. E Gri 8 C1
Elm Dr. Hove 165 E1
Elm Dr. M Sea 197 F3
Elm Gr S. Barn 175 F3
Elm Gr. Barn 175 F4
Elm Gr. Bog R 195 F2
Elm Gr. Bri 188 A4
Elm Gr. Hors 35 E1
Elm Gr. Lan 183 D3
Elm Gr. S Hay 189 D2
Elm Gr. Sels 206 B4
Elm Gr. Wing 181 E2
Elm Grove La. Stey 141 D2
Elm Park. Ferr 180 B1
Elm Pl. Rust 179 D1
Elm Rd. Hav 168 A4
Elm Rd. Por S 185 F4
Elm Rd. Wgate 175 E4
Elm Rd. Wing 182 B1
Elm Rise. Find 160 B3
Elm Tree Cl. Horl 1 C2
Elm Tree Cl. Sels 206 B4
Elmbank Dr. Brom 33 F2
Elmcroft Pl. Wgate 175 D3
Elmer Cl. M Sea 197 F3
Elmer Ct. M Sea 198 A3
Elmer Rd. M Sea 197 E3
Elmgrove Rd. Lit 178 B1
Elmhurst Cl. Ang 179 F3
Elmhurst La. Five O 54 A3
Elmleigh. Mid 90 B4
Elmore Rd. Bri 187 F3
Elms Dr. Lan 183 D3
Elms La. W Wit 191 E1
Elms Lea Ave. Bri 166 B2
Elms Ride. W Wit 191 D1
Elms Way. W Wit 191 D1
Elmsfield. Sels 206 B4
Elmstead Gdns. W Wit 191 D1
Elmstead Park Rd. W Wit 191 D1
Elmstone Cl. Lan 183 D3
Elmwood Ave. Bog R 196 A3
Elrington Rd. Hove 166 A1
Elsie Rd. Wing 181 F1
Elspring Mead. Wick 178 A2
Elstead Cres. Bri 167 D3
Elstead Rd. Els 88 B3
Elsted Cl. Cra 16 C4
Elsted Rd. Ste 89 D4
Elverlands Cl. Ferr 201 E4
Ely Cl. Cra 17 E1
Ely Cl. Wing 181 E2
Ely Cl. Wing 202 B4
Ely Gdns. Bog R 195 D2
Ely Rd. Wing 181 E2
Emerald Quay. S Sea 184 C3
Emlyn Rd. Horl 1 B2
Emms La. Bar G 76 B4
Empire Villa. Sal 1 C4
Emsbrook Dr. Ems 147 F1
Emsworth Common Rd. Ems 147 F3
Emsworth House Cl. Ems 147 F1
Emsworth Rd. Hav 147 D1
Emsworth Rd. Tho I 169 D2

Enfield Rd. Cra 17 D1
Engalee. E Gri 8 A1
Englefield. Hors 34 B1
English Cl. Hove 186 B4
Ennerdale Cl. Cra 16 C2
Ennerdale Dr. Lan 182 C3
Ensign Way. Lit 178 C1
Enterprise Rd. Maid 106 B3
Epping Wlk. Cra 17 F2
Epsom Rd. Cra 17 F2
Erica Way. Copt 5 F1
Erica Way. Hors 35 D3
Eridge Cl. Cra 18 A3
Eridge Rd. Hove 165 F1
Erin Way. Bur H 104 B2
Eriskay Ct. Wing 180 C3
Eriswell Rd. Wing 182 A1
Erles Rd. Lip 24 A2
Ernest Cl. Ems 147 F1
Erringham Rd. S Sea 163 E1
Erroll Rd. Hove 186 A3
Erskine Cl. Cra 16 B1
Esher Cl. Bog R 194 C1
Esher Dr. Lit 178 B1
Eskbank Ave. Bri 166 C4
Esmond Cl. Ems 168 C4
Esmonde Cl. Lit 178 B1
Esplanade The. Bog R 196 A1
Esplanade The. Wing 182 B1
Esplanade. Wing 182 A1
Essex Cotts. Bri 188 A2
Essex Rd. Bog R 196 A3
Essex St. Bri 188 A2
Estcots Dr. E Gri 8 C1
Estuary The. Lit 178 B1
Ethel St. Hove 186 C4
Ethelred Rd. Wing 181 F2
Ethelwulf Rd. Wing 181 F2
Eton Cl. Bog R 195 E2
Eton Dr. E Wit 202 B4
Eton Rd. Wing 181 F2
Ettrick Cl. Chic 172 C3
Ettrick Rd. Chic 172 C3
Evans Cl. Cra 18 A3
Evans Pl. Bog R 196 A3
Evelyn Ave. Rust 200 A4
Evelyn Rd. Wing 182 A2
Evelyn Terr. Bri 188 A3
Evelyn Wlk. Cra 17 E2
Eversfield Rd. Hors 35 E1
Ewart St. Bri 187 F3
Ewens Gdns. Barn 175 F4
Ewhurst Cl. Cra 17 D3
Ewhurst Rd. Bri 167 D1
Ewhurst Rd. Cra 17 D4
Exbury Rd. Hav 147 D3
Excalibur Cl. Cra 16 B3
Exceat Cl. Bri 188 B3
Exchange Rd. Cra 17 E3
Exeter Cl. Bog R 195 E2
Exeter Cl. Cra 17 E1
Exeter Cl. Ems 147 F1
Exeter Rd. Chic 151 E1
Exeter St. Bri 187 E4
Exford Wlk. Wing 181 D3
Exmoor Cl. Wing 181 E4
Exmoor Cres. Wing 181 E4
Exmoor Dr. Wing 181 E4
Exton Rd. Chic 172 C2
Exton Rd. Hav 147 D3
Eyles Cl. Hors 34 C2

Fabians Way. Hen 121 D3
Fair View. Hors 34 C2
Fairbanks. Hay H 83 E2
Faircox La. Hen 121 D3
Fairdene. Sock 164 B1
Fairfield Ave. Horl 1 C1
Fairfield Cl. Ard 61 F4
Fairfield Cl. Bos 171 D3
Fairfield Cl. Bur H 104 B2
Fairfield Cl. Ems 147 F1
Fairfield Cl. S Sea 163 F1
Fairfield Cotts. Cow 79 E1
Fairfield Cres. Hur 123 F3
Fairfield Gdns. Por S 164 C1
Fairfield Rd. Ash 118 C2
Fairfield Rd. Bos 170 C3
Fairfield Rd. Bur H 104 B2
Fairfield Rd. E Gri 21 E4
Fairfield Rise. Petw 93 E4
Fairfield Way. Ash 118 C2
Fairfield Way. Hay H 83 D4
Fairford Cl. Hay H 83 E3
Fairholme Dr. Yap 176 C1
Fairlands. Bog R 195 F3
Fairlands. E Pre 179 F1
Fairlawn Cres. E Gri 7 F1
Fairlawn Dr. E Gri 7 F1
Fairlawn Dr. Wing 182 A2
Fairlawn. Rust 179 D1
Fairlawns. Horl 1 C1
Fairlawns. S Sea 184 C4
Fairlea Cl. Bur H 104 B2
Fairlea Rd. Ems 147 F2
Fairlead. Lit 199 E4
Fairlie Gdns. Bri 166 B2
Fairlight Pl. Bri 188 A4
Fairmile Bottom. Hou 156 A4
Fairstone Ct. Horl 1 C2
Fairview Ave. Wing 181 D1
Fairview Rd. Lan 183 E4
Fairview Rise. Bri 166 A3
Fairway Cl. Copt 5 F1
Fairway Cres. Por S 165 D1
Fairway The. Mid 90 B3
Fairway The. Row C 126 B1
Fairway. Copt 5 F1
Fairway. Cra 16 A3
Fairway. Lit 199 F4
Faithfull Cres. Stor 116 C1
Falcon Cl. Cra 17 D4
Falcon Cl. S Sea 185 D3
Falcon Dr. Grays 8 C2
Falcon Gdns. Wick 178 A2
Falkland Ave. Lit 178 B1
Falklands Cl. Bog R 196 A3
Falklands Dri. Hors 35 F2
Fallow Deer Cl. Hors 35 F2
Fallowfield Cl. Hove 165 E1
Fallowfield Cres. Hove 165 E1
Fallowfield Way. Horl 1 C2
Falmer Ave. Wing 181 D1
Falmer Cl. Cra 17 D2
Falmer Cl. Wing 181 D1
Falmer Hill. Bri 167 F3
Falmer House Rd. Bri 167 F3
Faraday Ave. E Gri 21 E3
Faraday Cl. Wing 181 D3
Faraday Ct. Cra 4 B1
Faraday Rd. Cra 4 B1
Faresmead. Bog R 195 E1
Farhalls Cres. Hors 35 E3
Farlington Ave. Hay H 83 E3
Farlington Cl. Hay H 83 E3
Farm Ave. Hors 34 C2
Farm Cl. Bar G 54 B1
Farm Cl. Cra 17 F4
Farm Cl. E Gri 21 F4
Farm Cl. Hass 124 B2
Farm Cl. Hen 121 E3
Farm Cl. Lox 30 C2
Farm Cl. M Sea 197 F3
Farm Cl. Por S 164 C1
Farm Cl. Warm 34 B4
Farm Cnr. M Sea 197 F3
Farm La. Sou 169 F4
Farm Rd. E Wit 202 C3
Farm Rd. Hove 187 D3
Farm Rd. Wit 203 D3
Farm View. Ems 147 F2
Farm Way. Bur H 105 D1
Farm Way. Rust 178 C1
Farm Way. Sock 185 F4
Farm Yd. Bri 187 E3
Farman St. Hove 187 D3
Farmeadow Way. Ems 168 B4
Farmfield Dr. Hoo 4 A4
Farmleigh Cl. Cra 18 A4
Farmway Cl. Hove 165 D1
Farncombe Rd. Wing 182 B1
Farndell Cl. Chic 173 D4
Farne Cl. Bir 192 B2
Farne La. Bir 192 B2
Farnefold Rd. Stey 141 D2
Farnham Ave. Key 124 C3
Farnham Cl. Cra 38 A4
Farnham La. Hasl 25 F4
Farnham Rd. She 64 A4
Farnhurst Rd. Barn 175 F3
Farnlea Rd. Bur H 105 D3
Faroes The. Lit 178 C1
Farriers Cl. Bil 75 D4
Farringdon Rd. Hav 147 D2
Fasnet Way. Lit 178 C1
Fast Ct Way. Rust 179 E1
Faulkners Way. Bur H 104 C3
Fay Rd. Hors 35 D3
Faygate La. Fay 15 E2
Faygate La. Rusp 15 E2
Felbridge Ave. Cra 18 A4
Felbridge Cl. E Gri 8 A2
Felbridge Ct. E Gri 7 F2
Felbridge Rd. Cra D 7 D2
Felcot Rd. Cra D 7 D2
Felcourt La. Dor P 8 A4
Felcourt Rd. Dor P 8 A4
Fellcott Way. Hors 34 B1
Felpham Gdns. Bog R 196 C3
Felpham Rd. Bog R 196 B2
Felpham Way. Bog R 196 C3
Felride. Hay H 83 E2
Fenchurch Rd. Cra 18 A2
Fenhurst Cl. Hors 34 B1
Fennel Cres. Cra 16 C2
Fennel Wlk. S Sea 163 F1
Fereday Cl. Lan 183 E3
Fermandy La. Cra D 6 C1
Fern Cl. Pete 64 B2
Fern Rd. Stor 117 D1
Fern Way. Hors 35 D3
Ferndale Rd. Bur H 105 D1
Ferndale Rd. Chic 151 F2
Ferndale Rd. Hove 187 D4
Ferndale Wlk. Ang 179 F3
Fernden La. Hasl 26 A1
Fernden La. Lur 47 E3
Ferndown Gdns. Bog R 196 C3
Ferndown. Cra 5 D1
Ferndown. Cra 5 D1
Ferndown. Horl 1 C3
Fernhill Cl. Cra D 6 C1
Fernhill Rd. Burs 5 D4
Fernhill Rd. Cra 5 D4
Fernhurst Cl. Bri 166 C3
Fernhurst Cl. Cra 16 C4
Fernhurst Cres. Bri 166 C3
Fernhurst Dr. Wing 180 C1
Fernhurst Gdns. Bog R 195 D1
Fernwood Rise. Bri 166 A3
Feroners Cl. Cra 17 F2
Ferrier Cl. Rai (K) 76 A4
Ferring Cl. Cra 16 C4
Ferring Cl. Ferr 201 E4
Ferring Gdns. Bog R 196 C3
Ferring Grange Gdns. Ferr 180 B1
Ferring La. Ferr 180 B2
Ferring Marine. Ferr 201 E4
Ferring St. Ferr 180 B1
Ferringham La. Ferr 180 B1
Ferringham Way. Ferr 201 E4
Ferry App. Woolw 2 B4
Ferry Rd. Cli 177 F1
Ferry Rd. Cli 198 C4
Ferry Rd. S Sea 184 B3
Fetherston Rd. Lan 183 E4
Feversham Cl. S Sea 184 C3
Fiddlers Cl. Gree 22 B4
Field Cl. Bur H 104 B2
Field Cl. Lan 183 D3
Field Cl. Walb 155 D1
Field House. Rust 179 E1
Field Pl. Lip 24 A2
Field Pl. Lit 178 A1
Field Rd. E Wit 202 C4
Field Row. Wing 182 A1
Fieldend. Hors 35 F3
Fieldings The. Horl 1 C2
Fieldings The. Sour 77 E4
Fields End Cl. Hay H 83 E2
Fields The. Wgate 175 D3
Fieldview. Horl 1 C2
Fieldway. Dit 125 D2
Fieldway. Hasl 26 A4
Fieldway. Hay H 83 E4
Fiennes Way. Sev 98 C2
Fifth Ave. Hav 147 D1
Fifth Ave. Lan 183 E4
Fifth Ave. Wing 182 A4
Filbert Cres. Cra 16 C3
Filey Cl. Cra 16 B2
Filton Walk. Wing 181 D3
Finch Gdns. Bog R 195 F4
Fincham Cl. E Pre 179 E1
Finchdean Rd. Row C 126 B1
Finches Cl. Lan 183 D3
Finches Cl. Par G 100 C2
Finches Cl. Wick 178 A2
Finches Ct. Hay H 61 F1
Finches Gdns. Hay H 83 F4
Finches La. W Chi C 117 D4
Finches Park Rd. Hay H 83 F4
Findon By Pass. Find 160 A3
Findon Cl. Hove 165 E2
Findon Dr. Bog R 197 D3
Findon Rd. Bri 188 B3
Findon Rd. Cra 16 C4
Findon Rd. Wing 160 B1
Findon Way. Bro H 34 A2
Finians Field. Bar G 54 B1
Finisterre Way. Lit 199 F4
Finsbury Cl. Cra 17 D1
Finsbury Rd. Bri 188 A3
Finsbury Way. Bex 19 D3
Fir Tree Ave. Hasl 25 D3
Fir Tree Cl. Cra 3 F1
Fir Tree Cl. W Chi C 117 D3
Fir Tree La. W Chi C 117 D3
Fir Tree Rd. S Hay 189 D2
Fir Tree Way. Key 124 C2
Fircroft Ave. Lan 183 E4
Fircroft Cl. Bri 166 B2
Fircroft Cl. Wing 181 E3
Fircroft Cres. Rust 179 D2
Firlands. Hay H 83 E2
Firlands. Horl 1 C2
Firle Cl. Cra 17 E4
Firle Rd. Bri 188 A3
Firle Rd. Lan 162 A1
Firs Ave W. Bog R 196 C3
Firs Ave. Bog R 196 C3
Firsdown Cl. Wing 160 B1
Firsdown Rd. Wing 160 B1
Firside Gr. Sid 18 A2
First Ave. Bir 192 B1
First Ave. Bog R 196 C2
First Ave. E Wit 202 C3
First Ave. Hav 147 D1
First Ave. Hove 187 D3
First Ave. Lan 183 E4
First Ave. M Sea 197 E3
First Ave. Sou 169 E4
First Ave. Wing 182 A4
Firtoft Cl. Bur H 104 C2
Firtree Cl. Low B 57 F2
Fish La. Bog R 195 E1
Fish La. Sels 206 A4
Fishbourne Rd E. Chic 172 A3
Fishbourne Rd W. Chic 172 A3
Fishbourne Rd. Fise 171 F3
Fisher Cl. Cra 17 E2
Fisher La. N Mun 194 A4
Fisher La. Pla 28 C4
Fisherman's Wlk. Sels 206 C4
Fishermans The. Ems 169 D4
Fishermans Wlk. Bog R 195 D1
Fishermans Wlk. S Hay 189 F1
Fishermans Wlk. S Sea 184 A3
Fishers Cl. Lit 199 F4
Fishers Ct. Hors 35 D2
Fishery La. S Hay 189 E1
Fitch Dr. Bri 167 E1
Fitchet Cl. Cra 3 F1
Fittleworth Cl. Wing 180 C2
Fittleworth Dr. Bog R 197 D3
Fittleworth Gdn. Rust 179 D1
Fittleworth Rd. Wis G 73 E3
Fitzalan Rd. Aru 156 C1
Fitzalan Rd. Hors 35 F2
Fitzalan Rd. Lit 199 E4
Fitzalian Mews. Aru 156 C1
Fitzwilliam Cl. Bog R 195 E2
Five Acres. Cra 17 E4
Five Acres. Hamb 149 F3
Five Oaks Rd. Five O 54 A4
Five Oaks Rd. Slin 33 F1
Flag Sq. S Sea 184 B3
Flansham La. Bog R 197 D3
Flansham Park. Bog R 197 D3
Flatt Rd. Hamb 170 A4
Flax Mean. Bog R 196 C3
Flaxman Ave. Chic 172 A3
Fleet Cl. Lit 178 C1
Fleet The. Fit 94 C2
Fleming Centre The. Cra 4 B1
Fleming Way. Cra 4 B1
Fletcher Cl. Bog R 194 C1
Fletcher Cl. Cra 17 E2
Fletcher Cl. Run 173 D1
Fletcher Pl. Run 173 D1
Fletcher Rd. Wing 182 B3
Fletcher Way. Ang 179 E3
Fletcher's La. Bos 171 D1
Fletchers Cl. Hors 35 E1
Fletchers Field. Lip 24 A2
Fletchers La. S End 193 D2
Fletchers. Sour 55 E2
Fletching Cl. Bri 188 B3
Flexford Gdns. Hav 147 D2
Flimwell Cl. Bri 188 B2
Flimwell Cl. Bri 188 B3
Flint Cl. Por S 164 C1
Florence Ave. Hove 186 A4
Florence Cl. Bir 192 A2
Florence Pl. Bri 166 C1
Florence Rd. Bri 187 F4
Florence Rd. Chic 173 D3
Florets The. Upp B 141 F1
Florida Cl. Ferr 201 E4
Florida Gdns. Ferr 201 E4
Florida Rd. Ferr 201 E4
Florlandia Cl. Lan 182 C3
Flower Farm Cl. Hen 121 D3
Foamcourt Waye. Ferr 180 B1
Folders Cl. Bur H 105 D1
Folders La. Bur H 105 D1
Follett Cl. Bog R 195 E1
Folley La. Sut 113 E2
Fonthill Rd. Hove 186 C4
Fontwell Ave. Fon 154 B1
Fontwell Cl. Fon 154 C1
Fontwell Cl. Rust 199 F4
Fontwell Cl. Wing 181 F4
Fontwell Dr. Wing 181 F4
Fontwell Rd. Cra 17 F2
Fontwell Rd. Sels 206 C4
Ford Airfield Ind Est. Yap 176 C2
Ford La. Asht H 120 A4
Ford La. F 177 D2
Ford La. Yap 176 C2
Ford Rd. Aru 156 C1
Ford Rd. Cli 177 E3
Ford Rd. F 177 E3
Ford Rd. Tor 177 E3
Fordingbridge Cl. Hors 35 D1
Fordingbridge Cl. Maid 88 B1
Fordwater Gdns. Yap 176 C1
Fordwater La. Chic 151 F1
Fordwater Rd. Chic 151 F2
Fordwater Rd. E Lav 151 F3
Foredown Cl. Por S 164 C1
Foredown Dr. Por S 165 D1
Foredown Rd. Por S 164 C2
Foreland Ct. S Hay 189 E1
Forest Cl. Cra D 19 F4
Forest Cl. Hors 35 F2
Forest Cl. Man H 57 D3
Forest Cnr. Liss F 43 D4
Forest Lane Cl. Lip 23 F2
Forest Oaks. Hors 35 F2
Forest Rd. Bri 167 E3
Forest Rd. Colg 37 E3
Forest Rd. For R 22 C1
Forest Rd. Hors 36 B3
Forest Rd. Liss F 43 D3
Forest Rd. Mid 90 A3
Forest Rd. Wing 182 A3
Forest Ridge. Sha 41 F3
Forest Rise. Liss F 43 D3
Forest View Rd. E Gri 21 E3
Forest View. Cra 17 F2
Forester Rd. Cra 17 D2
Forestfield. Cra 17 F2
Forestfield. Hors 35 F2
Forestside Ave. Hav 147 D3
Forge Cl. Bro H 34 A2
Forge Cl. Chic 172 B2
Forge Cl. Chic 172 B2
Forge Cl. E Pre 179 E1
Forge Cl. Por S 164 C1
Forge La. Bro H 34 A2
Forge La. Cra 17 F4
Forge Rd. Cra 17 F4
Forge The. Sour 55 E1
Forge The. Warm 34 B4
Forge Way. Bil 75 D4
Forge Way. Bur H 104 C2
Forge Way. Padd W 139 E2
Forrester Rd. Par G 100 C2
Fort Haven. S Sea 185 D3
Fort Rd. Lit 178 A1
Fosters. Rust 200 B4
Foundry Cl. Hors 35 E2
Foundry La. Hasl 25 F3
Foundry La. Hors 35 E2
Foundry Rd. Yap 176 B2
Foundry St. Bri 187 F3
Fountains Cl. Bri 167 D1
Fountains Cl. Cra 16 C2
Four Marks Green. Hav 147 D3
Fourth Ave. Hav 147 D1
Fourth Ave. Hove 186 C3
Fourth Ave. Lan 183 E4
Fourth Ave. M Sea 197 D2
Fourth Ave. Wing 182 A4
Fowey Cl. S Sea 184 C3
Fowler Cl. Cra 18 A2
Fox Cl. Cra 3 F1
Fox Ct. Stor 116 C1
Fox Dell. Stor 116 C1
Fox Hill Cl. Hay H 83 E1
Fox Hill Village. Hay H 83 E1
Fox Hill. Hay H 83 E1
Fox Lea. Find 160 B3
Fox Rd. E 68 C1
Fox Rd. Hasl 25 E3
Fox Way. Por S 164 C1
Foxbury La. Wbou 148 B2
Foxdale Dr. Ang 179 E2
Foxes Cl. Sour 77 E4
Foxes Croft. Barn 176 A3
Foxfield Cotts. Sour 77 E4
Foxfields. W Chi C 117 D4
Foxglove Ave. Hors 35 E3
Foxglove Wlk. Cra 16 C2
Foxhole La. Bol 80 C1
Foxhunters Rd. Por S 164 B2
Foxleigh Chase. Hors 35 E3
Foxley La. Wing 181 E4
Foxwarren Cl. E Wit 202 B4
Foxwarren. Hay H 83 D3
Foxwells. Bal 39 F1
Framfield Cl. Cra 16 C4
Framptons The. E Pre 179 F1
France La. Pat 159 D1
Francis Edwards Way. Cra 16 B1
Francis Rd. Hay H 83 F4
Francis St. Bri 187 F4
Franciscan Way. Lit 178 A1
Frandor Rd. Bog R 195 E3
Frankland Mead. Was 139 E3
Frankland Terr. Ems 169 D4
Franklands Cl. Bur H 104 C1
Franklands Cl. Wing 160 C1
Franklands Gdns. Bur H 124 C4
Franklands Way. Bur H 124 C4
Franklin Pl. Chic 172 C4
Franklin Rd. Bri 188 A4
Franklin Rd. Cra 18 A3
Franklin Rd. Por S 186 A4
Franklin Rd. S Sea 164 A1
Franklin Rd. Wing 181 E4
Franklin St. Bri 188 A4
Franklynn Rd. Hay H 83 E2
Frankton Ave. Hay H 83 E2
Frant Rd. Hove 165 F1
Fraydene. Sou 169 E4
Fraser Cl. Sels 206 C3
Fraser Gdns. Sou 148 C1
Frederick Gdns. Bri 187 F3
Frederick Pl. Bri 187 F3
Frederick Rd. Chic 172 A4
Frederick St. Bri 187 F3
Freefolk Green. Hav 147 D3
Freehold St. S Sea 184 B4
Freehold Terr. Bri 167 D1
Freeks La. Bur H 104 C2
Freeks La. Bur H 104 C3
Freeman Rd. Warm 34 B4
Freemans Cl. Bil 75 D4
Freemans Rd. Por S 185 F4
French Gdns. Hay H 83 F3
Frenches Mead. Bil 75 D4
Frenches. Stor 117 D1
Freshbrook Cl. Lan 183 E3

Freshbrook Rd. Lan 183 E3
Freshfield Bank. For R 22 B1
Freshfield La. Dan 63 E1
Freshfield La. Hor K 85 D4
Freshfield Rd. Bri 188 A3
Freshfield St. Bri 188 A3
Freshfield Way. Bri 188 A3
Freshfield. Bri 188 A3
Freshfields Cl. Cra 17 F3
Freshfields Cl. Lan 183 D3
Freshfields R. Lan 183 D3
Friar Cl. Bri 166 C2
Friar Cres. Bri 166 C2
Friar Rd. Bri 166 C2
Friar Wlk. Bri 166 B2
Friars Cl. Hass 124 B2
Friars Oak Rd. Hass 124 B3
Friars Rookery. Cra 17 E3
Friars Wlk. Wing 181 E2
Friary Cl. M Sea 197 E3
Friary La. Chic 172 C3
Friary Way. Cra 17 E3
Friday St. Hors 14 B3
Friday St. Rusp 14 B3
Friday St. Warm 34 B4
Friends Cl. Cra 4 A1
Friston Cl. Bri 167 E2
Friston Wlk. Cra 16 C4
Friswell Pl. Bex 19 E4
Frith Park. E Gri 8 B2
Frith Rd. Bog R 195 F2
Frith Rd. Hove 186 C4
Frobisher Cl. Wing 181 D2
Frobisher Way. Rust 200 B4
Frobisher Way. Wing 181 D2
Froxfield Rd. Hav 147 D3
Fry Cl. Cra 16 C1
Fry Cres. Bur H 104 B3
Fryern Cl. Stor 117 D1
Fryern Rd. Stor 117 D2
Fryland La. Win 101 F2
Fulfords Hill. Itc 54 C4
Fulfords Rd. Itc 54 C4
Fulham Cl. Cra 16 C1
Fuller Cl. Wad 178 A1
Fullerton Cl. Hav 147 D3
Fulmar Cl. Cra 16 A3
Fulmar Cl. Hove 166 A1
Fulmar Dr. E Gri 8 C2
Furlongs The. Stey 141 D1
Furnace Dr. Cra 17 E2
Furnace Farm Rd. Cra 17 F2
Furnace Par. Cra 17 F2
Furnace Pl. Cra 17 F2
Furnace Rd. Cra D 7 D2
Furners La. Hen 121 F3
Furners Mead. Hen 121 E3
Furnston Gr. Sou 148 C1
Furse Feld. Bog R 195 F1
Furze Cl. Wing 160 A1
Furze Common Rd. Tha 117 F3
Furze Hill. Hove 187 D3
Furze La. E Gri 7 F2
Furze Rd. Rud 32 A4
Furze Rd. Wing 160 B1
Furze View. Five O 53 F3
Furzedown Cres. Hav 147 D3
Furzedown. Lit 199 E4
Furzefield Chase. Dor P 8 B3
Furzefield Cl. Ang 179 E4
Furzefield Rd. E Gri 8 A2
Furzefield Rd. Hors 35 F3
Furzefield. Cra 17 D4
Furzefield. Shi G 202 B3
Furzeholme. Wing 160 B1
Furzen La. Ell G 11 F2
Furzen La. Oak 12 A2
Fyning La. Rog 66 A3

Gabion Ave. Pur 6 C3
Gables Cl. SE12 16 B2
Gables The. Hors 35 D2
Gables The. Sour 77 E4
Gableson Ave. Bri 165 F2
Gage Cl. Cra D 7 D1
Gage Ridge. For R 22 B1
Gaggle Wood. Man H 57 D3
Gainsboro Rd. Bog R 196 A2
Gainsborough Ave. Wing 182 B4
Gainsborough Dr. Sels 206 B4
Gainsborough Rd. Cra 17 E2
Gaisford Cl. Wing 182 A2
Gaisford Rd. Wing 181 F2
Galahad Rd. Cra 16 B3
Gales Dr. Cra 17 E3
Gales Pl. Cra 17 E3
Galliers Cl. Bri 166 C3
Galsworthy Cl. Wing 180 C2
Galsworthy Rd. Wing 180 C2
Gander Cl. Bur H 104 C3
Gander Green. Hay H 83 E4
Gander Hill. Hay H 83 E4
Gannon Rd. Wing 182 B2
Garbitts La. Rog 65 F2
Garden Ave. E Wit 202 C3
Garden Centre Rd. Bri 167 F3
Garden Cl. Ang 179 F4
Garden Cl. E Gri 21 E4
Garden Cl. Lan 183 D3
Garden Cl. Por S 186 A4
Garden Cl. S Sea 163 F1
Garden Cl. Stor 117 D1
Garden Ct. Bog R 195 E1
Garden House La. Gri 21 E4
Garden Mead. W Hoa 41 E3
Garden Wlk. Cra 17 D3
Garden Wlk. Hors 35 D2
Garden Wood Cl. W Chi C 117 D3
Garden Wood Rd. E Gri 7 F1
Gardener Rd. Sock 185 F4
Gardonor St. Por S 185 F4
Gardeners Cl. Warm 34 B4
Gardeners Green. Rusp 15 D3
Gardens The. Fit 94 C2
Gardens The. Hav 147 D1
Gardens The. Por S 186 A4
Gardens The. Sock 185 E4
Gardner La. Cra D 19 F4
Gardner St. Bri 187 F3
Garland Ave. Ems 147 F2
Garland Cl. Chic 172 C3
Garland Rd. E Gri 8 A1
Garland Sq. Tan 153 D1
Garrett Cl. Cra 18 A2
Garrick Rd. Wing 182 B2
Garrick Wlk. Cra 17 E2
Garrones The. Cra 18 B4
Garson Rd. Sou 169 E4
Garton Cl. Cra 16 B3
Gaskyns Cl. Rud 32 A4
Gasson Wood Rd. Cra 16 B2
Gaston Way. M Lav 151 E4
Gatcombe Cl. Maid 88 C1
Gatcombe Cl. Wing 180 C3
Gateford Dr. Hors 35 E3
Gatehouse La. Bur H 104 A2
Gatehouse La. Tro 66 C2
Gatesmead. Hay H 83 E4
Gattons The. Bur H 104 B2
Gatwick Metro Centre. Ho 1 C2
Gatwick Rd. Cra 4 C2
Gatwick Way. Cra 4 B4
Gaugemaster Way. F 177 E3
Gaulder Cl. Hav 147 D2
Gay St. Gay S 97 D2
Gay Street La. N Hea 96 B3
Gayhurst Spinney. Tha 117 F3
Gaywood Wlk. Wing 181 D3
Geddes Pl. Bex 19 E4
Geddes Way. Pete 64 B2
Gemini Cl. Cra 16 B2
Genoa Cl. Lit 178 C1
George Denyer Cl. Hasl 26 A4
George Iv Wlk. Bog R 196 C3
George Pinion Ct. Hors 34 C2
George St. Bri 187 F3
George St. Chic 172 C4
George St. Hove 186 C3
George St. Por S 185 F4
George St. Sock 186 A4
George V Ave. Lan 183 F3
George V Ave. Wing 181 E1
Georges La. Stor 118 A1
Georgia Ave. Wing 182 A2
Georgian Cl. Cra 18 A3
Georgian Gdns. Rust 179 E1
Gerald Cl. Bur H 105 D2
Gerald Rd. Wing 181 E1
Gerard St. Bri 187 F4
Ghyll Cres. Hors 56 B4
Giblets La. Hors 35 E4
Gibson Rd. Tan 153 D1
Giffards Cl. E Gri 8 B1
Gifford Rd. Bos 171 D4
Gilbert Rd. Chic 172 B4
Gilberts The. Lit 199 F4
Giles Cl. Yap 176 B1
Gilham La. For R 22 B1
Gillam's La. Hasl 24 C3
Gillett Cl. Hors 35 F2
Gilligan Cl. Hors 34 C1
Gilligans The. Bur H 104 B3
Gillmans Ind Est. Bil 75 D3
Gillway. Sels 206 C4
Gilmore Rd. Chic 173 D3
Gilpin Cl. Fise 171 F3
Gilwynes. Bog R 195 E1
Ginhams Rd. Cra 16 C3
Glade The. Bog R 205 F4
Glade The. Cra 17 F2
Glade The. Hors 35 F2
Glade The. S Hay 189 E1
Glades The. E Gri 8 C1
Gladonian Rd. Wick 178 A2
Gladstone Pl. Bri 188 A4
Gladstone Rd. Bur H 105 D2
Gladstone Rd. Hors 35 D2
Gladstone Rd. Por S 185 F4
Gladstone Rd. Yap 176 B1
Gladstone Terr. Wick 178 A2
Gladys Rd. Hove 186 A4
Glamis Ct. Bog R 196 A2
Glamis St. Bog R 196 A2
Glanville Wlk. Cra 16 C2
Glaseby La. Was 139 D2
Glasshouse La. Petw 72 C3
Glastonbury Rd. Hove 186 A3
Glatting La. Sut 113 E1
Glaziers La. E 68 C1
Gleave Cl. E Gri 8 C1
Glebe Cl. Cra 17 E4
Glebe Cl. Lan 183 E4
Glebe Cl. Nor 153 F1
Glebe Cl. Sock 185 E4
Glebe Field Rd. W Ich 191 F3
Glebe Rd. Cuc 82 B3
Glebe Rd. Fer 46 C3
Glebe Rd. Wing 181 F3
Glebe The. Copt 5 F2
Glebe The. Fel 7 F2
Glebe The. Hay H 83 F4
Glebe The. Horl 1 B2
Glebe The. Tan 153 D1
Glebe Villas. Hove 186 A4
Glebe Way. Lan 183 E4
Glebe Way. Wis G 74 A4
Glebelands Cl. S Sea 184 C4
Glebelands. Cra D 19 F4
Glebelands. Lox 30 B2
Glebelands. Pul 96 A1
Glebeside Ave. Wing 181 F3
Glebeside Cl. Wing 181 F3
Glen Cres. Sels 206 B4
Glen Dale. Row C 126 B1
Glen Gdns. Ferr 180 B1
Glen Rise Cl. Bri 165 F3
Glen Rise. Bri 165 F3
Glen The. Sour 55 F1
Glen The. Wing 181 F4
Glen Vue. E Gri 8 B1
Glenbarrie Way. Ferr 180 B2
Glencathara Rd. Bog R 195 F2
Glendale Cl. Hors 35 F3
Glendale Rd. Bur H 104 C1
Glendale Rd. Hove 187 D4
Glendor Rd. Hove 186 B3
Glendyne Cl. E Gri 21 F4
Glendyne Way. E Gri 21 F4
Gleneagles Ct. Cra 17 D3
Glenelg Cl. Bog R 195 E3
Glenfalls Ave. Bri 166 C4
Glenlea Hollow. Hasl 25 E4
Glenleigh Park. Hav 147 D1
Glenvien Cl. Cra 17 E4
Glenview Pk. Cra 17 E4
Glenville Rd. Rust 200 A4
Glenway. Bog R 196 A2
Glenwood Ave. Bog R 196 A2
Glenwood Rd. Sou 148 C1
Gleton Ave. Hove 165 D1
Gloster Dr. Bog R 194 C1
Gloucester Cl. E Gri 21 F4
Gloucester La. Lit 178 A1
Gloucester Pas. Bri 187 F3
Gloucester Pl. Bri 187 F3
Gloucester Pl. Lit 178 A1
Gloucester Pl. Wing 182 A1
Gloucester Rd. Bog R 196 B2
Gloucester Rd. Bri 187 F3
Gloucester Rd. Bur H 104 B2
Gloucester Rd. Cra 17 E1
Gloucester Rd. Lit 178 A1
Gloucester St. Bri 187 F3
Gloucester Way. Chic 151 E1
Glover's Rd. Charl 3 D4
Glovers Field. Hasl 25 E3
Glynde Ave. Wing 180 C1
Glynde Cl. Ferr 180 B1
Glynde Cres. Bog R 196 C3
Glynde Pl. Hors 35 D1
Glynde Rd. Bri 188 A3
Goda Rd. Lit 178 B1
Goddard Cl. Cra 17 F2
Godolphin Ct. Cra 17 D3
Godstalls La. Stey 141 D1
Godwin Cl. Ems 147 F2
Godwin Rd. Hove 165 D1
Godwin Way. Fise 171 F4
Goffs Cl. Cra 17 D3
Goffs La. Cra 16 C3
Goffs Park Rd. Cra 17 D2
Goldcrest Ave. Wick 178 A2
Goldcrest Cl. Horl 1 B2
Golden Acre. Bog R 205 F4
Golden Acre. E Pre 200 C4
Golden Acre. W King 200 C4
Golden Ave Cl. W King 200 C4
Golden Ave. E Pre 179 F1
Golden Ave. W King 179 F1
Golden Fields. Lip 24 A2
Golden Hill. Bur H 105 D2
Golden La. Asht H 120 A3
Golden La. Bri 187 D3
Golden Sq. Hen 121 E2
Golden Sq. Petw 93 E4
Goldenfields Cl. Lip 24 A2
Goldfinch Cl. Cra 17 D4
Goldfinch Cl. Hors 35 D4
Golding La. Man H 57 D4
Golding's Hill. Man H 57 D4
Goldring Cl. S Hay 189 D2
Goldsmid Rd. Hove 187 E4
Goldsmith Rd. Rai (K) 62 A1
Goldsmith Rd. Wing 182 B2
Goldstone Cl. Hove 165 F1
Goldstone Cres. Hove 165 F1
Goldstone Ct. Hove 165 F2
Goldstone La. Hove 186 C4
Goldstone Rd. Hove 186 C4
Goldstone St. Hove 186 C4
Goldstone Villas. Hove 186 C4
Goldstone Way. Hove 165 F1
Golf Dr. Bri 166 C2
Golf Links La. Sels 204 B1
Golk Links Rd. Bog R 196 C3
Goodacres. Barn 176 A3
Goodhew Cl. Yap 176 C2
Goodman Cl. Bog R 195 D1
Goodwin Cl. Cra 16 B2
Goodwins Cl. E Gri 8 A2
Goodwood Ave. Bog R 196 B3
Goodwood Cl. Cra 17 F2
Goodwood Cl. Mid 90 B3
Goodwood Cl. Rust 179 E1
Goodwood Ct. Sou 169 F4
Goodwood Gdns. Run 173 E1
Goodwood Rd. Wing 181 F4
Goodwood Way. Bri 167 E2
Goose Green Cl. Hors 35 D3
Goosegreen La. Tha 98 A1
Gordon Ave W. Bog R 196 A3
Gordon Ave. Bog R 196 A2
Gordon Ave. Bog R 196 A3
Gordon Ave. Chic 172 B2
Gordon Ave. S Sea 184 C4
Gordon Cl. Hay H 83 E3
Gordon Rd. Bri 166 B1
Gordon Rd. Bur H 105 D2
Gordon Rd. Hay H 83 E3
Gordon Rd. Her 169 D4
Gordon Rd. Hors 35 D2
Gordon Rd. Lan 183 D3
Gordon Rd. Por S 185 F4
Gordon Rd. S Sea 184 C4
Gordon Rd. Sock 186 A4
Gordon Rd. Wing 182 A2
Goring Rd. Stey 141 E1
Goring Rd. Wing 181 D1
Goring St. Wing 180 C2
Goring Way. Ferr 180 B1
Goring Way. Par G 100 C2
Goring Way. Wing 180 C1
Goring's Mead. Hors 35 D1
Gorling Cl. Cra 16 B3
Gorringe Cl. S Sea 185 D4
Gorringes Brook. Hors 35 D3
Gorse Ave. Bog R 197 D3
Gorse Ave. K Gor 201 D4
Gorse Ave. Wing 181 F3
Gorse Bank Cl. Stor 118 A2
Gorse Cl. Copt 5 F1
Gorse Cl. Cra 16 C1
Gorse Cl. Por S 164 B2
Gorse End. Hors 35 D3
Gorse La. Wing 160 B1
Gorse Rd. Hav 147 D2
Gorse Rd. Pete 64 B2
Gorselands. Bil 75 E4
Gosden Cl. Cra 17 F3
Gosden Rd. Lit 178 B1
Gospond Rd. Barn 175 F3
Gossamer La. Bog R 195 D2
Gossops Dr. Cra 16 B3
Gossops Green La. Cra 16 C3
Goudhurst Cl. Cra 18 B3
Goudhurst Keep. Cra 18 B3
Gower Rd. Hay H 83 E2
Gowers Cl. Ard 61 F4
Grace Rd. Cra 16 C1
Graffham Cl. Bri 188 B3
Graffham Cl. Chic 151 F2
Graffham Cl. Cra 16 C4
Grafton Ave. Bog R 197 D3
Grafton Cl. Rust 178 C1
Grafton Dr. Lan 183 D3
Grafton Gdns. Lan 183 D3
Grafton Gdns. Lan 183 D3
Grafton Pl. Wing 182 A1
Grafton Rd. Sels 206 B3
Grafton Rd. Wing 182 A1
Grafton St. Bri 187 F2
Graham Ave. Bri 166 B3
Graham Ave. Por S 164 B2
Graham Cl. Por S 164 B2
Graham Cres. Por S 164 B2
Graham Rd. Wing 182 A1
Graham Rd. Yap 176 B1
Grailands Cl. Fer 47 D3
Granary Cl. Horl 1 C3
Granary Way. Hors 34 C1
Granary Way. Wick 178 A3
Grand Ave. Hove 187 D3
Grand Ave. Key 124 C2
Grand Ave. Lan 183 E4
Grand Ave. Wick 178 A2
Grand Ave. Wing 181 F1
Grand Junction Rd. Bri 187 F2
Grand Par. Bri 187 F3
Grand Par. S Hay 189 D1
Grange Cl. Bri 166 B1
Grange Cl. Bur H 105 D3
Grange Cl. Bur H 105 D3
Grange Cl. Cra 17 F4
Grange Cl. Ferr 180 B1
Grange Cl. Hav 147 D1
Grange Cres. Cra D 19 F4
Grange Ct. Bog R 195 E1
Grange La. Sels 204 C1
Grange Park Rd. Ferr 180 B1
Grange Rd. Cra D 19 F4
Grange Rd. Hove 186 B4
Grange Rd. Mid 90 B4
Grange Rd. Sock 185 E4
Grangefield Way. Bog R 195 D1
Grangeway The. Rust 179 D1
Grangeways. Bri 166 B3
Granston Way. Cra D 20 A4
Grant Cl. Sels 206 B4
Grant St. Bri 187 F4
Grantham Rd. Bri 166 C1
Grantsmead. Lan 183 E4
Granville Cl. Hav 147 D1
Granville Rd. Hove 187 E4
Granville Rd. Lit 199 E4
Grasmere Ave. Lan 182 C3
Grasmere Gdns. Hors 35 F3
Grassmere Cl. Bog R 196 B2
Grassmere Cl. Lit 178 C2
Gratten La. Twi 102 C2
Grattons Dr. Cra 5 D1
Grattons The. Slin 33 E2
Gratwicke Cl. Bil 75 D4
Gratwicke Rd. Wing 182 A1
Gravel La. Chic 173 D3
Gravelly Cres. Lan 183 E3
Gravelye Cl. Hay H 83 F3
Gravelye La. Hay H 83 F2
Graveney Rd. Cra 18 A3
Graveney Rd. Cra 18 A3
Gravett Ct. Bur H 104 B1
Gravetye Cl. Cra 17 F2
Gravits La. Bog R 195 F2
Graydon Ave. Chic 172 B2
Grays Cl. Hasl 26 B4
Grayswood Ave. E Wit 202 C3
Grayswood Rd. Hasl 26 A4
Great College St. Bri 188 A2
Great Daux Roundabout. Warn 34 C4
Great Hanger. Pete 64 A2
Great Heathmead. Hay H 83 D3
Greatfield Way. Row C 126 A2
Greatham Rd. Wing 160 C1
Greatlake Ct. Horl 1 C2
Greatpin Croft. Fit 94 C2
Grebe Cl. Hors 35 D3
Grebe Cres. Hors 56 C4
Green Acres. Hors 35 D2
Green Bushes Cl. Rust 199 F4
Green Cl. Sock 185 E4
Green Field Cl. Sock 185 D4
Green Hedges Ave. E Gri 8 A1
Green Hedges Cl. E Gri 8 A1
Green La. Bos 171 D3
Green La. Burs 5 E3
Green La. Chic 172 C4
Green La. Chic 173 E2
Green La. Copt 6 B2
Green La. Cra 17 E4
Green La. Cra 18 A3
Green La. Hamb 170 C4
Green La. Hors 14 B2
Green La. Hun 193 E3
Green La. Kin G 25 F2
Green La. Run 173 E1
Green La. Sels 206 B3
Green La. W Gri 77 F1
Green Lane Cl. Aru 156 B1
Green Meadows. Hay H 83 F4
Green Park Cnr. Wiv 105 F2
Green Pk. Ferr 180 B2
Green Pond Cnr. Hav 147 D1
Green Ridge. Bri 165 F3
Green The. Bog R 205 F4
Green The. Copt 5 F2
Green The. Cra 17 D4
Green The. E Lavn 112 B3
Green The. Hove 166 A1
Green The. Par G 100 C2
Green The. Row C 126 B1
Green The. Stor 117 E1
Green Way The. Wing 180 C2
Green Way. M Sea 197 E3
Green Wlk. Cra 17 E4
Greenacres Ring. Ang 179 F3
Greenacres. Ash 118 C3
Greenacres. Bir 192 A3
Greenacres. Cra 17 F3
Greenacres. S Sea 184 B4
Greenacres. Stey 141 D1
Greencourt Dr. Bog R 195 F3
Greenfield Cl. Bri 166 C3
Greenfield Cl. Lip 24 A3
Greenfield Cl. Nye 87 F4
Greenfield Cres. Bri 166 C3
Greenfield Rd. Chic 173 D4
Greenfield Rd. Slin 33 F3
Greenfield Way. Stor 117 E1
Greenfield. Sut 113 E1
Greenfields Cl. Horl 1 B3
Greenfields Cl. Hors 35 F3
Greenfields Rd. Horl 1 B3
Greenfields Rd. Hors 35 F3
Greenfields Way. Hors 35 F3
Greenfields. Liss 43 D2

Greenfields. Wick 177 F2
Greenfinch Way. Hors 35 D4
Greengates. Lur 48 A1
Greenhill Park. Hay H 83 F1
Greenhill Way. Hay H 83 F1
Greenhurst La. Stor 117 E2
Greenland Cl. Wing 181 E4
Greenland Rd. Wing 181 E4
Greenland Wlk. Wing 181 E4
Greenlands Cl. Bur H 124 C4
Greenlands Dr. Bur H 124 C4
Greenlea Ave. Bog R 194 C1
Greenleas. Hove 165 D1
Greenoaks. Lan 183 E4
Greenstede Ave. E Gri 8 B1
Greentree La. Par G 101 D3
Greentrees Cl. Lan 183 D3
Greentrees Cres. Lan 183 D3
Greenway. Hors 34 C2
Greenways Cres. Ferr 180 B1
Greenways Cres. S Sea 163 F1
Greenways Wlk. Cra 17 D1
Greenways. Bog R 194 C1
Greenways. Hay H 83 E3
Greenways. Hen 121 D3
Greenways. Sock 164 B1
Greenwich Cl. Cra 17 D1
Greenwood Ave. Bog R 195 F3
Greenwood Cl. Bog R 195 F3
Greenwood Ct. Cra 16 C1
Greenwood Dr. Ang 179 E2
Greet Rd. Lan 183 D4
Grendon Cl. Horl 1 B3
Grenville Ave. Wing 181 D2
Grenville Cl. Lip 24 A2
Grenville Cl. Wing 181 D2
Grenville St. Bri 187 E3
Gresham Pl. Hen 121 D3
Gresham Wlk. Cra 17 E2
Grevatts La. M Sea 197 F4
Greville Green. Ems 147 F2
Grey Alders. Hay H 83 F3
Greyfriars Cl. Bog R 195 E2
Greyfriars Cl. Wing 181 F3
Greyfriars La. Stor 138 A4
Greyhound Slip. Cra 18 A4
Greynville Cl. Bog R 195 D1
Greystoke Mews. Ferr 180 B1
Greystoke Rd. Ferr 180 B1
Greystoke Rd. Ferr 180 B1
Greystone Ave. Bog R 195 E4
Greystone Ave. Wing 181 E3
Gribble La. Chic 173 F4
Grier Cl. Cra 16 B3
Griffin Cres. Wick 178 A2
Griffith's Ave. Lan 183 D4
Grinder's La. Dia P 99 E1
Grinstead Ave. Lan 183 E3
Grinstead La. Lan 183 E3
Grinstead La. Sha 20 C1
Grisedale Cl. Cra 17 D2
Groombridge Way. Hors 34 B1
Grooms The. Cra 18 A4
Groomsland Dr. Bil 75 D3
Grosvenor Gdns. Bog R 195 D2
Grosvenor Rd. Chic 172 B2
Grosvenor Rd. E Gri 8 A1
Grosvenor Rd. Wing 182 A1
Grosvenor St. Bri 187 F3
Grosvenor Way. Bog R 195 D2
Grouse Rd. Colg 37 D2
Grouse Rd. Low B 57 F4
Grove Cres. Lit 178 B1
Grove Hill. Bri 187 F3
Grove La. Petw 93 F3
Grove La. W Chi C 117 E3
Grove Park. Chic 172 A3
Grove Rd. Bur H 104 C2
Grove Rd. Chic 172 C3
Grove Rd. Hav 147 D1
Grove Rd. Horl 1 B2
Grove Rd. Sels 206 B3
Grove Rd. Wing 182 A3
Grove St. Bri 187 F3
Grove St. Petw 93 E4
Grove The. Bog R 196 C2
Grove The. Cra 17 D3
Grove The. Ferr 180 B1
Grove The. Hay H 83 F2
Grove The. Horl 1 C1
Grove The. Lip 23 F2
Grove The. Wbou 148 A2
Grovelands Cl. Bur H 104 B1
Grovelands The. Lan 183 E2
Grover Ave. Lan 183 D4
Grundles. Pete 64 A2
Guernsey Cl. Cra 16 C1
Guernsey Farm La. Bog R 197 D3
Guernsey Rd. Ferr 201 E4
Guilden Rd. Chic 172 C3
Guildford Cl. Sou 148 C1
Guildford Cl. Wing 181 F2
Guildford Pl. Chic 151 E1
Guildford Rd. Bri 187 E3
Guildford Rd. Hors 34 C1
Guildford Rd. Row 33 F4
Guildford Rd. Rud 31 F4
Guildford Rd. Rud 32 B4
Guildford Rd. Rust 179 E1
Guildford Rd. Slin 33 E4
Guildford Rd. Wing 181 F2
Guildford St. Bri 187 E3
Guildhall St. Chic 172 C4
Guillards Oak. Mid 90 B4
Guillods Cts. Gra 111 F4
Guinevere Rd. Cra 16 B3
Guinness Ct. Cra 17 D1
Gunning Cl. Cra 16 C2
Gunns Farm. Lip 24 A1
Gunwin Ct. Bog R 195 D1
Gutner La. N Hay 168 B1
Gwynne Gdns. E Gri 8 A1

Habin Hill. Rog 65 F2
Hackenden Cl. E Gri 8 B2
Hackenden La. E Gri 8 B2
Haddington Cl. Hove 186 C3
Haddington St. Hove 186 C4
Hadley Ave. Wing 182 B4
Hadley Cl. M Sea 197 E3
Hadlow Cl. Bri 188 A3
Hadlow Way. Lan 183 E3
Hadmans Cl. Hors 35 D1
Hadrian Ave. Sock 185 F4
Haglands Copse. W Chi C 117 D4
Haglands La. W Chi C 117 D4
Haig Ave. Bri 167 D3
Hailsham Cl. E Pre 179 F2
Hailsham Rd. Wing 181 F1
Hales Ct. Ten 186 B2
Halewick Cl. Lan 183 D4
Halewick La. Lan 183 D4
Haleybridge Wlk. Tan 153 D1
Half Moon Hill. Hasl 26 A3
Half Moon La. Wing 181 E4
Halfrey Cl. Fise 171 F4
Halfrey Rd. Fise 171 F4
Halifax Cl. Cra 5 E1
Halifax Dr. Wing 181 D3
Hall Ave. Wing 181 F4
Hall Cl. Wing 181 F4
Halland Cl. Cra 17 F4
Halland Rd. Bri 167 E2
Hallett Rd. Bri 188 A4
Hallett Rd. Hav 147 D1
Halley Cl. Cra 16 C1
Halliford Dr. Barn 176 A3
Halliwick Gdns. Bog R 196 C2
Hallsland. Cra D 20 A4
Hallyburton Rd. Hove 186 A4
Halnaker Barn La. Box 153 F2
Halnaker Barn La. Nor 153 F2
Halnaker Gdns. Bog R 195 D1
Halnaker Wlk. Cra 16 B2
Halsbury Cl. Wing 182 B2
Halsbury Rd. Wing 182 B2
Halsford Green. E Gri 7 F2
Halsford La. E Gri 7 F1
Halsford Park Rd. E Gri 8 A1
Halton Shaws. Hur 123 F3
Ham Bridge Tdng Est. Wing 182 C2
Ham Cl. Wing 182 C2
Ham La. Ovi 174 A4
Ham La. Sca H 84 B2
Ham La. Sou 169 E4
Ham Manor Cl. Ang 179 E2
Ham Manor Way. Ang 179 E2
Ham Rd. High 204 A3
Ham Rd. S Sea 184 B4
Ham Rd. Sid 204 A2
Ham Rd. Wing 182 C2
Ham Way. Wing 182 C2
Hamble Gdns. Wing 181 D4
Hamble Rd. Lan 182 C3
Hamble Way. Wing 181 D4
Hambleton Hill. Cra 17 D2
Hambrook Hill N. Hamb 149 D2
Hambrook Hill S. Hamb 149 D1
Hambrook. Bur H 105 D1
Hamilton Cl. Por S 164 C2
Hamilton Cl. Ste 67 E1
Hamilton Cl. Wing 182 B3
Hamilton Gdns. Bog R 195 D1
Hamilton Rd. Bri 187 E4
Hamilton Rd. Hors 34 C2
Hamilton Rd. Lan 183 D4
Hammer A. Bram 25 D3
Hammer Hill. Hasl 25 D2
Hammer Hill. Low B 57 D3
Hammer Hill. Sta 59 F2
Hammer La. Bram 25 D4
Hammer La. Chit 67 D2
Hammer La. Hasl 25 D4
Hammer Yd. Cra 17 D3
Hammerpond Rd. Hors 56 C4
Hammerpond Rd. Man H 57 E4
Hammerwood Rd. Ash W 22 A3
Hammingden La. W Hoa 41 E2
Hammond Dr. Wing 181 E4
Hammonds Ridge. Bur H 104 B1
Hammy Cl. S Sea 185 D4
Hammy La. S Sea 184 C4
Hammy Way. S Sea 184 C4
Hampden Cl. Cra 5 E1
Hampden Cl. M Sea 197 E3
Hampden Rd. Bri 188 A4
Hamper's La. Hors 35 F1
Hampers Ct. Hors 35 D1
Hampers Green. Petw 71 E1
Hampers La. Stor 117 F1
Hampshire Ave. Bog R 195 F3
Hampshire Ct. Bri 188 A2
Hampshire Hill. Nuth 56 C1
Hampstead Rd. Hove 166 A1
Hampstead Wlk. Cra 17 D1
Hampton Ct. Bog R 195 E2
Hampton Ct. Lit 178 A1
Hampton Fields. Wick 178 A1
Hampton Pl. Bri 187 E3
Hampton St. Bri 187 E3
Hampton Way. E Gri 21 E4
Hamsey Cl. Bri 188 B3
Hamsey Rd. Sha 41 F3
Hamshire. Sla 58 B3
Hamsland. Hor K 63 D2
Hamstead Meadow. Chid 170 B4
Hanbury La. Hay H 83 F3
Hanbury Rd. Cra 16 B3
Handcross Rd. Bal 39 D2
Handcross Rd. Low B 58 A3
Handford Way. Han 58 A3
Hanger Way. Pete 64 A2
Hangleton Cl. Hove 165 D1
Hangleton Gdns. Hove 165 D1
Hangleton Grange. Ferr 180 B2
Hangleton La. Ferr 180 A2
Hangleton La. Hove 165 D1
Hangleton Manor Cl. Hove 165 D1
Hangleton Rd. Hove 165 E1
Hangleton Valley Dr. Hove 165 D2
Hangleton Way. Hove 165 D2
Hanlye La. Cuc 82 C4
Hannah Sq. Chic 172 A4
Hannington Pl. Hur 123 F4
Hanover Cl. Bury 135 F4
Hanover Cl. Cra 17 E2
Hanover Cl. Sels 206 C4
Hanover Cres. Bri 187 F4
Hanover St. Bri 187 F4
Hanover Terr. Bri 187 F4
Hanover Wlk. Stor 117 D1
Harberton Cres. Chic 151 F2
Harbolets Rd. Tha 97 F3
Harbolets Rd. W Chi 97 F3
Harborough Cl. W Chi C 116 C4
Harborough Dr. W Chi C 116 C4
Harborough Gorse. W Chi C 116 C4
Harborough Hill. W Chi C 116 C4
Harborough Meadow. W Chi 116 C4
Harbour Court. Bos 171 D3
Harbour Rd. Bog R 205 E4
Harbour Rd. Bos 170 C2
Harbour View Rd. Bog R 205 F4
Harbour Way. Bos 171 D2
Harbour Way. Chid 170 B3
Harbour Way. Ems 169 D4
Harbour Way. S Sea 184 C3
Harcourt Way. Sels 206 C4
Hard The. M Sea 198 A3
Hard's Hill. Hors 56 A3
Hardbarrow Woods. Tha 117 F3
Hardham Cl. Cra 16 C4
Hardham Cl. Rust 199 F4
Hardham Rd. Chic 172 C2
Hardwick Cres. Dart 21 E3
Hardwick Rd. Hove 165 E2
Hardy Cl. Bog R 197 D3
Hardy Cl. Cra 18 A4
Hardy Cl. Hors 34 C2
Hardy Cl. S Sea 184 B3
Hare La. Cra 16 C4
Harebell Dr. Por S 164 C2
Harefield Ave. Wing 181 E2
Harefield Gdns. M Sea 197 E3
Harefield Rd. M Sea 197 E3
Hares La. Fun 149 E3
Haresfield Terr. Tan 153 D1
Haresfoot Cl. Fun 149 E3
Harewood Cl. Cra 4 C1
Harlands Cl. Hay H 83 D3
Harlands Rd. Hay H 83 D3
Harlech Cl. Wing 180 C3
Harmans Dr. E Gri 8 C1
Harmans Mead. E Gri 8 C1
Harmony Cl. Cra 16 B2
Harmony Dr. E Wit 202 C3
Harmsworth Cres. Hove 165 E2
Harold Rd. Cra 18 B3
Harold Rd. S Hay 189 D1
Harold Rd. Wbou 148 A2
Harrier Ct. Cra 5 D1
Harrier Way. Pete 64 B1
Harrington Pl. Bri 166 C1
Harrington Rd. Bri 166 B1
Harrington Villas. Bri 166 B1
Harriot's Hill. Map 78 C4
Harriots Cl. Nuth 56 C1
Harris Cl. Cra 16 C2
Harris Path. Cra 16 C2
Harrison Ct. Wing 182 B3
Harrison Rd. Wing 182 B3
Harrow Dr. E Wit 202 B4
Harrow La. She 64 A4
Harrow Rd. Wing 181 F2
Harrow Way. Thu 90 A1
Harrows The. Til 92 C4
Harrowsley Ct. Horl 1 C2
Harsfold Cl. Lit 199 F4
Harsfold Rd. Lit 199 F4
Hartfield Ave. Bri 166 C3
Hartfield Rd. For R 22 C1
Harting Cl. Wing 180 C2
Harting Ct. Cra 16 B2
Harting Down. Pete 64 A2
Harting Rd. Wick 178 A2
Hartings The. Bog R 197 D3
Hartington Pl. Bri 188 A4
Hartington Rd. Bri 188 A4
Hartington Terr. Bri 188 A4
Hartington Villas. Hove 186 C4
Hartland Ct. Sou 148 B1
Hartlands Cl. Bex 19 D3
Harvel Cl. Orp 35 E1
Harvest Cl. Hay H 83 F4
Harvest Hill. Ans 82 C2
Harvest Hill. E Gri 21 E4
Harvest Way. Cra 18 A2
Harvesters. Hors 35 D3
Harvey Cl. Cra 16 C1
Harvey Rd. Wing 181 E1
Harwarden Cl. Cra D 20 A4
Harwood Ave. Wing 181 D2
Harwood Park. Sal 1 C4
Harwood Rd. Hors 35 F2
Harwood Rd. Lit 178 A1
Harwood's La. E Gri 21 E3
Harwoods Cl. Gri 21 E4
Hasle Dr. Hasl 25 F3
Haslemere Gdns. S Hay 189 F1
Haslemere Rd. Fer 46 C4
Haslemere Rd. Kin G 46 C4
Haslemere Rd. Lip 24 A2
Haslemere Rd. Sou 148 B1
Haslett Ave E. Cra 17 F3
Haslett Ave W. Cra 17 D3
Haslingbourne La. Petw 93 E3
Hassocks Ct. Cra 16 B2
Hassocks Rd. Hur 123 F3
Haste Hill. Hasl 26 A3
Hastings Cl. Bog R 195 E2
Hastings Rd. Bri 188 A4
Hastings Rd. Cra 18 A3
Hastings Rd. Wing 181 F1
Hatch End. For R 22 B1
Hatch Hill. Kin G 25 F1
Hatch La. Kin G 25 F1
Hatch La. Liss 43 E2
Hatchetts Dr. Hasl 25 D4
Hatchgate Cl. Cuc 82 C3
Hatchgate La. Cuc 82 C3
Hatchgate. Hoo 1 B1
Hatchlands. Cuc 82 B3
Hater Bank Cl. Dart 20 A3
Hatfield Wlk. Cra 16 B1
Hatfield Wlk. Wing 181 D3
Hatherleigh Cl. Bog R 195 F3
Hatherleigh Gdns. Bog R 195 F3
Havant By Pass. Hav 168 A4
Havant Rd. Ems 168 C4
Havant Rd. N Hay 189 D4
Havelock Cl. Bog R 196 B2
Havelock Rd. Bog R 196 A2
Havelock Rd. Bri 166 B1
Haven Cl. SE9 17 D1
Haven Gdns. Cra D 6 C1
Haven Rd. Rud 32 A2
Haven Rd. S Hay 189 F1
Haven The. Lit 178 C1
Havengate. Hors 35 E3
Havenside. S Sea 184 B3
Havenstoke Cl. Chic 151 F1
Haversham Cl. Cra 17 E3
Hawke Cl. Rust 179 E1
Hawkesbourne Rd. Hors 35 E3
Hawkesmoor Rd. Cra 16 B2
Hawkhurst Rd. Bri 167 D3
Hawkhurst Wlk. Cra 17 F2
Hawkins Cl. Bog R 194 C1
Hawkins Cl. S Sea 164 A1
Hawkins Cres. S Sea 164 A1
Hawkins Rd. Cra 17 D2
Hawkins Rd. S Sea 164 A1
Hawks Pl. Bog R 195 F3
Hawksfold La E. Fer 46 C3
Hawksfold La W. Fer 46 C3
Hawkshaw Cl. Lip 24 A2
Hawkwood. Maid 88 B1
Hawley Rd. Lit 199 F4
Hawmead. Cra D 20 A4
Hawth Ave. Cra 17 E2
Hawth Cl. Cra 17 E2
Hawthorn Cl. Bur H 105 D3
Hawthorn Cl. Chic 172 B4
Hawthorn Cl. Cra 4 A1
Hawthorn Cl. Hors 35 D2
Hawthorn Cl. Rust 200 A4
Hawthorn Cres. Wing 182 A3
Hawthorn Gdns. Wing 182 A3
Hawthorn Rd. Bog R 195 F2
Hawthorn Rd. Wing 182 A3
Hawthorn Way. Por S 164 C2
Hawthorn Way. Stor 117 D1
Hawthorn Way. Stor 117 D1
Hawthorne Cl. Mid 90 A3
Hawthorne Gr. S Hay 189 D2
Hawthorne Pl. Eri 4 C3
Hawthorne Rd. Wick 178 A2
Hawthorns The. Bur H 104 C3
Hay Rd. Chic 172 C2
Haybarn Dr. Hors 35 E4
Haybourne Cl. Bri 188 B4
Haybourne Rd. Bri 188 B4
Haydon Cl. Bog R 195 D1
Hayes Cl. M Lav 151 E4
Hayes Cl. Por S 186 A4
Hayes La. Slin 33 D1
Hayes Wood Rd. Five O 53 E3
Hayley Rd. Lan 183 E4
Hayley's Gdns. Bog R 196 C2
Haylind Rd. Hay H 83 F3
Hayling Gdns. Wing 160 B1
Hayling Rise. Wing 160 B1
Haynes Rd. Wing 181 F2
Haynes Way. Wing 181 F2
Hayrick Cl. Thu 90 A1
Hayward Business Centre. Hav 147 D2
Haywards Cl. Bog R 196 C3
Haywards Rd. Bri 166 C3
Haywards Rd. Hay H 83 E2
Haywards. Cra 5 D1
Hazel Cl. Cra 4 A1
Hazel Cl. Cra D 20 A4
Hazel Cl. Por S 165 D2
Hazel Dr. Bur H 104 C1
Hazel Dr. Row C 126 A1
Hazel Gr. Aru 156 B1
Hazel Gr. Bog R 195 D2
Hazel Rd. Bog R 195 F3
Hazel Way. Cra D 20 A4
Hazelbank Cl. Lip 24 A2
Hazelbank Cl. Pete 64 A2
Hazelbank Mews. Lip 24 A2
Hazeldene Meads. Bri 166 A2
Hazeley Green. Hav 147 D3
Hazelgrove Rd. Hay H 83 E2
Hazelhurst Cres. Wing 160 B2
Hazelhurst Dr. Cra 18 B3
Hazelmead Dr. E Pre 179 F1
Hazelwick Ave. Cra 17 F4
Hazelwick Mill La. Cra 17 F4
Hazelwick Rd. Cra 17 F4
Hazelwood Cl. Stor 117 F1
Hazelwood Cl. Wing 182 B3
Hazelwood Rd. Par G 100 C2
Hazelwood. Cra 16 C3
Hazlehurst Cres. Hors 34 B1
Hazlewood Cl. Cra D 19 E4
Head Down. Pete 64 A2
Headley Cl. Cra 5 D1
Headley Rd. Lip 23 F3
Hearn Cl. Tan 153 D1
Hearnfield Rd. Wick 178 A2
Heartwood Chase. Hove 166 A1
Heartwood Chase. Hove 187 D4
Heath Cl. Bro H 34 B2
Heath Cl. Hay H 83 E2
Heath Cl. Hun 193 F4
Heath Cl. Man H 57 D3
Heath Hill Ave. Bri 167 F1
Heath Park Dr. Brom 34 A1
Heath Pl. Bog R 196 A4
Heath Rd E. Pete 64 A1
Heath Rd W. Pete 64 A1
Heath Rd. Hasl 25 D3
Heath Rd. Hay H 83 E3
Heath Rd. Pete 64 A2
Heath Way. Hors 35 D3
Heathcote Dr. E Gri 8 A1
Heather Bank. Hay H 83 D3
Heather Cl. Copt 5 F1
Heather Cl. Hors 35 D3
Heather Cl. W Ash 150 A2
Heather La. W Chi C 117 D3
Heather La. Wing 160 B1
Heather Rd. Pete 64 B2
Heather Way. Stor 117 E1
Heather Wlk. Cra 16 C2
Heatherlands. Horl 1 C2
Heatherstone Rd. Wing 182 C2
Heatherton Mews. Ems 147 F2
Heatherway. Fel 7 E4
Heatherwood. Mid 90 A4
Heathfield Ave. E Pre 179 E2
Heathfield Cl. Mid 90 B4
Heathfield Cl. Wing 181 E3
Heathfield Copse. W Chi C 116 C4
Heathfield Cres. Por S 164 B2
Heathfield Dr. Por S 164 B2
Heathfield Gdns. Mid 90 B4
Heathfield Green. Mid 90 B4
Heathfield Park. Mid 90 B4
Heathfield Rd. Pete 64 B2
Heathlee Rd. Dart 20 A3
Hebe Rd. S Sea 184 B4
Hechle Wood. Bog R 195 E1
Heckfield Cl. Hav 147 D3
Hedge End Wlk. Hav 147 D3
Hedge End. Barn 176 A3
Hedgehog La. Hasl 25 F3
Hedgerow Gdns. Ems 147 F2
Hedgerow The. Thu 90 A1
Hedgerows The. Grave 24 A1
Hedgers Hill. Aru 155 E1
Hedgers Hill. Walb 155 E1

Hedgeside. Cra 17 D1
Hedgeway. Bog R 197 D3
Heene Pl. Wing 182 A1
Heene Rd. Wing 181 F1
Heene Terr. Wing 181 F1
Heene Way. Wing 181 F1
Heghbrok Way. Bog R 195 F1
Heights The. Wing 160 C1
Helena Cl. Por S 165 D1
Hellingly Cl. Bri 188 B3
Helston Dr. Ems 147 F2
Helyer's Green. Wick 178 A2
Hemsby Wlk. Cra 17 F2
Henbane Ct. Cra 16 C1
Henderson Rd. Cra 16 C1
Henderson Way. Hors 55 E4
Henderson Wlk. Stey 141 D2
Hendon Ave. Lit 199 F4
Hendon St. Bri 188 A3
Henfield Cl. Bri 188 B3
Henfield Cl. Wing 180 C2
Henfield Rd. Sma D 142 B3
Henfield Rd. Upp B 142 A1
Henfield Way. Bog R 197 D3
Henfield Way. Hove 165 E2
Hengist Cl. Hors 34 C1
Henley Rd. Bri 188 B2
Henry Ave. Lit 178 C1
Henry Cl. Chic 173 D3
Henry St. Bog R 196 A2
Henshaw Cl. Cra 16 B2
Henty Cl. Cra 16 B2
Henty Cl. Walb 176 B4
Henty Cl. Wing 182 A2
Henty Gdns. Chic 172 B3
Henty Gdns. Chic 172 B3
Henty Rd. Ferr 201 E4
Henty Rd. Wing 182 A2
Henwood Down. Pete 64 A2
Hepplewhite Cl. Cra 16 C1
Herald Dr. Chic 172 C3
Herbert Rd. Bri 166 B1
Herbert Rd. Lan 162 A1
Herbert Rd. Somp 161 F1
Hercules Pl. Bog R 197 D3
Hereford Cl. Chic 151 E1
Hereford Cl. Cra 17 E1
Hereford St. Bri 188 A3
Herington Rd. Aru 156 B1
Herm Cl. Cra 16 C1
Herm Rd. Ferr 201 E4
Hermione Cl. Ferr 180 B2
Hermitage Cl. Run 173 D1
Hermitage La. E Gri 21 E4
Hermitage Rd. E Gri 8 A2
Hermitage The. Run 173 D1
Hermits Rd. Cra 17 E4
Hermongers La. Cox G 11 E1
Hernbrook Dr. Hors 56 B4
Herne Gdns. Rust 179 D1
Herne La. Rust 179 D1
Herne Rd. Pete 64 A2
Heron Cl. Bog R 195 F4
Heron Cl. Cra 17 D4
Heron Cl. M Lav 151 E4
Heron Mead. Bog R 205 E4
Heron Pl. E Gri 21 E4
Heron Quay. Her 169 D4
Heron Way. Hors 35 F1
Heron's Ct. Cl 200 A4
Herondale. Hasl 25 E3
Herons Cl. Dom 6 C3
Herons Cl. Kir 50 C1
Herons Lea. Dom 6 C3
Herons The. S Sea 184 C4
Heronswood Ct. Horl 1 C2
Herontye Dr. E Gri 21 E4
Herrick Cl. Cra 18 A4
Hersee Way. Sels 206 A4
Hertford Cl. Bog R 195 E2
Hertford Rd. Bri 166 C1
Hertford Rd. Wing 182 A2
Heston Ave. Bri 166 B4
Heston Gr. Bog R 195 D1
Hevers Ave. Horl 1 C2
Hewart's La. Bog R 195 D2
Hewitts. Hen 121 E2
Hewshott Gr. Lip 24 B3
Hewshott La. Bram 24 B3
Hexham Cl. Cra 18 B3
Heyshott Cl. Lan 183 E4
Hickling Wlk. Cra 17 F2
Hickman's Cl. Hay H 83 F4
Hickman's La. Hay H 83 F4
Hickstead La. Hic 103 D3
Hide Gdns. Rust 178 C1
High Bank. Hun 193 E4
High Bar La. Tha 117 E3
High Beech La. Hay H 61 E1
High Beeches La. Bal 38 C2
High Beeches La. Han 38 B1
High Cl. Por S 164 C1
High La. Hasl 26 A4
High Meadow. Coc 110 A4
High Oaks. Cra 16 C2
High Park Ave. Hove 165 E2
High Point. Hay H 83 F2
High Ridge Cl. Aru 156 B1
High Spinney. W Chi C 117 E3
High St. Amb 136 B4
High St. Ang 179 F3
High St. Ard 61 F4
High St. Aru 156 C2
High St. Bal 39 D3
High St. Bil 75 D4
High St. Bog R 196 A1
High St. Bog R 196 A2
High St. Bos 170 C2
High St. Bri 187 F3
High St. Chic 172 B4
High St. Cra 17 D3
High St. Cuc 82 B3
High St. Dit 125 D2
High St. E Gri 21 E4
High St. Ems 168 C4
High St. Find 160 B3
High St. Grays 8 B2
High St. Han 59 D4
High St. Hasl 26 A4
High St. Hay H 83 F4
High St. Hen 121 E2
High St. Horl 1 C2
High St. Hur 123 F3
High St. Lit 178 A1
High St. Ovi 174 A3
High St. Par G 100 C2
High St. Pen 151 E4
High St. Petw 93 E4
High St. Rusp 15 D4
High St. S Sea 184 B4
High St. Sels 206 B4
High St. Stey 141 D2
High St. Stor 117 D1
High St. Upp B 141 F1
High St. Wing 181 F3
High St. Wing 182 B1
High Titten. Amb 136 B3
High Trees. Bog R 195 E1
High Trees. Hay H 83 E3
High Trees. Hun 172 C1
High View. Wing 160 B1
Highams Hill. Cra 16 B3
Highbank. Bri 166 A3
Highbarn. Find 160 B4
Highbrook Cl. Bri 167 D2
Highbrook Cl. Hors 35 F3
Highbury Gr. Hasl 26 A4
Highclere Way. Wing 180 C3
Highcroft Ave. Bog R 196 A3
Highcroft Cl. Bog R 196 B3
Highcroft Cres. Bog R 196 B3
Highcroft Dr. Rud 11 E1
Highcroft Rd. Sha 41 F3
Highdown Ave. Wing 181 F3
Highdown Cl. Ferr 180 B2
Highdown Cl. Sock 164 B1
Highdown Ct. Cra 17 F2
Highdown Dr. Lit 178 B1
Highdown Dr. Wick 178 B2
Highdown Rd. Hove 187 E4
Highdown Way. Ferr 180 B2
Highdown Way. Hors 35 E3
Highdown. Sock 164 B1
Highercombe Rd. Hasl 26 B4
Highfield Cl. Ang 179 F3
Highfield Cl. E 68 C1
Highfield Cres. Bri 166 C3
Highfield Dr. Hur 123 F3
Highfield Farm. Ovi 174 A4
Highfield Gdns. Bog R 196 A3
Highfield Gdns. Liss 43 D2
Highfield Gdns. Rust 199 F4
Highfield La. Lip 24 B2
Highfield La. Ovi 174 A4
Highfield Rd. Bog R 196 A3
Highfield Rd. E Gri 8 A2
Highfield Rd. Wing 181 F3
Highfields. Bri 167 E3
Highfields. For R 22 B1
Highgate Ct. Cra 17 D1
Highgate Dr. Bog R 195 F3
Highgate Rd. For R 22 B1
Highground La. Barn 175 F2
Highgrove Gdns. Wing 181 F1
Highland Ave. Bog R 195 F2
Highland Cl. Ems 168 C4
Highland Ct. Hay H 83 E2
Highland Rd. Chic 151 F1
Highland Rd. Ems 168 C4
Highland Rd. Hay H 83 E2
Highlands Ave. Hors 35 E1
Highlands Cl. Key 124 C2
Highlands Cl. Wing 160 B1
Highlands Cres. Hors 35 E1
Highlands Dr. Bur H 104 C2
Highlands Rd. Hors 35 E1
Highlands Rd. Por S 164 C1
Highleigh Rd. High 193 D1
Highstanding La. W Lav 90 C3
Highstead La. Lic 69 F4
Highview Ave N. Bri 166 B3
Highview Ave S. Bri 166 B3
Highview Rd. Bri 166 B3
Highview Rd. Eas 175 E4
Highview Way. Bri 166 B3
Highview. Lan 162 A1
Highway Cl. Bri 167 D1
Highway The. Bri 167 E2
Highways. Por S 164 C1
Hilary Gdns. Chath 59 D3
Hilary Rd. Chic 172 B4
Hildon Cl. Wing 181 D3
Hill Barn La. Wing 182 A4
Hill Brow Rd. Hill B 43 D1
Hill Brow. Hove 165 F2
Hill Cl. Poy 144 A3
Hill Court. Hasl 25 F3
Hill Crest. Dor P 8 B3
Hill Drive. Hove 165 F2
Hill Farm La. Pul 95 F3
Hill Farm Way. Sock 164 B1
Hill House Hill. Lip 23 F3
Hill La. Bal 39 F1
Hill La. Barn 176 A2
Hill La. E Har 87 E1
Hill La. Har 87 E1
Hill Mead. Hors 34 C2
Hill Rd. Hasl 26 A3
Hill Rd. Lit 178 B1
Hill Terr. Aru 156 B1
Hill Top. Bri 165 F3
Hill View. Els 88 A2
Hillary Cl. E Gri 8 C2
Hillbank Cl. Por S 164 B2
Hillbarn Ave. Lan 162 A1
Hillbarn La. Coc 110 A3
Hillbrow Cl. Row C 126 A1
Hillbrow Rd. Bri 166 A2
Hillcrest Cl. Ash 118 C3
Hillcrest Cl. Cra 18 A3
Hillcrest Cl. Sca H 84 B2
Hillcrest Dr. Ash 118 C3
Hillcrest La. Sca H 84 B2
Hillcrest. Bri 166 A3
Hillcroft. Por S 164 B1
Hillfield Rd. Sels 206 B3
Hillhouse Cl. Tur H 19 F2
Hillhouse La. Cran 10 B1
Hillingdale. Cra 17 D1
Hillmead. Cra 16 B3
Hillrise Ave. Lan 183 D4
Hills Farm La. Hors 34 B1
Hills Pl. Hors 34 C1
Hills Rd. Stey 141 D1
Hillsboro Rd. Bog R 196 A2
Hillside Ave. Wing 181 F4
Hillside Cl. Cra 16 C2
Hillside Cl. E Gri 8 B2
Hillside Cres. Ang 179 F3
Hillside La. Sma D 142 B3
Hillside Rd. Hasl 25 E3
Hillside Rd. Lan 162 A1
Hillside Rd. Stor 117 F1
Hillside Way. Bri 166 A2
Hillside Wlk. Hay H 83 D3
Hillside Wlk. Stor 117 F1
Hillside. Bri 167 E1
Hillside. Cra D 19 F4
Hillside. For R 22 B2
Hillside. Hors 34 C1
Hillside. Por S 165 D1
Hillside. Sock 164 B1
Hilltop Rd. W Hoa 41 E3
Hillview Cres. E Pre 179 F1
Hillview Gdns. Cra 38 A4
Hillview Rd. Wing 160 B1
Hillview Rd. Wood 188 C4
Hillview Rise. Wing 160 B1
Hillybarn Rd. Rusp 3 D1
Hiltingbury Ave. Hav 147 D3
Hilton Park. E Wit 202 C4
Hinde Rd. Bog R 197 D2
Hinde Rd. M Sea 197 D2
Hindhead Cl. Cra 17 D2
Hindhead Rd. Hasl 25 E4
Hinton Cl. Bri 167 D1
Hipley Rd. Hav 147 D2
Hoadlands. Pete 64 A2
Hobart Cl. Wing 181 D4
Hobbs Ind Est. Fel 7 D4
Hobbs Rd. Cra 16 C1
Hobbs Way. Rust 179 D1
Hobdens La. Ard 61 F4
Hoblands. Hay H 83 F2
Hobs Acre. Upp B 141 F1
Hocken Mead. Cra 18 A4
Hodges Cl. Hav 147 D2
Hodshrove La. Bri 167 E2
Hodshrove Rd. Bri 167 E2
Hoe Court. Lan 162 C1
Hoe La. Bog R 196 C4
Hoe La. Bos 171 E2
Hoe La. Walb 177 D4
Hoewood. Sma D 142 B4
Hog La. Amb 136 B4
Hog's Hill. Cra 17 D2
Hogarth Rd. Cra 17 E2
Hogarth Rd. Hove 186 B4
Hoggarth Cl. Pete 64 E4
Hogspudding La. Newd 2 A4
Hogwood Rd. Ifo 30 A2
Holbein Rd. Cra 17 E2
Holdens Farm Caravan Park. Earn 203 D4
Holdens The. Bos 170 C3
Holders. Alb 123 D3
Holdfast La. Hasl 26 B4
Hole St. Ash 118 C2
Hole St. Wist 119 F4
Holford Green. Sels 206 C4
Holland Cl. Bog R 195 E3
Holland Mews. Hove 187 D3
Holland Rd. Hove 187 D3
Holland Rd. Stey 141 E2
Holland St. Bri 187 F3
Hollands La. Hen 121 D2
Hollands Rd. Hen 121 D3
Hollands Way. E Gri 8 C2
Hollands Way. Warm 34 B4
Hollin Ct. Cra 4 B1
Hollingbourne Cres. Cra 38 A4
Hollingbury Copse. Bri 166 C2
Hollingbury Cres. Bri 166 C1
Hollingbury Gdns. Wing 160 C1
Hollingbury Park Ave. Bri 166 C1
Hollingbury Pl. Bri 166 C1
Hollingbury Rd. Bri 166 C1
Hollingbury Rise W. Bri 166 C1
Hollingbury Rise. Bri 166 C1
Hollingbury Terr. Bri 166 C1
Hollingdean Rd. Bri 188 A4
Hollingdean St. Bri 166 C1
Hollingdean Terr. Bri 166 C1
Hollist La. E 68 B1
Hollist La. E Har 87 E2
Hollist La. Wool 68 B1
Hollow La. Dor 9 D3
Hollow La. S Hay 189 D2
Hollow The. Bury 135 F4
Hollow The. Cra 16 B3
Hollow The. Hay H 83 F3
Hollow The. W Chi 97 D1
Hollow The. W Hoa 41 E3
Hollow The. Was 139 E4
Holly Cl. Bri 166 B2
Holly Cl. Cra 17 F4
Holly Cl. Hors 35 F3
Holly Cl. Stor 117 D1
Holly Cl. W Chi 97 D1
Holly Cl. Wing 181 D3
Holly Ct. Stor 117 D1
Holly Dr. Tod 178 B2
Holly Mews. Hur 123 F3
Holly Rd. Hay H 83 F2
Hollybank La. Ems 147 F2
Hollybrook School La. Hors 35 E4
Hollybush Rd. Cra 17 E4
Hollycombe Cl. Lip 24 A1
Hollyridge. Hasl 25 F3
Hollywater Rd. Lip 23 D4
Holmans. Ard 61 F4
Holmbury Cl. Cra 17 D2
Holmbush Cl. Hay H 83 E1
Holmbush Cl. Hors 35 D3
Holmbush Cl. S Sea 164 A1
Holmbush Ind Est. Mid 90 B3
Holmbush La. Wcote H 143 E4
Holmbush Way. Mid 90 A3
Holmbush Way. Sock 164 B1
Holmcroft Gdns. Find 160 B3
Holmcroft. Cra 17 E3
Holmes Ave. Hove 165 E1
Holmes La. Lit 199 F4
Holmes La. Rust 199 F4
Holmesdale Rd. Bur H 104 C1
Holming End. Hors 35 F3
Holmsted Hill. Whi G 59 F1
Holmwood Cl. W Wit 191 D1
Holt Down. Pete 64 A2
Holt Gdns. Row C 126 A2
Holt The. Bur H 105 D1
Holt The. Was 139 E4
Holtview Rd. Wood 188 C4
Holtye Ave. E Gri 8 C2
Holtye Rd. E Gri 8 C2
Holtye Wlk. Cra 17 F2
Holyrood Pl. Cra 16 C1
Holyrood. E Gri 21 F4
Home Cl. Cra 18 A4
Home Farm Rd. Bri 167 D2
Home Platt. Sha 41 F3
Home Rd. Bri 166 B1
Homefield Ave. Bog R 197 D3
Homefield Cl. Horl 1 C2
Homefield Cl. Rust 178 C1
Homefield Cres. Walb 155 D1
Homefield Rd. Wbou 148 A2
Homefield Rd. Wing 182 B2
Homelands Ave. E Pre 200 C4
Homelands Copse. Fer 47 D4
Homestead Mews. Ferr 180 B1
Homestead The. E Pre 179 F1
Homewood. Find 160 B4
Homing Gdns. Bog R 195 F4
Honer La. Bog R 194 A2
Honer La. S Mun 194 A3
Honey Croft. Hove 165 D2
Honey La. Ang 179 F3
Honeybridge La. Asht H 119 F4
Honeysuckle La. Cra 4 A1
Honeysuckle La. Find 160 A2
Honeysuckle Wlk. Hors 35 F3
Honeywood La. Oak 12 B3
Honeywood Rd. Hors 35 F2
Hooe The. Lit 178 C1
Hook La. Ald 174 C4
Hook La. Bog R 194 C1
Hook La. Bog R 196 A2
Hook La. Bos 171 E1
Hook La. W Hoa 41 D2
Hook La. Wgate 175 D3
Hooklands La. Bro C 98 C2
Hooks The. Hen 121 E2
Hop Garden La. N Mun 194 A4
Hop Gdn The. S Har 87 D2
Hopgarton The. Bog R 195 E2
Hophurst Cl. Cra D 19 F4
Hophurst Dr. Cra D 19 F4
Hophurst Hill. Cra D 7 D1
Hordens The. Bar G 54 B1
Horley Lodge La. Sal 1 C4
Horley Pl. Bri 188 B3
Horley Rd. Charl 3 F4
Horley Row. Horl 1 C2
Hormare Cres. Stor 117 D1
Horn La. Hen 121 F1
Horn La. Sma D 142 C4
Hornbeam Cl. Bog R 195 E1
Hornbeam Cl. Hors 35 E1
Hornbeam Rd. Hav 147 D2
Hornbrook Co. Hors 56 B4
Hornby Rd. Bri 167 F1
Horndean Cl. Cra 5 D1
Horndean Cl. Cra 5 D1
Horndean Rd. Ems 147 F2
Hornet Rd. Tho I 169 D2
Hornet The. Chic 172 C3
Hornpark Cl. SE12 16 B3
Horns La. Bog R 194 B1
Hornshill La. Rud 31 E4
Horse Hill. Hoo 1 A2
Horse Shoe The. Sels 206 B4
Horsebridge Hill. Petw 73 E1
Horsebridge Rd. Hav 147 D2
Horsefield Rd. Sels 206 B4
Horseshoe Cl. Cra 18 A4
Horseshoe Cl. Thu 90 A1
Horsgate La. Cuc 82 C3
Horsham By-pass. Hors 34 C3
Horsham Cl. Bri 188 B3
Horsham Rd W. Lit 178 B1
Horsham Rd. Asht H 120 A1
Horsham Rd. Cra 16 C2
Horsham Rd. Cran 10 A1
Horsham Rd. Cran 10 C4
Horsham Rd. Find 160 B4
Horsham Rd. Five O 53 F3
Horsham Rd. Han 58 C4
Horsham Rd. Hors 14 C2
Horsham Rd. Kin 14 A4
Horsham Rd. Lit 178 B1
Horsham Rd. Oak 12 A3
Horsham Rd. Pea P 37 F3
Horsham Rd. Row 12 B1
Horsham Rd. Rusp 14 C2
Horsham Rd. Stey 141 D4
Horsmere Green La. Cli 177 D1
Horsted La. Dan 63 F2
Horsted La. Sha 41 F2
Horton Rd. Bri 166 C1
Hoskins Pl. E Gri 8 C2
Hotham Way. Bog R 196 A2
Houghton Bridge. Amb 136 A2
Houghton La. Bury 135 F3
Hova Villas. Hove 186 C3
Hove Park Gdns. Ove 186 C4
Hove Park Rd. Hove 166 A1
Hove Park Villas. Hove 186 C4
Hove Park Way. Hove 166 A1
Hove Pl. Hove 186 C3
Hove Sea Wall. Hove 187 D3
Hove St. Hove 186 C3
Howard Ave. Bur H 104 B2
Howard Ave. E Wit 202 A4
Howard Pl. Bri 187 E4
Howard Pl. Lit 178 A1
Howard Rd. Aru 156 C1
Howard Rd. Bri 188 A4
Howard Rd. Cra 16 A1
Howard Rd. Cra 16 B1
Howard Rd. Hors 35 F2
Howard Rd. Lan 162 A1
Howard Rd. Lit 178 A1
Howard St. Wing 182 A2
Howard Terr. Bri 187 E4
Howards Way. Rust 199 F4
Hoylake Cl. Cra 16 A3
Hoyle La. Hey 111 D4
Hudson Cl. Wing 181 D3
Hudson Dr. Rust 200 B4
Hudson Rd. Cra 17 D2
Hudson Rd. Hay H 83 E3
Huffwood Tdng Est. Bil 75 D4
Huffwood Tdng Est. Par G 100 C2
Hughes Cl. Bog R 195 E2
Humber Ave. Wing 181 D4
Humber Cl. Lit 199 E4
Humber Cl. Wing 181 D4
Humber Rd. Dart 20 C3
Humphrys Rd. Wing 182 A1
Hundred Acre La. Dit 105 F1
Hundred Acre La. Wiv G 105 F2
Hungers La. Petw 93 D3
Hunstanton Cl. Cra 16 A3
Hunter Rd. Cra 17 D2

Hunter Rd. Tho I ... 169 D2
Hunter's Mead. Alb ... 123 D3
Hunters Chase. Lip ... 23 F3
Hunters Cl. Bog R ... 195 D1
Hunters Mead. Par G ... 100 C2
Hunters Race. Chic ... 151 D2
Hunters Way. Chic ... 151 E2
Huntingdon Way. Bur H ... 105 D3
Huntsbottom La. Liss ... 43 D2
Hurley Rd. Wing ... 181 E3
Hurst Ave. Hors ... 35 D2
Hurst Ave. Wing ... 181 E1
Hurst Cl. Amb ... 136 B4
Hurst Cl. Cra ... 16 B2
Hurst Cotts. Amb ... 136 B4
Hurst Cres. Por S ... 185 F4
Hurst Ct. Hors ... 35 D2
Hurst Farm Rd. E Gri ... 21 D4
Hurst Gdns. Hur ... 123 E4
Hurst Hill. Bri ... 167 D3
Hurst Hill. Hors ... 14 C1
Hurst Rd. Hass ... 124 A2
Hurst Rd. Horl ... 1 B2
Hurst Rd. Hors ... 35 D2
Hurst Rd. Rust ... 179 E1
Hurst Wickham Cl. Hur ... 124 A3
Hurstfield Cl. Hay H ... 83 F1
Hurstlands. Bil ... 75 D4
Hurston Cl. Wing ... 181 F4
Hurston Gr. Stor ... 116 C2
Hurston La. Stor ... 116 C2
Hurstwood Ave. Sou ... 148 C1
Hurstwood La. Hay H ... 83 F1
Hurstwood La. Hor K ... 42 A1
Hutchins Way. Horl ... 1 B3
Hutton Rd. Bri ... 166 C2
Hyde Dr. Cra ... 16 B3
Hyde La. Upp B ... 141 F1
Hyde Sq. Upp B ... 141 F1
Hyde St. Upp B ... 141 F1
Hyde The. Bri ... 188 B4
Hylands Cl. Cra ... 17 F3
Hylden Cl. Wood ... 188 C4
Hylters's La. Chil ... 109 D1
Hyperion Ct. Cra ... 16 B2
Hyperion Wlk. Horl ... 1 C1
Hythe Cl. Wing ... 181 F1
Hythe Rd. Bri ... 166 C1
Hythe Rd. Wing ... 181 F1

Icarus Way. Bog R ... 197 D3
Iden Cl. Bri ... 188 B3
Iden Hurst. Hur ... 123 F4
Ifield Ave. Cra ... 3 F1
Ifield Dr. Cra ... 16 C4
Ifield Rd. Charl ... 3 E3
Ifield Rd. Cra ... 17 D3
Ifield St. Cra ... 16 B4
Ifield Wood. Rusp ... 3 D1
Ifield Wood. Rusp ... 16 A4
Ifold Bridge La. Ifo ... 30 A2
Ifoldhurst. Ifo ... 30 A1
Ilex Cl. Rust ... 200 A4
Ilex Way. M Sea ... 197 E3
Ilex Way. Wing ... 180 C1
Ilex Wlk. S Hay ... 189 E1
Imberholme La. E Gri ... 7 F1
Imberhorne La. E Gri ... 20 C4
Imberhorne Way. E Gri ... 7 F2
Imperial Arc. Bri ... 187 E3
Industrial Estate. Pul ... 95 F1
Infirmary Terr. Chic ... 172 B4
Ingham Dr. Bri ... 167 D3
Inglegreen Cl. Ferr ... 201 E4
Ingleside Cres. Lan ... 183 E3
Ingleside Rd. Lan ... 183 E3
Inglewood Cl. Bog R ... 195 D1
Inglewood Dr. Bog R ... 194 C1
Ingram Cl. Hors ... 34 C1
Ingram Cl. Rust ... 178 C1
Ingram Cl. Stey ... 141 D1
Ingram Cres. Hove ... 186 B4
Ingram Rd. Stey ... 141 D1
Ingram's Green La. Els ... 89 D3
Ingram's Green La. Tre ... 89 D3
Inham's La. W Sto ... 150 C3
Inholmes Cl. Bur H ... 105 D2
Inholmes Park Rd. Bur H ... 104 C2
Ink Pen La. For R ... 22 B1
Inlands Rd. Sou ... 169 F4
Inmans La. She ... 64 A3
Innerwyke Cl. Bog R ... 196 C3
Innes Rd. Hors ... 35 E2
Institute Wlk. E Gri ... 8 B1
Inval Hill. Hasl ... 26 A4
Inverness Rd. Bri ... 188 A4
Inwood Cres. Bri ... 166 B1
Inwood Rd. Liss ... 43 D2
Iona Cl. Cra ... 16 C2
Iona Way. Hay H ... 83 E2
Iping La. Mil ... 67 E2
Iping La. Ste ... 67 E2
Irene Ave. Lan ... 183 D4
Irvine Rd. Lit ... 199 E4
Irving Wlk. Cra ... 17 E2
Irwin Dr. Hors ... 34 C2
Isaac's La. Bur H ... 104 B4
Isaac's La. Hay H ... 82 C2
Isabel Cres. Hove ... 186 B4
Isfield Rd. Bri ... 167 D1
Island Cl. N Hay ... 168 A2
Island La. Sels ... 206 A4
Island Loop. Sels ... 206 A4
Islingwood Pl. Bri ... 188 A3
Islingword Rd. Bri ... 188 A4
Islingword St. Bri ... 187 F3
Itchen Rd. Hav ... 147 D3
Itchenor Rd. S Hay ... 189 F1
Itchenor Rd. Shi G ... 191 F2
Itchenor Rd. W Ich ... 191 F2
Itchingfield Rd. Itc ... 54 C3
Ithica Cl. S Hay ... 189 D2
Ivanhoe Cl. Cra ... 4 A1
Ivanhoe Pl. Bog R ... 197 D3
Iveagh Cl. Cra ... 17 D1
Ivory Pl. Bri ... 187 F3
Ivory Wlk. Cra ... 16 B2
Ivy Arch Rd. Wing ... 182 A2
Ivy Cl. Ash ... 118 C3
Ivy Cl. Sour ... 55 E1
Ivy Cl. Wgate ... 175 D4
Ivy Cres. Bog R ... 196 A3
Ivy Dene La. Ash W ... 22 A3
Ivy La. Bog R ... 196 A3
Ivy La. Wgate ... 175 D4
Ivy Pl. Hove ... 187 D3
Ivy Pl. Wing ... 181 F1
Ivy Villas. Gree ... 22 B3
Ivydale Rd. Bog R ... 195 F2
Ivydene Cres. Chid ... 170 A4
Ivydore Ave. Wing ... 181 D4
Ivydore Cl. Wing ... 181 D4

Jackdaw Cl. Cra ... 17 D4
Jackdaw La. Hors ... 35 E3
Jacket's Hill. Stor ... 117 F3
Jackrells La. Sour ... 55 F2
Jackson St. Bri ... 187 F4
Jacobean Cl. Cra ... 18 A3
James Cl. Wing ... 181 E3
James St. Sels ... 206 B3
James Watt Way. Cra ... 4 C2
Jane Murray Way. Bur H ... 104 B1
Janes Cl. Bur H ... 105 D3
Janes La. Bur H ... 105 D3
Janes La. Lod ... 70 B2
Janes La. Wiv ... 105 E2
Japonica Cl. S Sea ... 163 F1
Jarvis La. Stey ... 141 D2
Jarvis Rd. Aru ... 156 B1
Javelin Ct. Cra ... 5 D1
Javelin Rd. Tho I ... 169 D2
Jay Cl. Sour ... 55 F1
Jay Gdns. SE9 ... 34 A4
Jay's La. Lur ... 27 D2
Jays Cl. Lit ... 178 A1
Jays The. Bur H ... 104 B2
Jays The. Lit ... 178 A1
Jeans Ct. Cra ... 16 C1
Jefferies La. Wing ... 181 D1
Jeffreys Ave. Chic ... 151 F1
Jengers Mead. Bil ... 53 D1
Jenner Rd. Cra ... 4 B2
Jeremy's La. Ward ... 81 D3
Jeremy's La. Whi G ... 81 D3
Jerrard Rd. Tan ... 153 D1
Jersey Rd. Cra ... 16 C1
Jersey Rd. Ferr ... 201 E4
Jersey St. Bri ... 187 F3
Jervis Ave. Rust ... 179 D1
Jesmond Cl. Hove ... 186 B4
Jesmond Rd. Hove ... 186 B4
Jesters. Bur H ... 105 D4
Jetty The. M Sea ... 197 F3
Jevington Cl. Wing ... 180 C3
Jevington Dr. Bri ... 167 D1
Jew St. Bri ... 187 F3
Jewel Wlk. Cra ... 16 C2
Jib Cl. Lit ... 178 C2
Jireh Ct. Hay H ... 83 E3
Job's La. God G ... 103 E3
Job's La. Hic ... 103 E3
Jobes. Bal ... 39 E1
Jobson's La. Lur ... 27 E1
Jockey Mead. Hors ... 34 C1
John Arundel Rd. Chic ... 172 B4
John St. Bog R ... 196 A2
John St. Bri ... 187 F3
John St. S Sea ... 184 B4
Johnson Dr. Bur H ... 105 D2
Johnson Way. Yap ... 176 C1
Johnson Wlk. Cra ... 17 E2
Jolesfield Ct. Cra ... 16 B2
Jolesfield. W Gri ... 100 B3
Jolliffe Rd. E Wit ... 202 A4
Jordans Cl. Cra ... 17 D4
Jordans Cres. Cra ... 4 A1
Jordans The. E Gri ... 21 E4
Joyce Cl. Wick ... 178 A2
Joyce Page Cl. SE7 ... 1 C3
Joys Croft. Chic ... 172 C4
Jubilee Ave. Rust ... 179 D1
Jubilee Rd. Bur H ... 104 B1
Jubilee Rd. Chic ... 172 C4
Jubilee Rd. Por S ... 185 F4
Jubilee Rd. Rud ... 32 A4
Jubilee St. Bri ... 187 F3
Jubilee Terr. Chic ... 172 C4
Jubilee Way. Stor ... 117 E2
Jubilee Wlk. Cra ... 17 F3
Jubille Cl. Hay H ... 83 F2
Juggs La. W Chi ... 97 E1
Juggs The. W Chi ... 97 E1
Julian Rd. Hove ... 187 E4
Junction Cl. Bur H ... 105 D2
Junction Cl. Yap ... 176 C1
Junction Pl. Hasl ... 25 E3
Junction Rd. Bri ... 187 E3
Junction Rd. Bur H ... 104 C2
June Cl. Bog R ... 205 E4
June La. Mid ... 90 B4
June Meadows. Mid ... 90 A4
Juniper Cl. M Sea ... 197 E3
Juniper Cl. Por S ... 164 C2
Juniper Cl. Wing ... 181 D3
Juniper Rd. Cra ... 4 A1
Juniper Wlk. S Sea ... 164 A1
Jupp's La. Wing ... 181 D2
Jura Cl. Cra ... 16 C2
Jury La. S End ... 193 D3
Juxon Cl. Chic ... 172 C3
Juxon Cl. Cra ... 16 B2

Karenza Ct. Hors ... 35 E2
Katrina Gdns. S Hay ... 189 D3
Kearsley Dr. Wing ... 160 C1
Keats Cl. Hors ... 35 E4
Keats Pl. E Gri ... 8 A1
Keats Wlk. Bog R ... 195 F2
Keble Cl. Bog R ... 195 E2
Keble Cl. Copt ... 5 D1
Keefe Cl. Burh ... 73 F3
Keelson Way. Lit ... 178 C1
Keepers Wood. Chic ... 151 E2
Kelly Rd. Hove ... 166 A1
Kelsey Ave. Sou ... 148 C1
Kelsey Cl. Horl ... 1 B2
Kelsey Cl. Liss ... 43 D3
Kelso Cl. Cra ... 18 B4
Kelso Cl. Lan ... 182 C4
Kelso Cl. Wing ... 181 E2
Kelvin La. Cra ... 4 B1
Kelvin Way. Cra ... 4 B1
Kemnal Park. Hasl ... 26 A4
Kemp St. Bri ... 187 F3
Kemp Town Pl. Bri ... 188 A2
Kemps. Hur ... 123 E4
Kempshott Rd. Hors ... 34 C2
Kendal Cl. Lit ... 178 C2
Kendal Rd. Hove ... 186 B4
Kendal Rd. Lan ... 183 D3
Kenilworth Cl. Bri ... 167 F1
Kenilworth Cl. Cra ... 16 C1
Kenilworth Rd. Bog R ... 195 F2
Kenlegh. Bog R ... 195 E1
Kenmara Cl. Cra ... 4 C1
Kenmure Ave. Bri ... 166 C4
Kennedy Ave. E Gri ... 8 A2
Kennedy Rd. Hors ... 35 D1
Kennel Hill. Cha ... 131 E1
Kennel Hill. Wham ... 152 B4
Kennel La. Hoo ... 1 A1
Kennel La. W Gri ... 78 B1
Kennet Cl. Cra ... 16 B3
Kennet Cl. Wing ... 181 D4
Kensington Gdns. Bri ... 187 F3
Kensington Pl. Bri ... 187 F3
Kensington Rd. Chic ... 173 D3
Kensington Rd. Cra ... 17 D1
Kensington St. Bri ... 187 F3
Kent Cl. S Sea ... 185 D4
Kent Rd. Chic ... 172 C4
Kent Rd. Lit ... 178 A1
Kent St. Cow ... 101 F4
Kent St. Win ... 102 A3
Kentish Gdns. T W ... 167 D2
Kenton Rd. Hove ... 186 A4
Kents Rd. Hay H ... 83 E2
Kentstreet La. Cow ... 80 A1
Kentstreet La. Cow ... 101 F4
Kentwyn's Dr. Hors ... 56 B4
Kenwards. Bri ... 167 D4
Kenwyn Rd. Dart ... 20 C3
Kerves La. Hors ... 56 A3
Kestrel Cl. Cra ... 17 D4
Kestrel Cl. E Wit ... 202 C3
Kestrel Cl. Hors ... 35 E3
Kestrel Cl. Hove ... 167 D4
Kestrel Ct. Bog R ... 205 E4
Kestrel Way. Wick ... 178 A2
Kestrels The. S Sea ... 184 C4
Keswick Cl. Cra ... 16 A2
Keswick Cl. Wing ... 181 D3
Keswick Dr. Maid ... 88 B1
Ketch Rd. Lit ... 199 F4
Ketche's La. Fle ... 85 E4
Ketche's La. Hor K ... 85 E4
Kew Berry Ct. Hav ... 147 D3
Kew Gdns. Bog R ... 195 E2
Kew St. Bri ... 187 E3
Kewbarn La. Hen ... 121 E1
Kewell's Cnr. Bir ... 192 B3
Keymer Cres. Wing ... 181 D1
Keymer Ct. Bur H ... 104 C1
Keymer Gdns. Bur H ... 104 C1
Keymer Park. Key ... 124 C2
Keymer Rd. Bri ... 166 C3
Keymer Rd. Bur H ... 104 C1
Keymer Rd. Cra ... 17 D2
Keymer Rd. Dit ... 125 D2
Keymer Rd. Hass ... 124 B2
Keymer Rd. Key ... 124 C2
Keymer Road. Bur H ... 104 C1
Keymer Way. Wing ... 181 D1
Keynor La. Sid ... 204 B4
Keysford La. Hay H ... 62 B2
Kidborough Rd. Cra ... 16 B2
Kidbrook. Hay H ... 83 F3
Kidbrooke Rise. For R ... 22 B1
Kidders La. Hen ... 121 D4
Kidmans Cl. Hors ... 35 E3
Kidworth Cl. Horl ... 1 B3
Kilmore Cl. Find ... 160 B3
Kiln Cl. Cra D ... 19 F4
Kiln Fields. Hasl ... 26 A4
Kiln La. Hay H ... 83 F3
Kiln La. Horl ... 1 C3
Kiln Rd. Cra D ... 19 F4
Kiln The. Bur H ... 105 D2
Kilnfield. Rud ... 32 A4
Kilnmead Cl. Cra ... 17 E4
Kilnmead. Cra ... 17 E4
Kilnwood Cl. Sels ... 206 B4
Kilnwood La. Rusp ... 15 F2
Kilwich Cl. M Sea ... 197 D3
Kimber Cl. Lan ... 183 D3
Kimberley Rd. Bri ... 167 D1
Kimberley Rd. Cra ... 17 F4
Kimbridge Cres. Hav ... 147 D3
Kimbridge Rd. E Wit ... 202 C3
Kindersley Cl. E Gri ... 8 C2
Kinfauns Dr. Wing ... 160 A1
King Alfred Cl. Stey ... 141 D2
King Edward Ave. Wing ... 182 B2
King Edward Cl. Hors ... 55 F4
King Edward Cl. Wing ... 182 B2
King Edward Rd. Hors ... 55 D3
King George Ave. E Gri ... 8 A2
King George Rd. S Sea ... 185 D4
King George Vi Ave. Hove ... 165 F2
King George Vi Dr. Hove ... 165 F2
King James's La. Hen ... 121 E2
King Pl. Bri ... 187 F3
King St. Aru ... 156 C2
King St. Bri ... 187 F3
King St. E Gri ... 8 B1
King St. Ems ... 169 D4
King St. Wbou ... 148 A2
King St. Wing ... 182 A2
King's Arms Hill. Aru ... 137 F1
King's Ave. Chic ... 172 B2
King's Barn La. Bra ... 141 E2
King's Cliff. Bri ... 188 A2
King's Dr. E ... 68 B4
King's Espl. Hove ... 186 C3
King's Gdns. Hove ... 186 C3
King's La. Cow ... 101 F4
King's Mews. Hove ... 187 D3
King's Par. Bog R ... 195 F1
King's Rd. Bri ... 187 E3
King's Rd. Ems ... 168 C4
King's Rd. Hors ... 35 E2
King's Stone Ave. Bra ... 141 E2
King's Terr. Ems ... 168 C4
Kingfisher Cl. Cra ... 4 C1
Kingfisher Cl. Row C ... 126 A1
Kingfisher Cl. Row C ... 126 A1
Kingfisher Cl. Wing ... 181 D3
Kingfisher Ct. M Sea ... 197 E3
Kingfisher Rise. E Gri ... 21 E4
Kingfisher Way. Hors ... 35 D3
Kings Barn Villas. Stey ... 141 E2
Kings Cl. Lan ... 183 E3
Kings Cl. Row C ... 126 A1
Kings Cl. Yap ... 176 C2
Kings Copse. E Gri ... 21 E4
Kings Cres. S Sea ... 184 A3
Kings Ct. Hors ... 35 E2
Kings Ct. Sels ... 206 B4
Kings Dr. Bog R ... 205 F4
Kings Dr. Key ... 124 B2
Kings Dr. S Sea ... 184 A3
Kings Gap. S Sea ... 184 A3
Kings La. Cold ... 115 D3
Kings La. Pul ... 96 B1
Kings La. Sour ... 55 F2
Kings Platt. Shi ... 99 D4
Kings Rd. Hasl ... 25 F3
Kings Rd. Hay H ... 83 E2
Kings Rd. Horl ... 1 C2
Kings Rd. Lan ... 183 E3
Kings Rd. S Hay ... 189 D3
Kings Rd. Sock ... 164 B1
Kings Ride. Bur H ... 105 D1
Kings Way. Bur H ... 105 D1
Kings Wlk. S Sea ... 184 A3
Kingsbridge La. Shi ... 99 D4
Kingsbury Rd. Bri ... 187 F4
Kingsbury St. Bri ... 187 F4
Kingscote Hill. Cra ... 16 C2
Kingsey Ave. Ems ... 168 C4
Kingsfernsden La. Pete ... 64 A3
Kingsfield. Stor ... 117 E1
Kingsfold Cl. Bil ... 75 D3
Kingsfold Ct. Kin ... 13 F3
Kingsham Ave. Chic ... 172 C3
Kingsham Rd. Chic ... 172 C3
Kingsland Cl. Stor ... 117 E1
Kingsland Rd. Wing ... 182 A3
Kingslea. Hors ... 35 E2
Kingsley Cl. Horl ... 1 B3
Kingsley Cl. Wing ... 182 B2
Kingsley Rd. Bri ... 166 A1
Kingsley Rd. Cra ... 16 C2
Kingsley Rd. Horl ... 1 B3
Kingsmead Cl. Hors ... 35 F3
Kingsmead Cl. Stey ... 141 D1
Kingsmead Gdns. M Sea ... 197 F3
Kingsmead Pl. Bro H ... 34 A2
Kingsmead Rd. Bro H ... 34 A2
Kingsmead Rd. M Sea ... 197 F3
Kingsmead. Bog R ... 196 B2
Kingsmere. Bri ... 166 B1
Kingsmill Rd. Barn ... 176 A3
Kingspit La. Petw ... 94 A4
Kingsthorpe Rd. Hove ... 186 B4
Kingston Bay Rd. S Sea ... 185 D3
Kingston Bwy. S Sea ... 164 A1
Kingston Cl. Hove ... 165 E1
Kingston Cl. S Sea ... 185 D4
Kingston La. E King ... 201 D4
Kingston La. E Pre ... 179 F1
Kingston La. S Sea ... 185 D4
Kingston La. W King ... 179 F1
Kingston La. W King ... 201 D4
Kingston Way. S Sea ... 164 A1
Kingsway. Bog R ... 195 D1
Kingsway. Hove ... 186 B3
Kingsway. N Hay ... 168 A2
Kingsway. Sels ... 206 C3
Kingswood Cl. Cra ... 38 A4
Kingswood St. Bri ... 187 F3
Kingswood. W Chi C ... 116 C4
Kingswood. W Chi C ... 117 D4
Kinnell Cl. Ems ... 168 C4
Kipling Ave. Wing ... 180 C2
Kipling Cl. Cra ... 18 A4
Kipling Ct. Hors ... 35 F2
Kipling Way. E Gri ... 8 A1
Kippens La. W Gri ... 77 F1
Kirdford Cl. Bur H ... 105 D1
Kirdford Cl. Cra ... 16 C4
Kirdford Cl. Rust ... 199 F4
Kirdford Rd. Aru ... 156 C1
Kirkby Cl. Box ... 153 D2
Kirkland Cl. Rust ... 178 C1
Kites Cl. Cra ... 17 D3
Kithurst Cl. Cra ... 17 D2
Kithurst Cl. E Pre ... 200 B4
Kithurst Cl. Wing ... 180 C2
Kithurst Cres. Wing ... 180 C2
Kithurst Farm Rd. Stor ... 137 F4
Kithurst La. Stor ... 117 D1
Kithurst Park. Stor ... 116 C1
Kittiwake Cl. Cra ... 16 A2
Kitwood Green. Hav ... 147 D3
Knap La. Sels ... 206 B4
Knepp Cl. Bri ... 167 E1
Knepp Cl. Cra ... 18 A3
Knight's Hill. Cha ... 131 E3
Knighton Cl. Cra ... 5 D1
Knighton Cl. Cra ... 5 D1
Knightons La. Pla ... 29 F4
Knights Park. Roc ... 44 B1
Knightscroft Ave. Rust ... 200 A4
Knightscroft Cl. Rust ... 199 F4
Knightwood Ave. Hav ... 147 D3
Knob Hill. Warm ... 13 F1
Knock Hundred La. Hasl ... 25 D4
Knockhundred Row. Mid ... 90 B4
Knole Cl. Cra ... 18 A4
Knole Gr. E Gri ... 8 A2
Knoll Cl. Hove ... 165 D1
Knowle Cl. Copt ... 6 A2
Knowle Dr. Copt ... 5 F2
Knowle La. Cran ... 10 A3
Knowles Cl. Hen ... 121 E3
Knowles Meadow. Hill B ... 43 D1
Knoyle Rd. Bri ... 166 B1
Kymer Gdns. Key ... 124 C2
Kynon Gdns. M Sea ... 197 D3
Kyoto Ct. Bog R ... 195 F2

Laburnham Wlk. Rust ... 179 D1
Laburnum Ave. Hove ... 165 E1
Laburnum Cl. Ferr ... 180 B1
Laburnum Cl. Lan ... 183 D2
Laburnum Gr. Bog R ... 196 A3
Laburnum Gr. Chic ... 172 C3
Laburnum Gr. S Hay ... 189 D2
Laburnum Way. Hay H ... 83 F2
Lacebark Cl. Sid ... 18 A2
Lackenhurst La. Bar G ... 76 C3
Ladbroke Rd. Horl ... 1 C3
Ladies Mile Cl. Bri ... 166 B3
Ladies Mile Rd. Bri ... 166 B3
Lady Margaret Rd. Cra ... 16 C4
Lady Margaret Wlk. Cra ... 16 C4
Ladydell Rd. Wing ... 182 B2
Ladymead Cl. Cra ... 18 A2
Ladymead. Bur H ... 105 D3
Ladysmith Rd. Bri ... 188 A4
Lagoon Rd. Bog R ... 205 E4
Lagwood Cl. Hass ... 124 B2
Laine Cl. Bri ... 166 B2

Laines Rd. Stey 141 D1
Lake Rd. Chic 173 D3
Lake View Rd. Cra D 7 D2
Lake View Rd. Dor P 8 B3
Lake View. Bog R 194 C1
Lakers Lea. Lox 30 B1
Lakers Meadow. Bil 75 D4
Lakes La. Barn 176 B3
Lakeside. Hors 35 D3
Lakeside. Mid 90 B3
Lambert's La. Mid 90 B4
Lambeth Cl. Cra 16 C1
Lambleys La. Somp 161 E1
Lambleys La. Wing 182 B4
Lambourn. E Gri 8 B2
Lambourne Cl. Bri 167 D1
Lambourne Cl. Cra 17 E2
Lambourne La. Mil 45 E1
Lambourne Rd. Bri 167 D1
Lambs Cres. Hors 35 E3
Lambs Farm Cl. Hors 35 F3
Lambs Farm Rd. Hors 35 F3
Lambs Green Rd. Rusp 15 E3
Lammas Cl. Wick 178 B2
Lamorna Gdns. Ferr 201 E4
Lamorna Gdns. Wgate 175 D3
Lamorna Gr. Wing 182 A3
Lanark Cl. Hors 35 E1
Lancaster Cl. Cra 5 D1
Lancaster Dr. E Gri 8 C2
Lancaster Rd. Bri 187 E4
Lancaster Rd. Wing 181 E1
Lancastrian Grange. Chic 172 B4
Lancelot Cl. Cra 16 B3
Lancing Cl. Cra 16 C4
Lancing Cl. Lan 183 D3
Lancing Ct. Hors 35 F2
Lancing Park. Lan 183 D2
Landen Park. Horl 1 B3
Landseer Dr. Sels 206 C4
Landseer Rd. Hove 186 C4
Lane End Dr. Ems 168 C4
Lane End Rd. M Sea 197 F3
Lane The. Chic 151 F1
Lane The. Ifo 30 A2
Lanercost Rd. Cra 17 D3
Lanfranc Rd. Wing 181 F2
Langbury Cl. Ferr 180 A2
Langbury La. Ferr 180 B2
Langdale Ave. Chic 173 D2
Langdale Cl. Lan 183 D3
Langdale Gdns. Hove 186 B3
Langdale Rd. Cra 16 A2
Langdale Rd. Hove 186 B3
Langham Gdns. Wing 181 F1
Langhurst Cl. Hors 14 A2
Langhurst La. Rusp 15 F4
Langhurstwood Rd. Hors 14 A2
Langley Dr. Cra 17 D4
Langley Gr. Bog R 195 D1
Langley La. Cra 16 C4
Langley Par. Cra 4 A1
Langley Pl. Cra 4 A1
Langley Wlk. Cra 4 A1
Langmead Cl. Cli 198 B4
Langridge Dr. E Gri 21 E4
Langridge La. Hay H 83 F3
Langridge Way. Bur H 104 B3
Langrish Cl. Hav 147 D3
Langshott La. Horl 1 C2
Langshott. Horl 1 C3
Langton Cl. Sels 206 B3
Langton La. Hur 123 E4
Langton Rd. Chic 172 B4
Langton Rd. Wing 182 A2
Lansbury Rd. Cra 16 C1
Lansdown Cl. Hors 35 F3
Lansdowne Cl. Ang 179 E3
Lansdowne Cl. Wing 181 F1
Lansdowne Ct. Wing 181 F1
Lansdowne Pl. Hove 187 D3
Lansdowne Rd. Ang 179 E3
Lansdowne Rd. Hove 187 D3
Lansdowne Rd. Wick 178 A2
Lansdowne Rd. Wing 181 F1
Lansdowne Sq. Hove 187 D3
Lansdowne St. Hove 187 D3
Lansdowne Way. Ang 179 E3
Lanyards. Lit 178 C2
Lanyon Cl. Hors 35 F3
Lapwing Cl. Hors 35 E2
Larch Cl. Bog R 196 A4
Larch Cl. Lip 23 F2
Larch End. Hors 34 C2
Larch End. W Chi C 117 D4
Larch Gr. Sid 18 A2
Larches The. Hors 36 A3
Larches Way. Cra D 19 F4
Larchfield Cl. Bog R 195 D1
Large Acres. Sels 206 B4
Lark Hill. Hove 165 E2
Lark Rise. Cra 17 D4
Lark Rise. Lip 23 F3
Larke Cl. S Sea 185 D4
Larkfield Cl. Lan 183 E3
Larkfield Way. Bri 166 C2
Larkins Rd. Cra 4 A4
Lasham Green. Hav 147 D3
Lashmar Rd. E Pre 179 F1
Lashmere. Copt 6 A2
Laski Ct. Cra 16 C1
Latham Rd. Sels 206 B3
Latimer Cl. Cra 4 A1
Latimer Rd. Wing 181 E1
Laud Dr. Cra 18 A3
Lauder Cl. Sou 148 B1
Laughton Rd. Hors 35 E3
Laurel Cl. Bur H 105 D3
Laurel Cl. Cra 17 F2
Laurel Cl. Wing 181 D3
Laurel Dene. E Gri 8 B1
Laurel Gr. Bog R 196 A3
Laurel Mt. Pul 96 A1
Laurel Wlk. Hors 35 E1
Laurels The. Hen 121 E3
Laurie Gray Ave. Burh 73 F3
Lauriston Rd. Bri 166 B1
Lavant Cl. Cra 16 B3
Lavant Cl. Wing 180 C2
Lavant Down Rd. M Lav 151 E4
Lavant Rd. Chic 151 E2
Lavant Straight. Wham 152 B2
Lavender Hill. S Sea 163 F1
Lavender St. Bri 187 F3
Lavington Cl. Cra 16 C4
Lavington Rd. Wing 181 F3
Lavinia Court. Wing 181 D2
Lavinia Way. E Pre 179 F1
Lawn The. Bog R 195 E1
Lawns Rd. Cran 10 C2
Lawns The. E Pre 200 C4
Lawns The. Lan 183 D4
Lawrence Ave. Rust 179 D1
Lawrence Rd. Hove 186 B4
Lawrie La. Hay H 83 F3
Laws Cl. Cra 16 B3
Lawson Hunt Ind Park. Bro H 34 A2
Lawyer's La. Hen 121 D2
Laylands Rd. Sock 185 F4
Layne The. M Sea 197 F3
Lazy Acre. Sou 169 E4
Le May Cl. Horl 1 C2
Lea Cl. Cra 16 B3
Lea Farm La. Stop 95 D1
Leahurst Court Rd. Bri 166 B2
Leamon Cl. M Sea 197 E3
Leander Rd. Bos 171 D3
Leas Ct. Bog R 196 A3
Leas The. Rust 179 E2
Leatherbottle La. Chic 173 D4
Lechford Rd. Horl 1 C1
Leckford Rd. Hav 147 D3
Leconfield Rd. Lan 183 D3
Ledbury Way. Bog R 194 C1
Ledgers Meadow. Cuc 82 B3
Ledra Dr. Bog R 205 F4
Lee St. Horl 1 B2
Leechpond Hill. Low B 57 E1
Leechpool La. Hors 35 F2
Leeds Cl. Sour 55 F1
Leeds Cl. Sour 55 F1
Leeds Cl. Wing 180 C3
Leercroft. Bog R 195 E1
Leeward Cl. Wing 181 E3
Leeward Rd. Lit 178 C1
Leeward Rd. Wing 181 E3
Leggyfield Ct. Hors 34 C3
Legion Rd. S Hay 189 D2
Legion Way. E Wit 202 C3
Legsheath La. E Gri 21 D1
Legsheath La. For R 42 B4
Leicester St. Bri 187 F3
Leicester Villas. Hove 186 A4
Leigh Rd. Chic 172 B3
Leigh Rd. Wing 182 A3
Leighlands. Cra 18 A4
Leighton Ave. Wing 182 B3
Leighton Rd. Hor K 63 D3
Leighton Rd. Hove 186 C4
Leinster Gdns. M Sea 197 D2
Leith View Rd. Hors 35 F3
Lemmington Way. Hors 35 E4
Lenham Forstal Rd. Len 129 E2
Lenhurst Way. Wing 181 E2
Lennox Rd. Chic 172 C4
Lennox Rd. Hove 186 B4
Lennox Rd. S Sea 184 C4
Lennox Rd. Wing 182 A2
Lennox St. Bog R 196 A1
Lennox St. Bri 187 F3
Leonardslee Ct. Cra 17 F2
Leonora Dr. Bog R 194 C1
Leopold Cl. Bog R 196 C3
Leopold Rd. Bri 187 E3
Leopold Rd. Cra 17 D3
Lesser Foxholes. S Sea 163 D1
Letchworth Cl. Ferr 180 B1
Letchworth Ct. Cra 16 B2
Letchworth Ct. Cra 16 B2
Level Mare La. Nor 154 B1
Leveret La. Cra 16 C4
Leverton Ave. M Sea 197 D2
Lewes Cl. Bog R 195 E2
Lewes Cl. Cra 18 A3
Lewes Cres. Bri 188 B2
Lewes Rd. Ash W 22 A3
Lewes Rd. Bri 167 D1
Lewes Rd. Dan 63 F2
Lewes Rd. Dit 125 D1
Lewes Rd. E Gri 21 F4
Lewes Rd. For R 22 A2
Lewes Rd. For R 22 B1
Lewes Rd. Hay H 83 F2
Lewes Rd. Hay H 83 F4
Lewes Rd. Hor K 63 D3
Lewes Rd. Sca H 84 B2
Lewes Rd. Wmes 146 B4
Lewes St. Bri 187 F3
Lewin Cl. Lan 183 E4
Lewis Ct. Wing 180 C3
Lewis Rd. Chic 172 C4
Lewis Rd. Ems 148 A2
Lewis Rd. Lan 183 D4
Lewis Rd. Sels 206 B4
Lewis's Bldgs. Bri 187 E3
Lewisham Cl. Cra 17 D1
Ley Rd. Bog R 196 C2
Leybourne Cl. Bri 167 F1
Leybourne Cl. Cra 17 D1
Leybourne Rd. Bri 167 F1
Leyfield. Alb 123 D3
Leylands Park. Bur H 104 C3
Leylands Rd. Bur H 104 C2
Leys The. Fer 46 C3
Leys The. Sin 131 D4
Leyton Lea. Cuc 82 B3
Library Pl. Wing 182 B1
Lichfield Gdns. Bog R 195 E2
Lidsey Rd. Woo 175 D2
Lilac Cl. M Sea 197 E3
Lilac Cl. Wing 180 C3
Limbourne La. Fit 94 C2
Limbrick Cl. Wing 181 D2
Limbrick La. Wing 181 D2
Limbrick Way. Wing 181 D2
Lime Ave. Hors 35 F2
Lime Cl. Bram 24 A4
Lime Cl. Chic 172 C4
Lime Cl. Copt 5 F2
Lime Cl. Cra 4 A1
Lime Gr. Ang 179 E2
Lime Kiln Rd. Man H 57 D3
Lime Rd. Find 160 B3
Lime Tree Ave. Wing 160 B1
Lime Tree Cl. E Pre 179 E1
Limes Ave. Horl 1 C1
Limes The. Fel 7 F3
Limes The. Yap 176 B2
Limmard Way. M Sea 197 D2
Limmer La. Bog R 196 C2
Limney Rd. Bri 188 B4
Linacre Dr. Cox G 11 D2
Lincett Dr. Wing 181 E2
Linch Rd. Wool 67 F3
Linchmere Pl. Cra 16 C4
Linchmere Rd. Hasl 25 D3
Linchmere Rd. Lin 24 C2
Lincoln Ave. Bog R 195 D2
Lincoln Cl. Cra 17 E2
Lincoln Cotts. Bri 187 F3
Lincoln Green. Chic 151 E1
Lincoln Rd. Por S 185 F4
Lincoln Rd. Wing 181 E2
Lincoln St. Bri 187 F4
Lincoln Wood. Hay H 83 D3
Linden Ave. E Gri 8 A1
Linden Cl. Cra 17 F2
Linden Gr. Hay H 83 F4
Linden Gr. S Hay 189 D2
Linden Park. Lit 178 A1
Linden Rd. Bog R 196 A2
Linden Rd. Lit 178 A1
Lindens Cl. Ems 147 F1
Lindens The. Copt 5 F2
Lindfield Rd. Ard 62 A3
Lindsey Ct. Bog R 196 C3
Lindum Rd. Wing 181 E3
Lindum Way. Wing 181 E3
Lineside Ind Est. Wick 177 F1
Lineside Way. Wick 177 F1
Lingfield Cl. Wing 181 E3
Lingfield Copse. Tha 117 E3
Lingfield Dr. Cra 18 B4
Lingfield Rd. E Gri 8 A2
Lingfield Way. Sels 206 C4
Link Hill. Stor 116 C1
Link La. Pul 96 A1
Link Rd. Wing 181 F4
Link The. Cra 17 D4
Link Way. Bog R 194 C1
Links Ave. Bog R 196 B2
Links Cl. Por S 186 A4
Links Cl. Row C 126 A1
Links La. Row C 126 A1
Links Rd. Lan 183 E3
Links Rd. Por S 186 A4
Linkway The. Bri 166 C1
Linkway. Cra 5 D4
Linnet Cl. Pete 64 B1
Linton Ave. Bri 188 B3
Linton Rd. Hove 186 B4
Lintott Gdns. Hors 35 E2
Lion Cl. Hasl 25 E4
Lion Green. Hasl 25 E3
Lion La. Hasl 25 E4
Lion La. Tur H 19 F2
Lion Mead. Hasl 25 E3
Lion Mews. Hove 186 B4
Lion Rd. Bog R 194 C1
Lion St W. Bog R 196 A2
Lion St. Chic 172 C3
Lionel Ave. Bog R 197 D3
Liphook Cl. Bri 167 D1
Liphook Rd. Hasl 25 E3
Lisher Rd. Lan 183 E4
Lisle Way. Ems 147 F2
Lismore Cres. Cra 16 C2
Lister Ave. E Gri 21 E3
Listers. Ward 58 B1
Litten Terr. Chic 172 C4
Little Ashfield. Mid 90 B4
Little Babbsham. Bog R 195 E1
Little Bentswood Cl. Hay H 83 E3
Little Bentswood. Hay H 83 E3
Little Boultons. Hun 193 E4
Little Breach. Chic 151 E1
Little Bridges Cl. Sour 55 E1
Little Cl. Sour 77 E4
Little Copse Rd. Hass 124 B2
Little Crabtree. Cra 17 D4
Little Ct Cl. Mid 90 A4
Little Dipper's. Pul 96 A1
Little Dr. Ferr 180 B1
Little Dro. Stey 141 D1
Little East St. Bil 53 D1
Little East St. Bri 187 F2
Little Finches. Par G 100 C2
Little George St. Bri 187 F3
Little Haven La. Hors 35 E3
Little High St. S Sea 184 B4
Little High St. Wing 182 A2
Little Hill. W Chi C 117 D4
Little King St. E Gri 8 B1
Little London. Chic 172 C3
Little Oak. Par G 100 C1
Little Paddocks Way. Ferr 180 B1
Little Paddocks. Ferr 180 B1
Little Preston St. Bri 187 E3
Little Western St. Hove 187 E3
Littlecote. Petw 93 E4
Littlecroft Caravan Park. Bir 192 A1
Littlefield Cl. Sels 206 B4
Littlefield Rd. Chic 172 C3
Littlegreen Ave. Hav 147 D2
Littlehampton Rd. E King 180 A2
Littlehampton Rd. Ferr 180 B2
Littlehampton Rd. Wing 181 E3
Littleheath Rd. Nor 154 B2
Littlestone Rd. Wing 181 E3
Littleworth La. Cow 78 C1
Littleworth La. Par G 100 C3
Liverpool Gdns. Wing 182 A1
Liverpool Rd. Wing 182 A1
Liverpool St. Bri 187 F3
Liverpool Terr. Wing 182 A1
Livesay Cres. Wing 182 A2
Livingstone Rd. Bur H 104 B2
Livingstone Rd. Cra 17 D2
Livingstone Rd. Hors 35 D1
Livingstone Rd. Hove 186 C4
Livingstone St. Bri 188 A3
Lizard Head. Lit 178 C1
Lloyd Goring Cl. Ang 179 E3
Lloyd Rd. Hove 187 D4
Lobster La. Sels 206 A4
Lock La. Bir 192 B3
Locke Rd. Lip 24 A2
Lockerley Rd. Hav 147 D2
Lockgate Rd. S End 193 D2
Locks Cres. Por S 164 C1
Locks Hill. Por S 164 C1
Locksash Cl. W Wit 191 D1
Locksash La. W Mar 128 A3
Lockwood Cl. Hors 35 F3
Lockwood Ct. Cra 17 E4
Loder Gdns. Wing 182 A3
Loder Pl. Bri 166 B1
Loder Rd. Bri 166 B1
Loders. Ard 61 F4
Lodge Cl. Cra 17 D3
Lodge Cl. E Gri 8 A1
Lodge Cl. M Sea 197 F3
Lodge Cl. Por S 164 B1
Lodge Ct. Bog R 195 E1
Lodge Ct. S Sea 163 E1
Lodge Hill La. Dit 125 D2
Lodge La. Key 124 C1
Lodge La. W Mar 127 E3
Lodgebury Cl. Sou 169 F4
Lodgelands. Ard 61 F3
Lodsworth Rd. Bog R 194 C2
Lombard St. Petw 93 E4
Lomond Ave. Bri 166 C4
London Cl. Wing 181 D4
London La. Cuc 82 B3
London Rd. Alb 144 B4
London Rd. Aru 156 B3
London Rd. Bal 39 F2
London Rd. Bal 60 C3
London Rd. Bog R 196 A2
London Rd. Bri 166 B3
London Rd. Bri 187 F4
London Rd. Bur H 124 B4
London Rd. Cold 115 E4
London Rd. Cra 1 B1
London Rd. Cra 4 B3
London Rd. Cuc 82 B4
London Rd. Dan 63 F2
London Rd. E Gri 8 A1
London Rd. Fon 154 C2
London Rd. For R 22 B2
London Rd. Hass 124 B3
London Rd. Hen 121 E3
London Rd. Hill B 43 D1
London Rd. Horl 1 B1
London Rd. Hors 35 D1
London Rd. Lip 24 A3
London Rd. Pul 96 A2
London Rd. She 64 C4
London Rd. Was 139 E4
London Rd. Wat 114 C3
London St. Wing 182 A2
London Terr. Bri 187 F4
Lonesome La. Sal 1 A4
Long Acre. Cra D 19 F4
Long Cl. Cra 18 A3
Long Copse La. Ems 148 A2
Long Copse La. Wbou 148 A2
Long Down. Pete 64 A2
Long Furlong. Find 160 A4
Long Furlong. Pat 159 E2
Long Hill. Crab 79 E4
Long Hill. Low B 57 E1
Long La. Aru 156 A2
Long La. E Mar 107 E2
Long Mead. Walb 155 D1
Long Meadow. Wing 160 C2
Long Park Cnr. Dit 125 D1
Longacre Cres. Cuc 82 B4
Longacre La. Sels 206 B3
Longacre. Liss 43 D2
Longacre. Sels 206 B3
Longbridge Rd. Cra 1 B1
Longbridge Rd. Horl 1 B1
Longbridge Wlk. Horl 1 B1
Longbrook. Bog R 196 B2
Longbury Cl. Orp 35 E1
Longdene Rd. Hasl 25 F3
Longfellow Cl. Hors 35 E4
Longfellow Rd. Wing 181 F2
Longfield Rd. Ems 147 F2
Longfield Rd. Hors 55 F4
Longford Rd. Bog R 196 A2
Longfurlong La. Pat 159 E2
Longhurst Rd. Cra 16 C1
Longhurst. Bur H 105 D1
Longland Ave. Stor 117 D1
Longlands Glade. Wing 182 A4
Longlands Rd. E Wit 202 B3
Longlands Rd. Sou 169 E4
Longlands Spinney. Wing 182 A4
Longlands. Wing 182 A4
Longmeadow Gdns. Bir 192 B2
Longmere Rd. Cra 17 D4
Longmoor Rd. Lip 23 E2
Longport Rd. Bog R 196 C2
Longstock Rd. Hav 147 D3
Longwood View. Cra 17 F2
Loop The. M Sea 197 D2
Loose La. Lan 182 C3
Loppets Rd. Cra 17 E2
Lordings La. W Chi C 117 D4
Lordings Rd. Bil 74 C3
Loriners. Cra 17 D2
Lorna Rd. Hove 187 D4
Lorne Rd. Bri 187 F4
Lotts La. Lan 183 D3
Loudoun Rd. Lit 178 A1
Love La. She 64 A2
Love La. Stor 117 D1
Loveletts. Cra 16 C3
Lovells Cl. Bog R 194 C1
Lover's Wlk. Bri 187 E4
Lovers Wlk. Hen 121 E2
Loveys Rd. Yap 176 B1
Low Meadow. Hall 58 B1
Lowdell's La. E Gri 8 A2
Lowdells Cl. E Gri 8 A2
Lowdells Dr. E Gri 8 A2
Lower Barn Cl. Hors 35 E3
Lower Beach Rd. S Sea 184 B3
Lower Bevendean Ave. Bri 167 E1
Lower Bognor Rd. Bog R 195 D3
Lower Chalvington Pl. Bri 188 B3
Lower Church Rd. Bur H 104 B2
Lower Dene. E Gri 8 C1
Lower Dr. Sock 164 B1
Lower Faircox. Hen 121 D3
Lower Forecourt. Cra 4 C4
Lower Grove Rd. Hav 168 A4
Lower Hanger. Hasl 25 D3
Lower Heyshott. Pete 64 A2
Lower Hone La. Bos 170 C1
Lower Market St. Hove 187 D3
Lower Mead. Pete 64 A2
Lower Mere. E Gri 21 E4
Lower Rd. For R 22 B2
Lower Rock Gdns. Bri 187 F2
Lower Sq. For R 22 B2
Lower St. Fit 94 C1
Lower St. Hasl 26 A3
Lower St. Pul 95 F1
Lower Station Rd. Bil 75 D3
Lower Station Rd. Hen 121 D2
Lower Wardown. Pete 64 A2

Lowestoft Wlk. Cra 17 F2
Lowfield Heath Rd. Cra 3 E2
Lowfield Rd. Hay H 83 E2
Lowfield Rd. Slin 33 F3
Lowfield Way. Cra 4 B3
Lowlands Rd. Bur H 104 C3
Lowther Rd. Bri 166 C1
Lowther Rd. Wing 181 E4
Loxwood Ave. Wing 181 F3
Loxwood Rd. Alf 30 B4
Loxwood Rd. Ifo 29 F2
Loxwood Rd. Lox 31 E3
Loxwood Rd. Pla 29 F1
Loxwood Rd. Rud 31 E3
Loxwood Wlk. Cra 16 B4
Loxwood. E Pre 179 F2
Luard Ct. Hav 168 A4
Lucas Cl. E Gri 8 C1
Lucas Field. Hasl 25 E3
Lucas Grange. Hay H 83 D3
Lucas Rd. Warm 34 B4
Lucas Way. Hay H 83 D3
Lucas. Hor K 63 D3
Lucasters La. Hay H 83 D3
Lucastes Ave. Hay H 83 D3
Lucastes Rd. Hay H 83 D3
Lucerne Cl. Por S 164 C1
Lucerne Ct. Bog R 195 E1
Lucerne Rd. Bri 166 C1
Lucking La. M Sea 197 E3
Lucroft Rd. Bri 167 F3
Ludlow Cl. Bog R 195 E1
Ludlow Rise. Bri 167 F1
Luffs Meadow. N 48 C4
Lullington Ave. Hove 186 B4
Lulworth Cl. S Hay 189 D3
Lumley Path. Her 169 D4
Lumley Rd. Her 169 D4
Lumley Rd. Horl 1 C2
Lunces Hill. Wiv 105 E4
Lundy Cl. Cra 17 D2
Lundy Cl. Lit 199 F4
Lurgashall. Bur H 105 D1
Lutener Rd. E 68 C1
Luth The. Wis G 73 F4
Luther St. Bri 188 A4
Lutman St. Ems 147 F2
Lutyens Cl. Cra 16 B2
Luxford Cl. Hors 35 E3
Luxford Rd. Hay H 83 F4
Luxford's La. E Gri 21 F3
Lychpole Wlk. Wing 180 C2
Lye La. E Ash 150 B2
Lye La. W Sto 150 B3
Lyle Ct. Maid 105 F4
Lyle Ct. Maid 105 F4
Lymbourn Rd. Hav 147 D1
Lyminster Ave. Bri 166 C3
Lyminster Rd. Lym 178 A4
Lyminster Rd. Wick 178 A2
Lyn Rd. Wing 181 D3
Lynch Down. Fun 149 F3
Lynchet Cl. Bri 167 D1
Lynchet Down. Bri 167 D1
Lynchet Wlk. Bri 167 D1
Lynchets Cres. Hove 165 D2
Lynchmere Ave. Lan 183 D4
Lyndhurst Cl. Cra 17 D3
Lyndhurst Cl. S Hay 189 D1
Lyndhurst Rd. Chic 172 C3
Lyndhurst Rd. Hove 187 D4
Lyndhurst Rd. Wing 182 B2
Lynton Cl. E Gri 8 C1
Lynton Cl. Hur 123 F3
Lynton Park Ave. E Gri 8 C1
Lynton St. Bri 188 A4
Lynwick St. Rud 32 A4
Lynwood Ct. Hors 35 D2
Lyon Cl. Hov 187 D4
Lyon St. Bog R 196 A2
Lyons Cl. Slin 33 F3
Lyons Rd. Slin 33 E2
Lyons Way. Wing 182 B4
Lyons Way. Wing 182 B4
Lyoth La. Hay H 84 A2
Lyric Cl. Cra 18 A2
Lytton Dr. Cra 18 A4

M'tongue Ave. Bos 171 D4
Mackie Ave. Bri 166 C4
Mackie Ave. Key 124 C3
Macleod Rd. Hors 35 E1
Madehurst Cl. Bri 188 A3
Madehurst Cl. E Pre 200 B4
Madehurst Ct. Cra 16 B2
Madeira Ave. Bog R 196 B2
Madeira Ave. Hor 35 D1
Madeira Ave. Wing 182 B1
Madeira Pl. Bri 187 F2
Madeira Terr. Bri 188 A2
Madeline Rd. Pete 64 A2
Madenhurst Way. Lit 178 A1
Madgwick La. Wham 152 A1
Mafeking Rd. Bri 167 D1
Magdalene Cl. Cra 5 D1
Magnolia Cl. Wing 180 C3
Magpie Rd. Row C 126 B3
Magpie Wlk. Cra 17 E4
Maiden Bower Dr. Cra 18 A2
Maiden La. Cra 17 D4
Maidenbower Dr. Cra 18 A3
Maidment Cl. Hen 121 E3
Main Dr. M Sea 197 E3
Main Rd. Bir 192 B2
Main Rd. E Dean 132 A4
Main Rd. Her 169 E4
Main Rd. Sou 169 E4
Main Rd. Yap 176 B2
Maines Farm Rd. Upp B 141 F1
Mainstone Rd. Hove 186 B4
Maisemore Gdns. Ems 168 B4
Major Cl. Bri 166 C1
Malcolm Cl. Ferr 180 B1
Malcolm Gdns. Hoo 1 A1
Malcolm Rd. Tan 153 D1
Malden Way. Sels 206 B4
Maldon Rd. Bri 166 A1
Malham Cl. Cra 18 A2
Malin Rd. Lit 178 C1
Mallard Cl. Hasl 25 E3
Mallard Cl. Hors 35 D3
Mallard Cres. Bog R 205 E4
Mallard Pl. E Gri 21 E4
Mallard Rd. Row C 126 A1
Mallard Rd. Row C 126 A1
Mallion's La. Sta 59 E1
Mallion's La. Whi G 59 E1
Mallon Dene. Rust 200 A4
Mallory Rd. Hove 166 A1
Mallow Cl. Hors 35 E3
Malmayne Ct. Bog R 195 E2
Malthouse Cl. Aru 156 C1
Malthouse Cl. Lan 182 C4
Malthouse La. Bur H 104 A1
Malthouse La. Hur 124 A4
Malthouse La. W Ash 149 F2
Malthouse Meadows. Lip 24 A2
Malthouse Pas. Wick 178 A1
Malthouse Rd. Cra 17 D2
Malthouse Rd. Sels 206 B4
Maltings Green. Stey 141 D1
Maltings The. Chic 172 B3
Maltings The. Lip 24 A2
Maltravers Dr. Lit 199 E4
Maltravers Rd. Lit 199 E4
Maltravers St. Aru 156 C2
Malvern Cl. Wing 182 C2
Malvern Mews. Ems 147 F1
Malvern Rd. Cra 17 D3
Malvern Rd. Hill B 43 D1
Malvern St. Hove 186 C4
Malvern Way. Bog R 194 C1
Malwood Cl. Hav 147 D3
Manaton Cl. Hay H 83 E2
Manchester St. Bri 187 F2
Manet Sq. Bog R 195 F3
Manhood La. Sid 204 B4
Manitoba Way. Wing 181 D3
Manley's Hill. Stor 117 E1
Manning Cl. E Gri 8 A1
Manning Rd. Chic 173 D4
Manning Rd. Wick 178 A2
Mannings Cl. Cra 5 D1
Mannock Rd. Box 152 C1
Manor Ave. Key 124 C3
Manor Cl. Bog R 196 C2
Manor Cl. Bri 188 B3
Manor Cl. Bur H 105 D2
Manor Cl. Chic 172 B2
Manor Cl. E Pre 179 E1
Manor Cl. Hasl 25 E3
Manor Cl. Hen 121 E3
Manor Cl. Horl 1 B2
Manor Cl. Lan 183 E4
Manor Cl. Sock 185 F4
Manor Cl. Stor 117 D1
Manor Cl. Wing 181 F1
Manor Cres. Bri 188 B3
Manor Cres. Hasl 25 E3
Manor Dr. Cuc 82 B4
Manor Dr. Horl 1 B2
Manor Farm Cl. Sels 206 B4
Manor Farm Ct. Sels 206 B4
Manor Fields. Hors 35 F2
Manor Fields. Lip 24 A2
Manor Gdns. Bri 188 B3
Manor Gdns. Hur 123 E3
Manor Gdns. Sou 148 B1
Manor Green. Bri 188 B3
Manor Hall Rd. Sock 185 E4
Manor Hill. Bri 188 B3
Manor House Pl. Lan 183 E4
Manor La. Sels 206 C4
Manor Lea. Hasl 25 E3
Manor Lea. Wing 181 F1
Manor Lodge Rd. Row C 126 A1
Manor Paddock. Bri 188 B2
Manor Par. Wing 181 D4
Manor Park. Bog R 194 C1
Manor Pl. Bog R 196 A1
Manor Pl. Bri 188 B2
Manor Rd. Bri 188 B3
Manor Rd. Bur H 105 D2
Manor Rd. E Gri 8 A1
Manor Rd. E Pre 200 C4
Manor Rd. Hors 35 F3
Manor Rd. Hur 123 E3
Manor Rd. Lan 183 E4
Manor Rd. N Hay 189 D3
Manor Rd. Por S 164 C1
Manor Rd. Rust 178 C1
Manor Rd. Sels 206 B4
Manor Rd. Sou 148 B1
Manor Rd. Upp B 142 A1
Manor Rd. Wing 181 F1
Manor Royal. Cra 4 B1
Manor Way. Bog R 195 D1
Manor Way. Bri 188 B3
Manor Way. Hen 121 E3
Manor Way. Lan 183 E4
Manor Way. M Sea 197 F3
Manor Way. S Hay 189 D1
Manor Way. Sou 148 B1
Manorfields. Cra 16 A1
Mansell Rd. S Sea 184 C4
Manser Rd. Walb 155 E1
Mansfield Cl. Wing 182 C2
Mansfield Rd. Bog R 195 F3
Mansfield Rd. Hove 186 B4
Mansfield Rd. Wing 182 C2
Mansion Cl. Bur H 105 D2
Mant Cl. Stor 117 D1
Mant Rd. Petw 93 E4
Mantling Rd. Lit 178 A1
Manton Rd. Bri 167 E1
Maple Cl. Bil 53 D1
Maple Cl. Bur H 105 D3
Maple Cl. Cra 4 A1
Maple Cl. Ems 147 F1
Maple Cl. Hay H 83 F2
Maple Cl. Hors 35 F3
Maple Cl. M Sea 197 E3
Maple Cl. Wing 160 B1
Maple Dr. Bur H 104 B3
Maple Dr. E Gri 8 C1
Maple Gdns. Bog R 196 A4
Maple Gdns. Hove 165 E1
Maple Leaf. Cold 115 D3
Maple Rd. Bil 75 D4
Maple Rd. Walb 176 B4
Maple Wlk. Lan 182 C4
Maple Wlk. Rust 179 D1
Mapledown Cl. Sour 55 E1
Maplehurst La. Map 78 B2
Maplehurst La. W Gri 78 C2
Maplehurst Rd. Chic 151 F2
Maplehurst Rd. Por S 164 C1
Mapleleaf Dr. Sid 18 A2
Maples The. Ferr 201 E4
Mapsons La. Bir 192 C2
Mapsons La. High 192 C2
Marama Gdns. Lit 199 F4
March Sq. Chic 151 F2
Marchants Rd. Hur 123 F3
Marchants Way. Bur H 104 B3
Marches Rd. Kin 13 E2
Marches Rd. Warm 13 E2
Marchwood Gate. Chic 151 F2
Marchwood Mews. Chic 151 F2
Marchwood. Chic 151 F2
Marcuse Fields. Bos 170 C3
Mardale Rd. Wing 181 E3
Marden Ave. Chic 172 B2
Marden Way. Pete 64 A2
Mardens The. Cra 16 C4
Mardyke. S Sea 184 A3
Mare Hill Rd. Pul 96 B1
Maresfield Rd. Bri 188 B3
Margaret Cl. Bog R 195 E2
Margaret St. Bri 187 F2
Margery Rd. Hove 186 A4
Marina Cl. Her 169 D4
Marina Way. Bri 188 B2
Marine Ave. Hove 186 B3
Marine Cl. E Wit 202 B3
Marine Cl. Wing 181 F1
Marine Cres. Wing 181 D1
Marine Dr W. Bog R 195 F1
Marine Dr W. E Wit 202 A4
Marine Dr. Bri 188 C2
Marine Dr. E Wit 202 B4
Marine Dr. Sels 206 C4
Marine Dr. Wing 201 F4
Marine Gdns. Bri 187 F2
Marine Gdns. Sels 206 B3
Marine Par. Bog R 195 F1
Marine Par. Bri 188 A2
Marine Par. Wing 182 A1
Marine Pl. Wing 182 B1
Marine Sq. Bri 188 A2
Marine Terr Mews. Bri 188 A2
Marine View. Bri 187 F3
Marine Wlk. S Hay 189 E2
Mariners Cl. S Sea 184 A3
Mariners Wlk. Rust 200 A4
Marineside. E Wit 202 C3
Marion Rd. Cra 17 F2
Maris The. Rud 32 A4
Marisfield Pl. Sels 206 C4
Maritime Cl. Gree 22 B3
Maritime Cl. Roc 44 C2
Marjoram Pl. S Sea 163 F1
Market Ave. Chic 172 C3
Market Cl. Barn 175 F3
Market Pl. Hay H 83 E3
Market Rd. Chic 172 C3
Market Sq. Hors 35 D1
Market Sq. Mid 90 B4
Market Sq. Petw 93 E4
Market St. Bog R 196 A1
Market St. Bri 187 F3
Market St. Wing 182 A1
Markfield. Bog R 195 F3
Markway Cl. Ems 147 E1
Markwick Mews. Wing 182 B2
Marlborough Cl. Chic 173 D3
Marlborough Cl. Cra 17 D1
Marlborough Cl. Hors 35 D3
Marlborough Ct. Bog R 195 E3
Marlborough Dr. Bur H 105 D1
Marlborough Park. Hav 147 E2
Marlborough Pl. Bri 187 F3
Marlborough Rd. Lan 183 D2
Marlborough Rd. Wing 181 D1
Marlborough St. Bri 187 E3
Marlborough Way. Wing 181 D1
Marldell Cl. Hav 147 D3
Marle Ave. Bur H 104 C2
Marles La. Five O 53 D4
Marley Combe Rd. Hasl 25 E2
Marley Hanger. Kin G 25 F2
Marley La. Hasl 25 E2
Marley La. Lin 25 E2
Marley Way. Stor 117 E1
Marlinspike The. S Sea 184 C3
Marlow Ct. Cra 17 D4
Marlow Dr. Hay H 83 F2
Marlow Dr. Hay H 83 F2
Marlow Rd. Bri 188 B2
Marlowe Cl. Bog R 197 E3
Marlowe Cl. M Sea 197 E3
Marlowe Rd. Wing 182 B3
Marlpit Cl. E Gri 8 B2
Marlpit La. Chic 173 F4
Marlpit La. Wcote S 149 D2
Marlpit Rd. Sha 41 F3
Marlpost Rd. Sour 77 D4
Marmion Rd. Hove 186 B4
Marringdean Rd. Bil 75 E2
Marsh Ct. Cra 16 C1
Marsh La. Chid 170 A2
Marsh La. M Lav 151 E4
Marsh La. Mer 173 F1
Marsh La. Run 173 E1
Marsh La. Tan 153 F1
Marshall Ave. Bog R 195 F2
Marshall Ave. Wing 160 B2
Marshall Cl. Barn 175 F3
Marshall Rd. Cra 18 A2
Marshall Rd. S Hay 189 E1
Marshalls Row. Bri 187 F4
Marsham Way. Hall 58 B1
Marston Rd. Wing 182 B2
Martin Cl. Cra 17 D4
Martin Rd. Hav 147 D2
Martin Rd. Hove 165 D1
Martins La. Bir 192 B3
Martins The. Cra D 20 A4
Martlet Cl. Chic 172 C3
Martlet Rd. Petw 93 E4
Martlet Way. Bog R 205 E4
Martlets Cl. Hors 35 D3
Martlets Tdng Est. Wing 181 D2
Martlets The. Cra 17 E3
Martlets The. Lan 183 D3
Martlets The. Lit 199 F4
Martlets The. S Sea 184 B4
Martlets Way. Wing 181 D2
Martlets. W Chi C 117 D4
Martyn Cl. Hen 121 E3
Martyns Pl. E Gri 21 E4
Martyrs Ave. Cra 4 A1
Marvell Cl. Cra 18 A4
Marylands Cres. Bog R 196 B3
Masefield Rd. Cra 16 B2
Mash Barn La. Lan 183 F3
Mason Cl. E Gri 8 B1
Mason Rd. Cra 17 D2
Masons Field. Man H 57 D3
Massetts Rd. Horl 1 C1
Matlock Rd. Hove 166 A1
Matterdale Gdns. Maid 105 D3
Matterdale Gdns. Maid 105 D3
Matthews Dr. Cra 18 A2
Matthey Pl. Cra 5 D1
Maud Cashmore Way. Woolw 2 A4
Maudlin La. Stey 141 E1
Maudlyn Cl. Stey 141 E1
Maudlyn Park. Stey 141 D1
Maudlyn Parkway. Stey 141 D1
Mauldmare Cl. Bog R 195 E1
Maunsell Park. Cra 17 F3
Maversham House. Horl 1 C3
Maxton Wlk. Cra 16 C1
Maxwell Rd. Aru 156 B1
Maxwell Rd. Lit 178 A1
Maxwell Way. Cra 4 C1
May Cl. Bog R 196 A3
May Cl. Sid 204 B4
May Cl. Wing 181 D2
May Rd. Bri 188 A4
May Tree Ave. Wing 160 B2
May Tree Wlk. Hove 165 E1
Maybridge Cres. Wing 181 D2
Maybridge Sq. Wing 181 D2
Maybush Dr. Chid 170 A4
Maydwell Ave. Slin 32 C1
Mayes Cl. Cra 18 A3
Mayes Cl. Cra 18 A3
Mayes La. Warm 13 E1
Mayes La. Warm 13 E1
Mayfield Cl. Bog R 194 C2
Mayfield Cl. Bri 166 C3
Mayfield Cl. Wing 181 F4
Mayfield Cres. Bri 166 B3
Mayfield Rd. Bog R 195 F2
Mayfield. Cra 18 A3
Mayfield. E Pre 179 F2
Mayflower Cl. Cra 18 A3
Mayflower Ct. Hay H 83 E2
Mayflower Rd. Hay H 83 E2
Mayflower Sq. Bri 187 F4
Mayflower Way. Chic 172 C4
Mayflower Way. Rust 179 F2
Mayo Rd. Bri 187 F4
Maypole La. Barn 176 B3
Maypole La. Yap 176 B3
Maypole Rd. Ash W 22 B3
Maypole Rd. E Gri 8 A1
Maytree Cl. Ang 179 E2
Maytree Cl. Lan 182 C3
Mc Indoe Rd. E Gri 8 A2
Mc Kerchar Cl. Lan 183 E4
Mead La. Bog R 196 A2
Mead La. Stor 117 E1
Mead Rd. Cra 17 E4
Mead The. Lip 23 F3
Mead Way. Mid 90 B3
Meadow App. Copt 5 F2
Meadow Bank. Wis G 73 F4
Meadow Brook Ind Cen. Cra 4 C1
Meadow Cl. Copt 5 F2
Meadow Cl. Hors 35 F3
Meadow Cl. Hove 165 F2
Meadow Cl. Hun 193 F4
Meadow Cl. Lip 24 A2
Meadow Cl. Por S 164 C1
Meadow Cl. Sock 185 F4
Meadow Cl. Wing 182 C2
Meadow Cres. Wing 182 C2
Meadow Ct. Ems 168 C4
Meadow Ct. M Sea 197 D3
Meadow Dr. Hay H 83 F3
Meadow Farm La. Hors 35 E4
Meadow La. Bur H 104 B1
Meadow La. Hay H 83 F3
Meadow La. Lan 183 E3
Meadow La. W Wit 191 D1
Meadow Rd. Wing 182 C2
Meadow The. Copt 5 F2
Meadow Vale. Hasl 25 F3
Meadow Way. Bog R 194 C1
Meadow Way. Bog R 195 F3
Meadow Way. Ferr 180 B1
Meadow Way. Lip 24 A3
Meadow Way. Lit 178 B1
Meadow Way. Petw 93 E4
Meadow Way. Tan 153 D1
Meadow Way. Wgate 175 D3
Meadow Wlk. Liss 43 D2
Meadow Wlk. M Sea 197 F3
Meadowcroft Cl. Cra 16 B3
Meadowcroft Cl. E Gri 8 A1
Meadowcroft Cl. Horl 5 D4
Meadowfield Dr. Chic 172 C4
Meadowland. Sels 206 B3
Meadowlands. Cra 17 D3
Meadowlands. Hav 147 D1
Meadowlands. Row C 126 B2
Meadows Rd. E Wit 202 C4
Meadows The. E Pre 179 F1
Meadows The. Hove 165 D2
Meadows The. Walb 176 B4
Meadows. Hass 124 B3
Meadowside. Ang 179 F3
Meadowside. Horl 1 C2
Meadowside. Stor 117 D1
Meadowview Rd. Lan 183 D4
Meads Ave. Hove 165 D2
Meads Cl. Hove 165 D2
Meads The. Bri 167 D3
Meads The. E Gri 21 E4
Meads The. Hasl 25 E3
Meadsway. Sli 155 D2
Meadvale. Hors 34 B1
Meadway Cres. Hove 165 E1
Meadway Ct. Sock 185 D4
Meadway Ct. Wing 181 E2
Meadway The. Bri 188 B3
Meadway The. S Sea 184 C3
Meadway. Hasl 25 E3
Meadway. Rust 179 D1
Measham Cl. Ferr 180 B1
Meath Cl. S Hay 189 E1
Meath Green Ave. Horl 1 B3
Meath Green La. Horl 1 B3
Meath Green La. Sal 1 B4
Medina Pl. Hove 186 C3
Medina Terr. Hove 186 C3
Medina Villas. Hove 186 C3
Medlar Cl. Cra 4 A1
Medmerry Hill. Bri 167 E1
Medmerry. Sels 206 A4
Medway Cl. Wing 181 D4
Medway Ct. Hors 35 F3

Medway Dr. E Gri ... 21 D3
Medway Dr. For R ... 22 C1
Medway Rd. Cra ... 16 B3
Medway. Tur H ... 19 F3
Medwin Way. Hors ... 35 D1
Medwin Wlk. Hors ... 35 D1
Meeds Rd. Bur H ... 104 C1
Meeting House La. Bri ... 187 F3
Melbourne Ave. Wing ... 181 D1
Melbourne Rd. Chic ... 172 C4
Melbourne Rd. Wing ... 181 D1
Melbourne St. Bri ... 188 A4
Melbourne Way. Hors ... 35 E3
Melbourne Way. Wing ... 181 D1
Melksham Cl. Hors ... 35 E1
Melrose Ave. Por S ... 164 C1
Melrose Ave. Wing ... 181 E2
Melrose Cl. Bri ... 167 D1
Melrose Cl. Wing ... 181 E2
Melrose Pl. Stor ... 118 A2
Melton Ave. Stor ... 117 D2
Melton Cl. Stor ... 117 E2
Melton Dr. Stor ... 117 E2
Melville Rd. Hove ... 187 E4
Melville Way. Wing ... 181 D2
Mendip Cl. E Pre ... 179 F1
Mendip Cres. Wing ... 181 E4
Mendip Rd. Wing ... 181 E4
Mendip Wlk. Cra ... 16 C3
Mengham Ave. S Hay ... 189 D2
Mengham La. S Hay ... 189 D2
Mengham Rd. S Hay ... 189 D2
Merchant St. Bog R ... 196 A2
Mercury Cl. Cra ... 16 B2
Meredith Rd. Wing ... 182 B2
Merevale. Bri ... 166 C1
Mereworth Dr. Cra ... 18 A4
Mergers Mead. Cow ... 79 E1
Meridian Way. E Gri ... 8 B2
Merle Way. Fer ... 46 C3
Merlin Cl. Cra ... 16 B3
Merlin Cl. Hove ... 187 D4
Merlin Way. E Gri ... 8 C2
Merlin Way. M Sea ... 197 D3
Merrion Ave. Bog R ... 195 F3
Merrivale Ct. Sou ... 148 B1
Merry End. M Sea ... 197 D3
Merryfield Cres. Ang ... 179 F3
Merryfield Dr. Hors ... 34 C2
Merryfield Dr. Sels ... 206 C4
Merryfield Rd. Pete ... 64 A2
Merryfield Rd. Stor ... 117 D1
Merryfield Way. Stor ... 117 D1
Merryhills La. Lox ... 30 C3
Merryweather Rd. Bos ... 170 C3
Merrywood La. Stor ... 117 F2
Mersey Cl. Wing ... 181 D4
Mersey Rd. Wing ... 181 D4
Mersham Gdns. Wing ... 181 D1
Merton Ave. Rust ... 200 A4
Merton Cl. Bog R ... 195 E2
Merton Dr. Lit ... 178 A1
Merton Rd. Wing ... 182 B1
Metcalf Way. Cra ... 4 A1
Metcalf Way. Cra ... 4 A1
Meteor Rd. Tho I ... 169 D2
Mews Ct. E Gri ... 21 E3
Meyers Wood. Par G ... 100 C1
Meyners Cl. Hove ... 165 D2
Michael Cres. Horl ... 1 C1
Michael Fields. For R ... 22 B1
Michel Gr. E Pre ... 179 E1
Michell Cl. Hors ... 34 C1
Micklam Cl. Bog R ... 195 D1
Middle Mead. Lit ... 178 C1
Middle Meadow. Liss ... 43 D2
Middle Onslow Cl. Ferr ... 180 B2
Middle Park Way. Hav ... 147 D3
Middle Rd. Bri ... 166 B1
Middle Rd. Lan ... 183 D3
Middle Rd. Par G ... 100 C2
Middle Rd. S Sea ... 184 C4
Middle St. Bri ... 187 E3
Middle St. Hors ... 35 D1
Middle St. Petw ... 93 E4
Middle St. Por S ... 185 F3
Middle St. S Sea ... 184 B4
Middle Tyne. Wing ... 181 D3
Middle Way. Bur H ... 104 C2
Middle Way. K Gor ... 201 D4
Middlefield La. Coc ... 110 A3
Middlefield La. E Lav ... 152 A4
Middlefield. W Wit ... 190 C1
Middlefield. W Wit ... 191 D1
Middleton Ave. Hove ... 186 A3
Middleton Gdns. Tan ... 153 D1
Middleton Rd. Bog R ... 197 D3
Middleton Rd. Hors ... 34 C1
Middleton Rd. M Sea ... 197 E3
Middleton Rise. Bri ... 167 E3
Middleton Way. Cra ... 16 B3
Midfield Cl. Bur H ... 104 C2
Midfield Dr. Bur H ... 104 C2
Midfields Wlk. Bur H ... 104 C2
Midgley Rd. Cra ... 17 E4
Midholme. Rust ... 179 E1
Midhurst Cl. Cra ... 16 C4
Midhurst Cl. Ferr ... 180 B1
Midhurst Dr. Ferr ... 180 B1
Midhurst Dr. Wing ... 180 C1
Midhurst Rd. Fer ... 46 C2
Midhurst Rd. Hasl ... 25 F3
Midhurst Rd. Lip ... 24 A1
Midhurst Rd. Petw ... 93 E4
Midhurst Rise. Bri ... 166 C3
Midhurst Wlk. Hove ... 165 E2
Midway The. Bog R ... 196 C2
Mighell St. Bri ... 187 F3
Milbury Cl. Ferr ... 201 E4
Milcote Ave. Hove ... 186 B4
Mile Oak Cres. Sock ... 164 B1
Mile Oak Gdns. Por S ... 164 C1
Mile Oak Rd. Por S ... 164 B2
Mile Oak Rd. Sock ... 164 B1
Miles Cl. Yap ... 176 C1
Mill Ave. S Sea ... 163 E1
Mill Bay La. Hors ... 34 C1
Mill Cl. Crab ... 79 F4
Mill Cl. E Gri ... 21 E4
Mill Cl. Fise ... 171 F3
Mill Cl. Hasl ... 25 E3
Mill Cl. Horl ... 1 B2
Mill Cl. Por S ... 165 D1
Mill Cl. Rust ... 179 D1
Mill Copse Rd. Kin G ... 25 F2
Mill Dr. Hen ... 121 E2
Mill Dr. Hove ... 165 F1
Mill End La. Apu ... 172 A1
Mill End. Hen ... 121 E2
Mill End. Her ... 169 D4
Mill End. W Chi C ... 117 D4
Mill Farm Rd. Hors ... 35 F2
Mill Gdns. E Wit ... 202 B4
Mill Green Rd. Hay H ... 83 E3
Mill Hill Cl. Hay H ... 83 E4
Mill Hill Cl. S Sea ... 163 E1
Mill Hill Dr. S Sea ... 163 E1
Mill Hill Gdns. S Sea ... 163 E1
Mill Hill. S Sea ... 163 E2
Mill House Gdns. Wing ... 181 F1
Mill La. Amb ... 136 B3
Mill La. Aru ... 156 C2
Mill La. Ash ... 118 B2
Mill La. Bal ... 39 F1
Mill La. Clay ... 145 E4
Mill La. Coc ... 110 A4
Mill La. Cool ... 76 A2
Mill La. Copt ... 6 B2
Mill La. Cra ... 16 C4
Mill La. Crab ... 79 F4
Mill La. Dor ... 8 B4
Mill La. Fel ... 7 E3
Mill La. Fise ... 171 F3
Mill La. God G ... 103 F2
Mill La. Hey ... 90 C1
Mill La. Hoo ... 1 A2
Mill La. Itc ... 54 C4
Mill La. Kin G ... 26 A2
Mill La. Par G ... 100 B3
Mill La. Por S ... 165 D1
Mill La. Pye ... 145 D4
Mill La. Run ... 173 E1
Mill La. Rust ... 179 D1
Mill La. S Har ... 87 D2
Mill La. S Sea ... 184 B4
Mill La. Say C ... 103 E1
Mill La. Sels ... 206 A4
Mill La. She ... 64 B3
Mill La. Sid ... 204 C4
Mill La. Sli ... 155 D3
Mill La. Ste ... 67 F1
Mill La. Stor ... 117 D1
Mill La. Tro ... 66 C1
Mill La. Walb ... 155 D1
Mill La. Wbou ... 148 A1
Mill La. Wick ... 178 A3
Mill La. Wing ... 160 B1
Mill Mead. Ash ... 118 C2
Mill Park Rd. Bog R ... 194 C1
Mill Pond La. W Ash ... 149 F2
Mill Quay. Her ... 169 D4
Mill Rd Ave. Ang ... 179 E3
Mill Rd. Ang ... 179 E3
Mill Rd. Aru ... 157 D2
Mill Rd. Bri ... 166 A3
Mill Rd. Bur H ... 104 C2
Mill Rd. Cra ... 17 F4
Mill Rd. Lan ... 183 E4
Mill Rd. Liss ... 43 D3
Mill Rd. Sli ... 155 D2
Mill Rd. Sock ... 185 F4
Mill Rd. Stey ... 141 D2
Mill Rd. W Ash ... 149 F2
Mill Rd. W Chi C ... 117 D4
Mill Rd. Walb ... 155 D2
Mill Rd. Wbou ... 148 A2
Mill Rd. Wing ... 181 F1
Mill Rise. Bri ... 166 A3
Mill Rythe La. N Hay ... 189 D4
Mill Straight. Sour ... 77 E4
Mill Stream Meadow. Hay H ... 83 D4
Mill Vale Meadows. Mil ... 44 C2
Mill View Rd. Yap ... 176 B1
Mill Way. Bil ... 53 D1
Mill Way. E Gri ... 21 E4
Mill Wood. Bur H ... 104 C2
Millais Cl. Cra ... 16 B1
Millais Ct. Hors ... 35 F2
Millais. Hors ... 35 F2
Milland La. Mil ... 44 C2
Milland Rd. Mil ... 45 D1
Millbank The. Cra ... 16 B3
Millbank. Bur H ... 104 C2
Millbrook Cl. Liss ... 43 D2
Millbrook Dr. Hav ... 147 D3
Millcroft Ave. Sock ... 164 B1
Millcroft Gdns. Sock ... 164 B1
Millcroft. Bri ... 166 A3
Millcross Rd. Por S ... 164 C1
Miller's Rd. Bri ... 166 B1
Millers Gate. Hors ... 35 D3
Millers The. Yap ... 176 B1
Millers Way. Bur H ... 104 C2
Millfield Cl. Chic ... 173 D4
Millfield Cl. Rust ... 199 F4
Millfield Cotts. Bri ... 188 A2
Millfield. Lan ... 183 D4
Millfield. Sour ... 77 F4
Millstream Cl. Asht ... 164 C3
Millstream The. Hasl ... 25 E3
Millthorpe Rd. Hors ... 35 E2
Milne Cl. Cra ... 16 B2
Milner Rd. Bri ... 167 D1
Milnthorpe Rd. Hove ... 186 B4
Milnwood Rd. Hors ... 35 D2
Milton Ave. Lit ... 178 C1
Milton Cl. Lan ... 183 E3
Milton Cl. Lit ... 178 C1
Milton Cres. E Gri ... 21 D4
Milton Dr. Sock ... 185 E4
Milton Mount Ave. Cra ... 18 A4
Milton Rd. Bri ... 187 F4
Milton Rd. Cra ... 18 A4
Milton Rd. Hay H ... 83 D3
Milton Rd. Hors ... 35 D2
Milton Rd. Wing ... 182 A1
Milton St. Wing ... 182 A1
Mimmack Cl. Stey ... 141 D2
Mindleheim. E Gri ... 8 C1
Minnels The. Key ... 124 C2
Minsted Rd. Ste ... 89 E4
Mint Rd. Liss F ... 43 D3
Minton Rd. Bog R ... 196 C2
Miranda Wlk. Cra ... 16 B2
Mitchells Rd. Cra ... 17 E3
Mitford Wlk. Cra ... 16 C2
Moat La. Pul ... 96 A1
Moat Rd. E Gri ... 8 B1
Moat The. Pul ... 96 A1
Moat Way. Wing ... 181 E1
Moat Wlk. Cra ... 18 A4
Moatfield La. Cow ... 101 F4
Modena Rd. Hove ... 186 B4
Moggs Mead. Pete ... 64 A2
Mole Cl. Cra ... 16 C4
Mole The. Lit ... 178 C1
Molesworth St. Hove ... 186 B4
Molins Ct. Cra ... 16 C2
Monarch Cl. Cra ... 16 C2
Monastery La. Stor ... 117 D1
Monk Cl. Bri ... 167 D3
Monk's Hill. Wbou ... 148 A3
Monkmead Copse. W Chi C ... 117 D3
Monkmead La. W Chi C ... 116 C4
Monks Ave. Lan ... 183 E3
Monks Cl. Lan ... 183 E3
Monks La. Oak ... 12 B3
Monks La. Row ... 12 B3
Monks Wlk. Upp B ... 141 F1
Monksfield. Cra ... 17 E4
Monmouth St. Hove ... 186 C4
Mons Ave. Bog R ... 195 F3
Montagu Rd. Chic ... 172 B4
Montague Cl. S Sea ... 185 D4
Montague Gdns. Pete ... 64 A2
Montague Pl. Bri ... 188 A2
Montague Pl. Wing ... 182 A1
Montague Rd. E ... 68 C1
Montague St. Bri ... 188 A2
Montague St. Wing ... 182 A1
Montefiore Rd. Hove ... 187 E4
Montes Hill. Hay H ... 84 B4
Monteswood La. Hay H ... 84 C4
Monteswood La. Hor K ... 84 C4
Montford Cl. S Sea ... 185 D4
Montfort Rise. Sal ... 1 B4
Montgomery Dr. M Sea ... 197 D3
Montgomery Rd. Hav ... 147 D1
Montgomery St. Hove ... 186 C4
Montpelier Cres. Bri ... 187 E3
Montpelier Gate. Maid ... 88 B1
Montpelier Gdns. Was ... 139 E4
Montpelier Pl. Bri ... 187 E3
Montpelier Rd. Bri ... 187 E3
Montpelier Rd. E Pre ... 179 F1
Montpelier St. Bri ... 187 E3
Montpelier Terr. Bri ... 187 E3
Montpelier Villas. Bri ... 187 E3
Montreal St. Bri ... 187 F3
Montreal Way. Wing ... 181 D3
Montrose Cl. Wing ... 181 D1
Monument La. Wal ... 148 C4
Monument View. Bri ... 188 A3
Monxton Green. Hav ... 147 D3
Moon's La. Dor ... 9 D4
Moons La. Hors ... 35 E1
Moor Park Cres. Cra ... 16 A3
Moor Pl. E Gri ... 8 A1
Moor Rd. Hasl ... 25 D3
Moorfield. Hasl ... 25 E3
Moorfoot Rd. Wing ... 181 E4
Moorgreen Rd. Hav ... 147 D3
Moorhead Rd. Hors ... 35 F3
Moorhen Way. Bog R ... 195 F3
Moorings The. Lan ... 183 E4
Moorings The. Lit ... 178 C1
Moorings The. S Sea ... 185 D3
Moraunt Dr. M Sea ... 197 D3
Moraunt Dr. M Sea ... 197 E3
Morecambe Cl. Cra ... 16 B2
Morecambe Rd. Bri ... 166 C3
Morello Cl. Swan ... 36 C1
Moreton Rd. Bos ... 170 C3
Morland Ave. Wing ... 182 B4
Morley Dr. Hors ... 157 E1
Morley St. Bri ... 187 F3
Morleys. Ash ... 118 C2
Mornington Cres. Bog R ... 196 C3
Mornington Cres. Hove ... 186 A4
Morrell Ave. Hors ... 35 E3
Morris Way. W Chi W ... 117 D4
Mortimer Rd. Hove ... 186 B4
Morton Rd. E Gri ... 21 E4
Mosdell Rd. Sou ... 169 F4
Mosford Cl. Horl ... 1 B3
Moss Bank. Grays ... 8 A3
Moss Cl. Liss ... 43 D2
Mosse Gdns. Fise ... 171 F4
Moulsecoomb Way. Bri ... 167 E2
Mount Cl. Cra ... 18 A4
Mount La. Chic ... 172 B3
Mount Noddy. Ans ... 82 A2
Mount Pleasant. Aru ... 156 C2
Mount Pleasant. Bri ... 187 F3
Mount The. Rusp ... 2 C1
Mount Way. Lan ... 162 B1
Mount Zion Pl. Bri ... 187 E3
Mountbatten Cl. Cra ... 17 D1
Mountfields. Bri ... 167 D1
Mountview Rd. Lan ... 162 A1
Mountwood Rd. Sels ... 206 C4
Mountwood Rd. Sou ... 148 B1
Mouse La. Stey ... 140 C2
Mouse La. Wist ... 140 C2
Mouthey's La. E Ash ... 150 B1
Mowbray Dr. Cra ... 16 B2
Moyne Cl. Hove ... 165 E1
Moyne Rd. Cra ... 17 D1
Muccleshell Cl. Hav ... 147 D2
Mudberry La. Hamb ... 170 C4
Mudland Rd. Sid ... 204 C4
Muggeridge's Hill. Rusp ... 14 B4
Muirfield Cl. Cra ... 16 A3
Muirfield Cl. Wing ... 181 E3
Muirfield Rd. Wing ... 181 E3
Mulberry Cl. Bri ... 166 B2
Mulberry Cl. Ferr ... 180 B1
Mulberry Cl. Hors ... 35 D3
Mulberry Cl. Lan ... 183 E3
Mulberry Cl. S Sea ... 164 A1
Mulberry Cl. Wing ... 181 D2
Mulberry Ct. Bog R ... 205 F4
Mulberry Gdns. Wing ... 181 D1
Mulberry La. Dit ... 125 D2
Mulberry La. Wing ... 181 D1
Mulberry Rd. Cra ... 3 F1
Mullein Wlk. Cra ... 16 C1
Mumford Pl. Chic ... 172 C2
Munmere Way. Rust ... 179 E1
Munnion Rd. Ard ... 61 F4
Munns Dr. Bur H ... 104 C2
Muntham Dr. Bar G ... 54 B2
Murina Ave. Bog R ... 196 A3
Murray Ct. Cra ... 16 C1
Murray Ct. Hors ... 35 F2
Murray Rd. Sels ... 206 A3
Museum Hill. Hasl ... 26 A3
Musgrave Ave. E Gri ... 21 E4
Mustang Cl. Yap ... 176 C1
Muster Green N. Hay H ... 83 D2
Muster Green S. Hay H ... 83 D2
Muster Green. Hay H ... 83 D2
Mutton Hill. Dor ... 8 C4
Mutton's La. Stor ... 118 A2
My Lords La. S Hay ... 189 D2
Myrtle Cres. Lan ... 183 D3
Myrtle Gr. E Pre ... 179 E1
Myrtle La. Bil ... 75 D4
Myrtle Rd. Lan ... 183 D3
Mytten Bank. Cuc ... 82 B3
Mytten Cl. Cuc ... 82 B3

Nab Wlk. E Wit ... 202 B3
Nagels Cl. E Wit ... 202 C3
Naiad Gdns. Bog R ... 197 D3
Naldrett Cl. Hors ... 35 E2
Naldretts La. Rud ... 32 A3
Namrik Mews. Hove ... 186 C3
Nanson Rd. Bri ... 167 D3
Napier Way. Cra ... 4 C1
Nappers Wood. Fer ... 46 C3
Nash La. Sca H ... 84 C2
Nash Rd. Cra ... 17 E2
Nash Way. Walb ... 155 D1
Natal Rd. Bri ... 167 D1
Natts La. Bil ... 75 D3
Navarine Rd. Wing ... 182 C1
Neale Cl. E Gri ... 7 F2
Needlemakers. Chic ... 172 C3
Needles Cl. Hors ... 34 C1
Nell Ball. Pla ... 29 E1
Nelson Cl. Cra ... 18 A3
Nelson Cl. Lan ... 183 D4
Nelson Cl. Tan ... 153 D1
Nelson Rd. Bog R ... 195 F2
Nelson Rd. Hors ... 35 D2
Nelson Rd. Wing ... 181 D2
Nelson Row. F ... 177 E2
Nep Cl. Hen ... 121 E2
Nep Town Rd. Hen ... 121 E2
Nepcote La. Find ... 160 B3
Nepcote. Find ... 160 B3
Nepfield Cl. Find ... 160 B3
Neptune Cl. Cra ... 16 B2
Neptune Cl. Roc ... 45 D2
Neptune Ct. M Sea ... 197 D2
Neptune Way. Lit ... 199 F4
Nesbit Ct. Cra ... 16 B2
Nesbitt Rd. Bri ... 167 D1
Netherfield Cl. Hav ... 147 D1
Netherton Cl. Sels ... 206 B4
Netherton Cl. Sour ... 55 E2
Netherwood. Cra ... 16 C2
Netherwoods Rd. Bar G ... 76 C3
Netley Cl. Cra ... 38 A4
Nettleton Ave. Tan ... 153 D1
Nevile Cl. Cra ... 16 C2
Nevill Ave. Hove ... 165 E1
Nevill Cl. Hove ... 165 F1
Nevill Cotts. Dit ... 125 D1
Nevill Gdns. Hove ... 165 F1
Nevill Pl. Hove ... 165 F1
Nevill Rd. Hove ... 165 F1
Nevill Rd. W Mal ... 86 C3
Nevill Way. Hove ... 165 F1
Neville Gdns. Ems ... 147 F2
Neville Rd. Bog R ... 196 A2
Neville Rd. Chic ... 172 A4
New Barn Cl. Por S ... 164 C1
New Barn Cl. S Sea ... 163 F1
New Barn Hill. Wham ... 152 C4
New Barn La. Bog R ... 196 C3
New Barn La. W Chi C ... 116 C4
New Barn Rd. Amb ... 136 A3
New Barn Rd. S Sea ... 163 F1
New Beach Holiday Camp. Earn ... 203 E2
New Brighton Rd. Ems ... 147 F1
New Church Rd. Hove ... 186 B4
New Courtwick La. Wick ... 178 A2
New Cut. Aru ... 156 C2
New Cut. N Hay ... 168 A2
New Dorset St. Bri ... 187 E3
New England Rd. Bri ... 187 E4
New England Rd. Hay H ... 83 E3
New England Rise. Por S ... 164 C2
New England St. Bri ... 187 F4
New Farthingdale. Dor ... 8 C4
New Hall La. Sma D ... 142 B4
New La. Hav ... 147 D2
New Moorhead Dr. Hors ... 36 A3
New Par. Wing ... 182 B1
New Park Rd. Chic ... 172 C4
New Place Rd. Pul ... 96 A2
New Rd. Bar G ... 54 A1
New Rd. Bil ... 53 F1
New Rd. Box ... 152 B2
New Rd. Bri ... 187 F3
New Rd. Dit ... 124 C1
New Rd. E Dean ... 132 A4
New Rd. E Lav ... 151 F2
New Rd. Hasl ... 25 E3
New Rd. Hey ... 91 E2
New Rd. Key ... 124 B1
New Rd. Lit ... 199 D4
New Rd. Mid ... 90 B3
New Rd. Rust ... 179 E2
New Rd. S Amb ... 91 E3
New Rd. S Sea ... 184 B4
New Rd. Sou ... 169 F4
New Rd. Sour ... 55 E2
New Rd. Tan ... 153 D1
New Rd. Til ... 92 C4
New Rd. Upp ... 70 C1
New Rd. Upp B ... 141 F1
New Rd. Wbou ... 148 A2
New Rd. Wing ... 181 D4
New Salts Farm Rd. Lan ... 184 A3
New St. Cra ... 17 F4
New St. Hors ... 35 D1
New St. Petw ... 93 E4
New St. Wing ... 182 A1
New Steine Mews. Bri ... 187 F2
New Steine. Bri ... 187 F2
New Town Rd. Stor ... 116 C1
New Town. Chic ... 172 C3
New Town. Copt ... 5 F2
New Tyler Way. Maid ... 106 B4
New Way La. Hur ... 123 F2
Newark Pl. Bri ... 187 F3
Newark Rd. Cra ... 17 E4
Newbarn La. Bog R ... 195 E3
Newbarn La. Wal ... 148 C4
Newbridge Cl. Bro H ... 34 A2
Newbridge Rd. Bil ... 74 C4

Newbury La. Cuc 82 B3
Newdigate Rd. Rusp 15 D4
Newells La. Hamb 170 C4
Newells La. Low B 57 D1
Newells La. W Ash 149 E1
Newfield Rd. Liss F 43 D3
Newfield Rd. Sels 206 C4
Newhall Cl. Bog R 195 E2
Newham Cl. Stey 141 D2
Newham La. Stey 141 D1
Newhaven St. Bri 187 F3
Newhouse La. E Dean 132 A4
Newhouse La. Stor 118 A2
Newick Rd. Bri 167 E3
Newland Rd. Upp B 141 F1
Newland Rd. Wing 182 A2
Newland St. Wing 182 A2
Newlands Cl. Horl 1 B3
Newlands Cl. Key 124 C2
Newlands Cres. E Gri 8 A1
Newlands La. Chic 172 A4
Newlands Park. Copt 6 B2
Newlands Rd. Cra 17 D3
Newlands Rd. Hors 35 D2
Newlands. Bal 39 E1
Newling Way. Wing 160 B1
Newman's Rd. Lan 182 C4
Newmans Gdns. Lan 182 C4
Newmarket Rd. Bri 188 A4
Newmarket Rd. Cra 17 F2
Newmarket Terr. Bri 188 A4
Newmay Cl. Cra 18 A3
Newport Dr. Fise 171 F4
Newport Mews. Wing 182 C2
Newport Rd. Bur H 104 B2
Newport St. Bri 187 F4
Newpound La. Wis G 52 A1
Newpound. New C 52 B2
Newtimber Ave. Wing 180 C2
Newtimber Dr. Por S 164 C1
Newtimber Gdns. S Sea 163 E1
Newton Ave. E Gri 21 E3
Newton Rd. Cra 4 B1
Newton Rd. Hay H 84 A4
Newtown Ave. Bog R 195 F3
Newtown Cl. Hay H 83 F4
Newtown Crt. Hay H 83 E3
Newtown Rd. Hove 186 C4
Newtown Rd. Lip 24 A2
Nicholsfield. Lox 30 B2
Nicolson Dr. S Sea 184 B4
Nightingale Cl. Cra 17 D4
Nightingale Cl. E Gri 21 D4
Nightingale Cl. Row C 126 A1
Nightingale Cl. Stor 117 E1
Nightingale Ct. M Sea 197 E3
Nightingale La. Bur H 124 C4
Nightingale La. Stor 117 E1
Nightingale La. Wcote S 149 D2
Nightingale Park. Hav 147 D1
Nightingale Rd. Hors 35 D2
Nightingale Wlk. Bil 75 E4
Nightingales The. Bidd 175 D3
Nightingales. Find 160 B4
Nightingales. W Chi C 117 D4
Nile St. Bri 187 F3
Nile St. Ems 168 C4
Nimbus Cl. Lit 178 C1
Nimrod Ct. Cra 5 D1
Ninfield Ct. Cra 16 B1
Ninfield Pl. Bri 188 B4
Niven Cl. Cra 18 A3
Nizells Ave. Hove 187 E4
Noahs Ark La. Hay H 84 A4
Noel Green. Bur H 104 C2
Noel Rise. Bur H 104 C2
Nookery The. E Pre 179 F1
Nor'bren Ave. Bog R 195 F3
Norbury Cl. Lan 183 E4
Norbury Dr. Lan 183 E4
Nore Cres. Ems 147 E1
Nore Down Way. W Mar 127 F4
Nore Farm Ave. Ems 147 E1
Norfolk Bldgs. Bri 187 E3
Norfolk Cl. Bog R 196 A1
Norfolk Cl. Cra 16 B1
Norfolk Gdns. Lit 199 E4
Norfolk Mews. Bri 187 E3
Norfolk Pl. Bri 187 E3
Norfolk Pl. Lit 199 E4
Norfolk Rd. Bri 187 E3
Norfolk Rd. Hors 35 D1
Norfolk Sq. Bog R 196 A1
Norfolk Sq. Bri 187 E3
Norfolk St. Bog R 196 A1
Norfolk St. Bri 187 E3
Norfolk St. Wing 182 A2
Norfolk Terr. Bri 187 E3
Norfolk Terr. Hors 35 D1
Norfolk Way. M Sea 197 F3
Norman Cl. Lit 178 B1
Norman Cres. S Sea 163 E1
Norman Rd. Bur H 104 C2
Norman Rd. Hove 186 B3
Norman Rd. S Hay 189 D1
Norman Way. Stey 141 D2
Norman's Dr. Bog R 196 C3
Normandy Cl. Cra 18 A2
Normandy Cl. E Gri 21 E4
Normandy Dr. E Pre 200 C4
Normandy Gdns. Hors 35 D1
Normandy La. E Pre 200 C4
Normandy Rd. Wing 182 A2
Normandy. Hors 35 D1
Normanhurst Cl. Cra 17 E3
Normanhurst Cl. Rust 200 A4
Normanton Ave. Bog R 195 F2
Normanton St. Bri 188 A4
Norris Dns. Hav 168 A4
Norris The. E Pre 179 F1
North Ave E. M Sea 197 E3
North Ave S. M Sea 197 E3
North Ave. M Sea 197 E3
North Ave. Wing 181 E1
North Bank. Hass 124 B2
North Bay. Tho I 169 D2
North Bersted St. Bog R 195 F4
North Bound. Walb 155 D1
North Cl. Cra 17 E4
North Cl. Hav 168 A4
North Cl. Por S 164 C1
North Cres. S Hay 189 D2
North Ct. Hass 124 B2
North Dr. Ang 179 E2
North Dr. Bri 188 A3
North End Rd. Yap 176 B2
North End. Dit 125 D2
North Farm Rd. Lan 183 E3
North Gdns. Bri 187 E3
North Gdns. Hors 35 D1
North Ham Rd. Lit 178 A1
North Heath Cl. Hors 35 D3
North Heath La. Hors 35 E3
North Holmes Cl. Hors 35 F3
North La. Cha 110 C1
North La. E Pre 179 F1
North La. Por S 164 C2
North La. Rust 178 C1
North La. W Hoa 41 E3
North La. Wist 119 D1
North Mead. Cra 17 E4
North Pallant. Chic 172 C3
North Par. Hors 35 D2
North Pl. Bri 187 F3
North Pl. Lit 199 E4
North Rd. Bos 171 D4
North Rd. Bri 166 B1
North Rd. Bri 187 F3
North Rd. Cra 17 F4
North Rd. Hay H 83 F2
North Rd. Lan 183 E3
North Rd. Por S 164 C1
North Rd. Sels 206 B4
North South Rd. Bri 167 F4
North St Quadrant. Bri 187 E3
North St. Bri 187 F3
North St. Chic 172 C4
North St. Hors 35 D1
North St. Mid 90 B4
North St. Petw 71 E1
North St. Por S 186 A4
North St. S Sea 184 B4
North St. Stor 117 D1
North St. Tur H 19 F2
North St. Wbou 148 A2
North St. Wick 178 A2
North St. Wing 182 A2
North Walls. Chic 172 B4
North Way. Bog R 196 B2
North Way. Petw 93 E4
Northbourne Cl. S Sea 184 B4
Northbrook Cl. Wing 182 B3
Northbrook Rd. Wing 182 B3
Northcliff Rd. Bog R 196 B2
Northcote Rd. Bog R 195 F2
Northcourt Cl. Rust 179 E1
Northcourt Rd. Wing 182 A2
Northcroft. Hen 121 E3
Northdown Cl. Hors 35 E2
Northease Cl. Hove 165 D1
Northease Dr. Hove 165 E2
Northease Gdns. Hove 165 E2
Northend La. God G 103 E2
Northend La. Hic 103 E2
Northern Cres. E Wit 202 B4
Northfield Rd. Wing 181 F3
Northfield Rise. Hove 165 D2
Northfield Way. Bri 166 C2
Northfield. Sels 206 C4
Northfields La. Nor 154 A1
Northfields La. Nyt 175 D4
Northfolk Rd. Lit 199 E4
Northgate Ave. Cra 17 E4
Northgate Cl. Lan 183 D3
Northgate Pl. Cra 17 E4
Northgate Rd. Cra 17 D3
Northgate. Chic 172 C4
Northlands Ave. Hay H 83 F2
Northlands La. Stor 117 E2
Northlands Rd. Hors 14 B1
Northlands Rd. Warm 13 D1
Northney La. N Hay 168 B2
Northney Rd. N Hay 168 A2
Northside. M Lav 151 E4
Northumberland Gdns. Bro 34 B1
Northview Terr. Find 160 B3
Northway Rd. Wick 178 A2
Northway. Bur H 105 D2
Northwood La. N Hay 168 A1
Northwyke Cl. Bog R 197 D3
Northwyke Rd. Bog R 197 D3
Norton Cl. Hove 186 C3
Norton La. Eart 154 A3
Norton La. Nor 153 F1
Norton La. Nor 154 A2
Norton Rd. Hove 186 C3
Norton Rd. Lan 183 D3
Norway La. Lit 178 B2
Norway St. Por S 186 A4
Norwich Cl. Bri 167 F1
Norwich Dr. Bri 167 F1
Norwich Rd. Chic 151 E1
Norwich Rd. Cra 17 F2
Norwood La S. E Lavn 112 B3
Norwoodhill Rd. Charl 3 E4
Nowhurst La. Slin 33 F3
Nuffield Cl. Bog R 195 E2
Nursery Cl. Barn 175 F3
Nursery Cl. E Pre 200 C4
Nursery Cl. Ems 147 F2
Nursery Cl. Hay H 83 D3
Nursery Cl. Hur 123 E4
Nursery Cl. Lan 183 D4
Nursery Cl. Por S 164 B2
Nursery Cl. S Sea 184 C4
Nursery Gdns. Wick 178 A2
Nursery La. Fise 171 F4
Nursery La. Hoo 1 A1
Nursery La. Wing 182 A1
Nursery The. Bur H 105 D2
Nurserylands. Cra 16 C3
Nursling Cres. Hav 147 D3
Nutbourne La. Nutb 96 C2
Nutbourne La. Pul 96 C2
Nutbourne Rd. Nutb 96 C1
Nutbourne Rd. S Hay 189 F1
Nutbourne Rd. W Chi C 116 B4
Nutbourne Rd. Wing 181 F2
Nutcombe La. Hasl 25 E4
Nutcroft. Pul 96 A2
Nuthatch Cl. Row C 126 A1
Nuthatch Cl. Row C 126 A1
Nuthatch Way. Hors 35 D4
Nuthurst Cl. Bri 188 B3
Nuthurst Cl. Cra 16 C4
Nuthurst Pl. Bri 188 B3
Nuthurst Rd. Map 78 B3
Nuthurst Rd. Nuth 57 D2
Nuthurst St. Map 78 C4
Nuthurst St. Nuth 56 C1
Nutley Ave. Wing 181 D1
Nutley Cl. Hove 165 E2
Nutley Cl. Wing 181 D1
Nutley Cres. Wing 181 D1
Nutley Dr. Wing 181 D1
Nutwick Rd. Hav 147 D2
Nye La. Dit 125 E1
Nye La. Wmes 146 A4
Nye Rd. Bur H 105 D2
Nye's Hill. Win 80 B1
Nyes Cl. Hen 121 E3
Nyetimber Cl. Bog R 194 C1
Nyetimber Copse. W Chi C 117 D4
Nyetimber Cres. Bog R 194 C1
Nyetimber Hill. Bri 167 E1
Nyetimber La. Bog R 194 C1
Nyetimber La. W Chi C 116 C4
Nyetimber Mill. Bog R 194 C1
Nyetimbers The. Bog R 194 C1
Nyewood Gdns. Bog R 195 F2
Nyewood La. Bog R 195 F2
Nyewood Pl. Bog R 195 F1
Nymans Cl. Hors 35 F4
Nymans Ct. Cra 17 F2
Nyton Rd. Nyt 175 D2
Nyton Rd. Wgate 175 D4

Oak Ave. Chic 172 B4
Oak Ave. Stor 117 F2
Oak Bank. Hay H 83 E4
Oak Cl. Bog R 196 A3
Oak Cl. Bri 166 B2
Oak Cl. Chic 172 B4
Oak Cl. Copt 5 F2
Oak Cl. Sour 77 E4
Oak Cl. Stor 117 E1
Oak Cl. Wing 160 B1
Oak Croft. E Gri 21 F4
Oak Dell. Cra 18 A4
Oak End. Aru 156 B1
Oak End. W Chi C 117 D4
Oak Gr. Bog R 196 A3
Oak Gr. Lox 30 C2
Oak Hall Park. Bur H 104 C1
Oak La. Bro H 34 B2
Oak Meadow. Bir 192 B3
Oak Park Dr. Hav 147 D2
Oak Rd. Cra 17 D3
Oak Rd. Sour 55 E1
Oak Tree Ave. Hasl 25 D3
Oak Tree Cotts. Dan 63 F2
Oak Tree Dr. Ems 147 F2
Oak Tree Dr. Liss 43 D2
Oak Tree Farm. Hamb 149 D1
Oak Tree La. Wgate 175 D3
Oak Tree Way. Hors 35 E2
Oak View. Hun 193 E4
Oak Way. Cra 17 E4
Oakapple Cl. Cow 79 E1
Oakapple Cl. Cra 16 C1
Oakapple Rd. Sock 164 B1
Oakcroft Gdns. Lit 178 B2
Oakdale Rd. Hay H 83 E2
Oakdene Ave. Por S 164 B2
Oakdene Cl. Por S 164 B2
Oakdene Cres. Por S 164 B2
Oakdene Gdns. Por S 164 B2
Oakdene Rise. Por S 164 B2
Oakdene Way. Por S 164 B2
Oakenfield. Bur H 104 B3
Oakfield Ave. E Wit 202 B4
Oakfield Cl. Hay H 83 F4
Oakfield Rd. Cow 79 E1
Oakfield Way. E Gri 8 B2
Oakfield. Lod 69 F2
Oakfield. Pla 29 E1
Oakfields. Cra 18 A4
Oakfields. Oak 12 A4
Oakhaven. Cra 17 D2
Oakhill Rd. Hors 35 E1
Oakhurst Gdns. E Gri 8 A1
Oakhurst Gdns. Rust 179 E1
Oakhurst La. Lox 30 B4
Oakhurst. Hay H 83 D4
Oakhurst. Hen 121 E3
Oakhurst. Mid 90 A4
Oakhurst. Say C 103 D1
Oaklands La. Mid 90 B3
Oaklands La. W Lav 90 C3
Oaklands Rd. Hav 147 D1
Oaklands Rd. Hay H 83 D3
Oaklands Way. Chic 172 C4
Oaklands. Ard 61 F4
Oaklands. Bil 75 D4
Oaklands. Hasl 26 A4
Oakleigh Cl. Swan 37 D1
Oakleigh Cl. Swan 37 D1
Oakleigh Cl. Wing 182 C2
Oakleigh Rd. Hors 35 E2
Oakleigh Rd. Wing 182 C2
Oakley Cl. E Gri 21 F4
Oakley Gdns. E Pre 179 F1
Oakmead Rd. Bur H 104 B1
Oakmeadow Cl. Ems 148 A2
Oakroyd Cl. Bur H 105 D3
Oaks Cl. Hors 35 F3
Oaks The. E Gri 21 F4
Oaks The. Rust 179 E1
Oakshott Dr. Hav 147 D3
Oakway. Man H 57 D3
Oakwood Centre The. Hav 147 D2
Oakwood Cl. Bur H 104 C1
Oakwood Cl. Mid 90 B4
Oakwood Dr. Bur H 104 C1
Oakwood Gdns. Bog R 196 A2
Oakwood Industrial Park. Cra 4 C1
Oakwood Rd. Horl 1 C2
Oakwood Rd. S Hay 189 D2
Oakwood. Par G 100 C2
Oates Wlk. Cra 17 E2
Oathall Ave. Hay H 83 E3
Oathall Rd. Hay H 83 E3
Oatlands. Cra 16 C3
Oberon Way. Cra 16 B2
Ocean Cl. Ferr 201 E4
Ocean Dr. Ferr 201 E4
Ockenden La. Cuc 82 B3
Ockenden Way. Hass 124 B2
Ockley Ct. Bog R 196 A2
Ockley Hill. Key 124 C3
Ockley La. Bur H 124 C4
Ockley La. Key 124 C3
Ockley Rd. Bog R 196 A2
Ockley Way. Key 124 C3
Odge La. Sal 1 B4
Offington Ave. Wing 181 F4
Offington Corner. Wing 181 F4
Offington Ct. Wing 182 A3
Offington Dr. Wing 181 F4
Offington Gdns. Wing 181 F3
Offington La. Wing 181 F4
Okehurst La. Bil 52 C2
Okehurst La. Bill 53 D2
Okehurst Rd. Bil 52 C3
Old Bakery La. Bog R 196 A1
Old Barn Way. Sock 185 F4
Old Bridge Rd. Bos 171 D4
Old Brighton Rd S. Cra 4 B3
Old Brighton Rd. Cra 4 B2
Old Brighton Rd. Cra 38 A4
Old Brighton Rd. Pea P 37 F3
Old Broyle Rd. Chic 151 D1
Old Buddington La. E 68 B2
Old Coastguards. Bog R 196 B2
Old Copse Rd. Hav 147 D2
Old Cottage Cl. Tan 153 D1
Old Court Cl. Bri 166 B2
Old Crawley Rd. Hors A4 .... 36 A1
Old Dartford Rd. Farn 53 D4
Old Denne Gdns. Hors 35 D1
Old Farm Cl. Bog R 195 D1
Old Farm La. Wbou 148 B1
Old Farm Rd. Bri 166 B3
Old Fort Rd. S Sea 184 C3
Old Glebe. Fer 46 C3
Old Guildford Rd. Bro H 34 B2
Old Ham La. Len 110 B1
Old Ham La. Len 128 B4
Old Haslemere Rd. Hasl 26 A3
Old Hollow. Copt 5 E1
Old Hollow. Wor 18 A3
Old Horsham Rd. Cra 16 C2
Old London Rd. Bri 166 B3
Old Manor Cl. Cra 16 C4
Old Manor House Gdns.
Bog R 196 C3
Old Manor Rd. Rust 178 C1
Old Manor Way. Chis 34 A4
Old Market Ave. Chic 172 C3
Old Martyrs. Cra 4 A1
Old Mead Rd. Wick 178 A3
Old Mill Cl. Bri 166 B3
Old Mill Dr. Stor 117 D1
Old Mill La. She 64 B3
Old Mill Pl. Pul 96 A1
Old Mill Sq. Stor 117 D1
Old Millmeads. Hors 35 D3
Old Museum Ct. Hasl 26 A3
Old Orchard The. Rai (K) 62 B3
Old Park Cl. Cuc 82 C3
Old Pl. Bog R 195 E2
Old Point. M Sea 197 E2
Old Quarry The. Hasl 25 E2
Old Rd. E Gri 8 B1
Old Rectory Cl. Wbou 148 A2
Old Rectory Dr. Eas 175 E4
Old Rectory Gdns. Bog R 196 C2
Old Rectory Gdns. Sock 185 D4
Old Salts Farm Rd. Lan 183 F3
Old School Cl. Bir 192 B2
Old Shoreham Rd. Hove 186 B4
Old Shoreham Rd. Lan 163 D1
Old Shoreham Rd. Por S 185 F4
Old Shoreham Rd. S Sea 184 B4
Old Shoreham Rd. Soc 164 B1
Old Shoreham Rd. Sock 185 E4
Old Station Cl. Cra D 19 F4
Old Steine. Bri 187 F3
Old Wickham La. Hay H 83 E4
Old Worthing Rd. E Pre 179 F2
Older Way. Ang 179 E3
Oldfield Cl. Horl 1 B1
Oldfield Cres. Sock 185 D4
Oldfield Rd. Horl 1 B1
Oldhouse La. Con 75 F2
Oldhouse La. High 204 A4
Oldhouse La. W Mar 127 F3
Oldlands Ave. Bal 39 F1
Oldlands Ave. Key 124 C2
Oldlands Way. Bog R 196 B4
Oldwick Meadows. E Lav 151 E3
Olive Rd. Hove 186 A4
Oliver Rd. Grays 7 D1
Oliver Rd. Hors 34 C1
Oliver Whitby Rd. Chic 172 B4
Olivers Meadow. Wgate 175 D4
Olivier Cl. Bri 188 A3
Olivier Rd. Cra 18 A3
Onslow Dr. Ferr 180 B1
Onslow Rd. Hove 166 A1
Ontario Cl. Wing 181 D3
Ontario Gdns. Wing 181 D3
Ophir Rd. Wing 182 C2
Orange Row. Bri 187 F3
Orange Row. Ems 168 C4
Orchard Ave. Chic 172 B4
Orchard Ave. Hove 165 F1
Orchard Ave. Lan 183 E4
Orchard Ave. Sels 206 B3
Orchard Ave. Wing 181 F3
Orchard Cl. Els 88 A2
Orchard Cl. Ferr 180 B2
Orchard Cl. Hay H 83 D4
Orchard Cl. Horl 1 B2
Orchard Cl. Petw 93 E4
Orchard Cl. S Sea 184 B4
Orchard Cl. Sca H 84 B2
Orchard Cl. Sma D 142 B3
Orchard Cl. Sock 185 E4
Orchard Cl. Wing 181 F3
Orchard Cott. Cuc 82 B3
Orchard Cres. Fon 154 C2
Orchard Dell. W Chi 97 D1
Orchard Gdns. Chic 172 B4
Orchard Gdns. Hove 165 F1
Orchard Gdns. Rust 179 D1
Orchard Hill. Rud 32 A4
Orchard La. Dit 125 D2
Orchard La. Her 169 D4
Orchard La. Key 124 B2
Orchard La. W Ich 191 E4
Orchard Pl. Aru 156 C2
Orchard Rd. Bur H 104 B2
Orchard Rd. E Pre 179 F1
Orchard Rd. Hors 35 E1
Orchard Rd. Hove 165 F1
Orchard Rd. S Hay 189 D1
Orchard Side. Hun 193 F4
Orchard St. Chic 172 B4
Orchard St. Cra 17 D3
Orchard The. Bog R 195 D1
Orchard The. Hasl 25 E3
Orchard The. Hass 124 B2
Orchard Way. Barn 175 F3
Orchard Way. Bog R 195 F2

Orchard Way. Bog R 196 A3
Orchard Way. Bur H 104 B2
Orchard Way. E Gri 8 B1
Orchard Way. Fon 154 C2
Orchard Way. Hay H 83 D4
Orchard Way. Hur 123 E3
Orchard Way. Lan 183 E4
Orchard Way. Mid 90 B4
Orchard Way. Pul 96 A2
Orchard Way. Whi G 81 D4
Orchards The. Cra 16 A3
Orchards The. Hors 35 E3
Orchid Park. Hay H 84 A2
Orde Cl. Cra 5 D1
Oriel Cl. Barn 175 F3
Oriel Cl. Cra 5 D1
Oriental Pl. Bri 187 E3
Orion Ct. Cra 16 A2
Orkney Ct. Wing 180 C3
Orltons La. Rusp 2 B1
Orme Rd. Wing 182 A2
Ormerod Crt. Hay H 83 E3
Ormesby Cres. Bog R 196 C3
Ormesby Wlk. Cra 17 F2
Ormonde Ave. Chic 172 C3
Ormonde Way. S Sea 184 A3
Orpen Pl. Sels 206 C4
Orpen Rd. Hove 166 A1
Osborn Cres. Chic 151 F1
Osborne Cl. Lan 183 D3
Osborne Cres. Chic 173 D3
Osborne Dr. Lan 183 D3
Osborne Rd. Bri 166 C1
Osborne Villas. Hove 186 C3
Osmond Rd. Hove 187 E4
Osmonde Cl. Wing 182 A2
Osmund Cl. Cra 18 B3
Osmunda Bank. Dor P 8 B3
Osney Cl. Cra 17 D3
Osprey Dr. S Hay 189 D2
Osprey Gdns. Bog R 196 A4
Osprey Quay. Her 169 D4
Ostlers View. Bil 75 D4
Otard Cl. Sels 206 B4
Otford Cl. Cra 38 A4
Otter Cl. Chic 172 B4
Otway Cl. Cra 16 B2
Otway Rd. Chic 151 F1
Oulton Wlk. Cra 17 F2
Outerwyke Ave. Bog R 196 C3
Outerwyke Gdns. Bog R 196 C3
Outerwyke Rd. Bog R 196 C3
Outram Rd. Bog R 196 B2
Oval The. Find 160 B4
Oval The. Wing 181 F3
Oval Waye. Ferr 201 E4
Over St. Bri 187 F3
Overdene Dr. Cra 16 C3
Overdown Rd. Bog R 196 C3
Overdown Rise. Por S 164 B2
Overhill Dr. Bri 166 B3
Overhill Gdns. Bri 166 B3
Overhill Way. Bri 166 B3
Overhill. Sock 164 B1
Overmead. S Sea 184 B4
Overstrand Ave. Rust 200 A4
Overton Rd. Sou 148 C1
Overton Shaw. E Gri 8 B2
Oving Rd. Chic 173 D3
Oving Rd. Chic 173 F4
Owers Way. E Wit 202 B4
Owl Beech Pl. Hors 35 F2
Owlbeech Ct. Hors 35 F2
Owlbeech Way. Hors 35 F2
Owletts. Cra 18 A4
Owlscastle Cl. Hors 35 D3
Ownside. Bri 166 A3
Oxen Ave. S Sea 184 B4
Oxford Cl. E Wit 202 B4
Oxford Ct. Bri 187 F4
Oxford Ct. Mid 90 B4
Oxford Dr. Bog R 195 E2
Oxford Pl. Bri 187 F4
Oxford Rd. Cra 17 E1
Oxford Rd. Hors 35 E1
Oxford Rd. Wing 182 A2
Oxford St. Bog R 195 F1
Oxford St. Bri 187 F4

Packham Way. Bur H 104 B2
Paddock Cl. Fer 46 C3
Paddock Gdns. E Gri 21 E4
Paddock Green. Rust 179 E1
Paddock La. Sels 206 B4
Paddock The. Bog R 196 A3
Paddock The. Cra 18 A4
Paddock The. Hasl 25 F4
Paddock The. Hove 166 A1
Paddock The. Lym 178 A3
Paddock The. S Sea 163 D1
Paddock Way. Find 160 B3
Paddock Way. Ip 24 A3
Paddockhall Rd. Hay H 83 D3
Paddockhurst La. Bal 40 A2
Paddockhurst Rd. Cra 16 C3
Paddockhurst Rd. Tur H 19 E2
Paddockhurst Rd. Wor 18 C1
Paddocks The. Lan 183 E3
Paddocks The. Upp B 141 F2
Paddocks. Barn 175 F3
Padstow Wlk. Cra 16 B2
Padwick Rd. Hors 35 F1
Pages La. Wing 182 C2
Paget Cl. Hors 56 B4
Pagham Cl. Her 169 D4
Pagham Gdns. S Hay 189 F1
Pagham Rd. Bog R 194 C2
Pagham Rd. N Mun 194 C4
Pagham Rd. Run 173 E1
Pains Flat. Bur H 104 A4
Palace Pl. Bri 187 F3
Palatine Rd. Wing 181 D2
Pallant The. Wing 180 C2
Pallingham La. Petw 73 E1
Palm Ct. E Pre 200 C4
Palmeira Ave. Hove 187 D3
Palmeira Pl. Hove 187 D4
Palmeira Sq. Hove 187 D3
Palmer Cl. Horl 1 B3
Palmer Cl. Stor 117 E1
Palmer Pl. Run 173 D1
Palmer Rd. Ang 179 E3
Palmer Rd. Cra 18 A2
Palmer's Rd. Ems 147 F1
Palmers Way. Wing 160 A1
Palmerston Ave. Wing 181 D1
Palmerston Rd. S Hay 189 D2
Pankhurst Ave. Bri 188 A3
Pankhurst Ct. Cra 16 C1
Pannell Cl. E Gri 8 A1
Panton Cl. Ems 147 F2
Parade The. Bog R 205 F4
Parade The. Cra 17 E4
Parade The. E Gri 7 F2
Paradise La. Wbou 148 A2
Parchment St. Chic 172 B4
Parham Cl. Bri 188 A3
Parham Cl. Lit 178 A1
Parham Cl. Rust 199 F4
Parham Rd. Cra 16 B4
Parham Rd. Wing 160 B1
Parish La. Pea P 38 B3
Park Ave. Hove 186 B4
Park Ave. Key 124 C1
Park Ave. S Sea 184 C4
Park Ave. Sels 206 C4
Park Ave. Wing 182 B2
Park Cl. Bri 167 E3
Park Cl. Bur H 104 B2
Park Cl. Hove 165 E2
Park Cl. Hur 123 F3
Park Cl. Por S 164 C1
Park Cl. Wing 181 F4
Park Copse. Sels 205 D1
Park Cres. Ems 147 E1
Park Cres. For R 22 C1
Park Cres. Mid 90 B4
Park Cres. Por S 185 F4
Park Cres. Sels 206 C4
Park Cres. Wing 182 A1
Park Crescent Pl. Bri 187 F4
Park Crescent Rd. Bri 187 F4
Park Crescent Terr. Bri 187 F4
Park Ct. Bri 166 B3
Park Dr. Bog R 197 D3
Park Dr. Ferr 180 B1
Park Dr. Rust 179 D1
Park Dr. Yap 176 C1
Park Farm Cl. Hors 35 D4
Park Hill. Bri 188 A3
Park La. Ald 174 C3
Park La. Ash 118 A3
Park La. Ash W 22 A3
Park La. Bos 171 E2
Park La. Box 153 D3
Park La. Fer 46 C3
Park La. Fise 171 E3
Park La. Hay H 62 A1
Park La. Map 78 C3
Park La. Sels 204 C1
Park La. Sli 155 D2
Park La. Sock 185 D4
Park La. W Gri 100 A4
Park La. Wbou 148 B4
Park Par. Hay H 83 E2
Park Pl. Aru 156 C2
Park Rd. Barn 176 A3
Park Rd. Bog R 195 F1
Park Rd. Bri 167 E3
Park Rd. Bur H 104 C2
Park Rd. Burs 6 A4
Park Rd. Dor P 8 B3
Park Rd. E Gri 8 A1
Park Rd. Fay 15 E1
Park Rd. For R 22 C1
Park Rd. Han 58 C3
Park Rd. Hasl 26 A3
Park Rd. Hay H 83 E2
Park Rd. Hen 121 E2
Park Rd. Petw 93 E4
Park Rd. S Sea 184 C4
Park Rd. Sels 206 C4
Park Rd. Sla 58 C3
Park Rd. Slin 33 F3
Park Rd. Sou 148 B1
Park Rd. Wham 152 B3
Park Rd. Wing 182 B2
Park Rd. Yap 176 C1
Park Rise. Hors 34 C2
Park Rise. Hove 165 E2
Park Rise. Petw 93 E4
Park Road Terr. Bri 187 F3
Park St. Bri 188 A3
Park St. Hors 35 D1
Park St. Slin 33 D2
Park Terr E. Hors 35 D1
Park Terr W. Hors 35 D1
Park Terr. Bog R 195 F1
Park View Rd. Hove 165 F1
Park View. Hay H 83 E3
Park View. Horl 1 C2
Park Way Cl. Sock 185 E4
Park Way. Cra 18 A4
Park Way. E 68 C1
Park Way. Hors 35 D1
Parker Cl. Cra 18 A3
Parker's Cotts. E Lav 151 F3
Parkfield Ave. Bog R 195 D2
Parkfield Cl. Cra 16 B3
Parkfield Ct. Wing 181 F2
Parkfield Rd. Wing 181 F2
Parkfield. Hors 35 D2
Parkhurst Gr. Horl 1 B2
Parkhurst Gr. Horl 1 B2
Parkhurst Rd. Horl 1 B2
Parklands Ave. Bog R 195 F2
Parklands Ave. Wing 181 D1
Parklands Rd. Chic 172 B4
Parklands Rd. Key 124 B2
Parklands. S Sea 185 D4
Parklawn Ave. Horl 1 B3
Parkmore Terr. Bri 187 E4
Parkrise. Hove 165 E2
Parkside Ave. Lit 178 B1
Parkside. Cra 17 E3
Parkside. E Gri 8 A1
Parkside. Key 124 C2
Parkside. S Sea 163 F1
Parkway The. Rust 179 D1
Parkway. Bog R 195 F2
Parkway. Horl 1 C2
Parnell Cl. Cra 18 A2
Parry Dr. Rust 178 C1
Parsonage Estate. Rog 65 F2
Parsonage Rd. Hen 121 E3
Parsonage Rd. Hors 35 E2
Parsonage Way. Hors 35 E2
Parsons Cl. Hasl 26 A4
Parsons Cl. Horl 1 B2
Parsons Green. Hasl 26 A4
Parsons Hill. Aru 156 C2
Parsons Wlk. Hors 55 E4
Parsons Wlk. Walb 176 B4
Parthings La. Hors 55 E4
Passfield Rd. Pass 23 E4
Passfield Walk. Hav 147 D3
Paston Pl. Bri 188 A2
Pasture Hill Road. Hay H 83 D3
Pasture The. Cra 18 A3
Patcham By Pass. Bri 166 B3
Patchdene. Bri 166 B3
Patching Cl. Cra 16 B4
Patching Cl. Wing 180 C2
Patchings. Hors 35 E2
Paterson Wilson Rd. Lit 178 B1
Path Link. Cra 17 E4
Pathfield Cl. Rud 32 A4
Pathfield Rd. Rud 32 A4
Pathfields Cl. Hasl 26 A4
Pathfields. Hasl 26 A4
Patricia Ave. Wing 181 D1
Patricia Cl. Wing 181 D1
Patrick's Cl. Liss 43 D2
Patrick's Copse Rd. Liss 43 D2
Patrington Cl. Cra 16 C2
Patterdale Cl. Cra 17 D2
Pavement The. Cra 17 E3
Pavilion Bldgs. Bri 187 F3
Pavilion Par. Bri 187 F3
Pavilion Rd. Wing 181 F2
Pavilion St. Bri 187 F3
Pavilion Way. E Gri 21 E4
Pax Cl. Cra 16 B2
Paxmead Cres. Wing 182 B3
Payne Ave. Hove 186 B4
Payne Cl. Bog R 205 F4
Payne Cl. Cra 18 A4
Paynesfield. Bol 81 D2
Paythorne Cl. Sock 164 A1
Peace Cl. Bri 167 D1
Peacemaker Cl. Cra 16 B2
Peacheries The. Chic 173 D3
Peachey Rd. Sels 206 B3
Peacock La. Bri 166 B2
Peacock Wlk. Cra 16 C2
Peacock's Hill. Crab 79 D3
Peacocks La. Tha 98 A1
Peak La. W King 201 D4
Peak The. Row C 126 B1
Pearson Rd. Aru 156 B1
Pearson Rd. Cra 18 A3
Peartree Cl. Bur H 104 B2
Peartree Cnr. Cow 79 D1
Peary Cl. Hors 35 D3
Pease Croft. S Har 87 D2
Pease Pottage Hill. Cra 17 D1
Pebble Wlk. Lit 178 C2
Peckhams Copse La. Chic 173 D2
Peckhams Copse La. Run 173 D1
Peeks Brook La. Burs 5 E3
Peel Cl. Lit 178 A1
Peel Rd. Bri 188 B2
Peerley Cl. E Wit 202 C3
Peerley Rd. E Wit 202 C3
Pegasus Cl. Hasl 25 D3
Pegasus Ct. Cra 16 B2
Pegasus Way. E Gri 8 C2
Pegwell Cl. Cra 16 B2
Pelham Dr. Cra 16 C1
Pelham Pl. Cra 16 C1
Pelham Rd. Hay H 83 F3
Pelham Rd. Wing 181 F3
Pelham Sq. Bri 187 F3
Pelham St. Bri 187 F3
Pelham Terr. Ems 169 D4
Pemberton Cl. Lan 183 E4
Pembley Green. Copt 6 B2
Pembroke Ave. Hove 186 C4
Pembroke Ave. Wing 181 E1
Pembroke Cres. Hove 186 C4
Pembroke Gdns. Hove 186 C3
Pembroke Rd. Cra 5 D1
Pembroke Way. Bog R 195 E2
Pembury Cl. Hay H 83 F2
Pembury Cl. Wing 182 A2
Pembury Rd. Hav 168 A4
Pembury Rd. Wing 182 A2
Penbridge La. Shi 98 C3
Pende Cl. Lan 183 D4
Pendean. Bur H 105 D1
Pendine Ave. Wing 182 C2
Penfold La. Rust 179 D2
Penfold Rd. Cra 17 F1
Penfold Rd. Wing 182 B3
Penfold Way. Stey 141 D1
Penfolds Pl. Aru 156 C1
Penhill Rd. Lan 183 E3
Penhurst Pl. Bri 188 B3
Penland Cl. Hay H 83 D4
Penland Rd. Hay H 83 D4
Penlands Cl. Stey 141 D1
Penlands Rise. Stey 141 D1
Penlands Vale. Stey 141 D1
Penlands Way. Stey 141 D1
Penleigh Cl. Lan 183 E3
Penn Cl. Cra 4 A1
Penn Cl. M Sea 197 E3
Penn Cres. Hay H 83 F3
Penn Gdns. Ash 118 B3
Penn's Gt. Stey 141 D2
Pennels Cl. Mil 44 C1
Penny La. Her 169 D4
Pennyfields. Bog R 197 D3
Pensfold La. Rud 32 B3
Penshurst Cl. Cra 18 A4
Penstone Cl. Lan 183 D3
Penstone Park. Lan 183 E3
Pentland Rd. Wing 181 E4
Penwarden Way. Bos 171 D4
Penwith Dr. Hasl 25 D3
Penwood Green. Hav 147 D3
Peperham Rd. Hasl 26 A4
Pepper's La. Asht H 120 A3
Peppering La. Burp 157 F4
Pepperscoombe La. Upp B 141 F1
Perching Dro. Ful 143 E2
Percival Terr. Bri 188 A2
Percy Rd. Hors 34 C2
Peregrine Rd. Lit 178 B1
Perimeter Rd E. Cra 4 C3
Perimeter Rd N. Cra 4 A4
Perimeter Rd S. Cra 4 B3
Perimeter Rd. Cra 4 C4
Perkstead Ct. Cra 16 C2
Perrots La. Stey 141 D1
Perry Ave. E Gri 8 B2
Perryfield La. Crab 79 F3
Perryfield Rd. Cra 17 D3
Perrylands. Charl 3 E4
Perrymount Rd. Hay H 83 E3
Perth Cl. Cra 4 A1
Perth Way. Hors 35 E2
Pescott's Cl. Bir 192 B3
Peskett Cl. Bar G 54 B1
Peter Rd. Lan 183 D2
Peterborough Rd. Cra 17 E1
Peterhouse Cl. Bog R 195 E2
Peterlee Wlk. Cra 16 B1
Peterlee Wlk. Cra 16 B1
Petersfield Rd. Hav 147 D3
Petersfield Rd. Mid 90 B4
Petlands Gdns. Hay H 83 E2
Petlands Rd. Hay H 83 E2
Pett Cl. Bri 188 B3
Petworth Ave. Wing 181 D1
Petworth Ct. Cra 16 B2
Petworth Ct. Hasl 26 A3
Petworth Dr. Bur H 104 C2
Petworth Dr. Hors 35 E4
Petworth Rd. Bri 166 C3
Petworth Rd. Hasl 26 B3
Pevensey Cl. Cra 18 A3
Pevensey Gdns. Wing 181 F1
Pevensey Rd. Bog R 195 F2
Pevensey Rd. Bri 188 A4
Pevensey Rd. Sour 55 F1
Pevensey Rd. Wing 181 F1
Peverel Rd. Cra 16 B3
Peverel Rd. Wing 181 F2
Peveril Cl. Lan 182 C3
Peveril Dr. Lan 182 C3
Phoenix Cl. Chic 172 C3
Phoenix Cres. Sock 185 D4
Phoenix La. Ash W 22 B3
Phoenix Pl. Bri 187 F3
Phoenix Way. Sock 185 D4
Phrosso Rd. Wing 181 E1
Pickers Green. Hay H 83 F4
Pickhurst La. Pul 95 F4
Pickwell La. Ans 81 E2
Pickwell La. Bol 81 E2
Pict's La. Crab 79 F2
Picton St. Bri 188 A4
Pier Rd. Lit 199 D4
Pigbush La. Lox 30 C4
Pigeonhouse La. Rust 200 B4
Piggery Hall La. Shi G 191 E1
Pike The. Was 139 E4
Pilgrim Ct. Hay H 83 F3
Pilgrims Cl. Wing 181 F2
Pilgrims Way. N Mun 194 C1
Pilgrims Wlk. Wing 181 F2
Piltdown Rd. Bri 188 B3
Pimms Gdns. Bri 187 F3
Pine Cl. Bil 53 D1
Pine Cl. Cra 4 A1
Pine Cl. Mid 90 B3
Pine Cl. Stor 117 F2
Pine Ct. Ems 147 F2
Pine Gdns. Horl 1 C1
Pine Gr. Chic 151 D1
Pine Gr. E Gri 7 F2
Pine Gr. Hav 147 D1
Pine Shaw. Cra 18 A4
Pine Tree Cl. Hur 123 F3
Pine Trees Cl. Ang 179 E4
Pine Trees. Hass 124 A2
Pine View Cl. Hasl 26 A4
Pine Way Cl. E Gri 21 E4
Pine Wlk. Bog R 195 D2
Pine Wlk. Liss F 43 D3
Pineham Copse. Hay H 83 E2
Pinehurst Park. Bog R 195 D2
Pinehurst. Bur H 104 C1
Pinehurst. Hors 35 D2
Pinelands Rd. Par G 100 B1
Pines Ave. Wing 182 A4
Pines Rd. Lip 23 E2
Pines The. Ang 179 E2
Pines The. Hay H 83 F2
Pines The. Hors 36 A3
Pines The. Yap 176 B2
Pinetrees Cl. Copt 5 F2
Pinewood Cl. Bro H 34 A2
Pinewood Cl. E Pre 179 F1
Pinewood Ct. W Lav 90 C3
Pinewood Gdns. Bog R 195 F2
Pinewood Way. Mid 90 B3
Pinkhurst La. Slin 33 F1
Pinks La. Bir 192 A2
Pioneer Way. Swan 37 D1
Pipers Cl. Hove 165 D2
Pipers Cl. Sour 55 E1
Pipers La. Eber 49 F3
Pipers La. N 49 F4
Piries Pl. Hors 35 D1
Pit Rd. Hur 123 F3
Pitcroft La. Nur 86 A3
Pitcroft The. Chic 173 D4
Pitfold Ave. Hasl 25 D3
Pitfold Cl. Hasl 25 E3
Pitsham La. Mid 90 A2
Pitsham Wood. Mid 90 A3
Pivington La. Lit C 147 F3
Plainfields Ave. Bri 166 C4
Plainwood Cl. Chic 151 E1
Plaistow Cl. Bri 188 B3
Plaistow Rd. Ifo 30 A1
Plaistow Rd. Kir 50 C2
Plaistow Rd. Lox 30 B1
Plaistow Rd. Pla 29 D4
Plaistow Rd. Pla 50 C4
Plantain Cres. Cra 16 C1
Plantation Cl. Wing 181 E4
Plantation Rd. Hill B 43 D1
Plantation Rise. Wing 181 F4
Plantation The. E Pre 179 F1
Plantation The. Stor 116 C1
Plantation The. Wing 181 F4
Plantation Way. Stor 117 D1
Plantation Way. Wing 181 E4
Plat The. Hors 34 C2
Platt The. Dor 8 C4
Platt The. Hay H 83 F3
Plaw Hatch La. For R 42 B3
Plaw Hatch La. Sha 42 A3
Playden Ct. Cra 16 C2
Pleasant La. Tho I 169 E1
Pleyden Cl. Bri 188 B2
Plough Cl. Cra 16 B4
Plough La. Hors 35 E3
Plover Cl. Bog R 196 A4
Plover Cl. Cra 17 D4
Plover Cl. E Wit 202 C3
Plovers Rd. Hors 35 E2

Plummerden La. Hay H 62 B1
Plumpton Rd. Bri 188 A3
Plumtree Cross La. Bar G 54 C2
Plumtree Cross La. Itc 54 C3
Plymouth Ave. Bri 167 E1
Polecat La. Cops 78 A4
Polecat La. Nuth 56 A1
Poles La. Cra 4 A2
Poling Cl. Wing 180 C2
Poling Cnr. Pol 178 C4
Poling St. Pol 178 C4
Pollard's Hill. Sour 77 F3
Pollards Dr. Hors 35 E1
Pollards. Cra 16 C3
Polperro Cl. Ferr 180 B1
Pomper La. God G 103 F1
Pond Cl. Lox 30 B2
Pond Copse La. Lox 30 B3
Pond La. Wing 181 D4
Pond Rd. E Wit 202 C3
Pond Rd. S Sea 184 B4
Pond Rise. W Chi 97 E1
Pond Way. E Gri 8 C1
Pond Wood Rd. Cra 17 F4
Pondcroft Rd. Hay H 83 F4
Pondfield. Rud 32 A4
Pondtail Cl. Hors 35 D3
Pondtail Dr. Hors 35 D4
Pondtail Rd. Hors 35 D3
Pony Farm. Find 160 B3
Pook La. E Lav 151 F3
Pook La. Hav 168 A4
Pookbourne La. Hic 103 E2
Pool Valley. Bri 187 F2
Popes Mead. Hasl 26 A4
Poplar Ave. Hove 165 E2
Poplar Cl. Bri 166 B1
Poplar Cl. Cra 4 A1
Poplar Cl. Hove 165 E2
Poplar Gr. S Hay 189 D2
Poplar Rd. Wing 181 D3
Poplar Way. Mid 90 B3
Poplars The. Ferr 201 E4
Poplars The. Hors 35 E2
Poplars The. Yap 176 C2
Porchester Cl. Sour 55 F1
Port Hall Ave. Bri 187 E4
Port Hall Pl. Bri 187 E4
Port Hall Rd. Bri 187 E4
Port Hall St. Bri 187 E4
Porters Cl. Brenc 156 A1
Portfield Ave. Bri 166 C3
Portfield Way. Chic 173 D4
Portland Ave. Hove 186 B4
Portland Mews. Bri 188 A2
Portland Pl. Bri 188 A2
Portland Rd. Bur H 104 B2
Portland Rd. E Gri 21 E4
Portland Rd. Hove 186 B4
Portland Rd. Wing 182 A1
Portland St. Bri 187 E3
Portland Villas. Hove 186 A4
Portland's Cl. She 64 A3
Portsmouth La. Hay H 83 E4
Portsmouth Rd. Bos 171 E3
Portsmouth Rd. Bram 24 B4
Portsmouth Rd. Fise 171 F3
Portsmouth Rd. Lip 23 F1
Portsmouth Wood Cl. Hay H 83 E4
Portsmouth Wood. Hay H 83 E4
Portway. Stey 141 D1
Post Horn Cl. For R 22 C1
Post Horn La. For R 22 C1
Post Office La. N Mun 194 A4
Post Office La. Run 173 D1
Post View. Stor 138 B4
Potters Croft. Hors 35 E1
Potters Field. Liss 43 D2
Potters Green. Cow 79 E1
Potters La. Bur H 104 B1
Potters Mead. Wick 178 A2
Pottery La. Hamb 170 A4
Potts La. Pul 96 A1
Poulner Cl. Bog R 196 C3
Poulter's A. Wing 181 F3
Poulter's Cnr. Wing 181 F3
Pound Cl. Lox 30 B3
Pound Cl. Petw 93 E4
Pound Farm Rd. Chic 173 D3
Pound Hill Par. Cra 18 A3
Pound Hill Pl. Cra 18 A3
Pound La. Cow 101 D4
Pound La. Man H 57 D3
Pound La. Shi 77 D1
Pound La. Upp B 141 F1
Pound Lea. S Hay 189 D3
Pound Pl. Petw 93 E4
Pound Rd. W Wit 190 C1
Pound Rd. Walb 155 D1
Pound St. Petw 93 E4
Pound The. Bog R 195 E1
Pound The. Bur H 104 B2
Poundfield La. Ifo 29 F2
Povey Cross Rd. Cra 1 B1
Povey Cross Rd. Hoo 1 B1
Poveys Cl. Bur H 104 A2
Powell Cl. Horl 1 B2
Powis Gr. Bri 187 E3
Powis Rd. Bri 187 E3
Powis Sq. Bri 187 E3
Powis Villas. Bri 187 E3
Poynes Rd. Horl 1 B3
Poynings Dr. Hove 165 E2
Poynings Rd. Cra 16 A3
Poynter Rd. Hove 186 C4
Poyntz Cl. Chic 172 B2
Pratton Ave. Lan 183 D4
Precinct The. Bog R 195 E2
Prescott Gdns. Bur H 104 C2
Preston Ave. Rust 179 D1
Preston Circ. Bri 187 F4
Preston Dro. Bri 166 B1
Preston Paddock. Rust 179 E1
Preston Park Ave. Bri 166 B1
Preston Rd. Bri 187 E4
Preston St. Bri 187 E3
Prestonville Rd. Bri 187 E4
Prestwick Cl. Cra 16 A3
Prestwood Cl. Cra 3 F1
Prestwood Cl. SE18 3 E2
Prestwood La. Rusp 3 D2
Pretoria Ave. Mid 90 B4
Pretoria Rd. Mid 90 B4
Price Way. Ard 61 F4
Priest Croft Cl. Cra 16 C3
Priestley Way. Bog R 197 D3
Priestley Way. Cra 4 C2
Priestley Way. M Sea 197 D3
Prime Cl. Walb 176 B4
Primrose Ave. Horl 1 C1
Primrose Cl. Cra 16 C2
Primrose La. For R 22 C1
Primrose La. Rake 43 E2
Prince Albert St. Bri 187 F3
Prince Ave. Lan 183 F3
Prince Charles Cl. Sock 164 B1
Prince Regent's Cl. Bri 188 B2
Prince William Cl. Wing 181 F4
Prince's Cres. Bri 187 F4
Prince's Rd. Bri 187 F4
Prince's St. Bri 187 F3
Princes Ave. Hove 186 C3
Princes Cres. Hove 186 C3
Princes Croft. Bog R 194 C1
Princes Pl. Bri 187 F3
Princes Sq. Hove 186 C3
Princes's Terr. Bri 188 B2
Princess Anne Rd. Rud 32 A3
Princess Ave. Bog R 195 F1
Princess Ave. Wing 181 E2
Princess Margaret Rd. Rud 32 A4
Princess Rd. Cra 17 D3
Prings La. Low B 57 D1
Prings La. Map 79 D4
Prinsep Rd. Hove 186 C4
Prinstead La. Sou 169 E4
Priors Acre. Box 153 D2
Priors Cl. Sou 148 C1
Priors Cl. Upp B 141 F1
Priors Leaze La. Hamb 149 D1
Priors Waye. Bog R 194 C1
Priors Wlk. Cra 17 E3
Priors Wood. Hasl 25 E3
Priory Cl. Bog R 205 F4
Priory Cl. Box 153 D2
Priory Cl. Horl 1 B2
Priory Cl. Lan 182 C4
Priory Cl. Wing 181 F2
Priory Field. Upp B 141 F1
Priory La. Chic 172 C4
Priory Rd. Aru 156 B1
Priory Rd. Bur H 104 C1
Priory Rd. Chic 172 C4
Priory Rd. For R 42 C4
Priory Rd. Hass 124 B3
Priory Rd. Rust 178 C1
Priory Way. Hay H 83 E2
Promenade The. Ems 168 C4
Prospect La. Hav 147 D3
Prospect La. Row C 147 D4
Prospect Pl. Cra 17 D3
Prospect Pl. Wing 182 A1
Providence Pl. Bri 187 F4
Providence Terr. Wing 182 B2
Providence The. Chic 172 B4
Pruetts La. She 64 C4
Pryors Green. Bog R 195 D1
Pryors La. Bog R 195 D1
Puckshott Way. Hasl 26 A4
Puffin Rd. Cra 16 A3
Pulborough Cl. Bri 188 B4
Pulborough Rd. Stor 116 C1
Pulborough Way. Bog R 197 D3
Pulens Cres. Pete 64 B2
Pulens La. Pete 64 A2
Punch Copse Rd. Cra 17 E4
Punches La. S Mun 194 A3
Punnetts Ct. Cra 16 B1
Purbeck Pl. Lit 178 A1
Purcell Rd. Cra 16 B2
Purton Rd. Hors 34 C2
Putmans Lane. S Har 86 C4
Puttock Cl. Hasl 25 D3
Pycroft Cl. N Hay 168 B2
Pyecombe Ct. Cra 16 B2
Pyecombe St. Pye 144 C3
Pyrford Cl. Bog R 194 C1
Quadrangle The. Find 160 B2
Quadrant The. Key 124 C2
Quadrant The. Wing 181 D2
Quail Cl. Hors 35 D4
Quail Cl. Hors 35 F3
Quakers La. Hay H 83 F3
Quantock Cl. Wing 181 E4
Quantock Rd. Wing 181 E4
Quarries The. Man H 57 D3
Quarry Bank Rd. Bri 166 C1
Quarry Cl. Bur H 105 D2
Quarry Cl. Hors 35 E3
Quarry Hill. Hay H 83 D3
Quarry Rise. E Gri 8 C2
Quarry Way. Sour 55 E1
Quarterbrass Farm Rd. Hors 35 D4
Quashetts The. Wing 182 A3
Quay La. Gree 22 B4
Quayside. Lit 177 F1
Quebec St. Bri 187 F3
Queen Alexandra Ave. Hove 165 F2
Queen Borough Gdns. Chis 34 C3
Queen Caroline Cl. Hove 165 F2
Queen Elizabeth Ave. Bur H 104 B1
Queen Elizabeth Rd. Rud 32 A4
Queen Mary Ave. Hove 165 F2
Queen Sq. Bri 187 E3
Queen St. Aru 156 C1
Queen St. Ems 169 D4
Queen St. Hors 35 D1
Queen St. Lit 178 A1
Queen St. Wing 182 A2
Queen Victoria Ave. Hove 165 F2
Queen's Ave. Chic 172 B2
Queen's Gdns. Bri 187 F3
Queen's Gdns. Chic 172 B2
Queen's Gdns. Hove 187 D3
Queen's Park Rd. Bri 188 A3
Queen's Park Rise. Bri 188 A3
Queen's Park Terr. Bri 188 A3
Queen's Pl. Bri 187 F4
Queen's Pl. Hove 187 D3
Queen's Pl. S Sea 184 B4
Queen's Rd Quadrant. Bri 187 E3
Queen's Rd. Bri 187 E3
Queen's Rd. E Gri 8 B1
Queen's Rd. Horl 1 C2
Queen's Rd. Wing 182 A1
Queen's Sq. Bog R 196 A2
Queen's Wlk. E Gri 8 B1
Queens Cres. Bur H 104 C1
Queens Dr. Key 124 B2
Queens Field E. Bog R 195 E2
Queens Field W. Bog R 195 E2
Queens Field Wlk. Bog R 195 E2
Queens Gate. Cra 4 C4
Queens La. Aru 156 C1
Queens Rd. Hay H 83 E3
Queens Rd. Lan 183 E3
Queens Rd. Sock 164 B1
Queens Sq. Cra 17 D3
Queens St. Ste 67 F1
Queensbury Mews. Bri 187 E3
Queensmead. Bog R 205 E4
Queensway. Bog R 195 E1
Queensway. Bog R 196 A2
Queensway. Bri 188 A3
Queensway. Cra 17 E3
Queensway. E Gri 8 B1
Queensway. Hors 35 D1
Queensway. N Hay 168 A2
Querneby Cl. S Sea 185 D4
Quickset Cotts. Shi G 191 E2

Racecourse Way. Cra 4 B4
Rackfield. Hasl 25 D4
Rackham Cl. Cra 17 D2
Rackham Cl. Wing 181 E3
Rackham Rd. Rust 199 F4
Rackham Rd. Wing 181 E3
Rackham St. Amb 136 C4
Rackham St. Rac 136 C4
Racton Rd. Ems 148 A2
Radburn Pl. Swans 23 D3
Radford Rd. Bog R 195 F3
Radford Rd. Cra 5 D2
Radinden Dr. Hove 166 A1
Radinden Manor Rd. Hove 187 D4
Radley Ave. Stor 116 C1
Radnor Cl. Wing 181 E2
Radnor Cres. SE18 3 E2
Radnor Rd. Wing 181 E2
Ragget's Hill. Ans 81 E2
Raglan Ave. Wing 181 E3
Railey Rd. Cra 17 E4
Railway App. E Gri 8 B1
Railway App. Wing 182 A2
Railway Mews. Hove 186 C4
Railway St. Bri 187 E3
Rainbow Way. Stor 117 E2
Rake Rd. Liss 43 D2
Rakers Ridge. Hors 35 D3
Raleigh Cl. Eri 5 E2
Raleigh Cres. Wing 181 D2
Raleigh Rd. Bog R 195 D2
Raleigh Way. Wing 181 D2
Ralls La. S Hay 189 E1
Rambledown La. W Chi C 117 D3
Ramblers Way. Cra 16 C1
Ramillies Gdns. Bog R 197 D3
Ramsay Rd. S Hay 189 D2
Ramsey Cl. Horl 1 B2
Ramsey Cl. Hors 35 D3
Ramsey Ct. Cra 16 C1
Ramshill. Pete 64 A2
Randiddles Cl. Hur 123 F2
Ranelagh Villas. Hove 186 C4
Ranmore Cl. Cra 38 A4
Ransome Cl. Cra 16 B2
Ranworth Cl. Bog R 196 B3
Rapeland Hill. Hors 14 B1
Raphael Rd. Hove 186 B4
Rascals Cl. Sour 77 E4
Ratham La. W Ash 150 A1
Rathbone Ct. Pul 96 A1
Rathlin Rd. Cra 16 C2
Raughmere Dr. E Lav 151 E2
Raven Cl. Hors 35 E3
Raven La. Cra 17 D4
Raven's Rd. S Sea 184 B4
Ravencroft Cres.. SE9 17 D1
Ravendene Ct. Cra 17 D3
Ravens Way. Bog R 195 F3
Ravensbourne Ave. S Sea 163 E1
Ravensbourne Cl. S Sea 163 E1
Ravenscroft Ct. Hors 35 D2
Ravenscroft. Stor 138 A4
Ravenswood Rd. Bur H 104 C2
Raworth Cl. Cra 18 A2
Raycroft Cl. Bog R 195 E1
Rayden Cl. Lit 178 B1
Reading Rd. Bri 188 B2
Readon Cl. Pete 64 A2
Reapers Cl. Hors 35 D3
Record Rd. Ems 147 F1
Rectory Cl. Ash 118 C3
Rectory Cl. Pul 96 A1
Rectory Cl. S Sea 185 D4
Rectory Cl. Stor 117 D1
Rectory Farm Rd. Lan 182 C4
Rectory Gdns. Wing 182 A3
Rectory La. Ang 179 E3
Rectory La. Ash 118 B3
Rectory La. Bram 24 A4
Rectory La. Charl 3 D4
Rectory La. Cra 16 B4
Rectory La. Pul 96 A1
Rectory La. Sels 204 C2
Rectory Rd. S Sea 185 D4
Rectory Rd. Stor 117 D1
Rectory Rd. Wing 181 F3
Rectory Wlk. Lan 183 D4
Rectory Wlk. Stor 117 D1
Red Admiral St. Hors 35 E3
Red Deer Cl. Hors 35 F2
Red La. Shi 77 D1
Red Lion St. Mid 90 B4
Red Oak Ct. E 68 C1
Red River Ct. Hors 34 C3
Redcross St. Bri 187 F3
Redditch Cl. Cra 16 B1
Redehall Rd. Burs 6 A4
Redford Ave. Hors 34 C2
Redgarth Ct. E Gri 7 F2
Redgill La. N Cha 85 F1
Redgrave Dr. Cra 18 A3
Redhill Cl. Bri 166 A3
Redhill Dr. Bri 166 A2
Redhill Rd. Row C 126 A1
Redkiln Cl. Hors 35 E2
Redkiln Way. Hors 35 E2
Redlands La. Ems 148 A2
Redlands La. Shi G 191 E2
Redlynch Cl. Hav 147 D2
Redmoor Estate. Bir 192 B2
Redvers Rd. Bri 167 D1
Redwing Cl. Hors 35 E2
Redwing Cl. Wick 178 A2
Redwing Rd. Chath 60 B2
Redwood Cl. Cra 17 E4
Redwood Cl. Wing 181 D3
Redwood Dr. Hay H 83 D2
Redwood Pl. Bog R 195 E1
Reed Pond Wlk. Hay H 83 F2
Reed's La. Alb 122 C4
Reedings. Cra 16 A2
Reeds La. Rake 43 E3
Reeds La. Say C 103 D1
Reef Cl. Lit 199 E4
Reeves Hill. Bri 167 D3
Refectory Rd. Bri 167 F4
Regal Dr. E Gri 21 E4
Regency Ct. Bri 166 B2
Regency Mews. Bri 187 E3
Regency Sq. Bri 187 E3
Regent Arc. Bri 187 F3
Regent Hill. Bri 187 E3
Regent Row. Bri 187 E3
Regent St. Bri 187 F3
Regents Cl. Cra 17 D1
Regents Way. Bog R 195 E2
Regis Ct. Bog R 196 A2
Reigate Cl. Cra 5 D1
Reigate Rd. Bri 166 A1
Reigate Rd. Hoo 1 A2
Reigate Rd. Sal 1 A3
Reigate Rd. Wing 181 E2
Renoir Ct. Bog R 195 F3
Renoir Mews. Bog R 195 F3
Renton Cl. Bil 75 D4
Reservoir La. Pete 64 A3
Rest-a-wyle Ave. S Hay 189 D3
Rew La. Chic 151 E2
Reynard Cl. Hors 35 F3
Reynolds Pl. Cra 17 D4
Reynolds Rd. Cra 17 D4
Reynolds Rd. Hove 186 B4
Rhodes Way. Cra 17 E2
Rices Hill. E Gri 8 B1
Richardson Rd. Hove 186 B4
Richmond Ave W. Bog R 195 F2
Richmond Ave. Bog R 195 F1
Richmond Ave. Chic 151 F1
Richmond Cl. Rust 179 E1
Richmond Ct. Wing 182 A1
Richmond Pl. Bri 187 F3
Richmond Rd N. Bog R 196 A2
Richmond Rd. Bog R 196 A2
Richmond Rd. Bri 187 F4
Richmond Rd. Hors 35 D2
Richmond Rd. Wham 152 B2
Richmond Rd. Wing 182 A1
Richmond Sq. E Gri 8 A2
Richmond St. Bri 187 F3
Richmond Way. E Gri 21 E4
Rickfield. Cra 16 C3
Rickman's La. Pla 29 E1
Rickwood. Horl 1 C2
Ride The. Bri 166 B1
Ride The. Ifo 30 A1
Ridge Cl. Por S 164 C2
Ridge Rd. Fal 167 F4
Ridge Rd. Wmes 146 C1
Ridge View. Bri 167 E3
Ridge Way. Hay H 83 F1
Ridgehurst Dr. Hors 34 B1
Ridgeside Ave. Bri 166 B3
Ridgeside. Cra 17 E3
Ridgeway Cl. Sock 164 B1
Ridgeway The. Bur H 104 C2
Ridgeway The. Chic 172 B4
Ridgeway The. Fer 46 C3
Ridgeway The. Horl 1 C1
Ridgeway The. Hors 34 C2
Ridgeway. E Gri 21 E4
Ridgeway. Sock 164 B1
Ridgewick Rd. Bri 167 D3
Ridgway The. Bog R 196 C2
Ridings The. Bog R 195 D1
Ridings The. Bur H 105 D1
Ridings The. Cra 18 A4
Ridings The. E Pre 200 B4
Ridings The. Liss 43 D2
Ridings The. Padd W 139 E2
Ridings The. Stey 141 D1
Ridleys. W Hoa 41 E3
Rife La. Sels 206 A4
Rife Way. Bog R 196 B2
Rife Way. Ferr 180 B1
Rifeside Gdns. Ferr 180 B2
Rigden Rd. Hove 166 A1
Riley Rd. Bri 167 D1
Rill Wlk. E Gri 8 C1
Rillside. Cra 17 F2
Ring Rd N. Cra 5 D4
Ring Rd S. Cra 5 D4
Ring Rd. Lan 162 B1
Ringley Ave. Horl 1 C1
Ringley Oak. Hors 35 E2
Ringley Rd. Hors 35 E2
Ringmer Rd. Bri 167 E2
Ringmer Rd. Wing 181 E3
Ringwood Cl. Cra 17 D2
Ripley Rd. Wing 181 E2
Ripon Gdns. Bog R 195 E2
Rise The. Cra 18 A3
Rise The. E Gri 21 E4
Rise The. Hay H 83 F3
Rise The. Par G 100 C2
Rise The. Por S 164 B1
Ritchie Cl. S Hay 189 D2
Rival Moor Rd. Pete 64 B1
River Cl. S Sea 184 B3
River La. Lod 70 A2
River La. Upp 70 B1
River Mead. Cra 3 F1
River Mead. Hors 34 C1
River Rd. Aru 156 C1
River Rd. Lit 178 A1
River St. Wbou 148 A3
River Way. Hav 147 D2
Riverhill La. Petw 94 B4
Rivermead. Pul 96 A1
Riverside Ind Est. Lit 177 F1
Riverside Rd. S Sea 184 B3
Riverside. Chic 172 C4
Riverside. For R 22 B2
Riverside. Horl 1 C1
Riverside. Hors 34 C1
Riverside. S Sea 184 B3
Riverside. Stor 117 D1
Riverside. Upp B 141 F1
Rixons Cl. Hor K 63 D3
Rixons Orch. Hor K 63 D3
Robell Way. Stor 117 E2
Robert St. Bri 187 F3
Robert Way. Hors 35 E4

Roberts Cl. Sour 55 E2
Roberts Rd. Lan 183 E2
Robertson Rd. Bri 166 A1
Robin Cl. Cra 17 D4
Robin Cl. Sour 55 F1
Robin Dene. Bri 188 B2
Robin Hood La. Bro H 34 B3
Robin Hood La. Hors 34 C3
Robin Hood Roundabout. Hors 34 C3
Robin's Cl. Sels 206 B4
Robins Dr. Bog R 195 D2
Robinson Cl. Lan 183 E3
Robinson Rd. Cra 17 D3
Robinswood Ct. Hors 35 E2
Robson Rd. Wing 181 E1
Rochester Cl. Chic 151 E1
Rochester Cl. Wing 180 C3
Rochester Gdns. Hove 187 D3
Rochester St. Bri 188 A3
Rochester Way. Bog R 195 E2
Rock Gdns. Bog R 196 A1
Rock Gr. Bri 188 A2
Rock La. Stor 118 B1
Rock Pl. Bri 187 F2
Rock Rd. Stor 118 A2
Rock St. Bri 188 B2
Rockingham Cl. Wing 181 E3
Rocks La. Bal 39 E1
Rocky La. Hay H 83 D1
Rodmell Rd. Wing 181 E3
Rodney Cl. Bog R 195 D2
Rodney Cres. F 177 D2
Roebuck Cl. Hors 35 F2
Roedale Rd. Bri 166 C1
Roedean Cres. Bri 188 C2
Roedean Path. Bri 188 C2
Roedean Rd. Bri 188 C2
Roedean Rd. Wing 181 E3
Roedean Vale. Bri 188 C2
Roedean Way. Bri 188 C2
Roedeer Copse. Hasl 25 E3
Roffey Cl. Horl 1 B2
Roffey Cnr. Hors 35 F2
Roffeys Cl. Copt 5 F2
Rogate Cl. Lan 182 C4
Rogate Cl. Wing 181 F3
Rogate Rd. Wing 181 F3
Roger's La. Find 160 B2
Rogers Mead. N Hay 168 A2
Rolfe Dr. Bur H 105 D2
Rollaston Park. Yap 176 C1
Romaine Cl. Bur H 105 D3
Roman Acre. Lit 178 A1
Roman Cres. Sock 185 E4
Roman Rd. Bra 141 E2
Roman Rd. Hove 186 A3
Roman Rd. Sock 185 E4
Roman Way. Bil 53 D1
Roman Way. Fise 171 F3
Roman Way. Sock 185 E4
Roman Wlk. Lan 182 C4
Romany Cl. Por S 185 F4
Romany Rd. Wing 180 C3
Romney Broadwalk. Bog R 195 F3
Romney Garth. Sels 206 C4
Romney Rd. Wing 181 E1
Romsey Cl. Bri 167 D1
Rona Cl. Cra 16 C2
Rook Way. Hors 35 E3
Rookcross La. Dia P 99 F3
Rookery La. Sid 204 C4
Rookery The. Her 148 A1
Rookery Way. Hay H 83 E1
Rooksbury Croft. Hav 147 D3
Rookwood La. W Wit 191 D2
Rookwood Rd. W Wit 191 D1
Roosthole Hill. Man H 57 D4
Rope Wlk. Lit 178 A1
Rope Wlk. S Sea 184 B4
Ropes La. Fer 47 D3
Ropetackle. S Sea 184 B4
Rosamund Rd. Cra 17 F2
Rose Ave. M Sea 197 E3
Rose Cottage La. Sta 59 F3
Rose Ct. Bog R 195 D2
Rose Green Rd. Bog R 195 D2
Rose Hill Cl. Bri 187 F4
Rose Hill Terr. Bri 187 F4
Rose Hill. Bri 187 F4
Rose Terr. Barn 176 A3
Rose Wlk. Wing 181 E1
Rosebarn Cl. Bur H 105 D1
Rosebery Ave. Wing 181 E1
Rosecroft Cl. Lan 183 E3
Rosedale Cl. Cra 16 C2
Rosehill. Bil 53 D1
Roseleigh Gdns. Sca H 84 B2
Rosemary Ave. Bra 141 E2
Rosemary Cl. Bra 141 E2
Rosemary Cl. Cuc 82 C3
Rosemary Cl. Petw 93 E4
Rosemary Cl. Stor 117 D1
Rosemary Ct. Hasl 26 A4
Rosemary Dr. S Sea 163 F1
Rosemary La. Alf 30 A4
Rosemary La. Charl 3 E4
Rosemary La. Horl 1 C2
Rosemary La. Petw 93 E4
Rosier Way. Bil 75 E3
Ross Cl. Bog R 194 C1
Ross Cl. Cra 17 E2
Rossalyn Cl. Bog R 194 C2
Rossiter Rd. Lan 183 E4
Rosslyn Ave. S Sea 184 C4
Rosslyn Ct. S Sea 184 B4
Rosslyn Green. Maid 88 B1
Rosslyn Rd. S Sea 184 B4
Rossmore Cl. Cra 5 D1
Rossmore Cl. Cra 5 D1
Rosvara Ave. Wgate 175 D4
Rothbury Rd. Hove 186 A4
Rother Cl. Pete 64 B2
Rother Cl. Stor 117 E2
Rother Cres. Cra 16 B3
Rother La. Tro 66 C1
Rotherbank Farm La. Liss F 43 D3
Rotherbridge La. Petw 93 E3
Rotherfield Cl. Bri 166 C3
Rotherfield Cres. Bri 166 C3
Rothermead. Petw 93 E4
Rothervale. Horl 1 B3
Rothesay Cl. Wing 181 E2
Rothley Chase. Hay H 83 E2
Rotten Row. S End 193 E2
Rough Field. E Gri 8 A2
Rough Way. Hors 35 E3
Round Hill Cres. Bri 187 F4
Round Hill Rd. Bri 187 F4
Round Hill St. Bri 187 F4
Roundabout Copse. W Chi C 117 D3
Roundabout La. W Chi C 117 D3
Roundabouts The. Liss 43 D3
Roundabouts. W Chi C 117 D3
Roundhouse Meadow. Ems 169 D4
Roundle Ave. Bog R 196 C3
Roundle Rd. Bog R 197 D3
Roundle Sq. Bog R 196 C3
Roundle Square Rd. Bog R 196 C3
Roundstone By Ps Rd. E King 180 A2
Roundstone By Ps Rd. E Pre 179 F2
Roundstone Cres. E Pre 179 F1
Roundstone Dr. E Pre 179 F1
Roundstone La. Ang 179 F2
Roundstone La. E Pre 179 F2
Roundstone Way. Sels 206 C4
Roundway The. Rust 200 A4
Roundway. Bri 167 E3
Roundwood La. Hay H 83 E4
Rowan Ave. Hove 165 E1
Rowan Cl. Cra 17 E3
Rowan Cl. Hay H 83 F2
Rowan Cl. Hors 35 F3
Rowan Cl. Por S 164 C1
Rowan Cl. Stor 117 E1
Rowan Dr. Bil 53 D1
Rowan Lea. Chath 60 B2
Rowan Rd. Hav 147 D2
Rowan Tree Cl. Liss 43 D2
Rowan Way. Bog R 196 A4
Rowan Way. Hors 36 A3
Rowan Wlk. Cra D 20 A4
Rowans The. Wing 181 F1
Rowanwood Ave. Sid 18 B2
Rowhill La. Bal 60 B3
Rowhook Hill. Row 33 E4
Rowhook Rd. Row 33 F4
Rowin Cl. S Hay 189 E1
Rowland Cl. Copt 6 B3
Rowlands Rd. Hors 35 F3
Rowlands Rd. Wing 181 F1
Rowner Rd. Bil 74 C4
Rowplatt La. Fel 7 E2
Roxburgh Cl. Wing 181 E4
Royal Bldgs. Lan 183 D2
Royal Cl. Chic 173 D3
Royal Cres Mews. Bri 188 A2
Royal Cres. Bri 188 A2
Royal Gdns. Row C 126 A1
Royal George Rd. Bur H 104 B2
Royce Cl. W Wit 191 D1
Royce Rd. Cra 4 C2
Royce Way. W Wit 191 D1
Royston Cl. Cra 4 C1
Roystons The. E Pre 200 B4
Ruckmans La. Oak 12 C4
Rucrofts Cl. Bog R 195 E2
Rudford Ind Est. Hor G 177 D1
Rudgwick Ave. Wing 180 C1
Rudgwick Cl. Rust 199 F4
Rudgwick Rd. Cra 16 B4
Rudwick's Cl. M Sea 197 D2
Rudwick's Way. M Sea 197 D2
Rufwood. Cra D 19 F4
Rugby Pl. Bri 188 B2
Rugby Rd. Bri 166 C1
Rugby Rd. Wing 181 F2
Ruislip Gdns. Bog R 195 D1
Rumbolds Cl. Chic 173 D3
Rumbolds Hill. Mid 90 B4
Rumbolds La. Hay H 83 D1
Runcorn Cl. Cra 16 B1
Runcton La. N Mun 194 B4
Runcton La. Run 173 E1
Runcton La. S Mun 194 B3
Runshooke Ct. Cra 16 C2
Rusbridge Cl. Bog R 195 D2
Rushams Rd. Hors 34 C2
Rushes The. Hay H 84 A2
Rushetts Pl. Cra 4 A1
Rushetts Rd. Cra 3 F1
Rushlake Cl. Bri 167 E3
Rushlake Rd. Bri 167 E3
Rushwood Cl. Hay H 83 F2
Ruskin Cl. Cra 5 D1
Ruskin Cl. Sels 206 C4
Ruskin Pl. Hove 186 B4
Ruskin Rd. Hove 186 B4
Ruskin Rd. Wing 182 B2
Rusper Keep. Cra 16 B4
Rusper Rd S. Wing 181 E3
Rusper Rd. Bri 167 D3
Rusper Rd. Cra 16 B3
Rusper Rd. Hors 14 C1
Rusper Rd. Newd 2 A2
Rusper Rd. Rusp 14 B4
Rusper Rd. Rusp 16 B3
Rusper Rd. Wing 181 E3
Ruspers. Bur H 105 D1
Russ Hill. Charl 3 D3
Russel Way. Pete 64 A1
Russell Cl. Wing 182 B3
Russell Cres. Bri 187 E4
Russell Pl. Bri 187 E3
Russell Rd. Bri 187 E3
Russell Rd. E Wit 202 B4
Russell Sq. Bri 187 E3
Russell St. Chic 173 D3
Russell Way. Cra 17 F3
Russell's Cl. E Pre 179 F1
Russells Cres. Horl 1 C1
Russells Dr. Lan 183 E3
Rustington Rd. Bri 166 C3
Rustlings Cl. Hay H 83 F3
Ruston Ave. Rust 179 D1
Ruston Park. Rust 179 E1
Rutherford Way. Cra 4 C2
Rutherwick Cl. Horl 1 B2
Ruthven Cl. Cuc 82 B4
Rutland Gdns. Hove 186 B4
Rutland Rd. Hove 186 C4
Rutland Way. Chic 173 D4
Rydal Cl. Cra 16 A2
Rydal Cl. Lit 178 C2
Ryde Rd. Bri 188 A4
Ryders Way. Hors 35 E4
Rye Ash. Cra 17 F4
Rye Cl. Wing 181 F1
Rye Farm La. Bar G 54 C1
Ryecroft Cl. Wing 181 D1
Ryecroft Dr. Hors 34 C2
Ryecroft Gdns. Wing 181 D1
Ryecroft La. Stor 117 D1
Ryecroft Meadow. Man H 57 D3
Ryecroft Rd. Bol 81 D2
Ryecroft. Grave 42 A4
Ryecroft. Hav 147 D1
Ryecroft. Hay H 83 E2
Ryedale Ct. Dunt 81 D2
Ryefield Cl. Pete 64 B2
Ryelands Dr. Bri 167 D2
Ryelands. Cra 16 C3
Ryst Wood Rd. For R 22 C1

Sabre Rd. Tho I 169 D2
Sack La. Shr 175 E1
Sackville Cl. E Gri 8 A2
Sackville Cres. Wing 182 B2
Sackville Gdns. E Gri 8 A2
Sackville Gdns. Hove 186 B3
Sackville La. E Gri 7 F2
Sackville Rd. Hove 186 C4
Sackville Rd. Wing 182 B2
Sackville Way. Wing 182 B2
Saddle La. Sels 206 B4
Saddler Row. Cra 17 D2
Saddler's Row. Petw 93 E4
Saddlers Cl. Bur H 105 D1
Saddlers Cl. Thu 90 A1
Sadler St. Bog R 196 A1
Sadler Way. Bri 188 B3
Sadlers Walk. Ems 169 D4
Saffron Cl. Cra 16 C2
Saffron Cl. S Sea 164 A1
Saffrons The. Bur H 104 B3
St Agnes Rd. E Gri 8 B1
St Alban's Rd. Hav 147 D2
St Andrew's Cl. Ferr 180 B1
St Andrew's Cl. Ovi 174 A3
St Andrew's Rd. Bri 166 C1
St Andrew's Rd. Por S 186 A4
St Andrew's Rd. S Hay 189 D1
St Andrew's Rd. Wing 181 E2
St Andrews Ct. Chic 172 C3
St Andrews Rd. Bur H 105 D2
St Andrews Rd. Cra 16 A3
St Ann's Hill. Mid 90 B4
St Annes Rd. Cra 5 D1
St Anselm's Rd. Wing 181 F2
St Anthony's Way. Rust 179 D1
St Anthony's Wlk. Bog R 195 D2
St Ary's R. E Pre 179 E1
St Aubin Cl. Cra 16 B1
St Aubins Rd. Ferr 201 E4
St Aubyn's Cres. Sock 185 F4
St Aubyn's Rd. Por S 185 F4
St Aubyn's Rd. Sock 186 A4
St Aubyns S. Hove 186 C3
St Aubyns. Hove 186 C3
St Augustine Rd. Lit 199 E4
St Augustine's Cl. Sca H 84 B2
St Bernards Ct. Lan 183 E3
St Blaises Rd. Box 153 D2
St Botolph's Rd. Wing 181 F2
St Brelades Rd. Cra 16 B1
St Catherine's Rd. Lit 199 D4
St Catherines Rd. Cra 5 D1
St Christopher's Green. Hasl 25 F3
St Christopher's Rd. Hasl 25 F3
St Christopher's Rd. Hur 123 F3
St Christophers Cl. Hors 35 D2
St Clare's Gdns. Bog R 195 F3
St Clement Rd. Cra 16 B1
St Cuthman's Rd. Stey 141 D2
St Cuthmans Cl. Bri 188 B3
St Cyriacs. Chic 172 C4
St Dunstan's Rd. Wing 181 F2
St Edmund Cl. Cra 4 A1
St Edmund's Rd. Hay H 83 E2
St Edward's Cl. E Gri 8 A1
St Elmo Rd. Wing 181 F2
St Flora's Rd. Lit 178 B1
St Francis Wlk. Cra 16 B2
St Gabriels Rd. Bil 75 E4
St George's Ave. Hav 147 D1
St George's Cl. Sels 206 C4
St George's Dr. Chic 172 B2
St George's Gdns. Hors 35 E2
St George's La. Hur 123 F3
St George's Mews. Bri 187 F3
St George's Pl. Bri 187 F3
St George's Pl. Hur 123 F3
St George's Rd. Wing 182 B1
St George's Terr. Bri 188 A2
St Georges Cl. Horl 1 C2
St Georges Ct. Cra 17 D4
St Georges Rd. Bri 188 A2
St Georges Rd. Par G 100 B2
St Georges Wkl. Eas 175 E4
St Giles Cl. S Sea 184 C4
St Helen's Cres. Hove 165 D2
St Helen's Dr. Hove 165 D2
St Helen's Rd. Bri 188 A4
St Helier Cl. Cra 16 C1
St Helier Rd. Ferr 201 E4
St Heliers Ave. Hove 186 B4
St Hermans Rd. S Hay 189 E1
St Hilda's Cl. Cra 5 D1
St Hilda's Cl. Horl 1 C2
St Hilda's Cl. Sels 206 B3
St Hill Rd. E Gri 21 D3
St Hugh's Cl. Cra 5 D1
St Itha Cl. Sels 206 B3
St Itha Rd. Sels 206 B3
St James Ave. Lan 183 E4
St James Rd. E Gri 8 B1
St James Wlk. Cra 17 D1
St James' Ind Est. Chic 173 D4
St James' Rd. Ems 147 F1
St James's Ave. Bri 187 F3
St James's Cl. Bir 192 B3
St James's Pl. Bri 187 F3
St James's Rd. Chic 173 D4
St James's Sq. Chic 173 D4
St James's St. Bri 187 F2
St James's Street Mews. Bri 187 F3
St Joan Cl. Cra 4 A1
St John Cl. Hors 35 E1
St John's Ave. Bur H 104 B2
St John's Ave. Wing 181 D1
St John's Cl. Bog R 195 E2
St John's Cl. E Gri 8 B1
St John's Cl. Mid 90 B4
St John's Cl. Wing 181 D1
St John's Cres. Bro H 34 B2
St John's Pl. Bri 187 F3
St John's Pl. Hove 187 D3
St John's Rd. Cra 17 D3
St John's Rd. E Gri 8 B1
St John's Rd. Hay H 83 E1
St John's Rd. Sou 148 B1
St John's St. Chic 172 C3
St Johns Cl. Wgate 175 D3
St Johns Rd. Bur H 104 C2
St Johns Rd. Hove 187 D3
St Joseph's Cl. Hove 186 C4
St Josephs Way. Hay H 83 E2
St Julian's La. S Sea 185 D4
St Julians Cl. S Sea 185 D4
St Keyna Ave. Hove 186 A3
St Lawrence Ave. Wing 181 F2
St Lawrence Way. Hur 123 F4
St Leodegar's Way. Hun 172 C1
St Leonard's Ave. Hove 186 A4
St Leonard's Ave. S Hay 189 D2
St Leonard's Gdns. Hove 186 A3
St Leonard's Rd. Bri 188 A4
St Leonard's Rd. Hors 35 E1
St Leonard's Rd. Hove 186 A4
St Leonards Dr. Cra 17 F2
St Leonards Park. E Gri 8 B1
St Louie Cl. Sock 185 F4
St Luke's Cl. Wing 182 C2
St Luke's Rd. Bri 188 A3
St Luke's Terr. Bri 188 A3
St Malo Cl. Ferr 201 E4
St Margaret's Ave. Dor P 8 B3
St Margaret's Pl. Bri 187 E3
St Margaret's Rd. E Gri 8 B2
St Margarets Rd. S Hay 189 D2
St Mark's Cres. Wing 182 C2
St Mark's Mews. Bri 188 B2
St Mark's St. Bri 188 B2
St Marks La. Hors 35 E3
St Martin's La. Lit 178 A1
St Martin's Pl. Bri 188 A4
St Martin's Sq. Chic 172 C3
St Martin's St. Bri 187 F4
St Martin's St. Chic 172 C3
St Martins. Lit 178 A1
St Mary Magdalene St. Bri 187 F4
St Mary's Cl. Lit 178 B1
St Mary's Cl. M Lav 151 E4
St Mary's Cl. Pul 96 A1
St Mary's Cl. S Sea 184 B4
St Mary's Dr. Cra 17 F4
St Mary's Gdns. Chic 172 C4
St Mary's Gdns. Hors 35 D1
St Mary's Gdns. Lit 178 B1
St Mary's Pl. Bri 187 F2
St Mary's Rd W. Bur H 104 B2
St Mary's Rd. Box 153 D2
St Mary's Rd. Bur H 104 B2
St Mary's Rd. S Hay 189 D2
St Mary's Rd. S Sea 184 B4
St Mary's Sq. Bri 188 A2
St Mary's Way. Lit 178 B1
St Marys Cl. Bog R 196 A3
St Marys Gate Mews. Aru 156 C2
St Marys Meadow. Yap 176 B2
St Matthew's Rd. Wing 182 A2
St Maur's Rd. Ferr 180 B1
St Michael's Ct. Wing 181 F1
St Michael's Pl. Bri 187 E3
St Michael's Rd. Por S 185 F4
St Michael's Rd. Wing 181 F1
St Michaels Rd. E Gri 8 B1
St Michaels Way. Par G 100 C2
St Nicholas Ct. M Sea 197 E3
St Nicholas Gdns. Roc 44 A2
St Nicholas Rd. Bri 187 E3
St Nicholas Rd. M Lav 151 E3
St Nicholas Rd. Por S 185 F4
St Nicholas' La. M Sea 197 E3
St Nicolas La. S Sea 184 A4
St Osmund Rd. Ferr 180 B1
St Pancras. Chic 172 C4
St Patrick's La. Rake 43 E3
St Patrick's Rd. Hove 186 C4
St Paul's Ave. Wing 182 C2
St Paul's Cl. Hay H 83 E3
St Paul's Rd. Chic 172 B4
St Paul's St. Bri 187 F4
St Pauls Gdns. Chic 172 B4
St Peter's Ave. N Hay 168 B2
St Peter's Cl. Cow 79 E1
St Peter's Cl. Hove 165 E1
St Peter's Cres. Sels 206 B4
St Peter's Pl. Bri 187 F3
St Peter's Rd. Cra 17 D3
St Peter's Rd. Por S 185 F4
St Peter's Sq. Ems 168 C4
St Peter's St. Bri 187 F4
St Peter's. Chic 172 C4
St Peters Cl. Bog R 195 E2
St Peters Rd. Bur H 104 C2
St Peters Rd. N Hay 168 B2
St Raphael's Rd. Wing 181 E1
St Richard's Dr. Bog R 195 D2
St Richard's Rd. Por S 185 F4
St Richard's Rd. Sock 185 F4
St Richard's Way. Bog R 195 D2
St Richard's Wlk. Chic 172 B3
St Richards Rd. Wgate 175 E4
St Roche's Cl. M Lav 151 E4
St Sampson Rd. Cra 16 B1
St Stephens Cl. Hasl 25 E3
St Stephens Cl. Hasl 26 A4
St Swithun's Cl. E Gri 8 B1
St Thomas Dr. Bog R 205 E4
St Thomas's Rd. Wing 181 F2
St Valerie Rd. Wing 181 F1
St Vincent Cl. Cra 18 A3
St Wilfred's Rd. Wing 182 A2
St Wilfreds Cl. Sels 206 C4
St Wilfreds View. Sels 206 A4
St Wilfrid Rd. Chic 172 A4
St Wilfrid's Way. Hay H 83 E2
St Wilfrids Rd. Bur H 104 C2
St Winefride's Rd. Lit 199 E4
St Winifreds Cl. Bog R 196 A1
Sake Ride La. Hen 121 F4
Salehurst Rd. Cra 18 B3
Salfords Way. Sal 1 C4
Salisbury Rd. Cra 17 E1
Salisbury Rd. Hors 55 F4
Salisbury Rd. Hove 187 D3
Salisbury Rd. Wing 182 A1
Salisbury Way. Chic 151 E1
Salt Box Cl. Bar G 54 B1
Saltdean Cl. Cra 17 D2
Salterns Cl. S Hay 189 E2

Salterns La. S Hay 189 E2
Salthill La. Chic 172 A4
Salthill Rd. E Ash 150 C1
Salthill Rd. Fise 171 F4
Saltings The. Bir 192 B2
Saltings The. Lan 183 E3
Saltings The. Lit 178 C1
Saltings The. S Sea 184 A3
Saltings Way. Upp B 141 F1
Salvington Cl. Wing 181 D4
Salvington Gdns. Wing 181 E3
Salvington Hill. Wing 160 B1
Salvington Rd. Cra 16 B2
Salvington Rd. Wing 181 E4
Samaritan Cl. Cra 16 B2
Samphire Cl. Cra 16 C2
San Feliu Ct. E Gri 8 C1
Sanctuary La. Stor 118 A1
Sand Hills La. Bar G 54 B2
Sandeman Way. Hors 56 B4
Sanderlings The. S Hay 189 D1
Sanderson Way. Tud 137 D3
Sandfield Ave. Wick 178 A2
Sandgate La. Stor 117 F1
Sandgate Rd. Bri 166 C1
Sandhawes Hill. E Gri 8 C2
Sandhill La. Cra D 19 F4
Sandown Ave. Wing 181 D1
Sandown Cl. Wing 181 D1
Sandown Rd. Bri 188 A4
Sandown Rd. Sock 185 D4
Sandpiper Cl. Cra 16 A2
Sandridge La. Hay H 61 E1
Sandringham Cl. E Gri 21 F4
Sandringham Cl. E Wit 202 C3
Sandringham Cl. Hove 165 F2
Sandringham Dr. Hove 165 F2
Sandringham Rd. Chic 173 D3
Sandringham Rd. Cra 16 C1
Sandringham Way. Bog R 195 F2
Sandrock. Hasl 26 A3
Sandrock. Mid 90 A4
Sandrocks Way. Hay H 83 E1
Sands La. Sma D 142 B3
Sands The. Ash 118 C3
Sandwich Rd. Wing 181 E1
Sandy Beach Estate. S Hay 189 F1
Sandy Cl. Pete 64 B2
Sandy La. Bram 25 D4
Sandy La. Cra D 19 F4
Sandy La. E Ash 150 A2
Sandy La. E Gri 8 B1
Sandy La. Fit 94 C1
Sandy La. Hen 121 D2
Sandy La. Rake 43 F2
Sandy La. W Hoa 41 E3
Sandy Point La. Sels 206 A4
Sandy Point Rd. S Hay 189 F1
Sandy Rd. Bog R 205 F4
Sandy Rise. Cold 115 D3
Sandygate La. Low B 57 F2
Sandymount Ave. Bog R 195 F3
Sandymount Cl. Bog R 196 A3
Sangers Dr. Horl 1 B2
Sanyhils Ave. Bri 166 B4
Sarel Way. Horl 1 C3
Sargent Cl. Cra 17 E1
Sarisbury Cl. Bog R 196 C3
Sark Cl. Cra 16 C1
Sark Gdns. Ferr 180 B1
Satellite Business Village The.
Cra 4 B1
Satinwood Cl. M Sea 197 E3
Saturn Cl. Cra 16 B2
Saucelands Rd. Bro C 98 B4
Saunders Cl. Cra 17 F4
Saunders Hill. Bri 167 D4
Savernake Wlk. Cra 17 F2
Savill Rd. Hay H 83 F4
Saville Gdns. Bil 75 D4
Sawyers Cl. Bur H 105 D1
Saxon Cl. Bog R 205 E4
Saxon Cl. E Pre 179 F2
Saxon Cres. Hors 34 C2
Saxon Meadow. Tan 153 D1
Saxon Rd. Bra 141 E2
Saxon Rd. Cra 18 B3
Saxon Rd. Hove 186 A3
Saxons. S Sea 163 E1
Saxony Rd. Wing 182 A2
Sayer Cl. Stone 22 B3
Sayers The. E Gri 8 A1
Scallows Cl. Cra 17 F4
Scallows Rd. Cra 17 F4
Scamps Hill. Hay H 84 A3
Scant Rd E. Hamb 149 E1
Scant Rd W. Hamb 149 E1
Scarborough Rd. Bri 166 A1
School A. Aru 156 C1
School Cl. Bur H 104 B1
School Cl. Fit 94 C2
School Cl. Hors 35 F3
School Cl. Sock 185 E4
School Dell. W Ash 149 F2
School Hill. Find 160 B3
School Hill. Sli 155 D3
School Hill. Stor 117 E1
School Hill. Warm 34 B4
School La. Ash W 22 B3
School La. Asht H 120 A3
School La. Bos 171 D3
School La. Com 106 C1
School La. Dan 63 F3
School La. Eas 175 E4
School La. Ems 168 C4
School La. Fit 94 C2
School La. Pye 145 D3
School La. Run 173 D1
School La. Sels 206 B4
School La. She 64 A3
School La. Sou 169 F4
School La. Ste 67 E1
School La. Stey 141 D2
School La. Stor 117 D1
School La. Sut 113 E2
School La. Was 139 E4
School La. Wbou 148 A3
School Rd. Amb 136 B4
School Rd. Hasl 25 E3
School Rd. Hove 186 B4
School Rd. Upp B 141 F1
Schooner Ct. Lit 178 C1
Scory Cl. Cra 16 C2
Scotland La. Hasl 26 A3
Scotland St. Bri 187 F3
Scotlands Cl. Hasl 25 F3
Scotney Cl. Wing 180 C3
Scott Cl. Bog R 196 A1
Scott Rd. Cra 17 E2
Scott Rd. Hove 186 B4
Scott St. Bog R 196 A1
Scratchings La. Eber 49 F3
Sea Ave. Rust 200 A4
Sea Cl. M Sea 197 E3
Sea Cl. Wing 181 E1
Sea Dr. Ferr 201 E4
Sea Dr. M Sea 197 D2
Sea Front Estate. S Hay 189 D1
Sea Front. S Hay 189 D1
Sea Grove Ave. S Hay 189 D1
Sea La Cl. E Pre 179 E1
Sea La. Bog R 205 E4
Sea La. E King 201 D4
Sea La. E Pre 200 B4
Sea La. Ferr 180 B1
Sea La. K Gor 201 D4
Sea La. M Sea 197 E3
Sea La. Rust 178 C1
Sea La. Wing 181 D1
Sea Lane Cl. Ferr 180 B1
Sea Lane Gdns. Ferr 180 B1
Sea Pl. Wing 181 E1
Sea Rd. Bog R 196 B2
Sea Rd. E Pre 200 C4
Sea Rd. Lit 199 F4
Sea Rd. Rust 199 F4
Sea View Rd. S Hay 189 E2
Sea View Rd. Wing 181 F1
Sea Way. Bog R 205 E4
Sea Way. M Sea 197 E2
Sea Way. M Sea 197 F3
Seafarers Walk. S Hay 189 F1
Seafield Ave. Wing 181 D1
Seafield Cl. E Wit 202 B3
Seafield Cl. Rust 200 A4
Seafield Rd. Hove 186 C3
Seafield Rd. Rust 200 A4
Seafield Way. E Wit 202 C3
Seafields. E Wit 202 C3
Seafields. Ems 168 C4
Seafields. Wit 203 D3
Seaford Rd. Cra 16 C1
Seaford Rd. Hove 186 A3
Seagate Ct. E Wit 202 B3
Seagate Wlk. Lit 199 F4
Seagull La. Ems 147 F1
Seahaven Gdns. S Sea 184 A3
Seal Rd. Sels 206 B3
Seal Sq. Sels 206 B3
Seamill Park Ave. Wing 182 C2
Seamill Park Cres. Wing 182 C2
Seamill Way. Wing 182 C2
Searle's View. Hors 35 E3
Seaside Ave. Lan 183 E3
Seaside Cl. Lan 183 E3
Seaside Rd. Lan 183 E3
Seaton Cl. Wick 178 A2
Seaton La. Wick 178 A2
Seaton Park. Wick 178 A2
Seaton Rd. Wick 178 A2
Seaview Ave. E Pre 200 C4
Seaview Ave. K Gor 201 D4
Seaview Ct. Lan 183 D2
Seaview Ct. Sels 206 A3
Seaview Rd. E Pre 200 C4
Seaview Rd. Wood 188 C4
Seaward Dr. W Wit 191 D1
Seawaves Cl. E Pre 179 F1
Second Ave. Bir 192 B1
Second Ave. Bog R 196 C2
Second Ave. E Wit 202 C3
Second Ave. Hav 147 D1
Second Ave. Hove 187 D3
Second Ave. Lan 183 E4
Second Ave. Sou 169 E4
Second Ave. Wing 182 A4
Sedbury Rd. Lan 183 D4
Seddon Ct. Cra 16 C1
Sedgefield Cl. Cra 18 B4
Sedgewick Cl. Cra 18 A3
Sedgewick La. Hors 56 B3
Sedgewick Rd. Bri 167 D3
Sefter Rd. Bog R 194 C2
Sefton Ave. Bog R 195 D2
Sefton Cl. Wing 181 D3
Sefton Rd. Por S 164 B2
Selangor Ave. Ems 147 E1
Selba Dr. Bri 167 E2
Selborne Cl. Pete 64 A3
Selborne Pl. Hove 187 D4
Selborne Rd. Hove 187 D3
Selborne Rd. Lit 199 E4
Selborne Rd. Wing 182 B2
Selborne Way. E Pre 200 B4
Selbourne Cl. Cra 5 D1
Selbourne Ct. Cra 5 D1
Selby Ct. Hay H 83 E2
Selden La. Ang 158 C1
Selden La. Wing 182 B1
Selden Rd. Wing 182 B1
Selden's Way. Wing 181 E4
Seldens Mews. Wing 181 E3
Selham Cl. Bri 167 D3
Selham Cl. Chic 151 F2
Selham Cl. Cra 16 C4
Selham Dr. Bri 167 D3
Selham Rd. Mid 90 B4
Selham Rd. S Amb 91 D3
Selham Rd. W Lav 90 C3
Selhurst Cl. E Pre 179 E1
Selhurstpark Rd. E Dean 132 B2
Selkirk Cl. Wing 181 E2
Selmeston Pl. Bri 188 B3
Selsey Ave. Bog R 195 F1
Selsey Cl. S Hay 189 F1
Selsey Cl. Wing 181 E3
Selsey Ct. Cra 16 C1
Selsey Rd. Chic 172 B2
Selsey Rd. Cra 16 C1
Selsey Rd. Don 193 D3
Selsey Rd. S End 193 E2
Selsey Rd. S End 193 E3
Selsey Rd. Sid 204 B4
Selsfield Dr. Bri 167 D2
Selsfield Rd. Ard 40 C3
Selsfield Rd. Sel C 19 F1
Selsfield Rd. Tur H 19 F2
Selsfield Rd. W Hoa 41 D4
Selsmore Ave. S Hay 189 E2
Selsmore Rd. S Hay 189 D2
Selway La. Lit 178 B1
Selwyn Ave. Wick 178 A2
Selwyn Cl. Bog R 195 E2
Selwyn Cl. Cra 5 D1
Semley Rd. Bri 166 C1
Semley Rd. Hass 124 B2
Sergison Cl. Hay H 83 D3
Sergison Rd. Hay H 83 D3
Sermanbury Rd. Wing 181 F2
Serrin Way. Hors 35 E3
Servite Cl. Bog R 195 F2
Sevelands Cl. Bri 188 B4
Seventh Ave. Lan 183 E3
Severals Rd. Mid 90 A4
Severals Rd. Ste 89 F4
Severn Rd. Cra 18 A3
Seville St. Bri 188 A4
Sewill Cl. Charl 3 E4
Sextant Ct. Lit 178 C1
Seymour Rd. Cra 16 C1
Seymour Sq. Bri 188 A2
Seymour St. Bri 188 A2
Shackleton Rd. Cra 17 E2
Shadwells Cl. Lan 183 E4
Shadwells Rd. Lan 183 E4
Shaftesbury Ave. Wing 181 E2
Shaftesbury Pl. Bri 187 F4
Shaftesbury Rd. Bri 187 F4
Shaftesbury Rd. Rust 200 A4
Shaftsbury Rd. Cra 18 A2
Shakespeare Rd. Wing 182 A1
Shakespeare St. Hove 186 C4
Shaldon Rd. Hav 147 D3
Shalesbrook La. For R 22 C1
Shalford Hill. Kin G 26 A1
Shamrock Cl. Bos 171 D3
Shamrock Cl. Chic 172 C4
Shandon Rd. Wing 182 A3
Shandon Way. Wing 182 A3
Shandys Cl. Hors 34 C1
Shanklin Rd. Bri 188 A4
Shannon Cl. Lit 199 F4
Shardeloes Rd. Ang 179 E3
Sharon Cl. Cra 17 F2
Sharps Rd. Hav 147 D3
Sharpthorne Cl. Cra 16 B3
Sharpthorne Cres. Por S 165 D1
Sharrow Cl. Hay H 83 E3
Shaw Cl. M Sea 197 E3
Shaw's La. Sour 55 D1
Shawfield Rd. Hav 147 D1
Shaws Rd. Cra 17 E4
Shear Hill. Pete 64 A3
Shearwater Dr. Bog R 196 A3
Sheddingdean Cl. Bur H 104 C2
Sheep Fold Ave. Rust 179 E1
Sheep La. Mid 90 B4
Sheep Pen La. Stey 141 D2
Sheepbell Cl. Por S 164 C2
Sheepdown Cl. Petw 93 F4
Sheepdown Dr. Petw 93 F4
Sheepwash La. E Lav 151 E3
Sheepwash La. W Wit 191 E2
Sheffield Cl. Cra 17 F2
Sheffield Mill La. Dan 85 F4
Shelby Rd. Wing 181 D3
Sheldon Cl. Cra 18 A3
Sheldon Cl. SE12 16 B3
Shell La. Bal 61 D4
Shellbridge Rd. Sli 155 E2
Shellbridge Rd. Walb 155 E2
Shelldale Ave. Por S 185 F4
Shelldale Cres. Por S 185 F4
Shelldale Rd. Por S 185 F4
Shelley Cl. Cra 18 A4
Shelley Dr. Bro H 34 A2
Shelley Rd. Bog R 195 F2
Shelley Rd. E Gri 8 A1
Shelley Rd. Hors 34 C2
Shelley Rd. Hove 186 B4
Shelley Rd. Wing 182 A1
Shelleys Ct. Hors 35 F2
Shenfield Way. Bri 166 C2
Shenstone. Hay H 83 F4
Shepherd Cl. Cra 17 E2
Shepherd's Hill. Hasl 26 A3
Shepherd's Mead. Wing 160 C1
Shepherds Croft. Bri 166 A2
Shepherds Mead. Bur H 104 B2
Shepherds Way. Hors 35 F3
Shepherds Way. Lip 24 A2
Shepherds Wlk. Hass 124 B3
Shepherdsgrove La. Hamm 9 F2
Sheppey Cl. Cra 17 D2
Sheppeys. Hay H 83 D1
Sheraton Wlk. Cra 16 C1
Sherborne Rd. Chic 172 B4
Sherbourne Cl. Hove 165 D2
Sherbourne Rd. Hove 165 D2
Sherbourne Way. Hove 165 D2
Sherbrooke Cl. Wing 181 D3
Sherfield Ave. Hav 147 D3
Sheridan Cl. E Gri 8 A1
Sheridan Rd. Wing 182 B3
Sheridan Terr. Hove 186 C4
Sherlock Ave. Chic 172 B4
Shermanbury Dr. Stor 117 D1
Sherwood Cl. Bog R 195 F3
Sherwood Cl. Liss F 43 D4
Sherwood Dr. Hay H 83 D3
Sherwood Rd. Bog R 195 F3
Sherwood Wlk. Cra 17 F2
Shetland Cl. Cra 18 B4
Shetland Ct. Wing 180 C3
Shingle Rd. S Sea 184 C3
Shingle Wlk. E Wit 202 B3
Shinwell Wlk. Cra 16 C1
Ship St Cl. Bri 187 F3
Ship St. Bri 187 E3
Ship St. E Gri 21 E4
Ship St. S Sea 184 B4
Ship Street Gdns. Bri 187 E3
Shipfield. Bog R 195 E1
Shipley Ct. Lip 23 F2
Shipley Rd. Cra 16 C3
Shipley Rd. Shi 77 E3
Shipley Rd. Sour 77 E3
Shipleybridge La. Bur 5 E2
Shipleybridge La. Copt 5 E2
Shire Parade. Cra 18 A4
Shire Pl. Cra 18 A4
Shires. Padd W 139 E2
Shirley Ave. Hove 165 F1
Shirley Cl. Bog R 205 F4
Shirley Cl. Cra 16 B1
Shirley Cl. Rust 200 A4
Shirley Cl. S Sea 185 D4
Shirley Cl. Wing 181 F4
Shirley Dr. Bog R 196 C3
Shirley Dr. Hove 166 A1
Shirley Dr. Wing 181 F3
Shirley Rd. Hove 187 D4
Shirley St. Hove 186 C4
Shirleys Gdns. Bog R 196 C3
Shirleys. Dit 125 E1
Shooting Fields. Stey 141 D2
Shopfield Cl. Rust 179 D1
Shopsdam Rd. Lan 183 E2
Shopwhyke Rd. Chic 173 E4
Shore Rd. Bos 170 C2
Shore Rd. E Wit 202 B4
Shorecroft. Bog R 195 E1
Shoreham By-ps. S Sea 163 F1
Shoreham Rd. Upp B 162 C4
Shoreside Wlk. E Wit 202 B4
Short Cl. Cra 4 A1
Short Furlong. Lit 178 B1
Short Gallop. Cra 18 A4
Shortgate Rd. Bri 167 E2
Shortsfield Cl. Hors 35 D3
Shottermill Rd. Hasl 25 E3
Shottermill. Hors 35 F4
Shripney La. Bog R 195 F4
Shripney La. Shr 175 D1
Shripney Rd. Bog R 196 B4
Shripney Rd. Shr 175 D1
Shrubbs Dr. M Sea 197 E3
Sickle Rd. Hasl 25 F3
Sidehill Dr. Por S 164 B1
Sidengreen La. Wham 152 B1
Sidings The. Rud 32 A4
Sidlesham Cl. S Hay 189 F1
Sidlesham La. Bir 192 C2
Silchester Dr. Cra 16 C2
Silkin Wlk. Cra 16 C1
Sillwood Pl. Bri 187 E3
Sillwood Rd. Bri 187 E3
Sillwood St. Bri 187 E3
Sillwood Terr. Bri 187 E3
Silver Birch Cl. Liss 43 D2
Silver Birch Dr. M Sea 197 E3
Silver Birch Dr. Wing 181 D3
Silver Birches. Hay H 83 F2
Silver Birches. Sma D 142 B4
Silver Glade. W Chi C 117 E3
Silver La. Bil 75 D4
Silver Way. Wit 203 D2
Silver Wood Copse.
W Chi C 116 C4
Silverdale Ave. Hove 187 D4
Silverdale Cl. Bog R 205 F4
Silverdale Dr. Lan 183 D3
Silverdale Dr. SE9 17 D1
Silverdale Rd. Bur H 105 D1
Silverdale Rd. Hove 187 D4
Silverdale. Cold 115 D3
Silverdale. Key 124 C2
Silverston Ave. Bog R 195 F1
Silvertrees. Ems 147 F1
Silvertrees. Ems 148 A1
Simmons Green. S Hay 189 E2
Sinclair Cl. Rai (K) 62 A1
Sinclair Rd. Cra 18 A2
Sincox La. Bro C 98 A3
Singleton Cl. Bog R 194 C1
Singleton Cres W. Ferr 180 B2
Singleton Cres. Ferr 180 B1
Singleton Cres. Wing 180 C1
Singleton Rd. Bri 166 C3
Singleton Rd. Bro H 34 A2
Singleton Way. Bur H 105 D1
Sinnocks. W Chi 97 E1
Sir George's Pl. Stey 141 D2
Siskin Cl. Hors 35 E3
Sissinghurst Cl. Cra 18 A4
Six Acres Cl. Bar G 54 B1
Skelmersdale Wlk. Cra 16 B1
Skeyne Dr. Pul 96 A1
Skiff La. Kir 51 E2
Skiff La. Lox 51 E4
Skipton Way. Horl 1 C3
Slade La. Rog 65 E3
Slattisfield Cl. Sels 206 C4
Slaugham Ct. Cra 16 B2
Slaugham La. Sla 58 C2
Slaugham La. Ward 58 B1
Sleets Rd. Bro H 34 B2
Slider's La. Dan 85 F4
Slider's La. Fle 85 F4
Slimbridge Rd. Bur H 104 B2
Slindon Bottom Rd. Fon 154 C2
Slindon Cl. Wing 182 A3
Slindon Rd. Wing 182 A3
Slinfold Cl. Bri 188 A3
Slinfold Wlk. Cra 16 C3
Slip Rd. Cra 4 C4
Slipper Rd. Her 169 D4
Slonk Hill Rd. S Sea 163 F1
Sloughbrook Cl. Hors 35 E3
Sloughgreen La. Whi G 59 E1
Slugwash La. Hay H 84 A1
Slugwash La. Wiv 105 F3
Small's La. Cra 17 D3
Smallcuts Ave. Sou 148 B1
Smallfield Rd. Horl 1 C2
Smallmead. Horl 1 C2
Smalls Mead. Cra 17 D3
Smith Cl. Cra 17 D2
Smith La. Tho I 169 E1
Smithbarn Cl. Horl 1 C2
Smithbarn. Hors 35 F1
Smithers Hill La. Cool 76 C1
Smithers Hill. Cool 98 C4
Smock Alley. W Chi C 117 E4
Smokejack Hill. Oak 12 A4
Smokyhouse La. S Amb 91 F3
Smolletts. E Gri 21 D4
Smuggler Way. Bar G 54 B1
Smuggler's La. Bos 170 C1
Smugglers Wharf. Stone 22 B3
Smugglers Wlk. Wing 181 E1
Smugglers' La. Bar G 54 B2
Smugglers' La. Oak 13 E4
Snapes Rd. Stor 117 E2
Snell Hatch. Cra 16 C3
Snipe La. Kin G 25 F1
Snow Hill. Copt 6 C2
Snow Hill. Dom 6 B2
Snowdrop Cl. Cra 16 C1
Snowdrop La. Hay H 84 A2
Snowflakes La. Hay H 84 D3
Snowhill La. Dom 6 B3
Soane Cl. Cra 16 B2
Soldridge Cl. Hav 147 D3
Solent Cl. Lit 178 C2

Solent Rd. E Wit 202 B3
Solent Way. Sels 206 B3
Solway Ave. Bri 166 B4
Solway Cl. Lit 178 C1
Somergate. Hors 34 B1
Somerhill Ave. Hove 187 D4
Somerhill Rd. Hove 187 D3
Somerley La. Bir 192 B1
Somerley La. Earn 203 D4
Somersbury La. Ell G 11 E4
Somerset Cl. Wing 181 F3
Somerset Gdns. Bog R 196 A3
Somerset Rd. E Pre 179 F1
Somerset Rd. Ferr 201 E4
Somerset St. Bri 188 A3
Somerstown. Chic 172 B4
Somerton Green. Bog R 196 B3
Somerville Dr. Cra 5 D1
Sompting Ave. Wing 182 A3
Sompting By-ps. Wing 182 B4
Sompting Cl. Bri 188 B4
Sompting Rd. Lan 183 D3
Sompting Rd. Wing 182 B3
Sopers La. Stey 141 D1
Sorrel Cl. Cra 16 C1
Sorrel Rd. Hors 35 E3
South Acre. S Har 87 D2
South Ash. Stey 141 D2
South Ave. Bog R 195 E2
South Ave. Bri 188 A3
South Ave. Hur 123 F3
South Ave. Wing 181 E1
South Bank. Chic 172 B2
South Bank. Hass 124 B2
South Bay. Tho I 169 D2
South Cl. Bur H 104 B2
South Cl. Cra 17 E4
South Cl. Hav 168 A4
South Cote Ave. E Wit 202 B4
South Dr. Bog R 197 D3
South Dr. Bur H 104 B2
South Dr. Ferr 201 E4
South Dr. Rust 179 D2
South Farm Rd. Wing 182 A3
South Gr. Pet W 93 E4
South Grove. Hors 35 D1
South Holmes Rd. Hors 35 F2
South La. Hou 135 F2
South La. Sou 148 B2
South La. Sou 148 C1
South La. Til 92 B4
South Lodge Cl. Bur H 104 B2
South Pallant. Chic 172 C3
South Par. Horl 1 B2
South Pas. Lit 199 E4
South Pier Rd. Cra 4 C4
South Rd. Bog R 196 B3
South Rd. Bri 166 B1
South Rd. Hay H 83 E2
South Rd. Lip 24 A1
South St. Bri 187 E3
South St. Chic 172 C3
South St. Cuc 82 B3
South St. Dit 125 D2
South St. Ems 168 C4
South St. Hors 35 D1
South St. Lan 183 E3
South St. Mid 90 B4
South St. Par G 100 C2
South St. Por S 164 C1
South St. Wing 181 F2
South St. Wing 182 A1
South Strand. E Pre 200 C4
South Terr. Lit 199 E4
South View Terr. Hen 121 E2
South View. Dit 125 E3
South View. E Pre 200 C4
South Way. Bog R 195 F3
South Wlk. M Sea 197 E3
South Woodlands. Bri 166 B3
Southall Ave. Bri 167 D1
Southampton St. Bri 188 A3
Southbourne Ave. Her 169 D4
Southbrook Rd. W Ash 149 F1
Southbrook. Cra 17 D1
Southcourt Cl. Rust 179 E1
Southcourt Rd. Wing 182 A2
Southdean Cl. M Sea 197 E3
Southdean Dr. M Sea 197 E3
Southdown Ave. Bri 166 C1
Southdown Ave. Por S 186 A4
Southdown Cl. Hay H 83 D1
Southdown Cl. Hors 35 F3
Southdown Cl. Mid 90 A3
Southdown Pl. Bri 166 C1
Southdown Rd. Bog R 196 A2
Southdown Rd. Bri 166 C1
Southdown Rd. Por S 164 C1
Southdown Rd. S Sea 184 B4
Southdown Rd. Sock 185 E4
Southdown Terr. Stey 141 E2
Southdown View Cl. Wing 182 B3
Southdown View Rd. Wing 182 B3
Southdown Way. Stor 117 E2
Southdownview Way. Wing 182 B3
Southern Rd. Sels 206 B3
Southern Ring Rd. Bri 167 F3
Southey Rd. Wing 182 A1
Southfield Rd. Wing 182 A3
Southfields Cl. Chic 172 B2
Southfields Rd. Lit 178 B1
Southgate Ave. Cra 17 E2
Southgate Dr. Cra 17 E2
Southgate Rd. Cra 17 D2
Southgate. Chic 172 B3
Southland La. W Chi C 117 E4
Southland Rd. SE18 3 E2
Southlands Ave. Horl 1 C2
Southlands Hill. Man H 57 D3
Southlands Park. Mid 90 B3
Southlands. E Gri 21 E4
Southleigh Rd. Hav 147 D2
Southmount. Bri 166 C1
Southon Cl. Por S 164 B2
Southover Pl. Bri 187 F4
Southover Rd. Bog R 196 A2
Southover St. Bri 187 F3
Southover Way. Hun 193 F4
Southsea Ave. Wing 181 E1
Southside. Pul 96 A1
Southview Cl. S Sea 185 D4
Southview Cl. Sock 164 B1
Southview Dr. Wing 181 F1
Southview Gdns. Wing 181 F1
Southview Rd. Bog R 196 C2
Southview Rd. Find 160 B3
Southview Rd. Sock 185 E4
Southwark Cl. Cra 16 C1
Southwark Wlk. Bog R 195 E2
Southwater Cl. Bri 188 A3
Southwater Cl. Wing 181 D2
Southwater St. Sour 55 F2
Southway. Bur H 104 A2
Southway. Lit 199 E4
Southways Ave. Wing 182 B3
Southwick Cl. E Gri 8 A1
Southwick Sq. Sock 185 E4
Southwick St. Sock 185 E4
Southwold Cl. Wing 160 B1
Southwood Rd. S Hay 189 E1
Spark's La. Whi G 60 B1
Sparks Ct. Lit 178 A1
Sparrows La. Ash 118 C3
Spatham La. Dit 125 E3
Spear Hill. Ash 118 C4
Speedwell Way. Hors 35 E3
Spencer Ave. Hove 165 D2
Spencer Cl. S Hay 189 D2
Spencer Rd. Ems 147 F2
Spencer Rd. Lan 183 D3
Spencer St. Bog R 196 A2
Spencer's Rd. Hors 34 C2
Spencers Pl. Hors 34 C2
Spencers Rd. Cra 17 D3
Spey Cl. Wing 181 D4
Spicers Cl. Bur H 104 B3
Spierbridge Rd. Stor 117 D1
Spiers Way. Horl 1 C1
Spindle Cl. Hav 147 E2
Spindle Warren. Hav 147 E2
Spindle Way. Cra 17 E3
Spinnais Gr. Sock 185 D3
Spinnais Gr. Sock 185 D4
Spinnaker Cl. Lit 178 C1
Spinney Cl. Cra D 20 A4
Spinney Cl. Hors 35 F3
Spinney Cl. Hur 123 F3
Spinney La W. Ich 191 F3
Spinney La. W Chi C 117 D3
Spinney N. Pul 96 A1
Spinney The. Bog R 195 E2
Spinney The. Cra 16 C2
Spinney The. E Pre 200 C4
Spinney The. Hasl 26 A4
Spinney The. Hass 124 B3
Spinney The. Hay H 83 D4
Spinney The. Hay H 83 E2
Spinney The. Horl 1 C3
Spinney The. Hove 166 A2
Spinney The. Pul 96 A1
Spinney The. W Ich 191 F3
Spinney Wlk. Barn 175 F3
Spitalfield La. Chic 172 C4
Spithandle La. Asht H 120 A2
Spithandle La. Wist 119 E1
Spooners Rd. Hors 35 F2
Sportscentre Rd. Br1 167 F3
Spring Copse. Copt 6 A2
Spring Gdns. Ash 118 B1
Spring Gdns. Bri 187 F3
Spring Gdns. Copt 6 A2
Spring Gdns. Ems 169 D4
Spring Gdns. Sock 185 E4
Spring La. Clay 145 E4
Spring La. Hay H 61 F1
Spring La. Slin 33 F3
Spring Meadow. For R 22 B1
Spring Meadows. Mid 90 B3
Spring Plat. Cra 18 A3
Spring Rd (East). Hort 54 A2
Spring St. Bri 187 E3
Spring Way. E Gri 8 C2
Springate Rd. Sock 185 E4
Springfarm Rd. Hasl 25 E3
Springfield Cl. Bir 192 B3
Springfield Cl. M Lav 151 E4
Springfield Cl. Rust 179 E1
Springfield Cres. Hors 34 C1
Springfield Ct. Hors 35 D1
Springfield Gdns. Wing 181 F4
Springfield La. Colg 36 C3
Springfield Park Rd. Hors 34 C1
Springfield Rd. Bri 187 F4
Springfield Rd. Cra 17 D3
Springfield Rd. Hors 35 D1
Springfield. Bog R 194 C1
Springfield. Chic 151 E1
Springfield. E Gri 8 A2
Springhills. Hen 121 E2
Spronkett's La. Bol 80 B2
Sproule Cl. Yap 176 C1
Sproutes La. Cool 98 A4
Spur Rd. Chic 173 D3
Spurgeon Cl. Cra 17 D4
Spy La. Lox 30 C2
Square Dr. Kin G 25 F1
Square The. Barn 175 F3
Square The. Bri 166 B3
Square The. Cra 17 D3
Square The. Find 160 B3
Square The. Lip 23 F2
Square The. S Har 87 D2
Square The. Sou 169 E4
Square The. Stor 117 D1
Square The. Was 139 D2
Square The. Wbou 148 A2
Squire Way. Hen 121 E2
Squires Cl. Cra D 19 F4
Squirrel Cl. Cra 3 F1
Stable Field. M Sea 197 F3
Stable La. Find 160 B3
Stace Way. Cra 18 B4
Stackfield Rd. Cra 16 B3
Stafford Rd. Bri 187 E4
Stafford Rd. Cra 3 F1
Stafford Way. Key 124 C2
Staffords Cl. Rust 178 C1
Staffords Pl. Horl 1 C1
Stagelands. Cra 4 A1
Stairbridge La. Hic 103 E4
Stakers La. Sour 55 F1
Stalham Way. Bog R 196 C3
Stall House La. N Hea 96 C4
Stammers Hill. Ful 143 E2
Stan Hill. Charl 3 D4
Stanbridge Cl. Cra 16 B3
Stanbridge Rd. Hav 147 D2
Stanbridge Way. Ard 61 F4
Stanbrook Cl. Bog R 195 E2
Stanbury Cl. Bos 171 D4
Standean Cl. Bri 167 D3
Standen Cl. E Gri 7 F2
Standen Pl. Hors 35 F4
Standgrove Pl. Ard 61 F3
Standstead Cl. Row C 126 B1
Stane St. Bil 53 E2
Stane St. Bil 74 C2
Stane St. Chic 173 D4
Stane St. Pul 96 B3
Stane St. Wham 152 B1
Stane Street Cl. Pul 96 A2
Stanford Ave. Bri 166 C1
Stanford Ave. Hass 124 B2
Stanford Cl. Bog R 196 B3
Stanford Cl. Hass 124 B2
Stanford Cl. Hove 166 A1
Stanford Rd. Bri 187 E4
Stanford Way. Bro H 34 A2
Stanhope Rd. Lit 178 B1
Stanhope Rd. Wing 182 A2
Stanier Cl. Cra 17 F3
Stanley Ave S. Por S 164 B2
Stanley Ave. Por S 164 B2
Stanley Cl. Bog R 196 A2
Stanley Cl. Cra 17 D2
Stanley Rd. Bri 187 F4
Stanley Rd. Ems 169 D4
Stanley Rd. Por 185 F4
Stanley Rd. Wick 178 A2
Stanley Rd. Wing 182 A2
Stanley St. Bri 187 F3
Stanley Wlk. Hors 35 D1
Stanmer Park Rd. Bri 166 C1
Stanmer St. Bri 166 C1
Stanmer Villas. Bri 166 C1
Stanmore Gdns. Bog R 195 E1
Stanover La. Bog R 196 C4
Stansfield Ct. Rust 179 D1
Stansted Cres. Hav 147 D3
Stanton Dr. Chic 151 F2
Stanwater La. Ste 67 E2
Staple La. M Lav 151 E4
Staplecross Ct. Cra 16 C2
Staplefield Dr. Bri 167 E2
Staplefield Rd. Cuc 82 A4
Staplefield Rd. Han 59 D4
Staplefield Rd. Sta 59 D3
Staples Barn La. Hen 121 D3
Staples Hill. Par G 100 B2
Stapleton Ct. Bog R 195 D1
Stapley Rd. Hove 165 D1
Star Rd. Par G 100 C1
Station App. Grays 8 B2
Station App. Hass 124 B2
Station App. Hor K 62 C4
Station App. Horl 1 C1
Station App. Hove 186 C4
Station Approach Rd. Cra 4 C4
Station Cl. Hors 35 D1
Station Cotts. Hass 124 B2
Station Hill. Cra 17 F4
Station Par. Rust 179 E1
Station Rd. Ang 179 E2
Station Rd. Aru 157 D1
Station Rd. Bil 75 D4
Station Rd. Bog R 196 A2
Station Rd. Bos 171 D4
Station Rd. Bri 166 A2
Station Rd. Bur H 104 C1
Station Rd. Cow 78 C1
Station Rd. Cox G 11 D2
Station Rd. Cra 17 D3
Station Rd. Cra D 19 F4
Station Rd. Cran 10 C2
Station Rd. Dun 93 E2
Station Rd. E Gri 8 A1
Station Rd. E Pre 179 E1
Station Rd. For R 22 B2
Station Rd. Hen 121 D3
Station Rd. Hor K 63 D3
Station Rd. Horl 1 C2
Station Rd. Hors 35 D2
Station Rd. Hors 55 D4
Station Rd. Lip 24 A1
Station Rd. Lox 30 B2
Station Rd. Mid 90 A4
Station Rd. Petw 93 E3
Station Rd. Por S 186 A4
Station Rd. Pul 95 F1
Station Rd. Rud 32 A4
Station Rd. Rust 179 D1
Station Rd. Sha 41 F3
Station Rd. Sock 185 E4
Station Rd. Sour 55 E1
Station Rd. Stey 141 E2
Station Rd. Warm 13 F1
Station Rd. Wing 182 A2
Station St. Bri 187 F3
Station Way. Cra 17 E3
Stavely Gdns. Chic 151 E2
Stead Cl. S Hay 189 D2
Stean Furlong. Wick 178 A2
Stedham La. Ste 67 F2
Stedham La. Wool 67 F2
Steels La. Chid 170 B3
Steep Cl. Find 160 B3
Steep La. Find 160 B3
Steepdown Rd. Lan 183 D4
Steeple View. Wing 181 F3
Steers Hill. Rusp 15 D3
Steers La. Cra 5 D2
Stein Rd. Sou 148 B1
Stein Rd. Sou 169 E4
Steine Gdns. Bri 187 F3
Steine La. Bri 187 F3
Steine St. Bri 187 F2
Stemp Dr. Bil 75 D4
Stephen Cl. Cra 4 A1
Stephens Rd. Bri 166 C1
Stephenson Dr. E Gri 21 E4
Stephenson Pl. Cra 17 F3
Stephenson Way. Cra 17 F3
Stepney Cl. Cra 18 A2
Sterling Par. Rust 179 D1
Sternway. Lit 178 C1
Stevenage Rd. Cra 16 B2
Stevens Ct. Hove 186 B4
Stevenson Rd. Bri 188 A3
Stewards' Rise. Aru 156 B1
Steyne Gdns. Wing 182 B1
Steyne St. Bog R 196 A2
Steyne The. Bog R 196 A1
Steyne The. Wing 182 B1
Steyning Ave. Hove 165 E2
Steyning By-ps. Stey 141 D3
Steyning Cl. Cra 17 E4
Steyning Cl. Lan 183 D4
Steyning Cl. Wing 181 D2
Steyning Cres. Stor 117 D1
Steyning Rd. S Sea 163 D2
Steyning Rd. W Gri 100 A4
Steyning Way. Bog R 196 B4
Stile Gdns. Hasl 25 E4
Stirling Cl. Bur H 105 D2
Stirling Cl. Cra 18 A3
Stirling Court Rd. Bur H 105 D2
Stirling Pl. Hove 186 C3
Stirling Rd. Chic 172 C3
Stirling Way. Bog R 195 E1
Stirling Way. Hors 35 E2
Stirrup Way. Cra 18 A4
Stoatley Hollow. Hasl 25 F4
Stoatley Rise. Hasl 25 F4
Stockbridge Cl. Hav 147 D3
Stockbridge Gdns. Chic 172 B2
Stockbridge Rd. Chic 172 B3
Stockcroft Rd. Bal 39 F1
Stocker Rd. Bog R 195 F1
Stockfield. Horl 1 C2
Stocklands Cl. Cuc 82 B4
Stocks La. Chic 151 F2
Stocks La. E Lav 151 F2
Stocks La. E Wit 202 C3
Stocks Mead. Was 139 E4
Stockwell Rd. E Gri 21 E3
Stodham La. Liss 43 D1
Stodham La. She 64 C4
Stoke Abbott Rd. Wing 182 A1
Stoke Rd. N Sto 136 A2
Stokers Cl. Cra 4 B4
Stone Cl. Wing 181 E3
Stone Hill. E Gri 21 D2
Stone La. Wing 181 E3
Stone St. Bri 187 E3
Stoneage Cl. Bog R 196 A4
Stonebridge Ct. Cra 17 D1
Stonebridge Ct. Hors 34 C1
Stonechat Cl. Pete 64 B1
Stonecroft Cl. Hove 165 E2
Stonecrop Cl. Cra 16 C2
Stonecross La. Hay H 62 B2
Stonecross Lea. Path 60 C3
Stonecross Rd. Bri 167 E2
Stonedene Cl. For R 22 C1
Stonefield Cl. Cra 17 D3
Stonefield Way. Bur H 104 B3
Stonefields. Rust 179 D1
Stoneham Rd. Hove 186 B4
Stonehill Cr. Bog R 194 C2
Stonehouse La. Cow 78 C1
Stonehouse Rd. Lip 24 A2
Stonehurst Ct. Bri 188 A3
Stonehurst Rd. Wing 181 F3
Stoneleigh Ave. Bri 166 B3
Stoneleigh Cl. Bri 166 B3
Stoneleigh Cl. E Gri 8 B1
Stonepark Dr. For R 22 C1
Stonepit La. Hen 120 C3
Stonepound Rd. Hass 124 B2
Stonery Cl. Por S 164 C1
Stonery Rd. Por S 164 C1
Stoney La. Bal 39 F3
Stoney La. Earn 203 D2
Stoney La. S Sea 185 D4
Stoney Stile Cl. Bog R 195 D1
Stoneybrook. Hors 34 B1
Stoneycroft Wlk. Cra 16 A3
Stopham Cl. Wing 181 F3
Stopham Rd. Cra 18 A2
Stopham Rd. Pul 95 E1
Stor Meadow. Stor 117 D1
Storrington Cl. Fise 171 F4
Storrington Cl. Hove 165 E1
Storrington Rd. Stor 117 F3
Storrington Rd. Stor 139 D4
Storrington Rd. Tha 117 F2
Storrington Rd. Was 139 D4
Storrington Rise. Wing 160 B2
Story Rd. Chic 173 D4
Stour Cl. Ton 118 B1
Stour Cl. Wing 181 D4
Stour Rd. Wing 181 D4
Straaudley Ct. Rust 179 E1
Strachey Ct. Cra 16 C1
Strand Cl. Cra 18 A2
Strand The. Ferr 201 E4
Strand The. S Hay 189 E1
Strand The. Wing 181 D2
Strand Way. Bog R 196 C2
Strange Gdns. Bog R 195 E1
Strathfield Cl. Hay H 83 E2
Strathmore Cl. Wing 181 E2
Strathmore Rd. Cra 3 F1
Strathmore Rd. Wing 181 E2
Stratton Ct. Bog R 196 B3
Stream Cl. Bos 170 C3
Stream La. Nutb 96 C1
Stream La. W Chi 97 D1
Stream Pk. E Gri 7 F2
Streel's La. Eber 49 E2
Street End La. S End 193 E2
Street End Rd. S End 193 E2
Street Hill. Wor 18 A3
Street La. Ard 61 F4
Street The. Box 153 D2
Street The. Bra 141 E1
Street The. Bury 135 F4
Street The. Charl 3 E4
Street The. E Pre 179 E1
Street The. E Pre 179 F1
Street The. Lan 183 E4
Street The. Nutb 96 C1
Street The. Pat 159 D1
Street The. Pla 29 E1
Street The. Rust 179 D1
Street The. S Sea 163 E1
Street The. Slin 33 D2
Street The. Ste 67 F1
Street The. Tha 117 F4
Street The. W Ich 191 E4
Street The. Walb 176 B4
Street The. Ward 80 B4
Street The. Was 139 E4
Street The. Wmes 146 B4
Streetfield Rd. Slin 33 D2
Stretch Hill. Fit 94 C3
Strettington La. Box 152 C2
Strettington Lane End. Box 152 C1
Strettons Copse. Mil 44 C1
Strickland Cl. Cra 16 B3
Stringer Way. Bri 166 B2
Strood La. Warm 34 A4
Stroud Green Dr. Bog R 195 F3
Stroud La. Fer 47 E3
Stroudley Cl. Cra 17 F3

Strouds La. Bog R 195 E3
Strudgate Cl. Cra 17 F2
Stuart Cl. Cra 18 A3
Stuart Cl. Wing 182 B2
Stuart Way. E Gri 21 E4
Stuarts Meadow. Gra 112 A4
Stubcroft La. E Wit 202 C4
Stubcroft La. Shi G 191 F1
Stubfield. Hors 34 C2
Stubpond La. Fel 7 D4
Stumblemead. Bal 39 F1
Stumblets. Cra 18 A4
Stumps End. Bos 171 D2
Stumps La. Bos 171 D2
Sturgeon St. Woolw 2 B4
Sturges Rd. Bog R 196 A2
Sturt Ave. Hasl 25 E3
Sturt Rd. Hasl 25 E3
Subworth Cl. Hay H 83 D4
Sudbury Cl. Bog R 195 D1
Sudeley Pl. Bri 188 A2
Sudeley St. Bri 188 A2
Sudeley Terr. Bri 188 A2
Sudley Gdns. Bog R 196 A2
Sudley Rd. Bog R 196 A2
Suffolk Cl. Horl 1 C1
Suffolk St. Hove 186 B4
Sugar La. Hor K 63 D2
Sugden Rd. Wing 182 B2
Sullington Cl. Bri 167 E2
Sullington Copse. Stor 117 E1
Sullington Gdns. Wing 160 B2
Sullington Hill. Cra 17 D2
Sullington La. Sul 141 F4
Sullington Mead. Bro H 34 B2
Sullington Way. S Sea 184 C4
Sullivan Dr. Cra 16 B2
Sultan Rd. Ems 147 F1
Summer Cl. Sock 185 F4
Summer La. Bog R 194 B1
Summerdale Rd. Hove 165 D1
Summerdown Cl. Wing 180 C3
Summerfield Rd. W Wit 191 D1
Summerfields. Find 160 B3
Summerhill Cl. Bog R 197 D3
Summerhill Cl. Hay H 83 E4
Summerhill Dr. Bog R 197 D3
Summerhill Dr. Hay H 83 F4
Summerhill Grange. Hay H 83 E4
Summerhill La. Hay H 83 E4
Summerlands Wlk. Hav 147 D3
Summerley La. Bog R 196 C3
Summersdale Rd. Chic 151 F1
Summersdeane. Sock 164 B1
Summersvere Cl. Cra 4 C1
Summers. Ard 61 F4
Sun Brow. Hasl 25 F3
Sun Park Cl. Bog R 195 F3
Sundale La. M Sea 197 E3
Sunderland Cl. Tan 153 D1
Sundew Cl. Cra 16 C1
Sunningdale Ct. Cra 17 D2
Sunningdale Gdns. Bog R 195 F4
Sunningdale Rd. Wing 181 E3
Sunninghill Ave. Hove 165 E1
Sunninghill Cl. Hove 165 E1
Sunny Ave. Cra D 19 F4
Sunny Cl. Wing 181 E1
Sunny Way. Bos 170 C3
Sunnybox La. Sli 155 E2
Sunnydale Ave. Bri 166 C3
Sunnydale Cl. Bri 166 C3
Sunnyhill Cl. Cra D 19 F4
Sunnymead Cl. M Sea 197 F3
Sunnymead Cl. Sels 206 C3
Sunnymead Dr. Sels 206 B3
Sunnymead. Cra 17 D3
Sunnywood Dr. Hay H 83 D2
Sunoak Rd. Man H 57 D4
Sunset La. W Chi C 117 D3
Sunte Ave. Hay H 83 E4
Sunte Cl. Hay H 83 E4
Sunvale Ave. Hasl 25 D3
Sunvale Cl. Hasl 25 F4
Surrenden Cl. Bri 166 B2
Surrenden Cres. Bri 166 B2
Surrenden Holt. Bri 166 B2
Surrenden Park. Bri 166 C2
Surrenden Rd. Bri 166 B2
Surrender Rise. Cra 38 A4
Surrey St. Aru 156 C1
Surrey St. Bri 187 E3
Surrey St. Lit 178 A1
Surrey St. Wing 182 A1
Surrey Wharf. Aru 156 C1
Surry St. S Sea 184 B4
Sussex Dr. Bog R 194 C1
Sussex Gdns. Hay H 83 F2
Sussex Gdns. Rust 179 D1
Sussex Manor Busn Pk. Cra 4 C1
Sussex Mews. Bri 188 B2
Sussex Mews. Lan 182 C4
Sussex Pl. Bri 187 F3
Sussex Rd. Hay H 83 E2
Sussex Rd. Hove 186 C3
Sussex Rd. Pete 64 A1
Sussex Rd. Wing 182 A2
Sussex Sq. Bri 188 B2
Sussex St. Bog R 196 A2
Sussex St. Bri 187 F3
Sussex St. Wick 178 A2
Sussex Terr. Bri 187 F3
Sussex Way. Bur H 104 B3
Sutherland Cl. Bog R 196 A2
Sutherland Cl. Rust 199 F4
Sutherland Ct. Bog R 196 A2
Sutherland Rd. Bri 188 A3
Sutton Ave. Rust 200 A4
Sutton Cl. Bog R 196 B3
Swainsthorpe Cl. Hay H 83 E2
Swaledale Cl. Cra 17 D2
Swallow Cl. Hav 147 D2
Swallow Rd. Cra 17 D4
Swallowfield Cl. Man H 57 D3
Swallows Cl. Lan 184 A3
Swallows Green Dr. Wing 181 D3
Swallows La. Dia P 99 E3
Swallows La. Shi 99 E3
Swallowtail Rd. Hors 35 E3
Swan Barn Cl. Hasl 26 A3
Swan Cl. Ems 169 D4
Swan Cl. Sour 55 F1
Swan Cl. Stor 117 D1
Swan Dene. Bog R 205 E4
Swan La. Charl 3 E4
Swan Sq. Hors 35 D1
Swan Wlk. Hors 35 D1
Swan Yd. Hors 35 D1
Swanborough Dr. Bri 188 B4
Swanborough Pl. Bri 188 B4
Swanbourne Cl. Lan 183 E4
Swanbourne Rd. Wick 178 A2
Swanfield Dr. Chic 173 D4
Swann Cl. Bur H 105 D2
Swann Way. Bro H 34 B2
Swans Ghyll. For R 22 B2
Swansea Gdns. Bog R 195 F1
Swarraton Rd. Hav 147 D2
Sweetlands. Key 124 C3
Swift La. Cra 17 D4
Swift Rd. Tho I 169 D2
Swillage La. Ang 158 C1
Swindon Rd. Hors 34 C2
Swiss Gdns. S Sea 184 B4
Swissland Hill. Dor P 8 B4
Sycamore Ave. Hors 36 A3
Sycamore Cl. Ang 179 E2
Sycamore Cl. Cra 4 A1
Sycamore Dr. E Gri 8 C1
Sycamore Rd. Bog R 196 A4
Sydney Rd. Hay H 83 E3
Sydney St. Bri 187 F3
Sylvan Cl. Hay H 83 F2
Sylvan Rd. Cra 17 F2
Sylvan Rd. Lan 182 C3
Sylvan Way. Bog R 195 F2
Sylvester Way. Hove 165 D2
Sylvia Cl. Bog R 194 C1
Symbister Rd. Por S 186 A4
Syresham Gdns. Hay H 83 E2
Tabard Gate. N Mun 194 C1
Tack Lee Rd. Yap 176 B2
Talbot Cres. Bri 167 D3
Talbot La. Hors 35 D1
Talbot Rd. Lit 178 A1
Tallis Cl. Cra 16 B2
Talman Cl. Cra 16 B3
Tamar Ave. Wing 181 D4
Tamar Cl. Cra 18 A3
Tamar Cl. Wing 181 D4
Tamar Way. Tan 153 D1
Tamarisk Cl. Bog R 196 A3
Tamarisk Way. E Pre 200 B4
Tamarisk Way. Ferr 180 B1
Tamarisk Wlk. E Wit 202 B3
Tamworth Rd. Hove 186 B4
Tanbridge Pl. Hors 34 C1
Tandridge Rd. Hove 186 B3
Tangle Oak. Fel 7 E2
Tangley Wlk. Hav 147 D3
Tangmere Gdns. Bog R 195 D1
Tangmere Rd. Bri 166 C3
Tangmere Rd. Chic 173 F4
Tangmere Rd. Cra 16 B3
Tangmere Rd. Tan 153 D1
Tankerdale La. She 64 B4
Tanners Field. Wiv 105 F3
Tanners La. Hasl 26 A4
Tanners Mead. Sta 59 E3
Tansy Mead. Stor 116 C1
Tanyard Ave. E Gri 21 F4
Tanyard Cl. Hors 35 E1
Tanyard Cl. Hors 35 E1
Tanyard La. Dan 63 F1
Tanyard La. Stey 141 D2
Tanyard Way. Horl 1 C2
Tarham Cl. Horl 1 B3
Tarmount La. S Sea 184 B4
Tarner Rd. Bri 187 F3
Tarragon Way. S Sea 164 A1
Tarrant St. Aru 156 C2
Tarrant Wharf. Aru 156 C1
Tarring Gate. Wing 181 F2
Tarring Rd. Wing 181 F2
Tasman Cl. Rust 200 A4
Tasman Way. Wing 181 D3
Tate Cres. Bur H 104 B3
Tate's Way. Rud 32 A4
Tatham Ct. Cra 16 C1
Taunton Gr. Bri 167 F1
Taunton Rd. Bri 167 E1
Taunton Way. Bri 167 F1
Taverner Pl. Chic 172 C3
Tavistock Down. Bri 167 D1
Tavistock Gdns. Hav 147 D1
Tavy Cl. Wing 181 D3
Tavy Rd. Wing 181 D3
Taw Cl. Wing 181 D4
Taylor's La. Bos 171 D2
Taylors Field. Mid 90 B4
Taylors Rise. Mid 90 B3
Teal Cl. Hors 35 D3
Teal Cl. S Hay 189 D2
Teasel Cl. Cra 16 C2
Teazle Cl. Pete 64 B1
Teesdale. Cra 17 D2
Teg Cl. Por S 165 D1
Teg Down. Pete 64 A2
Teign Wlk. Wing 181 D4
Telegraph St. Bri 188 A2
Telford Pl. Cra 17 E3
Telgarth Rd. Ferr 201 E4
Telham Ct. Cra 16 B2
Templars Cl. M Sea 197 D3
Templars The. Wing 182 B4
Temple Cl. Cra 18 A3
Temple Cl. Woolw 2 C4
Temple Gdns. Bri 187 E3
Temple Rd. Liss F 43 D3
Temple St. Bri 187 E3
Templesheen Rd. M Sea 197 F3
Ten Acres. Wing 182 C2
Tenacre Cl. Chic 172 C4
Tenantry Down Rd. Bri 188 B4
Tennis Rd. Hove 186 B3
Tennyson Ave. Lit 178 C1
Tennyson Cl. Cra 17 F4
Tennyson Cl. Hors 35 E3
Tennyson Rd. Bog R 195 F2
Tennyson Rd. Wing 182 A1
Tennyson Rise. E Gri 8 A1
Tennyson's La. Hasl 26 B2
Tenterden Cl. SE9 34 A4
Terminus Pl. Bri 187 E4
Terminus Pl. Lit 178 A1
Terminus Rd. Bri 187 E4
Terminus Rd. Chic 172 B3
Terminus Rd. Lit 178 A1
Terminus St. Bri 187 E3
Tern Rd. Cra 16 A3
Terrace The. Lan 183 E2
Terringes Ave. Wing 181 E3
Terry Rd. Cra 16 C1
Terwick Rise. Rog 66 A3
Test Rd. Lan 182 C3
Testers Cl. Sour 77 F4
Teville Pl. Wing 182 A2
Teville Rd. Wing 182 A2
Thackeray Rd. Wing 182 B2
Thakeham Cl. E Pre 179 F2
Thakeham Cl. Wing 180 C1
Thakeham Dr. Wing 180 C1
Thakeham Rd. Stor 117 E1
Thakenham Copse. Stor 117 F2
Thalassa Rd. Wing 182 C2
Thames Cl. Bri 187 F3
Thames Cl. Lit 199 F4
Thames Way. Wing 181 D4
Thatcher Cl. Cra 17 D2
Thatchers Cl. Bur H 105 D1
Thatchers Cl. Horl 1 C3
Thatchers Cl. Hors 35 E2
Thatchway Cl. Lit 178 A1
Thatchway The. Ang 179 E3
Thatchway The. Rust 200 A4
Theatre La. Chic 172 C3
Thelton Ave. Bro H 34 A2
Theobalds Rd. Bur H 105 D3
Theobalds Rd. Wiv 105 E4
Thesiger Cl. Wing 182 C2
Thesiger Rd. Wing 182 C2
Theydon Cl. Cra 17 F2
Thicket La. Box 153 F3
Thicket La. Eart 153 F3
Third Ave. Bog R 196 C2
Third Ave. E Wit 202 C3
Third Ave. Earn 203 E4
Third Ave. Hav 147 D1
Third Ave. Hove 186 C3
Third Ave. Lan 183 E4
Third Ave. Wing 182 A4
Thirlmere Cres. Lan 182 C3
Thirlmere Rd. Cra 16 A2
Thirlmere Way. Bog R 196 C3
Thompson Rd. Bri 167 D1
Thorgate Rd. Wick 177 F2
Thorn Cl. Pete 64 B1
Thorn Rd. Wing 182 A1
Thornbush Cres. Por S 164 C2
Thorncroft Rd. Lit 178 B1
Thorndean Rd. Bri 167 D2
Thornden. Cow 79 E1
Thorndene Ave. Bog R 195 F2
Thorndyke Cl. Cra 18 A3
Thorney Dr. Sels 206 A4
Thorney Old Park. Tho I 169 E1
Thorney Rd. Her 169 D4
Thorney Rd. Tho I 169 D4
Thornham La. Tho I 169 E3
Thornhill Ave. Bri 166 C4
Thornhill Cl. Hove 165 E1
Thornhill Rise. Por S 164 C2
Thornhill Way. Por S 164 C2
Thornlea Park. Wick 178 A3
Thornscroft. Stey 141 D2
Thornton Cl. Horl 1 B2
Thornton Meadow. Wis G 73 F4
Thornton Pl. Horl 1 B2
Threal's La. W Chi C 117 E3
Three Acres. Hors 34 C1
Three Bridges Rd. Cra 17 F3
Three Gates La. Hasl 26 B4
Thrusloes. Bog R 195 E2
Thurlestone Ct. Maid 89 D2
Thurlow Rd. Wing 182 B2
Thurne Way. Rud 32 A4
Thyme Cl. S Sea 164 A1
Ticehurst Cl. Cra 18 B3
Ticehurst Rd. Bri 188 B3
Tideway. Lit 199 F4
Tideys Mill. Par G 100 B2
Tidy St. Bri 187 F3
Tilbury Pl. Bri 187 F3
Tilbury Way. Bri 187 F3
Tilers Cl. Bur H 105 D2
Tilgate Cl. Bri 188 A3
Tilgate Dr. Cra 17 E1
Tilgate Par. Cra 17 E2
Tilgate Pl. Cra 17 E2
Tilgate Way. Cra 17 E2
Tilletts La. Warm 34 B4
Tillinghurst La. Ard 40 C1
Tillotson Cl. Cra 18 A3
Tillstone St. Bri 187 F3
Tilmore Gdns. Pete 64 A3
Tiltwood Dr. Cra D 20 A4
Timber Cl. Wing 181 D3
Timber Ct. Hors 35 D2
Timber Mill. Sour 55 E1
Timberham Way. Cra 4 B4
Timberlaine Tdng Est. Wing 182 B3
Timberlands. Cra 16 C1
Timberlands. Stor 117 E1
Timberlea Cl. Ash 118 C3
Timberleys. Lit 178 B2
Timbermill Ct. Hasl 25 E3
Timbers The. Man H 57 D3
Tindal Cl. Bur H 105 D2
Tinghall. Bog R 195 E2
Tinsley Green. Cra 4 C2
Tinsley La N. Cra 4 C2
Tinsley La S. Cra 17 F4
Tinsley La. Cra 4 C1
Tintagel Gdns. Roc 44 A2
Tintern Cl. Bri 166 C1
Tintern Rd. Cra 16 C2
Tinwood La. Box 153 E3
Tipper La. S Har 87 D2
Tiptoe Green. Hav 147 D3
Tiree Path. Cra 16 C2
Tisbury Rd. Hove 187 D3
Titch Hill. Somp 161 F1
Titchborne St. Bri 187 F3
Titchfield Cl. Bur H 105 D1
Tithe Barn Cl. Bog R 195 D1
Tithe Barn Way. Bog R 194 C1
Tithe Green. Rust 178 C1
Tithe Orch. Fel 7 E4
Titian Rd. Hove 186 B4
Titmus Dr. Cra 17 E1
Titnore La. Wing 180 C3
Titnore Way. Wing 180 C3
Tivoli Cres N. Bri 166 A1
Tivoli Cres. Bri 166 A1
Tivoli Pl. Hove 166 A1
Tivoli Rd. Bri 166 A1
Toat Hill. Five O 54 B4
Toat La. Pul 95 F4
Toddington La. Tod 178 B2
Todds Cl. Horl 1 B3
Toftwood Cl. Cra 18 A3
Tollgate Hill. Cra 38 A4
Tollgate La. Cuc 82 B4
Tollhouse Cl. Chic 172 B3
Tompset's Bank. For R 22 B1
Tongdean Ave. Hove 166 A1
Tongdean Ct. Bri 166 A2
Tongdean La. Bri 166 A2
Tongdean Rd. Hove 166 A2
Tongdean Rise. Bri 166 A2
Toomey Rd. Stey 141 D3
Top Rd. Sha 41 F3
Top Rd. Sli 155 D3
Top St. Bol 81 D2
Tophill Cl. Por S 164 B1
Tor Way. Pete 64 A2
Torberry Dr. Pete 64 A2
Toronto Cl. Wing 181 D3
Toronto Terr. Bri 187 F3
Torrance Cl. Hove 165 E1
Torridge Cl. Wing 181 D4
Torton Hill Rd. Aru 156 B1
Tote La. Ste 67 F3
Totland Rd. Bri 188 A4
Tottington Dr. Sma D 142 B3
Tottington Way. S Sea 163 F1
Tournerbury La. S Hay 189 D2
Tower Cl. Chic 172 B4
Tower Cl. E Gri 8 B1
Tower Cl. Hors 55 F4
Tower Hill. Hors 55 F4
Tower House Cl. Cuc 82 B4
Tower Pl. E Wit 202 B4
Tower Rd. Bri 188 A3
Tower Rd. Fay 36 C4
Tower Rd. Lan 183 D3
Tower Rd. Lip 23 F2
Tower Rd. Wing 182 B2
Tower St. Chic 172 B4
Tower St. Ems 168 C4
Towerhouse Gdns. Aru 156 C2
Towers Rd. Upp B 141 F1
Town Barn Rd. Cra 17 D4
Town Cross Ave. Bog R 196 A2
Town La. She 64 A3
Town La. Sin 131 D3
Town Mead. Cra 17 D4
Townfield Corner. Grave 24 C2
Townfield. Kir 50 C1
Townsend Cres. Lit 178 B1
Townshed Cl. Sid 35 E3
Tozer Way. Chic 172 C3
Trafalgar Ct. Bri 187 F3
Trafalgar La. Bri 187 F3
Trafalgar Rd. Hors 35 D2
Trafalgar Rd. Por S 185 F4
Trafalgar St. Bri 187 F3
Trafalgar Terr. Bri 187 F3
Treadcroft Dr. Hors 35 E3
Treadwheel Rd. Row C 126 A3
Tredcroft Rd. Hove 166 A1
Treemans Rd. Hor K 62 C1
Treemans Rd. Hor K 85 D4
Treetops. Sour 77 F4
Treeview. Cra 17 D1
Trefoil Cl. Hors 35 E3
Trefoil Cres. Cra 16 C1
Tregarth Rd. Chic 151 F1
Treharne Cl. Wing 181 D4
Treloar Rd. S Hay 189 F1
Trenear Cl. Hors 35 E1
Trent Cl. Cra 16 B2
Trent Cl. Lan 183 D3
Trent Rd. Wing 181 E1
Tretawn Gdns. Sels 206 C3
Trevanne Plat. Cra 18 A4
Trevor Cl. Wing 182 A1
Treyford Cl. Cra 16 B3
Triangle Rd. Hay H 83 E2
Triangle The. Lan 183 D2
Trident Cl. Roc 45 D2
Trinity Cl. Cra 18 A4
Trinity Rd. Hur 123 F3
Trinity St. Bri 187 F4
Trinity Way. Bog R 195 E2
Tripp Hill. Fit 114 B4
Tripp Hill. Wat 114 B4
Tristram Cl. Lan 182 C4
Triton Pl. Bog R 197 D3
Trivett Cl. Stone 22 A3
Troon Cl. Cra 16 A3
Trotton Rd. Els 88 C4
Trotton Rd. Tro 88 C4
Trout Rd. Hasl 25 E3
Troymede. Bal 39 F1
True Blue Prec. Wick 178 A2
Truggers. Han 59 D4
Truleigh Dr. Por S 164 C2
Truleigh Rd. Upp B 141 F1
Truleigh Way. S Sea 163 F1
Trundle Cl. M Lav 151 E3
Trundle Mead. Hors 35 D3
Trundle View Cl. Barn 175 F3
Truro Cl. Chic 151 E1
Truro Cres. Bog R 195 E2
Trusler's Hill. Alb 122 B3
Tryndell Way. Bog R 196 C2
Tudor Ave. Ems 147 F2
Tudor Cl. Cra 18 A3
Tudor Cl. E Gri 21 E4
Tudor Cl. Find 160 B3
Tudor Cl. Hove 165 E1
Tudor Cl. M Sea 197 D3
Tudor Cl. Pul 96 B1
Tudor Dr. Wgate 175 D4
Tudor Gdns. Bur H 104 B2
Tudor Village. Stor 118 A2
Tuff's Hard. Bos 192 A4
Tufts Field. Mid 90 A3
Tufts Meadow. Mid 90 B3
Tuggles Plat. Warm 34 B4
Tullett Rd. Cra 17 F1
Tunbridge Cres. Lip 23 F3
Tunbridge La. Bram 23 F3
Tunnmeade. Cra 16 B3
Tuppenny La. Her 169 E4
Turnbull Rd. Chic 172 C4
Turner Ct. E Gri 8 C2
Turner Rd. Wing 182 B3
Turner Way. Sels 206 C4
Turner Wlk. Cra 17 E2
Turner's Hill Rd. E Gri 20 C3
Turners Hill Rd. Copt 6 B2
Turners Hill Rd. Cra 18 B3

Turners Hill Rd. Cra D 19 F4
Turners Hill Rd. Tur H 19 E2
Turners Hill Rd. Wor 18 C3
Turners Mead. Stor 116 C1
Turners Mill Cl. Hay H 83 D4
Turners Mill Rd. Hay H 83 D3
Turners Way. Bur H 104 B2
Turnpike Cl. Chic 172 B2
Turnpike Piece. Bri 167 F3
Turnpike Pl. Cra 17 D4
Turnpike Rd. Amb 136 B4
Turton Cl. Bri 188 A3
Tuscan Ave. M Sea 197 E3
Tushmore Ave. Cra 4 B1
Tushmore Cres. Cra 4 B1
Tushmore La. Cra 17 E4
Tussock Cl. Cra 16 C2
Tweed La. Cra 3 E1
Twineham Cl. Bri 188 B4
Twineham La. Twi 102 C1
Twitten Cl. Sock 185 E4
Twitten La. Fel 7 E2
Twitten The. Alb 123 D3
Twitten The. Cra 17 D3
Twitten The. Dit 125 D2
Twitten The. Sock 185 E4
Twitten The. Upp B 141 F1
Twitten Way. Wing 181 F2
Twittens The. Bur H 104 C2
Two Barns La. M Lav 151 D4
Two Mile Ash Rd. Bar G 54 C1
Two Mile Ash Rd. Hors 55 E3
Two Mile Ash Rd. Sour 55 D2
Twyford Cl. Wing 181 E3
Twyford Gdns. Wing 181 E3
Twyford Rd. Bri 167 D3
Twyford Rd. Wing 181 E3
Twyne Cl. Cra 16 B2
Tye La. Walb 155 E1
Tylden Way. Hors 35 E3
Tyler Rd. Cra 17 D2
Tyler's Green. Cuc 82 C3
Tyler's Green. Hay H 82 C2
Tylston Meadow. Lip 23 F3
Tyne Cl. Cra 18 A3
Tyne Cl. Wing 181 D4
Tyne Way. Bog R 195 D2
Tynings The. Lan 183 E3
Tythe Barn Rd. Sels 206 B3
Tythe Barn. Bol 81 D2
Tytherley Green. Hav 147 D3

Uckfield Cl. Bri 188 B3
Ullswater Dr. Lit 178 C2
Ullswater Gr. Bog R 196 C3
Ullswater Rd. Lan 182 C3
Underdown Rd. Sock 185 D4
Underhill La. Clay 145 E4
Underhill La. Wmes 146 A4
Undermill Rd. Upp B 141 F1
Underwood Cl. Cra D 19 F4
Underwood Rd. Hasl 25 E4
Union Pl. Wing 182 A1
Union Rd. Bri 187 F4
Union St. Bri 187 F3
Upfield Cl. Horl 1 C1
Upfield. Horl 1 C1
Uphill Way. Hun 193 F4
Uplands Ave. Wing 181 E4
Uplands Cl. Hasl 26 A4
Uplands Rd. Bri 167 D1
Uplands Rd. Row C 126 B2
Uppark Gdns. Hors 35 E3
Uppark Gdns. Hors 35 E3
Uppark Way. Bog R 197 D3
Upper Abbey Rd. Bri 188 A2
Upper Bedford St. Bri 188 A2
Upper Bevendean Ave. Bri 167 E1
Upper Bognor Rd. Bog R 196 B2
Upper Boundstone La. Lan 183 D4
Upper Brighton Rd. Lan 183 D4
Upper Brighton Rd. Wing 182 B4
Upper Chalvington Pl. Bri 188 B3
Upper Cl. For R 22 B1
Upper Dr The. Hove 187 D4
Upper Dr. E Pre 200 C4
Upper Forecourt. Cra 4 C4
Upper Gardner St. Bri 187 F3
Upper Gloucester Rd. Bri 187 E3
Upper Hamilton Rd. Bri 187 E4
Upper Heyshott. Pete 64 A2
Upper High St. Wing 182 B2
Upper Hollingdean Rd. Bri 166 C1
Upper Kingston La. S Sea 164 A1
Upper Lewes Rd. Bri 187 F4
Upper Market St. Hove 187 D3
Upper North St. Bri 187 E3
Upper Park Pl. Bri 187 F3
Upper Rock Gdns. Bri 187 F3
Upper Shoreham Rd. S Sea 164 A1
Upper Sq. For R 22 B2
Upper St James's St. Bri 188 A2
Upper St Johns Rd. Bur H 104 C2
Upper St. Fit 94 C2
Upper Stapleheld Comm. Sta 59 F3
Upper Station Rd. Hen 121 D3
Upper Sudeley St. Bri 188 A2
Upper Wardown. Pete 64 A2
Upper Wellington Rd. Bri 188 A4
Upper West Dr. Ferr 180 B1
Upper Winfield Ave. Bri 166 B3
Upperfield. E 68 B1
Upperton Rd. Til 93 D4
Upperton Rd. Upp 71 D1
Upton Ave. Sock 164 B1
Upton Gdns. Wing 181 E2
Upton Rd. Chic 172 B2
Upton Rd. Wing 181 E2
Upways Cl. Sels 204 B1
Ursula Ave N. Sels 206 B3
Ursula Ave. Sels 206 B3
Ursula Sq. Sels 206 B3

Vachery La. Cran 10 B4
Vale Ave. Bri 166 B4
Vale Ave. Wing 160 B1
Vale Dr. Hors 34 C2
Vale Dr. Wing 160 B1
Vale Gdns. Por S 185 F4
Vale Rd. Hay H 83 E1
Vale Rd. Hay H 83 E1
Vale Rd. Por S 186 A4
Vale Wlk. Wing 160 B1
Valebridge Cl. Bur H 105 D3
Valebridge Dr. Bur H 105 D3
Valebridge Rd. Bur H 105 D3
Valencia Rd. Wing 181 F2
Valentine Cl. Wing 181 F4
Valentine Dr. Bur H 104 B2
Valentines Gdns. Bog R 195 D1
Valentines Lea. N 48 C4
Valerie Cl. Por S 165 D1
Valetta Park. Ems 168 C4
Valetta Rd. Tho I 169 E1
Valewood Cl. Bar G 54 A1
Valewood La. Bar G 54 A1
Valewood Rd. Kin G 26 A2
Valiant Rd. Tho I 169 E1
Vallance Cl. Bur H 104 B2
Vallance Gdns. Hove 186 C3
Vallance Rd. Hove 186 C3
Valley Cl. Bri 166 A2
Valley Dr. Bri 166 A2
Valley Rd. Lan 183 D4
Valley Rd. Por S 164 C1
Valley Side. Lip 23 F3
Van Dyck Pl. Bog R 195 F3
Van Gogh Pl. Bog R 195 F3
Vanbrugh Cl. Cra 16 B2
Vancouver Cl. Wing 181 D3
Vancouver Dr. Cra 4 A1
Vancouver Rd. Wing 181 D3
Vann Bridge Cl. Fer 46 C3
Vann Rd. Fer 46 C3
Vanners. Cra 17 E4
Vanzell Rd. E 68 C1
Varndean Cl. Bri 166 B2
Varndean Dr. Bri 166 B2
Varndean Gdns. Bri 166 B2
Varndean Rd. Bri 166 B2
Varsity Rd. Tho I 169 E1
Velyn Ave. Chic 172 C3
Ventnor Villas. Hove 186 C3
Venus La. Bog R 205 E4
Veras Wlk. Stor 118 A1
Verbama Way. E Gri 8 C1
Vere Rd. Bri 187 F4
Vermont Dr. E Pre 179 F1
Vermont Way. E Pre 179 F1
Vernon Cl. Hors 35 F2
Vernon Cl. Rust 179 D1
Vernon Terr. Bri 187 E4
Veronica Cl. E Pre 200 C4
Veronica Way. Bri 187 F2
Verwood Rd. Hav 147 D3
Viaduct Rd. Bri 187 F4
Vicarage Fields. Wing 181 D4
Vicarage La. Bog R 196 C2
Vicarage La. E Pre 179 E1
Vicarage La. Hasl 25 E3
Vicarage La. Hoo 1 B2
Vicarage La. Sca H 84 B2
Vicarage La. Stey 141 D2
Vicarage Rd. Cra D 19 F4
Victor Ct. Cra 5 D1
Victor Rd. Tho I 169 E1
Victoria Ave. Bur H 104 B2
Victoria Ave. E 68 C1
Victoria Cl. Bur H 104 B1
Victoria Cl. Horl 1 C2
Victoria Cl. Mid 90 B4
Victoria Cotts. Hove 186 C3
Victoria Ct. Hors 35 D1
Victoria Dr. Bog R 196 A2
Victoria Gdns. Bur H 104 B1
Victoria Gdns. Wgate 175 D4
Victoria Gr. Hove 187 D3
Victoria Park Gdns. Wing 182 A2
Victoria Pl. Bri 187 E3
Victoria Rd S. Bog R 195 F1
Victoria Rd Spur. Horl 1 C1
Victoria Rd. Bal 39 F1
Victoria Rd. Bog R 195 F1
Victoria Rd. Bri 187 E3
Victoria Rd. Bur H 104 B1
Victoria Rd. Chic 173 D4
Victoria Rd. Cra 17 D3
Victoria Rd. Ems 147 F1
Victoria Rd. Hay H 83 E2
Victoria Rd. Horl 1 C1
Victoria Rd. N Hay 168 B2
Victoria Rd. Por S 186 A4
Victoria Rd. S Sea 184 B4
Victoria Rd. Sock 185 D4
Victoria Rd. Wing 182 A2
Victoria St. Bri 187 E3
Victoria St. Hors 35 D1
Victoria Way. Bur H 104 B1
Victoria Way. E Gri 21 E4
Victory Rd. Hors 34 C2
View Terr. Dor 8 C4
View The. Bog R 205 F4
Village St. She 64 A3
Vincent Cl. Hors 35 E1
Vincent Cl. Lan 183 D3
Vincent Rd. Sels 206 A3
Vine Pl. Bri 187 E3
Vine St. Bri 187 F3
Vineries Cl. Wing 181 F3
Vineries The. Bur H 105 D2
Vines Cross Rd. Bri 188 B4
Vinnetrow Rd. Chic 173 E2
Vinson Rd. Liss 43 D2
Viscount Dr. Bog R 205 F4
Vivienne Cl. Cra 4 A1
Vowels La. Sel C 20 A1
Vulcan Cl. Cra 17 D1
Vulcan Rd. Tho I 169 E1

Wad The. W Wit 190 C1
Waddington Cl. Cra 16 C2
Wade Court Rd. Hav 168 A4
Wade La. Hav 168 A4
Wadeys The. Bil 75 D4
Wadham Cl. Cra 5 D1
Wadhurst Cl. Bog R 195 F2
Wadhurst Dr. Wing 180 C1
Wadhurst Rise. Bri 188 B3
Wadlands Brook Rd. Dor P 8 A3
Wagg Cl. E Gri 8 C1
Wain End. Hors 35 D3
Wainwrights. Cra 17 D2
Wakefield Rd. Bri 187 F4
Wakefield Way. Bog R 195 E2
Wakehams Green Dr. Cra 5 D1
Wakehurst Dr. Cra 17 D2
Wakehurst La. Ard 61 F4
Wakehurst Mews. Hors 34 B1
Wakehurst Pl. Rust 179 D1
Wakestone La. Petw 72 C1
Walberton Cl. Bog R 196 C3
Waldby Ct. Cra 16 C2
Waldegrave Rd. Bri 166 C1
Walders Rd. Rust 178 C1
Waldron Ave. Bri 167 D3
Walesbeech. Cra 17 F3
Walker Cl. Cra 18 A2
Walker Rd. Cra 18 A2
Walker Rd. Cra 18 A2
Wall Hill Rd. Ash W 22 B3
Wall Hill Rd. For R 22 B3
Wallace Ave. Wing 181 E1
Wallace Rd. Rust 179 D2
Wallage La. Cra D 19 E3
Wallage La. Wor 19 D3
Wallfield. Bog R 195 E1
Wallis Ct. Cra 4 B1
Wallis Way. Hors 35 F2
Wallner Cres. Bog R 197 D3
Wallrock Wlk. Ems 147 F2
Walmer Cres. Bri 167 F1
Walnut Ave. Chic 172 B4
Walnut Ave. Rust 178 C1
Walnut Cl. Bri 166 B2
Walnut La. Cra 4 A1
Walnut Tree Dr. Wcote S 148 C2
Walnut Tree Way. Wing 180 C3
Walpole Ave. Wing 181 D1
Walpole Rd. Bri 188 A3
Walpole Terr. Bri 188 A3
Walsham Cl. Bog R 196 B3
Walsingham Rd. Hove 186 B3
Waltham Park Rd. Cold 114 C3
Walton Ave. Bog R 196 B2
Walton Bank. Bri 167 E3
Walton Cl. Wing 181 E3
Walton Heath. Cra 18 A4
Walton La. Bos 171 D3
Walton Lodge. Wing 181 E3
Walton Rd. Bog R 196 A2
Wandle Cl. Cra 18 A3
Wandle Rd. Cra 18 A3
Wandleys Cl. Fon 154 B1
Wandleys Dr. Fon 154 B1
Wandleys La. Fon 154 C1
Wansford Way. M Sea 197 D2
Wantley Hill Estate. Hen 121 E3
Wantley La. Stor 117 E1
Wantley Rd. Wing 160 C1
Warble Heath Cl. M Lav 151 E3
Warblers Way. Bog R 195 F4
Warbleton Cl. Bri 188 B3
Warblington Ave. Hav 147 D1
Warblington Rd. Ems 168 C4
Warburton Cl. E Gri 21 F4
Ward Cres. Ems 148 A2
Warden Ct. Cuc 82 B3
Warenne Rd. Hove 165 D2
Warleigh Rd. Bri 187 F4
Warmdene Ave. Bri 166 B3
Warmdene Cl. Bri 166 B3
Warmdene Rd. Bri 166 B3
Warmdene Way. Bri 166 B3
Warnborough Ct. Hav 147 D3
Warner Rd. Wing 182 B2
Warner's La. Sels 206 A4
Warners La. Sels 206 A4
Warnham Rd. Bro H 34 A2
Warnham Rd. Cra 17 F2
Warnham Rd. Hors 34 C3
Warnham Rd. Wing 181 D1
Warnham Rise. Bri 166 C3
Warninglid La. Low B 58 A2
Warninglid La. Ward 58 B1
Warren Cl. Fel 7 E2
Warren Cl. Wood 188 C4
Warren Cres. E Pre 179 F1
Warren Croft. Stor 116 C1
Warren Ct. Lan 183 D3
Warren Dr. Cra 16 C4
Warren Farm La. Chic 151 E1
Warren Gdns. Wing 181 F4
Warren Rd. Bri 188 B4
Warren Rd. Liss F 43 D4
Warren Rd. Wing 181 F4
Warren Rd. Wood 188 C4
Warren Rise. Wood 188 C4
Warren Side. S Har 87 D2
Warren The. Bur H 105 D1
Warren The. Ferr 201 E4
Warren The. Pen 151 E4
Warren Way. Barn 176 A3
Warrington Cl. Cra 16 B1
Warrington Cl. Cra 16 B2
Warrs Hill La. N Cha 85 E1
Warwick Cl. Bog R 194 C1
Warwick Gdns. Wing 182 B1
Warwick Pl. Bog R 197 D3
Warwick Pl. Wing 182 B1
Warwick Rd. Wing 182 B1
Warwick St. Wing 182 B1
Warwick Wlk. S Sea 163 E1
Washington Bostal. Was 139 D3
Washington Rd. Cra 16 B2
Washington Rd. Ems 147 F1
Washington Rd. Hay H 83 F3
Washington Rd. Stey 140 C3
Washington Rd. Stor 117 E1
Washington Rd. Wist 140 B4
Washington St. Bri 187 F4
Washington St. Chic 172 B4
Wassand Cl. Cra 17 F3
Water La. Ang 179 F3
Water La. Lit 178 A1
Water La. Pat 180 A4
Water La. Stor 117 E1
Water La. Wist 140 A4
Water Lane Ind Est. Stor 117 E2
Water Lea. Cra 17 F3
Waterbury Hill. Hor K 62 C3
Waterdyke Ave. Sock 185 E4
Waterfield Cl. Hors 35 E2
Waterfield Gdns. Cra 16 B2
Wateringbury Cl. Orp 35 E2
Waterloo Pl. Bri 187 F3
Waterloo Rd. Bog R 196 C2
Waterloo Sq. Bog R 196 A1
Waterloo St. Hove 187 D3
Waterplat The. Chic 173 D4
Waters Edge. Bog R 195 E1
Watersedge Gdns. Ems 168 C4
Watersfield Rd. Wing 181 F3
Waterside Cl. Cra 16 B2
Waterside Ct. Roc 45 D1
Waterside Dr. Chic 172 B2
Waterside. E Gri 8 C1
Waterside. Horl 1 C3
Waterside. Pass 23 E4
Waterstone Cl. W Ich 191 E4
Waterworks Dr. For R 22 B2
Waterworks Rd. She 64 A3
Watery La. Chic 172 C2
Watery La. Fun 149 F2
Watery La. W Ash 149 F2
Watling Cl. Sock 185 E4
Watling Rd. Sock 185 E4
Waveney Wlk. Cra 17 F2
Waverley Cres. Bri 167 D1
Waverley Rd. Bog R 195 F2
Waverley Rd. Rust 179 D1
Wavertree Rd. Wing 181 D2
Way The. E Pre 200 C4
Wayfield Ave. Hove 165 E1
Wayland Ave. Bri 166 A2
Wayside Ave. Wing 181 D4
Wayside. Bri 166 A3
Wayside. Cra 16 B2
Weald Ave. Hove 186 B4
Weald Cl. Hors 56 B4
Weald Cl. Hur 123 E3
Weald Dr. Cra 17 F2
Weald Dr. S Sea 184 B3
Weald Rd. Bur H 104 B2
Weald Rise. Hay H 83 E1
Weald The. E Gri 8 B2
Wealden Way. Hay H 83 D2
Wealdon Cl. Sour 77 E4
Wear Cl. Wing 181 D4
Wear Rd. Wing 181 D4
Weare St. Oak 13 D4
Weaver Cl. Cra 16 B3
Weavers Cl. Bur H 105 D1
Weavers Cl. E 68 B1
Weavers Green. Hav 147 E2
Weavers Hill. Ang 179 F3
Weavers La. Hen 121 E2
Weavers Ring. Ang 179 F3
Webb Cl. Bog R 205 F4
Webb Cl. Cra 16 C1
Webb Cl. S Hay 189 D1
Webb La. S Hay 189 D1
Weddell Rd. Cra 17 E2
Wedges The. Bar G 54 A3
Wedgwood Rd. Bog R 196 C2
Weirbrook. Cra 17 F2
Welbeck Ave. Hove 186 B3
Welbeck Cl. Bur H 105 D2
Welbeck Dr. Bur H 105 D2
Welkin The. Hay H 83 F4
Well La. Hasl 26 A3
Well Rd. Bog R 205 E4
Welland Cl. Wing 181 D4
Welland Rd. Wing 181 D4
Weller Cl. Cra 18 A3
Wellesley Ave. Wing 181 D1
Wellfield. Ash W 22 A4
Wellhouse La. Bur H 124 C4
Wellingham La. Wing 160 B1
Wellington Cl. Cra 5 E1
Wellington Gdns. Sels 206 B4
Wellington Rd. Bog R 196 A2
Wellington Rd. Bri 188 A4
Wellington Rd. Chic 151 F1
Wellington Rd. Hors 35 D1
Wellington Rd. Por S 186 A3
Wellington St. Bri 188 A4
Wellington Town Rd. E Gri 8 A1
Wellington Way. Horl 1 B3
Wells Cl. Hors 34 B1
Wells Cres. Bog R 195 E2
Wells Cres. Chic 151 E1
Wells Lea. E Gri 8 A2
Wells Meadow. E Gri 8 A2
Wells Rd. Cra 17 E1
Wellsfield. W Wit 191 D1
Wellswood Gdns. Row C 126 B2
Wellsworth La. Row C 126 B2
Wellwood Cl. Hors 35 F2
Welwyn Cl. Cra 16 B1
Wembley Ave. Lan 183 D3
Wembley Gdns. Lan 183 D3
Wenban Rd. Wing 182 A2
Wenceling Cotts. Lan 184 A3
Wendy Ridge. Rust 178 C1
Wenlock Cl. Cra 16 C2
Wensley Gdns. Ems 147 F1
Wensleydale. Cra 17 D2
Wentworth Cl. Barn 175 F4
Wentworth Cl. Wing 181 E4
Wentworth Dr. Cra 18 A4
Wentworth St. Bri 187 F2
Wesley Cl. Cra 16 B2
Wesley Cl. Horl 1 C3
Wessex Ave. Bog R 195 F1
Wessex Ave. E Wit 202 C4
Wessex Wlk. S Sea 163 E1
West Ashling Rd. Hamb 149 E2
West Ashling Rd. Wcote S 149 D2
West Ave. Bog R 195 E2
West Ave. Cra 17 F4
West Ave. Lan 183 F3
West Ave. M Sea 197 E3
West Ave. Wing 181 F1
West Beach Rd. E 202 A4
West Beach Rd. S Sea 184 A3
West Beach. E Wit 202 B4
West Bldgs. Wing 182 A1
West Bracklesham Dr. E Wit 202 C3
West Broyle Dr. Chic 151 D1
West Burton Rd. W Bur 114 B1
West Burton Rd. W Bur 135 D4
West Chiltington La. Bar G 54 A1
West Chiltington La. Con 75 F2
West Chiltington La. W Chi 97 E4
West Chiltington Rd. Pul 96 B1
West Chiltington Rd. Tha 97 F1
West Chiltington Rd. W Chi 97 F1
West Chiltington Rd. W Chi C 116 C4
West Cl. Bog R 196 C2
West Cl. Fer 46 C3
West Cl. M Sea 197 D3
West Comm. Hay H 83 E4
West Common Dr. Hay H 83 F4
West Dr. Ang 179 D2
West Dr. Bog R 194 C1
West Dr. Bri 188 A3
West Dr. Ferr 201 E4
West Dr. M Sea 197 F3
West End La. Hen 120 C3
West End Way. Lan 183 D2
West Front Rd. Bog R 205 E4
West Furlong La. Hur 123 F3
West Green Dr. Cra 17 D3

West Haye Rd. S Hay 189 E1
West Head. Lit 199 E4
West Hill Pl. Bri 187 E3
West Hill Rd. Bri 187 E3
West Hill St. Bri 187 E3
West Hill. Dor P 8 B3
West Hill. E Gri 21 D4
West Hill. Wing 160 B1
West Hoathly Rd. E Gri 21 D3
West La. E Gri 21 D4
West La. Lan 183 E4
West La. N Hay 168 A1
West Leigh. E Gri 21 E4
West Mallion. Hay H 83 E2
West Mare La. Pul 96 B1
West Mead. Rust 200 B4
West Meade. Mil 44 C1
West Meads Dr. Bog R 195 E2
West Onslow Cl. Ferr 180 B2
West Pallant. Chic 172 C3
West Par. Hors 35 D2
West Par. Wing 181 F1
West Park Cres. Bur H 104 A2
West Park Rd. Dom 6 C3
West Park Rd. Han 58 C4
West Rd. Ems 168 C4
West Rd. Poy 144 B4
West Rd. Pye 144 C3
West Rd. Sock 185 F4
West Ridings. E Pre 200 B4
West Sands Caravan Park.
Sels 206 A4
West Sands La. Sels 206 A4
West Side. Til 92 C4
West St. Bil 75 D4
West St. Bog R 196 A1
West St. Bri 187 E3
West St. Bur H 104 B2
West St. Chic 172 B3
West St. Cra 17 D3
West St. Dit 125 D2
West St. Dor 8 C4
West St. E Gri 21 E4
West St. Ems 168 C4
West St. Hasl 26 A3
West St. Hors 35 D1
West St. Lan 182 C4
West St. Mid 90 B4
West St. Por S 186 A4
West St. S Sea 184 B4
West St. Sels 206 A3
West St. Stor 117 D1
West St. Wing 182 A1
West Stoke Rd. Chic 151 D2
West Stoke Rd. W Sto 150 C2
West Tyne. Wing 181 D3
West View Dr. Yap 176 B1
West View Gdns. E Gri 21 E4
West View. Hay H 83 F3
West Walberton La. Fon 154 C1
West Walberton La. Walb 155 D1
West Way. Chic 151 D1
West Way. Cra 17 F4
West Way. Hove 165 E1
West Way. Lan 183 F3
West Way. Slin 33 F3
West Way. Wing 160 A1
Westbourne Ave. Ems 148 A1
Westbourne Ave. Wing 182 A2
Westbourne Cl. Ems 148 A1
Westbourne Gdns. Hove 186 C4
Westbourne Gr. Hove 186 C4
Westbourne Pl. Hove 186 C3
Westbourne Rd. Ems 148 A2
Westbourne St. Hove 186 C4
Westbourne Villas. Hove 186 B3
Westbrook Cl. Bos 170 C3
Westbrook Field. Bos 170 C3
Westbrooke. Wing 182 A1
Westburton La. Bury 135 E4
Westburton La. W Bur 135 E4
Westcott Cl. Cra 38 A4
Westcourt Pl. Wing 182 A2
Westcourt Rd. Wing 182 A2
Westdean Rd. Wing 181 F3
Westdene Dr. Bri 166 A3
Westdown Ct. Wing 181 F2
Westergate Cl. Ferr 180 B1
Westergate Mews. Wgate 175 D4
Westergate Rd. Bri 167 E2
Westergate St. Wgate 175 D3
Western Ave. Ems 168 C4
Western Cl. Lan 183 D2
Western Ct. Lit 199 E4
Western Espl. Hove 186 B3
Western Par. Ems 168 C4
Western Pl. Wing 182 A1
Western Rd N. Lan 183 D3
Western Rd. Bri 187 E3
Western Rd. Bur H 104 B2
Western Rd. Hay H 83 E2
Western Rd. Hur 123 E3
Western Rd. Lan 182 C3
Western Rd. Lit 199 E4
Western Rd. S Sea 184 B4
Western Rd. Sels 206 B3
Western Row. Wing 182 A1
Western St. Bri 187 D3
Western Terr. Bri 187 E3
Westfield Ave. E Pre 200 C4
Westfield Cl. Bri 166 C2
Westfield Cres. Bri 166 C3
Westfield Rd. Charl 3 E3
Westfield Rd. Cra 16 C3
Westfield. Bog R 195 F4
Westgate. Chic 172 A3
Westhampnett Rd. Chic 173 D4
Westhill Dr. Bur H 104 B2
Westingway. Bog R 195 F2
Westlake Cl. Wing 181 E3
Westland Ave. Wing 181 F2
Westland's Copse La. Upp 70 C2
Westlands La. Bir 192 A3
Westlands Rd. Hay H 83 F3
Westlands Rd. Hun 193 F4
Westlands. Ferr 180 B1
Westlands. Lit 178 C1
Westlands. Rust 178 C1
Westleas. Horl 1 B3
Westloats Gdns. Bog R 195 F3
Westloats La. Bog R 195 F3
Westmead Rd. Chic 172 A3
Westminster Dr. Bog R 195 E2
Westminster Rd. Cra 18 A3
Westmoreland Wlk. S Sea 163 E1
Westmorland Dr. Bog R 196 C3
Westmount Cl. Sock 185 D4
Weston La. Fun 149 E3
Weston Rd. Pete 64 A2
Weston's Hill. Itc 54 C3
Westons Cl. Hors 35 D4
Westpark La. Wing 181 E1
Westup Rd. Bal 39 E1
Westview Terr. Find 160 B3
Westward Cl. Bos 171 D3
Westward La. W Chi C 117 D3
Westway Cl. Por S 164 B2
Westway Gdns. Por S 164 B2
Westway. Bog R 196 A2
Westway. Copt 5 F2
Westway. Cra 4 C4
Westway. Wick 178 A2
Westwood Cl. Brom 33 F1
Westwood Cl. Ems 148 A2
Wey Hill. Hasl 25 F3
Wey Lodge Cl. Lip 24 A2
Weycombe Rd. Hasl 26 A4
Weydown Rd. Hasl 25 F4
Weylands Cl. Lip 24 A3
Weysprings. Hasl 25 F3
Whapple The. Lit 199 F4
Wharf Rd. Hove 186 A3
Wharf Rd. Lit 178 A1
Wharf Road S. Grays 8 B2
Wharf The. Mid 90 B4
Wheatcroft. Wick 178 A2
Wheatear Dr. Pete 64 B1
Wheatfield Rd. Sels 206 C4
Wheatfield Way. Bri 167 E2
Wheatfield Way. Horl 1 C2
Wheatlands Ave. S Hay 189 F1
Wheatlands Cl. S Hay 189 F1
Wheatley Cl. Stone 22 A3
Wheatsheaf Cl. Hors 35 E3
Wheatsheaf La. Cuc 82 C3
Wheatstone Cl. Cra 4 C2
Wheelbarrow Castle. E 68 C1
Wheeler R. Cra 17 F2
Wheelwright La. Bur H 105 D1
Whichelo Pl. Bri 188 A3
Whichers Cl. Row C 147 D4
Whichers Gate Rd. Row C 147 D4
Whipping Rd. Bri 188 A4
Whippingham St. Bri 188 A4
Whistler Ave. Chic 151 F1
Whistler Cl. Cra 17 E2
White Acre. Wick 178 A2
White City. Mid 90 B4
White Friars. Sev 98 B2
White Hart Ct. Hors 35 D2
White Horse Sq. Stey 141 D2
White Horse Yd. Stor 117 D1
White Horses Way. Lit 178 C1
White Ladies Cl. Hav 147 D1
White Oak Gdns. Sid 18 A2
White Oak Wlk. Hav 147 D3
White St. Bri 187 F3
White Styles Rd. Lan 182 C4
White's Cl. Hur 123 F4
Whitebeam Rd. Wing 181 D3
Whitebeam Way. Tan 153 D1
Whitechimney Row. Wbou 148 A2
Whitecroft. Horl 1 C2
Whitecross St. Bri 187 F3
Whitehall Dr. Cra 16 B3
Whitehawk Cl. Bri 188 B3
Whitehawk Cres. Bri 188 B3
Whitehawk Hill Rd. Bri 188 A3
Whitehawk Rd. Bri 188 B3
Whitehawk Way. Bri 188 B3
Whitehawk Way. Bri 188 B4
Whitehorn Rd. Hay 189 D2
Whitehorse Rd. Hors 35 F3
Whitelands. Bog R 196 C3
Whitelea Rd. Wick 178 A1
Whitelot Cl. Sock 164 B1
Whitelot Way. Sock 164 B1
Whiteman's Cl. Cuc 82 B4
Whitemans Green. Cuc 82 A4
Whiterock Pl. Sock 185 E4
Whites La. Fer 46 B2
Whiteside Cl. Chic 172 C4
Whitethorn Dr. Bri 165 F2
Whitethroat La. Bal 60 A3
Whiteways Cl. Bog R 195 F3
Whiteways Cl. Lit 178 A1
Whiteways. Bog R 195 F3
Whitfield Cl. Bog R 196 B3
Whitfield Rd. Hasl 26 A4
Whitgift Wlk. Cra 17 D2
Whitley Cl. Wbou 148 A3
Whitmore Way. Horl 1 A2
Whitsbury Rd. Hav 147 D3
Whittingehame Gdns. Bri 166 B2
Whittington College. Fel 7 F2
Whittington Ct. Ems 168 C4
Whittington Rd. Cra 17 E2
Whittle Way. Cra 4 C2
Whitworth Rd. Cra 4 A1
Whyke Cl. Chic 172 C2
Whyke La. Chic 172 C3
Whyke Rd. Chic 172 C3
Whylands Ave. Wing 181 D4
Whylands Cl. Wing 181 D4
Whylands Cres. Wing 181 D4
Whytings. Man H 57 D3
Wick Cl. Bog R 196 C3
Wick Farm Rd. Lit 178 A1
Wick La. Bog R 196 C3
Wick La. E 68 C2
Wick Par. Wick 178 A2
Wick St. Wick 178 A2
Wickham Cl. Hay H 83 E4
Wickham Cl. Horl 1 B2
Wickham Dr. Hur 123 F3
Wickham Dr. Hur 124 A3
Wickham Hill. Hur 124 A2
Wickham Way. Hay H 83 E4
Wickhurst Cl. Por S 164 B1
Wickhurst Gdns. Hors 34 B2
Wickhurst La. Bro H 34 A1
Wickhurst Rd. Por S 164 C1
Wickhurst Rise. Por S 164 B2
Wickor Cl. Ems 148 A1
Wickor Way. Ems 148 A2
Wicks Rd. Bil 75 D4
Widdicombe Way. Bri 167 E1
Widewater Cl. Lan 184 A3
Widgeon Way. Hors 35 D3
Wierton Rd. Bou Mon 125 D3
Wigmore Cl. Bri 166 C1
Wigmore Rd. Wing 182 A3
Wilberforce Cl. Cra 38 A4
Wilbury Ave. Hove 187 D4
Wilbury Cres. Hove 187 D4
Wilbury Gdns. Hove 187 D4
Wilbury Gr. Hove 187 D3
Wilbury Rd. Hove 187 D3
Wilbury Villas. Hove 187 D4
Wilby Ave. Sock 164 B1
Wild Park Cl. Bri 167 E2
Wilderness Rd. Hur 123 F3
Wilderness Rise. Dor P 8 C3
Wilderness The. Hay H 83 F4
Wilderwick Rd. Dor 8 C3
Wilderwick Rd. E Gri 8 C2
Wildmoor Wlk. Hav 147 D3
Wildwood La. Cran 10 A3
Wilfrid Rd. Hove 165 D1
Wilkinson Ct. Cra 16 C1
Willett Cl. Dun 112 C4
William Allen La. Hay H 83 F3
William Morris Way. Cra 38 A4
William Rd. Chic 173 D3
William St. Bog R 196 A2
William St. Bri 187 F3
William St. Sock 185 F4
Williams Rd. Bos 171 D4
Williams Rd. S Sea 185 D4
Willingdon Rd. Bri 167 E1
Willoughby Way. SE7 1 B3
Willow Ave. Rust 179 E1
Willow Brean. Horl 1 B3
Willow Brook. Wick 178 A2
Willow Cl. Cra 17 E4
Willow Cl. E Gri 8 A2
Willow Cl. Hav 147 D1
Willow Cl. Lan 184 A3
Willow Cl. Lip 24 A2
Willow Cl. Stey 141 D2
Willow Cl. W Chi C 117 D3
Willow Cnr. Charl 3 E4
Willow Cres. Wing 181 D3
Willow Ct. Chic 172 A3
Willow Ct. Wing 181 F2
Willow Dr. Bil 75 D4
Willow Gdns. Hur 123 F4
Willow Gdns. Lip 24 A2
Willow Gdns. Wbou 148 A2
Willow Mead. E Gri 21 E4
Willow Park. Hay H 83 F2
Willow Rd. Hors 35 F3
Willow Rd. Liss 43 D2
Willow Ridge. Tur H 19 F2
Willow Way. Ash 118 C2
Willow Way. Bog R 194 C1
Willow Way. Hur 123 E4
Willow Wlk. Petw 93 E4
Willowbed Ave. Chic 172 C2
Willowbed Dr. Chic 173 D2
Willowbrook Park. Lan 183 F3
Willowbrook Rd. Wing 182 C2
Willowbrook Way. Key 124 C2
Willowhale Ave. Bog R 195 D1
Willowhale Green. Bog R 195 D1
Willowhayne Ave. E Pre 200 C4
Willowhayne Cl. E Pre 200 C4
Willowhayne Cres. E Pre 200 C4
Willows The. Bur H 104 C3
Willows The. F 177 E3
Willows The. Hors 35 D3
Willows The. Lan 183 E3
Willows The. Pul 95 F1
Willows The. Rust 179 D1
Willows The. Sels 206 B4
Willowside. Snod 72 B3
Wills Cl. Yap 176 C1
Wills Ct. Yap 176 C1
Wilman Gdns. Bog R 195 D1
Wilmington Cl. Bri 166 C3
Wilmington Cl. Key 124 B2
Wilmington Par. Bri 166 B3
Wilmington Way. Bri 166 C3
Wilmington Way. Hay H 83 F3
Wilmot Rd. S Sea 185 D4
Wilson Ave. Bri 188 B3
Wilson Cl. Chic 172 A4
Wilton Cl. Par G 100 C2
Wilverley Ave. Hav 147 D2
Wimblehurst Rd. Hors 35 D2
Wimland Hill. Hors 15 D1
Wimlands La. Rusp 15 E2
Wimlands Rd. Hors 15 D2
Wimlands Rd. Rusp 15 D2
Winchelsea Gdns. Wing 181 F1
Winchester Ct. Sour 55 F1
Winchester Dr. Chic 172 B4
Winchester Rd. Cra 17 E1
Winchester Rd. Rust 179 E1
Winchester Rd. Wing 182 A1
Winchester St. Bri 187 F4
Wincombe Rd. Bri 166 A1
Winden Ave. Chic 172 C3
Windermere Cres. Wing 181 D3
Windermere Rd. Hay H 83 E2
Windlesham Ave. Bri 187 E3
Windlesham Cl. Por S 164 C1
Windlesham Gdns. Bri 187 E4
Windlesham Gdns. E Pre 179 F1
Windlesham Gdns. S Sea 184 B4
Windlesham Rd. Bri 187 E3
Windlesham Rd. S Sea 184 B4
Windmill Ave. Key 124 B2
Windmill Cl. Ash 118 C3
Windmill Cl. Bog R 194 C1
Windmill Cl. Horl 1 C2
Windmill Cl. Hors 35 F2
Windmill Cl. Hove 165 E1
Windmill Cl. Upp B 141 F1
Windmill Copse. Stor 117 E1
Windmill Ct. Cra 17 D4
Windmill Ct. E Wit 202 B4
Windmill Dr. Bri 166 A3
Windmill Dr. Bur H 104 C2
Windmill Dr. Rust 179 D1
Windmill Field. Bos 170 C3
Windmill La. Ash W 22 A4
Windmill La. E Gri 8 A2
Windmill La. Hen 121 E2
Windmill Platt. Han 59 D4
Windmill Rd. Lit 199 D4
Windmill Rd. Sock 164 B1
Windmill St. Bri 187 F3
Windmill Terr. Bri 187 F3
Windrum Cl. Hors 55 E4
Windrush Cl. Cra 16 B2
Windrush Cl. Wing 181 D4
Windsor Cl. Bog R 195 E2
Windsor Cl. Cra 17 D1
Windsor Cl. Hove 165 F2
Windsor Cl. Sour 55 F1
Windsor Dr. E Wit 202 B4
Windsor Pl. E Gri 21 F4
Windsor Rd. Chic 173 D3
Windsor Rd. Sels 206 B3
Windsor Rd. Wing 182 B2
Windsor St. Bri 187 E3
Windward Cl. Lit 178 C1
Windyridge. Cra 16 C3
Wineham La. Win 102 A3
Winfield Ave. Bri 166 B3
Winfield Cl. Bri 166 B3
Winfield Cl. Por S 164 C2
Wingle Tye Rd. Bur H 124 C4
Winkhurst Way. Bur H 105 D1
Winnet Way. Sour 55 F1
Winsor Cl. S Hay 189 E1
Winston Cl. Bog R 195 E3
Winston Cl. Stone 22 A3
Winston Cres. Bog R 195 E3
Winston Rd. Lan 183 D2
Winter Knoll The. Lit 178 B1
Winterbourne Cl. Wing 180 C3
Winterbourne Rd. Chic 151 F1
Winterbourne Way. Wing 180 C3
Winterfold. Cra 17 F2
Winterpit Cl. Man H 57 D3
Winterpit La. Man H 57 D3
Winters La. E 68 C2
Winterton Ct. Hors 35 D1
Winterton Way. S Sea 184 C3
Winton Pl. Wing 182 A2
Wire Mill La. Fel 7 E4
Wisborough Ct. Cra 16 B2
Wisborough Gdns. Wis G 74 A4
Wisborough La. Stor 117 E1
Wisden Ave. Bur H 104 B3
Wish Ct. Hove 186 B4
Wish Rd. Hove 186 B3
Wiston Ave. Chic 172 B2
Wiston Ave. Wing 181 F3
Wiston Cl. Wing 181 F3
Wiston Ct. Cra 16 B2
Wiston Rd N. Bri 188 B4
Wiston Rd S. Bri 188 B3
Wiston Way. Bri 188 B4
Witchampton Cl. Hav 147 D3
Withdean Ave. Bri 166 A1
Withdean Ave. Wing 201 F4
Withdean Cl. Bri 166 A2
Withdean Court Ave. Bri 166 A2
Withdean Cres. Bri 166 B2
Withdean Rd. Bri 166 A2
Withdean Rise. Bri 166 A2
Wither Dale. Horl 1 B2
Withey Meadows. Hoo 1 B1
Withy Bush. Bur H 104 B3
Withypitts E. Tur H 19 F2
Withypitts. Tur H 19 F2
Wittering Rd. S Hay 189 F1
Wivelsfield Green Rd. Wiv 105 F3
Wivelsfield Rd. Hay H 83 E1
Woburn Pl. Bri 167 E3
Woburn Rd. Cra 16 C2
Wold Cl. Cra 16 B2
Woldhurstlea Cl. Cra 16 C2
Wolseley Rd. Bri 167 D3
Wolseley Rd. Por S 185 F4
Wolstenbury Rd. Rust 179 D2
Wolstonbury Cl. Cra 17 D2
Wolstonbury Cl. Hur 123 F2
Wolstonbury Rd. Hove 187 E4
Wolstonbury Way. Bur H 104 C1
Wolstonbury Wlk. S Sea 163 E1
Wolverstone Dr. Bri 167 D1
Wolverton Cl. Horl 1 B1
Wolverton Gdns. Hoo 1 B1
Wonston Ct. Hav 147 E3
Wood Cl. Sal 1 C4
Wood End. Hors 36 A3
Wood La. Sma D 142 B4
Wood Ride. Hay H 83 D2
Wood St. Bog R 195 F1
Wood St. Bri 187 F3
Wood St. E Gri 8 A1
Wood View. Aru 156 C1
Woodard Rd. Lan 183 E4
Woodards View. S Sea 184 A3
Woodberry La. Row C 147 F4
Woodbourne Ave. Bri 166 C2
Woodbourne Cl. Liss 43 D2
Woodbridge Park. E Pre 179 F1
Woodbury Ave. E Gri 8 C1
Woodbury Ave. E Gri 8 C1
Woodbury Cl. E Gri 21 F4
Woodcock Hill. Fel 7 E3
Woodcot Cres. Hav 147 D3
Woodcote La. Wick 178 A3
Woodcote Rd. For R 22 B1
Woodcote. Gra 111 F4
Woodcourt. Cra 17 D1
Woodcrest Rd. Bur H 104 B1
Woodcroft Rd. Cra 16 A2
Woodcroft. Bur H 104 B3
Wooddale La. Bil 53 E1
Woodend Cl. Cra 17 F4
Woodend. Bog R 195 F2
Woodend. W Sto 150 A3
Woodfield Cl. Bog R 205 F4
Woodfield Cl. Cra 17 E4
Woodfield Cl. Tan 153 D1
Woodfield Park Rd. Her 169 D4
Woodfield Rd. Cra 17 E4
Woodfield. Rud 32 A4
Woodfield. Sour 55 E1
Woodgason La. N Hay 189 E4
Woodgate Cl. Woo 175 D3
Woodgate Park. Wgate 175 D3
Woodgate Rd. Woo 175 D3
Woodgates Cl. Hors 35 E2
Woodhall Cl. Cuc 82 B4
Woodhay Wlk. Hav 147 D3
Woodhorn La. Ovi 174 A3
Woodhouse La. Row C 126 A3
Woodhouse La. Row C 126 B3
Woodhouse Rd. Hove 186 B4
Wooding Gr. Cra 16 C1
Woodington Cl. Hav 147 D3
Woodland Ave. Bur H 105 D2
Woodland Ave. Hove 165 F2
Woodland Ave. Wing 160 B1
Woodland Cl. Bur H 105 D2
Woodland Cl. Five O 53 E3
Woodland Cl. Hors 35 F2
Woodland Cl. Hove 165 F1

Woodland Cotts. Rust 179 D1
Woodland Ct. Hove 165 F2
Woodland Dr. Cra D 19 F4
Woodland Dr. Hove 165 F2
Woodland La. Colg 37 D2
Woodland Rd. Sels 206 B3
Woodland Way. Bri 166 B2
Woodland Way. Gree 22 B4
Woodland Way. Hors 35 F2
Woodlands Ave. Ems 147 F2
Woodlands Ave. Rust 179 D1
Woodlands Cl. Ang 179 F4
Woodlands Cl. Cla 159 E3
Woodlands Cl. Cra D 19 F4
Woodlands Cl. Hass 124 B2
Woodlands Cl. Rust 179 D1
Woodlands La. Chic 172 B4
Woodlands La. Hasl 25 E4
Woodlands La. Liss 43 D2
Woodlands La. Stor 118 A2
Woodlands La. W Mar 127 F1
Woodlands Rd. Bog R 195 F3
Woodlands Rd. E Gri 8 C2
Woodlands Rd. Hass 124 B2
Woodlands Rd. Hay H 83 E2
Woodlands Rd. Lit 199 E4
Woodlands The. Bri 166 B3
Woodlands Way. Bil 75 E3
Woodlands Way. Sour 77 E4
Woodlands Wlk. Man H 57 D3
Woodlands. Cra 18 A4
Woodlands. Hove 166 A1
Woodlark Gdns. Pete 64 B2
Woodlea Rd. Wing 181 F2
Woodleigh Cl. Hav 147 E2
Woodleigh Rd. Bur H 105 D2
Woodmancote La. Hamb 149 D1
Woodmancote Rd. Wing 181 F2
Woodmans Hill. Cra 17 D1
Woodmatch. Sour 55 E1
Woodpecker Cl. Hav 147 D1
Woodpecker La. Stor 117 E1
Woodpecker Rd. Petw 93 E4
Woodpecker Way. Wing 181 D3
Woodridge Cl. Hay H 83 F2
Woodroffe Wlk. Ems 147 F2
Woodroyd Ave. Hoo 1 B1
Woodroyd Gdns. Horl 1 B1
Woodruff Ave. Hove 166 A1
Woods Hill Cl. Ash W 22 A3
Woods Hill La. Ash W 22 A3
Woods Way. Wing 181 D2
Woodside Ave. Hove 166 A1
Woodside Cl. Par G 101 D2
Woodside Cl. Stor 117 E1
Woodside Rd. Cra 17 E4
Woodside Rd. Wing 181 F2
Woodside School Rd. Bri 167 D1
Woodside. Barn 175 F3
Woodside. Hors 35 F2
Woodstock Cl. Hors 35 D3
Woodstock. E Gri 8 A1
Woodview Cl. Bri 167 D3
Woodview. S Sea 163 E1
Woodwards Cl. Bur H 104 C1
Woodwards. Cra 17 D1
Wool La. Mid 90 B4
Woolbeding La. Wool 67 F2
Woolborough Cl. Cra 17 E4
Woolborough La. Cra 4 B1
Woolborough Rd. Cra 17 E4
Woolmer Hill Rd. Hasl 25 D4
Woolmer St. Ems 147 F2
Woolstaplers The. Chic 172 B3
Wophams La. Apu 193 D4
Wophams La. Don 193 D4
Worcester Cl. Bog R 195 E2
Worcester Rd. Chic 151 E1
Worcester Rd. Cra 17 E1
Worcester Villas. Hove 186 A4
Wordsworth Cl. Cra 17 F4
Wordsworth Gdns. Bog R 197 D3
Wordsworth Pl. Hors 35 E4
Wordsworth Rd. Wing 182 A1
Wordsworth Rise. E Gri 8 A1
Wordsworth St. Hove 186 C4
Worldham Rd. Hav 147 D3
Worms La. M Sea 197 E4
Worsted La. E Gri 21 F4
Worth Park Ave. Cra 18 A4
Worth Rd. Cra 18 A3
Worthing Rd. Ang 179 D2
Worthing Rd. Dia P 99 F3
Worthing Rd. E Pre 179 E1
Worthing Rd. Hors 55 F4
Worthing Rd. Lit 178 B2
Worthing Rd. Sour 55 E1
Worthing Rd. W Gri 99 F3
Worthing Rd. Wick 178 A2
Wouldham Rd. Grays 8 A2
Wray Cl. Ash W 22 A3
Wraysbury Park Dr. Ems 147 F2
Wren Cl. Hors 35 D4
Wren Cl. Pul 95 F2
Wren Cres. Bog R 195 F3
Wroxham Way. Bog R 196 B3
Wroxham Wlk. Cra 17 F2
Wyatt Cl. Wis G 51 F1
Wyatt Ct. E Wit 202 B4
Wyatts La. Hor K 63 D3
Wyberlye Rd. Bur H 104 C2
Wyborn Cl. S Hay 189 D1
Wychperry Rd. Hay H 83 D3
Wychwood Cl. Bog R 195 E1
Wychwood Gdns. Wing 182 C2
Wychwood Wlk. Bog R 195 E1
Wycliffe Ct. Cra 16 B2
Wyde Feld. Bog R 195 E1
Wye Cl. Cra 38 A4
Wyeford Cl. Hav 147 D3
Wyke Ave. Wing 182 B1
Wyke La N. Bog R 197 D3
Wykeham Cl. Stey 141 D2
Wykeham Rd. Wing 182 A1
Wykeham Way. Bur H 105 D1
Wykwood. Lip 24 A2
Wyld Green La. Liss 43 D3
Wyncombe Cl. Fit 94 C2
Wyndham Lea. W Chi C 117 D3
Wyndham Rd. Petw 93 E4
Wyndham St. Bri 187 F2
Wynnes Mews. Hove 186 C4
Wyshe The. Pye 145 D3
Wythering Cl. Bog R 205 E4
Wythwood. Hay H 83 E1

Yapton La. Barn 176 B3
Yapton La. Walb 176 B4
Yapton Rd. Barn 176 A3
Yapton Rd. Cli 177 D1
Yapton Rd. M Sea 197 E4
Yapton Rd. Yap 176 B2
Yarbrook. M Lav 151 E4
Yardlea Cl. Row C 126 A1
Yardley St. Bri 187 F4
Yarmouth Cl. Cra 17 F2
Yarrow Cl. Hors 35 E3
Yattendon Rd. Horl 1 C2
Yeoman Rd. Wing 180 C3
Yeoman Wy. Wing 180 C2
Yeomans Acre. Bog R 195 E2
Yeomans La. Lip 23 F2
Yew La. E Gri 7 F2
Yew Tree Cl. Cow 79 E1
Yew Tree Cl. Horl 1 C2
Yew Tree Cl. Lan 183 E3
Yew Tree Pl. Liss 43 D2
Yew Tree Rd. Charl 3 E4
Yew Tree Rd. N Hay 189 D4
Yewlands Wlk. Cra 16 A2
York Ave. E Gri 21 E4
York Ave. Hove 187 E3
York Chase. Chic 151 E1
York Cl. Hors 35 E2
York Cl. Sour 55 F1
York Gdns. Lit 178 A1
York Gr. Bri 187 E4
York Hill. Bri 187 F4
York Pl. Bri 187 F3
York Rd. Bog R 196 A1
York Rd. Bur H 104 A1
York Rd. Chic 173 D3
York Rd. Cra 17 E1
York Rd. Hove 187 E3
York Rd. Lit 178 A1
York Rd. Sels 206 B3
York Rd. Wing 182 B1
York Villas. Bri 187 E4
Yorkhurst Hill. Cha 110 B1
Young St. Chic 151 F1
Youngsmere Cl. Bri 166 C3

Zion Gdns. Bri 187 E3

STREET ATLASES

CSA94

	Hardback (Quantity / Total)	Softback	Pocket (Quantity / Total)	
	£12.99	£8.99	£4.99	
East Essex	£__.__ ISBN 0-540-05848-3	£__.__ ISBN 0-540-05866-1	£__.__ ISBN 0-540-05850-5	£__.__
West Essex	£__.__ ISBN 0-540-05849-1	£__.__ ISBN 0-540-05867-X	£__.__ ISBN 0-540-05851-3	£__.__
North Hampshire	£__.__ ISBN 0-540-05852-1	£__.__ ISBN 0-540-05853-X	£__.__ ISBN 0-540-05854-8	£__.__
South Hampshire	£__.__ ISBN 0-540-05855-6	£__.__ ISBN 0-540-05856-4	£__.__ ISBN 0-540-05857-2	£__.__
Nottinghamshire	£__.__ ISBN 0-540-05858-0	£__.__ ISBN 0-540-05859-9	£__.__ ISBN 0-540-05860-2	£__.__
East Sussex	£__.__ ISBN 0-540-05875-0	£__.__ ISBN 0-540-05874-2	£__.__ ISBN 0-540-05873-4	£__.__
West Sussex	£__.__ ISBN 0-540-05876-9	£__.__ ISBN 0-540-05877-7	£__.__ ISBN 0-540-05878-5	£__.__
	£10.99		£4.99	
Berkshire	£__.__ ISBN 0-540-05738-X		£__.__ ISBN 0-540-05835-1	£__.__
Buckinghamshire	£__.__ ISBN 0-540-05660-X		£__.__ ISBN 0-540-05711-8	£__.__
Hertfordshire	£__.__ ISBN 0-540-05720-7		£__.__ ISBN 0-540-05840-8	£__.__
East Kent	£__.__ ISBN 0-540-05661-8			£__.__
West Kent	£__.__ ISBN 0-540-05662-6			£__.__
Oxfordshire	£__.__ ISBN 0-540-05665-0			£__.__
Warwickshire	£__.__ ISBN 0-540-05642-1			£__.__
	£10.99		£3.99	
Surrey	£__.__ ISBN 0-540-05694-4		£__.__ ISBN 0-540-05708-8	£__.__

I enclose a cheque/postal order for £__.__ *made payable to* ***Reed Book Services*** *or please debit my* ◂*Access* ◂*American Express* ◂*Visa account by* £__.__

Name

Address

Postcode

Account number

Expiry date

Signature

Please tick this box if you do not wish your name to be used by other carefully selected organisations that may wish to send you information about other products and services

◆ ***Free postage and packing*** ◆ *All available titles will normally be dispatched within 5 working days of receipt of order, but please allow up to 28 days for delivery.*

Registered office: Michelin House, 81 Fulham Road, London SW3 6RB. Registered in England No 1974080